Java 11 Cookbook
Second Edition

A definitive guide to learning the key concepts of modern
application development

Nick Samoylov
Mohamed Sanaulla

BIRMINGHAM - MUMBAI

Java 11 Cookbook
Second Edition

Commissioning Editor: Richa Tripathi
Acquisition Editor: Denim Pinto
Content Development Editor: Pooja Parvatkar
Technical Editor: Mehul Singh
Copy Editor: Safis Editing
Project Coordinator: Ulhas Kambali
Proofreader: Safis Editing
Indexer: Rekha Nair
Graphics: Tom Scaria
Production Coordinator: Arvindkumar Gupta

First published: August 2017
Second edition: September 2018

Production reference: 1210918

Published by Packt Publishing Ltd.
Livery Place
35 Livery Street
Birmingham
B3 2PB, UK.

ISBN 978-1-78913-235-9

www.packtpub.com

mapt.io

Mapt is an online digital library that gives you full access to over 5,000 books and videos, as well as industry leading tools to help you plan your personal development and advance your career. For more information, please visit our website.

Why subscribe?

- Spend less time learning and more time coding with practical eBooks and Videos from over 4,000 industry professionals

- Improve your learning with Skill Plans built especially for you

- Get a free eBook or video every month

- Mapt is fully searchable

- Copy and paste, print, and bookmark content

Packt.com

Did you know that Packt offers eBook versions of every book published, with PDF and ePub files available? You can upgrade to the eBook version at www.packt.com and as a print book customer, you are entitled to a discount on the eBook copy. Get in touch with us at customercare@packtpub.com for more details.

At www.packt.com, you can also read a collection of free technical articles, sign up for a range of free newsletters, and receive exclusive discounts and offers on Packt books and eBooks.

Contributors

About the authors

Nick Samoylov graduated as an engineer-physicist from Moscow Institute of Physics and Technology, has worked as a theoretical physicist, and learned how to program as a tool for testing his mathematical models using FORTRAN and C++. After the demise of the USSR, Nick created and successfully ran a software company, but was forced to close it under pressure from governmental and criminal rackets. In 1999, with his wife Luda and two daughters, he emigrated to the USA and has been living in Colorado since then, working as a Java programmer.

In his free time, Nick likes to read (mostly non-fiction), write (fiction novels and blogs), and hike the Rocky Mountains.

Mohamed Sanaulla is a full-stack developer with more than 8 years, experience in developing enterprise applications and Java-based backend solutions for e-commerce applications.

His interests include enterprise software development, refactoring and redesigning applications, designing and implementing RESTful web services, troubleshooting Java applications for performance issues, and TDD.

He has strong expertise in Java-based application development, ADF (a JSF-based Java EE web framework), SQL, PL/SQL, JUnit, designing RESTful services, Spring, Spring Boot, Struts, Elasticsearch, and MongoDB. He is also a Sun Certified Java Programmer for the Java 6 platform. He is a moderator for JavaRanch and likes to share his findings on his blog.

I would like to thank my family for their encouragement, support, and for putting up with my absence while I was busy compiling this book. I would also like to thank the Packt Publishing team for giving me the opportunity to author the book.

About the reviewer

Aristides Villarreal Bravo is a Java developer, a member of the NetBeans Dream Team, and a Java User Groups leader. He lives in Panama. He has organized and participated in various conferences and seminars related to Java, JavaEE, NetBeans, the NetBeans platform, free software, and mobile devices. He is the author of *jmoordb* and tutorials and blogs about Java, NetBeans, and web development. Aristides has participated in several interviews on sites about topics such as NetBeans, NetBeans DZone, and JavaHispano. He is a plugin developer for NetBeans.

I would like to thank my mother, father, and all my family and friends.

Packt is searching for authors like you

If you're interested in becoming an author for Packt, please visit authors.packtpub.com and apply today. We have worked with thousands of developers and tech professionals, just like you, to help them share their insight with the global tech community. You can make a general application, apply for a specific hot topic that we are recruiting an author for, or submit your own idea.

Table of Contents

Preface

This cookbook offers a range of software development examples that are illustrated by simple and straightforward code, providing step-by-step resources and time-saving methods to help you solve data problems efficiently. Starting with the installation of Java, each recipe addresses a specific problem and is accompanied by a discussion that explains the solution and offers insight into how it works. We cover major concepts about the core programming language, as well as common tasks involved in building a wide variety of software. You will follow recipes to learn about new features of the latest Java 11 release to make your application modular, secure, and fast.

Who this book is for

The intended audience includes beginners, programmers with intermediate experience, and even experts; all will be able to access these recipes, which demonstrate the latest features released with Java 11.

What this book covers

Chapter 1, *Installation and a Sneak Peek into Java 11*, helps you to set up the development environment for running your Java programs and gives a brief overview of the new features and tools in Java 11.

Chapter 2, *Fast Track to OOP – Classes and Interfaces*, covers Object-Oriented Programming (OOP) principles and design solutions, including inner classes, inheritance, composition, interfaces, enumerations, and the Java 9 changes to Javadocs.

Chapter 3, *Modular Programming*, introduces Jigsaw as a major feature and a huge leap for the Java ecosystem. This chapter demonstrates how to use tools, such as jdeps and jlink, to create simple modular applications and related artifacts, such as modular JARs, and finally, how to modularize your pre-Jigsaw applications.

Chapter 4, *Going Functional*, introduces a programming paradigm called functional programming. The topics covered include functional interfaces, lambda expressions, and lambda-friendly APIs.

Chapter 5, *Streams and Pipelines*, shows how to leverage streams and chain multiple operations on a collection to create a pipeline, use factory methods to create collection objects, create and operate on streams, and create an operation pipeline on streams, including parallel computations.

Chapter 6, *Database Programming*, covers both basic and commonly used interactions between a Java application and a database, right from connecting to the database and performing CRUD operations to creating transactions, storing procedures, and working
with large objects.

Chapter 7, *Concurrent and Multithreaded Programming*, presents different ways of incorporating concurrency and some best practices, such as synchronization and immutability. The chapter also discusses the implementation of some commonly used patterns, such as divide-conquer and publish-subscribe, using the constructs provided by Java.

Chapter 8, *Better Management of the OS Process*, elaborates on the new API enhancements regarding the Process API.

Chapter 9, *RESTful Web Services Using Spring Boot*, deals with creating simple RESTful web services using Spring Boot, deploying them to Heroku, dockerizing Spring Boot-based RESTful web service applications, and monitoring Spring Boot applications using Prometheus.

Chapter 10, *Networking*, shows you how to use different HTTP client API libraries; namely, the new HTTP client API shipped with latest JDK, the Apache HTTP client, and the Unirest HTTP client API.

Chapter 11, *Memory Management and Debugging*, explores managing the memory of a Java application, including an introduction to the garbage collection algorithm used in Java 9, and some new features that help in advanced application diagnostics. We'll also show how to manage resources by using the new try-with-resources construct and the new stack-walking API.

Chapter 12, *The Read-Evaluate-Print Loop (REPL) Using JShell*, shows you how to work with the new REPL tool and JShell, provided as part of the JDK.

Chapter 13, *Working with New Date and Time APIs*, demonstrates how to construct time zone-dependent and independent date and time instances, how to create a date- and time-based period between date instance, how to represent epoch time, how to manipulate and compare date and time instances, how to work with different calendar systems, and how to format dates using the `DateTimeFormatter`.

Chapter 14, *Testing*, explains how to unit test your APIs before they are integrated with other components, including stubbing dependencies with some dummy data and mocking dependencies. We will also show you how to write fixtures to populate test data and then how to test your application behavior by integrating different APIs and testing them.

Chapter 15, *The New Way of Coding with Java 10 and Java 11*, demonstrates how to use local variable type inference and when and how to use local variable syntax for lambda parameters.

Chapter 16, *GUI Programming Using JavaFX*, explains how to use JavaFX for creating a GUI using FXML Markup, and CSS. It will demonstrate creating a bar chart, a pie chart, a line chart, an area chart. It will also show how to embed HTML in an application and a media source and how to add effects to controls. Also, we will learn about the newly released Robot API in the OpenJFX 11 update.

To get the most out of this book

In order to get the most out of this book, some knowledge of Java and the ability to run Java programs is required. Also, it helps to have your favorite editor or, even better, an IDE installed and configured for use in the recipes. Because the book is essentially a collection of recipes, with each recipe being based on specific examples, the benefits of the book will be lost if the reader does not execute the examples provided. Readers will get even more from this book if they reproduce every example that is provided in their IDE, execute it, and compare their result with the one shown in the book.

Download the example code files

You can download the example code files for this book from your account at www.packt.com. If you purchased this book elsewhere, you can visit www.packt.com/support and register to have the files emailed directly to you.

You can download the code files by following these steps:

1. Log in or register at www.packt.com.
2. Select the **SUPPORT** tab.
3. Click on **Code Downloads & Errata**.
4. Enter the name of the book in the **Search** box and follow the onscreen instructions.

Once the file is downloaded, please make sure that you unzip or extract the folder using the latest version of:

- WinRAR/7-Zip for Windows
- Zipeg/iZip/UnRarX for Mac
- 7-Zip/PeaZip for Linux

The code bundle for the book is also hosted on GitHub at `https://github.com/ PacktPublishing/Java-11-Cookbook-Second-Edition`. We also have other code bundles from our rich catalog of books and videos available at `https://github.com/ PacktPublishing/`. Check them out!

Conventions used

There are a number of text conventions used throughout this book.

`CodeInText`: Indicates code words in text, database table names, folder names, filenames, file extensions, pathnames, dummy URLs, user input, and Twitter handles. Here is an example: "Use the `allProcesses()` method on the `ProcessHandle` interface to get a stream of the currently active processes"

A block of code is set as follows:

```
public class Thing {
   private int someInt;
   public Thing(int i) { this.someInt = i; }
   public int getSomeInt() { return someInt; }
   public String getSomeStr() {
      return Integer.toString(someInt); }
}
```

When we wish to draw your attention to a particular part of a code block, the relevant lines or items are set in bold:

```
Object[] os = Stream.of(1,2,3).toArray();
Arrays.stream(os).forEach(System.out::print);
System.out.println();
String[] sts = Stream.of(1,2,3)
                     .map(i -> i.toString())
                     .toArray(String[]::new);
Arrays.stream(sts).forEach(System.out::print);
```

Any command-line input or output is written as follows:

```
jshell> ZoneId.getAvailableZoneIds().stream().count()
$16 ==> 599
```

Bold: Indicates a new term, an important word, or words that you see onscreen. For example, words in menus or dialog boxes appear in the text like this. Here is an example: "Right-click on **My Computer** and then click on **Properties**. You will see your system information."

Warnings or important notes appear like this.

Tips and tricks appear like this.

Sections

In this book, you will find several headings that appear frequently (*Getting ready*, *How to do it...*, *How it works...*, *There's more...*, and *See also*). To give clear instructions on how to complete a recipe, use these sections as follows:

Getting ready

This section tells you what to expect in the recipe and describes how to set up any software or any preliminary settings required for the recipe.

How to do it...

This section contains the steps required to follow the recipe.

How it works...

This section usually consists of a detailed explanation of what happened in the previous section.

There's more...

This section consists of additional information about the recipe in order to make you more knowledgeable about the recipe.

See also

This section provides helpful links to other useful information for the recipe.

Get in touch

Feedback from our readers is always welcome.

General feedback: If you have questions about any aspect of this book, mention the book title in the subject of your message and email us at customercare@packtpub.com.

Errata: Although we have taken every care to ensure the accuracy of our content, mistakes do happen. If you have found a mistake in this book, we would be grateful if you would report this to us. Please visit www.packt.com/submit-errata, selecting your book, clicking on the Errata Submission Form link, and entering the details.

Piracy: If you come across any illegal copies of our works in any form on the internet, we would be grateful if you would provide us with the location address or website name. Please contact us at copyright@packtpub.com with a link to the material.

If you are interested in becoming an author: If there is a topic that you have expertise in and you are interested in either writing or contributing to a book, please visit authors.packtpub.com.

Reviews

Please leave a review. Once you have read and used this book, why not leave a review on the site that you purchased it from? Potential readers can then see and use your unbiased opinion to make purchase decisions, we at Packt can understand what you think about our products, and our authors can see your feedback on their book. Thank you!

For more information about Packt, please visit packt.com.

Installation and a Sneak Peek into Java 11

1

In this chapter, we will cover the following recipes:

- Installing JDK 18.9 on Windows and setting up the PATH variable
- Installing JDK 18.9 on Linux (Ubuntu, x64) and configuring the PATH variable
- Compiling and running a Java application
- What's new in JDK 18.9
- Using application class-data sharing

Introduction

Every quest for learning a programming language begins with setting up the environment to experiment with our learning. Keeping in sync with this philosophy, in this chapter, we will show you how to set up your development environment and then run a simple modular application to test our installation. After that, we'll give you an introduction to the new features and tools in JDK 18.9. Then, we will compare JDK 9, 18.3, and 18.9. We'll end the chapter with a new feature introduced in JDK 18.3 that allows application-class-data sharing.

Installing JDK 18.9 on Windows and setting up the PATH variable

In this recipe, we will look at installing JDK on Windows and how to set up the PATH variable to be able to access the Java executables (such as javac, java, and jar) from anywhere within the command shell.

How to do it...

1. Visit http://jdk.java.net/11/ and accept the early-adopter license agreement, which looks like this:

> **License agreement**
> You must accept the Early Adopter Development License Agreement in order to download this software.
>
> ◯ Accept License Agreement
> ◯ Decline License Agreement

2. After accepting the license, you will get a grid of the available JDK bundles based on the OS and architecture (32/64-bit). Click to download the relevant JDK executable (.exe) for your Windows platform.
3. Run the JDK executable (.exe) and follow the onscreen instructions to install JDK on your system.
4. If you have chosen all the defaults during the installation, you will find JDK installed in C:/Program Files/Java for 64 bit and C:/Program Files (x86)/Java for 32 bit.

Now that we have finished installing JDK, let's see how we can set the PATH variable.

The tools provided with JDK, namely javac, java, jconsole, and jlink, are available in the bin directory of your JDK installation. There are two ways you could run these tools from the Command Prompt:

1. Navigate to the directory where the tools are installed and run them, as follows:

```
cd "C:\Program Files\Java\jdk-11\bin"
javac -version
```

2. Export the path to the directory so that the tools are available from any directory in the command prompt. To achieve this, we have to add the path to the JDK tools in the `PATH` environment variable. The command prompt will search for the relevant tool in all the locations declared in the `PATH` environment variable.

Let's see how you can add the JDK bin directory to the `PATH` variable:

1. Right-click on **My Computer** and then click on **Properties**. You will see your system information. Search for **Advanced system settings** and click on it to get a window, as shown in the following screenshot:

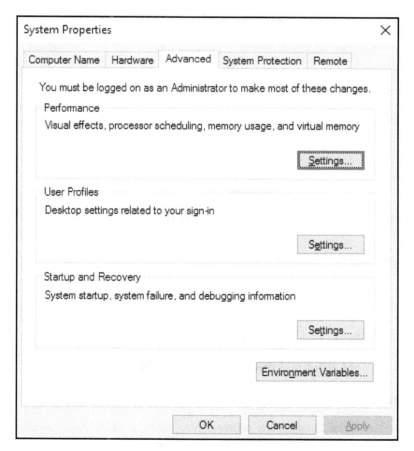

2. Click on **Environment Variables** to view the variables defined in your system. You will see that there are quite a few environment variables already defined, as shown in the following screenshot (the variables will differ across systems; in the following screenshot, there are a few predefined variables and a few variables added by me):

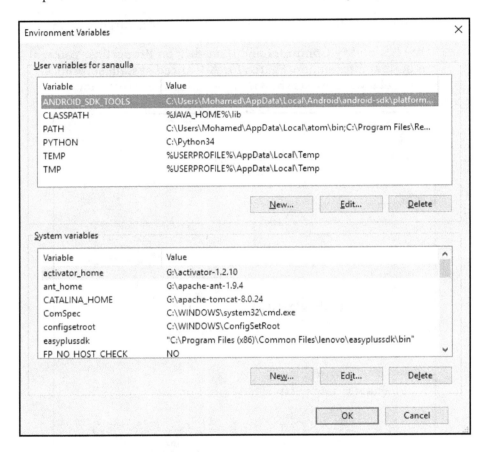

The variables defined under **System variables** are available across all the users of the system, and those defined under **User variables for <user name>** are available only to the specific user.

3. A new variable, with the name JAVA_HOME, and its value as the location of the JDK 9 installation. For example, it would be C:\Program Files\Java\jdk-11 (for **64** bit) or C:\Program Files (x86)\Java\jdk-11 (for **32** bit):

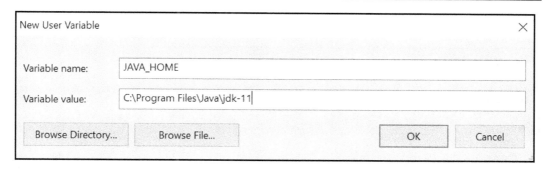

4. Update the PATH environment variable with the location of the bin directory of your JDK installation (defined in the JAVA_HOME environment variable). If you already see the PATH variable defined in the list, then you need to select that variable and click on **Edit**. If the PATH variable is not seen, click on **New**.

5. Any of the actions in the previous step will give you a popup, as shown in the following screenshot (on Windows 10):

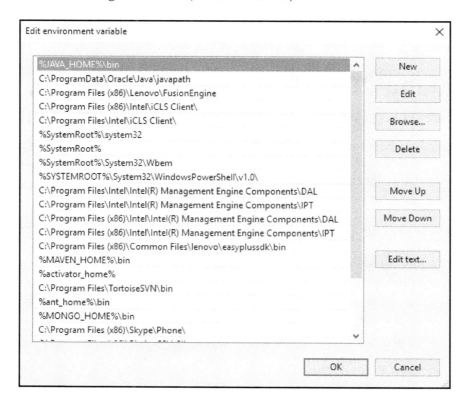

The following screenshot shows the other Windows versions:

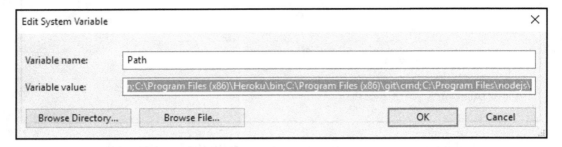

6. You can either click on **New** in the first screenshot and insert the `%JAVA_HOME%\bin` value, or you can append the value against the **Variable value** field by adding `;  %JAVA_HOME%\bin`. The semicolon (`;`) in Windows is used to separate multiple values for a given variable name.
7. After setting the values, open the command prompt and run `javac -version`. You should be able to see `javac 11-ea` as the output. If you don't see it, it means that the bin directory of your JDK installation has not been correctly added to the `PATH` variable.

Installing JDK 18.9 on Linux (Ubuntu, x64) and configuring the PATH variable

In this recipe, we will look at installing JDK on Linux (Ubuntu, x64), and how to configure the `PATH` variable to make the JDK tools (such as `javac`, `java`, and `jar`) available from any location within the Terminal.

How to do it...

1. Follow steps 1 and 2 of the *Installing JDK 18.9 on Windows and setting up the PATH variable* recipe to reach the downloads page.
2. Copy the download link (`tar.gz`) for the JDK for the Linux x64 platform from the downloads page.
3. Download the JDK by using `$> wget <copied link>`, for example, `$> wget https://download.java.net/java/early_access/jdk11/26/BCL/jdk-11-ea+26_linux-x64_bin.tar.gz`.

4. Once the download completes, you should have the relevant JDK available, for example, `jdk-11-ea+26_linux-x64_bin.tar.gz`. You can list the contents by using `$> tar -tf jdk-11-ea+26_linux-x64_bin.tar.gz`. You can even pipe it to `more` to paginate the output: `$> tar -tf jdk-11-ea+26_linux-x64_bin.tar.gz | more`.

5. Extract the contents of the `tar.gz` file under `/usr/lib` by using `$> tar -xvzf jdk-11-ea+26_linux-x64_bin.tar.gz -C /usr/lib`. This will extract the contents into a directory, `/usr/lib/jdk-11`. You can then list the contents of JDK 11 by using `$> ls /usr/lib/jdk-11`.

6. Update the `JAVA_HOME` and `PATH` variables by editing the `.bash_aliases` file in your Linux home directory:

```
$> vim ~/.bash_aliases
export JAVA_HOME=/usr/lib/jdk-11
export PATH=$PATH:$JAVA_HOME/bin
```

Source the `.bashrc` file to apply the new aliases:

```
$> source ~/.bashrc
$> echo $JAVA_HOME
/usr/lib/jdk-11
$>javac -version
javac 11-ea
$> java -version
java version "11-ea" 2018-09-25
Java(TM) SE Runtime Environment 18.9 (build 11-ea+22)
Java HotSpot(TM) 64-Bit Server VM 18.9 (build 11-ea+22, mixed
mode)
```

 All the examples in this book are run against JDK installed on Linux (Ubuntu, x64), except for places where we have specifically mentioned that these are run on Windows. We have tried to provide run scripts for both platforms.

Compiling and running a Java application

In this recipe, we will write a very simple modular `Hello world` program to test our JDK installation. This simple example prints `Hello world` in XML; after all, it's the world of web services.

Getting ready

You should have JDK installed and the PATH variable updated to point to the JDK installation.

How to do it...

1. Let's define the model object with the relevant properties and annotations that will be serialized into XML:

```
@XmlRootElement
@XmlAccessorType(XmlAccessType.FIELD)
class Messages{
  @XmlElement
  public final String message = "Hello World in XML";
}
```

In the preceding code, @XmlRootElement is used to define the root tag, @XmlAccessorType is used to define the type of source for the tag name and tag values, and @XmlElement is used to identify the sources that become the tag name and tag values in the XML.

2. Let's serialize an instance of the Message class into XML using JAXB:

```
public class HelloWorldXml{
  public static void main(String[] args) throws JAXBException{
    JAXBContext jaxb =
JAXBContext.newInstance(Messages.class);
    Marshaller marshaller = jaxb.createMarshaller();
marshaller.setProperty(Marshaller.JAXB_FRAGMENT,Boolean.TRUE);
    StringWriter writer = new StringWriter();
    marshaller.marshal(new Messages(), writer);
    System.out.println(writer.toString());
  }
}
```

3. We will now create a module named com.packt. To create a module, we need to create a file named module-info.java, which contains the module definition. The module definition contains the dependencies of the module and the packages exported by the module to other modules:

```
module com.packt{
  //depends on the java.xml.bind module
  requires java.xml.bind;
```

```
        //need this for Messages class to be available to
java.xml.bind
    exports  com.packt to java.xml.bind;
}
```

 We will explain modules in detail in Chapter 3, *Modular Programming*. But this example is just to give you a taste of modular programming and to test your JDK installation.

The directory structure with the preceding files is as follows:

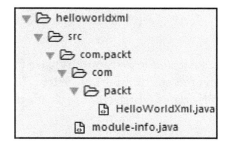

4. Let's compile and run the code. From the helloworddxml directory, create a new directory in which to place your compiled class files:

   ```
   mkdir -p mods/com.packt
   ```

   Compile the source, HelloWorldXml.java and module-info.java, into the mods/com.packt directory:

   ```
   javac -d mods/com.packt/ src/com.packt/module-info.java
   src/com.packt/com/packt/HelloWorldXml.java
   ```

5. Run the compiled code using java --module-path mods -m com.packt/com.packt.HelloWorldXml. You will see the following output:

   ```
   <messages><message>Hello World in XML</message></messages>
   ```

   Don't worry if you are not able to understand the options passed with the java or javac commands. You will learn about them in Chapter 3, *Modular Programming*.

What's new in Java 11?

The release of Java 9 was a milestone in the Java ecosystem. The modular framework developed under Project Jigsaw became part of Java SE release. Another major feature was the JShell tool, which is a REPL tool for Java. Many other new features introduced with Java 9 are listed in the release notes: `http://www.oracle.com/technetwork/java/javase/9all-relnotes-3704433.html`.

In this recipe, we will enumerate and discuss some of the new features introduced with JDK 18.3 and 18.9 (Java 10 and 11).

Getting ready

The Java 10 release (JDK 18.3) started a six-month release cycle—every March and every September—and a new release numbering system. It also introduced many new features, the most significant of which (for application developers) are the following:

- Local variable type inference that allows the declaration of a variable using the reserved `var` type (see `Chapter 15`, *The New Way of Coding with Java 10 and Java 11*)
- Parallel full garbage collection for the G1 garbage collector, which improves worst-case latencies
- A new method, `Optional.orElseThrow()`, that is now the preferred alternative to the existing `get()` method
- New APIs for creating unmodifiable collections: The `List.copyOf()`, `Set.copyOf()`, and `Map.copyOf()` methods of the `java.util` package and new methods of the `java.util.stream.Collectors` class: `toUnmodifiableList()`, `toUnmodifiableSet()`, and `toUnmodifiableMap()` (see `Chapter 5`, *Streams and Pipelines*)
- A default set of root Certification Authorities, making OpenJDK builds more appealing to developers
- A new Javadoc command-line option, `--add-stylesheet`, provides support for the use of multiple stylesheets in the generated documentation
- Extending the existing class-data sharing feature to allow application classes to be placed in the shared archive that improves startup time and reduces the footprint (see the *Using application class-data sharing* recipe)

- An experimental just-in-time compiler, Graal, can be used on the Linux/x64 platform
- A clean garbage-collector (GC) interface that makes it simpler to add a new GC to HotSpot without perturbing the current code base and makes it easier to exclude a GC from a JDK build
- Enabling HotSpot to allocate the object heap on an alternative memory device, such as an NVDIMM memory module, specified by the user
- Thread-local handshakes, for executing a callback on threads without performing a global VM safepoint
- Docker awareness: JVM will know whether it is running in a Docker container on a Linux system and can extract container-specific configuration information instead of querying the operating system
- Three new JVM options, to give Docker container users greater control over the system memory

See the full list of Java 10's new features in the release notes: `https://www.oracle.com/technetwork/java/javase/10-relnote-issues-4108729.html`.

We will discuss the new features of JDK 18.9 in more detail in the next section.

How to do it...

We have picked a few features that we feel are the most important and useful for an application developer.

JEP 318 – Epsilon

Epsilon is a so-called no-op garbage collector that basically does nothing. Its use cases include testing for performance, memory pressure, and the virtual machine interface. It also could be used for short-lived jobs or the jobs that do not consume much memory and do not require garbage collection.

We discussed this feature in more details in the recipe *Understand Epsilon, a low-overhead garbage collector* recipe in `Chapter 11`, *Memory Management and Debugging*.

JEP 321 – HTTP Client (Standard)

JDK 18.9 standardizes the incubated HTTP API client introduced in JDK 9 and updated in JDK 10. Based on CompleteableFuture, it supports nonblocking requests and responses. The new implementation is asynchronous and provides a better traceable data flow.

Chapter 10, *Networking,* explains this feature in more detail in several recipes.

JEP 323 – Local-Variable Syntax for Lambda Parameters

A local-variable syntax for lambda parameters has the same syntax as a local-variable-declaration using the reserved var type introduced in Java 11. See the *Using local variable syntax for lambda parameters* recipe in Chapter 15, *The New Way of Coding with Java 10 and Java 11,* for more details.

JEP 333 – ZGC

The **Z Garbage Collector** (**ZGC**) is an experimental low-latency garbage collector. Its pause times should not exceed 10 ms and there should be no more than 15% application throughput reduction compared to using the G1 collector. ZGC also lays a foundation for future features and optimizations. Linux/x64 will be the first platform to get ZGC support.

New API

There are several additions to the standard Java API:

- `Character.toString(int codePoint)`: Returns a `String` object representing the character specified by the provided Unicode code point:

  ```
  var s = Character.toString(50);
  System.out.println(s);  //prints: 2
  ```

- CharSequence.compare(CharSequence s1, CharSequence s2):
  Compares two CharSequence instances lexicographically. Returns the
  difference between the position of the second parameter and the position of
  the first parameter in the ordered list:

  ```
  var i = CharSequence.compare("a", "b");
  System.out.println(i);   //prints: -1

  i = CharSequence.compare("b", "a");
  System.out.println(i);   //prints: 1

  i = CharSequence.compare("this", "that");
  System.out.println(i);   //prints: 8

  i = CharSequence.compare("that", "this");
  System.out.println(i);   //prints: -8
  ```

- The repeat(int count) method of the String class: Returns a String
  value composed of count times repeated in the String source value:

  ```
  String s1 = "a";
  String s2 = s1.repeat(3); //prints: aaa
  System.out.println(s2);

  String s3 = "bar".repeat(3);
  System.out.println(s3); //prints: barbarbar
  ```

- The isBlank() method of the String class: Returns true if the
  String value is empty or contains only white spaces, otherwise false. In
  our example, we have contrasted it with the isEmpty() method, which
  returns true if, and only if, length() is zero:

  ```
  String s1 = "a";
  System.out.println(s1.isBlank());   //false
  System.out.println(s1.isEmpty());   //false

  String s2 = "";
  System.out.println(s2.isBlank());   //true
  System.out.println(s2.isEmpty());   //true

  String s3 = "   ";
  System.out.println(s3.isBlank());   //true
  System.out.println(s3.isEmpty());   //false
  ```

- The `lines()` method of the `String` class: Returns a `Stream` object that emits lines extracted from the source `String` value, separated by line terminators – \n, \r, or \r\n:

```
String s = "l1 \nl2 \rl3 \r\nl4 ";
s.lines().forEach(System.out::print); //prints: l1 l2 l3 l4
```

- Three methods of the `String` class that remove leading space, trailing space, or both from the source `String` value:

```
String s = " a b ";
System.out.println("'" + s.strip() + "'");          // 'a b'
System.out.println("'" + s.stripLeading() + "'"); // 'a b '
System.out.println("'" + s.stripTrailing() + "'");// ' a b'
```

- Two `Path.of()` methods that construct a `java.nio.file.Path` object:

```
Path filePath = Path.of("a", "b", "c.txt");
System.out.println(filePath);       //prints: a/b/c.txt

try {
    filePath = Path.of(new URI("file:/a/b/c.txt"));
    System.out.println(filePath);  //prints: /a/b/c.txt
} catch (URISyntaxException e) {
    e.printStackTrace();
}
```

- The `asMatchPredicate()` method of the `java.util.regex.Pattern` class, which creates an object of the `java.util.function.Predicate` functional interface, which then allows us to test a `String` value for matching the compiled pattern. In the following example, we test whether a `String` value starts with the a character and ends with the b character:

```
Pattern pattern = Pattern.compile("^a.*z$");
Predicate<String> predicate = pattern.asMatchPredicate();
System.out.println(predicate.test("abbbbz")); // true
System.out.println(predicate.test("babbbz")); // false
System.out.println(predicate.test("abbbbx")); // false
```

There's more...

There are quite a few other changes introduced in JDK 18.9:

- The Java EE and CORBA modules are removed
- JavaFX is separated and removed from the Java standard libraries
- The Pack200 and Unpack200 tools and the Pack200 API in `util.jar` are deprecated
- The Nashorn JavaScript engine, along with the JJS tool, are deprecated with the intent to remove them in the future
- The Java class file format is extended to support a new constant pool form, `CONSTANT_Dynamic`
- Aarch64 intrinsics are improved, with the implementation of new intrinsics for the `java.lang.Math` sin, cos, and log functions, on Aarch64 processorsJEP 309—Dynamic Class-File Constants
- Flight Recorder provides a low-overhead data-collection framework for troubleshooting both Java applications and the HotSpot JVM
- The Java launcher can now run a program supplied as a single file of Java source code, so these programs can run directly from the source
- A low-overhead heap profiling, providing a way to sample Java heap allocations, is accessible via JVM Tool Interface
- **Transport Layer Security** (**TLS**) 1.3 increases security and improves performance
- Support of Unicode version 10.0 in the `java.lang.Character`, `java.lang.String`, `java.awt.font.NumericShaper`, `java.text.Bidi`, `java.text.Break Iterator`, and `java.text.Normalizer` classes

Read the Java 11 (JDK 18.9) release notes for more details and other changes.

Using application class-data sharing

This feature has existed in Java since Java 5. It was extended in Java 9 as a commercial feature by allowing not only bootstrap classes but also application classes to be placed in the archive shared by JVMs. In Java 10, this feature became part of the open JDK. It decreases startup time and, when several JVMs are running on the same machine with the same application being deployed, reduces memory consumption.

Getting ready

The advantages of loading classes from the shared archive became possible for two reasons:

- The classes stored in the archive are preprocessed, which means that the JVM memory mapping is stored in the archive too. It reduces the overhead of class-loading when a JVM instance starts.
- The memory region can even be shared between the JVM instances running on the same computer, which reduces overall memory consumption by eliminating the need to replicate the same information in each instance.

The new JVM functionality allows us to create a list of classes to be shared, then use this list to create a shared archive, and use the shared archive to fast-load archived classes into memory.

How to do it...

1. By default, JVM can create an archive using the list of classes that comes with JDK. For example, run the following command:

   ```
   java -Xshare:dump
   ```

   It will create the shared archive as a `classes.jsa` file. On a Linux system, this file is placed in the following folder:

   ```
   /Library/Java/JavaVirtualMachines/jdk-11.jdk/Contents/Home/lib/ser
   ver
   ```

   On a Windows system, it is placed in the following folder:
   ```
   C:\Program Files\Java\jdk-11\bin\server
   ```

   If this folder is accessible by the system admin only, run the command as an admin.

   Please notice that not all classes can be shared. For example, the `.class` files located in the directory on the classpath and classes loaded by custom class loaders cannot be added to the shared archive.

2. To tell the JVM to use the default shared archive, use the following command:

```
java -Xshare:on -jar app.jar
```

The preceding command maps the content of the archive at a fixed address. This memory-mapping operation may occasionally fail when the required address space is not available. If that happens when the -Xshare:on option is used, the JVM exits with an error. Alternatively, the -Xshare:auto option can be used, which just disables the feature and loads the classes from the classpath if the shared archive cannot be used for whatever reason.

3. The simplest way to create a list of loaded application classes is by using the following command:

```
java -XX:+UseAppCDS -XX:DumpLoadedClassList=classes.txt -jar
app.jar
```

The preceding command records all the loaded classes in the classes.txt file. If you would like to make your application load faster, stop the JVM just after the application has been started. If you need it to load certain classes faster but these classes are not loaded at the application startup automatically, make sure that the use cases that require these classes are executed.

4. Alternatively, you can manually edit the classes.txt file and add/remove any classes you need to put in the shared archive. Create this file once automatically and see the format. It is a simple text file that lists one class in each line.

5. Once the list is created, use the following command to generate the shared archive:

```
java -XX:+UseAppCDS -Xshare:dump -
XX:SharedClassListFile=classes.txt -XX:SharedArchiveFile=app-
shared.jsa --class-path app.jar
```

Notice that the shared archive file has a name other than classes.jsa, so the default shared archive is not overwritten.

6. Use the created archive by executing the following command:

```
java -XX:+UseAppCDS -Xshare:on -XX:SharedArchiveFile=app-
shared.jsa -jar app.jar
```

Again, you can use the `-Xshare:auto` option to avoid an unexpected exit of the JVM.

The effect of the shared archive usage depends on the number of classes in it and other particulars of the application. So, we recommend you experiment and test various configurations before committing to a certain list of classes in production.

Fast Track to OOP - Classes and Interfaces

2

In this chapter, we will cover the following recipes:

- Implementing **Object-Oriented Design (OOD)**
- Using inner classes
- Using inheritance and aggregation
- Coding to an interface
- Creating interfaces with default and static methods
- Creating interfaces with private methods
- A better way to work with nulls using `Optional`
- Using the utility class `Objects`

The recipes in this chapter do not require any prior knowledge of OOD. However, some experience of writing code in Java would be beneficial. The code samples in this chapter are fully functional and compatible with Java 11. For better understanding, we recommend that you try to run the presented examples.

We also encourage you to adapt the tips and recommendations in this chapter to your needs in the context of your team experience. Consider sharing your newfound knowledge with your colleagues and discuss how the described principles can be applied to your domain and your current project.

Introduction

This chapter gives you a quick introduction to the concepts of **object-oriented programming (OOP)** and covers some enhancements that have been introduced since Java 8. We will also try to cover a few good OOD practices wherever applicable and demonstrate them using specific code examples.

One can spend many hours reading articles and practical advice on OOD in books and on the internet. Doing this can be beneficial for some people. But, in our experience, the fastest way to get hold of OOD is to try its principles early in your own code. That is exactly the goal of this chapter—to give you a chance to see and use the OOD principles so that the formal definition makes sense immediately.

One of the main criteria of well-written code is the clarity of the intent. A well-motivated and clear design helps achieve this. The code is run by a computer, but it is maintained—read and modified—by humans. Keeping this in mind will assure the longevity of your code and perhaps even a few thanks and mentions with appreciation from those who have to deal with it later.

In this chapter, you will learn how to use the five basic OOP concepts:

- **Object/class**: Keeping data and methods together
- **Encapsulation**: Hiding data and/or methods
- **Inheritance**: Extending another class data and/or methods
- **Interface**: Hiding the implementation and coding for a type
- **Polymorphism**: Using the base class type reference that points to a child class object

If you search the internet, you may notice that many other concepts and additions to them, as well as all OOD principles, can be derived from the five concepts listed previously. This means that a solid understanding of them is a prerequisite to a successful design of an object-oriented system.

Implementing object-oriented design (OOD)

In this recipe, you will learn the first two OOP concepts—object/class and encapsulation. These concepts are at the foundation of OOD.

Getting ready

The term *object* usually refers to an entity that couples data and procedures that can be applied to this data. Neither data nor procedures are required, but one of them is—and, typically, both are—always present. The data is called object fields (or properties), while procedures are called methods. Field values describe the object's *state*. Methods describe the object's *behavior*. Every object has a type, which is defined by its class—the template used for the object's creation. An object is also said to be an instance of a class.

A *class* is a collection of definitions of fields and methods that will be present in each of its instances—the objects created based on this class.
Encapsulation is the hiding of those fields and methods that should not be accessible by other objects.

Encapsulation is achieved by using the `public`, `protected`, or `private` Java keywords, called *access modifiers,* in the declaration of the fields and methods. There is also a default level of encapsulation when no access modifier is specified.

How to do it...

1. Create an `Engine` class with the `horsePower` field. Add the `setHorsePower(int horsePower)` method, which sets this field's value, and the `getSpeedMph(double timeSec, int weightPounds)` method, which calculates the speed of a vehicle based on the period of time passed since the vehicle began moving, the vehicle weight, and the engine power:

```java
public class Engine {
   private int horsePower;
   public void setHorsePower(int horsePower) {
      this.horsePower = horsePower;
   }
   public double getSpeedMph(double timeSec, int weightPounds){
      double v = 2.0 * this.horsePower * 746 * timeSec *
                                   32.17 / weightPounds;
      return Math.round(Math.sqrt(v) * 0.68);
   }
}
```

2. Create the `Vehicle` class:

```java
public class Vehicle {
    private int weightPounds;
    private Engine engine;
    public Vehicle(int weightPounds, Engine engine) {
        this.weightPounds = weightPounds;
        this.engine = engine;
    }
    public double getSpeedMph(double timeSec){
        return this.engine.getSpeedMph(timeSec, weightPounds);
    }
}
```

3. Create the application that will use the preceding classes:

```java
public static void main(String... arg) {
    double timeSec = 10.0;
    int horsePower = 246;
    int vehicleWeight = 4000;
    Engine engine = new Engine();
    engine.setHorsePower(horsePower);
    Vehicle vehicle = new Vehicle(vehicleWeight, engine);
    System.out.println("Vehicle speed (" + timeSec + " sec)="
                    + vehicle.getSpeedMph(timeSec) + " mph");
}
```

As you can see, the `engine` object was created by invoking the default constructor of the `Engine` class without parameters and with the new Java keyword that allocates memory for the newly created object on the heap.

The second object, `vehicle`, was created with the explicitly defined constructor of the `Vehicle` class with two parameters. The second parameter of the constructor is the `engine` object, which carries the `horsePower` value set to `246` using the `setHorsePower(int horsePower)` method.

The `engine` object contains the `getSpeedMph(double timeSec, int weightPounds)` method, which can be called by any object (because it is `public`), as is done in the `getSpeedMph(double timeSec)` method of the `Vehicle` class.

How it works...

The preceding application produces the following output:

```
Vehicle speed (10.0 sec) = 117.0 mph
```

It's worth noticing that the getSpeedMph(double timeSec) method of
the Vehicle class relies on the presence of a value assigned to the engine field. This
way, the object of the Vehicle class *delegates* the speed calculation to the object of
the Engine class. If the latter is not set (null passed in the Vehicle() constructor,
for example), NullPointerException will be thrown at the runtime and, if not
handled by the application, will be caught by JVM and force it to exit. To avoid this,
we can place a check for the presence of the engine field value in the Vehicle()
constructor:

```
if(engine == null){
    throw new RuntimeException("Engine" + " is required parameter.");
}
```

Alternatively, we can place a check in the getSpeedMph(double timeSec) method
of the Vehicle class:

```
if(getEngine() == null){
    throw new RuntimeException("Engine value is required.");
}
```

This way, we avoid the ambiguity of NullPointerException and tell the user
exactly what the source of the problem was.

As you may have noticed, the getSpeedMph(double timeSec, int
weightPounds) method can be removed from the Engine class and can be fully
implemented in the Vehicle class:

```
public double getSpeedMph(double timeSec){
    double v =  2.0 * this.engine.getHorsePower() * 746 *
                            timeSec * 32.17 / this.weightPounds;
    return Math.round(Math.sqrt(v) * 0.68);
}
```

To do this, we would need to add the `getHorsePower()` public method to the `Engine` class in order to make it available for usage by the `getSpeedMph(double timeSec)` method in the `Vehicle` class. For now, we leave the `getSpeedMph(double timeSec, int weightPounds)` method in the `Engine` class.

This is one of the design decisions you need to make. If you think that an object of the `Engine` class is going to be passed around and used by the objects of different classes (not only `Vehicle`), you would need to keep the `getSpeedMph(double timeSec, int weightPounds)` method in the `Engine` class. Otherwise, if you think that only the `Vehicle` class is going to be responsible for the speed calculation (which makes sense, since it is the speed of a vehicle, not of an engine), you should implement this method inside the `Vehicle` class.

There's more...

Java provides a capability to extend a class and allows the subclass to access all non-private fields and methods of the base class. For example, you can decide that every object that could be asked about its speed belongs to a subclass that is derived from the `Vehicle` class. In such a case, the `Car` class may look like this:

```
public class Car extends Vehicle {
  private int passengersCount;
  public Car(int passengersCount, int weightPounds, Engine engine){
    super(weightPounds, engine);
    this.passengersCount = passengersCount;
  }
  public int getPassengersCount() {
    return this.passengersCount;
  }
}
```

Now, we can change our test code by replacing the `Vehicle` class object with the object of the `Car` class:

```
public static void main(String... arg) {
  double timeSec = 10.0;
  int horsePower = 246;
  int vehicleWeight = 4000;
  Engine engine = new Engine();
  engine.setHorsePower(horsePower);
  Vehicle vehicle = new Car(4, vehicleWeight, engine);
```

```
System.out.println("Car speed (" + timeSec + " sec) = " +
                        vehicle.getSpeedMph(timeSec) + " mph");
}
```

When the preceding code is executed, it produces the same value as with an object of the Vehicle class:

```
Car speed (10.0 sec) = 117.0 mph
```

Because of polymorphism, a reference to the object of the Car class can be assigned to the reference of its base class, Vehicle. The Car class object has two types—its own type, Car, and the type of the base class, Vehicle.

In Java, a class can also implement multiple interfaces, and the object of such a class would have a type of each of the implemented interfaces, too. We will talk about this in the subsequent recipes.

Using inner classes

In this recipe, you will learn about three types of inner classes:

- **Inner class**: This is a class defined inside another (enclosing) class. Its accessibility from outside the enclosing class is regulated by the public, protected, and private access modifiers. An inner class can access the private members of the enclosing class, and the enclosing class can access the private members of its inner class, but a private inner class or private members of a non-private inner class cannot be accessed from outside the enclosing class.
- **Method-local inner class**: This is a class defined inside a method. Its accessibility is restricted to within the method.
- **Anonymous inner class**: This is a class without a declared name that's defined during object instantiation based on the interface only or the extended class.

Getting ready

When a class is used by one, and only one, other class, the designer might decide that there is no need to make such a class public. For example, let's assume that the `Engine` class is only used by the `Vehicle` class.

How to do it...

1. Create the `Engine` class as an inner class of the `Vehicle` class:

```
public class Vehicle {
  private int weightPounds;
  private Engine engine;
  public Vehicle(int weightPounds, int horsePower) {
    this.weightPounds = weightPounds;
    this.engine = new Engine(horsePower);
  }
  public double getSpeedMph(double timeSec){
    return this.engine.getSpeedMph(timeSec);
  }
  private int getWeightPounds(){ return weightPounds; }
  private class Engine {
    private int horsePower;
    private Engine(int horsePower) {
      this.horsePower = horsePower;
    }
    private double getSpeedMph(double timeSec){
      double v = 2.0 * this.horsePower * 746 *
                  timeSec * 32.17 / getWeightPounds();
      return Math.round(Math.sqrt(v) * 0.68);
    }
  }
}
```

2. Notice that the `getSpeedMph(double timeSec)` method of the `Vehicle` class can access the `Engine` class, even though it is declared private. It can even access the `getSpeedMph(double timeSec)` private method of the `Engine` class. And the inner class can access all private elements of the enclosing class, too. That is why the `getSpeedMph(double timeSec)` method of the `Engine` class can access the private `getWeightPounds()` method of the enclosing `Vehicle` class.

3. Look closer at the usage of the inner `Engine` class. Only the `getSpeedMph(double timeSec)` method of the `Engine` class is used. If the designer believes that it is going to be the case in the future too, they could reasonably decide to make the `Engine` class a method-local inner class, which is the second type of an inner class:

```java
public class Vehicle {
    private int weightPounds;
    private int horsePower;
    public Vehicle(int weightPounds, int horsePower) {
        this.weightPounds = weightPounds;
        this.horsePower = horsePower;
    }
    private int getWeightPounds() { return weightPounds; }
    public double getSpeedMph(double timeSec){
        class Engine {
            private int horsePower;
            private Engine(int horsePower) {
                this.horsePower = horsePower;
            }
            private double getSpeedMph(double timeSec){
                double v = 2.0 * this.horsePower * 746 *
                        timeSec * 32.17 / getWeightPounds();
                return Math.round(Math.sqrt(v) * 0.68);
            }
        }
        Engine engine = new Engine(this.horsePower);
        return engine.getSpeedMph(timeSec);
    }
}
```

In the preceding code example, it does not make sense to have an `Engine` class at all. The speed-calculation formula can be just used directly, without the mediation of the `Engine` class. But there are cases when this might be not so easy to do. For example, the method-local inner class may need to extend some other class in order to inherit its functionality, or the created `Engine` object may need to go through some transformation, so creation is required. Other considerations may require a method-local inner class.

In any case, it is a good practice to make all the functionality that is not required to be accessed from outside the enclosing class inaccessible. Encapsulation—hiding the state and behavior of objects—helps avoid unexpected side effects resulting from an accidental change or overriding object behavior. It makes the results more predictable. That's why a good design exposes only the functionality that must be accessed from the outside. And it is usually the enclosing class functionality that motivated the class creation in the first place, not the inner class or other implementation details.

How it works...

Whether the `Engine` class is implemented as an inner class or a method-local inner class, the test code looks the same:

```java
public static void main(String arg[]) {
    double timeSec = 10.0;
    int engineHorsePower = 246;
    int vehicleWeightPounds = 4000;
    Vehicle vehicle =
            new Vehicle(vehicleWeightPounds, engineHorsePower);
    System.out.println("Vehicle speed (" + timeSec + " sec) = "
                    + vehicle.getSpeedMph(timeSec) + " mph");
}
```

If we run the preceding program, we get the same output:

```
Car speed (10.0 sec) = 117.0 mph
```

Now, let's assume that we need to test a different implementation of the `getSpeedMph()` method:

```java
public double getSpeedMph(double timeSec){ return -1.0d;  }
```

If this speed-calculation formula does not make sense to you, you are correct, it does not. We did it to make the result predictable and different from the result of the previous implementation.

There are many ways to introduce this new implementation. We can change the code of the `getSpeedMph(double timeSec)` method in the `Engine` class, for example. Or, we can change the implementation of the same method in the `Vehicle` class.

In this recipe, we will do this by using the third type of inner class, called the anonymous inner class. This approach is especially handy when you want to write as little new code as possible, or you want to quickly test the new behavior by temporarily overriding the old one. The usage of an anonymous class would then look like the following:

```
public static void main(String... arg) {
    double timeSec = 10.0;
    int engineHorsePower = 246;
    int vehicleWeightPounds = 4000;
    Vehicle vehicle =
        new Vehicle(vehicleWeightPounds, engineHorsePower) {
            public double getSpeedMph(double timeSec){
                return -1.0d;
            }
        };
    System.out.println("Vehicle speed (" + timeSec + " sec) = "
                    + vehicle.getSpeedMph(timeSec) + " mph");
}
```

If we run this program, this would be the result:

```
Vehicle speed (10.0 sec) = -1.0 mph
```

As you can see, the anonymous class implementation has overridden the Vehicle class implementation. The new anonymous class has only one method in it—the getSpeedMph() method which returns the hardcoded value. But we could override other methods of the Vehicle class or add new ones too. We just wanted to keep the example simple for demonstration purposes.

By definition, an anonymous inner class has to be an expression that is part of a statement that ends (as any statement) with a semicolon. Such an expression is composed of the following parts:

- The new operator
- The name of the implemented interface or extended class followed by parentheses, (), that represents the default constructor or a constructor of the extended class (the latter is our case, with the extended class being Vehicle)
- The class body with methods

Like any inner class, an anonymous inner class can access any member of the enclosing class with a caveat—to be used by an inner anonymous class, the fields of the enclosing class have to be either declared `final` or become `final` implicitly, which means that their values cannot be changed. A good modern IDE will warn you about the violation of this constraint if you try to change such a value.

Using these features, we can modify our sample code and provide more input data for the newly implemented `getSpeedMph(double timeSec)` method without passing them as method parameters:

```java
public static void main(String... arg) {
  double timeSec = 10.0;
  int engineHorsePower = 246;
  int vehicleWeightPounds = 4000;
  Vehicle vehicle =
    new Vehicle(vehicleWeightPounds, engineHorsePower){
      public double getSpeedMph(double timeSec){
        double v = 2.0 * engineHorsePower * 746 *
            timeSec * 32.17 / vehicleWeightPounds;
        return Math.round(Math.sqrt(v) * 0.68);
      }
    };
  System.out.println("Vehicle speed (" + timeSec + " sec) = "
                + vehicle.getSpeedMph(timeSec) + " mph");
}
```

Notice that the `timeSec`, `engineHorsePower`, and `vehicleWeightPounds` variables are accessible by the `getSpeedMph(double timeSec)` method of the inner class and cannot be modified. If we run the preceding code, the result will be the same as before:

```
Car speed (10.0 sec) = 117.0 mph
```

In the case of an interface with only one abstract method (called the functional interface), instead of an anonymous inner class, another construct can be used, called a *lambda expression*. It provides a shorter notation. We are going to discuss the functional interface and lambda expressions in Chapter 4, *Going Functional*.

There's more...

An inner class is a non-static nested class. Java also allows us to create a static nested class that can be used when an inner class does not require access to non-static fields and methods of the enclosing class. Here is an example (the `static` keyword is added to the `Engine` class):

```
public class Vehicle {
  private Engine engine;
  public Vehicle(int weightPounds, int horsePower) {
    this.engine = new Engine(horsePower, weightPounds)
  }
  public double getSpeedMph(double timeSec){
    return this.engine.getSpeedMph(timeSec);
  }
  private static class Engine {
    private int horsePower;
    private int weightPounds;
    private Engine(int horsePower, int weightPounds) {
      this.horsePower = horsePower;
    }
    private double getSpeedMph(double timeSec){
      double v = 2.0 * this.horsePower * 746 *
                      timeSec * 32.17 / this.weightPounds;
      return Math.round(Math.sqrt(v) * 0.68);
    }
  }
}
```

Because a static class couldn't access a non-static member, we were forced to pass the weight value to the `Engine` class during its construction, and we removed the `getWeightPounds()` method as it's no longer needed.

Using inheritance and aggregation

In this recipe, you will learn more about two important OOP concepts, inheritance and polymorphism, which have been mentioned already and used in the examples of the previous recipes. Together with aggregation, these concepts make the design more extensible.

Getting ready

 Inheritance is the ability of one class to get ownership of the non-private fields and methods of another class.

The extended class is called the base class, superclass, or parent class. The new extension of the class is called a subclass or child class.

 Polymorphism is the ability to use the base class type for the reference to an object of its subclass.

To demonstrate the power of inheritance and polymorphism, let's create classes that represent cars and trucks, each with the weight, engine power, and speed it can reach (as a function of time) with the maximum load. In addition, a car, in this case, will be characterized by the number of passengers, while a truck's important feature will be its payload.

How to do it...

1. Look at the `Vehicle` class:

```java
public class Vehicle {
  private int weightPounds, horsePower;
  public Vehicle(int weightPounds, int horsePower) {
    this.weightPounds = weightPounds;
    this.horsePower = horsePower;
  }
  public double getSpeedMph(double timeSec){
    double v = 2.0 * this.horsePower * 746 *
            timeSec * 32.17 / this.weightPounds;
    return Math.round(Math.sqrt(v) * 0.68);
  }
}
```

The functionality implemented in the `Vehicle` class is not specific to a car or to a truck, so it makes sense to use this class as a base class for the `Car` and `Truck` classes, so each of them gets this functionality as its own.

2. Create the `Car` class:

```
public class Car extends Vehicle {
  private int passengersCount;
  public Car(int passengersCount, int weightPounds,
                                   int horsepower){
    super(weightPounds, horsePower);
    this.passengersCount = passengersCount;
  }
  public int getPassengersCount() {
    return this.passengersCount;
  }
}
```

3. Create the `Truck` class:

```
public class Truck extends Vehicle {
  private int payload;
  public Truck(int payloadPounds, int weightPounds,
                                   int horsePower){
    super(weightPounds, horsePower);
    this.payload = payloadPounds;
  }
  public int getPayload() {
    return this.payload;
  }
}
```

Since the `Vehicle` base class has neither an implicit nor explicit constructor without parameters (because we have chosen to use an explicit constructor with parameters only), we had to call the base class constructor `super()` as the first line of the constructor of every subclass of the `Vehicle` class.

How it works...

Let's write a test program:

```
public static void main(String... arg) {
  double timeSec = 10.0;
  int engineHorsePower = 246;
  int vehicleWeightPounds = 4000;
  Vehicle vehicle = new Car(4, vehicleWeightPounds, engineHorsePower);
  System.out.println("Passengers count=" +
                            ((Car)vehicle).getPassengersCount());
  System.out.println("Car speed (" + timeSec + " sec) = " +
                            vehicle.getSpeedMph(timeSec) + " mph");
```

```
    vehicle = new Truck(3300, vehicleWeightPounds, engineHorsePower);
    System.out.println("Payload=" +
                            ((Truck)vehicle).getPayload() + " pounds");
    System.out.println("Truck speed (" + timeSec + " sec) = " +
                            vehicle.getSpeedMph(timeSec) + " mph");
}
```

Notice that the `vehicle` reference of the `Vehicle` type points to the object of the `Car` subclass and later to the object of the `Truck` subclass. This is possible thanks to polymorphism, according to which an object has a type of every class in its line of inheritance, including all the interfaces.

If you need to invoke a method that exists only in the subclass, you have to cast such a reference to the subclass type, as was done in the previous example.

The results of the preceding code are as follows:

```
Passengers count=4
Car speed (10.0 sec) = 117.0 mph
Payload=3300 pounds
Truck speed (10.0 sec) = 117.0 mph
```

We should not be surprised to see the same speed calculated for both the car and the truck because the same weight and engine power are used to calculate the speed of each. But, intuitively, we feel that a heavily loaded truck should not be able to reach the same speed as a car in the same period of time. To verify this, we need to include the total weight of the car (with the passengers and their luggage) and that of the truck (with the payload) in the calculations of the speed. One way to do this is to override the `getSpeedMph(double timeSec)` method of the `Vehicle` base class in each of the subclasses.

We can add the `getSpeedMph(double timeSec)` method to the `Car` class, which will override the method with the same signature in the base class. This method will use car-specific weight calculation:

```
public double getSpeedMph(double timeSec) {
   int weight = this.weightPounds + this.passengersCount * 250;
   double v = 2.0 * this.horsePower * 746 * timeSec * 32.17 / weight;
   return Math.round(Math.sqrt(v) * 0.68);
}
```

In the preceding code, we have assumed that a passenger with luggage weighs 250 pounds total on average.

Similarly, we can add the `getSpeedMph(double timeSec)` method to the `Truck` class:

```
public double getSpeedMph(double timeSec) {
    int weight = this.weightPounds + this.payload;
    double v = 2.0 * this.horsePower * 746 * timeSec * 32.17 / weight;
    return Math.round(Math.sqrt(v) * 0.68);
}
```

The results of these modifications (if we run the same test class) will be as follows:

```
Passengers count=4
Car speed (10.0 sec) = 105.0 mph
Payload=3300 pounds
Truck speed (10.0 sec) = 86.0 mph
```

The results confirm our intuition—a fully loaded car or truck does not reach the same speed as an empty one.

The new methods in the subclasses override `getSpeedMph(double timeSec)` of the `Vehicle` base class, although we access it via the base class reference:

```
Vehicle vehicle =   new Car(4, vehicleWeightPounds, engineHorsePower);
System.out.println("Car speed (" + timeSec + " sec) = " +
                          vehicle.getSpeedMph(timeSec) + " mph");
```

The overridden method is dynamically bound, which means that the context of the method invocation is determined by the type of the actual object being referred to. Since, in our example, the reference `vehicle` points to an object of the `Car` subclass, the `vehicle.getSpeedMph(double timeSec)` construct invokes the method of the subclass, not the method of the base class.

There is obvious code redundancy in the two new methods, which we can refactor by creating a method in the `Vehicle` base class and then use it in each of the subclasses:

```
protected double getSpeedMph(double timeSec, int weightPounds) {
    double v = 2.0 * this.horsePower * 746 *
                              timeSec * 32.17 / weightPounds;
    return Math.round(Math.sqrt(v) * 0.68);
}
```

Since this method is used by subclasses only, it can be `protected` and thus, accessible only to the subclasses.

Now, we can change the `getSpeedMph(double timeSec)` method in the `Car` class, as follows:

```
public double getSpeedMph(double timeSec) {
   int weightPounds = this.weightPounds + this.passengersCount * 250;
   return getSpeedMph(timeSec, weightPounds);
}
```

In the preceding code, there was no need to use the `super` keyword while calling the `getSpeedMph(timeSec, weightPounds)` method because a method with such a signature exists only in the `Vehicle` base class, and there is no ambiguity about it.

Similar changes can be made in the `getSpeedMph(double timeSec)` method of the `Truck` class:

```
public double getSpeedMph(double timeSec) {
   int weightPounds = this.weightPounds + this.payload;
   return getSpeedMph(timeSec, weightPounds);
}
```

Now, we need to modify the test class by adding casting, otherwise there will be a runtime error because the `getSpeedMph(double timeSec)` method does not exist in the `Vehicle` base class:

```
public static void main(String... arg) {
    double timeSec = 10.0;
    int engineHorsePower = 246;
    int vehicleWeightPounds = 4000;
    Vehicle vehicle = new Car(4, vehicleWeightPounds,
    engineHorsePower);
    System.out.println("Passengers count=" +
    ((Car)vehicle).getPassengersCount());
    System.out.println("Car speed (" + timeSec + " sec) = " +
                  ((Car)vehicle).getSpeedMph(timeSec) + " mph");
    vehicle = new Truck(3300, vehicleWeightPounds, engineHorsePower);
    System.out.println("Payload=" +
                  ((Truck)vehicle).getPayload() + " pounds");
    System.out.println("Truck speed (" + timeSec + " sec) = " +
                  ((Truck)vehicle).getSpeedMph(timeSec) + " mph");
   }
}
```

As you may have expected, the test class produces the same values:

```
Passengers count=4
Car speed (10.0 sec) = 105.0 mph
Payload=3300 pounds
Truck speed (10.0 sec) = 86.0 mph
```

To simplify the test code, we can drop casting and write the following instead:

```java
public static void main(String... arg) {
    double timeSec = 10.0;
    int engineHorsePower = 246;
    int vehicleWeightPounds = 4000;
    Car car = new Car(4, vehicleWeightPounds, engineHorsePower);
    System.out.println("Passengers count=" + car.getPassengersCount());
    System.out.println("Car speed (" + timeSec + " sec) = " +
                                    car.getSpeedMph(timeSec) + " mph");
    Truck truck =
                new Truck(3300, vehicleWeightPounds, engineHorsePower);
    System.out.println("Payload=" + truck.getPayload() + " pounds");
    System.out.println("Truck speed (" + timeSec + " sec) = " +
                                    truck.getSpeedMph(timeSec) + " mph");
}
```

The speed values produced by this code remain the same.

Yet, there is an even simpler way to achieve the same effect. We can add the getMaxWeightPounds() method to the base class and each of the subclasses. The Car class will now look as follows:

```java
public class Car extends Vehicle {
    private int passengersCount, weightPounds;
    public Car(int passengersCount, int weightPounds, int horsePower){
        super(weightPounds, horsePower);
        this.passengersCount = passengersCount;
        this.weightPounds = weightPounds;
    }
    public int getPassengersCount() {
        return this.passengersCount;
    }
    public int getMaxWeightPounds() {
        return this.weightPounds + this.passengersCount * 250;
    }
}
```

And here's what the new version of the `Truck` class looks like now:

```
public class Truck extends Vehicle {
  private int payload, weightPounds;
  public Truck(int payloadPounds, int weightPounds, int horsePower) {
    super(weightPounds, horsePower);
    this.payload = payloadPounds;
    this.weightPounds = weightPounds;
  }
  public int getPayload() { return this.payload; }
  public int getMaxWeightPounds() {
    return this.weightPounds + this.payload;
  }
}
```

We also need to add the `getMaxWeightPounds()` method to the base class so that it can be used for the speed calculations:

```
public abstract class Vehicle {
  private int weightPounds, horsePower;
  public Vehicle(int weightPounds, int horsePower) {
    this.weightPounds = weightPounds;
    this.horsePower = horsePower;
  }
  public abstract int getMaxWeightPounds();
  public double getSpeedMph(double timeSec){
    double v = 2.0 * this.horsePower * 746 *
                          timeSec * 32.17 / getMaxWeightPounds();
    return Math.round(Math.sqrt(v) * 0.68);
  }
}
```

Adding an abstract method, `getMaxWeightPounds()`, to the `Vehicle` class makes the class abstract. This has a positive side effect—it enforces the implementation of the `getMaxWeightPounds()` method in each subclass. Otherwise, a subclass cannot be instantiated and has to be declared abstract too.

The test class remains the same and produces the same results:

```
Passengers count=4
Car speed (10.0 sec) = 105.0 mph
Payload=3300 pounds
Truck speed (10.0 sec) = 86.0 mph
```

But, to be honest, we did it just to demonstrate one possible way of using an abstract method and class. In fact, an even simpler solution would be to pass the maximum weight as a parameter into the constructor of the `Vehicle` base class. The resulting classes will look like this:

```
public class Car extends Vehicle {
  private int passengersCount;
  public Car(int passengersCount, int weightPounds, int horsepower){
    super(weightPounds + passengersCount * 250, horsePower);
    this.passengersCount = passengersCount;
  }
  public int getPassengersCount() {
    return this.passengersCount; }
}
```

We added the weight of the passengers to the value we pass to the constructor of the superclass; this is the only change in this subclass. Here is a similar change in the `Truck` class:

```
public class Truck extends Vehicle {
  private int payload;
  public Truck(int payloadPounds, int weightPounds, int horsePower) {
    super(weightPounds + payloadPounds, horsePower);
    this.payload = payloadPounds;
  }
  public int getPayload() { return this.payload; }
}
```

The `Vehicle` base class remains the same as the original one:

```
public class Vehicle {
  private int weightPounds, horsePower;
  public Vehicle(int weightPounds, int horsePower) {
    this.weightPounds = weightPounds;
    this.horsePower = horsePower;
  }
  public double getSpeedMph(double timeSec){
    double v = 2.0 * this.horsePower * 746;
    v = v * timeSec * 32.174 / this.weightPounds;
    return Math.round(Math.sqrt(v) * 0.68);
  }
}
```

The test class does not change and produces the same results:

```
Passengers count=4
Car speed (10.0 sec) = 105.0 mph
Payload=3300 pounds
Truck speed (10.0 sec) = 86.0 mph
```

This last version—passing the maximum weight to the constructor of the base class—will now be the starting point for further code demonstrations.

Aggregation makes the design more extensible

In the preceding example, the speed model was implemented in the `getSpeedMph(double timeSec)` method of the `Vehicle` class. If we need to use a different speed model (which includes more input parameters and is more tuned to certain driving conditions, for example), we would need to change the `Vehicle` class or create a new subclass to override the method. In the case where we need to experiment with dozens or even hundreds of different models, this approach becomes untenable.

Also, in real life, modeling based on machine learning and other advanced techniques become so involved and specialized, that it is quite common that the modeling of car acceleration is done by a different team, not the team that assembles the vehicle model.

To avoid the proliferation of subclasses and code-merge conflicts between vehicle builders and speed-model developers, we can create a more extensible design using aggregation.

 Aggregation is an OOD principle for implementing the necessary functionality using the behavior of classes that are not part of the inheritance hierarchy. That behavior can exist independent of the aggregated functionality.

We can encapsulate the speed calculations inside the `SpeedModel` class in the `getSpeedMph(double timeSec)` method:

```java
public class SpeedModel{
  private Properties conditions;
  public SpeedModel(Properties drivingConditions){
    this.drivingConditions = drivingConditions;
  }
  public double getSpeedMph(double timeSec, int weightPounds,
                                            int horsePower){
    String road =
        drivingConditions.getProperty("roadCondition","Dry");
    String tire =
        drivingConditions.getProperty("tireCondition","New");
    double v = 2.0 * horsePower * 746 * timeSec *
                                  32.17 / weightPounds;
    return Math.round(Math.sqrt(v)*0.68)-road.equals("Dry")? 2 : 5)
                              -(tire.equals("New")? 0 : 5);
  }
}
```

An object of this class can be created and then set as the value of the `Vehicle` class field:

```java
public class Vehicle {
  private SpeedModel speedModel;
  private int weightPounds, horsePower;
  public Vehicle(int weightPounds, int horsePower) {
    this.weightPounds = weightPounds;
    this.horsePower = horsePower;
  }
  public void setSpeedModel(SpeedModel speedModel){
    this.speedModel = speedModel;
  }
  public double getSpeedMph(double timeSec){
    return this.speedModel.getSpeedMph(timeSec,
                  this.weightPounds, this.horsePower);
  }
}
```

The test class changes as follows:

```
public static void main(String... arg) {
    double timeSec = 10.0;
    int horsePower = 246;
    int vehicleWeight = 4000;
    Properties drivingConditions = new Properties();
    drivingConditions.put("roadCondition", "Wet");
    drivingConditions.put("tireCondition", "New");
    SpeedModel speedModel = new SpeedModel(drivingConditions);
    Car car = new Car(4, vehicleWeight, horsePower);
    car.setSpeedModel(speedModel);
    System.out.println("Car speed (" + timeSec + " sec) = " +
                          car.getSpeedMph(timeSec) + " mph");
}
```

The result of the preceding code is as follows:

```
Car speed (10.0 sec) = 100.0 mph
```

We isolated the speed-calculating functionality in a separate class and can now modify or extend it without changing any class of the Vehicle inheritance hierarchy. This is how the aggregation design principle allows you to change the behavior without changing the implementation.

In the next recipe, we will show you how the OOP concept of interface unlocks more power of aggregation and polymorphism, making the design simpler and even more expressive.

Coding to an interface

In this recipe, you will learn the last of the OOP concepts, called interface, and further practice the usage of aggregation and polymorphism as well as inner classes and inheritance.

Getting ready

An interface defines the signatures of the methods one can expect to see in the class that implements the interface. It is the public face of the functionality that's accessible to a client and is thus often called an **Application Program Interface (API)**. It supports polymorphism and aggregation, and facilitates a more flexible and extensible design.

An interface is implicitly abstract, which means it cannot be instantiated. No object can be created based on an interface only, without implementing it. It is used to contain abstract methods (without body) only. But since Java 8, it is possible to add default and private methods to an interface, which is the capability we are going to discuss in the following recipes.

Each interface can extend multiple other interfaces and, similar to class inheritance, inherit all default and abstract methods of the extended interfaces. Static members cannot be inherited because they belong to a specific interface.

How to do it...

1. Create interfaces that describe the API:

```java
public interface SpeedModel {
    double getSpeedMph(double timeSec, int weightPounds,
                                       int horsePower);
}
public interface Vehicle {
    void setSpeedModel(SpeedModel speedModel);
    double getSpeedMph(double timeSec);
}
public interface Car extends Vehicle {
    int getPassengersCount();
}
public interface Truck extends Vehicle {
    int getPayloadPounds();
}
```

2. Use factories, which are classes that generate objects that implement certain interfaces. A factory hides from the client code the details of the implementation, so the client deals with an interface only. It is especially helpful when an instance creation requires a complex process and/or significant code duplication. In our case, it makes sense to have a `FactoryVehicle` class that creates objects of classes that implement the `Vehicle`, `Car`, or `Truck` interface. We will also create the `FactorySpeedModel` class, which generates objects of a class that implements the `SpeedModel` interface. Such an API allows us to write the following code:

```java
public static void main(String... arg) {
    double timeSec = 10.0;
    int horsePower = 246;
    int vehicleWeight = 4000;
    Properties drivingConditions = new Properties();
    drivingConditions.put("roadCondition", "Wet");
    drivingConditions.put("tireCondition", "New");
    SpeedModel speedModel   = FactorySpeedModel.
                    generateSpeedModel(drivingConditions);
    Car car = FactoryVehicle.
                    buildCar(4, vehicleWeight, horsePower);
    car.setSpeedModel(speedModel);
    System.out.println("Car speed (" + timeSec + " sec) = "
                    + car.getSpeedMph(timeSec) + " mph");
}
```

3. Observe that the code behavior is the same as in the previous examples:

```
Car speed (10.0 sec) = 100.0 mph
```

However, the design is much more extensible.

How it works...

We have already seen one possible implementation of the `SpeedModel` interface. Here is another way to do it by aggregating the object of the `SpeedModel` type inside the `FactorySpeedModel` class:

```
public class FactorySpeedModel {
  public static SpeedModel generateSpeedModel(
  Properties drivingConditions){
    //if drivingConditions includes "roadCondition"="Wet"
    return new SpeedModelWet(...);
    //if drivingConditions includes "roadCondition"="Dry"
    return new SpeedModelDry(...);
  }
  private class SpeedModelWet implements SpeedModel{
    public double getSpeedMph(double timeSec, int weightPounds,
                                              int horsePower){
      //method code goes here
    }
  }
  private class SpeedModelDry implements SpeedModel{
    public double getSpeedMph(double timeSec, int weightPounds,
                                              int horsePower){
      //method code goes here
    }
  }
}
```

We put comments as pseudocode, and the . . . symbol instead of the actual code, for brevity.

As you can see, the factory class may hide many different private classes, each containing a specialized model for particular driving conditions. Each model produces a different result.

An implementation of the `FactoryVehicle` class may look like this:

```
public class FactoryVehicle {
  public static Car buildCar(int passengersCount,
                        int weightPounds, int horsePower){
    return new CarImpl(passengersCount, weightPounds,horsePower);
  }
  public static Truck buildTruck(int payloadPounds,
                        int weightPounds, int horsePower){
    return new TruckImpl(payloadPounds, weightPounds,horsePower);
  }
}
```

The `CarImpl` private nested class may look as follows inside the `FactoryVehicle` class:

```
private static class CarImpl extends VehicleImpl implements Car {
   private int passengersCount;
   private CarImpl(int passengersCount, int weightPounds,
                                             int horsePower){
     super(weightPounds + passengersCount * 250, horsePower);
     this.passengersCount = passengersCount;
   }
   public int getPassengersCount() {
     return this.passengersCount;
   }
}
```

Similarly, the `TruckImpl` class can be a private nested class of the `FactoryImpl` class:

```
private static class TruckImpl extends VehicleImpl implements Truck
{
   private int payloadPounds;
   private TruckImpl(int payloadPounds, int weightPounds,
                                             int horsePower){
     super(weightPounds+payloadPounds, horsePower);
     this.payloadPounds = payloadPounds;
   }
   public int getPayloadPounds(){ return payloadPounds; }
}
```

We can place the `VehicleImpl` class as a private inner class of the `FactoryVehicle` class too, so the `CarImpl` and `TruckImpl` classes can access it, but not any other class outside of `FactoryVehicle`:

```
private static abstract class VehicleImpl implements Vehicle {
   private SpeedModel speedModel;
   private int weightPounds, horsePower;
   private VehicleImpl(int weightPounds, int horsePower){
     this.weightPounds = weightPounds;
     this.horsePower = horsePower;
   }
   public void setSpeedModel(SpeedModel speedModel){
     this.speedModel = speedModel;
   }
   public double getSpeedMph(double timeSec){
     return this.speedModel.getSpeedMph(timeSec, weightPounds,
                                             horsePower);
   }
```

```
    }
```

As you can see, an interface describes how to invoke object behavior, while factories can generate different implementations for different requests without changing the code of the client application.

There's more...

Let's try to model a crew cab—a truck with multiple passenger seats that combines the properties of a car and a truck. Java does not allow multiple inheritances. This is another case where an interface comes to the rescue.

The CrewCab class may look like this:

```
public class CrewCab extends VehicleImpl implements Car, Truck {
    private int payloadPounds;
    private int passengersCount;
    private CrewCabImpl(int passengersCount, int payloadPounds,
                            int weightPounds, int horsePower) {
       super(weightPounds + payloadPounds + passengersCount * 250,
                                                      horsePower);
       this.payloadPounds = payloadPounds;
       this. passengersCount = passengersCount;
    }
    public int getPayloadPounds(){ return payloadPounds; }
    public int getPassengersCount() {
       return this.passengersCount;
    }
}
```

This class implements both interfaces—Car and Truck—and passes the combined weight of the vehicle, payload, and passengers with their luggage to the base class constructor.

We can also add the following method to FactoryVehicle:

```
public static Vehicle buildCrewCab(int passengersCount,
                 int payload, int weightPounds, int horsePower){
    return new CrewCabImpl(passengersCount, payload,
                                    weightPounds, horsePower);
}
```

The double nature of the `CrewCab` object can be demonstrated in the following test:

```java
public static void main(String... arg) {
    double timeSec = 10.0;
    int horsePower = 246;
    int vehicleWeight = 4000;
    Properties drivingConditions = new Properties();
    drivingConditions.put("roadCondition", "Wet");
    drivingConditions.put("tireCondition", "New");
    SpeedModel speedModel =
        FactorySpeedModel.generateSpeedModel(drivingConditions);
    Vehicle vehicle = FactoryVehicle.
            buildCrewCab(4, 3300, vehicleWeight, horsePower);
    vehicle.setSpeedModel(speedModel);
    System.out.println("Payload = " +
            ((Truck)vehicle).getPayloadPounds()) + " pounds");
    System.out.println("Passengers count = " +
                        ((Car)vehicle).getPassengersCount());
    System.out.println("Crew cab speed (" + timeSec + " sec) = "
                    + vehicle.getSpeedMph(timeSec) + " mph");
}
```

As you can see, we can cast the object of the `CrewCub` class to each of the interfaces it implements. If we run this program, the results will be as follows:

```
Payload = 3300 pounds
Passengers count = 4
Crew cab speed (10.0 sec) = 76.0 mph
```

Creating interfaces with default and static methods

In this recipe, you will learn about two new features that were first introduced in Java 8—the default and static methods in an interface.

Getting ready

A default method in an interface allows us to add a new method signature without changing the classes that have implemented this interface before a new method signature was added. The method is called *default* because it provides functionality in case this method is not implemented by the class. If, however, the class implements it, the interface's default implementation is ignored and overridden by the class implementation.

A static method in an interface can provide functionality in the same way a static method in a class can. Similarly to a class static method, which can be called without class instantiation, an interface static method can also be called using a dot-operator applied to the interface, `SomeInterface.someStaticMethod()`.

A static method of an interface cannot be overridden by the class that implements this interface, and it cannot hide any static method of any class, including the class that implements this interface.

For example, let's add some functionality to the system we have used already in our examples. So far, we have created an amazing piece of software that calculates the speed of a vehicle. If the system becomes popular (as it should), we would like it to be friendlier to the readers who prefer a metric system of units, instead of the miles and pounds we have used in our speed calculations. To address such a need after our speed-calculating software has become popular, we have decided to add more methods to the `Car` and `Truck` interfaces, but we do not want to break the existing implementations.

The default interface method was introduced exactly for such a situation. Using it, we can release a new version of the `Car` and `Truck` interfaces without the need to coordinate the release with the corresponding modification of the existing implementations, that is, the `CarImpl`, `TruckImpl`, and `FactoryVehicle` classes.

How to do it...

As an example, we will change the `Truck` interface. The `Car` interface can be modified in a similar fashion:

1. Enhance the `Truck` interface by adding the `getPayloadKg()` method, which returns the truck payload in kilograms. You can do this without forcing a change in the `TruckImpl` class that implements the `Truck` interface—by adding a new default method to the `Truck` interface:

```
public interface Truck extends Vehicle {
    int getPayloadPounds();
    default int getPayloadKg(){
        return (int) Math.round(0.454 * getPayloadPounds());
    }
}
```

Notice how the new `getPayloadKg()` method uses the existing `getPayloadPounds()` method as if the latter is implemented inside the interface too, although, in fact, it is implemented in a class that implements the `Truck` interface. The magic happens during runtime when this method becomes dynamically bound to the instance of the class that implements this interface.

We could not make the `getPayloadKg()` method static because it would not be able to access the non-static `getPayloadPounds()` method, and we must use the `default` keyword because only the default or static method of an interface can have a body.

2. Write the client code that uses the new method:

```
public static void main(String... arg) {
    Truck truck = FactoryVehicle.buildTruck(3300, 4000, 246);
    System.out.println("Payload in pounds: " +
                                    truck.getPayloadPounds());
    System.out.println("Payload in kg: " +
                                    truck.getPayloadKg());
}
```

3. Run the preceding program and check out the output:

```
Payload in pounds: 3300
Payload in kg: 1498
```

4. Notice that the new method works even without changing the class that implemented it.

5. When you decide to improve the implementation of the `TruckImpl` class, you can do it by adding the corresponding method, for example:

```
class TruckImpl extends VehicleImpl implements Truck {
    private int payloadPounds;
    private TruckImpl(int payloadPounds, int weightPounds,
                                        int horsePower) {
      super(weightPounds + payloadPounds, horsePower);
      this.payloadPounds = payloadPounds;
    }
    public int getPayloadPounds(){ return payloadPounds; }
    public int getPayloadKg(){ return -2; }
}
```

We have implemented the `getPyloadKg()` method as `return -2` in order to make it obvious which implementation is used.

6. Run the same demo program. The results will be as follows:

```
Payload in pounds: 3300
Payload in kg: -2
```

As you can see, this time, the method implementation in the `TruckImpl` class was used. It has overridden the default implementation in the `Truck` interface.

7. Enhance the `Truck` interface with the ability to enter the payload in kilograms without changing the implementation of `FactoryVehicle` and the `Truck` interface. Also, we do not want to add a setter method. With all of these limitations, our only recourse is to add `convertKgToPounds(int kgs)` to the `Truck` interface, and it has to be `static` since we are going to use it before the object that implements the `Truck` interface is constructed:

```
public interface Truck extends Vehicle {
    int getPayloadPounds();
    default int getPayloadKg(){
      return (int) Math.round(0.454 * getPayloadPounds());
    }
    static int convertKgToPounds(int kgs){
      return (int) Math.round(2.205 * kgs);
    }
}
```

How it works...

Those who prefer the metric system of units can now take advantage of the new method:

```
public static void main(String... arg) {
  int horsePower = 246;
  int payload = Truck.convertKgToPounds(1500);
  int vehicleWeight = Truck.convertKgToPounds(1800);
  Truck truck = FactoryVehicle.
          buildTruck(payload, vehicleWeight, horsePower);
  System.out.println("Payload in pounds: " +
                              truck.getPayloadPounds());
  int kg = truck.getPayloadKg();
  System.out.println("Payload converted to kg: " + kg);
  System.out.println("Payload converted back to pounds: " +
                          Truck.convertKgToPounds(kg));
}
```

The results will be as follows:

```
Payload in pounds: 3308
Payload converted to kg: 1502
Payload converted back to pounds: 3312
```

The value of 1,502 is close to the original 1,500, while 3,308 is close to 3,312. The difference is caused by the error of an approximation during the conversion.

Creating interfaces with private methods

In this recipe, you will learn about a new feature that was introduced in Java 9, the private interface method, which is of two types—static and non-static.

Getting ready

A private interface method must have an implementation (a body with a code). A private interface method not used by other methods of the same interface does not make sense. The purpose of a private method is to contain functionality that is common between two or more methods with a body in the same interface or to isolate a section of code in a separate method for better structure and readability. A private interface method cannot be overridden—not by a method of any other interface, nor by a method in a class that implements the interface.

A non-static private interface method can only be accessed by non-static methods of the same interface. A static private interface method can be accessed by non-static and static methods of the same interface.

How to do it...

1. Add the `getWeightKg(int pounds)` method implementation:

```
public interface Truck extends Vehicle {
    int getPayloadPounds();
    default int getPayloadKg(){
        return (int) Math.round(0.454 * getPayloadPounds());
    }
    static int convertKgToPounds(int kilograms){
        return (int) Math.round(2.205 * kilograms);
    }
    default int getWeightKg(int pounds){
        return (int) Math.round(0.454 * pounds);
    }
}
```

2. Remove the redundant code by using the private interface method:

```java
public interface Truck extends Vehicle {
    int getPayloadPounds();
    default int getPayloadKg(int pounds){
        return convertPoundsToKg(pounds);
    }
    static int convertKgToPounds(int kilograms){
        return (int) Math.round(2.205 * kilograms);
    }
    default int getWeightKg(int pounds){
        return convertPoundsToKg(pounds);
    }
    private int convertPoundsToKg(int pounds){
        return (int) Math.round(0.454 * pounds);
    }
}
```

How it works...

The following code demonstrates the new addition:

```java
public static void main(String... arg) {
    int horsePower = 246;
    int payload = Truck.convertKgToPounds(1500);
    int vehicleWeight = Truck.convertKgToPounds(1800);
    Truck truck =
        FactoryVehicle.buildTruck(payload, vehicleWeight, horsePower);
    System.out.println("Weight in pounds: " + vehicleWeight);
    int kg = truck.getWeightKg(vehicleWeight);
    System.out.println("Weight converted to kg: " + kg);
    System.out.println("Weight converted back to pounds: " +
                                        Truck.convertKgToPounds(kg));
}
```

The results of the test do not change:

```
Weight in pounds: 3969
Weight converted to kg: 1802
Weight converted back to pounds: 3973
```

There's more...

With the `getWeightKg(int pounds)` method accepting the input parameter, the method name can be misleading because it does not capture the weight unit of the input parameter. We could try and name it `getWeightKgFromPounds(int pounds)` but it does not make the method function clearer. After realizing it, we decided to make the `convertPoundsToKg(int pounds)` method public and to remove the `getWeightKg(int pounds)` method at all.

Since the `convertPoundsToKg(int pounds)` method does not require access to the object fields, it can be static, too:

```
public interface Truck extends Vehicle {
  int getPayloadPounds();
  default int getPayloadKg(int pounds){
    return convertPoundsToKg(pounds);
  }
  static int convertKgToPounds(int kilograms){
    return (int) Math.round(2.205 * kilograms);
  }
  static int convertPoundsToKg(int pounds){
    return (int) Math.round(0.454 * pounds);
  }
}
```

Fans of the metric system are still able to convert pounds into kilograms and back. Besides, since both converting methods are static, we do not need to create an instance of the class that implements the `Truck` interface in order to do the conversion:

```
public static void main(String... arg) {
  int payload = Truck.convertKgToPounds(1500);
  int vehicleWeight = Truck.convertKgToPounds(1800);
  System.out.println("Weight in pounds: " + vehicleWeight);
  int kg = Truck.convertPoundsToKg(vehicleWeight);
  System.out.println("Weight converted to kg: " + kg);
  System.out.println("Weight converted back to pounds: " +
                                Truck.convertKgToPounds(kg));
}
```

The results do not change:

```
Weight in pounds: 3969
Weight converted to kg: 1802
Weight converted back to pounds: 3973
```

A better way to work with nulls using Optional

In this recipe, you will learn how to use the `java.util.Optional` class for representing optional values instead of using `null` references. It was introduced in Java 8 and further enhanced in Java 9—where three more methods were added—`or()`, `ifPresentOrElse()`, and `stream()`. We will demonstrate all of them.

Getting ready

The `Optional` class is a wrapper around a value, which can be `null` or a value of any type. It was intended to help to avoid the dreaded `NullPointerException`. But, so far, the introduction of `Optional` helped to accomplish it only to a degree and mostly in the area of streams and functional programming.

The vision that motivated the creation of the `Optional` class was to call the `isPresent()` method on an `Optional` object and then apply the `get()` method (to get the contained value) only when the `isPresent()` method returns `true`. Unfortunately, when one cannot guarantee that the reference to the `Optional` object itself is not `null`, one needs to check it in order to avoid `NullPointerException`. If so, then the value of using `Optional` diminishes, because with even less amount of code writing we could check for `null` the value itself and avoid wrapping inside `Optional` whatsoever? Let's write the code that illustrates what we have been talking about.

Let's assume that we would like to write a method that checks the lottery result and, if the ticket you have bought with your friend wins, calculates your 50% share. The traditional way to do it would be:

```
void checkResultInt(int lotteryPrize){
    if(lotteryPrize <= 0){
        System.out.println("We've lost again...");
    } else {
        System.out.println("We've won! Your half is " +
                    Math.round(((double)lotteryPrize)/2) + "!");
    }
}
```

But, to demonstrate how to use `Optional`, we will assume that the result is of the `Integer` type. Then, we also need to check for `null`, if we are not sure that the passed-in value cannot be `null`:

```
void checkResultInt(Integer lotteryPrize){
    if(lotteryPrize == null || lotteryPrize <= 0){
        System.out.println("We've lost again...");
    } else {
        System.out.println("We've won! Your half is " +
                Math.round(((double)lotteryPrize)/2) + "!");
    }
}
```

Using the `Optional` class does not help to avoid the check for `null`. It even requires an additional check, `isPresent()`, to be added so that we can avoid `NullPointerException` while getting the value:

```
void checkResultOpt(Optional<Integer> lotteryPrize){
    if(lotteryPrize == null || !lotteryPrize.isPresent()
                                    || lotteryPrize.get() <= 0){
        System.out.println("We lost again...");
    } else {
        System.out.println("We've won! Your half is " +
                Math.round(((double)lotteryPrize.get())/2) + "!");
    }
}
```

Apparently, the preceding usage of `Optional` does not help to improve the code or make the coding easier. Using `Optional` in Lambda expressions and stream pipelines has more potential because the `Optional` object provides methods that can be invoked via the dot-operator and can be plugged into the fluent-style processing code.

How to do it...

1. Create an `Optional` object using any of the methods that have been demonstrated, as follows:

```
Optional<Integer> prize1 = Optional.empty();
System.out.println(prize1.isPresent()); //prints: false
System.out.println(prize1);   //prints: Optional.empty

Optional<Integer> prize2 = Optional.of(1000000);
System.out.println(prize2.isPresent()); //prints: true
```

```
System.out.println(prize2);  //prints: Optional[1000000]

//Optional<Integer> prize = Optional.of(null);
                                //NullPointerException

Optional<Integer> prize3 = Optional.ofNullable(null);
System.out.println(prize3.isPresent());  //prints: false
System.out.println(prize3);      //prints: Optional.empty
```

Notice that a `null` value can be wrapped inside an `Optional` object by using the `ofNullable()` method.

2. It is possible to compare two `Optional` objects by using the `equals()` method, which compares them by value:

```
Optional<Integer> prize1 = Optional.empty();
System.out.println(prize1.equals(prize1)); //prints: true

Optional<Integer> prize2 = Optional.of(1000000);
System.out.println(prize1.equals(prize2)); //prints: false

Optional<Integer> prize3 = Optional.ofNullable(null);
System.out.println(prize1.equals(prize3)); //prints: true

Optional<Integer> prize4 = Optional.of(1000000);
System.out.println(prize2.equals(prize4)); //prints: true
System.out.println(prize2 == prize4); //prints: false

Optional<Integer> prize5 = Optional.of(10);
System.out.println(prize2.equals(prize5)); //prints: false

Optional<String> congrats1 = Optional.empty();
System.out.println(prize1.equals(congrats1));//prints: true

Optional<String> congrats2 = Optional.of("Happy for you!");
System.out.println(prize1.equals(congrats2));//prints: false
```

Please note that an empty `Optional` object is equal to an object that wraps the `null` value (the `prize1` and `prize3` objects in the preceding code). The `prize2` and `prize4` objects in the preceding code are equal because they wrap the same value, although they are different objects and the references do not match (`prize2 != prize4`). Also, notice that empty objects that wrap different types are equal (`prize1.equals(congrats1)`), which means that the `equals()` method of the `Optional` class does not compare the value type.

3. Use the `or(Suppier<Optional<T>> supplier)` method of the `Optional` class to reliably return a non-null value from the `Optional` object. If the object is empty and contains `null`, it returns another value contained in the `Optional` object that was produced by the provided `Supplier` function.

For example, if the `Optional<Integer> lotteryPrize` object can contain a `null` value, the following construct will return zero every time the `null` value is encountered:

```
int prize = lotteryPrize.or(() -> Optional.of(0)).get();
```

3. Use the `ifPresent(Consumer<T> consumer)` method to ignore the `null` value and to process the non-null value using the provided `Consumer<T>` function. For example, here is the `processIfPresent(Optional<Integer>)` method, which processes the `Optional<Integer> lotteryPrize` object:

```
void processIfPresent(Optional<Integer> lotteryPrize){
    lotteryPrize.ifPresent(prize -> {
        if(prize <= 0){
            System.out.println("We've lost again...");
        } else {
            System.out.println("We've won! Your half is " +
                    Math.round(((double)prize)/2) + "!");
        }
    });
```

We can simplify the preceding code by creating
the `checkResultAndShare(int prize)` method:

```
void checkResultAndShare(int prize){
    if(prize <= 0){
        System.out.println("We've lost again...");
    } else {
        System.out.println("We've won! Your half is " +
                    Math.round(((double)prize)/2) + "!");
    }
}
```

Now, the `processIfPresent()` method looks much simpler:

```
void processIfPresent(Optional<Integer> lotteryPrize){
    lotteryPrize.ifPresent(prize ->
checkResultAndShare(prize));
}
```

4. If you do not want to ignore the `null` value and process it as well, you can
   use the `ifPresentOrElse(Consumer<T> consumer, Runnable
   processEmpty)` method to apply the `Consumer<T>` function to a non-null
   value, and use the `Runnable` functional interface to process the `null`
   value:

```
void processIfPresentOrElse(Optional<Integer> lotteryPrize){
    Consumer<Integer> weWon =
                    prize -> checkResultAndShare(prize);
    Runnable weLost =
            () -> System.out.println("We've lost again...");
    lotteryPrize.ifPresentOrElse(weWon, weLost);
}
```

As you can see, we have reused the `checkResultAndShare(int
prize)` method we just created.

5. Using the `orElseGet(Supplier<T> supplier)` method allows us to
   replace an empty or `null` value (contained in the `Optional` object) with
   the value produced by the provided `Supplier<T>` function:

```
void processOrGet(Optional<Integer> lotteryPrize){
    int prize = lotteryPrize.orElseGet(() -> 42);
    lotteryPrize.ifPresentOrElse(p -> checkResultAndShare(p),
        () -> System.out.println("Better " + prize
                                    + " than nothing..."));
}
```

6. Use the `orElseThrow()` method if you need to throw an exception in case an `Optional` object is empty or contains a `null` value:

```
void processOrThrow(Optional<Integer> lotteryPrize){
    int prize = lotteryPrize.orElseThrow();
    checkResultAndShare(prize);
}
```

An overloaded version of the `orElseThrow()` method allows us to specify an exception and the message you would like to throw when the value contained in the `Optional` object is `null`:

```
void processOrThrow(Optional<Integer> lotteryPrize){
    int prize = lotteryPrize.orElseThrow(() ->
            new RuntimeException("We've lost again..."));
    checkResultAndShare(prize);
}
```

7. Use the `filter()`, `map()`, and `flatMap()` methods to process `Optional` objects in a stream:

```
void useFilter(List<Optional<Integer>> list){
    list.stream().filter(opt -> opt.isPresent())
        .forEach(opt -> checkResultAndShare(opt.get()));
}
void useMap(List<Optional<Integer>> list){
    list.stream().map(opt -> opt.or(() -> Optional.of(0)))
        .forEach(opt -> checkResultAndShare(opt.get()));
}
void useFlatMap(List<Optional<Integer>> list){
    list.stream().flatMap(opt ->
            List.of(opt.or(()->Optional.of(0))).stream())
        .forEach(opt -> checkResultAndShare(opt.get()));
}
```

In the preceding code, the `useFilter()` method processes only those stream elements that have non-null values. The `useMap()` method processes all stream elements but replaces `Optional` objects without any value or by wrapping the `null` value with an `Optional` object that wraps zero. The last method uses `flatMap()`, which requires returning a stream from the provided function. Our example is quite useless in this respect because the function we pass as a `flatMap()` parameter produces a stream of one object, so using `map()` (as in the previous `useMap()` method) is a better solution here. We only did this for demonstrating how the `flatMap()` method can be plugged into the stream pipeline.

How it works...

The following code demonstrates the functionality of the described `Optional` class. The `useFlatMap()` method accepts a list of `Optional` objects, creates a stream, and process each emitted element:

```
void useFlatMap(List<Optional<Integer>> list){
    Function<Optional<Integer>,
      Stream<Optional<Integer>>> tryUntilWin = opt -> {
        List<Optional<Integer>> opts = new ArrayList<>();
        if(opt.isPresent()){
            opts.add(opt);
        } else {
            int prize = 0;
            while(prize == 0){
                double d = Math.random() - 0.8;
                prize = d > 0 ? (int)(1000000 * d) : 0;
                opts.add(Optional.of(prize));
            }
        }
        return opts.stream();
    };
    list.stream().flatMap(tryUntilWin)
        .forEach(opt -> checkResultAndShare(opt.get()));
}
```

Each element of the original list first enters the `flatMap()` method as an input into the `tryUntilWin` function. This function first checks if the value of the `Optional` object is present. If yes, the `Optional` object is emitted as a single element of a stream and is processed by the `checkResultAndShare()` method. But if the `tryUntilWin` function determines that there is no value in the `Optional` object or the value is `null`, it generates a random double number in the range between -0.8 and 0.2. If the value is negative, an `Optional` object is added to the resulting list with a value of zero and a new random number is generated. But if the generated number is positive, it is used for the prize-value calculation, which is added to the resulting list that's wrapped inside an `Optional` object. The resulting list of `Optional` objects is then returned as a stream, and each element of the stream is processed by the `checkResultAndShare()` method.

Now, let's run the preceding method for the following list:

```
List<Optional<Integer>> list = List.of(Optional.empty(),
                                   Optional.ofNullable(null),
                                   Optional.of(100000));
useFlatMap(list);
```

The results will be as follows:

```
We've lost again...
We've lost again...
We've won! Your half is 68833!
We've lost again...
We've won! Your half is 50813!
We've won! Your half is 50000!
```

As you can see, when the first list element, `Optional.empty()`, was processed, the `tryUntilWin` function succeeded in getting a positive `prize` value from the third attempt. The second `Optional.ofNullable(null)` object caused two attempts until the `tryUntilWin` function succeeded. The last object successfully went through and awarded you and your friend 50,000 each.

There's more...

An object of the `Optional` class is not serializable and, thus, cannot be used as a field of an object. This is another indication that the designer of the `Optional` class intended to be used in a stateless process.

It makes the stream processing pipeline more compact and expressive, focusing on the actual values instead of checking if there are empty elements in the stream.

Using the utility class Objects

In this recipe, you will learn how the `java.util.Objects` utility class allows for the better processing of objects related functionality related to object comparison, calculating a hash value, and checking for `null`. It was a long time coming, as the programmers wrote the same code for checking an object for `null` again and again.

Getting ready

The `Objects` class has only 17 methods, all of which are static. For a better overview, we have organized them into seven groups:

- `compare()`: One method compares two objects using the provided `Comparator`
- `toString()`: Two methods that convert an `Object` to a `String` value
- `checkIndex()`: Three methods that allow us to check whether the index and the length of a collection or an array are compatible
- `requireNonNull()`: Five methods throw an exception if the provided object is `null`
- `hash()`, `hashCode()` : Two methods that calculate a hash value for a single object or an array of objects
- `isNull()`, `nonNull()`: Two methods that wrap the `obj == null` or `obj != null` expressions
- `equals()`, `deepEquals()`: Two methods that compare two objects that can be null or arrays

We are going to write code that uses these methods in the preceding sequence.

How to do it...

1. The `int compare(T a, T b, Comparator<T> c)` method uses the
    provided comparator for comparing the two objects:

    *   Returns 0 when the objects are equal
    *   Returns a negative number when the first object is smaller than
        the second one
    *   Returns a positive number otherwise

    The non-zero return value of the `int compare(T a, T b,
    Comparator<T> c)` method depends on the implementation. In the case
    of `String`, smaller and bigger are defined according to their ordering
    position (smaller is placed in front of bigger in the ordered list), and the
    returned value is the difference between the positions of the first and the
    second parameter in the list, ordered according to the provided comparator:

    ```
    int res =
            Objects.compare("a", "c", Comparator.naturalOrder());
    System.out.println(res);        //prints: -2
    res = Objects.compare("a", "a", Comparator.naturalOrder());
    System.out.println(res);        //prints: 0
    res = Objects.compare("c", "a", Comparator.naturalOrder());
    System.out.println(res);        //prints: 2
    res = Objects.compare("c", "a", Comparator.reverseOrder());
    System.out.println(res);        //prints: -2
    ```

    The `Integer` values, on the other hand, return just −1 or 1 when the values
    are not equal:

    ```
    res = Objects.compare(3, 5, Comparator.naturalOrder());
    System.out.println(res);        //prints: -1
    res = Objects.compare(3, 3, Comparator.naturalOrder());
    System.out.println(res);        //prints: 0
    res = Objects.compare(5, 3, Comparator.naturalOrder());
    System.out.println(res);        //prints: 1
    res = Objects.compare(5, 3, Comparator.reverseOrder());
    System.out.println(res);        //prints: -1
    res = Objects.compare("5", "3", Comparator.reverseOrder());
    System.out.println(res);        //prints: -2
    ```

Please notice how, in the last line in the preceding code block, the result changes when we compare numbers as `String` literals.

When both objects are `null`, the `compare()` method considers them equal:

```
res = Objects.compare(null,null,Comparator.naturalOrder());
System.out.println(res);        //prints: 0
```

But it throws `NullPointerException` when only one of the objects is null:

```
//Objects.compare(null, "c", Comparator.naturalOrder());
//Objects.compare("a", null, Comparator.naturalOrder());
```

If you need to compare an object with null, you are better off using `org.apache.commons.lang3.ObjectUtils.compare(T o1, T o2)`.

2. The `toString(Object obj)` method is helpful when an `obj` object reference is the `null` value:

- `String toString(Object obj)`: Returns the result of calling `toString()` on the first parameter when it is not `null` and `null` when the first parameter value is `null`
- `String toString(Object obj, String nullDefault)`: Returns the result of calling `toString()` on the first parameter when it is not `null` and the second parameter value, `nullDefault`, when the first parameter value is `null`

The usage of the `toString(Object obj)` method is straightforward:

```
System.out.println(Objects.toString("a")); //prints: a
System.out.println(Objects.toString(null)); //prints: null
System.out.println(Objects.toString("a", "b")); //prints: a
System.out.println(Objects.toString(null, "b"));//prints: b
```

3. The `checkIndex()` overloaded method checks whether the index and the length of a collection or an array are compatible:

- `int checkIndex(int index, int length)`: Throws `IndexOutOfBoundsException` if the provided `index` is bigger than `length - 1`, for example:

```
List<Integer> list = List.of(1, 2);
try {
    Objects.checkIndex(3, list.size());
} catch (IndexOutOfBoundsException ex){
    System.out.println(ex.getMessage());
        //prints: Index 3 out-of-bounds for length 2
}
```

- `int checkFromIndexSize(int fromIndex, int size, int length)`: Throws `IndexOutOfBoundsException` if the provided `index + size` is bigger than `length - 1`, for example:

```
List<Integer> list = List.of(1, 2);
try {
    Objects.checkFromIndexSize(1, 3, list.size());
} catch (IndexOutOfBoundsException ex){
    System.out.println(ex.getMessage());
//prints:Range [1, 1 + 3) out-of-bounds for length 2
}
```

- `int checkFromToIndex(int fromIndex, int toIndex, int length)`: Throws `IndexOutOfBoundsException` if the provided `fromIndex` is bigger than `toIndex`, or `toIndex` is bigger than `length - 1`, for example:

```
List<Integer> list = List.of(1, 2);
try {
    Objects.checkFromToIndex(1, 3, list.size());
} catch (IndexOutOfBoundsException ex){
    System.out.println(ex.getMessage());
    //prints:Range [1, 3) out-of-bounds for length 2
}
```

4. The five methods of the `requireNonNull()` group check the value of the first parameter, `obj`. If the value is `null`, they either throw `NullPointerException` or return the provided default value:

- `T requireNonNull(T obj)`:
  Throws `NullPointerException` without a message if the parameter is `null`, for example:

```
String obj = null;
try {
  Objects.requireNonNull(obj);
} catch (NullPointerException ex){
  System.out.println(ex.getMessage());//prints: null
}
```

- `T requireNonNull(T obj, String message)`:
  Throws `NullPointerException` with the provided message if the first parameter is `null`, for example:

```
String obj = null;
try {
  Objects.requireNonNull(obj,
                         "Parameter 'obj' is null");
} catch (NullPointerException ex){
  System.out.println(ex.getMessage());
                  //prints: Parameter 'obj' is null
}
```

- `T requireNonNull(T obj, Supplier<String> messageSupplier)`: If the first parameter is `null`, returns the message generated the provided function or, if the generated message or the function itself is `null`, throws `NullPointerException`, for example:

```
String obj = null;
Supplier<String> supplier = () -> "Message";
try {
  Objects.requireNonNull(obj, supplier);
} catch (NullPointerException ex){
  System.out.println(ex.getMessage());
                           //prints: Message
}
```

- `T requireNonNullElse(T obj, T defaultObj)`: Returns the first parameter (if it is non-null), the second parameter (if it is non-null), throws `NullPointerException` (if both parameters is null), for example:

```
String object = null;
System.out.println(Objects
        .requireNonNullElse(obj, "Default value"));
                        //prints: Default value
```

- `T requireNonNullElseGet(T obj, Supplier<T> supplier)`: Returns the first parameter (if it is non-null), the object produced by the provided supplier function (if it is non-null and `supplier.get()` is non-null), throws `NullPointerException` (if both parameters are null or the first parameter and supplier.get() are null), for example:

```
Integer obj = null;
Supplier<Integer> supplier = () -> 42;
try {
    System.out.println(Objects
            .requireNonNullElseGet(obj, supplier));
} catch (NullPointerException ex){
    System.out.println(ex.getMessage()); //prints: 42
}
```

5. The `hash()` or `hashCode()` method is typically used to override the default `hashCode()` implementation:

- `int hashCode(Object value)`: Calculates a hash value for a single object, for example:

```
System.out.println(Objects.hashCode(null));
                                        //prints: 0
System.out.println(Objects.hashCode("abc"));
                                        //prints: 96354
```

- `int hash(Object... values)`: Calculates a hash value for an array of objects, for example:

```
System.out.println(Objects.hash(null));  //prints: 0
System.out.println(Objects.hash("abc"));
                                        //prints: 96385
String[] arr = {"abc"};
System.out.println(Objects.hash(arr));
```

```
                                          //prints: 96385
Object[] objs = {"a", 42, "c"};
System.out.println(Objects.hash(objs));
                                         //prints: 124409
System.out.println(Objects.hash("a", 42, "c"));
                                         //prints: 124409
```

Please note that the `hashCode(Object value)` method
returns a different hash value
(`96354`) than the `Objects.hash(Object...`
`values)` method (`96385`), even though they calculate
the hash value for the same single object.

6. The `isNull()` and `nonNull()` methods are just wrappers around Boolean
    expressions:

    - `boolean isNull(Object obj)`: Returns the same value as `obj`
      `== null`, for example:

      ```
      String obj = null;
      System.out.println(obj == null);     //prints: true
      System.out.println(Objects.isNull(obj));
                                           //prints: true
      obj = "";
      System.out.println(obj == null);     //prints: false
      System.out.println(Objects.isNull(obj));
                                           //prints: false
      ```

    - `boolean nonNull(Object obj)`: Returns the same value
      as `obj != null`, for example:

      ```
      String obj = null;
      System.out.println(obj != null);     //prints: false
      System.out.println(Objects.nonNull(obj));
                                           //prints: false
      obj = "";
      System.out.println(obj != null);     //prints: true
      System.out.println(Objects.nonNull(obj));
                                           //prints: true
      ```

7. The `equals()` and `deepEquals()` methods allow us to compare two objects by their state:

- `boolean equals(Object a, Object b)`: Compares two objects using the `equals(Object)` method and handles the case when one of them or both are `null`, for example:

```
String o1 = "o";
String o2 = "o";
System.out.println(Objects.equals(o1, o2));
                                    //prints: true
System.out.println(Objects.equals(null, null));
                                    //prints: true
Integer[] ints1 = {1,2,3};
Integer[] ints2 = {1,2,3};
System.out.println(Objects.equals(ints1, ints2));
                                    //prints: false
```

In the preceding example, `Objects.equals(ints1, ints2)` returns `false` because arrays cannot override the `equals()` method of the `Object` class and are compared by references, not by value.

- `boolean deepEquals(Object a, Object b)`: Compares two arrays by the value of their elements, for example:

```
String o1 = "o";
String o2 = "o";
System.out.println(Objects.deepEquals(o1, o2));
                                    //prints: true
System.out.println(Objects.deepEquals(null, null));
                                    //prints: true
Integer[] ints1 = {1,2,3};
Integer[] ints2 = {1,2,3};
System.out.println(Objects.deepEquals(ints1,ints2));
                                    //prints: true
Integer[][] iints1 = {{1,2,3},{1,2,3}};
Integer[][] iints2 = {{1,2,3},{1,2,3}};
System.out.println(Objects.
        deepEquals(iints1, iints2)); //prints: true
```

As you can see,
the `deepEquals()` method returns `true` when the
corresponding values of the arrays are equal. But if the arrays
have different values or a different order of the same values,
the method returns `false`:

```
Integer[][] iints1 = {{1,2,3},{1,2,3}};
Integer[][] iints2 = {{1,2,3},{1,3,2}};
System.out.println(Objects.
        deepEquals(iints1, iints2)); //prints: false
```

How it works...

The `Arrays.equals(Object a, Object
b)` and `Arrays.deepEquals(Object a, Object b)` methods behave the same
way as the `Objects.equals(Object a, Object
b)` and `Objects.deepEquals(Object a, Object b)` methods:

```
Integer[] ints1 = {1,2,3};
Integer[] ints2 = {1,2,3};
System.out.println(Arrays.equals(ints1, ints2));
                                    //prints: true
System.out.println(Arrays.deepEquals(ints1, ints2));
                                    //prints: true
System.out.println(Arrays.equals(iints1, iints2));
                                    //prints: false
System.out.println(Arrays.deepEquals(iints1, iints2));
                                    //prints: true
```

In fact, the `Arrays.equals(Object a, Object
b)` and `Arrays.deepEquals(Object a, Object b)` methods are used in the
implementation of the `Objects.equals(Object a, Object
b)` and `Objects.deepEquals(Object a, Object b)` methods.

To summarize, if you would like to compare two objects, a and b, by the values of their fields, then:

- If they are not arrays and a is not `null`, use `a.equals(Object b)`
- If they are not arrays and each or both objects can be `null`,
  use `Objects.equals(Object a, Object b)`
- If both can be arrays and each or both can be `null`,
  use `Objects.deepEquals(Object a, Object b)`

The `Objects.deepEquals(Object a, Object b)` method seems to be the safest one, but it does not mean that you must always use it. Most of the time, you will know whether the compared objects can be `null` or can be arrays, so you can safely use other methods, too.

3
Modular Programming

In this chapter, we will cover the following recipes:

- Using jdeps to find dependencies in a Java application
- Creating a simple modular application
- Creating a modular JAR
- Using a module JAR with pre-Project Jigsaw JDK applications
- Bottom-up migration
- Top-down migration
- Using services to create loose coupling between the consumer and provider modules
- Creating a custom modular runtime image using jlink
- Compiling for older platform versions
- Creating multi-release JARs
- Using Maven to develop a modular application
- Making your library module-path-friendly
- How to open a module for reflection

Introduction

Modular programming enables one to organize code into independent, cohesive modules, which can be combined to achieve the desired functionality. This allows us to create code that is:

- More cohesive, because the modules are built with a specific purpose, so the code that resides there tends to cater to that specific purpose.
- Encapsulated, because modules can interact with only those APIs that have been made available by the other modules.

- Reliable, because the discoverability is based on the modules and not on the individual types. This means that if a module is not present, the dependent module cannot be executed until it is discoverable by the dependent module. This helps to prevent runtime errors.
- Loosely coupled. If you use service interfaces, the module interface and the service interface implementation can be loosely coupled.

So, the thought process in designing and organizing the code will now involve identifying the modules, code, and configuration files that go into the module and the packages in which the code is organized within the module. After that, we have to decide upon the public APIs of the module, thereby making them available for use by dependent modules.

Coming to the development of the **Java Platform Module System**, it is being governed by **Java Specification Request (JSR)** 376 (`https://www.jcp.org/en/jsr/detail?id=376`). The JSR mentions that a module system should address the following fundamental issues:

- **Reliable configuration**: Provide an alternative to the classpath for declaring dependency between components such that developers can prevent their applications from throwing surprises on runtime due to missing dependencies in the classpath.
- **Strong encapsulation**: Provide more strict access-control such that something private to a component is private in true sense i.e not accessible even via Reflection and allow the developer to selectively expose parts in the component for use by other components.

The JSR lists the advantages that result from addressing the preceding issues:

- **A scalable platform**: The specification in JSR 376 will allow leveraging the different profiles introduced in JSR 337 in the right way by allowing the creation of profiles using different components/modules created in the new platform. This modular platform will also allow other developers to package different components of the Java Platform to create custom runtime thereby giving them an option to create runtime just enough for their use.
- **Greater platform integrity**: The strong encapsulation will prevent the purposeful or accidental use of the Java internal APIs thereby giving greater platform integrity.

- **Improved performance**: With the clear dependency between components, it now becomes much easier to optimize the individual components based on the components they interact within in the Java SE platform and outside of it.

In this chapter, we will look at a few important recipes that will help you get started with modular programming.

Using jdeps to find dependencies in a Java application

The first step in modularizing your application is to identify its dependencies. A static analysis tool called `jdeps` was introduced in JDK 8 to enable developers to find the dependencies of their applications. There are multiple options supported in the command, which enables developers to check for dependencies in the JDK internal APIs, show the dependencies at the package level, show the dependencies at the class level, and filter the dependencies, among other options.

In this recipe, we will look at how to make use of the `jdeps` tool by exploring its functionality and using the multiple command-line options it supports.

Getting ready

We need a sample application that we can run against the `jdeps` command to find its dependencies. So, we thought of creating a very simple application that uses the Jackson API to consume JSON from the REST API: `http://jsonplaceholder.typicode.com/users`.

In the sample code, we also added a call to the deprecated JDK internal API, called `sun.reflect.Reflection.getCallerClass()`. This way, we can see how `jdeps` helps in finding dependencies for the JDK internal APIs.

The following steps will help you to set up the prerequisites for this recipe:

1. You can get the complete code for the sample from `Chapter03/1_json-jackson-sample`. We have built this code against Java 9 and also using Java 8, and it compiles well. So, you only need to install Java 9 to compile it. If you try to compile with JDK 11, you will face an error due to the deprecated internal API, which is no longer available.

2. Once you have the code, compile it by using the following:

```
# On Linux
javac -cp 'lib/*' -d classes
      -sourcepath src $(find src -name *.java)

# On Windows
javac -cp lib*;classes
        -d classes src/com/packt/model/*.java
                   src/com/packt/*.java
```

 Note: If your `javac` is pointing to JDK 11, you can declare environment variables such as `JAVA8_HOME` or `JAVA9_HOME` that are pointing to your JDK 8 and JDK9 installations, respectively. This way, you can compile using:

```
# On Linux
"$JAVA8_HOME"/bin/javac -cp 'lib/*'
   -d classes -sourcepath src $(find src -name *.java)

# On Windows
"%JAVA8_HOME%"\bin\javac -cp lib\*;classes
        -d classes src\com\packt\*.java
                   src\com\packt\model\*.java
```

You will see a warning for the use of an internal API, which you can safely ignore. We added this with a purpose to demonstrate the capability of `jdeps`. Now, you should have your compiled class files in the classes directory.

3. You can create an executable JAR and run the sample program by running the JAR using the following commands:

```
# On Linux:
  jar cvfm sample.jar manifest.mf -C classes .
  "$JAVA8_HOME"/bin/java -jar sample.jar
# On Windows:
  jar cvfm sample.jar manifest.mf -C classes .
  "%JAVA8_HOME%"\bin\java -jar sample.jar
```

4. We have provided the `run.bat` and `run.sh` scripts
   in `Chapter03/1_json-jackson-sample`. You can compile and run using
   these scripts as well.

A `sample.jar` file gets created in the current directory if you have used `run.bat` or
`run.sh` or the preceding commands to create JAR. If the JAR hasn't been created, you
can use the `build-jar.bat` or `build.-jar.sh` script to compile and build the JAR.

So, we have a sample non-modular application that we will analyze using `jdeps` to
find its dependencies, and also the names of the modules it possibly depends on.

How to do it...

1. The simplest way to use `jdeps` is as follows:

```
# On Linux
jdeps -cp classes/:lib/* classes/com/packt/Sample.class

# On Windows
jdeps -cp "classes/;lib/*" classes/com/packt/Sample.class
```

The preceding command is equivalent to the following:

```
# On Linux
jdeps -verbose:package -cp classes/:lib/*
        classes/com/packt/Sample.class

# On Windows
jdeps -verbose:package -cp "classes/;lib/*"
classes/com/packt/Sample.class
```

The output for the preceding code is as follows:

```
Sample.class -> JDK removed internal API
Sample.class -> lib\jackson-core-2.9.6.jar
Sample.class -> lib\jackson-databind-2.9.6.jar
Sample.class -> java.base
   com.packt                           -> com.fasterxml.jackson.core.type      jackson-core-2.9.6.jar
   com.packt                           -> com.fasterxml.jackson.databind       jackson-databind-2.9.6.jar
   com.packt                           -> java.io                              java.base
   com.packt                           -> java.lang                            java.base
   com.packt                           -> java.lang.invoke                     java.base
   com.packt                           -> java.net                             java.base
   com.packt                           -> java.util                            java.base
   com.packt                           -> java.util.function                   java.base
   com.packt                           -> java.util.stream                     java.base
   com.packt                           -> sun.reflect                          JDK internal API (JDK removed internal API)
```

In the preceding command, we use `jdeps` to list the dependencies for the class file, `Sample.class`, at the package level. We have to provide `jdeps` with the path to search for the dependencies of the code being analyzed. This can be done by setting the `-classpath`, `-cp`, or `--class-path` option of the `jdeps` command.

 The `-verbose:package` option lists the dependencies at the package level.

2. Let's list the dependencies at the class level:

```
# On Linux
jdeps -verbose:class -cp classes/:lib/*
        classes/com/packt/Sample.class

# On Windows
jdeps -verbose:class -cp "classes/;lib/*"
classes/com/packt/Sample.class
```

The output of the preceding command is as follows:

```
Sample.class -> JDK removed internal API
Sample.class -> lib\jackson-core-2.9.6.jar
Sample.class -> lib\jackson-databind-2.9.6.jar
Sample.class -> java.base
   com.packt.Sample                           -> com.fasterxml.jackson.core.type.TypeReference    jackson-core-2.9.6.jar
   com.packt.Sample                           -> com.fasterxml.jackson.databind.ObjectMapper      jackson-databind-2.9.6.jar
   com.packt.Sample                           -> java.io.PrintStream                              java.base
   com.packt.Sample                           -> java.lang.Class                                  java.base
   com.packt.Sample                           -> java.lang.Exception                              java.base
   com.packt.Sample                           -> java.lang.Object                                 java.base
   com.packt.Sample                           -> java.lang.String                                 java.base
   com.packt.Sample                           -> java.lang.StringBuilder                          java.base
   com.packt.Sample                           -> java.lang.System                                 java.base
   com.packt.Sample                           -> java.lang.invoke.CallSite                        java.base
   com.packt.Sample                           -> java.lang.invoke.LambdaMetafactory               java.base
   com.packt.Sample                           -> java.lang.invoke.MethodHandle                    java.base
   com.packt.Sample                           -> java.lang.invoke.MethodHandles                   java.base
   com.packt.Sample                           -> java.lang.invoke.MethodHandles$Lookup            java.base
   com.packt.Sample                           -> java.lang.invoke.MethodType                      java.base
   com.packt.Sample                           -> java.net.URL                                     java.base
   com.packt.Sample                           -> java.util.List                                   java.base
   com.packt.Sample                           -> java.util.function.Consumer                      java.base
   com.packt.Sample                           -> java.util.stream.Stream                          java.base
   com.packt.Sample                           -> sun.reflect.Reflection                           JDK internal API (JDK removed internal API)
```

In this case, we make use of the `-verbose:class` option to list the dependencies at the class level, which is why you can see that the `com.packt.Sample` class depends on `com.packt.model.Company`, `java.lang.Exception`, `com.fasterxml.jackson.core.type.TypeReference`, and so on.

3. Let's get the summary of the dependencies:

```
# On Linux
jdeps -summary -cp classes/:lib/*
                        classes/com/packt/Sample.class


# On Windows
jdeps -summary -cp "classes/;lib/*"
                        classes/com/packt/Sample.class
```

The output is as follows:

```
Sample.class -> JDK removed internal API
Sample.class -> lib\jackson-core-2.9.6.jar
Sample.class -> lib\jackson-databind-2.9.6.jar
Sample.class -> java.base
```

4. Let's check for the dependency on the JDK internal API:

```
# On Linux
jdeps -jdkinternals -cp classes/:lib/*
                        classes/com/packt/Sample.class


# On Windows
jdeps -jdkinternals -cp "classes/;lib/*"
                        classes/com/packt/Sample.class
```

The following is the output of the preceding command:

```
Sample.class -> JDK removed internal API
   com.packt.Sample                           -> sun.reflect.Reflection        JDK internal API (JDK removed internal API)
classes -> JDK removed internal API
   com.packt.Sample                           -> sun.reflect.Reflection        JDK internal API (JDK removed internal API)

Warning: JDK internal APIs are unsupported and private to JDK implementation that are
subject to be removed or changed incompatibly and could break your application.
Please modify your code to eliminate dependence on any JDK internal APIs.
For the most recent update on JDK internal API replacements, please check:
https://wiki.openjdk.java.net/display/JDK8/Java+Dependency+Analysis+Tool

JDK Internal API                    Suggested Replacement
----------------                    ---------------------
sun.reflect.Reflection              Use java.lang.StackWalker @since 9
```

 The StackWalker API is the new API for traversing the call stack, which was introduced in Java 9. This is the replacement for the `sun.reflect.Reflection.getCallerClass()` method. We will discuss this API in `Chapter 11`, *Memory Management and Debugging*.

5. Let's run `jdeps` on the JAR file, `sample.jar`:

```
# On Linux and Windows
        jdeps -s -cp lib/* sample.jar
```

The output we get is the following:

```
sample.jar -> JDK removed internal API
sample.jar -> lib\jackson-core-2.9.6.jar
sample.jar -> lib\jackson-databind-2.9.6.jar
sample.jar -> java.base
```

The preceding information obtained after investigating the `sample.jar` using `jdeps` is quite useful. It clearly states the dependencies of our JAR files and is very useful when we try to migrate this application to a modular application.

6. Let's find whether there are any dependencies on a given package name:

```
# On Linux and Windows
        jdeps -p java.util sample.jar
```

The output is as follows:

```
sample.jar -> java.base
   com.packt                    -> java.util      java.base
```

The -p option is used to find dependencies on the given package name. So, we get to know that our code depends on the `java.util` package. Let's try this with another package name:

```
jdeps -p java.util.concurrent sample.jar
```

There is no output, which means that our code doesn't depend on the `java.util.concurrent` package.

7. We would want to run the dependency check only for our code. Yes, this is possible. Suppose we run `jdeps -cp lib/* sample.jar`; you will see even the library JARs being analyzed. We wouldn't want that, right? Let's just include the classes of the `com.packt` package:

```
# On Linux
jdeps -include 'com.packt.*' -cp lib/* sample.jar

# On Windows
jdeps -include "com.packt.*" -cp lib/* sample.jar
```

The output is as follows:

```
sample.jar -> JDK removed internal API
sample.jar -> lib\jackson-core-2.9.6.jar
sample.jar -> lib\jackson-databind-2.9.6.jar
sample.jar -> java.base
   com.packt                    -> com.fasterxml.jackson.core.type    jackson-core-2.9.6.jar
   com.packt                    -> com.fasterxml.jackson.databind     jackson-databind-2.9.6.jar
   com.packt                    -> com.packt.model                    sample.jar
   com.packt                    -> java.io                            java.base
   com.packt                    -> java.lang                          java.base
   com.packt                    -> java.lang.invoke                   java.base
   com.packt                    -> java.net                           java.base
   com.packt                    -> java.util                          java.base
   com.packt                    -> java.util.function                 java.base
   com.packt                    -> java.util.stream                   java.base
   com.packt                    -> sun.reflect                        JDK internal API (JDK removed internal API)
   com.packt.model              -> java.lang                          java.base
```

8. Let's check whether our code is dependent on a specific package:

```
# On Linux
jdeps -p 'com.packt.model' sample.jar

# On Windows
jdeps -p "com.packt.model" sample.jar
```

The output is as follows:

```
sample.jar -> sample.jar
   com.packt                    -> com.packt.model       sample.jar
```

9. We can use `jdeps` to analyze the JDK modules. Let's pick the `java.httpclient` module for analysis:

```
jdeps -m java.xml
```

Here is the output:

```
java.xml
 [jrt:/java.xml]
   requires mandated java.base
java.xml -> java.base
   com.sun.java_cup.internal.runtime          -> java.io                                        java.base
   com.sun.java_cup.internal.runtime          -> java.lang                                      java.base
   com.sun.java_cup.internal.runtime          -> java.lang.invoke                               java.base
   com.sun.java_cup.internal.runtime          -> java.util                                      java.base
   com.sun.org.apache.bcel.internal           -> com.sun.org.apache.bcel.internal.classfile     java.xml
   com.sun.org.apache.bcel.internal           -> com.sun.org.apache.bcel.internal.util          java.xml
   com.sun.org.apache.bcel.internal           -> java.lang                                      java.base
   com.sun.org.apache.bcel.internal           -> java.lang.invoke                               java.base
   com.sun.org.apache.bcel.internal           -> java.util                                      java.base
   com.sun.org.apache.bcel.internal.classfile -> com.sun.org.apache.bcel.internal               java.xml
   com.sun.org.apache.bcel.internal.classfile -> com.sun.org.apache.bcel.internal.generic       java.xml
   com.sun.org.apache.bcel.internal.classfile -> com.sun.org.apache.bcel.internal.util          java.xml
   com.sun.org.apache.bcel.internal.classfile -> java.io                                        java.base
   com.sun.org.apache.bcel.internal.classfile -> java.lang                                      java.base
   com.sun.org.apache.bcel.internal.classfile -> java.lang.invoke                               java.base
   com.sun.org.apache.bcel.internal.classfile -> java.lang.reflect                              java.base
   com.sun.org.apache.bcel.internal.classfile -> java.util                                      java.base
   com.sun.org.apache.bcel.internal.classfile -> java.util.zip                                  java.base
   com.sun.org.apache.bcel.internal.classfile -> jdk.xml.internal                               java.xml
   com.sun.org.apache.bcel.internal.generic   -> com.sun.org.apache.bcel.internal               java.xml
   com.sun.org.apache.bcel.internal.generic   -> com.sun.org.apache.bcel.internal.classfile     java.xml
   com.sun.org.apache.bcel.internal.generic   -> com.sun.org.apache.bcel.internal.util          java.xml
   com.sun.org.apache.bcel.internal.generic   -> java.io                                        java.base
   com.sun.org.apache.bcel.internal.generic   -> java.lang                                      java.base
   com.sun.org.apache.bcel.internal.generic   -> java.lang.invoke                               java.base
   com.sun.org.apache.bcel.internal.generic   -> java.lang.reflect                              java.base
   com.sun.org.apache.bcel.internal.generic   -> java.util                                      java.base
   com.sun.org.apache.bcel.internal.util      -> com.sun.org.apache.bcel.internal               java.xml
   com.sun.org.apache.bcel.internal.util      -> com.sun.org.apache.bcel.internal.classfile     java.xml
   com.sun.org.apache.bcel.internal.util      -> com.sun.org.apache.bcel.internal.generic       java.xml
   com.sun.org.apache.bcel.internal.util      -> java.io                                        java.base
   com.sun.org.apache.bcel.internal.util      -> java.lang                                      java.base
   com.sun.org.apache.bcel.internal.util      -> java.lang.invoke                               java.base
   com.sun.org.apache.bcel.internal.util      -> java.lang.ref                                  java.base
   com.sun.org.apache.bcel.internal.util      -> java.util                                      java.base
   com.sun.org.apache.bcel.internal.util      -> java.util.regex                                java.base
-- More --
```

We can also find out whether a given module is dependent on another module by using the `--require` option, as follows:

```
# On Linux and Windows
        jdeps --require java.logging -m java.sql
```

Here is the output:

```
java.sql
 [jrt:/java.sql]
   requires mandated java.base
   requires transitive java.logging
   requires transitive java.transaction.xa
   requires transitive java.xml
java.sql -> java.logging
   java.sql                              -> java.util.logging      java.logging
   javax.sql                             -> java.util.logging      java.logging
```

In the preceding command, we tried to find out whether the `java.sql` module is dependent on the `java.logging` module. The output we get is the dependency summary of the `java.sql` module and the packages in the `java.sql` module, which make use of the code from the `java.logging` module.

How it works...

The `jdeps` command is a static-class dependency analyzer and is used to analyze the static dependencies of the application and its libraries. The `jdeps` command, by default, shows the package-level dependencies of the input files, which can be `.class` files, a directory, or a JAR file. This is configurable and can be changed to show class-level dependencies. There are multiple options available to filter out the dependencies and to specify the class files to be analyzed. We have seen a regular use of the `-cp` command-line option. This option is used to provide the locations to search for the analyzed code's dependencies.

We have analyzed the class file, JAR files, and the JDK modules, and we also tried out different options of the `jdeps` command. There are a few options, such as `-e`, `-regex`, `--regex`, `-f`, `--filter`, and `-include`, which accept a regular expression (regex). It's important to understand the output of the `jdeps` command. There are two parts of information for every class/JAR file being analyzed:

1. The summary of the dependency for the analyzed file (JAR or class file). This consists of the name of the class or the JAR file on the left and the name of the dependent entity on the right. The dependent entity can be a directory, a JAR file, or a JDK module, as follows:

```
Sample.class -> classes
Sample.class -> lib/jackson-core-2.9.6.jar
Sample.class -> lib/jackson-databind-2.9.6.jar
Sample.class -> java.base
Sample.class -> jdk.unsupported
```

2. A more verbose dependency information of the contents of the analyzed file at the package or class level (depending on the command-line options). This consists of three columns—column 1 contains the name of the package/class, column 2 contains the name of the dependent package, and column 3 contains the name of the module/JAR where the dependency is found. A sample output looks like the following:

```
com.packt   -> com.fasterxml.jackson.core.type
                jackson-core-2.9.6.jar
com.packt   -> com.fasterxml.jackson.databind
                jackson-databind-2.9.6.jar
com.packt   -> com.packt.model   sample.jar
```

There's more...

We have seen quite a few options of the `jdeps` command. There are a few more related to filtering the dependencies and filtering the classes to be analyzed. Apart from that, there are a few options that deal with module paths.

The following are the options that can be tried out:

- `-e`, `-regex`, `--regex`: These find dependencies matching the given pattern.
- `-f`, `-filter`: These exclude dependencies matching the given pattern.
- `-filter:none`: This allows no filtering that's applied via `filter:package` or `filter:archive`.
- `-filter:package`: This excludes dependencies within the same package. This is the default option. For example, if we added `-filter:none` to `jdeps sample.jar`, it would print the dependency of the package to itself.
- `-filter:archive`: This excludes dependencies within the same archive.
- `-filter:module`: This excludes dependencies in the same module.
- `-P`, `-profile`: This is used to show the profile of the package, whether it is in compact1, compact2, compact3, or full JRE.
- `-R`, `-recursive`: These recursively traverse all the runtime dependencies; they are equivalent to the `-filter:none` option.

Creating a simple modular application

You should be wondering what this modularity is all about, and how to create a modular application in Java. In this recipe, we will try to clear up the confusion around creating modular applications in Java by walking you through a simple example. Our goal is to show you how to create a modular application; hence, we picked a simple example so as to focus on our goal.

Our example is a simple advanced calculator, which checks whether a number is prime, calculates the sum of prime numbers, checks whether a number is even, and calculates the sum of even and odd numbers.

Getting ready

We will divide our application into two modules:

- The `math.util` module, which contains the APIs for performing the mathematical calculations
- The `calculator` module, which launches an advanced calculator

How to do it...

1. Let's implement the APIs in the `com.packt.math.MathUtil` class, starting with the `isPrime(Integer number)` API:

```
public static Boolean isPrime(Integer number){
    if ( number == 1 ) { return false; }
    return IntStream.range(2,num).noneMatch(i -> num % i == 0 );
}
```

2. Implement the `sumOfFirstNPrimes(Integer count)` API:

```
public static Integer sumOfFirstNPrimes(Integer count){
    return IntStream.iterate(1,i -> i+1)
                    .filter(j -> isPrime(j))
                    .limit(count).sum();
}
```

3. Let's write a function to check whether the number is even:

```
public static Boolean isEven(Integer number){
    return number % 2 == 0;
}
```

4. The negation of `isEven` tells us whether the number is odd. We can have functions to find the sum of the first *N* even numbers and the first *N* odd numbers, as shown here:

```
public static Integer sumOfFirstNEvens(Integer count){
    return IntStream.iterate(1,i -> i+1)
                    .filter(j -> isEven(j))
                    .limit(count).sum();
}

public static Integer sumOfFirstNOdds(Integer count){
    return IntStream.iterate(1,i -> i+1)
                    .filter(j -> !isEven(j))
                    .limit(count).sum();
}
```

We can see in the preceding APIs that the following operations are repeated:

- An infinite sequence of numbers starting from 1
- Filtering the numbers based on some condition
- Limiting the stream of numbers to a given count
- Finding the sum of numbers thus obtained

Based on our observation, we can refactor the preceding APIs and extract these operations into a method, as follows:

```
Integer computeFirstNSum(Integer count,
                                IntPredicate filter){
    return IntStream.iterate(1,i -> i+1)
                    .filter(filter)
                    .limit(count).sum();
}
```

Here, `count` is the limit of numbers we need to find the sum of, and `filter` is the condition for picking the numbers for summing.

Let's rewrite the APIs based on the refactoring we just did:

```
public static Integer sumOfFirstNPrimes(Integer count){
    return computeFirstNSum(count, (i -> isPrime(i)));
```

```
    }

    public static Integer sumOfFirstNEvens(Integer count){
        return computeFirstNSum(count, (i -> isEven(i)));
    }

    public static Integer sumOfFirstNOdds(Integer count){
        return computeFirstNSum(count, (i -> !isEven(i)));
    }
```

You must be wondering about the following:

- The `IntStream` class and the related chaining of the methods
- The use of `->` in the code base
- The use of the `IntPredicate` class

If you are indeed wondering, then you need not worry, as we will cover these things in `Chapter 4`, *Going Functional*, and `Chapter 5`, *Streams and Pipelines.*

So far, we have seen a few APIs around mathematical computations. These APIs are part of our `com.packt.math.MathUtil` class. The complete code for this class can be found at `Chapter03/2_simple-modular-math-util/math.util/com/packt/math`, in the codebase downloaded for this book.

Let's make this small utility class part of a module named `math.util`. The following are some conventions we use to create a module:

1. Place all the code related to the module under a directory named `math.util` and treat this as our module root directory.
2. In the root folder, insert a file named `module-info.java`.
3. Place the packages and the code files under the root directory.

What does `module-info.java` contain? The following:

- The name of the module
- The packages it exports, that is, the one it makes available for other modules to use
- The modules it depends on
- The services it uses
- The service for which it provides implementation

As mentioned in `Chapter 1`, *Installation and a Sneak Peek into Java 11*, the JDK comes bundled with a lot of modules, that is, the existing Java SDK has been modularized! One of those modules is a module named `java.base`. All of the user-defined modules implicitly depend on (or require) the `java.base` module (think of every class implicitly extending the `Object` class).

Our `math.util` module doesn't depend on any other module (except, of course, the `java.base` module). However, it makes its API available for other modules (if not, then this module's existence is questionable). Let's go ahead and put this statement into code:

```
module math.util{
   exports com.packt.math;
}
```

We are telling the Java compiler and runtime that our `math.util` module is *exporting* the code in the `com.packt.math` package to any module that depends on `math.util`.

 The code for this module can be found at `Chapter03/2_simple-modular-math-util/math.util`.

Now, let's create another module calculator that uses the `math.util` module. This module has a `Calculator` class whose work is to accept the user's choice for which mathematical operation to execute and then the input required to execute the operation. The user can choose from five available mathematical operations:

- Prime number check
- Even number check
- Sum of *N* primes
- Sum of *N* evens
- Sum of *N* odds

Let's see this in code:

```
private static Integer acceptChoice(Scanner reader){
   System.out.println("***********Advanced Calculator***********");
   System.out.println("1. Prime Number check");
   System.out.println("2. Even Number check");
   System.out.println("3. Sum of N Primes");
   System.out.println("4. Sum of N Evens");
   System.out.println("5. Sum of N Odds");
```

```
System.out.println("6. Exit");
System.out.println("Enter the number to choose operation");
return reader.nextInt();
}
```

Then, for each of the choices, we accept the required input and invoke the corresponding MathUtil API, as follows:

```
switch(choice){
  case 1:
    System.out.println("Enter the number");
    Integer number = reader.nextInt();
    if (MathUtil.isPrime(number)){
      System.out.println("The number " + number +" is prime");
    }else{
      System.out.println("The number " + number +" is not prime");
    }
  break;
  case 2:
    System.out.println("Enter the number");
    Integer number = reader.nextInt();
    if (MathUtil.isEven(number)){
      System.out.println("The number " + number +" is even");
    }
  break;
  case 3:
    System.out.println("How many primes?");
    Integer count = reader.nextInt();
    System.out.println(String.format("Sum of %d primes is %d",
        count, MathUtil.sumOfFirstNPrimes(count)));
  break;
  case 4:
    System.out.println("How many evens?");
    Integer count = reader.nextInt();
    System.out.println(String.format("Sum of %d evens is %d",
        count, MathUtil.sumOfFirstNEvens(count)));
  break;
  case 5:
    System.out.println("How many odds?");
    Integer count = reader.nextInt();
    System.out.println(String.format("Sum of %d odds is %d",
        count, MathUtil.sumOfFirstNOdds(count)));
  break;
}
```

The complete code for the `Calculator` class can be found at `Chapter03/2_simple-modular-math-util/calculator/com/packt/calculator/Calculator.java`.

Let's create the module definition for our `calculator` module in the same way we created it for the `math.util` module:

```
module calculator{
   requires math.util;
}
```

In the preceding module definition, we mentioned that the `calculator` module depends on the `math.util` module by using the `required` keyword.

 The code for this module can be found at `Chapter03/2_simple-modular-math-util/calculator`.

Let's compile the code:

```
javac -d mods --module-source-path . $(find . -name "*.java")
```

The preceding command has to be executed from `Chapter03/2_simple-modular-math-util`.

Also, you should have the compiled code from across both the modules, `math.util` and `calculator`, in the `mods` directory. Just a single command and everything including the dependency between the modules is taken care of by the compiler. We didn't require build tools such as `ant` to manage the compilation of modules.

The `--module-source-path` command is the new command-line option for `javac`, specifying the location of our module source code.

Let's execute the preceding code:

```
java --module-path mods -m calculator/com.packt.calculator.Calculator
```

The `--module-path` command, similar to `--classpath`, is the new command-line option `java`, specifying the location of the compiled modules.

After running the preceding command, you will see the calculator in action:

```
***********Advanced Calculator***********
1. Prime Number check
2. Even Number check
3. Sum of N Primes
4. Sum of N Evens
5. Sum of N Odds
6. Exit
Enter the number to choose operation
1
Enter the number
11
The number 11 is prime
***********Advanced Calculator***********
1. Prime Number check
2. Even Number check
3. Sum of N Primes
4. Sum of N Evens
5. Sum of N Odds
6. Exit
Enter the number to choose operation
3
How many primes?
5
Sum of 5 primes is 28
***********Advanced Calculator***********
1. Prime Number check
2. Even Number check
3. Sum of N Primes
4. Sum of N Evens
5. Sum of N Odds
6. Exit
Enter the number to choose operation
6
```

Congratulations! With this, we have a simple modular application up and running.

We have provided scripts to test out the code on both Windows and Linux platforms. Please use run.bat for Windows and run.sh for Linux.

How it works...

Now that you have been through the example, we will look at how to generalize it so that we can apply the same pattern in all our modules. We followed a particular convention to create the modules:

```
|application_root_directory
|--module1_root
|----module-info.java
|----com
|------packt
|--------sample
|----------MyClass.java
|--module2_root
|----module-info.java
|----com
|------packt
|--------test
|----------MyAnotherClass.java
```

We place the module-specific code within its folders with a corresponding `module-info.java` file at the root of the folder. This way, the code is organized well.

Let's look into what `module-info.java` can contain. From the Java language specification (http://cr.openjdk.java.net/~mr/jigsaw/spec/lang-vm.html), a module declaration is of the following form:

```
{Annotation} [open] module ModuleName { {ModuleStatement} }
```

Here's the syntax, explained:

- `{Annotation}`: This is any annotation of the form `@Annotation(2)`.
- `open`: This keyword is optional. An open module makes all its components accessible at runtime via reflection. However, at compile-time and runtime, only those components that are explicitly exported are accessible.
- `module`: This is the keyword used to declare a module.
- `ModuleName`: This is the name of the module that is a valid Java identifier with a permissible dot (`.`) between the identifier names—similar to `math.util`.
- `{ModuleStatement}`: This is a collection of the permissible statements within a module definition. Let's expand this next.

A module statement is of the following form:

```
ModuleStatement:
    requires {RequiresModifier} ModuleName ;
    exports PackageName [to ModuleName {, ModuleName}] ;
    opens PackageName [to ModuleName {, ModuleName}] ;
    uses TypeName ;
    provides TypeName with TypeName {, TypeName} ;
```

The module statement is decoded here:

- `requires`: This is used to declare a dependency on a module. `{RequiresModifier}` can be **transitive**, **static**, or both. Transitive means that any module that depends on the given module also implicitly depends on the module that is required by the given module transitively. Static means that the module dependence is mandatory at compile time, but optional at runtime. Some examples are `requires math.util`, `requires transitive math.util`, and `requires static math.util`.
- `exports`: This is used to make the given packages accessible to the dependent modules. Optionally, we can force the package's accessibility to specific modules by specifying the module name, such as `exports com.package.math to claculator`.
- `opens`: This is used to open a specific package. We saw earlier that we can open a module by specifying the `open` keyword with the module declaration. But this can be less restrictive. So, to make it more restrictive, we can open a specific package for reflective access at runtime by using the `opens` keyword—`opens com.packt.math`.
- `uses`: This is used to declare a dependency on a service interface that is accessible via `java.util.ServiceLoader`. The service interface can be in the current module or in any module that the current module depends on.
- `provides`: This is used to declare a service interface and provide it with at least one implementation. The service interface can be declared in the current module or in any other dependent module. However, the service implementation must be provided in the same module; otherwise, a compile-time error will occur.

We will look at the `uses` and `provides` clauses in more detail in the *Using services to create loose coupling between the consumer and provider modules* recipe.

The module source of all modules can be compiled at once using the `--module-source-path` command-line option. This way, all the modules will be compiled and placed in their corresponding directories under the directory provided by the `-d` option. For example, `javac -d mods --module-source-path . $(find . -name "*.java")` compiles the code in the current directory into a `mods` directory.

Running the code is equally simple. We specify the path where all our modules are compiled into using the command-line option `--module-path`. Then, we mention the module name along with the fully qualified main class name using the command-line option `-m`, for example, `java --module-path mods -m calculator/com.packt.calculator.Calculator`.

See also

The *Compiling and running a Java application* recipe in `Chapter 1`, *Installation and a Sneak Peek into Java 11*

Creating a modular JAR

Compiling modules into a class is good, but it is not suitable for sharing binaries and deployment. JARs are better formats for sharing and deployment. We can package the compiled module into JARs, and the JARs that contain `module-info.class` at its top level are called **modular JARs**. In this recipe, we will look at how to create modular JARs, and we'll also look at how to execute the application, which is composed of multiple modular JARs.

Getting ready

We have seen and created a simple modular application in the *Creating a simpler modular application* recipe. In order to build a modular JAR, we will make use of the sample code available at `Chapter03/3_modular_jar`. This sample code contains two modules: `math.util` and `calculator`. We will create modular JARs for both the modules.

How to do it...

1. Compile the code and place the compiled classes in a directory, say, `mods`:

   ```
   javac -d mods --module-source-path . $(find . -name *.java)
   ```

2. Build a modular JAR for the `math.util` module:

   ```
   jar --create --file=mlib/math.util@1.0.jar --module-version 1.0
   -C mods/math.util .
   ```

    Do not forget the dot (.) at the end of the preceding code.

3. Build a modular JAR for the `calculator` module, specifying the main class to make the JAR executable:

   ```
   jar --create --file=mlib/calculator@1.0.jar --module-version 1.0
   --main-class com.packt.calculator.Calculator -C mods/calculator
   .
   ```

   The critical piece in the preceding command is the `--main-class` option. This enables us to execute the JAR without providing the main class information during execution.

4. Now, we have two JARs in the `mlib` directory: `math.util@1.0.jar` and `calculator@1.0.jar`. These JARs are called modular JARs. If you want to run the example, you can use the following command:

   ```
   java -p mlib -m calculator
   ```

5. A new command-line option for the JAR command has been introduced in Java 9, called `-d`, or `--describe-module`. This prints the information about the module that the modular JAR contains:

   ```
   jar -d --file=mlib/calculator@1.0.jar
   ```

The output of `jar -d` for `calculator@1.0.jar` is as follows:

```
calculator@1.0
   requires mandated java.base
   requires math.util
   conceals com.packt.calculator
   main-class com.packt.calculator.Calculator

jar -d --file=mlib/math.util@1.0.jar
```

The output of `jar -d` for `math.util@1.0.jar` is as follows:

```
math.util@1.0
   requires mandated java.base
   exports com.packt.math
```

We have provided the following scripts to try out the recipe code on Windows:

- `compile-math.bat`
- `compile-calculator.bat`
- `jar-math.bat`
- `jar-calculator.bat`
- `run.bat`

We have provided the following scripts to try out the recipe code on Linux:

- `compile.sh`
- `jar-math.sh`
- `jar-calculator.sh`
- `run.sh`

You have to run the scripts in the order they have been listed.

Using a module JAR with pre-Project Jigsaw JDK applications

It would be amazing if our modular JARs could be run with pre-Project Jigsaw JDK applications. This way, we will not be concerned with writing another version of our API for pre-JDK 9 applications. The good news is that we can use our modular JARs just as if they were ordinary JARs, that is, JARs without `module-info.class` at their root. We will see how to do so in this recipe.

Getting ready

For this recipe, we will need a modular jar and a non-modular application. Our modular code can be found at `Chapter03/4_modular_jar_with_pre_java9/math.util` (this is the same `math.util` module that we created in our *Creating a simple modular application* recipe). Let's compile this modular code and create a modular JAR by using the following commands:

```
javac -d classes --module-source-path . $(find math.util -name *.java)
mkdir mlib
jar --create --file mlib/math.util.jar -C classes/math.util .
```

We have also provided a `jar-math.bat` script at `Chapter03/4_modular_jar_with_pre_java9`, which can be used to create modular JARs on Windows. We have our modular JAR. Let's verify it by using the `-d` option of the `jar` command:

```
jar -d --file mlib/math.util@1.0.jar
math.util@1.0
    requires mandated java.base
    exports com.packt.math
```

How to do it...

Now, let's create a simple application, which is non-modular. Our application will consist of one class named `NonModularCalculator`, which borrows its code from the `Calculator` class, in the *Creating a simple modular application* recipe.

You can find the `NonModularCalculator` class definition in the `com.packt.calculator` package under the `Chapter03/4_modular_jar_with_pre_java9/calculator` directory. As it is non-modular, it doesn't need a `module-info.java` file. This application makes use of our modular JAR `math.util.jar` to execute some mathematical calculations.

At this point, you should have the following:

- A modular JAR named `math.util@1.0.jar`
- A non-modular application consisting of the `NonModularCalculator` package

Now, we need to compile our `NonModularCalculator` class:

```
javac -d classes/ --source-path calculator $(find calculator -name
*.java)
```

After running the previous command, you will see a list of errors saying that the `com.packt.math` package doesn't exist, the `MathUtil` symbol cannot be found, and so on. You've guessed it; we didn't provide the location of our modular JAR for the compiler. Let's add the modular `jar` location using the `--class-path` option:

```
javac --class-path mlib/* -d classes/ --source-path calculator $(find
calculator -name *.java)
```

Now, we have successfully compiled our non-modular code, which was dependent on the modular JAR. Let's run the compiled code:

```
java -cp classes:mlib/* com.packt.calculator.NonModularCalculator
```

Congratulations! You have successfully used your modular JAR with a non-modular application. Amazing, right?

We have provided the following scripts at `Chapter03/4_modular_jar_with_pre_java9` to run the code on the Windows platform:

- `compile-calculator.bat`
- `run.bat`

Bottom-up migration

Now that Java 9 is out of the door, the much-awaited modularity feature is now available to be adopted by developers. At some point or another, you will be involved in migrating your application to Java 9 and, hence, trying to modularize it. A change of such magnitude, which involves third-party libraries and rethinking the code structure, would require proper planning and implementation. The Java team has suggested two migration approaches:

- Bottom-up migration
- Top-down migration

Before going into learning about bottom-up migration, it's important to understand what an unnamed module and an automatic module are. Suppose you are accessing a type that's not available in any of the modules; in such a case, the module system will search for the type on the classpath, and if found, the type becomes part of an unnamed module. This is similar to the classes we write that do not belong to any package, but Java adds them to an unnamed package so as to simplify the creation of new classes.

So, an unnamed module is a catch-all module without a name that contains all those types that are not part of any modules, but are found in the classpath. An unnamed module can access all the exported types of all the named modules (user-defined modules) and built-in modules (Java platform modules). On the other hand, a named module (user-defined module) will not be able to access the types in the unnamed module. In other words, a named module cannot declare dependency on an unnamed module. If you want to declare a dependency, how would you do that? An unnamed module doesn't have a name!

> With the concept of unnamed modules, you can take your Java 8 application as is and run it on Java 9 (except for any deprecated internal APIs, which might not be available for user code in Java 9).

You may have seen this if you have tried out the *Using jdeps to find dependencies in a Java application* recipe, where we had a non-modular application and were able to run it on Java 9. However, running as is on Java 9 would defeat the purpose of introducing the modular system.

If a package is defined in both named and unnamed modules, the one in the named module would be given preference over the one in the unnamed module. This helps to prevent package conflicts when they come from both named and unnamed modules.

Automatic modules are those that are automatically created by the JVM. These modules are created when we introduce the classes packaged in JARs in the module path instead of the classpath. The name of this module will be derived from the name of the JAR without the `.jar` extension and, hence, is different from unnamed modules. Alternatively, one can provide the name for these automatic modules by providing the module name against `Automatic-Module-Name` in the JAR manifest file. These automatic modules export all the packages present in it and also depend on all the automatic and named (user/JDK) modules.

Based on this explanation, modules can be classified into the following:

- **Unnamed modules**: The code available on the classpath and not available on the module path is placed in an unnamed module.
- **Named modules**: All those modules that have a name associated with them—these can be user-defined modules and JDK modules.
- **Automatic modules**: All those modules that are implicitly created by JVM based on the JAR files present in the module path.
- **Implicit modules**: Modules which are implicitly created. They are the same as automatic modules.
- **Explicit modules**: All modules which are created explicitly by the user or JDK.

But the unnamed module and automatic module are a good first step to start your migration. So, let's get started!

Getting ready

We need a non-modular application that we will eventually modularize. We have already created a simple application, whose source code is available at `Chapter03/6_bottom_up_migration_before`. This simple application has three parts to it:

- A math utility library that contains our favorite mathematical APIs: prime checker, even number checker, sum of primes, sum of evens, and sum of odds. The code for this is available at `Chapter03/6_bottom_up_migration_before/math_util`.

- A banking utility library that contains APIs to compute simple interest and compound interest. The code for this is available at `Chapter03/6_bottom_up_migration_before/banking_util`.
- Our calculator app helps us with our mathematical and banking calculations. To make this more interesting, we will output the results in JSON and for this, we will make use of Jackson JSON API. The code for this is available at `Chapter03/6_bottom_up_migration_before/calculator`.

After you have copied or downloaded the code, we will compile and build the respective JARs. So, use the following commands to compile and build the JARs:

```
#Compiling math util

javac -d math_util/out/classes/ -sourcepath math_util/src $(find
math_util/src -name *.java)
jar --create --file=math_util/out/math.util.jar
-C math_util/out/classes/ .

#Compiling banking util

javac -d banking_util/out/classes/ -sourcepath banking_util/src $(find
banking_util/src -name *.java)
jar --create --file=banking_util/out/banking.util.jar
-C banking_util/out/classes/ .

#Compiling calculator

javac -cp
calculator/lib/*:math_util/out/math.util.jar:banking_util/out/banking.
util.jar -d calculator/out/classes/ -sourcepath calculator/src $(find
calculator/src -name *.java)
```

Let's also create a JAR for this (we will make use of the JAR to build the dependency graph, but not for running the app):

```
jar --create --file=calculator/out/calculator.jar -C
calculator/out/classes/ .
```

Please note that our Jackson JARs are in the calculator/lib, so you don't need to worry about downloading them. Let's run our calculator using the following command:

```
java -cp
calculator/out/classes:calculator/lib/*:math_util/out/math.util.jar:ba
nking_util/out/banking.util.jar com.packt.calculator.Calculator
```

You will see a menu asking for the choice of operation, and then you can play around with different operations. Now, let's modularize this application!

We have provided `package-*.bat` and run.bat to the package and run the application on Windows. You can use `package-*.sh` and `run.sh` for the package and run the application on Linux.

How to do it...

The first step in modularizing your application is to understand its dependency graph. Let's create a dependency graph for our application. For that, we make use of the `jdeps` tool. If you are wondering what the `jdeps` tool is, stop right now and read the *Using jdeps to find dependencies in a Java application* recipe. OK, so let's run the `jdeps` tool:

```
jdeps -summary -R -cp
calculator/lib/*:math_util/out/*:banking_util/out/*
calculator/out/calculator.jar
```

We are asking `jdeps` to give us a summary of the dependencies of our `calculator.jar` and then do this recursively for each dependency of `calculator.jar`. The output we get is as follows:

```
banking.util.jar -> java.base
calculator.jar -> banking_util/out/banking.util.jar
calculator.jar -> calculator/lib/jackson-databind-2.8.4.jar
calculator.jar -> java.base
calculator.jar -> math_util/out/math.util.jar
jackson-annotations-2.8.4.jar -> java.base
jackson-core-2.8.4.jar -> java.base
jackson-databind-2.8.4.jar -> calculator/lib/jackson-
annotations-2.8.4.jar
jackson-databind-2.8.4.jar -> calculator/lib/jackson-core-2.8.4.jar
jackson-databind-2.8.4.jar -> java.base
jackson-databind-2.8.4.jar -> java.logging
jackson-databind-2.8.4.jar -> java.sql
jackson-databind-2.8.4.jar -> java.xml
math.util.jar -> java.base
```

The preceding output is hard to understand and the same can be diagrammatically, as follows:

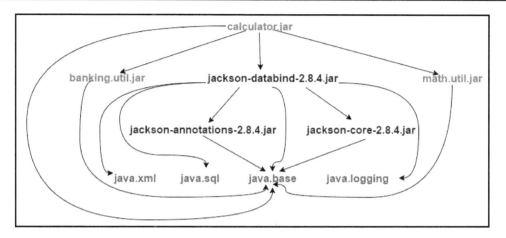

In bottom-up migration, we start by modularizing the leaf nodes. In our graph, the java.xml, java.sql, java.base, and java.logging leaf nodes are already modularized. Let's modularize banking.util.jar.

 All the code for this recipe is available
at Chapter03/6_bottom_up_migration_after.

Modularizing banking.util.jar

1. Copy BankUtil.java from
   Chapter03/6_bottom_up_migration_before/banking_util/src/co
   m/packt/banking
   to Chapter03/6_bottom_up_migration_after/src/banking.util/c
   om/packt/banking. There are two things to take a note of:
   - We have renamed the folder from banking_util to
     banking.util. This is to follow the convention of placing
     module-related code under the folder bearing the module name.
   - We have placed the package directly under the banking.util
     folder and not under src. Again, this is to follow the convention.
     We will be placing all our modules under the src folder.

2. Create the module definition file `module-info.java` under `Chapter03/6_bottom_up_migration_after/src/banking.util` with the following definition:

```
module banking.util{
    exports com.packt.banking;
}
```

3. From within the `6_bottom_up_migration_after` folder, compile the java code of the modules by running the command:

```
javac -d mods --module-source-path src
$(find src -name *.java)
```

4. You will see that the java code in the module `banking.util` is compiled into the mods directory.

5. Let's create a modular JAR for this module:

```
jar --create --file=mlib/banking.util.jar -C mods/banking.util
```

If you are wondering what a modular JAR is, feel free to read through the *Creating a modular JAR* recipe in this chapter.

Now that we have modularized `banking.util.jar`, let's use this modular `jar` in place of the non-modular JAR used in the *Getting ready* section earlier. You should execute the following from the `6_bottom_up_migration_before` folder because we haven't yet completely modularized the app:

```
java --add-modules ALL-MODULE-PATH --module-path
../6_bottom_up_migration_after/mods/banking.util -cp
calculator/out/classes:calculator/lib/*:math_util/out/math.util.jar
com.packt.calculator.Calculator
```

The `--add-modules` option tells the Java runtime to include the modules either by module name or by predefined constants, namely `ALL-MODULE-PATH`, `ALL-DEFAULT`, and `ALL-SYSTEM`. We made use of `ALL-MODULE-PATH` to add the module that is available on our module path.

The `--module-path` option tells the Java runtime the location of our modules.

You will see that our calculator is running as usual. Try out a simple interest calculation, a compound interest calculation, to check if the `BankUtil` class is found. So, our dependency graph now looks like this:

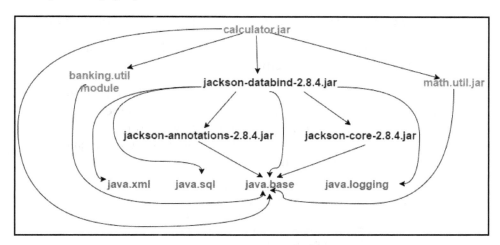

Modularizing math.util.jar

1. Copy `MathUtil.java` from
   `Chapter03/6_bottom_up_migration_before/math_util/src/com/packt/math`
   to `Chapter03/6_bottom_up_migration_after/src/math.util/com/packt/math`.

2. Create the module definition file, `module-info.java`, under
   `Chapter03/6_bottom_up_migration_after/src/math.util` with the
   following definition:

   ```
   module math.util{
      exports com.packt.math;
   }
   ```

3. From within the `6_bottom_up_migration_after` folder, compile the
   Java code of the modules by running the following command:

   ```
   javac -d mods --module-source-path src $(find src -name *.java)
   ```

4. You will see that the Java code in the `math.util` and `banking.util` modules is compiled into the `mods` directory.

5. Let's create a modular JAR for this module:

```
jar --create --file=mlib/math.util.jar -C mods/math.util .
```

If you are wondering what a modular `jar` is, feel free to read through the *Creating a modular JAR* recipe in this chapter.

6. Now that we have modularized `math.util.jar`, let's use this modular `jar` in place of the non-modular `jar` that we used in the *Getting ready* section earlier. You should execute the following from the `6_bottom_up_migration_before` folder because we haven't completely modularized the app yet:

```
java --add-modules ALL-MODULE-PATH --module-path
../6_bottom_up_migration_after/mods/banking.util:
../6_bottom_up_migration_after/mods/math.util
-cp calculator/out/classes:calculator/lib/*
com.packt.calculator.Calculator
```

Our app is running fine, and the dependency graph looks as follows:

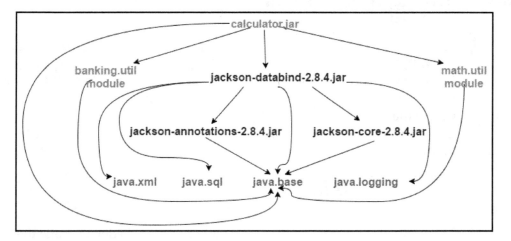

We cannot modularize `calculator.jar` because it depends on another non-modular code, `jackson-databind`, and we cannot modularize `jackson-databind` as it is not maintained by us. This means that we cannot achieve 100% modularity for our application. We introduced you to Unnamed modules at the beginning of this recipe. All our non-modular code in the classpath are grouped in unnamed modules, which means all jackson-related code can still remain in the unnamed module and we can try to modularize `calculator.jar`. But we cannot do so because `calculator.jar` cannot declare a dependency on `jackson-databind-2.8.4.jar` (because it is an unnamed module and named modules cannot declare dependency on unnamed modules).

A way to get around this is to make the jackson-related code as automatic modules. We can do this by moving the jars related to jackson:

- `jackson-databind-2.8.4.jar`
- `jackson-annotations-2.8.4.jar`
- `jackson-core-2.8.4.jar`

We'll move them under the `6_bottom_up_migration_after` folder using the following commands:

```
$ pwd
/root/java9-samples/Chapter03/6_bottom_up_migration_after
$ cp ../6_bottom_up_migration_before/calculator/lib/*.jar mlib/
$ mv mlib/jackson-annotations-2.8.4.jar mods/jackson.annotations.jar
$ mv mlib/jackson-core-2.8.4.jar mods/jackson.core.jar
$ mv mlib/jackson-databind-2.8.4.jar mods/jackson.databind.jar
```

The reason for renaming the jars is that the name of the module has to be a valid identifier (should not be only numeric, should not contain -, and other rules) separated with .. As the names are derived from the name of the JAR files, we had to rename the JAR files to conform to the Java identifier rules.

Create a new `mlib` directory, if it is not present, under `6_bottom_up_migration_after`.

Now, let's run our calculator program again using the following command:

```
java --add-modules ALL-MODULE-PATH --module-path
../6_bottom_up_migration_after/mods:../6_bottom_up_migration_after/mli
b -cp calculator/out/classes com.packt.calculator.Calculator
```

The application will run as usual. You will notice that our -cp option value is getting smaller as all the dependent libraries have been moved as modules in the module path. The dependency graph now looks like this:

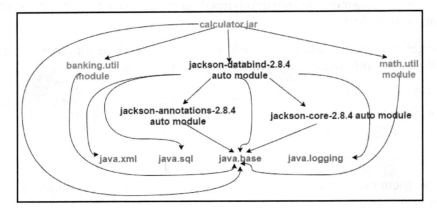

Modularizing calculator.jar

The last step in the migration is to modularize `calculator.jar`. Follow these steps to modularize it:

1. Copy the `com` folder from `Chapter03/6_bottom_up_migration_before/calculator/src` to `Chapter03/6_bottom_up_migration_after/src/calculator`.

2. Create the module definition file, `module-info.java`, under `Chapter03/6_bottom_up_migration_after/src/calculator`, with the following definition:

   ```
   module calculator{
       requires math.util;
       requires banking.util;
       requires jackson.databind;
       requires jackson.core;
       requires jackson.annotations;
   }
   ```

3. From within the `6_bottom_up_migration_after` folder, compile the Java code of the modules by running the following command:

```
javac -d mods --module-path mlib:mods --module-source-path src
$(find src -name *.java)
```

4. You will see that the Java code in all our modules is compiled into the mods directory. Please note that you should have the automatic modules (that is, jackson-related JARs) already placed in the `mlib` directory.

5. Let's create a modular JAR for this module and also mention which is the `main` class:

```
jar --create --file=mlib/calculator.jar --main-
class=com.packt.calculator.Calculator -C mods/calculator .
```

6. Now, we have a modular JAR for our calculator module, which is our main module as it contains the `main` class. With this, we have also modularized our complete application. Let's run the following command from the folder: `6_bottom_up_migration_after`:

```
java -p mlib:mods -m calculator
```

So, we have seen how to modularize a non-modular application using a bottom-up migration approach. The final dependency graph looks something like this:

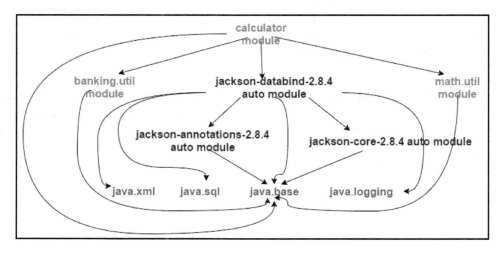

The final code for this modular application can be found at `Chapter03/6_bottom_up_migration_after`.

We could have done modification in line, that is, modularize the code in the same directory, 6_bottom_up_migration_before. But we prefer to do it separately in a different directory, 6_bottom_up_migration_after, so as to keep it clean and not disturb the existing codebase.

How it works...

The concept of unnamed modules helped us to run our non-modular application on Java 9. The use of both module path and classpath helped us to run the partly modular application while we were doing the migration. We started with modularizing those codebases that were not dependent on any non-modular code, and any codebase that we couldn't modularize, we converted into automatic modules, thereby enabling us to modularize the code which was dependent on such a code base. Eventually, we ended up with a completely modular application.

Top-down migration

The other technique for migration is top-down migration. In this approach, we start with the root JAR in the dependency graph of the JARs.

JARs indicate a codebase. We have assumed that the codebase is available in the form of JARs and hence the dependency graph that we get has nodes, which are JARs.

Modularizing the root of the dependency graph would mean that all other JARs on which this root depends have to be modular. Otherwise, this modular root cannot declare a dependency on unnamed modules. Let's consider the example non-modular application we introduced in our Bottom-Up Migration recipe. The dependency graph looks something like this:

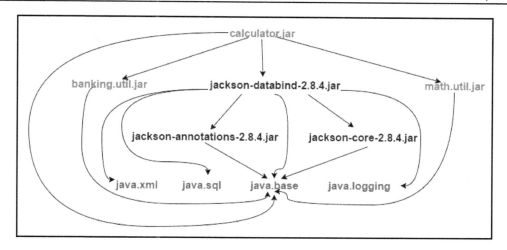

We extensively make use of automatic modules in top-down migration. Automatic modules are modules that are implicitly created by the JVM. These are created based on the non-modular JARs available in the module path.

Getting ready

We will make use of the calculator example that we introduced in the previous recipe, *Bottom-up migration*. Go ahead and copy the non-modular code from Chapter03/7_top_down_migration_before. Use the following commands if you wish to run it and see whether it's working:

```
$ javac -d math_util/out/classes/ -sourcepath math_util/src $(find
math_util/src -name *.java)

$ jar --create --file=math_util/out/math.util.jar
-C math_util/out/classes/ .

$ javac -d banking_util/out/classes/ -sourcepath banking_util/src
$(find banking_util/src -name *.java)

$ jar --create --file=banking_util/out/banking.util.jar
-C banking_util/out/classes/ .

$ javac -cp
calculator/lib/*:math_util/out/math.util.jar:banking_util/out/banking.
util.jar -d calculator/out/classes/ -sourcepath calculator/src $(find
calculator/src -name *.java)
```

```
$ java -cp
calculator/out/classes:calculator/lib/*:math_util/out/math.util.jar:ba
nking_util/out/banking.util.jar com.packt.calculator.Calculator
```

 We have provided `package-*.bat` and `run.bat` to the package and run the code on Windows, and used `package-*.sh` and `run.sh` on the package and run the code on Linux.

How to do it...

We will be modularizing the application under the `Chapter03/7_top_down_migration_after` directory. Create two directories, `src` and `mlib`, under `Chapter03/7_top_down_migration_after`.

Modularizing the calculator

1. We cannot modularize the calculator until we have modularized all its dependencies. But modularizing its dependencies might be easier at times and not so at other times, especially in cases where the dependency is from a third party. In such scenarios, we make use of automatic modules. We copy the non-modular JARs under the folder `mlib` and ensuring that the name of the JAR is in the form `<identifier>(.<identifier>)*`, where `<identifier>` is a valid Java identifier:

```
$ cp ../7_top_down_migration_before/calculator/lib/jackson-
annotations-
2.8.4.jar mlib/jackson.annotations.jar

$ cp ../7_top_down_migration_before/calculator/lib/jackson-core-
2.8.4.jar
mlib/jackson.core.jar

$ cp ../7_top_down_migration_before/calculator/lib/jackson-
databind-
2.8.4.jar mlib/jackson.databind.jar

$ cp
../7_top_down_migration_before/banking_util/out/banking.util.jar
mlib/

$ cp ../7_top_down_migration_before/math_util/out/math.util.jar
mlib/
```

We have provided the `copy-non-mod-jar.bat` and `copy-non-mod-jar.sh` scripts to copy the jars easily.

Let's see what we copied into `mlib`:

```
$ ls mlib
banking.util.jar   jackson.annotations.jar   jackson.core.jar
jackson.databind.jar   math.util.jar
```

 `banking.util.jar` and `math.util.jar` will exist only if you have compiled and JAR-ed the code in the `Chapter03/7_top_down_migration_before/banking_util` and `Chapter03/7_top_down_migration_before/math_util` directories. We did this in the *Getting ready* section earlier.

2. Create a new `calculator` folder under `src`. This will contain the code for the `calculator` module.

3. Create `module-info.java` under the `Chapter03/7_top_down_migration_after/src/calculator` directory that contains the following:

```
module calculator{
    requires math.util;
    requires banking.util;
    requires jackson.databind;
    requires jackson.core;
    requires jackson.annotations;
}
```

4. Copy the `Chapter03/7_top_down_migration_before/calculator/src/com` directory and all the code under it to `Chapter03/7_top_down_migration_after/src/calculator`.

5. Compile the calculator module:

```
#On Linux
javac -d mods --module-path mlib --module-source-path src $(find
src -name *.java)

#On Windows
javac -d mods --module-path mlib --module-source-path src
srccalculatormodule-info.java
srccalculatorcompacktcalculatorCalculator.java
srccalculatorcompacktcalculatorcommands*.java
```

6. Create the modular JAR for the `calculator` module:

```
jar --create --file=mlib/calculator.jar --main-
class=com.packt.calculator.Calculator -C mods/calculator/ .
```

7. Run the `calculator` module:

```
java --module-path mlib -m calculator
```

We will see that our calculator is executing correctly. You can try out different operations to verify if all of them are executing correctly.

Modularizing banking.util

As this doesn't depend on other non-module code, we can directly convert this into a module by following these steps:

1. Create a new `banking.util` folder under `src`. This will contain the code for the `banking.util` module.

2. Create `module-info.java` under the `Chapter03/7_top_down_migration_after/src/banking.util` directory, which contains the following:

```
module banking.util{
   exports com.packt.banking;
}
```

3. Copy
   the `Chapter03/7_top_down_migration_before/banking_util/src/` `com` directory and all the code under it
   to `Chapter03/7_top_down_migration_after/src/banking.util`.

4. Compile the modules:

```
#On Linux
javac -d mods --module-path mlib --module-source-path src $(find
src -name *.java)

#On Windows
javac -d mods --module-path mlib --module-source-path src
srcbanking.utilmodule-info.java
srcbanking.utilcompacktbankingBankUtil.java
```

5. Create a modular JAR for the `banking.util` module. This will replace the
   non-modular `banking.util.jar` already present in `mlib`:

```
jar --create --file=mlib/banking.util.jar -C mods/banking.util/
```

6. Run the `calculator` module to test whether the `banking.util` modular
   JAR has been created successfully:

```
java --module-path mlib -m calculator
```

7. You should see the calculator getting executed. Play around with different
   operations to ensure that there are no "class not found" issues.

Modularizing math.util

1. Create a new `math.util` folder under `src`. This will contain the code for
   the `math.util` module.

2. Create `module-info.java` under
   the `Chapter03/7_top_down_migration_after/src/math.util` direct
   ory, which contains the following:

```
module math.util{
  exports com.packt.math;
}
```

3. Copy
   the `Chapter03/7_top_down_migration_before/math_util/src/com`
   directory and all the code under it
   to `Chapter03/7_top_down_migration_after/src/math.util`.

4. Compile the modules:

```
#On Linux
javac -d mods --module-path mlib --module-source-path src $(find
src -name *.java)
```

```
#On Windows
javac -d mods --module-path mlib --module-source-path src
srcmath.utilmodule-info.java
srcmath.utilcompacktmathMathUtil.java
```

5. Create a modular JAR for the `banking.util` module. This will replace the
   non-modular `banking.util.jar` already present in `mlib`:

```
jar --create --file=mlib/math.util.jar -C mods/math.util/ .
```

6. Run the `calculator` module to test whether the `math.util` modular JAR
   has been created successfully.

```
java --module-path mlib -m calculator
```

7. You should see the calculator getting executed. Play around with different
   operations to ensure that there are no *class not found* issues.

With this, we have completely modularized the application, baring the Jackson
libraries which we have converted to automatic modules.

We prefer the top-down approach for migration. This is because we don't have to deal
with classpath and module-path at the same time. We can make everything into
automatic modules and then use the module-path as we keep migrating the non-
modular JARs into modular JARs.

Using services to create loose coupling between the consumer and provider modules

Generally, in our applications, we have some interfaces and multiple implementations of those interfaces. Then, at runtime, depending on certain conditions, we make use of specific implementations. This principle is called **Dependency Inversion**. This principle is used by dependency injection frameworks, such as Spring, to create objects of concrete implementations and assign (or inject) into the references of the abstract interface type.

For a long time, Java (since Java 6) has supported service-provider loading facilities via the `java.util.ServiceLoader` class. Using Service Loader, you can have a **service provider interface** (**SPI**) and multiple implementations of the SPI simply called service provider. These service providers are located in the classpath and loaded at runtime. When these service providers are located within modules, and as we no longer depend on the classpath scanning to load the service provider, we need a mechanism to tell our modules about the service provider and the service provider interface for which it is providing an implementation. In this recipe, we will look at this mechanism by using a simple example.

Getting ready

There is nothing specific we need to set up for this recipe. In this recipe, we will take a simple example. We have one `BookService` abstract class, which supports CRUD operations. Now, these CRUD operations can work on a SQL DB, MongoDB, a filesystem, and so on. This flexibility can be provided by using the service provider interface and the `ServiceLoader` class to load the required service provider implementation.

How to do it...

We have four modules in this recipe:

- `book.service`: This is the module that contains our service provider interface, that is, the service
- `mongodb.book.service`: This is one of the service provider modules

- `sqldb.book.service`: This is the other service provider module
- `book.manage`: This is the service consumer module

The following steps demonstrate how to make use of `ServiceLoader` to achieve loose coupling:

1. Create a `book.service` folder under the `Chapter03/8_services/src` directory. All our code for the `book.service` module will be under this folder.

2. Create a new package, `com.packt.model`, and a new class, `Book`, under the new package. This is our model class, which contains the following properties:

   ```
   public String id;
   public String title;
   public String author;
   ```

3. Create a new package, `com.packt.service`, and a new class, `BookService`, under the new package. This is our main service interface, and the service providers will provide an implementation for this service. Apart from the abstract methods for CRUD operations, one method worth mentioning is `getInstance()`. This method uses the `ServiceLoader` class to load any one service provider (the last one, to be specific) and then use that service provider to get an implementation of `BookService`. Let's see the following code:

   ```
   public static BookService getInstance(){
     ServiceLoader<BookServiceProvider> sl =
           ServiceLoader.load(BookServiceProvider.class);
     Iterator<BookServiceProvider> iter = sl.iterator();
     if (!iter.hasNext())
       throw new RuntimeException("No service providers found!");
     BookServiceProvider provider = null;
     while(iter.hasNext()){
       provider = iter.next();
       System.out.println(provider.getClass());
     }
     return provider.getBookService();
   }
   ```

The first `while` loop is just for demonstrating that the `ServiceLoader` loads all the service providers and we pick one of the service providers. You can conditionally return the service provider as well, but that all depends on the requirements.

4. The other important part is the actual service provider interface. The responsibility of this is to return an appropriate instance of the service implementation. In our recipe, `BookServiceProvider` in the `com.packt.spi` package is a service provider interface:

```
public interface BookServiceProvider{
   public BookService getBookService();
}
```

5. We create `module-info.java` under the `Chapter03/8_services/src/book.service` directory, which contains the following:

```
module book.service{
   exports com.packt.model;
   exports com.packt.service;
   exports com.packt.spi;
   uses com.packt.spi.BookServiceProvider;
}
```

The `uses` statement in the preceding module definition specifies the service interface that the module discovers using `ServiceLoader`.

6. Now let's create a service provider module called `mongodb.book.service`. This will provide an implementation for our `BookService` and `BookServiceProvider` interface in the `book.service` module. Our idea is that this service provider will implement the CRUD operations using the MongoDB datastore.

7. Create a `mongodb.book.service` folder under the `Chapter03/8_services/src` directory.

8. Create a `MongoDbBookService` class in the `com.packt.mongodb.service` package, which extends the `BookService` abstract class and provides an implementation of our abstract CRUD operation methods:

```
public void create(Book book){
   System.out.println("Mongodb Create book ... " + book.title);
}

public Book read(String id){
   System.out.println("Mongodb Reading book ... " + id);
   return new Book(id, "Title", "Author");
}
```

```
public void update(Book book){
  System.out.println("Mongodb Updating book ... " +
      book.title);
}

public void delete(String id){
  System.out.println("Mongodb Deleting ... " + id);
}
```

9. Create a `MongoDbBookServiceProvider` class in the `com.packt.mongodb` package, which implements the `BookServiceProvider` interface. This is our service-discovery class. Basically, it returns a relevant instance of the `BookService` implementation. It overrides the method in the `BookServiceProvider` interface, as follows:

```
@Override
public BookService getBookService(){
  return new MongoDbBookService();
}
```

10. The module definition is quite interesting. We have to declare in the module definition that this module is a service provider for the `BookServiceProvider` interface, and that can be done as follows:

```
module mongodb.book.service{
  requires book.service;
  provides com.packt.spi.BookServiceProvider
          with com.packt.mongodb.MongoDbBookServiceProvider;
}
```

The `provides .. with ..` statement is used to specify the service interface and one of the service providers.

11. Now let's create a service consumer module called `book.manage`.

12. Create a new `book.manage` folder under `Chapter03/8_services/src` which will contain the code for the module.

13. Create a new class called `BookManager` in the `com.packt.manage` package. The main aim of this class is to get an instance of `BookService` and then execute its CRUD operations. The instance returned is decided by the service providers loaded by the `ServiceLoader`. The `BookManager` class looks something like this:

```
public class BookManager{
  public static void main(String[] args){
```

```
        BookService service = BookService.getInstance();
        System.out.println(service.getClass());
        Book book = new Book("1", "Title", "Author");
        service.create(book);
        service.read("1");
        service.update(book);
        service.delete("1");
    }
}
```

14. Let's compile and run our main module by using the following commands:

```
$ javac -d mods --module-source-path src
$(find src -name *.java)
$ java --module-path mods -m
book.manage/com.packt.manage.BookManager
class com.packt.mongodb.MongoDbBookServiceProvider
class com.packt.mongodb.service.MongoDbBookService
Mongodb Create book ... Title
Mongodb Reading book ... 1
Mongodb Updating book ... Title
Mongodb Deleting ... 1
```

In the preceding output, the first line states the service providers that are available and the second line states which BookService implementation we are using.

15. With one service provider, it looks simple. Let's go ahead and add another module, sqldb.book.service, whose module definition would be as follows:

```
module sqldb.book.service{
    requires book.service;
    provides com.packt.spi.BookServiceProvider
            with com.packt.sqldb.SqlDbBookServiceProvider;
}
```

16. The SqlDbBookServiceProvider class in the com.packt.sqldb package is an implementation of the BookServiceProvider interface, as follows:

```
@Override
public BookService getBookService(){
    return new SqlDbBookService();
}
```

17. The implementation of CRUD operations is done by the `SqlDbBookService` class in the package `com.packt.sqldb.service` package.

18. Let's compile and run the main module, this time with two service providers:

```
$ javac -d mods --module-source-path src
$(find src -name *.java)
$ java --module-path mods -m
book.manage/com.packt.manage.BookManager
class com.packt.sqldb.SqlDbBookServiceProvider
class com.packt.mongodb.MongoDbBookServiceProvider
class com.packt.mongodb.service.MongoDbBookService
Mongodb Create book ... Title
Mongodb Reading book ... 1
Mongodb Updating book ... Title
Mongodb Deleting ... 1
```

The first two lines print the class names of the available service providers and the third line prints which `BookService` implementation we are using.

Creating a custom modular runtime image using jlink

Java comes in two flavors:

- Java runtime only, also known as JRE: This supports the execution of Java applications
- Java development kit with Java runtime, also called JDK: This supports the development and execution of Java applications

Apart from this, there were three compact profiles introduced in Java 8 with the aim of providing runtimes with a smaller footprint in order to run on embedded and smaller devices shown as follows:

Full SE API	Beans	JNI	JAX-WS
	Preferences	Accessibility	IDL
	RMI-IIOP	CORBA	Print Service
	Sound	Swing	Java 2D
	AWT	Drag and Drop	Input Methods
	Image I/O		
compact3	Security[1]	JMX	
	XML JAXP[2]	Management	Instrumentation
compact2	JDBC	RMI	XML JAXP
compact1	Core (`java.lang.*`)	Security	Serialization
	Networking	Ref Objects	Regular Expressions
	Date and Time	Input/Output	Collections
	Logging	Concurrency	Reflection
	JAR	ZIP	Versioning
	Internationalization	JNDI	Override Mechanism
	Extension Mechanism	Scripting	

1. Adds kerberos, acl, and sasl to compact1 Security.
2. Adds crypto to compact2 XML JAXP.

The preceding image shows the different profiles and the features supported by them.

A new tool, called `jlink` was introduced in Java 9 that enables the creation of modular runtime images. These runtime images are nothing but a collection of a set of modules and their dependencies. There is a Java enhancement proposal, JEP 220, governing the structure of this runtime image.

In this recipe, we will use `jlink` to create a runtime image consisting of our `math.util`, `banking.util`, and `calculator` modules, along with the Jackson automatic modules.

Getting ready

In the *Creating a simple modular application* recipe, we created a simple modular application consisting of the following modules:

- `math.util`
- `calculator`: Consists of the main class

We will reuse the same set of modules and code to demonstrate the use of the `jlink` tool. For the convenience of our readers, the code can be found at `Chapter03/9_jlink_modular_run_time_image`.

How to do it...

1. Let's compile the modules:

   ```
   $ javac -d mods --module-path mlib --module-source-path
     src $(find src - name *.java)
   ```

2. Let's create the modular JAR for all the modules:

   ```
   $ jar --create --file mlib/math.util.jar -C mods/math.util .
   ```

   ```
   $ jar --create --file=mlib/calculator.jar --main-
   class=com.packt.calculator.Calculator -C mods/calculator/ .
   ```

3. Let's use `jlink` to create a runtime image consisting of the `calculator` and `math.util` modules and their dependencies:

   ```
   $ jlink --module-path mlib:$JAVA_HOME/jmods --add-modules
   calculator,math.util --output image --launcher
   launch=calculator/com.packt.calculator.Calculator
   ```

   The runtime image gets created at the location specified with the `--output` command-line option.

4. The runtime image created under the directory image contains the `bin` directory, among other directories. This `bin` directory consists of a shell script named `calculator`. This can be used to launch our application:

   ```
   $ ./image/bin/launch

   ***********Advanced Calculator***********
   1. Prime Number check
   2. Even Number check
   3. Sum of N Primes
   4. Sum of N Evens
   5. Sum of N Odds
   6. Exit
   Enter the number to choose operation
   ```

We cannot create a runtime image of modules that contain automatic modules. Jlink gives an error if the JAR files are not modular or if there is no `module-info.class`.

Compiling for older platform versions

We have, at some point, used the `-source` and `-target` options to create a java build. The `-source` option is used to indicate the version of Java language accepted by the compiler, and the `-target` option is used to indicate the version supported by the class files. Often, we forget to use the `-source` option and by default, `javac` compiles against the latest available Java version. Due to this, there are chances of newer APIs being used and as a result, the build doesn't run as expected on the target version.

To overcome the confusion of providing two different command-line options, a new command-line option, `--release`, was introduced in Java 9. This acts as a substitute to the `-source`, `-target` and `-bootclasspath` options. `-bootclasspath` is used to provide the location of the bootstrap class files for a given version, *N*.

Getting ready

We have created a simple module, called demo, that contains a very simple class called `CollectionsDemo` that just puts a few values in the map and iterates over them as follows:

```
public class CollectionsDemo{
  public static void main(String[] args){
    Map<String, String> map = new HashMap<>();
    map.put("key1", "value1");
    map.put("key2", "value3");
    map.put("key3", "value3");
    map.forEach((k,v) -> System.out.println(k + ", " + v));
  }
}
```

Let's compile and run it to see its output:

```
$ javac -d mods --module-source-path src srcdemomodule-info.java
srcdemocompacktCollectionsDemo.java
$ java --module-path mods -m demo/com.packt.CollectionsDemo
```

The output we get is as follow:

```
key1, value1
key2, value3
key3, value3
```

Now let's compile this to run on Java 8 and then run it on Java 8.

How to do it...

1. As the older versions of Java, Java 8 and before, don't support modules, so we would have to get rid of module-info.java if we were compiling on an older version. That is why we did not include module-info.java during our compilation. We compiled using the following code:

   ```
   $ javac --release 8 -d mods srcdemocompacktCollectionsDemo.java
   ```

   You can see that we are using the --release option, targeting Java 8 and not compiling module-info.java.

2. Let's create a JAR file because it becomes easier to transport the java build instead of copying all the class files:

   ```
   $jar --create --file mlib/demo.jar --main-class
   com.packt.CollectionsDemo -C mods/ .
   ```

3. Let's run the preceding JAR in Java 9:

   ```
   $ java -version
   java version "9"
   Java(TM) SE Runtime Environment (build 9+179)
   Java HotSpot(TM) 64-Bit Server VM (build 9+179, mixed mode)

   $ java -jar mlib/demo.jar
   key1, value1
   key2, value3
   key3, value3
   ```

4. Let's run the JAR in Java 8:

   ```
   $ "%JAVA8_HOME%"binjava -version
   java version "1.8.0_121"
   Java(TM) SE Runtime Environment (build 1.8.0_121-b13)
   Java HotSpot(TM) 64-Bit Server VM (build 25.121-b13, mixed mode)
   ```

```
$ "%JAVA8_HOME%"binjava -jar mlibdemo.jar
key1, value1
key2, value3
key3, value3
```

What if we did not use the -release option while building on Java 9? Let's try that as well:

1. Compile without using the --release option and create a JAR out of the resulting class files:

```
$ javac -d mods srcdemocompacktCollectionsDemo.java
$ jar --create --file mlib/demo.jar --main-class
com.packt.CollectionsDemo -C mods/ .
```

2. Let's run the JAR on Java 9:

```
$ java -jar mlib/demo.jar
key1, value1
key2, value3
key3, value3
```

It works as expected.

3. Let's run the JAR on Java 8:

```
$ "%JAVA8_HOME%"binjava -version
java version "1.8.0_121"
Java(TM) SE Runtime Environment (build 1.8.0_121-b13)
Java HotSpot(TM) 64-Bit Server VM (build 25.121-b13, mixed mode)
```

The output is as follow:

```
$ java -jar mlibdemo.jar

Exception in thread "main" java.lang.UnsupportedClassVersionError:

com/packt/CollectionsDemo has been compiled by a more recent version
of the Java Runtime (class file version 53.0), this version of the
Java Runtime only recognizes class file versions up to 52.0
```

It is clearly stating that there is a mismatch in the version of the class file. As it was compiled for Java 9 (version 53.0), it doesn't run on Java 8 (version 52.0).

How it works...

The data required for compiling to a target older version is stored in
the $JDK_ROOT/lib/ct.sym file. This information is used by the --release option
to locate bootclasspath. The ct.sym file is a ZIP file containing stripped-down
class files corresponding to class files from the target platform versions (taken
verbatim from http://openjdk.java.net/jeps/247).

Creating multi-release JARs

Prior to Java 9, it was hard for the developers of a library to adopt the new features
introduced in the language without releasing a new library version. But in Java 9,
multi-release JARs provide such a functionality where you can bundle certain class
files to run when a higher version of Java is being used.

In this recipe, we will show you how to create such a multi-release JAR.

How to do it...

1. Create the required Java code for the Java 8 platform. We will add two
   classes, CollectionUtil.java and FactoryDemo.java, in
   the src8compackt directory:

```
public class CollectionUtil{
  public static List<String> list(String ... args){
    System.out.println("Using Arrays.asList");
    return Arrays.asList(args);
  }

  public static Set<String> set(String ... args){
    System.out.println("Using Arrays.asList and set.addAll");
    Set<String> set = new HashSet<>();
    set.addAll(list(args));
    return set;
  }
}

public class FactoryDemo{
  public static void main(String[] args){
    System.out.println(CollectionUtil.list("element1",
            "element2", "element3"));
    System.out.println(CollectionUtil.set("element1",
```

```
                    "element2", "element3"));
        }
    }
```

2. We wish to make use of the `Collection` factory methods that were introduced in Java 9. So, we will create another subdirectory under `src` to place our Java-9-related code: `src9compackt`. This is where we will add another `CollectionUtil` class:

```
public class CollectionUtil{
    public static List<String> list(String ... args){
        System.out.println("Using factory methods");
        return List.of(args);
    }
    public static Set<String> set(String ... args){
        System.out.println("Using factory methods");
        return Set.of(args);
    }
}
```

3. The preceding code uses the Java 9 collection factory methods. Compile the source code using the following commands:

```
javac -d mods --release 8 src8compackt*.java
javac -d mods9 --release 9 src9compackt*.java
```

Make a note of the `--release` option that's used to compile the code for different java versions.

4. Now let's create the multi-release JAR:

```
jar --create --file mr.jar --main-class=com.packt.FactoryDemo
-C mods . --release 9 -C mods9 .
```

While creating the JAR, we have also mentioned that, when running on Java 9, we make use of the Java-9-specific code.

5. We will run `mr.jar` on Java 9:

```
java -jar mr.jar
[element1, element2, element3]
Using factory methods
[element2, element3, element1]
```

6. We will run `mr.jar` on Java 8:

```
#Linux
$ /usr/lib/jdk1.8.0_144/bin/java -version
java version "1.8.0_144"
Java(TM) SE Runtime Environment (build 1.8.0_144-b01)
Java HotSpot(TM) 64-Bit Server VM (build 25.144-b01, mixed mode)
$ /usr/lib/jdk1.8.0_144/bin/java -jar mr.jar
Using Arrays.asList
[element1, element2, element3]
Using Arrays.asList and set.addAll
Using Arrays.asList
[element1, element2, element3]

#Windows
$ "%JAVA8_HOME%"binjava -version
java version "1.8.0_121"
Java(TM) SE Runtime Environment (build 1.8.0_121-b13)
Java HotSpot(TM) 64-Bit Server VM (build 25.121-b13, mixed mode)
$ "%JAVA8_HOME%"binjava -jar mr.jar
Using Arrays.asList
[element1, element2, element3]
Using Arrays.asList and set.addAll
Using Arrays.asList
[element1, element2, element3]
```

How it works...

Let's look at the layout of the content in `mr.jar`:

```
jar -tvf mr.jar
```

The contents of the JAR is as follows:

```
    0 Sat Jul 29 00:24:08 UTC 2017 META-INF/
  117 Sat Jul 29 00:24:08 UTC 2017 META-INF/MANIFEST.MF
    0 Sat Jul 29 00:19:40 UTC 2017 com/
    0 Sat Jul 29 00:19:40 UTC 2017 com/packt/
  966 Sat Jul 29 00:23:54 UTC 2017 com/packt/CollectionUtil.class
  678 Sat Jul 29 00:23:54 UTC 2017 com/packt/FactoryDemo.class
    0 Sat Jul 29 00:19:46 UTC 2017 META-INF/versions/9/
    0 Sat Jul 29 00:19:46 UTC 2017 META-INF/versions/9/com/
    0 Sat Jul 29 00:19:46 UTC 2017 META-INF/versions/9/com/packt/
  862 Sat Jul 29 00:24:02 UTC 2017 META-INF/versions/9/com/packt/CollectionUtil.class
```

In the preceding layout, we have `META-INF/versions/9`, which contains the Java 9-specific code. Another important thing to note is the contents of the `META-INF/MANIFEST.MF` file. Let's extract the JAR and view its contents:

```
jar -xvf mr.jar

$ cat META-INF/MANIFEST.MF
Manifest-Version: 1.0
Created-By: 9 (Oracle Corporation)
Main-Class: com.packt.FactoryDemo
Multi-Release: true
```

The new `Multi-Release` manifest attribute is used to indicate whether the JAR is a multi-release JAR.

Using Maven to develop a modular application

In this recipe, we will look at using Maven, the most popular build tool in the Java ecosystem, to develop a simple modular application. We will reuse the idea we introduced in the *Services* recipe in this chapter.

Getting ready

We have the following modules in our example:

- `book.manage`: This is the main module that interacts with the data source
- `book.service`: This is the module that contains the service-provider interface
- `mongodb.book.service`: This is the module that provides an implementation to the service-provider interface
- `sqldb.book.service`: This is the module that provides another implementation to the service-provider interface

In the course of this recipe, we will create a maven project and include the preceding JDK modules as maven modules. So let's get started.

How to do it...

1. Create a folder to contain all the modules. We have called it
   `12_services_using_maven` with the following folder structure:

```
12_services_using_maven
        |---book-manage
        |---book-service
        |---mongodb-book-service
        |---sqldb-book-service
        |---pom.xml
```

2. The `pom.xml` for the parent is as follows:

```xml
<?xml version="1.0" encoding="UTF-8"?>
<project xmlns="http://maven.apache.org/POM/4.0.0"
 xmlns:xsi="http://www.w3.org/2001/XMLSchema-instance"
 xsi:schemaLocation="http://maven.apache.org/POM/4.0.0
 http://maven.apache.org/xsd/maven-4.0.0.xsd">
  <modelVersion>4.0.0</modelVersion>
  <groupId>com.packt</groupId>
  <artifactId>services_using_maven</artifactId>
  <version>1.0</version>
  <packaging>pom</packaging>
  <modules>
    <module>book-service</module>
    <module>mongodb-book-service</module>
    <module>sqldb-book-service</module>
    <module>book-manage</module>
  </modules>
  <build>
    <plugins>
      <plugin>
        <groupId>org.apache.maven.plugins</groupId>
        <artifactId>maven-compiler-plugin</artifactId>
        <version>3.6.1</version>
        <configuration>
          <source>9</source>
          <target>9</target>
          <showWarnings>true</showWarnings>
          <showDeprecation>true</showDeprecation>
        </configuration>
      </plugin>
    </plugins>
  </build>
</project>
```

3. Let's create the structure for the `book-service` Maven module as follows:

```
book-service
  |---pom.xml
  |---src
    |---main
      |---book.service
        |---module-info.java
        |---com
          |---packt
            |---model
              |---Book.java
            |---service
              |---BookService.java
            |---spi
              |---BookServiceProvider.java
```

4. The content of `pom.xml` for the `book-service` Maven module is:

```xml
<?xml version="1.0" encoding="UTF-8"?>
<project xmlns="http://maven.apache.org/POM/4.0.0"
xmlns:xsi="http://www.w3.org/2001/XMLSchema-instance"
xsi:schemaLocation="http://maven.apache.org/POM/4.0.0
http://maven.apache.org/xsd/maven-4.0.0.xsd">
  <modelVersion>4.0.0</modelVersion>
  <parent>
    <groupId>com.packt</groupId>
    <artifactId>services_using_maven</artifactId>
    <version>1.0</version>
  </parent>
  <artifactId>book-service</artifactId>
  <version>1.0</version>
  <build>
    <sourceDirectory>src/main/book.service</sourceDirectory>
  </build>
</project>
```

5. Here is `module-info.java`:

```java
module book.service{
  exports com.packt.model;
  exports com.packt.service;
  exports com.packt.spi;
  uses com.packt.spi.BookServiceProvider;
}
```

6. Here is `Book.java`:

```java
public class Book{
  public Book(String id, String title, String author){
    this.id = id;
    this.title = title
    this.author = author;
  }
  public String id;
  public String title;
  public String author;
}
```

7. Here is `BookService.java`:

```java
public abstract class BookService{
public abstract void create(Book book);
public abstract Book read(String id);
public abstract void update(Book book);
public abstract void delete(String id);
public static BookService getInstance(){
  ServiceLoader<BookServiceProvider> sl =
      ServiceLoader.load(BookServiceProvider.class);
  Iterator<BookServiceProvider> iter = sl.iterator();
  if (!iter.hasNext())
    throw new RuntimeException("No service providers
found!");
  BookServiceProvider provider = null;
  while(iter.hasNext()){
    provider = iter.next();
    System.out.println(provider.getClass());
  }
  return provider.getBookService();
  }
}
```

8. Here is `BookServiceProvider.java`:

```java
public interface BookServiceProvider{
  public BookService getBookService();
}
```

On similar lines, we define the other three Maven modules, `mongodb-book-service`, `sqldb-book-service`, and `book-manager`. The code for this can be found at `Chapter03/12_services_using_maven`.

We can compile the classes and build the required JAR files using the following command:

```
mvn clean install
```

We have provided `run-with-mongo.*` to use `mongodb-book-service` as the service-provider implementation and `run-with-sqldb.*` to use `sqldb-book-service` as the service-provider implementation.

The complete code for this recipe can be found at `Chapter03/12_services_using_maven`.

Making your library module-path-friendly

For an application to be fully modular, it should have itself modularized as well as its dependents. Now, making a third party modular is not in the hands of the application developer. One approach is to include the third-party `jar` in the module path and use the name of the `jar` as the name of the module to declare the dependency. In such cases, the `jar` becomes an automatic module. This is OK, but often the name of the `jar` is not module-name-friendly or doesn't conform to the syntax of a valid module name. In such cases, we make use of another support added in JDK 9 wherein one can define the name of the `jar` in the `MANIFEST.mf` file of the `jar`, and the library consumer can then declare a dependency on the defined name. This way, in the future, the library developer can modularize their library while still using the same module name.

In this recipe, we will show you how to provide a name for the automatic module created from the non-modular `jar`. First, we will show you how to achieve this using maven and then in the *There's more...* section, we will see how to create a JAR without using any build tools.

Getting ready

You would need at least JDK 9 to run this recipe, but we will be using JDK 11 in the Maven build plugin. You will also need to install Maven to be able to use it. You can search on the internet to find the installation procedure for Maven.

How to do it...

1. Generate an empty project using Maven:

   ```
   mvn archetype:generate -DgroupId=com.packt.banking -
   DartifactId=13_automatic_module -DarchetypeArtifactId=maven-
   archetype-quickstart -DinteractiveMode=false
   ```

2. Update the dependencies in the pom.xml file located in the 13_automatic_module directory by copying the following dependencies:

   ```
   <dependencies>
     <dependency>
       <groupId>junit</groupId>
       <artifactId>junit</artifactId>
       <version>4.12</version>
       <scope>test</scope>
     </dependency>
     <dependency>
       <groupId>org.assertj</groupId>
       <artifactId>assertj-core</artifactId>
       <version>3.10.0</version>
       <scope>test</scope>
     </dependency>
   </dependencies>
   ```

3. We need to configure maven-compiler-plugin to be able to compile for JDK 11. So, we will add the following plugin configuration right after <dependencies></dependencies>:

   ```
   <build>
     <plugins>
       <plugin>
         <groupId>org.apache.maven.plugins</groupId>
         <artifactId>maven-compiler-plugin</artifactId>
         <version>3.6.1</version>
         <configuration>
           <source>11</source>
   ```

```
        <target>11</target>
        <showWarnings>true</showWarnings>
        <showDeprecation>true</showDeprecation>
      </configuration>
    </plugin>
  </plugins>
</build>
```

4. Configure `maven-jar-plugin` to provide the automatic module name by providing the name in the new `<Automatic-Module-Name>` tag, as shown here:

```
<plugin>
  <groupId>org.apache.maven.plugins</groupId>
  <artifactId>maven-jar-plugin</artifactId>
  <configuration>
    <archive>
      <manifestEntries>
        <Automatic-Module-Name>com.packt.banking</Automatic-
Module-
          Name>
      </manifestEntries>
    </archive>
  </configuration>
</plugin>
```

5. We will add an API to calculate simple interest in the `com.packt.banking.Banking` class, which is shown as follows:

```
public class Banking {
  public static Double simpleInterest(Double principal,
                        Double rateOfInterest, Integer years){
    Objects.requireNonNull(principal, "Principal cannot be null");
    Objects.requireNonNull(rateOfInterest,
                        "Rate of interest cannot be null");
    Objects.requireNonNull(years, "Years cannot be null");
    return ( principal * rateOfInterest * years ) / 100;
  }
}
```

6. We also added a test, which you can find
   at `Chapter03\13_automatic_module\src\test\java\com\packt\ba`
   `nking` in the code downloaded for this chapter. Let's run the `mvn`
   `package` command to build a JAR. If everything goes fine, you will see the
   following:

```
-------------------------------------------------------------------
 T E S T S
-------------------------------------------------------------------
Running com.packt.banking.BankingTest
Tests run: 1, Failures: 0, Errors: 0, Skipped: 0, Time elapsed: 0.902 sec

Results :

Tests run: 1, Failures: 0, Errors: 0, Skipped: 0

[INFO]
[INFO] --- maven-jar-plugin:2.4:jar (default-jar) @ 13_automatic_module ---
[INFO] -------------------------------------------------------------------
[INFO] BUILD SUCCESS
[INFO] -------------------------------------------------------------------
[INFO] Total time: 12.037 s
[INFO] Finished at: 2018-08-05T23:15:26+03:00
[INFO] Final Memory: 14M/50M
[INFO] -------------------------------------------------------------------
```

7. You can use any compression utility, such as 7z, to view the contents of the
   JAR, especially the `Manifest.MF` file, whose contents are as follows:

```
Manifest-Version: 1.0
Archiver-Version: Plexus Archiver
Created-By: Apache Maven 3.3.9
Built-By: sanaulla
Build-Jdk: 11-ea
Automatic-Module-Name: com.packt.banking
```

The code for these steps can be found at `Chapter03\13_automatic_module`.

How it works...

So far, we have created a Java library JAR with an automatic module name. Now, let's see how to use this non-modular JAR as an automatic module in a modular application. The complete code for this can be found at Chapter03\13_using_automatic_module.

Let's copy the jar file created in the How to do it... section, which you can find in 13_automatic_module\target\13_automatic_module-1.0.jar, into the 13_using_automatic_module\mods folder. This enables our upcoming modular application to make use of the com.packt.banking module that was shipped with the jar.

After copying the jar, we need to create a module definition for our module and declare its dependencies in module-info.java, placed in 13_using_automatic_module\src\banking.demo:

```
module banking.demo{
    requires com.packt.banking;
}
```

Next is to create the main com.packt.demo.BankingDemo class, which will make use of the banking utilities. This will be created in the 13_using_automatic_module\src\banking.demo\com\packt\demo path, as follows:

```
package com.packt.demo;
import com.packt.banking.Banking;
public class BankingDemo{
  public static void main(String[] args) {
    Double principal = 1000.0;
    Double rateOfInterest = 10.0;
    Integer years = 2;
    Double simpleInterest = Banking.simpleInterest(principal,
                                    rateOfInterest, years);
        System.out.println("The simple interest is: " +
                                        simpleInterest);
    }
}
```

We can compile the preceding code using the following command, executed from `13_using_automatic_module`:

```
javac -d mods -p mods --module-source-path src src\banking.demo\*.java
src\banking.demo\com\packt\demo\*.java
```

And then run the preceding code using the following command, executed from the same location:

```
java --module-path mods -m banking.demo/com.packt.demo.BankingDemo
```

You will see the following output:

```
The simple interest is: 200.0
```

Note: You can make use of the `run.bat` or `run.sh` scripts to compile and run the code.

So, with this, we have:

- Created a non-modular JAR with an automatic module name.
- Used the non-modular JAR as an automatic module by declaring a dependency on it by using its automatic module name.

You will also see that we have totally removed the use of classpath, instead of using only the module path; this is our first step toward a completely modular application.

There's more...

We will show you how to create a JAR of your banking utility, along with the automatic module name if you don't use Maven. The code for this can be found at `Chapter03\13_automatic_module_no_maven`. We will still have the same `Banking .java` copied into the `13_automatic_module_no_maven\src\com\packt\banking` directory.

Next, we need to define a `manifest.mf` manifest file that will contain the following automatic module name:

```
Automatic-Module-Name: com.packt.banking
```

We can compile the preceding class by issuing the following command from `Chapter03\13_automatic_module_no_maven`:

```
javac -d classes src/com/packt/banking/*.java
```

And then build a `jar` by issuing the following command from the same location:

```
jar cvfm banking-1.0.jar manifest.mf -C classes .
```

We have also provided scripts for creating your `jar`. You can use `build-jar.bat` or `build-jar.sh` to compile and create a `jar`. Now, you can copy `banking-1.0.jar` to `Chapter03\13_using_automatic_module\mods` and replace `13_automati_module-1.0.jar`. Then, run the code in `Chapter03\13_using_automatic_module` using the `run.bat` or `run.sh` scripts, depending on your platform. You will still see the same output as in the previous section.

How to open a module for reflection

The module system introduces strict encapsulation of classes within its module and a strictness level that, if the class isn't explicitly allowed for reflection, then its private members cannot be accessed via reflection. Most of the libraries, such as hibernate and Jackson, rely on reflection to achieve their purpose. A strict encapsulation offered by the module system would break these libraries on the new JDK 9 and later right away.

In order to support such important libraries, the Java team decided to introduce features wherein the module developer can declare a few packages or complete packages that are open for inspection by reflection. In this recipe, we will look at how exactly to achieve that.

Getting ready

You need JDK 9 or later installed. We will be using the Jackson API in this recipe, and its `jar` files can be found at `Chapter03/14_open_module_for_rflxn/mods` of the code download for this book. These `jar` files are important as we will create a JSON string from a Java object using the Jackson API. These Jackson APIs will be used as automatic modules.

How to do it...

1. Create a `Person` class
   in `14_open_module_for_rflxn/src/demo/com/packt/demo` with the
   following definition:

   ```java
   package com.packt.demo;

   import java.time.LocalDate;

   public class Person{
       public Person(String firstName, String lastName,
           LocalDate dob, String placeOfBirth){
           this.firstName = firstName;
           this.lastName = lastName;
           this.dob = dob;
           this.placeOfBirth = placeOfBirth;
       }
       public final String firstName;
       public final String lastName;
       public final LocalDate dob;
       public final String placeOfBirth;
   }
   ```

2. Create a `OpenModuleDemo` class that creates an instance of the `Person` class
   and uses `com.fasterxml.jackson.databind.ObjectMapper` to
   serialize it into JSON. The serialization of the new date-time APIs requires
   some configuration changes to the `ObjectMapper` instance, which has also
   been done in the static initialization block, as follows:

   ```java
   package com.packt.demo;

   import java.time.LocalDate;

   import com.fasterxml.jackson.databind.ObjectMapper;
   import com.fasterxml.jackson.databind.SerializationFeature;
   import com.fasterxml.jackson.datatype.jsr310.JavaTimeModule;

   public class OpenModuleDemo{
       final static ObjectMapper MAPPER = new ObjectMapper();
       static{
           MAPPER.registerModule(new JavaTimeModule());
           MAPPER.configure(SerializationFeature.
                           WRITE_DATES_AS_TIMESTAMPS, false);
       }
       public static void main(String[] args)
   ```

```
        throws Exception {
        Person p = new Person("Mohamed", "Sanaulla",
            LocalDate.now().minusYears(30), "India");
        String json = MAPPER.writeValueAsString(p);
        System.out.println("The Json for Person is: ");
        System.out.println(json);
    }
}
```

3. Create `module-info.java` in `14_open_module_for_rflxn/src/demo`, which declares the name of the module, its dependencies, and another interesting thing called `opens`. `opens` is the solution to allow reflection from external libraries, as shown here:

```
module demo{
    requires com.fasterxml.jackson.annotation;
    requires com.fasterxml.jackson.core;
    requires com.fasterxml.jackson.databind;
    requires com.fasterxml.jackson.datatype.jsr310;
    opens com.packt.demo;
}
```

How it works...

There are two ways of opening up a module for inspection by reflection:

- Declaring open on the module level:

```
open module demo { }
```

- Declaring opens on the individual package level:

```
module demo {
    opens com.packt.demo;
}
```

The latter is more restrictive (that is, making only a package available for reflection) than the former. There is another way to achieve this, and that is by exporting the specific package to the right Jackson package, as follows:

```
module demo{
    exports com.packt.demo to <relevant Jackson package here>
}
```

4
Going Functional

This chapter introduces a programming paradigm called functional programming and its applicability in Java 11. We will cover the following recipes:

- Using standard functional interfaces
- Creating a functional interface
- Understanding lambda expressions
- Using lambda expressions
- Using method references
- Leveraging lambda expressions in your programs

Introduction

Functional programming is the ability to treat a certain piece of functionality as an object and pass it as a parameter or the return value of a method. This feature is present in many programming languages, and Java acquired it with the release of Java 8.

It avoids creating a class, its object, and managing the object state. The result of a function depends only on the input data, no matter how many times it is called. This style makes the outcome more predictable, which is the most attractive aspect of functional programming.

Its introduction to Java also allows us to improve parallel programming capabilities in Java by shifting the responsibility of parallelism from the client code to the library. Before this, in order to process elements of Java collections, the client code had to acquire an iterator from the collection and organize the processing of the collection.

Some of the default methods of Java collections accept a function (an implementation of a functional interface) as a parameter and then apply it to each element of the collection. So, it is the library's responsibility to organize the processing. One example is the `forEach(Consumer)` method that is available in every `Iterable` interface, where `Consumer` is a functional interface. Another example is the `removeIf(Predicate)` method that is available for every `Collection` interface, where `Predicate` is a functional interface too. Also, the `sort(Comparator)` and `replaceAll(UnaryOperator)` methods were added to the `List` interface, and the `compute()` method was added to `Map`.

Lambda expressions take advantage of functional interfaces and significantly simplify their implementation, making the code shorter, clearer, and more expressive.

Throughout this chapter, we will discuss the advantages of functional programming, define and explain functional interfaces and lambda expressions, and demonstrate all the related features in code examples.

Making functions first-class citizens of the language adds more power to Java. But taking advantage of this language capability requires—from those not exposed to functional programming yet—a new way of thinking and organizing the code.

Explaining this new feature and sharing the best practices of using it is the purpose of this chapter.

Using standard functional interfaces

In this recipe, you will learn what a functional interface is and why it was added to Java, along with 43 ready-to-use functional interfaces of the standard Java library that comes with JDK 8 in the `java.util.function` package.

Without functional interfaces, the only way to pass a functionality into a method would be through writing a class, creating its object, and then passing it as a parameter. But even the least involved style—using an anonymous class—requires writing too much code. Using functional interfaces helps to avoid all of that.

Getting ready

Any interface that has one and only one abstract method is called a functional interface. To help avoid a runtime error, the @FunctionalInterface annotation can be added in front of the interface. It tells the compiler about the intent, so the compiler can check to see whether there is actually one abstract method in that interface, including those inherited from other interfaces.

In our demo code in the previous chapters, we've already had an example of a functional interface, even if we did not annotate it as functional:

```
public interface SpeedModel {
    double getSpeedMph(double timeSec, int weightPounds, int
horsePower);
    enum DrivingCondition {
      ROAD_CONDITION,
      TIRE_CONDITION
    }
    enum RoadCondition {
      //...
    }
    enum TireCondition {
      //...
    }
}
```

The presence of enum types or any implemented (default or static) methods does not make it a non-functional interface. Only abstract (not implemented) methods count. So, this is an example of a functional interface too:

```
public interface Vehicle {
    void setSpeedModel(SpeedModel speedModel);
    default double getSpeedMph(double timeSec){ return -1; };
    default int getWeightPounds(){ return -1; }
    default int getWeightKg(){
      return convertPoundsToKg(getWeightPounds());
    }
    private int convertPoundsToKg(int pounds){
      return (int) Math.round(0.454 * pounds);
    }
    static int convertKgToPounds(int kilograms){
      return (int) Math.round(2.205 * kilograms);
    }
}
```

To recap what you have already learned about a default method of an interface in `Chapter 2`, *Fast Track to OOP - Classes and Interfaces*, the `getWeightPounds()` method will return `-1` when called by `getWeightKg()` or directly, using the object of a class that implements the `Vehicle` interface. However, this is only true if the `getWeightPounds()` method is not implemented in a class. Otherwise, the class implementation will be used and return a different value.

In addition to default and static interface methods, a functional interface can include any and all abstract methods of the `java.lang.Object` base. In Java, every object is provided with the default implementation of `java.lang.Object` methods, so the compiler and Java runtime ignore such abstract methods.

For example, this is a functional interface, too:

```
public interface SpeedModel {
    double getSpeedMph(double timeSec, int weightPounds, int
horsePower);
    boolean equals(Object obj);
    String toString();
}
```

The following is not a functional interface, though:

```
public interface Car extends Vehicle {
    int getPassengersCount();
}
```

This is because the `Car` interface has two abstract methods—its own `getPassengersCount()` method and the `setSpeedModel(SpeedModel speedModel)` method inherited from the `Vehicle` interface.

We can try to add the `@FunctionalInterface` annotation to the `Car` interface:

```
@FunctionalInterface
public interface Car extends Vehicle {
    int getPassengersCount();
}
```

If we do that, the compiler generates the following error:

```
Error:(3, 1) java: Unexpected @FunctionalInterface annotation
        com.cookbook.api.Car is not a functional interface
        multiple non-overriding abstract methods found in interface com.cookbook.api.Car
```

Using the @FunctionalInterface annotation helps to not only catch errors at compile-time, but it also secures reliable communication of the design intent between programmers. It helps you or other programmers remember that this interface cannot have more than one abstract method, which is especially important when some code exists already that relies on such an assumption.

For the same reason, the Runnable and Callable interfaces (they've existed in Java since its earlier versions) were annotated as @FunctionalInterface in Java 8 to make this distinction explicit:

```
@FunctionalInterface
interface Runnable { void run(); }

@FunctionalInterface
interface Callable<V> { V call() throws Exception; }
```

How to do it...

Before you create your own functional interface, consider using one of the 43 functional interfaces provided in the java.util.function package first. Most of them are specializations of the Function, Consumer, Supplier, and Predicate interfaces.

The following are the steps you can follow to get familiar with functional interfaces:

1. Look at the Function<T,R> functional interface:

   ```
   @FunctionalInterface
   public interface Function<T,R>
   ```

   As you can see from the <T,R> generics, the only method of this interface takes a parameter of the T type and returns a value of the R type. According to the JavaDoc, this interface has the R apply(T t) method. We can create an implementation of this interface using an anonymous class:

   ```
   Function<Integer, Double> ourFunc =
       new Function<Integer, Double>() {
           public Double apply(Integer i){
               return i * 10.0;
           }
       };
   ```

The R apply(T t) method in our implementation accepts a value of the Integer type (or the int primitive, which is going to be auto-boxed), multiplies it by 10, and returns the value of the Double type so that we can use our new function as follows:

```
System.out.println(ourFunc.apply(1));   //prints: 10
```

In the recipe *Understanding lambda expressions* below, we will introduce a lambda expression and show you how its usage makes the implementation much shorter. But for now, we will continue using an anonymous class.

2. Look at the Consumer<T> functional interface. The name helps us to remember that the method of this interface accepts a value but does not return anything—it only consumes. Its only method is void accept(T). The implementation of this interface can look as follows:

```
Consumer<String> ourConsumer = new Consumer<String>() {
  public void accept(String s) {
    System.out.println("The " + s + " is consumed.");
  }
};
```

The void accept(T t) method in our implementation receives a value of the String type and prints it. For example, we can use it as follows:

```
ourConsumer.accept("Hello!");
                //prints: The Hello! is consumed.
```

3. Look at the Supplier<T> functional interface. The name helps you to remember that the method of this interface does not accept any value but does return something—only supplies. Its only method is T get(). Based on this, we can create a function:

```
Supplier<String> ourSupplier = new Supplier<String>() {
  public String get() {
    String res = "Success";
    //Do something and return result—Success or Error.
    return res;
  }
};
```

The T get() method in our implementation does something and then returns a value of the String type, so we can write the following:

```
System.out.println(ourSupplier.get());   //prints: Success
```

4. Look at the `Predicate<T>` functional interface. The name helps to remember that the method of this interface returns a Boolean—it predicates something. Its only method is `boolean test(T t)`, which means that we can create the following function:

```
Predicate<Double> ourPredicate = new Predicate<Double>() {
  public boolean test(Double num) {
    System.out.println("Test if " + num +
                       " is smaller than 20");
    return num < 20;
  }
};
```

Its `boolean test(T t)` method of our implementation accepts a value of the `Double` type as a parameter and returns the value of the `boolean` type, so we can use it as follows:

```
System.out.println(ourPredicate.test(10.0) ?
                   "10 is smaller" : "10 is bigger");
```

The result of this will be as follows:

```
Test if 10.0 is smaller than 20
10 is smaller
```

5. Look at the other 39 functional interfaces in the `java.util.function` package. Notice that they are variations of the four interfaces we have discussed already. These variations are created for the following reasons:

- For better performance by avoiding auto-boxing and unboxing via the explicit usage of the `int`, `double`, or `long` primitives
- For accepting two input parameters
- For a shorter notation

The following functional interfaces are just a few examples from the list of 39 interfaces.

The `IntFunction<R>` functional interface has the `R apply(int i)` abstract method. It provides a shorter notation (without generics for the parameter type) and avoids auto-boxing (by defining the `int` primitive as the parameter). Here's an example of its usage:

```
IntFunction<String> iFunc = new IntFunction<String>() {
  public String apply(int i) {
    return String.valueOf(i * 10);
  }
};
System.out.println(iFunc.apply(1));      //prints: 10
```

The `BiFunction<T,U,R>` functional interface has abstract method, `R apply(T,U)`. Here's an example of its implementation:

```
BiFunction<String, Integer, Double> biFunc =
                new BiFunction<String, Integer, Double >() {
   public Double apply(String s, Integer i) {
     return (s.length() * 10d) / i;
   }
};
System.out.println(biFunc.apply("abc", 2)); //prints: 15.0
```

The `BinaryOperator<T>` functional interface has an abstract method, `T apply(T, T)`. It provides a shorter notation by avoiding repeating the same type three times. Here's an example of its usage:

```
BinaryOperator<Integer> function = new
BinaryOperator<Integer>(){
     public Integer apply(Integer i, Integer j) {
       return i >= j ? i : j;
     }
};
  System.out.println(binfunc.apply(1, 2));     //prints: 2
```

The `IntBinaryOperator` functional interface has the `int applyAsInt(int,int)` abstract method. We can use it to reproduce the same functionality as in the previous example:

```
IntBinaryOperator intBiFunc = new IntBinaryOperator(){
     public int applyAsInt(int i, int j) {
        return i >= j ? i : j;
     }
};
System.out.println(intBiFunc.applyAsInt(1, 2)); //prints: 2
```

More examples of the usage of such specializations will be provided in the
following recipes.

How it works...

We can compose the whole method using only the functions:

```
void calculate(Supplier<Integer> source,
    Function<Integer, Double> process, Predicate<Double> condition,
            Consumer<Double> success, Consumer<Double> failure){
    int i = source.get();
    double res = process.apply(i);
    if(condition.test(res)){
        success.accept(res);
    } else {
        failure.accept(res);
    }
}
```

The preceding code gets the value from the source, processes it, and then decides
whether the result is successful—all based on the functions provided as parameters.
Now, let's create these functions and invoke the method. The source parameter we
decided to be as follows:

```
Supplier<Integer> source = new Supplier<Integer>() {
    public Integer get() {
        Integer res = 42;
        //Do something and return result value
        return res;
    }
};
```

In real-life code, this function could pull data from a database or any other source of
data. We keep it simple—with a hardcoded return value—in order to get a
predictable result.

The processing function and predicate will remain the same as before:

```
Function<Integer, Double> process = new Function<Integer, Double>(){
    public Double apply(Integer i){
        return i * 10.0;
    }
};
Predicate<Double> condition = new Predicate<Double>() {
    public boolean test(Double num) {
        System.out.println("Test if " + num +
```

```
                                           " is smaller than " + 20);
           return num < 20;
       }
};
```

And the consumers will be almost identical, except for the different prefix before printing the result:

```
Consumer<Double> success = new Consumer<Double>() {
    public void accept(Double d) {
        System.out.println("Success: " + d);
    }
};
Consumer<Double> failure = new Consumer<Double>() {
    public void accept(Double d) {
        System.out.println("Failure: " + d);
    }
};
```

We can now invoke the calculate method, as follows:

```
calculate(source, process, condition, success, failure);
```

And the result will be as follows:

```
Test if 420.0 is smaller than 20.0
Failure: 420.0
```

If we need to quickly test various combinations of the source value and the predicate condition, we can create the `testSourceAndCondition(int src, int limit)` method, as follows:

```
void testSourceAndCondition(int src, double condition) {
    Supplier<Integer> source = new Supplier<Integer>() {
        public Integer get() {
            Integer res = src;
            //Do something and return result value
            return res;
        }
    };
    Function<Integer, Double> process =
      new Function<Integer, Double>() {
        public Double apply(Integer i){
            return i * 10.0;
        }
    };
    Predicate<Double> condition = new Predicate<Double>() {
        public boolean test(Double num) {
```

```
            System.out.println("Test if " + num +
                              " is smaller than " + limit);
            return num < limit;
        }
    };
    Consumer<Double> success = new Consumer<Double>() {
        public void accept(Double d) {
            System.out.println("Success: " + d);
        }
    };
    Consumer<Double> failure = new Consumer<Double>() {
        public void accept(Double d) {
            System.out.println("Failure: " + d);
        }
    };
    calculate(source, process, cond, success, failure);
}
```

Notice how we pass the src value into the source supplier, and the limit value into the condition predicate. Now, we can run the testSourceAndCondition(int src, int limit) method with different input values in search of the combination of the src value and the limit value that brings success:

```
testSourceAndCondition(10, 20);
testSourceAndCondition(1, 20);
testSourceAndCondition(10, 200);
```

The result will be as follows:

```
Test if 100.0 is smaller than 20.0
Failure: 100.0
Test if 10.0 is smaller than 20.0
Success: 10.0
Test if 100.0 is smaller than 200.0
Success: 100.0
```

There's more...

Many of the functional interfaces in the `java.util.function` package have default methods that not only enhance their functionality but also allow you to chain the functions and pass the result of one as an input parameter to another. For example, we can use the `Function<T,V> andThen(Function<R,V> after)` default method of the `Function<T,R>` interface:

```
Function<Integer, Double> before = new Function<Integer, Double>(){
    public Double apply(Integer i){
        return i * 10.0;
    }
};
Function<Double, Double> after = new Function<Double, Double>(){
    public Double apply(Double d){
        return d + 10.0;
    }
};
Function<Integer, Double> process = before.andThen(after);
```

As you can see, our `process` function is now a combination of our original function (which multiplies the source value by 10.0) and a new function, `after`, that adds 10.0 to the result of the first function. If we call the `testSourceAndCondition(int source, int condition)` method as `testSourceAndCondition(42, 20)`, the result will be as follows:

```
Test if 430.0 is smaller than 20
Failure: 430.0
```

The `Supplier<T>` interface does not have methods that allow us to chain several functions, but the `Predicate<T>` interface has the `and(Predicate<T> other)` and `or(Predicate<T> other)` default methods, which allow us to construct more complex Boolean expressions. The `Consumer<T>` interface has the `andThen(Consumer<T> after)` default method, too.

Notice how the type of the input value of the `after` function has to match the result type of the `before` function:

```
Function<T,R> before = ...
Function<R,V> after = ...
Function<T,V> result = before.andThen(after);
```

The resulting function accepts a value of the T type and produces a value of the V type.

Another way to achieve the same result is to use the `Function<V,R>` `compose(Function<V,T> before)` default method:

```
Function<Integer, Double> process = after.compose(before);
```

Which of the methods—`andThen()` or `compose()`—to use depends on which of the functions is available to invoke the aggregating method. Then, one is considered a base, while another is a parameter.

If this coding looks a bit over-engineered and convoluted, that's because it is. We did it for demo purposes only. The good news is that lambda expressions presented in the next recipe allow us to achieve the same results in a much shorter and clearer way.

Functional interfaces of the `java.util.function` package have other helpful default methods. The one that stands out is the `identity()` method, which returns a function that always returns its input argument:

```
Function<Integer, Integer> id = Function.identity();
System.out.println(id.apply(4));   //prints: 4
```

The `identity()` method is very helpful when a method requires you to provide a certain function, but you do not want this function to modify the result.

Other default methods are mostly related to conversion, boxing, unboxing, and extracting the min and max of two parameters. We encourage you to walk through the API of all the functional interfaces of the `java.util.function` and get an idea of the possibilities.

Creating a functional interface

In this recipe, you will learn how to create and use a custom functional interface when none of the standard interfaces in the `java.util.function` package satisfies the requirements.

Getting ready

Creating a functional interface is easy. One just has to make sure there is only one abstract method in the interface, including methods inherited from other interfaces:

```java
@FunctionalInterface
interface A{
    void m1();
}

@FunctionalInterface
interface B extends A{
    default void m2(){};
}

//@FunctionalInterface
interface C extends B{
    void m3();
}
```

In the preceding example, interface C is not a functional interface because it has two abstract methods—m1(), inherited from interface A, and its own method, m3().

We have also already seen the SpeedModel functional interface:

```java
@FunctionalInterface
public interface SpeedModel {
   double getSpeedMph(double timeSec, int weightPounds, int
horsePower);
}
```

We have annotated it to express the intent and to be warned in case another abstract method will be added to the SpeedModel interface. And, to make it simpler, we have removed enum classes from it. This interface is used in the Vehicle interface:

```java
public interface Vehicle {
    void setSpeedModel(SpeedModel speedModel);
    double getSpeedMph(double timeSec);
}
```

And the reason the Vehicle implementation needs it is because SpeedModel is the source of the functionality that calculates the speed:

```java
public class VehicleImpl implements Vehicle {
    private SpeedModel speedModel;
    private int weightPounds, hoursePower;
    public VehicleImpl(int weightPounds, int hoursePower){
```

```
            this.weightPounds = weightPounds;
            this.hoursePower = hoursePower;
        }
        public void setSpeedModel(SpeedModel speedModel){
            this.speedModel = speedModel;
        }
        public double getSpeedMph(double timeSec){
            return this.speedModel.getSpeedMph(timeSec,
                                this.weightPounds, this.hoursePower);
        };
    }
```

As we mentioned in `Chapter 2`, *Fast Track to OOP – Classes and Interfaces*, such a design is called aggregation. It is a preferred way of composing the desired behavior as it allows for more flexibility.

With functional interfaces, such a design becomes even more flexible. To demonstrate it, let's implement our custom interface—`SpeedModel`.

How to do it...

The traditional approach would be to create a class that implements the `SpeedModel` interface:

```
public class SpeedModelImpl implements SpeedModel {
    public double getSpeedMph(double timeSec,
                        int weightPounds, int horsePower){
        double v = 2.0 * horsePower * 746 *
                        timeSec * 32.17 / weightPounds;
        return (double) Math.round(Math.sqrt(v) * 0.68);
    }
}
```

Then, we can use this implementation as follows:

```
Vehicle vehicle = new VehicleImpl(3000, 200);
SpeedModel speedModel = new SpeedModelImpl();
vehicle.setSpeedModel(speedModel);
System.out.println(vehicle.getSpeedMph(10.)); //prints: 122.0
```

To change the way the speed is calculated, we need to change the `SpeedModelImpl` class.

Alternatively, using the fact that `SpeedModel` is an interface, we can introduce changes faster and even avoid having the `SpeedModelImpl` class in the first place:

```
Vehicle vehicle = new VehicleImpl(3000, 200);
SpeedModel speedModel = new SpeedModel(){
    public double getSpeedMph(double timeSec,
                         int weightPounds, int horsePower){
        double v = 2.0 * horsePower * 746 *
                         timeSec * 32.17 / weightPounds;
        return (double) Math.round(Math.sqrt(v) * 0.68);
    }
};
vehicle.setSpeedModel(speedModel);
System.out.println(vehicle.getSpeedMph(10.)); //prints: 122.0
```

However, the preceding implementation does not take advantage of the interface being functional. If we comment out the annotation, we can add another method to the `SpeedModel` interface:

```
//@FunctionalInterface
public interface SpeedModel {
    double getSpeedMph(double timeSec,
                     int weightPounds, int horsePower);
    void m1();
}
Vehicle vehicle = new VehicleImpl(3000, 200);
SpeedModel speedModel = new SpeedModel(){
    public double getSpeedMph(double timeSec,
                         int weightPounds, int horsePower){
        double v = 2.0 * horsePower * 746 *
                         timeSec * 32.17 / weightPounds;
        return (double) Math.round(Math.sqrt(v) * 0.68);
    }
    public void m1(){}
    public void m2(){}
};
vehicle.setSpeedModel(speedModel);
System.out.println(vehicle.getSpeedMph(10.)); //prints: 122.0
```

As you can see from the preceding code, not only `SpeedModel` interface has another abstract method `m1()`, but the anonymous class has yet another method `m2()` that is not listed in the `SpeedModel` interface. So, an anonymous class does not require the interface to be functional. But lambda expression does.

How it works...

Using lambda expressions, we can rewrite the preceding code as follows:

```
Vehicle vehicle = new VehicleImpl(3000, 200);
SpeedModel speedModel =  (t, wp, hp) -> {
    double v = 2.0 * hp * 746 * t * 32.17 / wp;
    return (double) Math.round(Math.sqrt(v) * 0.68);
};
vehicle.setSpeedModel(speedModel);
System.out.println(vehicle.getSpeedMph(10.)); //prints: 122.0
```

We will discuss the lambda expressions format in the next recipe. For now, we would like only to point out the importance of functional interfaces for an implementation such as the preceding one. As you can see, there is only the name of the interface specified and no method name at all. That is possible because a functional interface has only one method that has to be implemented, and that is how JVM can figure it out and generate a functional interface implementation behind the scenes.

There's more...

It is possible to define a generic custom functional interface that looks similar to the standard functional interfaces. For example, we could create the following custom functional interface:

```
@FunctionalInterface
interface Func<T1,T2,T3,R>{
    R apply(T1 t1, T2 t2, T3 t3);
}
```

It allows three input parameters, which is exactly what we need to calculate the speed:

```
Func<Double, Integer, Integer, Double> speedModel = (t, wp, hp) -> {
    double v = 2.0 * hp * 746 * t * 32.17 / wp;
    return (double) Math.round(Math.sqrt(v) * 0.68);
};
```

Using this function instead of the `SpeedModel` interface, we could change
the `Vehicle` interface and its implementation as follows:

```
interface Vehicle {
    void setSpeedModel(Func<Double, Integer, Integer,
                                         Double> speedModel);
    double getSpeedMph(double timeSec);
}
class VehicleImpl  implements Vehicle {
    private Func<Double, Integer, Integer, Double> speedModel;
    private int weightPounds, hoursePower;
    public VehicleImpl(int weightPounds, int hoursePower){
        this.weightPounds = weightPounds;
        this.hoursePower = hoursePower;
    }
    public void setSpeedModel(Func<Double, Integer,
                                   Integer, Double> speedModel){
        this.speedModel = speedModel;
    }
    public double getSpeedMph(double timeSec){
        return this.speedModel.apply(timeSec,
                               weightPounds, hoursePower);
    };
}
```

The preceding code produces the same result as before—with the `SpeedModel`
interface.

The name of the custom interface and the name of its only method can be anything
we like. For example:

```
@FunctionalInterface
interface FourParamFunction<T1,T2,T3,R>{
    R caclulate(T1 t1, T2 t2, T3 t3);
}
```

Well, since we are going to create a new interface anyway, using
the `SpeedModel` name and the `getSpeedMph()` method name is probably a better
solution since it makes the code more readable. But there are cases when a generic
custom functional interface is a better choice. In such cases, you can use the preceding
definition and enhance it however you need to.

Understanding lambda expressions

We have mentioned lambda expressions several times already and stated that their usage in Java justified the introduction of functional interfaces in the `java.util.function` package. The lambda expression allows us to simplify function implementation by removing all boilerplate code of anonymous classes, leaving only minimally necessary information. We have also explained that this simplification is possible because a functional interface has only one abstract method, so the compiler and JVM match the provided functionality with the method signature and generate the functional interface implementation behind the scene.

Now, it's time to define the lambda expression syntax and see the range of possible forms of lambda expressions, before we start using them to make our code shorter and more readable than when we used anonymous classes.

Getting ready

In the 1930s, the mathematician Alonzo Church, in the course of his research into the foundations of mathematics, introduced lambda calculus—a universal model of computation that can be used to simulate any Turing machine. Well, at that time, the Turing machine hadn't been created. Only later, when Alan Turing invented his *a-machine* (automatic machine), also called the *universal Turing machine*, did he and Church join forces and produce a Church-Turing thesis that showed that lambda calculus and the Turing machine had very similar capabilities.

Church used the Greek letter *lambda* to describe anonymous functions, and it became an unofficial symbol of the field of programming language theory. The first programming language that took advantage of lambda calculus formalism was Lisp. Java added functional programming to its capabilities in 2014, with the release of Java 8.

A lambda expression is an anonymous method that allows us to omit modifiers, return types, and parameter types. That makes for a very compact notation. The syntax of a lambda expression includes the list of parameters, an arrow token (`->`), and a body. The list of parameters can be empty (just brackets, `()`), without brackets (if there is only one parameter), or a comma-separated list of parameters surrounded by brackets. The body can be a single expression without brackets or a statement block surrounded by brackets.

How to do it...

Let's look at a few examples. The following lambda expression has no input parameters and always returns 33:

```
() -> 33;
```

The following lambda expression accepts one parameter of the integer type, increments it by 1, and returns the result:

```
i -> i++;
```

The following lambda expression accepts two parameters and returns their sum:

```
(a, b) -> a + b;
```

The following lambda expression accepts two parameters, compares them, and returns the `boolean` result:

```
(a, b) -> a == b;
```

And the last lambda expression accepts two parameters, calculates, and prints the result:

```
(a, b) -> {
    double c = a +  Math.sqrt(b);
    System.out.println("Result: " + c);
}
```

As you can see, a lambda expression can include a code block of any size—similarly to any method. The preceding example does not return any value. Here is another example of a code block that returns the `String` value:

```
(a, b) -> {
    double c = a +  Math.sqrt(b);
    return c > 10.0 ? "Success" : "Failure";
}
```

How it works...

Let's look at that last example again. If there is a String m1(double x, double y) method defined in a *functional* interface, A, and if there is a m2(A a) method that accepts an object of the A type, we can invoke it as follows:

```
A a = (a, b) -> {
    double c = a +  Math.sqrt(b);
    return c > 10.0 ? "Success" : "Failure";
}
m2(a);
```

The preceding code means that the passed-in object has the following implementation of the m1() method:

```
public String m1(double x, double y){
    double c = a +  Math.sqrt(b);
    return c > 10.0 ? "Success" : "Failure";
}
```

The fact that m2(A a) has the A object as a parameter tells us that the code of m2(A a) probably uses at least one of the A interface methods (there may be also defaulted or static methods in the A interface). But, in general, there is no guarantee that the method uses the passed-in object because the programmer may have decided to stop using it and left the signature unchanged just to avoid breaking the client code, for example.

Nevertheless, the client must pass into the method an object that implements the A interface, which means its only abstract method has to be implemented. And that is what the lambda expression does. It defines the abstract method functionality using the minimal amount of code—a list of the input parameters and a code block of the method's implementation. This is all the compiler and JVM need to generate an implementation.

Writing such compact and efficient code became possible because of the combination of a lambda expression and functional interface.

There's more...

As in an anonymous class, the variable created outside but used inside a lambda expression becomes effectively final and cannot be modified. You can write the following code:

```
double v = 10d;
Function<Integer, Double> multiplyBy10 = i -> i * v;
```

However, you cannot change the value of the v variable outside the lambda expression:

```
double v = 10d;
v = 30d; //Causes compiler error
Function<Integer, Double> multiplyBy10 = i -> i * v;
```

You cannot change it inside the expression, either:

```
double v = 10d;
Function<Integer, Double> multiplyBy10 = i -> {
  v = 30d; //Causes compiler error
  return i * v;
};
```

The reason for this restriction is that a function can be passed and executed for different arguments in different contexts (different threads, for example), and the attempt to synchronize these contexts would frustrate the original idea of the distributed evaluation of functions.

Another lambda expression feature worth mentioning is its interpretation of the this keyword, which is quite different from its interpretation by an anonymous class. Inside an anonymous class, this refers to the instance of the anonymous class, but inside the lambda expression, this refers to the instance of the class that surrounds the expression. Let's demonstrate it, assuming that we have the following class:

```
class Demo{
    private String prop = "DemoProperty";
    public void method(){
        Consumer<String> consumer = s -> {
            System.out.println("Lambda accept(" + s
                                + "): this.prop=" + this.prop);
        };
        consumer.accept(this.prop);
        consumer = new Consumer<>() {
            private String prop = "ConsumerProperty";
```

```
        public void accept(String s) {
            System.out.println("Anonymous accept(" + s
                            + "): this.prop=" + this.prop);
        }
    };
    consumer.accept(this.prop);
  }
}
```

As you can see, in the `method()` code, the `Consumer` functional interface is implemented twice—using the lambda expression and using an anonymous class. Let's invoke this method in the following code:

```
Demo d = new Demo();
d.method();
```

The output will be as follows:

```
Lambda accept(DemoProperty): this.prop=DemoProperty
Anonymous accept(DemoProperty): this.prop=ConsumerProperty
```

The lambda expression is not an inner class and cannot be referred to by `this`. The lambda expression just does not have fields or properties. It is stateless. That's why in a lambda expression, the `this` keyword refers to the surrounding context. And that is another reason for the requirement that all the variables of the surrounding context used by the lambda expression must be final or effectively final.

Using lambda expressions

In this recipe, you will learn how to use lambda expressions in practice.

Getting ready

Creating and using lambda expressions is actually much simpler than writing a method. One just needs to list the input parameters, if any, and the code that does what has to be done.

Let's revisit our implementation of standard functional interfaces from the first recipe of this chapter and rewrite them using lambda expressions. Here's how we have implemented the four main functional interfaces using anonymous classes:

```
Function<Integer, Double> ourFunc = new Function<Integer, Double>(){
    public Double apply(Integer i){
        return i * 10.0;
    }
};
System.out.println(ourFunc.apply(1));        //prints: 10.0
Consumer<String> consumer = new Consumer<String>() {
    public void accept(String s) {
        System.out.println("The " + s + " is consumed.");
    }
};
consumer.accept("Hello!"); //prints: The Hello! is consumed.
Supplier<String> supplier = new Supplier<String>() {
    public String get() {
        String res = "Success";
        //Do something and return result—Success or Error.
        return res;
    }
};
System.out.println(supplier.get());        //prints: Success
Predicate<Double> pred = new Predicate<Double>() {
    public boolean test(Double num) {
        System.out.println("Test if " + num + " is smaller than 20");
        return num < 20;
    }
};
System.out.println(pred.test(10.0)? "10 is smaller":"10 is bigger");
                    //prints: Test if 10.0 is smaller than 20
                    //          10 is smaller
```

And here's how they look with lambda expressions:

```
Function<Integer, Double> ourFunc = i -> i * 10.0;
System.out.println(ourFunc.apply(1)); //prints: 10.0

Consumer<String> consumer =
        s -> System.out.println("The " + s + " is consumed.");
consumer.accept("Hello!");        //prints: The Hello! is consumed.

Supplier<String> supplier = () - > {
        String res = "Success";
        //Do something and return result—Success or Error.
        return res;
    };
```

```
System.out.println(supplier.get());  //prints: Success

Predicate<Double> pred = num -> {
    System.out.println("Test if " + num + " is smaller than 20");
    return num < 20;
};
System.out.println(pred.test(10.0)? "10 is smaller":"10 is bigger");
                        //prints: Test if 10.0 is smaller than 20
                        //        10 is smaller
```

The examples of specialized functional interfaces we have presented are as follows:

```
IntFunction<String> ifunc = new IntFunction<String>() {
    public String apply(int i) {
        return String.valueOf(i * 10);
    }
};
System.out.println(ifunc.apply(1));   //prints: 10
BiFunction<String, Integer, Double> bifunc =
        new BiFunction<String, Integer, Double >() {
            public Double apply(String s, Integer i) {
                return (s.length() * 10d) / i;
            }
        };

System.out.println(bifunc.apply("abc",2));      //prints: 15.0
BinaryOperator<Integer> binfunc = new BinaryOperator<Integer>(){
    public Integer apply(Integer i, Integer j) {
        return i >= j ? i : j;
    }
};
System.out.println(binfunc.apply(1,2));  //prints: 2
IntBinaryOperator intBiFunc = new IntBinaryOperator(){
    public int applyAsInt(int i, int j) {
        return i >= j ? i : j;
    }
};
System.out.println(intBiFunc.applyAsInt(1,2)); //prints: 2
```

And here's how they look with lambda expressions:

```
IntFunction<String> ifunc = i -> String.valueOf(i * 10);
System.out.println(ifunc.apply(1));              //prints: 10

BiFunction<String, Integer, Double> bifunc =
                    (s,i) -> (s.length() * 10d) / i;
System.out.println(bifunc.apply("abc",2));       //prints: 15.0
```

```
BinaryOperator<Integer> binfunc = (i,j) -> i >= j ? i : j;
System.out.println(binfunc.apply(1,2));            //prints: 2

IntBinaryOperator intBiFunc = (i,j) -> i >= j ? i : j;
System.out.println(intBiFunc.applyAsInt(1,2));  //prints: 2
```

As you can see, the code is less cluttered and more readable.

How to do it...

Those who have some traditional code-writing experience, when starting functional programming, equate functions with methods. They try to create functions first because that was how we all used to write traditional code—by creating methods. Yet, functions are just smaller pieces of functionality that modify some aspects of the behavior of the methods or provide the business logic for the otherwise non-business-specific code. In functional programming, as in traditional programming, methods continue to provide the code structure, while functions are the nice and helpful additions to it. So, in functional programming, creating a method comes first, before the functions are defined. Let's demonstrate this.

The following are the basic steps of code writing. First, we identify the well-focused block of code that can be implemented as a method. Then, after we know what the new method is going to do, we can convert some pieces of its functionality into functions:

1. Create the `calculate()` method:

```
void calculate(){
    int i = 42;        //get a number from some source
    double res = 42.0; //process the above number
    if(res < 42){ //check the result using some criteria
        //do something
    } else {
        //do something else
    }
}
```

The preceding pseudocode outlines the idea of the `calculate()` method's functionality. It can be implemented in a traditional style—by using methods, as follows:

```
int getInput(){
    int result;
    //getting value for result variable here
    return result;
}
double process(int i){
    double result;
    //process input i and assign value to result variable
}
boolean checkResult(double res){
    boolean result = false;
    //use some criteria to validate res value
    //and assign value to result
    return result;
}
void processSuccess(double res){
    //do something with res value
}
void processFailure(double res){
    //do something else with res value
}
void calculate(){
    int i = getInput();
    double res = process(i);
    if(checkResult(res)){
        processSuccess(res);
    } else {
        processFailure(res);
    }
}
```

But some of these methods may be very small, so the code becomes fragmented and less readable with so many additional indirections. This disadvantage becomes especially glaring in the case when the methods come from outside the class where the `calculate()` method is implemented:

```
void calculate(){
    SomeClass1 sc1 = new SomeClass1();
    int i = sc1.getInput();
    SomeClass2 sc2 = new SomeClass2();
    double res = sc2.process(i);
    SomeClass3 sc3 = new SomeClass3();
```

```
SomeClass4 sc4 = new SomeClass4();
if(sc3.checkResult(res)){
    sc4.processSuccess(res);
} else {
    sc4.processFailure(res);
}
}
```

As you can see, in the case where each of the external methods is small, the amount of plumbing code may substantially exceed the payload it supports. Besides, the preceding implementation creates many tight dependencies between classes.

2. Let's look at how we can implement the same functionality using functions. The advantage is that the functions can be as small as they need to be, but the plumbing code will never exceed the payload because there is no plumbing code. Another reason to use functions is when we need the flexibility to change sections of the functionality on the fly, for the algorithm's research purpose. And if these pieces of functionality have to come from outside the class, we do not need to build other classes just for the sake of passing a method into `calculate()`. We can pass them as functions:

```
void calculate(Supplier<Integer> souc e, Function<Integer,
        Double> process, Predicate<Double> condition,
    Consumer<Double> success, Consumer<Double> failure){
    int i = source.get();
    double res = process.apply(i);
    if(condition.test(res)){
        success.accept(res);
    } else {
        failure.accept(res);
    }
}
```

3. Here's how the functions may look:

```
Supplier<Integer> source = () -> 4;
Function<Integer, Double> before = i -> i * 10.0;
Function<Double, Double> after = d -> d + 10.0;
Function<Integer, Double> process = before.andThen(after);
Predicate<Double> condition = num -> num < 100;
Consumer<Double> success =
                d -> System.out.println("Success: "+ d);
Consumer<Double> failure =
                d -> System.out.println("Failure: "+ d);
```

```
calculate(source, process, condition, success, failure);
```

The result of the preceding code is going to be as follows:

```
Success: 50.0
```

How it works...

The lambda expression acts as a regular method, except when you think about testing each function separately. How to do it?

There are two ways to address this issue. First, since the functions are typically small, there is often no need to test them separately, and they are tested indirectly when the code that uses them is tested. Second, if you still think the function has to be tested, it is always possible to wrap it in the method that returns the function, so you can test that method as any other method. Here is an example of how it can be done:

```
public class Demo {
    Supplier<Integer> source(){ return () -> 4;}
    Function<Double, Double> after(){ return d -> d + 10.0; }
    Function<Integer, Double> before(){return i -> i * 10.0; }
    Function<Integer, Double> process(){return
before().andThen(after());}
    Predicate<Double> condition(){ return num -> num < 100.; }
    Consumer<Double> success(){
        return d -> System.out.println("Failure: " + d); }
    Consumer<Double> failure(){
        return d-> System.out.println("Failure: " + d); }
    void calculate(Supplier<Integer> souce, Function<Integer,
                Double> process, Predicate<Double> condition,
           Consumer<Double> success, Consumer<Double> failure){
        int i = source.get();
        double res = process.apply(i);
        if(condition.test(res)){
            success.accept(res);
        } else {
            failure.accept(res);
        }
    }
    void someOtherMethod() {
        calculate(source(), process(),
                        condition(), success(), failure());
    }
```

Now we can write the function unit tests as follows:

```
public class DemoTest {

    @Test
    public void source() {
        int i = new Demo().source().get();
        assertEquals(4, i);
    }
    @Test
    public void after() {
        double d = new Demo().after().apply(1.);
        assertEquals(11., d, 0.01);
    }
    @Test
    public void before() {
        double d = new Demo().before().apply(10);
        assertEquals(100., d, 0.01);
    }
    @Test
    public void process() {
        double d = new Demo().process().apply(1);
        assertEquals(20., d, 0.01);
    }
    @Test
    public void condition() {
        boolean b = new Demo().condition().test(10.);
        assertTrue(b);
    }
}
```

Typically, lambda expressions (and functions in general) are used for specializing otherwise generic functionalities—by adding business logic to a method. A good example is stream operations, which we are going to discuss in Chapter 5, *Streams and Pipelines*. The library authors have created them to be able to work in parallel, which required a lot of expertise. And now the library users can specialize the operations by passing into them the lambda expressions (functions) that provide the application's business logic.

There's more...

Since, as we have mentioned already, functions are often simple one-liners, they are often inlined when passed in as parameters, for example:

```
Consumer<Double> success = d -> System.out.println("Success: " + d);
Consumer<Double> failure = d-> System.out.println("Failure: " + d);
calculate(() -> 4, i -> i * 10.0 + 10, n -> n < 100, success,
failure);
```

But one should not push it too far, as such inlining may decrease code readability.

Using method references

In this recipe, you will learn how to use a method reference, with the constructor reference being one of the cases.

Getting ready

When a one-line lambda expression consists only of a reference to an existing method implemented somewhere else, it is possible to further simplify the lambda notation by using the *method reference*.

The syntax of the method reference is `Location::methodName`, where `Location` indicates where (in which object or class) the `methodName` method can be found. The two colons (`::`) serve as a separator between the location and the method name. If there are several methods with the same name at the specified location (because of the method overload), the reference method is identified by the signature of the abstract method of the functional interface implemented by the lambda expression.

How to do it...

The exact format of the method reference depends on whether the referred method is static or non-static. The method reference can also be *bound* or *unbound*, or to be more formal, the method reference can have a *bound receiver* or an *unbound receiver*. A receiver is an object or class that is used to invoke the method. It *receives* the call. It can be bound to a particular context or not (unbound). We will explain what this means during the demonstration.

The method reference can also refer to a constructor with or without parameters.

Please note that the method reference is applicable *only when the expression consists of only one method call and nothing else*. For example, a method reference can be applied to the `() -> SomeClass.getCount()` lambda expression. It will look like `SomeClass::getCount`. But the expression `() -> 5 + SomeClass.getCount()` cannot be replaced with method reference because there are more operations in this expression than just a method call.

Static unbound method reference

To demonstrate a static method reference, we will use the `Food` class with two static methods:

```
class Food{
    public static String getFavorite(){ return "Donut!"; }
    public static String getFavorite(int num){
        return num > 1 ? String.valueOf(num) + " donuts!" : "Donut!";
    }
}
```

Since the first method, `String getFavorite()`, does not accept any input parameters and returns a value, it can be implemented as a functional interface, `Supplier<T>`. The lambda expression that implements the function that consists of the call to the `String getFavorite()` static method looks like this:

```
Supplier<String> supplier = () -> Food.getFavorite();
```

Using the method reference, the preceding line changes to the following:

```
Supplier<String> supplier = Food::getFavorite;
```

As you can see, the preceding format defines the location of the method (as the `Food` class), the name of the method, and the value of the return type (as `String`). The name of the functional interface indicates that there are no input parameters, so the compiler and JVM can identify the method among the methods of the `Food` class.

A static method reference is unbound because there's no object being used to invoke the method. In the case of a static method, a class is the call receiver, not an object.

The second static method, `String getFavorite(int num)`, accepts one parameter and returns a value. It means we can use the `Function<T, R>` functional interface to implement the function that consists only of a call to this method:

```
Function<Integer, String> func = i -> Food.getFavorite(i);
```

But when the method reference is used, it changes to exactly the same form as the previous example:

```
Function<Integer, String> func = Food::getFavorite;
```

The difference is in the specified functional interface. It allows the compiler and Java runtime to identify the method to be used: the method is named `getFavorite()`, accepts the `Integer` value, and returns `String` value. And there is only one such method in the `Food` class. Actually, there is no need to even look at which value the method returns, because it is not possible to overload a method by the return value only. The signature of the method—name, and list of parameter types—is enough for the method's identification.

We can use the implemented functions as follows:

```
Supplier<String> supplier = Food::getFavorite;
System.out.println("supplier.get() => " + supplier.get());

Function<Integer, String> func = Food::getFavorite;
System.out.println("func.getFavorite(1) => " + func.apply(1));
System.out.println("func.getFavorite(2) => " + func.apply(2));
```

If we run the preceding code, the result is going to be as follows:

```
supplier.get() => Donut!
func.getFavorite(1) => Donut!
func.getFavorite(2) => 2 donuts!
```

Non-static bound method reference

To demonstrate a non-static bound method reference, let's enhance the `Food` class by adding a `name` field, two constructors, and two `String sayFavorite()` methods:

```
class Food{
    private String name;
    public Food(){ this.name = "Donut"; }
    public Food(String name){ this.name = name; }
    public static String getFavorite(){ return "Donut!"; }
    public static String getFavorite(int num){
        return num > 1 ? String.valueOf(num) + " donuts!" : "Donut!";
    }
    public String sayFavorite(){
        return this.name + (this.name.toLowerCase()
                            .contains("donut")?"? Yes!" : "? D'oh!");
```

```
    }
    public String sayFavorite(String name){
        this.name = this.name + " and " + name;
        return sayFavorite();
    }
}
```

Now, let's create three instances of the `Food` class:

```
Food food1 = new Food();
Food food2 = new Food("Carrot");
Food food3 = new Food("Carrot and Broccoli");
```

The preceding is the context—the code that surrounds the lambda expression we are going to create now. We use the local variables of the preceding context to implement three different suppliers:

```
Supplier<String> supplier1 = () -> food1.sayFavorite();
Supplier<String> supplier2 = () -> food2.sayFavorite();
Supplier<String> supplier3 = () -> food3.sayFavorite();
```

We used `Supplier<T>` because the `String, sayFavorite()` method does not require any parameter and just produces (supplies) the `String` value. Using the method reference, we can rewrite the preceding lambda expressions as follows:

```
Supplier<String> supplier1 = food1::sayFavorite;
Supplier<String> supplier2 = food2::sayFavorite;
Supplier<String> supplier3 = food3::sayFavorite;
```

The method `sayFavorite()` belongs to an object that was created in a certain context. In other words, this object (the call receiver) is bound to a certain context, which is why such method reference is called a *bound method reference* or *bound receiver method reference*.

We can pass the newly created functions as any other object and use them anywhere we need, for example:

```
System.out.println("new Food().sayFavorite() => " + supplier1.get());
System.out.println("new Food(Carrot).sayFavorite() => "
                                        + supplier2.get());
System.out.println("new Food(Carrot,Broccoli).sayFavorite() => "
                                        + supplier3.get());
```

The result will be as follows:

```
new Food().sayFavorite() => Donut? Yes!
new Food(Carrot).sayFavorite() => Carrot? D'oh!
new Food(Carrot,Broccoli).sayFavorite() => Carrot and Broccoli? D'oh!
```

Please note that the receiver remains bound to the context, so its state may change and affect the output. That is the significance of the distinction of being *bound*. Using such a reference, one has to be careful not to change the state of the receiver in the context of its origination. Otherwise, it may lead to unpredictable results. This consideration is especially pertinent for parallel processing when the same function can be used in different contexts.

Let's look at another case of a bound method reference using the second non-static method, `String sayFavorite(String name)`. First, we create an implementation of a functional interface, `UnaryOperator<T>`, using the same objects of the `Food` class that we used in the previous example:

```
UnaryOperator<String> op1 = s -> food1.sayFavorite(s);
UnaryOperator<String> op2 = s -> food2.sayFavorite(s);
UnaryOperator<String> op3 = s -> food3.sayFavorite(s);
```

The reason we have used the `UnaryOperator<T>` functional interface is that the `String sayFavorite(String name)` method accepts a parameter and produces the value of the same type. And that is the purpose of functional interfaces with the name `Operator` in them—to support cases when the input value and the result have the same type.

The method reference allows us to change the lambda expression as follows:

```
UnaryOperator<String> op1 = food1::sayFavorite;
UnaryOperator<String> op2 = food2::sayFavorite;
UnaryOperator<String> op3 = food3::sayFavorite;
```

Now we can use the preceding functions (operators) anywhere in the code, for example:

```
System.out.println("new Food()
        .sayFavorite(Carrot) => " + op1.apply("Carrot"));
System.out.println("new Food(Carrot)
    .sayFavorite(Broccoli) => " + op2.apply("Broccoli"));
System.out.println("new Food(Carrot, Broccoli)
        .sayFavorite(Donuts) => " + op3.apply("Donuts"));
```

The result of the preceding code is as follows:

```
new Food().sayFavorite(Carrot) => Donut and Carrot? Yes!
new Food(Carrot).sayFavorite(Broccoli) => Carrot and Broccoli? D'oh!
new Food(Carrot,Broccoli).sayFavorite(Donuts) => Carrot and Broccoli and Donuts? Yes!
```

Non-static unbound method reference

To demonstrate an unbound method reference to the String
sayFavorite() method, we will use the Function<T, R> functional interface
because we would like to use an object of the Food class (the call receiver) as a
parameter and get back a String value:

```
Function<Food, String> func = f -> f.sayFavorite();
```

The method reference allows us to rewrite the preceding lambda expression as
follows:

```
Function<Food, String> func = Food::sayFavorite;
```

Using the same objects of the Food class we created in the previous examples, we use
the newly created function in the following code, for example:

```
System.out.println("new Food()
            .sayFavorite() => " + func.apply(food1));
System.out.println("new Food(Carrot)
            .sayFavorite() => " + func.apply(food2));
System.out.println("new Food(Carrot, Broccoli)
            .sayFavorite() => " + func.apply(food3));
```

As you can see, the parameter (the call receiver object) comes from the current context
only, as any parameter does. Wherever the function is passed, it does not carry the
context with it. Its receiver is not bound to the context that was used for the function's
creation. That is why this method reference is called *unbound*.

The output of the preceding code is as follows:

```
new Food().sayFavorite() => Donut and Carrot? Yes!
new Food(Carrot).sayFavorite() => Carrot and Broccoli? D'oh!
new Food(Carrot,Broccoli).sayFavorite() => Carrot and Broccoli and Donuts? Yes!
```

And, to demonstrate another case of the unbound method reference, we will use the second method, `String sayFavorite(String name)`, with the same `Food` objects we have used all along. The functional interface we are going to implement this time is called `BiFunction<T,U,R>`:

```
BiFunction<Food, String, String> func = (f,s) -> f.sayFavorite(s);
```

The reason we select this functional interface is that it accepts two parameters—exactly what we need in this case—to have the receiver object and `String` value as parameters. The method reference version of the preceding lambda expression looks as follows:

```
BiFunction<Food, String, String> func = Food::sayFavorite;
```

We can use the preceding function by writing the following code, for example:

```
System.out.println("new Food()
   .sayFavorite(Carrot) => " + func.apply(food1, "Carrot"));
System.out.println("new Food(Carrot)
   .sayFavorite(Broccoli) => "
                      + func2.apply(food2, "Broccoli"));
System.out.println("new Food(Carrot,Broccoli)
   .sayFavorite(Donuts) => " + func2.apply(food3,"Donuts"));
```

The result is as follows:

```
new Food().sayFavorite(Carrot) => Donut and Carrot and Carrot? Yes!
new Food(Carrot).sayFavorite(Broccoli) => Carrot and Broccoli and Broccoli? D'oh!
new Food(Carrot,Broccoli).sayFavorite(Donuts) => Carrot and Broccoli and Donuts and Donuts? Yes!
```

Constructor method references

Using the method reference for a constructor is very similar to a static method reference because it uses a class as the call receiver, not an object (it has not been created yet). Here is the lambda expression that implements the `Supplier<T>` interface:

```
Supplier<Food> foodSupplier = () -> new Food();
```

And here is its version with the method reference:

```
Supplier<Food> foodSupplier = Food::new;
System.out.println("new Food()
  .sayFavorite() => " + foodSupplier.get().sayFavorite());
```

If we run the preceding code, we get the following output:

```
new Food().sayFavorite() => Donut? Yes!
```

Now, let's add another constructor to the `Food` class:

```
public Food(String name){
    this.name = name;
}
```

Once we do this, we can express the preceding constructor using the method reference:

```
Function<String, Food> createFood = Food::new;
Food food = createFood.apply("Donuts");
System.out.println("new Food(Donuts).sayFavorite() => "
                                    + food.sayFavorite());
food = createFood.apply("Carrot");
System.out.println("new Food(Carrot).sayFavorite() => "
                                    + food.sayFavorite());
```

Here is the output of the preceding code:

```
new Food(Donuts).sayFavorite() => Donuts? Yes!
new Food(Carrot).sayFavorite() => Carrot? D'oh!
```

In the same manner, we can add a constructor with two parameters:

```
public Food(String name, String anotherName) {
    this.name = name + " and " + anotherName;
}
```

Once we do that, we can express it via `BiFunction<String, String>`:

```
BiFunction<String, String, Food> createFood = Food::new;
Food food = createFood.apply("Donuts", "Carrots");
System.out.println("new Food(Donuts, Carrot)
        .sayFavorite() => " + food.sayFavorite());
food = constrFood2.apply("Carrot", "Broccoli");
System.out.println("new Food(Carrot, Broccoli)
        .sayFavorite() => " food.sayFavorite());
```

The result of the preceding code is as follows:

```
new Food(Donuts,Carrot).sayFavorite() => Donuts and Carrots? Yes!
new Food(Carrot,Broccoli).sayFavorite() => Carrot and Broccoli? D'oh!
```

To express a constructor that accepts more than two parameters, we can create a custom functional interface with any number of parameters. For example, we can use the following custom functional interface, which we discussed in the previous recipe:

```
@FunctionalInterface
interface Func<T1,T2,T3,R>{ R apply(T1 t1, T2 t2, T3 t3);}
```

Let's assume that we need to use the `AClass` class:

```
class AClass{
    public AClass(int i, double d, String s){ }
    public String get(int i, double d){ return ""; }
    public String get(int i, double d, String s){ return ""; }
}
```

We can write the following code by using the method reference:

```
Func<Integer, Double, String, AClass> func1 = AClass::new;
AClass obj = func1.apply(1, 2d, "abc");

Func<Integer, Double, String, String> func2 = obj::get;    //bound
String res1 = func2.apply(42, 42., "42");

Func<AClass, Integer, Double, String> func3 = AClass::get; //unbound
String res21 = func3.apply(obj, 42, 42.);
```

In the preceding code snippet, we created `func1` function that allows us to create an object of class `AClass`. The `func2` function applies to the resulting object `obj` the method `String get(int i, double d)` using the bound method reference because its call receiver (object `obj`) comes from a particular context (bound to it). By contrast, the `func3` function is implemented as an unbound method reference because it gets its call receiver (class `AClass`) not from a context.

There's more...

There are several simple but very helpful method references because it gets its call receiver that is often used in practice:

```
Function<String, Integer> strLength = String::length;
System.out.println(strLength.apply("3"));  //prints: 1

Function<String, Integer> parseInt = Integer::parseInt;
System.out.println(parseInt.apply("3"));    //prints: 3

Consumer<String> consumer = System.out::println;
consumer.accept("Hello!");                 //prints: Hello!
```

There are also a few useful methods for working with arrays and lists:

```
Function<Integer, String[]> createArray = String[]::new;
String[] arr = createArray.apply(3);
System.out.println("Array length=" + arr.length);

int i = 0;
for(String s: arr){ arr[i++] = String.valueOf(i); }
Function<String[], List<String>> toList = Arrays::<String>asList;
List<String> l = toList.apply(arr);
System.out.println("List size=" + l.size());
for(String s: l){ System.out.println(s); }
```

Here are the results of the preceding code:

```
Array length=3
List size=3
1
2
3
```

We leave it up to you to analyze how the preceding lambda expressions were created and used.

Leveraging lambda expressions in your programs

In this recipe, you will learn how to apply a lambda expression to your code. We will get back to the demo application and modify it by introducing a lambda expression where it makes sense.

Getting ready

Equipped with functional interfaces, lambda expressions, and the best practices of a lambda-friendly API design, we can substantially improve our speed-calculating application by making its design more flexible and user-friendly. Let's set up some background as close to a real-life problem as possible without making it too complex.

Driverless cars are in the news these days, and there is good reason to believe it is going be this way for quite some time. One of the tasks in this domain is the analysis and modeling of the traffic flow in an urban area based on real data. A lot of such data already exists and will continue to be collected in future. Let's assume that we have access to such a database by date, time, and geographical location. Let's also assume that the traffic data from this database comes in units, each capturing details about one vehicle and the driving conditions:

```
public interface TrafficUnit {
  VehicleType getVehicleType();
  int getHorsePower();
  int getWeightPounds();
  int getPayloadPounds();
  int getPassengersCount();
  double getSpeedLimitMph();
  double getTraction();
  RoadCondition getRoadCondition();
  TireCondition getTireCondition();
  int getTemperature();
}
```

The enum types—VehicleType, RoadCondition, and TireCondition—were already constructed in Chapter 2, *Fast Track to OOP - Classes and Interfaces*:

```
enum VehicleType {
  CAR("Car"), TRUCK("Truck"), CAB_CREW("CabCrew");
  private String type;
  VehicleType(String type){ this.type = type; }
  public String getType(){ return this.type; }
```

```
  }
enum RoadCondition {
  DRY(1.0),
  WET(0.2) { public double getTraction() {
    return temperature > 60 ? 0.4 : 0.2; } },
  SNOW(0.04);
  public static int temperature;
  private double traction;
  RoadCondition(double traction){ this.traction = traction; }
  public double getTraction(){return this.traction;}
}
enum TireCondition {
  NEW(1.0), WORN(0.2);
  private double traction;
  TireCondition(double traction){ this.traction = traction; }
  public double getTraction(){ return this.traction;}
}
```

The interface of accessing traffic data may look like this:

```
TrafficUnit getOneUnit(Month month, DayOfWeek dayOfWeek,
                int hour, String country, String city,
                String trafficLight);
List<TrafficUnit> generateTraffic(int trafficUnitsNumber,
                Month month, DayOfWeek dayOfWeek, int hour,
                String country, String city, String trafficLight);
```

Here is an example of the access to the preceding methods:

```
TrafficUnit trafficUnit = FactoryTraffic.getOneUnit(Month.APRIL,
            DayOfWeek.FRIDAY, 17, "USA", "Denver", "Main103S");
```

The number 17 is an hour of a day (5 pm) and Main1035 is a traffic light identification.

The call to the second method returns multiple results:

```
List<TrafficUnit> trafficUnits =
    FactoryTrafficModel.generateTraffic(20, Month.APRIL,
        DayOfWeek.FRIDAY, 17, "USA", "Denver", "Main103S");
```

The first parameter, `20`, is the number of the requested units of traffic.

As you can see, such a traffic factory provides data about traffic in a particular location at a particular time (between 5 pm and 6 pm in our example). Each call to the factory yields a different result, while the list of traffic units describes statistically-correct data (including the most probable weather conditions) in the specified location.

We will also change the interfaces of `FactoryVehicle` and `FactorySpeedModel` so they could build `Vehicle` and `SpeedModel` based on the `TrafficUnit` interface. The resulting demo code is as follows:

```
double timeSec = 10.0;
TrafficUnit trafficUnit = FactoryTraffic.getOneUnit(Month.APRIL,
            DayOfWeek.FRIDAY, 17, "USA", "Denver", "Main103S");
Vehicle vehicle = FactoryVehicle.build(trafficUnit);
SpeedModel speedModel =
            FactorySpeedModel.generateSpeedModel(trafficUnit);
vehicle.setSpeedModel(speedModel);
printResult(trafficUnit, timeSec, vehicle.getSpeedMph(timeSec));
```

The `printResult()` method has the following code:

```
void printResult(TrafficUnit tu, double timeSec, double speedMph){
    System.out.println("Road " + tu.getRoadCondition()
                    + ", tires " + tu.getTireCondition() + ": "
                        + tu.getVehicleType().getType()
                        + " speedMph (" + timeSec + " sec)="
                                    + speedMph + " mph");
}
```

The output of this code may look like this:

```
Road WET, tires NEW: Truck speedMph (10.0 sec)=22.0 mph
```

Since we use the "real" data now, every run of this program produces a different result, based on the statistical properties of the data. In a certain location, a car or dry weather would appear more often at that date and time, while in another location, a truck or snow would be more typical.

In this run, the traffic unit brought a wet road, new tires, and `Truck` with such an engine power and load that in 10 seconds it was able to reach a speed of 22 mph. The formula we used to calculate the speed (inside an object of `SpeedModel`) is familiar to you:

```
double weightPower = 2.0 * horsePower * 746 * 32.174 / weightPounds;
double speed = (double) Math.round(Math.sqrt(timeSec * weightPower)
                                          * 0.68 * traction);
```

Here, the `traction` value comes from `TrafficUnit`. In the class that implements the `TrafficUnit` interface, the `getTraction()` method looks like the following:

```
public double getTraction() {
   double rt = getRoadCondition().getTraction();
   double tt = getTireCondition().getTraction();
   return rt * tt;
}
```

The `getRoadCondition()` and `getTireCondition()` methods return the elements of the corresponding `enum` types we just described.

Now we are ready to improve our speed-calculating application using the lambda expressions discussed in the previous recipes.

How to do it...

Follow these steps to learn how to use lambda expressions:

1. Let's start building an API. We will call it `Traffic`. Without using functional interfaces, it might look like this:

```
public interface Traffic {
    void speedAfterStart(double timeSec, int
trafficUnitsNumber);
}
```

Its implementation may be as follows:

```
public class TrafficImpl implements Traffic {
    private int hour;
    private Month month;
    private DayOfWeek dayOfWeek;
    private String country, city, trafficLight;
    public TrafficImpl(Month month, DayOfWeek dayOfWeek, int
hour,
```

```
                      String country, String city, String
trafficLight){
     this.hour = hour;
     this.city = city;
     this.month = month;
     this.country = country;
     this.dayOfWeek = dayOfWeek;
     this.trafficLight = trafficLight;
   }
   public void speedAfterStart(double timeSec,
                                  int trafficUnitsNumber){
     List<TrafficUnit> trafficUnits =
       FactoryTraffic.generateTraffic(trafficUnitsNumber,
         month, dayOfWeek, hour, country, city,
trafficLight);
     for(TrafficUnit tu: trafficUnits){
        Vehicle vehicle = FactoryVehicle.build(tu);
        SpeedModel speedModel =
FactorySpeedModel.generateSpeedModel(tu);
        vehicle.setSpeedModel(speedModel);
        double speed = vehicle.getSpeedMph(timeSec);
        printResult(tu, timeSec, speed);
     }
   }
}
```

2. Let's write sample code that uses the `Traffic` interface:

```
Traffic traffic = new TrafficImpl(Month.APRIL,
  DayOfWeek.FRIDAY, 17, "USA", "Denver", "Main103S");
double timeSec = 10.0;
int trafficUnitsNumber = 10;
traffic.speedAfterStart(timeSec, trafficUnitsNumber);
```

We get results similar to the following:

```
Road WET, tires WORN: Truck speedMph (10.0 sec)=5.0 mph
Road DRY, tires WORN: Car speedMph (10.0 sec)=33.0 mph
Road DRY, tires WORN: Car speedMph (10.0 sec)=21.0 mph
Road WET, tires NEW: Truck speedMph (10.0 sec)=29.0 mph
Road DRY, tires NEW: Truck speedMph (10.0 sec)=66.0 mph
Road DRY, tires WORN: Car speedMph (10.0 sec)=17.0 mph
Road WET, tires WORN: CabCrew speedMph (10.0 sec)=3.0 mph
Road DRY, tires NEW: CabCrew speedMph (10.0 sec)=83.0 mph
Road DRY, tires NEW: Car speedMph (10.0 sec)=71.0 mph
Road WET, tires WORN: Car speedMph (10.0 sec)=12.0 mph
```

As mentioned before, since we are using real data, the same code does not produce exactly the same result every time. One should not expect to see the speed values of the preceding screenshot, but instead something that looks very similar.

3. Let's use a lambda expression. The preceding API is quite limited. For example, it does not allow you to test different speed-calculation formulas without changing `FactorySpeedModel`. Meanwhile, the `SpeedModel` interface has only one abstract method, called `getSpeedMph()` (which makes it a functional interface):

```
public interface SpeedModel {
   double getSpeedMph(double timeSec,
            int weightPounds, int horsePower);
}
```

We can take advantage of `SpeedModel` being a functional interface, and add another method to the `Traffic` interface that is able to accept the `SpeedModel` implementation as a lambda expression:

```
public interface Traffic {
   void speedAfterStart(double timeSec,
                        int trafficUnitsNumber);
   void speedAfterStart(double timeSec,
      int trafficUnitsNumber, SpeedModel speedModel);
}
```

The problem though is the `traction` value does not come as a parameter to the `getSpeedMph()` method, so we cannot implement it as a function passed as a parameter into the `speedAfterStart()` method. Look closer at the speed calculation by `FactorySpeedModel.generateSpeedModel(TrafficUnit trafficUnit)`:

```
double getSpeedMph(double timeSec, int weightPounds,
                                    int horsePower) {
    double traction = trafficUnit.getTraction();
    double v = 2.0 * horsePower * 746 * timeSec *
                                32.174 / weightPounds;
    return Math.round(Math.sqrt(v) * 0.68 * traction);
}
```

As you can see, the `traction` value is a multiplier to the calculated value of `speed` and that is the only dependency on traffic unit. We can remove traction from the speed model and apply traction after the speed is calculated using the speed model. It means we can change the implementation of `speedAfterStart()` of the `TrafficImpl` class, as follows:

```
public void speedAfterStart(double timeSec,
            int trafficUnitsNumber, SpeedModel speedModel) {
    List<TrafficUnit> trafficUnits =
      FactoryTraffic.generateTraffic(trafficUnitsNumber,
        month, dayOfWeek, hour, country, city, trafficLight);
    for(TrafficUnit tu: trafficUnits){
        Vehicle vehicle = FactoryVehicle.build(tu);
        vehicle.setSpeedModel(speedModel);
        double speed = vehicle.getSpeedMph(timeSec);
        speed = (double) Math.round(speed * tu.getTraction());
        printResult(tu, timeSec, speed);
    }
}
```

This change allows the users of the `Traffic` API pass `SpeedModel` as a function:

```
Traffic traffic = new TrafficImpl(Month.APRIL,
    DayOfWeek.FRIDAY, 17, "USA", "Denver", "Main103S");
double timeSec = 10.0;
int trafficUnitsNumber = 10;
SpeedModel speedModel = (t, wp, hp) -> {
    double weightPower = 2.0 * hp * 746 * 32.174 / wp;
    return (double) Math
                .round(Math.sqrt(t * weightPower) * 0.68);
```

```
};
traffic.speedAfterStart(timeSec, trafficUnitsNumber,
                                   speedModel);
```

4. The result of the preceding code is the same as when `SpeedModel` was generated by `FactorySpeedModel`. But now the API users can come up with their own speed-calculating function.

5. We can Annotate the `SpeedModel` interface as `@FunctionalInterface`, so everybody who tries to add another method to it would be dutifully warned and would not be able to add another abstract method without removing this annotation and being aware of the risk of breaking the code of the existing clients that have implemented this functional interface already.

6. We can enrich the API by adding various criteria that slice all of the possible traffic into segments.

For example, API users might want to analyze only cars, trucks, cars with an engine bigger than 300 horsepower, or trucks with an engine bigger than 400 horsepower. The traditional way to accomplish this would be by creating methods such as these:

```
void speedAfterStartCarEngine(double timeSec,
            int trafficUnitsNumber, int horsePower);
void speedAfterStartCarTruckOnly(double timeSec,
                              int trafficUnitsNumber);
void speedAfterStartEngine(double timeSec,
        int trafficUnitsNumber, int carHorsePower,
                              int truckHorsePower);
```

Instead, we can just add standard functional interfaces to the existing `speedAfterStart()` method of the `Traffic` interface and let the API user decide which slice of traffic to extract:

```
void speedAfterStart(double timeSec, int trafficUnitsNumber,
    SpeedModel speedModel, Predicate<TrafficUnit> limitTraffic);
```

The speedAfterStart() method implementation in
the TrafficImpl class would change as follows:

```
public void speedAfterStart(double timeSec,
           int trafficUnitsNumber, SpeedModel speedModel,
                   Predicate<TrafficUnit> limitTraffic) {
   List<TrafficUnit> trafficUnits =
     FactoryTraffic.generateTraffic(trafficUnitsNumber,
       month, dayOfWeek, hour, country, city, trafficLight);
   for(TrafficUnit tu: trafficUnits){
       if(limitTraffic.test(tu){
          Vehicle vehicle = FactoryVehicle.build(tu);
          vehicle.setSpeedModel(speedModel);
          double speed = vehicle.getSpeedMph(timeSec);
          speed = (double) Math.round(speed *
                                    tu.getTraction());
          printResult(tu, timeSec, speed);
      }
    }
}
```

The Traffic API users can then define the traffic they need as follows:

```
Predicate<TrafficUnit> limit = tu ->
   (tu.getHorsePower() < 250
       && tu.getVehicleType() == VehicleType.CAR) ||
   (tu.getHorsePower() < 400
       && tu.getVehicleType() == VehicleType.TRUCK);
traffic.speedAfterStart(timeSec,
           trafficUnitsNumber, speedModel, limit);
```

The results are now limited to cars with an engine smaller than 250 hp and
trucks with an engine smaller than 400 hp:

```
Road WET, tires WORN: Truck speedMph (10.0 sec)=3.0 mph
Road DRY, tires WORN: Car speedMph (10.0 sec)=25.0 mph
Road DRY, tires NEW: Truck speedMph (10.0 sec)=107.0 mph
Road DRY, tires NEW: Truck speedMph (10.0 sec)=72.0 mph
Road DRY, tires NEW: Car speedMph (10.0 sec)=86.0 mph
```

In fact, a `Traffic` API user can now apply any criteria for limiting the traffic as long as they are applicable to the values in the `TrafficUnit` object. A user can write, for example, the following:

```
Predicate<TrafficUnit> limitTraffic =
  tu -> tu.getTemperature() > 65
  && tu.getTireCondition() == TireCondition.NEW
  && tu.getRoadCondition() == RoadCondition.WET;
```

Alternatively, they can write any other combination of limits on the values that come from `TrafficUnit`. If a user decides to remove the limit and analyze all of the traffic, this code will do it too:

```
traffic.speedAfterStart(timeSec, trafficUnitsNumber,
                              speedModel, tu -> true);
```

7. If there is a need to select traffic units by speed, we can apply the predicate criteria after the speed calculations (notice how we replaced `Predicate` with `BiPredicate` since we need to use two parameters now):

```
public void speedAfterStart(double timeSec,
           int trafficUnitsNumber, SpeedModel speedModel,
              BiPredicate<TrafficUnit, Double> limitSpeed){
    List<TrafficUnit> trafficUnits =
      FactoryTraffic.generateTraffic(trafficUnitsNumber,
      month, dayOfWeek, hour, country, city, trafficLight);
    for(TrafficUnit tu: trafficUnits){
        Vehicle vehicle = FactoryVehicle.build(tu);
        vehicle.setSpeedModel(speedModel);
        double speed = vehicle.getSpeedMph(timeSec);
        speed = (double) Math.round(speed*tu.getTraction());
        if(limitSpeed.test(tu, speed)){
            printResult(tu, timeSec, speed);
        }
    }
}
```

The `Traffic` API users can now write the following code:

```
BiPredicate<TrafficUnit, Double> limit = (tu, sp) ->
   (sp > (tu.getSpeedLimitMph() + 8.0) &&
         tu.getRoadCondition() == RoadCondition.DRY) ||
   (sp > (tu.getSpeedLimitMph() + 5.0) &&
         tu.getRoadCondition() == RoadCondition.WET) ||
   (sp > (tu.getSpeedLimitMph() + 0.0) &&
         tu.getRoadCondition() == RoadCondition.SNOW);
traffic.speedAfterStart(timeSec,
              trafficUnitsNumber, speedModel, limit);
```

The predicate above selects traffic units that exceed the speed limit by more than a certain amount (which is different for different driving conditions). If needed, it can disregard the speed completely and limit traffic exactly the same way the previous predicate did. The only drawback of this implementation is that it is slightly less efficient because the predicate is applied after the speed calculations. This means that the speed calculation will be done for each generated traffic unit, not to a limited number, as in the previous implementation. If this is a concern, you might leave all the different signatures we have discussed in this recipe:

```
public interface Traffic {
   void speedAfterStart(double timeSec, int
trafficUnitsNumber);
   void speedAfterStart(double timeSec, int
trafficUnitsNumber,
                                       SpeedModel
speedModel);
   void speedAfterStart(double timeSec,
           int trafficUnitsNumber, SpeedModel speedModel,
                         Predicate<TrafficUnit>
limitTraffic);
   void speedAfterStart(double timeSec,
           int trafficUnitsNumber, SpeedModel speedModel,
                  BiPredicate<TrafficUnit,Double>
limitTraffic);
}
```

This way, the API user decides which of the methods to use, more flexible or more efficient, and decide whether the default speed-calculation implementation is acceptable.

There's more...

So far, we have not given the API user a choice of the output format. Currently, it is implemented as the `printResult()` method:

```
void printResult(TrafficUnit tu, double timeSec, double speedMph) {
    System.out.println("Road " + tu.getRoadCondition() +
                    ", tires " + tu.getTireCondition() + ": "
                        + tu.getVehicleType().getType() + " speedMph ("
                        + timeSec + " sec)=" + speedMph + " mph");
}
```

To make it more flexible, we can add another parameter to our API:

```
Traffic traffic = new TrafficImpl(Month.APRIL, DayOfWeek.FRIDAY, 17,
                                "USA", "Denver", "Main103S");
double timeSec = 10.0;
int trafficUnitsNumber = 10;
BiConsumer<TrafficUnit, Double> output = (tu, sp) ->
    System.out.println("Road " + tu.getRoadCondition() +
                    ", tires " + tu.getTireCondition() + ": "
                        + tu.getVehicleType().getType() + " speedMph ("
                        + timeSec + " sec)=" + sp + " mph");
traffic.speedAfterStart(timeSec, trafficUnitsNumber, speedModel,
    output);
```

Notice that we take the `timeSec` value-not as one of the function parameters, but from the enclosed scope of the function. We can do this because it remains constant (and can be effectively final) throughout the calculations. In the same manner, we can add any other object to the `output` function—a filename or another output device, for example—thus leaving all the output-related decisions to the API user. To accommodate this new function, the API implementation changes to the following:

```java
public void speedAfterStart(double timeSec, int trafficUnitsNumber,
        SpeedModel speedModel, BiConsumer<TrafficUnit, Double> output)
{
   List<TrafficUnit> trafficUnits =
      FactoryTraffic.generateTraffic(trafficUnitsNumber, month,
                       dayOfWeek, hour, country, city, trafficLight);
   for(TrafficUnit tu: trafficUnits){
      Vehicle vehicle = FactoryVehicle.build(tu);
      vehicle.setSpeedModel(speedModel);
      double speed = vehicle.getSpeedMph(timeSec);
      speed = (double) Math.round(speed * tu.getTraction());
      output.accept(tu, speed);
   }
}
```

It took us a while to come to this point—where the power of functional programming starts to shine and justify the effort of learning it. Yet, when used to process streams, as described in the next chapter, lambda expressions yield even more power.

5
Streams and Pipelines

In Java 8 and 9, the collections API got a major facelift with the introduction of streams and internal iteration by leveraging lambda expressions. In Java 10 (JDK 18.3), new methods—`List.copyOf`, `Set.copyOf`, and `Map.copyOf`—were added that allow us to create a new immutable collection from existing instances. Also, new methods— `toUnmodifiableList`, `toUnmodifiableSet`, and `toUnmodifiableMap`—were added to the `Collectors` class in the `java.util.stream` package, allowing the elements of `Stream` to be collected into an immutable collection. This chapter shows you how to use the streams and chain multiple operations to create a pipeline. Also, the reader will learn how these operations can be done in parallel. The list of recipes includes the following:

- Create immutable collections using the `of()` and `copyOf()` factory methods
- Create and operating on streams
- Use numeric streams for arithmetic operations
- Complete streams by producing collections
- Complete streams by producing maps
- Complete streams by grouping stream elements
- Create a stream operation pipeline
- Processing a stream in parallel

Introduction

Lambda expressions described and demonstrated in the previous chapter were introduced in Java 8. Together with functional interfaces, they added the functional programming capability to Java, allowing the passing of behavior (functions) as parameters to the libraries optimized for the performance of data processing. This way, an application programmer can concentrate on the business aspects of the developed system, leaving performance aspects to the specialists—the authors of the library.

One example of such a library is the `java.util.stream` package, which is going to be the focus of this chapter. This package allows you to have a declarative presentation of the procedures that can be subsequently applied to the data, also in parallel; these procedures are presented as streams, which are objects of the `Stream` interface. For a better transition from the traditional collections to streams, two default methods (`stream()` and `parallelStream()`) were added to the `java.util.Collection` interface, along with the addition of new factory methods of the stream generation to the `Stream` interface.

This approach takes advantage of the power of aggregation, as discussed in `Chapter 2`, *Fast Track to OOP - Classes and Interfaces*. Together with other design principles—encapsulation, interface, and polymorphism—it facilitates a highly extensible and flexible design, while lambda expressions allow you to implement it in a concise and succinct manner.

Today, when the machine learning requirements of massive data processing and the fine-tuning of operations have become ubiquitous, these new features reinforce the position of Java among a few modern programming languages of choice.

Creating immutable collections using the of() and copyOf() factory methods

In this recipe, we will revisit traditional methods of creating collections and compare them with the `List.of()`, `Set.of()`, `Map.of()`, and `Map.ofEntries()` factory methods that came with Java 9, and the `List.copyOf()`, `Set.copyOf()`, and `Map.copyOf()` methods that came with Java 10.

Getting ready

Before Java 9, there were several ways to create collections. Here is the most popular way that was used to create a List:

```
List<String> list = new ArrayList<>();
list.add("This ");
list.add("is ");
list.add("built ");
list.add("by ");
list.add("list.add()");
list.forEach(System.out::print);
```

If we run the preceding code, we get this:

```
This is built by list.add()
```

The shorter way of creating the List collection is by starting with an array:

```
Arrays.asList("This ", "is ", "created ", "by ",
              "Arrays.asList()").forEach(System.out::print);
```

The result is as follows:

```
This is created by Arrays.asList()
```

The Set collection used to be created similarly:

```
Set<String> set = new HashSet<>();
set.add("This ");
set.add("is ");
set.add("built ");
set.add("by ");
set.add("set.add() ");
set.forEach(System.out::print);
```

Alternatively, we can build Set by starting with an array:

```
new HashSet<>(Arrays.asList("This ", "is ", "created ", "by ",
                            "new HashSet(Arrays.asList()) "))
                 .forEach(System.out::print);
```

Here's an illustration of the results of the last two examples:

```
This set.add() is by built
This is by created new HashSet(Arrays.asList())
```

Notice that, unlike `List`, the order of elements in `Set` is not preserved. It depends on the hash code implementation and can change from computer to computer. But the order remains the same between the runs on the same computer. Please take note of this last fact, because we will come back to it later.

And this is how we used to create `Map` before Java 9:

```
Map<Integer, String> map = new HashMap<>();
map.put(1, "This ");
map.put(2, "is ");
map.put(3, "built ");
map.put(4, "by ");
map.put(5, "map.put() ");
map.entrySet().forEach(System.out::print);
```

The output of the preceding code is as follows:

```
1=This 2=is 3=built 4=by 5=map.put()
```

Although the preceding output preserves the order of the elements, it is not guaranteed for `Map` since it is based on the keys that are collected in `Set`.

Those who had to create collections that way often appreciated the JDK enhancement-Proposal 269 *Convenience Factory Methods for Collections* (JEP 269) that stated,

> *"Java is often criticized for its verbosity"* and its goal was to *"Provide static factory methods on the collection interfaces that will create compact, unmodifiable collection instances."*

In response to the criticism and the proposal, Java 9 introduced 12 `of()` static factory methods for each of the 3 interfaces—`List`, `Set`, and `Map`. The following are the factory methods of `List`:

```
static <E> List<E> of()  //Returns list with zero elements
static <E> List<E> of(E e1) //Returns list with one element
static <E> List<E> of(E e1, E e2)  //etc
```

```
static <E> List<E> of(E e1, E e2, E e3)
static <E> List<E> of(E e1, E e2, E e3, E e4)
static <E> List<E> of(E e1, E e2, E e3, E e4, E e5)
static <E> List<E> of(E e1, E e2, E e3, E e4, E e5, E e6)
static <E> List<E> of(E e1, E e2, E e3, E e4, E e5, E e6, E e7)
static <E> List<E> of(E e1, E e2, E e3, E e4, E e5,
                                      E e6, E e7, E e8)
static <E> List<E> of(E e1, E e2, E e3, E e4, E e5,
                                  E e6, E e7, E e8, E e9)
static <E> List<E> of(E e1, E e2, E e3, E e4, E e5,
                              E e6, E e7, E e8, E e9, E e10)
static <E> List<E> of(E... elements)
```

10 overloaded factory methods with a fixed number of elements are optimized for performance, and as stated in JEP 269 (http://openjdk.java.net/jeps/269), these methods

> *"avoid array allocation, initialization, and garbage collection overhead that is incurred by varargs calls."*

Using the of() factory methods makes the code much more compact:

```
List.of("This ", "is ", "created ", "by ", "List.of()")
.forEach(System.out::print);
System.out.println();
Set.of("This ", "is ", "created ", "by ", "Set.of() ")
.forEach(System.out::print);
System.out.println();
Map.of(1, "This ", 2, "is ", 3, "built ", 4, "by ", 5,"Map.of() ")
.entrySet().forEach(System.out::print);
```

The System.out.println() statement was added to inject a line break between the results:

```
This is created by List.of()
by This Set.of() created is
2=is 3=built 4=by 5=Map.of() 1=This
```

One of the 12 static factory methods in the Map interface is different from the other of() methods:

```
Map<K,V> ofEntries(Map.Entry<K,V>... entries)
```

Here is an example of its usage:

```
Map.ofEntries(
    entry(1, "This "),
    entry(2, "is "),
    entry(3, "built "),
    entry(4, "by "),
    entry(5, "Map.ofEntries() ")
).entrySet().forEach(System.out::print);
```

It produces the following output:

```
3=built 2=is 1=This 5=Map.ofEntries() 4=by
```

And there is no `Map.of()` factory method for an unlimited number of elements. One has to use `Map.ofEntries()` when creating a map with more than 10 elements.

In Java 10, the `List.copyOf()`, `Set.copyOf()`, and `Map.copyOf()` methods were introduced. They allow us to convert any collection into an immutable collection of the corresponding type.

How to do it...

As we have mentioned already, the `Set.of()`, `Map.of()`, and `Map.ofEntries()` methods do not preserve the order of the collection elements. This is different from the previous (before Java 9) instances of the `Set` and `Map` behavior of preserving the same order while running on the same computer. The `Set.of()`, `Map.of()`, and `Map.ofEntries()` methods change the elements' order between runs even on the same computer. The order remains the same only during the same run, no matter how many times the collection is iterated. Changing the elements' order from one run to another on the same computer helps programmers avoid the unwarranted reliance on a certain order.

Another feature of the collections generated by the `of()` static method of the `List`, `Set`, and `Map` interfaces is their immutability. What does this mean? Consider the following code:

```
List<String> list = List.of("This ", "is ", "immutable");
list.add("Is it?");      //throws UnsupportedOperationException
list.set(1, "is not "); //throws UnsupportedOperationException
```

As you can see, any attempt to add a new element or modify an existing element of a collection created using the `List.of()` method results in a `java.lang.UnsupportedOperationException` runtime exception.

In addition, the `List.of()` method does not accept a `null` element, so the following code throws a `java.lang.NullPointerException` runtime exception:

```
List<String> list = List.of("This ", "is ", "not ", "created ", null);
```

The collections created by `Set.of()` and `Map.of()` have the same behavior as the method `List.of()` described earlier:

```
Set<String> set = Set.of("a", "b", "c");
//set.remove("b");    //UnsupportedOperationException
//set.add("e");       //UnsupportedOperationException
//set = Set.of("a", "b", "c", null); //NullPointerException

Map<Integer, String> map = Map.of(1, "one", 2, "two", 3, "three");
//map.remove(2);                      //UnsupportedOperationException
//map.put(5, "five ");                //UnsupportedOperationException
//map = Map.of(1, "one", 2, "two", 3, null); //NullPointerException
//map = Map.ofEntries(entry(1, "one"), null); //NullPointerException
```

The `List.copyOf()`, `Set.copyOf()`, and `Map.copyOf()` methods provide another way to create an immutable collection based on another collection:

```
List<Integer> list = Arrays.asList(1,2,3);
list = List.copyOf(list);
//list.set(1, 0);      //UnsupportedOperationException
//list.remove(1);      //UnsupportedOperationException

Set<Integer> setInt = Set.copyOf(list);
//setInt.add(42);        //UnsupportedOperationException
//setInt.remove(3);    //UnsupportedOperationException

Set<String> set = new HashSet<>(Arrays.asList("a","b","c"));
set = Set.copyOf(set);
//set.add("d");        //UnsupportedOperationException
//set.remove("b");     //UnsupportedOperationException

Map<Integer, String> map = new HashMap<>();
map.put(1, "one ");
map.put(2, "two ");
map = Map.copyOf(map);
//map.remove(2);            //UnsupportedOperationException
//map.put(3, "three ");     //UnsupportedOperationException
```

Notice that the input parameter can be any collection that has elements of the same type or the type that extends the type of the elements of the passed-in collection:

```
class A{}
class B extends A{}

List<A> listA = Arrays.asList(new B(), new B());
Set<A> setA = new HashSet<>(listA);

List<B> listB = Arrays.asList(new B(), new B());
setA = new HashSet<>(listB);

//List<B> listB = Arrays.asList(new A(), new A()); //compiler error
//Set<B> setB = new HashSet<>(listA);              //compiler error
```

There's more...

It is not an accident that non-null values and immutability were enforced soon after lambda expressions and streams were introduced. As you will see in subsequent recipes, functional programming and stream pipelines encourage a fluent style of coding (using method chaining, as well as using the forEach() method in the examples of this recipe). Fluent style provides more compact and readable code. Removing the need for the check for the null value helps to keep it this way—compact and focused on the main processing procedures.

The immutability feature, in turn, aligns well with the *effectively final* concept for the variables used by lambda expressions. For example, a mutable collection allows us to work around this limitation:

```
List<Integer> list = Arrays.asList(1,2,3,4,5);
list.set(2, 0);
list.forEach(System.out::print);   //prints: 12045

list.forEach(i -> {
  int j = list.get(2);
  list.set(2, j + 1);
});
System.out.println();
list.forEach(System.out::print);    //prints: 12545
```

In the preceding code, the lambda expression used by the second `forEach()` operation maintains state in the third (with index 2) element of the original list. It makes it possible—intentionally or not—to introduce a state in a lambda expression and cause different outcomes of the same function in different contexts. This is especially dangerous in parallel processing because one cannot predict the state of each possible context. This is why immutability of a collection is a helpful addition that makes the code more robust and reliable.

Creating and operating on streams

In this recipe, we will describe how streams can be created and how the operations can be applied to the elements emitted by the streams. The discussion and examples are applicable for a stream of any type, including the specialized numeric streams: `IntStream`, `LongStream`, and `DoubleStream`. The behavior specific to the numeric streams is not presented because it is described in the next recipe, *Using numeric streams for arithmetic operations*.

Getting ready

There are many ways to create a stream:

- The `stream()` and `parallelStream()` methods of the `java.util.Collection` interface—this means that all the sub-interfaces, including `Set` and `List`, have these methods too
- Two overloaded `stream()` methods of the `java.util.Arrays` class, which convert arrays and subarrays to streams
- The `of()`, `generate()`, and `iterate()` methods of the `java.util.stream.Stream` interface
- The `Stream<Path> list()`, `Stream<String> lines()`, and `Stream<Path> find()` methods of the `java.nio.file.Files` class
- The `Stream<String> lines()` method of the `java.io.BufferedReader` class

After a stream is created, various methods (called operations) can be applied to its elements. A stream itself does not store data. Instead, it acquires data from the source (and provides or emits it to the operations) as needed. The operations can form a pipeline using the fluent style since many intermediate operations can return a stream too. Such operations are called *intermediate* operations. Examples of intermediate operations include the following:

- `map()`: Transforms elements according to a function
- `flatMap()`: Transforms each element into a stream according to a function
- `filter()`: Selects only elements matching a criterion
- `limit()`: Limits a stream to the specified number of elements
- `sorted()`: Transforms an unsorted stream into a sorted one
- `distinct()`: Removes duplicates
- Other methods of the `Stream` interface that return `Stream` too

The pipeline ends with a **terminal operation**. The processing of the stream elements actually begins only when a terminal operation is being executed. Then, all the intermediate operations (if present) start processing and the stream closes and cannot be reopened until the terminal operation is finished with the execution. Examples of terminal operations are:

- `forEach()`
- `findFirst()`
- `reduce()`
- `collect()`
- Other methods of the `Stream` interface that do not return `Stream`

Terminal operations return a result or produce a side effect, but they do not return the `Stream` object.

All the `Stream` operations support parallel processing, which is especially helpful in the case of a large amount of data processed on a multicore computer. All the Java Stream API interfaces and classes are in the `java.util.stream` package.

In this recipe, we are going to demonstrate sequential streams. Parallel-streams processing is not much different. One just has to watch that the processing pipeline does not use a context state that can vary across different processing environments. We will discuss parallel processing in another recipe later in this chapter.

How to do it...

In this section of the recipe, we will present methods to create a stream. Each class that implements the `Set` interface or the `List` interface has the `stream()` method and the `parallelStream()` method, which returns an instance of the `Stream` interface:

1. Consider the following examples of stream creation:

```
List.of("This", "is", "created", "by", "List.of().stream()")
.stream().forEach(System.out::print);
System.out.println();
Set.of("This", "is", "created", "by", "Set.of().stream()")
.stream().forEach(System.out::print);
System.out.println();
Map.of(1, "This ", 2, "is ", 3, "built ", 4, "by ", 5,
                        "Map.of().entrySet().stream()")
.entrySet().stream().forEach(System.out::print);
```

We used the fluent style to make the code more compact and interjected `System.out.println()` in order to start a new line in the output.

2. Run the preceding example and you should see the following result:

```
This is created by List.of().stream()

by created This is Set.of().stream()

4=by 5=Map.of().entrySet().stream()2=is 3=built 1=This
```

Notice that, `List` preserves the order of the elements, while the order of the `Set` elements changes at every run. The latter helps to uncover the defects based on the reliance on a certain order when the order is not guaranteed.

3. Look at the Javadoc of the `Arrays` class. It has two `stream()` overloaded static methods:

```
Stream<T> stream(T[] array)
Stream<T> stream(T[] array, int startInclusive, int
endExclusive)
```

4. Write an example of the usage of the last two methods:

```
String[] array = {"That ", "is ", "an ",
"Arrays.stream(array)"};
Arrays.stream(array).forEach(System.out::print);
System.out.println();
String[] array1 = { "That ", "is ", "an ",
                                "Arrays.stream(array,0,2)"
};
Arrays.stream(array1, 0, 2).forEach(System.out::print);
```

5. Run it and see the result:

```
That is an Arrays.stream(array)
That is
```

Notice that in the second example, only the first two elements—with indexes 0 and 1—were selected to be included in the stream, as it was intended.

6. Open the Javadoc of the `Stream` interface and see the `of()`, `generate()`, and `iterate()` static factory methods:

```
Stream<T> of(T t)            //Stream of one element
Stream<T> ofNullable(T t)    //Stream of one element
          // if not null. Otherwise, returns an empty Stream
Stream<T> of(T... values)
Stream<T> generate(Supplier<T> s)
Stream<T> iterate(T seed, UnaryOperator<T> f)
Stream<T> iterate(T seed, Predicate<T> hasNext,
                          UnaryOperator<T> next)
```

The first two methods are simple, so we skip their demo and start with the third method, `of()`. It can accept either an array or comma-delimited elements.

7. Write the example as follows:

```
String[] array = { "That ", "is ", "a ", "Stream.of(array)" };
Stream.of(array).forEach(System.out::print);
System.out.println();
Stream.of( "That ", "is ", "a ", "Stream.of(literals)" )
                                .forEach(System.out::print);
```

8. Run it and observe the output:

```
That is a Stream.of(array)
That is a Stream.of(literals)
```

9. Write the examples of the usage of the `generate()` and `iterate()` methods as follows:

```
Stream.generate(() -> "generated ")
.limit(3).forEach(System.out::print);
System.out.println();
System.out.print("Stream.iterate().limit(10): ");
Stream.iterate(0, i -> i + 1)
.limit(10).forEach(System.out::print);
System.out.println();
System.out.print("Stream.iterate(Predicate < 10): ");
Stream.iterate(0, i -> i < 10, i -> i + 1)
.forEach(System.out::print);
```

We had to put a limit on the size of the streams generated by the first two examples. Otherwise, they would be infinite. The third example accepts a predicate that provides the criterion for when the iteration has to stop.

10. Run the examples and observe the results:

```
Stream.generate().limit(3): generated generated generated
Stream.iterate().limit(10): 0123456789
Stream.iterate(Predicate < 10): 0123456789
```

11. Let's look at the example of the `Files.list(Path dir)` method, which returns `Stream<Path>` of all the entries of the directory:

```
System.out.println("Files.list(dir): ");
Path dir = FileSystems.getDefault()
    .getPath("src/main/java/com/packt/cookbook/ch05_streams/");
try(Stream<Path> stream = Files.list(dir)) {
        stream.forEach(System.out::println);
} catch (Exception ex){
        ex.printStackTrace();
}
```

The following is from the JDK API:

> *"This method must be used within a try-with-resources statement or similar control structure to ensure that the stream's open directory is closed promptly after the stream's operations are completed."*

And this is what we did; we used a try-with-resources statement. Alternatively, we could use a try-catch-finally construct, close the stream in the finally block, and the result would not change.

12. Run the preceding examples and observe the output:

```
Files.list(dir):
src/com/packt/cookbook/ch05_streams/api
src/com/packt/cookbook/ch05_streams/Chapter05Streams.java
src/com/packt/cookbook/ch05_streams/FactorySpeedModel.java
src/com/packt/cookbook/ch05_streams/FactoryTraffic.java
src/com/packt/cookbook/ch05_streams/FactoryVehicle.java
src/com/packt/cookbook/ch05_streams/Thing.java
```

Not all streams have to be closed explicitly, although the `Stream` interface extends `AutoCloseable` and one would expect that all streams have to be closed automatically using the try-with-resources statement. But that is not the case. The Javadoc for the `Stream` interface (`https://docs.oracle.com/javase/8/docs/api/java/util/stream/Stream.html`) says,

> "*Streams have a* `BaseStream.close()` *method and implement* `AutoCloseable`. *Most stream instances do not actually need to be closed after use, as they are backed by collections, arrays, or generating functions, which require no special resource management. Generally, only streams whose source is an I/O channel, such as those returned by* `Files.lines(Path)`, *will require closing.*"

This means that a programmer has to know the source of the stream, so make sure that the stream is closed if the API for the source requires it.

13. Write an example of the `Files.lines()` method's usage:

```
System.out.println("Files.lines().limit(3): ");
String file = "src/main/java/com/packt/cookbook/" +
                        "ch05_streams/Chapter05Streams.java";
try(Stream<String> stream=Files.lines(Paths.get(file)).limit(3)){
    stream.forEach(l -> {
        if( l.length() > 0 ) {
            System.out.println("    " + l);
        }
    });
} catch (Exception ex){
    ex.printStackTrace();
}
```

The intent of the preceding example was to read the first three lines of the specified file and print non-empty lines with an indentation of three spaces.

14. Run the preceding example and see the result:

```
Files.lines().limit(3):
    package com.packt.cookbook.ch05_streams;
    import com.packt.cookbook.ch05_streams.api.SpeedModel;
```

15. Write the code that uses the `Files.find()` method:

```
Stream<Path> find(Path start, int maxDepth, BiPredicate<Path,
    BasicFileAttributes> matcher, FileVisitOption... options)
```

16. Similar to the previous case, a stream generated by the `Files.find()` method has to be closed explicitly too. The `Files.find()` method walks the file tree rooted at a given starting file and at the requested depth and returns the paths to the files that match the predicate (which includes file attributes). Write the following code:

```
Path dir = FileSystems.getDefault()
  .getPath("src/main/java/com/packt/cookbook/ch05_streams/");
BiPredicate<Path, BasicFileAttributes> select =
    (p, b) -> p.getFileName().toString().contains("Factory");
try(Stream<Path> stream = Files.find(f, 2, select)){
        stream.map(path -> path.getFileName())
                                .forEach(System.out::println);
} catch (Exception ex){
  ex.printStackTrace();
}
```

17. Run the preceding example and you'll get the following output:

```
FactorySpeedModel.java
FactoryTraffic.java
FactoryVehicle.java
```

If necessary, `FileVisitorOption.FOLLOW_LINKS` could be included as the last parameter of the `Files.find()` method if we need to perform a search that would follow all symbolic links it might encounter.

18. The requirements for using the `BufferedReader.lines()` method, which returns `Stream<String>` of lines read from a file, is a little bit different. According to Javadoc (`https://docs.oracle.com/javase/8/docs/api/java/io/BufferedReader.html`),

"The reader must not be operated on during the execution of the terminal stream operation. Otherwise, the result of the terminal stream operation is undefined."

There are many other methods in the JDK that produce streams. But they are more specialized, and we will not demonstrate them here because of the shortage of space.

How it works...

Throughout the preceding examples, we have demonstrated several stream operations already—methods of the `Stream` interface. We used `forEach()` most often and `limit()` a few times. The first one is a terminal operation and the second one is an intermediate one. Let's look at other methods of the `Stream` interface now.

Here are the intermediate operations—methods that return `Stream` and can be connected in a fluent style:

```
//1
Stream<T> peek(Consumer<T> action)
//2
Stream<T> distinct()          //Returns stream of distinct elements
Stream<T> skip(long n)        //Discards the first n elements
Stream<T> limit(long n)       //Allows the first n elements to be
processed
Stream<T> filter(Predicate<T> predicate)
Stream<T> dropWhile(Predicate<T> predicate)
Stream<T> takeWhile(Predicate<T> predicate)
//3
Stream<R> map(Function<T, R> mapper)
IntStream mapToInt(ToIntFunction<T> mapper)
LongStream mapToLong(ToLongFunction<T> mapper)
DoubleStream mapToDouble(ToDoubleFunction<T> mapper)
//4
Stream<R> flatMap(Function<T, Stream<R>> mapper)
IntStream flatMapToInt(Function<T, IntStream> mapper)
LongStream flatMapToLong(Function<T, LongStream> mapper)
DoubleStream flatMapToDouble(Function<T, DoubleStream> mapper)
//5
```

```
static Stream<T> concat(Stream<T> a, Stream<T> b)
//6
Stream<T> sorted()
Stream<T> sorted(Comparator<T> comparator)
```

The signatures of the preceding methods typically include "`? super T`" for an input parameter and "`? extends R`" for the result (see the Javadoc for the formal definition). We simplified them by removing these notations in order to provide a better overview of the variety and commonality of the methods. To compensate, we would like to recap the meaning of the related generic notations since they are used extensively in the Stream API and might be the source of confusion.

Let's look at the formal definition of the `flatMap()` method because it has all of them:

```
<R> Stream<R> flatMap(Function<? super T,
                      ? extends Stream<? extends R>> mapper)
```

The `<R>` symbol in front of the method indicates to the compiler that it is a generic method (the one with its own type parameters). Without it, the compiler would be looking for the definition of the `R` type. The `T` type is not listed in front of the method because it is included in the `Stream<T>` interface definition (look at the top of the page where the interface is declared). The `? super T` notation means that the `T` type or its superclass is allowed here. The `? extends R` notation means that the `R` type or its subclass is allowed here. The same applies to `? extends Stream<...>`: the `Stream` type or its subclass is allowed here.

Now, let's get back to our (simplified) list of intermediate operations. We have broken them into several groups by similarity:

- The first group contains only one `peek()` method, which allows you to apply the `Consumer` function to each of the stream elements without affecting the element because the `Consumer` function does not return anything. It is typically used for debugging:

  ```
  int sum = Stream.of( 1,2,3,4,5,6,7,8,9 )
                  .filter(i -> i % 2 != 0)
                  .peek(i -> System.out.print(i))
                  .mapToInt(Integer::intValue)
                  .sum();
  System.out.println("sum = " + sum);
  ```

If you execute the preceding code, the result will be as follows:

- In the second group of intermediate operations listed above, the first three—distinct(), skip(), limit()—are self-explanatory. The filter(Predicate p) method is one of the most often used. It does what its name suggests—it removes from the stream those elements that do not match the criterion passed in as the Predicate function. We saw an example of its usage in the previous snippet of code: only the odd numbers were allowed to flow through the filter. The dropWhile() method discards the elements as long as the criterion is met (then allows the rest of the stream elements to flow to the next operation). The takeWhile() method does the opposite—it allows the elements to flow as long as the criterion is met (then discards the rest of the elements). Here is an example of these operations' usage:

```
System.out.println("Files.lines().dropWhile().takeWhile():");
String file = "src/main/java/com/packt/cookbook/" +
                        "ch05_streams/Chapter05Streams.java";
try(Stream<String> stream = Files.lines(Paths.get(file))){
    stream.dropWhile(l ->
                    !l.contains("dropWhile().takeWhile()"))
        .takeWhile(l -> !l.contains("} catc" + "h"))
        .forEach(System.out::println);
} catch (Exception ex){
    ex.printStackTrace();
}
```

This code reads the file where the preceding code is stored. We want it to print "Files.lines().dropWhile().takeWhile():" first, then print all the preceding lines except the last three. So, the preceding code discards all the first lines of the file that do not have the dropWhile().takeWhile() substring, then allows all the lines to flow until the } catch substring is found.

Notice that we had to write "} catc" + "h" instead of "} catch". Otherwise, the code would find contains(" catch") and would not go further.

The result of the preceding code in as follows:

```
Files.lines().dropWhile().takeWhile():
    System.out.println("Files.lines().dropWhile().takeWhile(): ");
    String file = "src/com/packt/cookbook/ch05_streams/Chapter05Streams.java";
    try(Stream<String> stream = Files.lines(Paths.get(file))){
        stream.dropWhile(l -> !l.contains("dropWhile().takeWhile()"))
            .takeWhile(l -> !l.contains("} catc"+"h"))
            .forEach(System.out::println);
```

- The group of map() operations is pretty straightforward too. Such an operation transforms each element of the stream by applying to it a function that was passed in as a parameter. We have already seen an example of the usage of the mapToInt() method. Here is another example of the map() operation:

```
Stream.of( "That ", "is ", "a ", "Stream.of(literals)" )
                .map(s -> s.contains("i"))
                .forEach(System.out::println);
```

In this example, we transform String literals into boolean. The result is as follows:

```
false
true
false
true
```

- The next group of intermediate operations, called flatMap(), provides more complex processing. A flatMap() operation applies the passed-in function (which returns a stream) to each of the elements so that the operation can produce a stream composed of the streams extracted from each of the elements. Here's an example of flatMap() usage:

```
Stream.of( "That ", "is ", "a ", "Stream.of(literals)" )
        .filter(s -> s.contains("Th"))
        .flatMap(s -> Pattern.compile("(?!^)").splitAsStream(s))
        .forEach(System.out::print);
```

The preceding code selects from the stream elements only literals that contain Th and converts them into a stream of characters, which are then printed out by forEach(). The result of this is as follows:

- The `concat()` method creates a stream from two input streams so that all the elements of the first stream are followed by all the elements of the second stream. Here's an example of this functionality:

```
Stream.concat(Stream.of(4,5,6), Stream.of(1,2,3))
                                .forEach(System.out::print);
```

The result is as follows:

In the case there are more than two stream concatenations, one can write the following:

```
Stream.of(Stream.of(4,5,6), Stream.of(1,2,3),
Stream.of(7,8,9))
  .flatMap(Function.identity())
  .forEach(System.out::print);
```

The result is as follows:

Notice that, in the preceding code, `Function.identity()` is a function that returns its input argument. We use it because we do not need to transform the input streams but just pass them as is to the resulting stream. Without using this `flatMap()` operation, the stream would consist of the `Stream` objects, not of their elements, and the output would show `java.util.stream.ReferencePipeline$Head@548b7f67ja va.util.stream.ReferencePipeline$Head@7ac7a4e4 java.util.stream.ReferencePipeline$Head@6d78f375`.

- The last group of intermediate operations is composed of the `sorted()` methods that sort the stream elements in a natural order (if they are of the `Comparable` type) or according to the passed-in `Comparator` object. It is a stateful operation (as well as `distinct()`, `limit()`, and `skip()`) that yields a non-deterministic result in the case of parallel processing (that is the topic of the recipe *Processing stream in parallel* below).

Now, let's look at terminal operations (we simplified their signature too by removing `? super T` and `? extends R`):

```
//1
long count()                       //Returns total count of elements
//2
Optional<T> max(Comparator<T> c) //Returns max according to Comparator
Optional<T> min(Comparator<T> c) //Returns min according to Comparator
//3
Optional<T> findAny()      //Returns any or empty Optional
Optional<T> findFirst()    //Returns the first element or empty Optional
//4
boolean allMatch(Predicate<T> p)    //All elements match Predicate?
boolean anyMatch(Predicate<T> p)    //Any element matches Predicate?
boolean noneMatch(Predicate<T> p)   //No element matches Predicate?
//5
void forEach(Consumer<T> action)    //Apply action to each element
void forEachOrdered(Consumer<T> action)
//6
Optional<T> reduce(BinaryOperator<T> accumulator)
T reduce(T identity, BinaryOperator<T> accumulator)
U reduce(U identity, BiFunction<U,T,U> accumulator,
                                  BinaryOperator<U> combiner)
//7
R collect(Collector<T,A,R> collector)
R collect(Supplier<R> supplier, BiConsumer<R,T> accumulator,
                                  BiConsumer<R,R> combiner)
//8
Object[] toArray()
A[] toArray(IntFunction<A[]> generator)
```

The first four groups are self-explanatory, but we need to say a few words about `Optional`. The Javadoc (`https://docs.oracle.com/javase/8/docs/api/java/util/Optional.html`) defines it as,

> *"A container object which may or may not contain a non-null value. If a value is present,* `isPresent()` *returns* `true` *and* `get()` *returns the value."*

It allows you to avoid `NullPointerException` or check for `null` (well, you have to call `isPresent()` instead anyway). It has its own methods—`map()`, `filter()`, and `flatMap()`. In addition, `Optional` has methods that include the `isPresent()` check implicitly:

- `ifPresent(Consumer<T> action)`: Performs the action with the value if present, otherwise does nothing
- `ifPresentOrElse(Consumer<T> action, Runnable emptyAction)`: Performs the provided action with the value if present, otherwise performs the provided empty-based action
- `or(Supplier<Optional<T>> supplier)`: Returns an `Optional` class describing the value if present, otherwise returns an `Optional` class produced by the provided function
- `orElse(T other)`: Returns the value if present, otherwise returns the provided `other` object
- `orElseGet(Supplier<T> supplier)`: Returns the value if present, otherwise returns the result produced by the provided function
- `orElseThrow(Supplier<X> exceptionSupplier)`: Returns the value if present, otherwise throws an exception produced by the provided function

Note that `Optional` is used as a return value in cases when `null` is a possible result. Here is an example of its usage. We reimplemented the stream-concatenating code using the `reduce()` operation that returns `Optional`:

```
Stream.of(Stream.of(4,5,6), Stream.of(1,2,3), Stream.of(7,8,9))
        .reduce(Stream::concat)
        .orElseGet(Stream::empty)
        .forEach(System.out::print);
```

The result is the same as in the previous implementation with the `flatMap()` method:

```
456123789
```

The next group of terminal operations is referred to as `forEach()`. These operations guarantee that the given function will be applied to each element of the stream. But `forEach()` does not say anything about the order, which might be changed for better performance. By contrast, `forEachOrdered()` guarantees not only the processing of all the elements of the stream, but also doing this in the order specified by its source, regardless of whether the stream is sequential or parallel. Here are a couple of examples of this:

```
Stream.of("3","2","1").parallel().forEach(System.out::print);
System.out.println();
Stream.of("3","2","1").parallel().forEachOrdered(System.out::print);
```

The result is as follows:

As you can see, in the case of parallel processing, `forEach()` does not guarantee the order, while `forEachOrdered()` does. Here is another example of using both `Optional` and `forEach()`:

```
Stream.of( "That ", "is ", "a ", null, "Stream.of(literals)" )
        .map(Optional::ofNullable)
        .filter(Optional::isPresent)
        .map(Optional::get)
        .map(String::toString)
        .forEach(System.out::print);
```

We could not use `Optional.of()` and used `Optional.ofNullable()` instead because `Optional.of()` would throw `NullPointerException` on null. In such a case, `Optional.ofNullable()` just returns `Optional` empty. The result is as follows:

```
That is a Stream.of(literals)
```

Now, let's talk about the next group of terminal operations, called `reduce()`. Each of the three overloaded methods returns a single value after processing all the stream elements. Among the most simple examples are finding a sum of the stream elements in case they are numbers, or max, min, and similar. But a more complex result can be constructed for a stream of objects of any type.

The first method, `Optional<T> reduce(BinaryOperator<T> accumulator)`, returns the `Optional<T>` object because it is the responsibility of the provided accumulator function to calculate the result, and the authors of the JDK implementation cannot guarantee that it will always contain a non-null value:

```
int sum = Stream.of(1,2,3).reduce((p,e) -> p + e).orElse(0);
System.out.println("Stream.of(1,2,3).reduce(acc): " +sum);
```

The passed-in function receives the result of the previous execution of the same function (as the first parameter, `p`) and the next element of the stream (as the second parameter, `e`). For the very first element, `p` gets its value, while `e` is the second element. You can print the `p` value as follows:

```
int sum = Stream.of(1,2,3)
        .reduce((p,e) -> {
            System.out.println(p);    //prints: 1 3
            return p + e;
        })
        .orElse(10);
System.out.println("Stream.of(1,2,3).reduce(acc): " + sum);
```

The output of the preceding code is as follows:

```
1
3
Stream.of(1,2,3).reduce(acc): 6
```

To avoid the extra step with `Optional`, the second method, `T reduce(T identity, BinaryOperator<T> accumulator)`, returns the value provided as the first parameter, `identity`, of the `T` type (which is the type of the elements of `Stream<T>`) in case the stream is empty. This parameter has to comply with the for all `t`, as `accumulator.apply(identity, t)` is equal to the `t` requirement (from Javadoc). In our case, it has to be `0` for it to comply with `0 + e == e`. Here is an example of how to use the second method:

```
int sum = Stream.of(1,2,3).reduce(0, (p,e) -> p + e);
System.out.println("Stream.of(1,2,3).reduce(0, acc): " + sum);
```

The result is the same as with the first `reduce()` method.

The third method, `U reduce(U identity, BiFunction<U,T,U> accumulator, BinaryOperator<U> combiner)`, converts the value of the `T` type into a value of the `U` type with the help of the `BiFunction<U,T,U>` function. `BiFunction<U,T,U>` is used as an accumulator so that the result (the `U` type) of its application to the previous element (the `T` type) becomes an input into the function along with the current element of the stream. Here is a code example:

```
String sum = Stream.of(1,2,3)
    .reduce("", (p,e) -> p + e.toString(), (x,y) -> x + "," + y);
System.out.println("Stream.of(1,2,3).reduce(,acc,comb): " + sum);
```

One naturally expects to see the result as 1, 2, 3. Instead, we see the following:

```
Stream.of(1,2,3).reduce(,acc,comb): 123
```

The reason for the preceding result is that the combiner was used because the stream was sequential. But let's make the stream parallel now:

```
String sum = Stream.of(1,2,3).parallel()
    .reduce("", (p,e) -> p + e.toString(), (x,y) -> x + "," + y);
System.out.println("Stream.of(1,2,3).reduce(,acc,comb): " + sum);
```

The result of the preceding code execution will be as follows:

```
Stream.of(1,2,3).parallel.reduce(,acc,comb): 1,2,3
```

This means that the combiner is called only for parallel processing in order to assemble (combine) the results of different sub-streams processed in parallel. This is the only deviation we have noticed so far from the declared intent of providing the same behavior for sequential and parallel streams. But there are many ways to accomplish the same result without using this third version of `reduce()`. For example, consider the following code:

```
String sum = Stream.of(1,2,3)
                    .map(i -> i.toString() + ",")
                    .reduce("", (p,e) -> p + e);
System.out.println("Stream.of(1,2,3).map.reduce(,acc): "
                    + sum.substring(0, sum.length()-1));
```

It produces the same result as the previous example:

```
Stream.of(1,2,3).map.reduce(,acc): 1,2,3
```

Now let's change it to a parallel stream:

```
String sum = Stream.of(1,2,3).parallel()
                    .map(i -> i.toString() + ",")
                    .reduce("", (p,e) -> p + e);
System.out.println("Stream.of(1,2,3).map.reduce(,acc): "
                    + sum.substring(0, sum.length()-1));
```

The result remains the same: 1, 2, 3.

The next group of intermediate operations, called `collect()`, consists of two methods:

```
R collect(Collector<T,A,R> collector)
R collect(Supplier<R> supplier, BiConsumer<R,T> accumulator,
                                BiConsumer<R,R> combiner)
```

The first one accepts `Collector<T,A,R>` as a parameter. It is much more popular than the second one because it is backed up by the `Collectors` class, which provides a wide variety of implementations of the `Collector` interface. We encourage you to go through the Javadoc of the `Collectors` class and see what it offers.

Let's discuss a few examples of using the `Collectors` class. First, we'll create a small demo class called `Thing`:

```
public class Thing {
  private int someInt;
  public Thing(int i) { this.someInt = i; }
  public int getSomeInt() { return someInt; }
  public String getSomeStr() {
    return Integer.toString(someInt); }
}
```

Now we can use it to demonstrate a few collectors:

```
double aa = Stream.of(1,2,3).map(Thing::new)
              .collect(Collectors.averagingInt(Thing::getSomeInt));
System.out.println("stream(1,2,3).averagingInt(): " + aa);

String as = Stream.of(1,2,3).map(Thing::new).map(Thing::getSomeStr)
                    .collect(Collectors.joining(","));
```

```
System.out.println("stream(1,2,3).joining(,): " + as);

String ss = Stream.of(1,2,3).map(Thing::new).map(Thing::getSomeStr)
                    .collect(Collectors.joining(",", "[", "]"));
System.out.println("stream(1,2,3).joining(,[,]): " + ss);
```

The result will be as follows:

```
stream(1,2,3).averagingInt(): 2.0
stream(1,2,3).joining(,): 1,2,3
stream(1,2,3).joining(,[,]): [1,2,3]
```

The joining collector is a source of joy for any programmer who has ever had to write code that checks whether the added element is the first, the last, or removes the last character (like we did in the example of the reduce() operation). The collector produced by the joining() method does this behind the scenes. All the programmer has to provide is the delimiter, prefix, and suffix.

Most programmers will never need to write a customs collector. But in the case there is a need, one can use the second method, collect(), of Stream, and provide the functions that compose the collector or use one of the two Collector.of() static methods that generate a collector that can be reused.

If you compare the reduce() and collect() operations, you'll notice that the primary purpose of reduce() is to operate on immutable objects and primitives. The result of reduce() is one value that is typically (but not exclusively) of the same type as the elements of the stream. collect(), by contrast, produces the result of a different type wrapped in a mutable container. The most popular usage of collect() is centered around producing List, Set, or Map objects using the corresponding Collectors.toList(), Collectors.toSet(), or Collectors.toMap() collector.

The last group of terminal operations consists of two toArray() methods:

```
Object[] toArray()
A[] toArray(IntFunction<A[]> generator)
```

The first returns Object[], the second, an array of the specified type. Let's look at the examples of their usage:

```
Object[] os = Stream.of(1,2,3).toArray();
Arrays.stream(os).forEach(System.out::print);
System.out.println();
```

```
String[] sts = Stream.of(1,2,3)
                    .map(i -> i.toString())
                    .toArray(String[]::new);
Arrays.stream(sts).forEach(System.out::print);
```

The output of these examples is as follows:

The first example is quite straightforward. It is worth noting that we cannot write the following:

```
Stream.of(1,2,3).toArray().forEach(System.out::print);
```

This is because `toArray()` is a terminal operation and the stream is closed automatically after it. That's why we have to open a new stream in the second line of our preceding code example.

The second example—with the overloaded `A[] toArray(IntFunction<A[]> generator)` method—is more complicated. The Javadoc (`https://docs.oracle.com/javase/8/docs/api/java/util/stream/Stream.html`) says,

> *"The generator function takes an integer, which is the size of the desired array, and produces an array of the desired size."*

This means that the method reference to a `toArray(String[]::new)` constructor in the last example is a shorter version of `toArray(size -> new String[size])`.

Using numeric streams for arithmetic operations

In addition to the `Stream` interface, the `java.util.stream` package also provides specialized interfaces—`IntStream`, `DoubleStream`, and `LongStream`—that are optimized for processing streams of corresponding primitive types. They are very convenient to use, and have numeric operations, such as `max()`, `min()`, `average()`, `sum()`.

The numeric interfaces have methods similar to the methods of the Stream interface, which means that everything we have talked about in the previous recipe, *Creating and operating on streams*, applies to numeric streams too. That is why, in this section, we will only talk about the methods that are not present in the `Stream` interface.

Getting ready

In addition to the methods described in the *Creating and operating on streams* recipe, the following methods can be used to create a numeric stream:

- The `range(int startInclusive, int endInclusive)` and `rangeClosed(int startInclusive, int endInclusive)` methods of the `IntStream` and `LongStream` interfaces
- Six overloaded `stream()` methods of the `java.util.Arrays` class, which convert arrays and subarrays to numeric streams

The list of intermediate operations specific to numeric streams includes the following:

- `boxed()`: Converts a numeric stream of a primitive type to a stream of the corresponding wrapping type
- `mapToObj(mapper)`: Converts a numeric stream of a primitive type to a stream of objects using the provided function mapper
- `asDoubleStream()` of the `LongStream` interface: Converts `LongStream` to `DoubleStream`
- `asLongStream()` and `asDoubleStream()` of the `IntStream` interface: Converts `IntStream` to the corresponding numeric stream

The list of terminal arithmetic operations specific to numeric streams includes the following:

- `sum()`: Calculates a sum of the numeric stream elements
- `average()`: Calculates an average of the numeric stream elements
- `summaryStatistics()`: Creates an object with various summary data about the elements of the stream

How to do it...

1. Experiment with the `range(int startInclusive, int endInclusive)` and `rangeClosed(int startInclusive, int endInclusive)` methods of the `IntStream` and `LongStream` interfaces:

```
IntStream.range(1,3).forEach(System.out::print); //prints: 12
LongStream.range(1,3).forEach(System.out::print); //prints: 12
IntStream.rangeClosed(1,3).forEach(System.out::print);  // 123
LongStream.rangeClosed(1,3).forEach(System.out::print); // 123
```

As you can see, the difference between the `range()` and `rangeClosed()` methods is the exclusion or inclusion of the value passed in as the second parameter. This also leads to the following results in the case where both parameters have the same value:

```
IntStream.range(3,3).forEach(System.out::print);
                                            //prints:
LongStream.range(3,3).forEach(System.out::print);
                                            //prints:
IntStream.rangeClosed(3,3).forEach(System.out::print);
                                            //prints: 3
LongStream.rangeClosed(3,3).forEach(System.out::print);
                                            //prints: 3
```

In the preceding examples, the `range()` method does not emit any element, while the `rangeClosed()` method emits only one element.

Please notice that neither of these methods generates an error when the first parameter is bigger than the second parameter. They just emit nothing and the following statements produce no output:

```
IntStream.range(3,1).forEach(System.out::print);
LongStream.range(3,1).forEach(System.out::print);
IntStream.rangeClosed(3,1).forEach(System.out::print);
LongStream.rangeClosed(3,1).forEach(System.out::print);
```

2. If you do not need the values of stream elements to be sequential, you can create an array of the values first and then generate a stream using one of six overloaded `stream()` static methods of the `java.util.Arrays` class:

```
IntStream stream(int[] array)
IntStream stream(int[] array, int startInclusive,
 int endExclusive)
LongStream stream(long[] array)
LongStream stream(long[] array, int startInclusive,
                                      int endExclusive)
DoubleStream stream(double[] array)
DoubleStream stream(double[] array, int startInclusive,
                                      int endExclusive)
```

Here are the examples of the usage of the `Arrays.stream()` method:

```
int[] ai = {2, 3, 1, 5, 4};
Arrays.stream(ai)
      .forEach(System.out::print);   //prints: 23154
Arrays.stream(ai, 1, 3)
      .forEach(System.out::print);   //prints: 31
long[] al = {2, 3, 1, 5, 4};
Arrays.stream(al)
      .forEach(System.out::print);   //prints: 23154
Arrays.stream(al, 1, 3)
      .forEach(System.out::print);   //prints: 31
double[] ad = {2., 3., 1., 5., 4.};
Arrays.stream(ad)
  .forEach(System.out::print);   //prints: 2.03.01.05.04.0
Arrays.stream(ad, 1, 3)
      .forEach(System.out::print);   //prints: 3.01.0
```

The last two pipelines can be improved to print out the elements of `DoubleStream` in a more human-friendly format by using the joining collector we discussed in the previous recipe, *Creating and operating on streams*:

```
double[] ad = {2., 3., 1., 5., 4.};
String res = Arrays.stream(ad).mapToObj(String::valueOf)
                    .collect(Collectors.joining(" "));
System.out.println(res);   //prints: 2.0 3.0 1.0 5.0 4.0
res = Arrays.stream(ad, 1, 3).mapToObj(String::valueOf)
                    .collect(Collectors.joining(" "));
System.out.println(res);              //prints: 3.0 1.0
```

Since the `Collector<CharSequence, ?, String>` joining collector accepts `CharSequence` as an input type, we had to convert the number into `String` using an intermediate operation, `mapToObj()`.

3. Use the `mapToObj(mapper)` intermediate operation to convert a primitive type element to a reference type. We saw an example of its usage in step 2. The mapper function can be as simple or as complex as it needs to be in order to achieve the necessary transformation.

   There is also a specialized operation, `boxed()`, without parameters that convert elements of a primitive numeric type to the corresponding wrapping type—`int` value to `Integer` value, `long` value to `Long` value, and `double` value to `Double` value. We can use it, for example, to achieve the same results as the last two examples of the usage of the `mapToObj(mapper)` operation:

```
double[] ad = {2., 3., 1., 5., 4.};
String res = Arrays.stream(ad).boxed()
                    .map(Object::toString)
                    .collect(Collectors.joining(" "));
System.out.println(res); //prints: 2.0 3.0 1.0 5.0 4.0
res = Arrays.stream(ad, 1, 3).boxed()
                    .map(Object::toString)
                    .collect(Collectors.joining(" "));
System.out.println(res); //prints: 3.0 1.0
```

4. There are also intermediate operations that convert an element of a numeric stream from one primitive type to another numeric primitive type: `asLongStream()` and `asDoubleStream()` in the `IntStream` interface, and `asDoubleStream()` in the `LongStream` interface. Let's look at examples of their usage:

```
IntStream.range(1, 3).asLongStream()
                .forEach(System.out::print); //prints: 12
IntStream.range(1, 3).asDoubleStream()
  .forEach(d -> System.out.print(d + " ")); //prints: 1.0 2.0
LongStream.range(1, 3).asDoubleStream()
  .forEach(d -> System.out.print(d + " ")); //prints: 1.0 2.0
```

You may have noticed that these operations are possible only for the widening primitive conversion: from the int type to long and double, and from long to double.

5. The terminal arithmetic operations specific to numeric streams are pretty straightforward. Here are examples of the sum() and average() operations with IntStream:

```
int sum = IntStream.empty().sum();
System.out.println(sum);                        //prints: 0
sum = IntStream.range(1, 3).sum();
System.out.println(sum);                        //prints: 3
double av = IntStream.empty().average().orElse(0);
System.out.println(av);                         //prints: 0.0
av = IntStream.range(1, 3).average().orElse(0);
System.out.println(av);                         //prints: 1.5
```

As you can see, the average() operation returns OptionalDouble. It is interesting to consider why the authors decided to return OptionalDouble for average() but not for sum(). This decision was probably made to map an empty stream to an empty OptionalDouble, but then the decision to return 0 when sum() applies to an empty stream seems inconsistent.

These operations behave the same way for LongStream and DoubleStream:

```
long suml = LongStream.range(1, 3).sum();
System.out.println(suml);                       //prints: 3
double avl = LongStream.range(1, 3).average().orElse(0);
System.out.println(avl);                        //prints: 1.5

double sumd = DoubleStream.of(1, 2).sum();
System.out.println(sumd);                       //prints: 3.0
double avd = DoubleStream.of(1, 2).average().orElse(0);
System.out.println(avd);                        //prints: 1.5
```

6. The summaryStatistics() terminal operation collects various summary data about the elements of the stream:

```
IntSummaryStatistics iss =
               IntStream.empty().summaryStatistics();
System.out.println(iss);    //count=0, sum=0,
  //min=2147483647, average=0.000000, max=-2147483648
iss = IntStream.range(1, 3).summaryStatistics();
System.out.println(iss);    //count=2, sum=3, min=1,
                            //average=1.500000, max=2
```

```
LongSummaryStatistics lss =
                LongStream.empty().summaryStatistics();
System.out.println(lss);  //count=0, sum=0,
                            //min=9223372036854775807,
        //average=0.000000, max=-9223372036854775808
lss = LongStream.range(1, 3).summaryStatistics();
System.out.println(lss);  //count=2, sum=3, min=1,
                            //average=1.500000, max=2

DoubleSummaryStatistics dss =
                DoubleStream.empty().summaryStatistics();
System.out.println(dss);  //count=0, sum=0.000000,
        //min=Infinity, average=0.000000, max=-Infinity
dss = DoubleStream.of(1, 2).summaryStatistics();
System.out.println(dss);  //count=2, sum=3.000000,
        //min=1.000000, average=1.500000, max=2.000000
```

The printouts added as comments to the preceding printing lines come from the `toString()` method of the `IntSummaryStatistics`, `LongSummaryStatistics`, or `DoubleSummaryStatistics` objects, correspondingly. Other methods of these objects include `getCount()`, `getSum()`, `getMin()`, `getAverage()`, and `getMax()`, which allow access to a particular aspect of the collected statistics.

Notice that in the case of an empty stream, the min (max) value is the smallest (biggest) possible value of the corresponding Java type:

```
System.out.println(Integer.MAX_VALUE);  // 2147483647
System.out.println(Integer.MIN_VALUE);  //-2147483648
System.out.println(Long.MAX_VALUE);     // 9223372036854775807
System.out.println(Long.MIN_VALUE);     //-9223372036854775808
System.out.println(Double.MAX_VALUE);   //1.7976931348623157E308
System.out.println(Double.MIN_VALUE);   //4.9E-324
```

Only `DoubleSummaryStatistics` shows Infinity and -Infinity as min and max values, instead of the actual numbers shown here. According to the Javadoc of these methods, `getMax()` returns "the maximum recorded value, `Double.NaN` if any recorded value was NaN or `Double.NEGATIVE_INFINITY` if no values were recorded" and `getMin()` returns "the minimum recorded value, `Double.NaN` if any recorded value was NaN or `Double.POSITIVE_INFINITY` if no values were recorded."

Also, please notice that in contrast with the `average()` terminal stream operation, the `getAverage()` method of any of the preceding summary statistics returns the arithmetic mean of streamed values, or zero if there were no values emitted from the stream, not the `Optional` object.

There's more...

The `IntSummaryStatistics`, `LongSummaryStatistics`, and `DoubleSummaryStatistics` objects can be created not only by the `summaryStatistics()` numeric stream terminal operation. Such an object can also be created by the `collect()` terminal operation applied to any `Stream` object, not just `IntStream`, `LongStream`, or `DoubleStream`.

Each of the summary statistics objects has the `accept()` and `combine()` methods, which allow us to create a `Collector` object that can be passed into the `collect()` operation and produce the corresponding summary statistics object. We will demonstrate this possibility by creating the `IntSummaryStatistics` object. The `LongSummaryStatistics` and `DoubleSummaryStatistics` objects can be created similarly.

The `IntSummaryStatistics` class has the following two methods:

- void accept (int value): Includes a new value into statistics summary
- void combine (`IntSummaryStatistics` other): Adds the collected statistics of the provided `other` object to the current one

These methods allow us to use the overloaded version of the R collect(Supplier<R> supplier, BiConsumer<R,? super T> accumulator, BiConsumer<R,R> combiner) operation on any `Stream` object, as follows:

```
IntSummaryStatistics iss = Stream.of(3, 1)
        .collect(IntSummaryStatistics::new,
                IntSummaryStatistics::accept,
                IntSummaryStatistics::combine
        );
System.out.println(iss);  //count=2, sum=4, min=1,
                          //average=2.000000, max=3
```

As you can see, the stream is not one of the specialized numeric streams. It just has numeric elements of the same type as the created summary statistics object. Nevertheless, we were able to create an object of the `IntSummaryStatistics` class. Similarly, it is possible to create objects of the `LongSummaryStatistics` and `DoubleSummaryStatistics` classes.

Please notice that the third parameter, `combiner`, is used only for parallel stream processing—it combines the results of sub-streams that are processed in parallel. To demonstrate this, we can change the preceding example as follows:

```
IntSummaryStatistics iss = Stream.of(3, 1)
    .collect(IntSummaryStatistics::new,
        IntSummaryStatistics::accept,
        (r, r1) -> {
            System.out.println("Combining...");  //is not printing
            r.combine(r1);
        }
    );
System.out.println(iss); //count=2, sum=4, min=1,
                         //average=2.000000, max=3
```

The `Combining...` line is not printing. Let's change the stream to a parallel one:

```
IntSummaryStatistics iss = Stream.of(3, 1)
    .parallel()
    .collect(IntSummaryStatistics::new,
        IntSummaryStatistics::accept,
        (r, r1) -> {
            System.out.println("Combining...");  //Now it prints!
            r.combine(r1);
        }
    );
System.out.println(iss); //count=2, sum=4, min=1,
                         //average=2.000000, max=3
```

If you run the preceding code now, you will see the `Combining...` line.

Another way to collect statistics is to use a `Collector` object created by one of the following methods of the `Collectors` class:

```
Collector<T, ?, IntSummaryStatistics>
                    summarizingInt (ToIntFunction<T> mapper)
Collector<T, ?, LongSummaryStatistics>
                    summarizingLong (ToLongFunction<T> mapper)
Collector<T, ?, DoubleSummaryStatistics>
                    summarizingDouble (ToDoubleFunction<T> mapper)
```

Again, we will use the first of the preceding methods to create the `IntSummaryStatistics` object. Let's assume we have the following `Person` class:

```
class Person {
    private int age;
    private String name;
    public Person(int age, String name) {
        this.name = name;
        this.age = age;
    }
    public int getAge() { return this.age; }
    public String getName() { return this.name; }
}
```

If there is a stream of `Person` class objects, we can collect statistics of the age of the persons (stream elements) as follows:

```
IntSummaryStatistics iss =
    Stream.of(new Person(30, "John"), new Person(20, "Jill"))
        .collect(Collectors.summarizingInt(Person::getAge));
System.out.println(iss);      //count=2, sum=50, min=20,
                              //average=25.000000, max=30
```

As you can see, we were able to collect statistics only on the field of an object that matches the type of the collected statistics. Neither the stream nor its elements are numeric.

Look in the Javadoc of the `java.util.stream.Collectors` class to see what other functionality it provides before trying to create a custom `Collector` object.

Completing streams by producing collections

You will learn and practice how to use the `collect()` terminal operation to repackage stream elements to a target collection structure.

Getting ready

There are two overloaded versions of the `collect()` terminal operation that allow us to create a collection of the stream elements:

- `R collect(Supplier<R> supplier, BiConsumer<R,T> accumulator, BiConsumer<R,R> combiner)`: Produces the R result using the passed-in functions applied to the stream elements of the T type. The provided supplier and accumulator work together as follows:

  ```
  R result = supplier.get();
  for (T element : this stream) {
      accumulator.accept(result, element);
  }
  return result;
  ```

  The provided combiner is used only for the processing of a parallel stream. It combines the results of the sub-streams processed in parallel.

- `R collect(Collector<T, A, R> collector)`: Produces the R result using the passed-in `Collector` object applied to the stream elements of the T type. The A type is an intermediate accumulation type of `Collector`. The `Collector` object can be built using the `Collector.of()` factory method, but we are not going to discuss it in this recipe because there are many factory methods available in the `java.util.stream.Collectors` class that cover the majority of the needs. Besides, after you learn how to use the `Collectors` class, you will be able to use the `Collector.of()` method too.

In this recipe, we are going to demonstrate how to use the following methods of the `Collectors` class:

- `Collector<T, ?, List<T>> toList()`: Creates a `Collector` object that collects the stream elements of the T type into a `List<T>` object
- `Collector<T, ?, Set<T>> toSet()`: Creates a `Collector` object that collects the stream elements of the T type into a `Set<T>` object
- `Collector<T, ?, C> toCollection(Supplier<C> collectionFactory)`: Creates a `Collector` object that collects the stream elements of the T type into a `Collection` of the C type produced by the `collectionFactor` supplier

- `Collector<T, ?, List<T>> toUnmodifiableList()`: Creates a `Collector` object that collects the stream elements of the `T` type into an immutable `List<T>` object
- `Collector<T, ?, Set<T>> toUnmodifiableSet()`: Creates a `Collector` object that collects the stream elements of the `T` type into an immutable `Set<T>` object

For our demonstrations, we are going to use the following `Person` class:

```
class Person {
    private int age;
    private String name;
    public Person(int age, String name) {
        this.age = age;
        this.name = name;
    }
    public int getAge() { return this.age; }
    public String getName() { return this.name; }
    @Override
    public boolean equals(Object o) {
        if (this == o) return true;
        if (!(o instanceof Person)) return false;
        Person person = (Person) o;
        return getAge() == person.getAge() &&
                Objects.equals(getName(), person.getName());
    }
    @Override
    public int hashCode() {
        return Objects.hash(getName(), getAge());
    }
    @Override
    public String toString() {
        return "Person{name:" + this.name + ",age:" + this.age + "}";
    }
}
```

How to do it...

We will walk you through the sequence of practical steps that demonstrate how to use the preceding methods and classes:

1. Write an example of the usage of the `R collect(Supplier<R> supplier, BiConsumer<R,T> accumulator, BiConsumer<R,R> combiner)` operation of the `Stream<T>` interface that produces the `List<T>` object:

```
List<Person> list =
    Stream.of(new Person(30, "John"), new Person(20, "Jill"))
    .collect(ArrayList::new,
            List::add,        //same as: (a,p)-> a.add(p),
            List::addAll      //same as: (r, r1)-> r.addAll(r1)
    );
System.out.println(list);
    //prints: [Person{name:John,age:30}, Person{name:Jill,age:20}]
```

In the preceding example, the comments to the accumulator and the combiner demonstrate how these functions can be presented as lambda expressions instead of just method references.

The first parameter, `Supplier<R>`, returns the container for the result. In our case, we have defined it as a constructor of the `ArrayList<Person>` class because it implements the `List<Person>` interface—the type of the object we would like to construct.

The accumulator takes the current result, `a` (which is going to be of the `List<Person>` type in our case), and adds to it the next stream element, `p` (the `Person` object in our case). The output of the example is shown as the last comment line.

The combiner combines the results of the sub-streams processed in parallel. It takes the first result, `r` (of any sub-stream that has finished processing first), and adds to it another result, `r1`, and so on. This means that the combiner is used for parallel processing only. To demonstrate this, let's modify the preceding code as follows:

```
List<Person> list =
    Stream.of(new Person(30, "John"), new Person(20, "Jill"))
        .collect(ArrayList::new,
                ArrayList::add,
            (r, r1)-> {
                System.out.println("Combining...");
```

```
                    r.addAll(r1);
              }
        );
System.out.println(list1);
 //prints: [Person{name:John,age:30}, Person{name:Jill,age:20}]
```

If you run the preceding example, you will not see the `Combining...` line printed out because `combiner` is not used for sequential stream processing.

Now, let's convert the stream into a parallel one:

```
List<Person> list =
    Stream.of(new Person(30, "John"), new Person(20, "Jill"))
        .parallel()
        .collect(ArrayList::new,
                ArrayList::add,
                (r, r1)-> {
                    System.out.println("Combining...");
                    r.addAll(r1);
                }
        );
System.out.println(list1);
   //prints: [Person{name:John,age:30}, Person{name:Jill,age:20}]
```

If you run the preceding code, the `Combining...` line will be displayed.

Nothing prevents you from modifying the provided functions any way you need to, as long as the input and return types of each function remain the same.

The `Set<Person>` object can be created the same way:

```
Set<Person> set =
  Stream.of(new Person(30, "John"), new Person(20, "Jill"))
        .collect(HashSet::new,
                Set::add,        //same as: (a,p)-> a.add(p),
                Set::addAll      //same as: (r, r1)-> r.addAll(r1)
        );
System.out.println(set);
   //prints: [Person{name:John,age:30}, Person{name:Jill,age:20}]
```

The created `List` or a `Set` object can be modified at any time:

```
list.add(new Person(30, "Bob"));
System.out.println(list);  //prints: [Person{name:John,age:30},
                           //          Person{name:Jill,age:20},
                           //          Person{name:Bob,age:30}]
list.set(1, new Person(15, "Bob"));
System.out.println(list);  //prints: [Person{name:John,age:30},
                           //          Person{name:Bob,age:15},
                           //          Person{name:Bob,age:30}]
set.add(new Person(30, "Bob"));
System.out.println(set);   //prints: [Person{name:John,age:30},
                           //          Person{name:Jill,age:20},
                           //          Person{name:Bob,age:30}]
```

We have mentioned it to contrast this behavior with the behavior of immutable collections, which we are going to discuss shortly.

2. Write an example of the usage of the `R collect(Collector<T, A, R> collector)` operation of the `Stream<T>` interface with the collector created by the `Collector<T, ?, List<T>>` `Collectors.toList()` and `Collector<T, ?, Set<T>>` `Collectors.toSet()` methods:

```
List<Person> list = Stream.of(new Person(30, "John"),
                              new Person(20, "Jill"))
        .collect(Collectors.toList());
System.out.println(list);  //prints: [Person{name:John,age:30},
                           //          Person{name:Jill,age:20}]

Set<Person> set1 = Stream.of(new Person(30, "John"),
                             new Person(20, "Jill"))
        .collect(Collectors.toSet());
System.out.println(set1); //prints: [Person{name:John,age:30},
                                      Person{name:Jill,age:20}]

Set<Person> set2 = Stream.of(new Person(30, "John"),
                             new Person(20, "Jill"),
                             new Person(30, "John"))
        .collect(Collectors.toSet());
System.out.println(set2); //prints: [Person{name:John,age:30},
                                      Person{name:Jill,age:20}]
set2.add(new Person(30, "Bob"));
System.out.println(set2); //prints: [Person{name:John,age:30},
                                      Person{name:Jill,age:20},
                                      Person{name:Bob,age:30}]
```

As was expected, Set does not allow duplicate elements defined by the equals() method implementation. In the case of the Person class, the equals() method compares both age and name, so a difference in any of these properties makes two Person objects not equal.

3. Write an example of the usage of the R collect(Collector<T, A, R> collector) operation of the Stream<T> interface with the collector created by the Collector<T, ?, C> Collectors.toCollection(Supplier<C> collectionFactory) method. The advantage of this collector is that it collects stream elements not just in List or Set, but in any object that implements a Collection interface. The target object that collects the stream elements of the T type is produced by the collectionFactor supplier:

```
LinkedList<Person> list = Stream.of(new Person(30, "John"),
                                    new Person(20, "Jill"))
        .collect(Collectors.toCollection(LinkedList::new));
System.out.println(list);   //prints:
[Person{name:John,age:30},
                            //
Person{name:Jill,age:20}]

LinkedHashSet<Person> set = Stream.of(new Person(30, "John"),
                                      new Person(20, "Jill"))
        .collect(Collectors.toCollection(LinkedHashSet::new));
System.out.println(set);   //prints: [Person{name:John,age:30},
                                      Person{name:Jill,age:20}]
```

4. Write an example of the usage of the `R collect(Collector<T, A, R> collector)` operation of the `Stream<T>` interface with the collector created by the `Collector<T, ?, List<T>>` `Collectors.toUnmodifiableList()` and `Collector<T, ?, Set<T>>` `Collectors.toUnmodifiableSet()` methods:

```
List<Person> list = Stream.of(new Person(30, "John"),
                               new Person(20, "Jill"))
        .collect(Collectors.toUnmodifiableList());
System.out.println(list);  //prints: [Person{name:John,age:30},
                           //          Person{name:Jill,age:20}]

list.add(new Person(30, "Bob"));  //UnsupportedOperationException
list.set(1, new Person(15, "Bob"));
//UnsupportedOperationException
list.remove(new Person(30, "John"));
//UnsupportedOperationException

Set<Person> set = Stream.of(new Person(30, "John"),
                            new Person(20, "Jill"))
        .collect(Collectors.toUnmodifiableSet());
System.out.println(set);  //prints: [Person{name:John,age:30},
                          //          Person{name:Jill,age:20}]

set.add(new Person(30, "Bob"));  //UnsupportedOperationException
```

As you can see from the comments in the preceding code, the objects created using collectors generated by the `Collector<T, ?, List<T>>` `Collectors.toUnmodifiableList()` and `Collector<T, ?, Set<T>> Collectors.toUnmodifiableSet()` methods create immutable objects. Such objects are very helpful when used in lambda expressions because this way we are guaranteed that they cannot be modified, so the same the expression—even if passed around and executed in different contexts—will produce the result that depends only on its input parameters and will not have unexpected side-effects caused by the modification of the `List` or `Set` object it uses.

For example:

```
Set<Person> set = Stream.of(new Person(30, "John"),
                            new Person(20, "Jill"))
        .collect(Collectors.toUnmodifiableSet());

Predicate<Person> filter = p -> set.contains(p);
```

The filter we have created in the preceding example can be used anywhere to select `Person` objects that belong to the provided set.

Completing streams by producing maps

You will learn and practice how to use the `collect()` terminal operation to repackage stream elements to target the `Map` structure. While discussing collectors, we will not include collectors that use grouping because they will be presented in the next recipe.

Getting ready

As we mentioned in the previous recipe, there are two overloaded versions of the `collect()` terminal operation, which allow us to create a collection of the stream elements:

- `R collect(Supplier<R> supplier, BiConsumer<R,T> accumulator, BiConsumer<R,R> combiner)`: Produces the `R` result using the passed-in functions applied to the stream elements of the `T` type
- `R collect(Collector<T, A, R> collector)`: Produces the `R` result using the passed-in `Collector` object applied to the stream elements of the `T` type

These operations can be also used to create a `Map` object, and in this recipe, we are going to demonstrate how to do so.

In support of the second of the preceding versions of the `collect()` operation, the `Collectors` class provides four groups of factory methods that create the `Collector` object. The first group includes the factory methods very similar to those that create the `Collector` object for collecting stream elements into `List` or `Set` discussed and demonstrated in the previous recipe:

- `Collector<T,?,Map<K,U>> toMap(Function<T,K> keyMapper, Function<T,U> valueMapper)`: **Creates a** `Collector` **object that collects** the stream elements of the `T` type into a `Map<K,U>` object using the provided functions (mappers) that produce a key and value from a stream element as an input parameter.

- `Collector<T,?,Map<K,U>> toMap(Function<T,K> keyMapper, Function<T,U> valueMapper, BinaryOperator<U> mergeFunction)`: **Creates a** `Collector` **object that collects the stream** elements of the `T` type into a `Map<K,U>` object using the provided functions (mappers) that produce a key and value from a stream element as an input parameter. The provided `mergeFunction` is used only for parallel stream processing; it merges the results of the sub-streams into the one final result—the `Map<K,U>` object.

- `Collector<T,?,M> toMap(Function<T,K> keyMapper, Function<T,U> valueMapper, BinaryOperator<U> mergeFunction, Supplier<M> mapFactory)`: **Creates** a `Collector` object that collects the stream elements of the `T` type into a `Map<K,U>` object using the provided functions (mappers) that produce a key and value from a stream element as an input parameter. The provided `mergeFunction` is used only for parallel stream processing; it merges the results of the sub-streams into the one final result—the `Map<K,U>` object. The provided `mapFactory` supplier creates an empty `Map<K,U>` object into which the results will be inserted.

- `Collector<T,?,Map<K,U>> toUnmodifiableMap(Function<T,K> keyMapper, Function<T,U> valueMapper)`: **Creates** a `Collector` object that collects the stream elements of the `T` type into an *immutable* `Map<K,U>` object using the provided functions (mappers) that produce a key and value from a stream element as an input parameter.

- `Collector<T,?,Map<K,U>> toUnmodifiableMap(Function<T,K> keyMapper, Function<T,U> valueMapper, BinaryOperator<U> mergeFunction)`: Creates a `Collector` object that collects the stream elements of the `T` type into an *immutable* `Map<K,U>` object using the provided functions (mappers) that produce a key and value from a stream element as an input parameter. The provided `mergeFunction` is used only for parallel stream processing; it merges the results of the sub-streams into the one final result—an immutable `Map<K,U>` object.

The second group includes three factory methods similar to the three `toMap()` methods we just listed. The only difference is that the collectors created by the `toConcurrentMap()` methods collect stream elements in a `ConcurrentMap` object:

- `Collector<T,?,ConcurrentMap<K,U>> toConcurrentMap(Function<T,K> keyMapper, Function<T,U> valueMapper)`: Creates a `Collector` object that collects the stream elements of the `T` type into a `ConcurrentMap<K,U>` object using the provided functions (mappers) that produce a key and value from a stream element as an input parameter.

- `Collector<T,?,ConcurrentMap<K,U>> toConcurrentMap(Function<T,K> keyMapper, Function<T,U> valueMapper, BinaryOperator<U> mergeFunction)`: Creates a `Collector` object that collects the stream elements of the `T` type into a `ConcurrentMap<K,U>` object using the provided functions (mappers) that produce a key and value from a stream element as an input parameter. The provided `mergeFunction` is used only for parallel stream processing; it merges the results of the sub-streams into the one final result—the `ConcurrentMap<K,U>` object.

- `Collector<T,?,M> toConcurrentMap(Function<T,K> keyMapper, Function<T,U> valueMapper, BinaryOperator<U> mergeFunction, Supplier<M> mapFactory)`: Creates a `Collector` object that collects the stream elements of the `T` type into a `ConcurrentMap<K,U>` object using the provided functions (mappers) that produce a key and value from a stream element as an input parameter. The provided `mergeFunction` is used only for parallel stream processing; it merges the results of the sub-streams into the one final result—the `ConcurrentMap<K,U>` object. The provided `mapFactory` supplier creates an empty `ConcurrentMap<K,U>` object into which the results will be inserted.

The need for this second group of factory methods arises from the fact that, for a parallel stream, the merging results of different sub-streams is an expensive operation. It is especially heavy when the results have to be merged into the resulting Map in the encountered order—that is what the collectors created by the toMap() factory methods do. These collectors create multiple intermediate results and then merge them by calling the collector's supplier and combiner multiple times.

When the order of the results-merging is not important, the collectors created by the toConcurrentMap() methods can be used as less heavy because they call the supplier only once, insert the elements in the *shared* resulting container, and never call the combiner.

So, the difference between the toMap() and toConcurrentMap() collectors manifest only during parallel stream processing. That's why it is often recommended to use the toMap() collectors for serial stream processing, and the toConcurrentMap() collectors for parallel stream processing (if the order of collecting the stream elements is not important).

The third group includes three groupingBy() factory methods, which we are going to discuss in the next recipe.

The fourth group includes three groupingByConcurrent() factory methods, which we are going to discuss in the next recipe, too.

For our demonstrations, we are going to use the same Person class we used to create collections in the previous recipe:

```java
class Person {
    private int age;
    private String name;
    public Person(int age, String name) {
        this.age = age;
        this.name = name;
    }
    public int getAge() { return this.age; }
    public String getName() { return this.name; }
    @Override
    public boolean equals(Object o) {
        if (this == o) return true;
        if (!(o instanceof Person)) return false;
        Person person = (Person) o;
        return getAge() == person.getAge() &&
                Objects.equals(getName(), person.getName());
    }
    @Override
```

```
public int hashCode() {
    return Objects.hash(getName(), getAge());
}
@Override
public String toString() {
    return "Person{name:" + this.name + ",age:" + this.age + "}";
}
}
```

How to do it...

We will walk you through the sequence of practical steps that demonstrate how to use the preceding methods and classes:

1. Write an example of the usage of the R collect(Supplier<R> supplier, BiConsumer<R,T> accumulator, BiConsumer<R,R> combiner) operation of the Stream<T> interface that produces the Map object. Create Map<String, Person> with a person's name as the key:

```
Map<String, Person> map = Stream.of(new Person(30, "John"),
                                    new Person(20, "Jill"))
        .collect(HashMap::new,
                (m,p) -> m.put(p.getName(), p),
                Map::putAll
        );
System.out.println(map); //prints:
{John=Person{name:John,age:30},
                                  //
Jill=Person{name:Jill,age:20}}
```

Or, to avoid redundant data in the resulting Map, we can use age field as the Map value:

```
Map<String, Integer> map = Stream.of(new Person(30, "John"),
                                     new Person(20, "Jill"))
        .collect(HashMap::new,
                (m,p) -> m.put(p.getName(), p.getAge()),
                Map::putAll
        );
System.out.println(map);          //prints: {John=30, Jill=20}
```

The combiner is called only for a parallel stream, as it is used to combine the results of different sub-stream processing. To prove it, we have replaced the method reference `Map::putAll` with the code block that prints the message `Combining...`:

```
Map<String, Integer> map = Stream.of(new Person(30, "John"),
                                      new Person(20, "Jill"))
        //.parallel()       //conversion to a parallel stream
        .collect(HashMap::new,
                 (m,p) -> m.put(p.getName(), p.getAge()),
                 (m,m1) -> {
                         System.out.println("Combining...");
                         m.putAll(m1);
                 }
        );
System.out.println(map);   //prints: {John=30, Jill=20}
```

The `Combining...` message will be displayed only if the conversion to a parallel stream is not commented out.

If we add another `Person` object with the same name, one of them is going to be overwritten in the resulting `Map`:

```
Map<String, Integer> map = Stream.of(new Person(30, "John"),
                                      new Person(20, "Jill"),
                                      new Person(15, "John"))
        .collect(HashMap::new,
                 (m,p) -> m.put(p.getName(), p.getAge()),
                 Map::putAll
        );
System.out.println(map);       //prints: {John=15, Jill=20}
```

If such a behavior is not desirable and we need to see all the values of all duplicate keys, we can change the resulting `Map` to have a `List` object as a value, so that in this list we can collect all the values that have the same key:

```
BiConsumer<Map<String, List<Integer>>, Person> consumer =
(m,p) -> {
    List<Integer> list = m.get(p.getName());
    if(list == null) {
        list = new ArrayList<>();
        m.put(p.getName(), list);
    }
    list.add(p.getAge());
};
Map<String, List<Integer>> map =
  Stream.of(new Person(30, "John"),
```

```
                         new Person(20, "Jill"),
                         new Person(15, "John"))
              .collect(HashMap::new, consumer, Map::putAll);
        System.out.println(map);
                         //prints: {John=[30, 15], Jill=[20]}
```

As you can see, we did not inline the `BiConsumer` function in
the `collect()` operation as a parameter because it is a multiline code now
and is easier to read this way.

Another way to collect multiple values for the same key, in this case, would
be to create `Map` with a `String` value as follows:

```
BiConsumer<Map<String, String>, Person> consumer2 = (m,p) -> {
  if(m.keySet().contains(p.getName())) {
    m.put(p.getName(), m.get(p.getName()) + "," + p.getAge());
  } else {
    m.put(p.getName(), String.valueOf(p.getAge()));
  }
};
Map<String, String> map = Stream.of(new Person(30, "John"),
                              new Person(20, "Jill"),
                              new Person(15, "John"))
          .collect(HashMap::new, consumer, Map::putAll);
System.out.println(map);      //prints: {John=30,15, Jill=20}
```

2. Write an example of the usage of the `R collect(Collector<T, A, R>
   collector)` operation of the `Stream<T>` interface with the collector
   created by the `Collector<T, ?, Map<K,U>>`
   `Collectors.toMap(Function<T,K> keyMapper,`
   `Function<T,U> valueMapper)` method:

```
Map<String, Integer> map = Stream.of(new Person(30, "John"),
                              new Person(20, "Jill"))
      .collect(Collectors.toMap(Person::getName, Person::getAge));
System.out.println(map);      //prints: {John=30, Jill=20}
```

The preceding solution works fine as long as there is no duplicate key encountered, as in the following case:

```
Map<String, Integer> map = Stream.of(new Person(30, "John"),
                                     new Person(20, "Jill"),
                                     new Person(15, "John"))
      .collect(Collectors.toMap(Person::getName, Person::getAge));
```

The preceding code throws `IllegalStateException` with the `Duplicate key John` (attempted merging values 30 and 15) message and there is no way for us to add a check for a duplicate key, as we have done before. So, if there is a chance for a duplicate key, one has to use the overloaded version of the `toMap()` method.

3. Write an example of the usage of the `R collect(Collector<T, A, R> collector)` operation of the `Stream<T>` interface with the collector created by the `Collector<T, ?, Map<K,U>>` `Collectors.toMap(Function<T,K> keyMapper, Function<T,U> valueMapper, BinaryOperator<U> mergeFunction)` method:

```
Function<Person, List<Integer>> valueMapper = p -> {
    List<Integer> list = new ArrayList<>();
    list.add(p.getAge());
    return list;
};
BinaryOperator<List<Integer>> mergeFunction = (l1, l2) -> {
    l1.addAll(l2);
    return l1;
};
Map<String, List<Integer>> map =
    Stream.of(new Person(30, "John"),
              new Person(20, "Jill"),
              new Person(15, "John"))
        .collect(Collectors.toMap(Person::getName,
                          valueMapper, mergeFunction));
System.out.println(map);
                //prints: {John=[30, 15], Jill=[20]}
```

That is the purpose of the `mergeFunction`—to combine values for a duplicate key. Instead of `List<Integer>`, we can also collect the values of a duplicate key in a `String` object:

```
Function<Person, String> valueMapper =
                          p -> String.valueOf(p.getAge());
BinaryOperator<String> mergeFunction =
                          (s1, s2) -> s1 + "," + s2;
Map<String, String> map =
   Stream.of(new Person(30, "John"),
             new Person(20, "Jill"),
             new Person(15, "John"))
          .collect(Collectors.toMap(Person::getName,
                        valueMapper, mergeFunction));
System.out.println(map3);//prints: {John=30,15, Jill=20}
```

4. Write an example of the usage of the `R collect(Collector<T, A, R> collector)` operation of the `Stream<T>` interface with the collector created by the `Collector<T, ?, M> Collectors.toMap(Function<T,K> keyMapper, Function<T,U> valueMapper, BinaryOperator<U> mergeFunction, Supplier<M> mapFactory)` method:

```
Function<Person, String> valueMapper =
                          p -> String.valueOf(p.getAge());
BinaryOperator<String> mergeFunction =
                          (s1, s2) -> s1 + "," + s2;
LinkedHashMap<String, String> map =
   Stream.of(new Person(30, "John"),
             new Person(20, "Jill"),
             new Person(15, "John"))
          .collect(Collectors.toMap(Person::getName,
            valueMapper, mergeFunction, LinkedHashMap::new));
System.out.println(map3);     //prints: {John=30,15, Jill=20}
```

As you can see, this version of the `toMap()` method allows us to specify the desired `Map` interface implementation (the `LinkedHashMap` class, in this case) instead of using the default one.

5. Write an example of the usage of the `R collect(Collector<T, A, R> collector)` operation of the `Stream<T>` interface with the collector created by the `Collector<T, ?, Map<K,U>> Collectors.toUnmodifiableMap(Function<T,K> keyMapper, Function<T,U> valueMapper)` method:

```
Map<String, Integer> map = Stream.of(new Person(30, "John"),
                                     new Person(20, "Jill"))
        .collect(Collectors.toUnmodifiableMap(Person::getName,
Person::getAge));
System.out.println(map);          //prints: {John=30, Jill=20}

map.put("N", new Person(42, "N")); //UnsupportedOperationExc
map.remove("John");                //UnsupportedOperationExc

Map<String, Integer> map = Stream.of(new Person(30, "John"),
                                     new Person(20, "Jill"),
                                     new Person(15, "John"))
   .collect(Collectors.toUnmodifiableMap(Person::getName,
      Person::getAge)); //IllegalStateExc: Duplicate key John
```

As you can see, the collector created by the `toUnmpdifiableMap()` method behaves the same as the collector created by the `Collector<T, ?, Map<K,U>> Collectors.toMap(Function<T,K> keyMapper, Function<T,U> valueMapper)` method, except that it produces an immutable `Map` object.

6. Write an example of the usage of the `R collect(Collector<T, A, R> collector)` operation of the `Stream<T>` interface with the collector created by the `Collector<T, ?, Map<K,U>> Collectors.toUnmodifiableMap(Function<T,K> keyMapper, Function<T,U> valueMapper, BinaryOperator<U> mergeFunction)` method:

```
Function<Person, List<Integer>> valueMapper = p -> {
    List<Integer> list = new ArrayList<>();
    list.add(p.getAge());
    return list;
};
BinaryOperator<List<Integer>> mergeFunction = (l1, l2) -> {
    l1.addAll(l2);
    return l1;
};
Map<String, List<Integer>> map =
    Stream.of(new Person(30, "John"),
```

```
                              new Person(20, "Jill"),
                              new Person(15, "John"))
            .collect(Collectors.toUnmodifiableMap(Person::getName,
                                        valueMapper, mergeFunction));
      System.out.println(map); //prints: {John=[30, 15], Jill=[20]}
```

The collector created by the `toUnmpdifiableMap()` method behaves the same as the collector created by the `Collector<T, ?, Map<K,U>>` `Collectors.toMap(Function<T,K> keyMapper, Function<T,U> valueMapper, BinaryOperator<U> mergeFunction)` method, except that it produces an immutable `Map` object. Its purpose is to handle the case of duplicate keys. The following is another way to combine the values of duplicate keys:

```
Function<Person, String> valueMapper =
                              p -> String.valueOf(p.getAge());
BinaryOperator<String> mergeFunction =
                              (s1, s2) -> s1 + "," + s2;
Map<String, String> map = Stream.of(new Person(30, "John"),
                              new Person(20, "Jill"),
                              new Person(15, "John"))
      .collect(Collectors.toUnmodifiableMap(Person::getName,
                                        valueMapper, mergeFunction));
      System.out.println(map);        //prints: {John=30,15, Jill=20}
```

7. Write an example of the usage of the `R collect(Collector<T, A, R> collector)` operation of the `Stream<T>` interface with the collector created by the `Collector<T, ?, ConcurrentMap<K,U>>` `Collectors.toConcurrentMap(Function<T,K> keyMapper, Function<T,U> valueMapper)` method:

```
ConcurrentMap<String, Integer> map =
                        Stream.of(new Person(30, "John"),
                              new Person(20, "Jill"))
            .collect(Collectors.toConcurrentMap(Person::getName,
                                        Person::getAge));
      System.out.println(map);        /prints: {John=30, Jill=20}

map.put("N", new Person(42, "N")); //UnsupportedOperationExc
map.remove("John");                //UnsupportedOperationExc

ConcurrentMap<String, Integer> map =
                        Stream.of(new Person(30, "John"),
                              new Person(20, "Jill"),
                              new Person(15, "John"))
      .collect(Collectors.toConcurrentMap(Person::getName,
```

```
Person::getAge)); //IllegalStateExc: Duplicate key John
```

As you can see, the collector created by the `toConcurrentMap()` method
behaves the same as the collector created by the `Collector<T, ?,`
`Map<K,U>> Collectors.toMap(Function<T,K> keyMapper,`
`Function<T,U> valueMapper)` and `Collector<T, ?, Map<K,U>>`
`Collectors.toUnmodifiableMap(Function<T,K> keyMapper,`
`Function<T,U> valueMapper)` methods, except that it produces a
mutable `Map` object and, when the stream is parallel, shares between sub-
streams the resulting `Map`.

8. Write an example of the usage of the `R collect(Collector<T, A, R>`
   `collector)` operation of the `Stream<T>` interface with the collector
   created by the `Collector<T, ?, ConcurrentMap<K,U>>`
   `Collectors.toConcurrentMap(Function<T,K> keyMapper,`
   `Function<T,U> valueMapper, BinaryOperator<U>`
   `mergeFunction)` method:

```java
Function<Person, List<Integer>> valueMapper = p -> {
    List<Integer> list = new ArrayList<>();
    list.add(p.getAge());
    return list;
};
BinaryOperator<List<Integer>> mergeFunction = (l1, l2) -> {
    l1.addAll(l2);
    return l1;
};
ConcurrentMap<String, List<Integer>> map =
  Stream.of(new Person(30, "John"),
            new Person(20, "Jill"),
            new Person(15, "John"))
        .collect(Collectors.toConcurrentMap(Person::getName,
                              valueMapper, mergeFunction));
System.out.println(map);
                        //prints: {John=[30, 15], Jill=[20]}
```

As you can see, the collector created by the `toConcurrentMap()` method
behaves the same as the collector created by the `Collector<T, ?,`
`Map<K,U>> Collectors.toMap(Function<T,K> keyMapper,`
`Function<T,U> valueMapper, BinaryOperator<U>`
`mergeFunction)` and `Collector<T, ?, Map<K,U>>`
`Collectors.toUnmodifiableMap(Function<T,K> keyMapper,`
`Function<T,U> valueMapper, BinaryOperator<U>`
`mergeFunction)` methods, except that it produces a mutable `Map` object

and, when the stream is parallel, shares the resulting `Map` between substreams. The following is another way to combine the values of duplicate keys:

```
Function<Person, String> valueMapper =
                              p -> String.valueOf(p.getAge());
BinaryOperator<String> mergeFunction =
                              (s1, s2) -> s1 + "," + s2;
ConcurrentMap<String, String> map =
                      Stream.of(new Person(30, "John"),
                                new Person(20, "Jill"),
                                new Person(15, "John"))
        .collect(Collectors.toConcurrentMap(Person::getName,
                              valueMapper, mergeFunction));
System.out.println(map);          //prints: {John=30,15, Jill=20}
```

9. Write an example of the usage of the `R collect(Collector<T, A, R> collector)` operation of the `Stream<T>` interface with the collector created by the `Collector<T, ?, M>` `Collectors.toConcurrentMap(Function<T,K> keyMapper, Function<T,U> valueMapper, BinaryOperator<U> mergeFunction, Supplier<M> mapFactory)` method:

```
ConcurrentSkipListMap<String, String> map =
                      Stream.of(new Person(30, "John"),
                                new Person(20, "Jill"),
                                new Person(15, "John"))
        .collect(Collectors.toConcurrentMap(Person::getName,
            valueMapper, mergeFunction, ConcurrentSkipListMap::new));
System.out.println(map4);          //prints: {Jill=20, John=30,15}
```

As you can see, this version of the `toConcurrentMap()` method allows us to specify the desired `Map` interface implementation (the `ConcurrentSkipListMap` class, in this case) instead of using the default one.

The collector created by the `toConcurrentMap()` method behaves the same as the collector created by the `Collector<T, ?, Map<K,U>>` `Collectors.toMap(Function<T,K> keyMapper,` `Function<T,U> valueMapper, BinaryOperator<U> mergeFunction,` `Supplier<M> mapFactory)` method, but when the stream is parallel, it shares between sub-streams the resulting `Map`.

Completing streams by producing maps using grouping collectors

In this recipe, you will learn about and practice how to use the `collect()` terminal operation to group elements by a property and store the result in a `Map` instance using a collector.

Getting ready

There are two sets of collectors that use grouping—similar to the *group by* functionality of SQL statements—to present stream data as a `Map` object. The first set includes three overloaded `groupingBy()` factory methods:

- `Collector<T, ?, Map<K,List<T>>> groupingBy(Function<T,K>` `classifier)`: Creates a `Collector` object that collects the stream elements of the `T` type into a `Map<K,List<T>>` object using the provided `classifier` function to map the current element to the key in the resulting map.
- `Collector<T,?,Map<K,D>> groupingBy(Function<T,K>` `classifier, Collector<T,A,D> downstream)`: Creates a `Collector` object that collects the stream elements of the `T` type into a `Map<K,D>` object using the provided `classifier` function to map the current element to the key in the intermediate map `Map<K,List<T>>`. It then uses the `downstream` collector to convert the values of the intermediate map into the values of the resulting map, `Map<K,D`.

- `Collector<T, ?, M> groupingBy(Function<T,K> classifier, Supplier<M> mapFactory, Collector<T,A,D> downstream):` Creates a `Collector` object that collects the stream elements of the `T` type into the `M` map object using the provided `classifier` function to map the current element to the key in the `Map<K,List<T>>` intermediate map. It then uses the `downstream` collector to convert the values of the intermediate map into the values of the resulting map of the type provided by the `mapFactory` supplier.

The second set of collectors includes three `groupingByConcurrent()` factory methods, which are created for concurrency handling during parallel stream processing. These collectors take the same arguments as the corresponding overloaded versions of the `groupingBy()` collectors listed earlier. The only difference is that the return type of the `groupingByConcurrent()` collectors are the instances of the `ConcurrentHashMap` class or its subclass:

- `Collector<T, ?, ConcurrentMap<K,List<T>>> groupingByConcurrent(Function<T,K> classifier)` : Creates a `Collector` object that collects the stream elements of the `T` type into a `ConcurrentMap<K,List<T>>` object using the provided `classifier` function to map the current element to the key in the resulting map.

- `Collector<T, ?, ConcurrentMap<K,D>> groupingByConcurrent(Function<T,K> classifier, Collector<T,A,D> downstream):` Creates a `Collector` object that collects the stream elements of the `T` type into a `ConcurrentMap<K,D>` object using the provided `classifier` function to map the current element to the key in the `ConcurrentMap<K,List<T>>` intermediate map. It then uses the `downstream` collector to convert the values of the intermediate map into the values of the resulting map, `ConcurrentMap<K,D>`.

- `Collector<T, ?, M> groupingByConcurrent(Function<T,K> classifier, Supplier<M> mapFactory, Collector<T,A,D> downstream):` Creates a `Collector` object that collects the stream elements of the `T` type into the `M` map object using the provided `classifier` function to map the current element to the key in the `ConcurrentMap<K,List<T>>` intermediate map. It then uses the `downstream` collector to convert the values of the intermediate map into the values of the resulting map of the type provided by the `mapFactory` supplier.

For our demonstrations, we are going to use the same `Person` class we used to create maps in the previous recipe:

```java
class Person {
    private int age;
    private String name;
    public Person(int age, String name) {
        this.age = age;
        this.name = name;
    }
    public int getAge() { return this.age; }
    public String getName() { return this.name; }
    @Override
    public boolean equals(Object o) {
        if (this == o) return true;
        if (!(o instanceof Person)) return false;
        Person person = (Person) o;
        return getAge() == person.getAge() &&
                Objects.equals(getName(), person.getName());
    }
    @Override
    public int hashCode() {
        return Objects.hash(getName(), getAge());
    }
    @Override
    public String toString() {
        return "Person{name:" + this.name + ",age:" + this.age + "}";
    }
}
```

We will also use the `Person2` class:

```java
class Person2 {
    private int age;
    private String name, city;
    public Person2(int age, String name, String city) {
        this.age = age;
        this.name = name;
        this.city = city;
    }
    public int getAge() { return this.age; }
    public String getName() { return this.name; }
    public String getCity() { return this.city; }
    @Override
    public boolean equals(Object o) {
        if (this == o) return true;
        if (!(o instanceof Person)) return false;
        Person2 person = (Person2) o;
```

```
                return getAge() == person.getAge() &&
                        Objects.equals(getName(), person.getName()) &&
                        Objects.equals(getCity(), person.getCity());
        }
        @Override
        public int hashCode() {
            return Objects.hash(getName(), getAge(), getCity());
        }
        @Override
        public String toString() {
            return "Person{name:" + this.name + ",age:" + this.age  +
                                        ",city:" + this.city + "}";
        }
    }
```

The `Person2` class is different from the `Person` class as it has an additional
field—city. It will be used to demonstrate the power of the grouping functionality.
And the `Person2` class variation—the `Person3` class—will be used to demonstrate
how to create the `EnumMap` object. The `Person3` class uses `enum City` as the value
type for its `city` property:

```
enum City{
    Chicago, Denver, Seattle
}

class Person3 {
    private int age;
    private String name;
    private City city;
    public Person3(int age, String name, City city) {
        this.age = age;
        this.name = name;
        this.city = city;
    }
    public int getAge() { return this.age; }
    public String getName() { return this.name; }
    public City getCity() { return this.city; }
    @Override
    public boolean equals(Object o) {
        if (this == o) return true;
        if (!(o instanceof Person)) return false;
        Person3 person = (Person3) o;
        return getAge() == person.getAge() &&
                Objects.equals(getName(), person.getName()) &&
                Objects.equals(getCity(), person.getCity());
    }
    @Override
```

```
public int hashCode() {
    return Objects.hash(getName(), getAge(), getCity());
}
@Override
public String toString() {
    return "Person{name:" + this.name + ",age:" + this.age  +
                                ",city:" + this.city + "}";
}
}
```

To make the examples less verbose, we are going to use the following methods to generate test streams:

```
Stream<Person> getStreamPerson() {
    return Stream.of(new Person(30, "John"),
                     new Person(20, "Jill"),
                     new Person(20, "John"));
}
Stream<Person2> getStreamPerson2(){
    return Stream.of(new Person2(30, "John", "Denver"),
                     new Person2(30, "John", "Seattle"),
                     new Person2(20, "Jill", "Seattle"),
                     new Person2(20, "Jill", "Chicago"),
                     new Person2(20, "John", "Denver"),
                     new Person2(20, "John", "Chicago"));
}
Stream<Person3> getStreamPerson3(){
    return Stream.of(new Person3(30, "John", City.Denver),
                     new Person3(30, "John", City.Seattle),
                     new Person3(20, "Jill", City.Seattle),
                     new Person3(20, "Jill", City.Chicago),
                     new Person3(20, "John", City.Denver),
                     new Person3(20, "John", City.Chicago));
}
```

How to do it...

We will walk you through the sequence of practical steps that demonstrate how to use the preceding methods and classes:

1. Write an example of the usage of the `R collect(Collector<T, A, R>`
   `collector)` operation of the `Stream<T>` interface with the collector
   created by the `Collector<T, ?,`
   `Map<K,List<T>>> groupingBy(Function<T,K>`
   `classifier)` method:

   ```
   Map<String, List<Person>> map = getStreamPerson()
           .collect(Collectors.groupingBy(Person::getName));
   System.out.println(map);
                   //prints: {John=[Person{name:John,age:30},
                   //                Person{name:John,age:20}],
                   //             Jill=[Person{name:Jill,age:20}]}
   ```

   This is the simplest version of the `Collector` object. You just define what is
   going to be the key of the resulting map, and the collector will add all the
   stream elements that have the same key value to the list of elements
   associated with that key in the resulting map.

   Here is another example:

   ```
   Map<Integer, List<Person>> map = getStreamPerson()
           .collect(Collectors.groupingBy(Person::getAge));
   System.out.println(map);
                   //prints: {20=[Person{name:Jill,age:20},
                   //                Person{name:John,age:20}],
                   //             30=[Person{name:John,age:30}]}
   ```

   If the stream elements have to be grouped by a combination of properties,
   you can create a class that can contain the necessary combination. The object
   of this class will serve as a complex key. For example, let's read the stream
   of the `Person2` elements and group them by age and name. This means that
   need a class that can carry two values. For example, here is such a class,
   called `TwoStrings`:

   ```
   class TwoStrings {
       private String one, two;
       public TwoStrings(String one, String two) {
           this.one = one;
           this.two = two;
       }
       public String getOne() { return this.one; }
   ```

---
[270]

```
public String getTwo() { return this.two; }
@Override
public boolean equals(Object o) {
    if (this == o) return true;
    if (!(o instanceof TwoStrings)) return false;
    TwoStrings twoStrings = (TwoStrings) o;
    return Objects.equals(getOne(), twoStrings.getOne())
        && Objects.equals(getTwo(), twoStrings.getTwo());
}
@Override
public int hashCode() {
    return Objects.hash(getOne(), getTwo());
}
@Override
public String toString() {
    return "(" + this.one + "," + this.two + ")";
}
}
```

We had to implement the `equals()` and `hashCode()` methods because an object of the `TwoStrings` class will be used as a key and its value has to be specific for each combination of the two values. We can use it now as follows:

```
Map<TwoStrings, List<Person2>> map = getStreamPerson2()
    .collect(Collectors.groupingBy(p ->
            new TwoStrings(String.valueOf(p.getAge()),
                                        p.getName())));
System.out.println(map);
//prints:
//    {(20,Jill)=[Person{name:Jill,age:20,city:Seattle},
//                Person{name:Jill,age:20,city:Chicago}],
//     (20,John)=[Person{name:John,age:20,city:Denver},
//                Person{name:John,age:20,city:Chicago}],
//     (30,John)=[Person{name:John,age:30,city:Denver},
//                Person{name:John,age:30,city:Seattle}]}
```

3. Write an example of the usage of the `R collect(Collector<T, A, R> collector)` operations of the `Stream<T>` interface with the collector created by
the `Collector<T, ?, Map<K, D>> groupingBy(Function<T, K> classifier, Collector<T, A, D> downstream)` method:

```
Map<String, Set<Person>> map = getStreamPerson()
    .collect(Collectors.groupingBy(Person::getName,
                            Collectors.toSet()));
System.out.println(map);
                //prints: {John=[Person{name:John,age:30},
                //                 Person{name:John,age:20}],
                //         Jill=[Person{name:Jill,age:20}]}
```

As you can see, the `List<Person>` values of the map produced by the `Collectors.groupingBy(Person::getName)` collector were later (downstream) changed to a set by the `Collectors.toSet()` collector.

Alternatively, each `List<Person>` value can be converted to just a count of the list elements, as follows:

```
Map<String, Long> map = getStreamPerson()
        .collect(Collectors.groupingBy(Person::getName,
Collectors.counting()));
System.out.println(map);    //prints: {John=2, Jill=1}
```

To count how many of the same `Person` objects (those that are equal according to the `equals()` method) are in the stream, we can use the identity function, which is defined as returning the input unchanged. For example:

```
Stream.of("a","b","c")
      .map(s -> Function.identity()
      .apply(s))
      .forEach(System.out::print);   //prints: abc
```

Using this function, we can count the number of same persons, as follows:

```
Map<Person, Long> map = Stream.of(new Person(30, "John"),
                                  new Person(20, "Jill"),
                                  new Person(30, "John"))
        .collect(Collectors.groupingBy(Function.identity(),
Collectors.counting()));
System.out.println(map);  //prints:
{Person{name:Jill,age:20}=1,
                              //
Person{name:John,age:30}=2}
```

We can also calculate an average age in each group of persons (a group is defined as having the same the resulting key value):

```
Map<String, Double> map = getStreamPerson()
        .collect(Collectors.groupingBy(Person::getName,
              Collectors.averagingInt(Person::getAge)));
System.out.println(map);  //prints: {John=25.0, Jill=20.0}
```

To list all the values of the age of the persons with the same name, we can use the downstream collector created by the `Collector<T, ?, R> Collectors.mapping (Function<T,U> mapper, Collector<U,A,R> downstream)` method:

```
Map<String, List<Integer>> map = getStreamPerson()
    .collect(Collectors.groupingBy(Person::getName,
          Collectors.mapping(Person::getAge,
                          Collectors.toList())));
System.out.println(map);
              //prints: {John=[30, 20], Jill=[20]}
```

Another variation of this solution is the following example, where for each age, a comma-delimited list of names is created:

```
Map<Integer, String> map = getStreamPerson()
  .collect(Collectors.groupingBy(Person::getAge,
          Collectors.mapping(Person::getName,
                          Collectors.joining(","))));
System.out.println(map);
              //prints: {20=Jill, John, 30=John}
```

And, finally, to demonstrate another technique, we can use the nested `groupingBy()` collectors to create a map that contains age as a key and a map of person's names to their cities as values:

```
Map<Integer, Map<String, String>> map = getStreamPerson2()
    .collect(Collectors.groupingBy(Person2::getAge,
            Collectors.groupingBy(Person2::getName,
                    Collectors.mapping(Person2::getCity,
                            Collectors.joining(",")))));
System.out.println(map);   //prints:
                           //   {20={John=Denver,Chicago,
                           //          Jill=Seattle,Chicago},
                           //    30={John=Denver,Seattle}}
```

Please note that we used the `Person2` stream in the preceding example.

4. Write an example of the usage of the `R collect(Collector<T, A, R> collector)` operation of the `Stream<T>` interface with the collector created by the `Collector<T, ?, M> groupingBy(Function<T,K> classifier, Supplier<M> mapFactory, Collector<T,A,D> downstream)` method:

```
LinkedHashMap<String, Long> map = getStreamPerson()
        .collect(Collectors.groupingBy(Person::getName,
                                LinkedHashMap::new,
                                Collectors.counting()));
System.out.println(map);   //prints: {John=2, Jill=1}
```

The code in the preceding example counts how many times each name is encountered in the stream of the `Person` objects and places the result in the container (`LinkedHashMap` in this case) defined by the `mapFactory` function (the second parameter of the `groupingBy()` method).

The following examples demonstrate how to tell the collector to use EnumMap based on enum City as a container of the final result:

```
EnumMap<City, List<Person3>> map = getStreamPerson3()
        .collect(Collectors.groupingBy(Person3::getCity,
                       () -> new EnumMap<>(City.class),
                            Collectors.toList())));
System.out.println(map);
 //prints: {Chicago=[Person{name:Jill,age:20,city:Chicago},
 //                  Person{name:John,age:20,city:Chicago}],
 //         Denver=[Person{name:John,age:30,city:Denver},
 //                  Person{name:John,age:20,city:Denver}],
 //        Seattle=[Person{name:Jill,age:20,city:Seattle},
 //                  Person{name:John,age:30,city:Seattle}]}
```

Please notice that we used the Person3 stream in the preceding examples. To simplify the result (to avoid displaying a city twice for the same result) and to group the persons by age (for each city), we can use the nested groupingBy() collector again:

```
EnumMap<City, Map<Integer, String>> map = getStreamPerson3()
     .collect(Collectors.groupingBy(Person3::getCity,
              () -> new EnumMap<>(City.class),
          Collectors.groupingBy(Person3::getAge,
          Collectors.mapping(Person3::getName,
                     Collectors.joining(","))))));
System.out.println(map);
                    //prints: {Chicago={20=Jill,John},
                    //          Denver={20=John, 30=John},
                    //          Seattle={20=Jill, 30=John}}
```

5. As examples of the second set of collectors, those created by the groupingByConcurrent() methods, all the preceding code snippets (except the last two with EnumMap) can be used by just replacing groupingBy() with groupingByConcurrent() and the resulting Map with the ConcurrentMap class or its subclass. For example:

```
ConcurrentMap<String, List<Person>> map1 =
   getStreamPerson().parallel()
      .collect(Collectors.groupingByConcurrent(Person::getName));
System.out.println(map1);
                  //prints: {John=[Person{name:John,age:30},
                  //                Person{name:John,age:20}],
                  //          Jill=[Person{name:Jill,age:20}]}

ConcurrentMap<String, Double> map2 =
   getStreamPerson().parallel()
```

```
        .collect(Collectors.groupingByConcurrent(Person::getName,
                    Collectors.averagingInt(Person::getAge)));
System.out.println(map2);        //prints: {John=25.0, Jill=20.0}

ConcurrentSkipListMap<String, Long> map3 =
    getStreamPerson().parallel()
        .collect(Collectors.groupingByConcurrent(Person::getName,
            ConcurrentSkipListMap::new, Collectors.counting()));
System.out.println(map3);        //prints: {Jill=1, John=2}
```

As we have mentioned before, the `groupingByConcurrent()` collectors can process sequential streams too, but they are designed to be used to process parallel stream data, so we have converted the preceding streams to parallel ones. The returned result is of the `ConcurrentHashMap` type or a subclass of it.

There's more...

The `Collectors` class also provides two collectors generated by the `partitioningBy()` method, which are specialized versions of the `groupingBy()` collectors:

- `Collector<T, ?, Map<Boolean,List<T>>> partitioningBy(Predicate<T> predicate)`: Creates a `Collector` object that collects the stream elements of the `T` type into a `Map<Boolean,List<T>>` object using the provided `predicate` function to map the current element to the key in the resulting map.

- `Collector<T, ?, Map<Boolean,D>> partitioningBy(Predicate<T> predicate, Collector<T,A,D> downstream)` : Creates a `Collector` object that collects the stream elements of the `T` type into a `Map<Boolean,D>` object using the provided `predicate` function to map the current element to the key in the `Map<K,List<T>>` intermediate map. It then uses the `downstream` collector to convert the values of the intermediate map into the values of the resulting map, `Map<Boolean,D>`.

Let's look at some examples. Here is how the first of the preceding methods can be used to collect the `Person` stream elements into two groups—one with names that contain the letter `i` and another with names that don't contain the letter `i`:

```
Map<Boolean, List<Person>> map = getStreamPerson()
   .collect(Collectors.partitioningBy(p-> p.getName().contains("i")));
System.out.println(map);  //prints: {false=[Person{name:John,age:30},
   //                                      Person{name:John,age:20}],
   //                                true=[Person{name:Jill,age:20}]}
```

To demonstrate the usage of the second method, we can convert each `List<Person>` value of the map created in the preceding example to the list size:

```
Map<Boolean, Long> map = getStreamPerson()
   .collect(Collectors.partitioningBy(p-> p.getName().contains("i"),
                                       Collectors.counting()));
System.out.println(map);  //prints: {false=2, true=1}
```

The same result can be achieved using collectors created by the `groupingBy()` methods:

```
Map<Boolean, List<Person>> map1 = getStreamPerson()
    .collect(Collectors.groupingBy(p-> p.getName().contains("i")));
System.out.println(map); //prints: {false=[Person{name:John,age:30},
   //                                      Person{name:John,age:20}],
   //                                true=[Person{name:Jill,age:20}]}

Map<Boolean, Long> map2 = getStreamPerson()
     .collect(Collectors.groupingBy(p-> p.getName().contains("i"),
                                     Collectors.counting()));
System.out.println(map2);  //prints: {false=2, true=1}
```

The collectors created by the `partitioningBy()` methods are considered a specialization of the collectors created by the `groupingBy()` methods, and are expected to allow us to write less code when stream elements are broken into two groups and stored in a map with Boolean keys. But, as you can see from the preceding code, that's not always the case. The `partitioningBy()` collectors in our examples require us to write exactly the same amount of code as the `groupingBy()` collectors.

Creating stream operation pipeline

In this recipe, you will learn how to build a pipeline from the `Stream` operations.

Getting ready

In the previous chapter, `Chapter 4`, *Going Functional*, while creating a lambda-friendly API, we ended up with the following API method:

```
public interface Traffic {
  void speedAfterStart(double timeSec,
    int trafficUnitsNumber, SpeedModel speedModel,
    BiPredicate<TrafficUnit, Double> limitTraffic,
    BiConsumer<TrafficUnit, Double> printResult);
}
```

The specified number of `TrafficUnit` instances were produced inside the `speedAfterStart()` method. They were limited by the `limitTrafficAndSpeed` function and were processed according to the `speedModel` function inside the `speedAfterStart()` method. The results were formatted by the `printResults` function.

It is a very flexible design that allows for quite a range of experimentation via the modification of functions that are passed to the API. In reality, though, especially during the early stages of data analysis, creating an API requires more code writing. It pays back only in the long run and only if the design flexibility allows us to accommodate new requirements with zero or very few code changes.

The situation radically changes during the research phase. When new algorithms are developed or when the need for processing a large amount of data presents its own challenges, transparency across all the layers of the developed system becomes a foundational requirement. Without it, many of today's successes in the analysis of big data would be impossible.

Streams and the pipelines address the problem of transparency and minimize the overhead of writing infrastructural code.

How to do it...

Let's recall how a user called the lambda-friendly API:

```
double timeSec = 10.0;
int trafficUnitsNumber = 10;

SpeedModel speedModel = (t, wp, hp) -> ...;
BiConsumer<TrafficUnit, Double> printResults = (tu, sp) -> ...;
BiPredicate<TrafficUnit, Double> limitSpeed = (tu, sp) -> ...;

Traffic api = new TrafficImpl(Month.APRIL, DayOfWeek.FRIDAY, 17,
                              "USA", "Denver", "Main103S");
api.speedAfterStart(timeSec, trafficUnitsNumber, speedModel,
                    limitSpeed, printResults);
```

As we have already noticed, such an API may not cover all the possible ways the model can evolve, but it is a good starting point that allows us to construct the stream and the pipeline of operations with more transparency and flexibility of experimentation.

Now, let's look at the API's implementation:

```
double timeSec = 10.0;
int trafficUnitsNumber = 10;

SpeedModel speedModel = (t, wp, hp) -> ...;
BiConsumer<TrafficUnit, Double> printResults = (tu, sp) -> ...;
BiPredicate<TrafficUnit, Double> limitSpeed = (tu, sp) -> ...;
List<TrafficUnit> trafficUnits = FactoryTraffic
      .generateTraffic(trafficUnitsNumber, Month.APRIL,
                       DayOfWeek.FRIDAY, 17, "USA", "Denver",
                       "Main103S");
for(TrafficUnit tu: trafficUnits){
  Vehicle vehicle = FactoryVehicle.build(tu);
  vehicle.setSpeedModel(speedModel);
  double speed = vehicle.getSpeedMph(timeSec);
  speed = Math.round(speed * tu.getTraction());
    if(limitSpeed.test(tu, speed)){
      printResults.accept(tu, speed);
    }
  }
```

We can convert the `for` loop into a stream of traffic units and apply the same functions directly to the elements of the stream. But first, we can request the traffic-generating system to supply us with a `Stream` instead of a `List` of data. It allows us to avoid storing all the data in memory:

```
Stream<TrafficUnit> stream = FactoryTraffic
    .getTrafficUnitStream(trafficUnitsNumber, Month.APRIL,
        DayOfWeek.FRIDAY, 17, "USA", "Denver", "Main103S");
```

We can now process an endless number of traffic units without storing in the memory more than one unit at a time. In the demo code, we still use `List`, so the streaming does not save us memory. But in real systems, such as those that collect data from various sensors, using streams helps to decrease or completely avoid memory-usage concerns.

We will also create a convenience method:

```
Stream<TrafficUnit>getTrafficUnitStream(int trafficUnitsNumber){
    return FactoryTraffic.getTrafficUnitStream(trafficUnitsNumber,
            Month.APRIL, DayOfWeek.FRIDAY, 17, "USA",
                                "Denver", "Main103S");
}
```

With this, we can write the following:

```
getTrafficUnitStream(trafficUnitsNumber).map(tu -> {
    Vehicle vehicle = FactoryVehicle.build(tu);
    vehicle.setSpeedModel(speedModel);
    return vehicle;
})
.map(v -> {
    double speed = v.getSpeedMph(timeSec);
    return Math.round(speed * tu.getTraction());
})
.filter(s -> limitSpeed.test(tu, s))
.forEach(tuw -> printResults.accept(tu, s));
```

We mapped (transform) `TrafficUnit` to `Vehicle`, then mapped `Vehicle` to speed, and then used the current `TrafficUnit` instance and the calculated speed to limit the traffic and print results. If you have this code in a modern editor, you will notice that it does not compile because, after the first map, the current `TrafficUnit` element is not accessible anymore—it is replaced by `Vehicle`. This means we need to carry the original elements and add new values along the way. To accomplish this, we need a container—some kind of traffic-unit wrapper. Let's create one:

```
class TrafficUnitWrapper {
  private double speed;
  private Vehicle vehicle;
  private TrafficUnit trafficUnit;
  public TrafficUnitWrapper(TrafficUnit trafficUnit){
    this.trafficUnit = trafficUnit;
  }
  public TrafficUnit getTrafficUnit(){ return this.trafficUnit; }
  public Vehicle getVehicle() { return vehicle; }
  public void setVehicle(Vehicle vehicle) {
    this.vehicle = vehicle;
  }
  public double getSpeed() { return speed; }
  public void setSpeed(double speed) { this.speed = speed; }
}
```

Now, we can build a pipeline that works:

```
getTrafficUnitStream(trafficUnitsNumber)
  .map(TrafficUnitWrapper::new)
  .map(tuw -> {
      Vehicle vehicle = FactoryVehicle.build(tuw.getTrafficUnit());
      vehicle.setSpeedModel(speedModel);
      tuw.setVehicle(vehicle);
      return tuw;
   })
  .map(tuw -> {
      double speed = tuw.getVehicle().getSpeedMph(timeSec);
      speed = Math.round(speed * tuw.getTrafficUnit().getTraction());
      tuw.setSpeed(speed);
      return tuw;
   })
  .filter(tuw -> limitSpeed.test(tuw.getTrafficUnit(),tuw.getSpeed()))
  .forEach(tuw -> printResults.accept(tuw.getTrafficUnit(),
                                        tuw.getSpeed()));
```

The code looks a bit verbose, especially the `Vehicle` and `SpeedModel` settings. We can hide this plumbing by moving them to the `TrafficUntiWrapper` class:

```
class TrafficUnitWrapper {
  private double speed;
  private Vehicle vehicle;
  private TrafficUnit trafficUnit;
  public TrafficUnitWrapper(TrafficUnit trafficUnit){
    this.trafficUnit = trafficUnit;
    this.vehicle = FactoryVehicle.build(trafficUnit);
  }
  public TrafficUnitWrapper setSpeedModel(SpeedModel speedModel) {
    this.vehicle.setSpeedModel(speedModel);
    return this;
  }
  pubic TrafficUnit getTrafficUnit(){ return this.trafficUnit; }
  public Vehicle getVehicle() { return vehicle; }
  public double getSpeed() { return speed; }
  public TrafficUnitWrapper setSpeed(double speed) {
    this.speed = speed;
    return this;
  }
}
```

Notice how we return `this` from the `setSpeedModel()` and `setSpeed()` methods. This allows us to preserve the fluent style. Now, the pipeline looks much cleaner:

```
getTrafficUnitStream(trafficUnitsNumber)
  .map(TrafficUnitWrapper::new)
  .map(tuw -> tuw.setSpeedModel(speedModel))
  .map(tuw -> {
      double speed = tuw.getVehicle().getSpeedMph(timeSec);
      speed = Math.round(speed * tuw.getTrafficUnit().getTraction());
      return tuw.setSpeed(speed);
  })
  .filter(tuw -> limitSpeed.test(tuw.getTrafficUnit(),tuw.getSpeed()))
  .forEach(tuw -> printResults.accept(tuw.getTrafficUnit(),
                                      tuw.getSpeed()));
```

If there is no need to keep the formula for the speed calculations easily accessible, we can move it to the `TrafficUnitWrapper` class by changing the `setSpeed()` method to `calcSpeed()`:

```
TrafficUnitWrapper calcSpeed(double timeSec) {
    double speed = this.vehicle.getSpeedMph(timeSec);
    this.speed = Math.round(speed * this.trafficUnit.getTraction());
    return this;
}
```

So, the pipeline becomes even less verbose:

```
getTrafficUnitStream(trafficUnitsNumber)
    .map(TrafficUnitWrapper::new)
    .map(tuw -> tuw.setSpeedModel(speedModel))
    .map(tuw -> tuw.calcSpeed(timeSec))
    .filter(tuw -> limitSpeed.test(tuw.getTrafficUnit(),
                                          tuw.getSpeed()))
    .forEach(tuw -> printResults.accept(tuw.getTrafficUnit(),
                                          tuw.getSpeed()));
```

Based on this technique, we can now create a method that calculates traffic density—the count of vehicles in each lane of a multilane road for the given speed limit in each of the lanes:

```
Integer[] trafficByLane(Stream<TrafficUnit> stream,
        int trafficUnitsNumber, double timeSec,
        SpeedModel speedModel, double[] speedLimitByLane) {
    int lanesCount = speedLimitByLane.length;
    Map<Integer, Integer> trafficByLane = stream
      .limit(trafficUnitsNumber)
      .map(TrafficUnitWrapper::new)
      .map(tuw -> tuw.setSpeedModel(speedModel))
      .map(tuw -> tuw.calcSpeed(timeSec))
      .map(speed -> countByLane(lanesCount,
                              speedLimitByLane, speed))
      .collect(Collectors.groupingBy(CountByLane::getLane,
            Collectors.summingInt(CountByLane::getCount)));
    for(int i = 1; i <= lanesCount; i++){
      trafficByLane.putIfAbsent(i, 0);
    }
    return trafficByLane.values()
                        .toArray(new Integer[lanesCount]);
}
```

The private `CountByLane` class used by the preceding method looks as follows:

```
private class CountByLane {
  int count, lane;
  private CountByLane(int count, int lane){
    this.count = count;
    this.lane = lane;
  }
  public int getLane() { return lane; }
  public int getCount() { return count; }
}
```

And here is how the private `TrafficUnitWrapper` class looks:

```
private static class TrafficUnitWrapper {
  private Vehicle vehicle;
  private TrafficUnit trafficUnit;
  public TrafficUnitWrapper(TrafficUnit trafficUnit){
    this.vehicle = FactoryVehicle.build(trafficUnit);
    this.trafficUnit = trafficUnit;
  }
  public TrafficUnitWrapper setSpeedModel(SpeedModel speedModel) {
    this.vehicle.setSpeedModel(speedModel);
    return this;
  }
  public double calcSpeed(double timeSec) {
    double speed = this.vehicle.getSpeedMph(timeSec);
    return Math.round(speed * this.trafficUnit.getTraction());
  }
}
```

The code of the `countByLane()` private method is as follows:

```
private CountByLane countByLane(int lanesNumber,
                               double[] speedLimit, double speed){
  for(int i = 1; i <= lanesNumber; i++){
    if(speed <= speedLimit[i - 1]){
      return new CountByLane(1, i);
    }
  }
  return new CountByLane(1, lanesNumber);
}
```

In Chapter 14, *Testing,* we will discuss this method of the TrafficDensity class in more detail and revisit this implementation to allow for better unit testing. This is why writing a unit test parallel to the code development brings higher productivity; it eliminates the need to change the code afterward. It also results in more testable (better-quality) code.

There's more...

The pipeline allows the easy addition of another filter, or any other operation for that matter:

```
Predicate<TrafficUnit> limitTraffic = tu ->
    tu.getVehicleType() == Vehicle.VehicleType.CAR
    || tu.getVehicleType() == Vehicle.VehicleType.TRUCK;

getTrafficUnitStream(trafficUnitsNumber)
    .filter(limitTraffic)
    .map(TrafficUnitWrapper::new)
    .map(tuw -> tuw.setSpeedModel(speedModel))
    .map(tuw -> tuw.calcSpeed(timeSec))
    .filter(tuw -> limitSpeed.test(tuw.getTrafficUnit(),
                                  tuw.getSpeed()))
    .forEach(tuw -> printResults.accept(tuw.getTrafficUnit(),
                                        tuw.getSpeed()));
```

It is especially important when many types of data have to be processed. It's worth mentioning that having a filter before the calculations are the best way to improve performance because it allows you to avoid unnecessary calculations.

Another major advantage of using a stream is that the process can be made parallel without extra coding. All you need to do is change the first line of the pipeline to getTrafficUnitStream(trafficUnitsNumber).parallel() (assuming the source does not generate the parallel stream, which can be identified by the .isParallel() operation). We will talk about parallel processing in more detail in the next recipe.

Processing streams in parallel

In the previous recipes, we demonstrated some of the techniques of parallel stream-processing. In this recipe, we will discuss processing in greater detail, and share the best practices and solutions for common problems.

Getting ready

It is tempting to just set up all the streams to be parallel and not think about it again. Unfortunately, parallelism does not always provide an advantage. In fact, it incurs an overhead because of the worker threads' coordination. Besides, some stream sources are sequential in nature and some operations may share the same (synchronized) resource. Even worse, the usage of a stateful operation in parallel processing can lead to an unpredictable result. It does not mean one cannot use a stateful operation for a parallel stream, but it requires careful planning and a clear understanding of how the state is shared between the sub-streams of parallel processing.

How to do it...

As was mentioned in the previous recipe, a parallel stream can be created by the `parallelStream()` method of a collection or the `parallel()` method applied to a stream. Conversely, the existing parallel stream can be converted into a sequential one by using the `sequential()` method.

As the first best practice, one should use a sequential stream by default and start thinking about the parallel one only if necessary and possible. The need usually comes up if the performance is not good enough and a large amount of data has to be processed. The possibilities are limited by the nature of the stream source and operations. For example, reading from a file is sequential and a file-based stream does not perform better in parallel. Any blocking operation also negates performance improvement in parallel.

One of the areas where sequential and parallel streams are different is ordering. Here is an example:

```
List.of("This ", "is ", "created ", "by ",
        "List.of().stream()").stream().forEach(System.out::print);
System.out.println();
List.of("This ", "is ", "created ", "by ",
        "List.of().parallelStream()")
                    .parallelStream().forEach(System.out::print);
```

The result is as follows:

```
This is created by List.of().stream()

created This is by List.of().parallelStream()
```

As you can see, `List` preserves the order of the elements but does not keep it in the case of parallel processing.

In the *Creating and operating on streams* recipe, we demonstrated that with the `reduce()` and `collect()` operations, a combiner is called only for a parallel stream. So, the combiner is not needed for a sequential stream processing, but it must be present while operating on a parallel one. Without it, the results of multiple workers are not correctly aggregated.

We have also demonstrated that the `sorted()`, `distinct()`, `limit()`, and `skip()` stateful operations yield non-deterministic results in the case of parallel processing.

If the order is important, we have shown that you can rely on the `forEachOrdered()` operation. It guarantees not only the processing of all the elements of the stream but also doing it in the order specified by its source, regardless of whether the stream is sequential or parallel.

A parallel stream can be created by the `parallelStream()` method or by the `parallel()` method. Once created, it uses a `ForkJoin` framework during processing: the original stream is broken into segments (sub-streams) that are then given to different worker threads for processing, then all the results (of each sub-stream processing) are aggregated and presented as the final results of the original stream processing. On a computer with only one processor, such an implementation does not have an advantage because the processor is shared. But on a multicore computer, worker threads can be executed by different processors. Even more, if one worker becomes idle, it can *steal* a part of the job from a busy one. The results are then collected from all the workers and aggregated for the terminal operation completion (that is when a combiner of a collect operation becomes busy).

Generally speaking, if there is a resource that is not safe for concurrent access, it is not safe to use during parallel stream-processing either. Consider these two examples (`ArrayList` is not known to be thread-safe):

```
List<String> wordsWithI = new ArrayList<>();
Stream.of("That ", "is ", "a ", "Stream.of(literals)")
        .parallel()
        .filter(w -> w.contains("i"))
        .forEach(wordsWithI::add);
System.out.println(wordsWithI);
System.out.println();

wordsWithI = Stream.of("That ", "is ", "a ", "Stream.of(literals)" )
                .parallel()
                .filter(w -> w.contains("i"))
                .collect(Collectors.toList());
System.out.println(wordsWithI);
```

If run several times, this code may produce the following result:

```
[Stream.of(literals)]

[is , Stream.of(literals)]
```

The `Collectors.toList()` method always generates the same list, which consists of `is` and `Stream.of(literals)`, while `forEach()` misses either `is` or `Stream.of(literals)` once in a while.

> If possible, try using collectors constructed by the `Collectors` class first and avoid shared resource during parallel computations.

Overall, using stateless functions is your best bet for parallel stream pipelines. If in doubt, test your code and, most importantly, run the same test many times to check whether the result is stable.

6
Database Programming

This chapter covers both basic and commonly used interactions between a Java application and a **database (DB)**, right from connecting to the DB and performing CRUD operations to creating transactions, storing procedures, and working with **large objects (LOBs)**. We will be covering the following recipes:

- Connecting to a database using JDBC
- Setting up the tables required for DB interactions
- Performing CRUD operations using JDBC
- Using the **Hikari Connection Pool (HikariCP)**
- Using prepared statements
- Using transactions
- Working with large objects
- Executing stored procedures
- Using batch operations for a large set of data
- Using **MyBatis** for CRUD operations
- Using the **Java Persistence API** and **Hibernate**

Introduction

It is difficult to imagine a complex software application that does not use some kind of structured and accessible data storage called a database. This is why any modern language implementation includes a framework that allows you to access the DB and **create, read, update, and delete (CRUD)** data in it. In Java, the **Java Database Connectivity (JDBC)** API provides access to any data source, from relational databases to spreadsheets and flat files.

Based on this access, an application can manipulate data in the database directly, using database language (SQL, for example), or indirectly, using an **Object-Relational Mapping (ORM)** framework, which allows for the mapping of objects in memory to the tables in the database. The **Java Persistence API (JPA)** is the ORM specification for Java. When an ORM framework is used, the CRUD operations on the mapped Java objects are translated into the database language automatically. The list of the most popular ORM frameworks includes Apache Cayenne, Apache OpenJPA, EclipseLink, jOOQ, MyBatis, and Hibernate, to name a few.

The `java.sql` and `javax.sql` packages that compose the JDBC API are included in the **Java Platform Standard Edition (Java SE)**. The `java.sql` package provides the API for accessing and processing data stored in a data source (usually a relational database). The `javax.sql` package provides the API for server-side data source access and processing. Specifically, it provides the `DataSource` interface for establishing a connection with a database, connection and statement pooling, distributed transactions, and rowsets. The `javax.persistence` package that contains interfaces that are compliant with JPA is not included in Java SE and has to be added as a dependency to the Maven configuration file `pom.xml`. The specific JPA implementation—the preferred ORM framework—has to be included as a Maven dependency too. We will discuss the usage of JDBC, JPA, and two ORM frameworks—Hibernate and MyBatis—in the recipes of this chapter.

To actually connect `DataSource` to a physical database, you also need a database-specific driver (provided by a database vendor, such as MySQL, Oracle, PostgreSQL, or SQL server database, for example). It may be written in Java or in a mixture of Java and **Java Native Interface (JNI)** native methods. This driver implements the JDBC API.

Working with a database involves eight steps:

1. Installing the database by following the vendor instructions.
2. Adding the dependency on a `.jar` to the application with the database-specific driver.
3. Creating a user, database, and database schema—tables, views, stored procedures, and so on.
4. Connecting to the database from the application.
5. Constructing an SQL statement directly using JDBC or indirectly using JPA.

6. Executing the SQL statement directly using JDBC or committing data changes using JPA.
7. Using the result of the execution.
8. Closing the database connection and other resources.

Steps 1 –3 are done only once at the database setup stage, before the application is run.

Steps 4 – 8 are performed by the application repeatedly, as needed.

Steps 5 – 7 can be repeated multiple times with the same database connection.

Connecting to a database using JDBC

In this recipe, you will learn how to connect to a database.

How to do it...

1. Select the database you would like to work with. There are good commercial databases and good open source databases. The only thing we are going to assume is that the database of your choice supports **Structured Query Language** (**SQL**), which is a standardized language that allows you to perform CRUD operations on a database. In our recipes, we will use the standard SQL and avoid constructs and procedures specific to a particular database type.

2. If the database is not installed yet, follow the vendor instructions and install it. Then, download the database driver. The most popular ones are of types 4 and 5, written in Java. They are very efficient and talk to the database server through a socket connection. If a `.jar` file with such a driver is placed on the classpath, it is loaded automatically. Type 4 and 5 drivers are database specific because they use a database native protocol for accessing the database. We are going to assume that you are using a driver of such a type.

If your application has to access several types of databases, then you need a driver of type 3. Such a driver can talk to different databases via a middleware application server.

Use drivers of type 1 and 2 only when there are no other driver types available for your database.

3. Set the downloaded .jar file with the driver on your application's classpath. Now, your application can access the database.
4. Your database might have a console, a GUI, or some other way to interact with it. Read the instructions and first create a user, that is, cook, and then a database, namely cookbook.

For example, here are the commands for PostgreSQL:

```
CREATE USER cook SUPERUSER;
CREATE DATABASE cookbook OWNER cook;
```

We selected the SUPERUSER role for our user; however, a good security practice is to assign such a powerful role to an administrator and create another application-specific user who can manage data but cannot change the database structure. It is good practice to create another logical layer, called a **schema**, that can have its own set of users and permissions. This way, several schemas in the same database could be isolated, and each user (one of them is your application) will have access only to a certain schema.

5. Also, at the enterprise level, the common practice is to create synonyms for the database schema so that no application can access the original structure directly. You can even create a password for each user, but, again, for the purpose of this book, this is not needed. So, we leave it to the database administrators to establish the rules and guidelines suitable for the particular working conditions of each enterprise.

Now, we connect our application to the database. In the following demonstration code, we will use, as you may have probably guessed by now, the open source PostgreSQL database.

How it works...

Here is the code fragment that creates a connection to the local PostgreSQL database:

```
String URL = "jdbc:postgresql://localhost/cookbook";
Properties prop = new Properties( );
//prop.put( "user", "cook" );
//prop.put( "password", "secretPass123" );
Connection conn = DriverManager.getConnection(URL, prop);
```

The commented lines show how you can set a user and password for your connection. Since, for this demonstration, we are keeping the database open and accessible to anyone, we could use an overloaded `DriverManager.getConnection(String url)` method. However, we will show the most general implementation that would allow anyone to read from a property file and pass other useful values (`ssl` as true/false, `autoReconnect` as true/false, `connectTimeout` in seconds, and so on) to the connection-creating method. Many keys for the passed-in properties are the same for all major database types, but some of them are database-specific.

Alternatively, for passing only a user and a password, we could use the third overloaded version, namely `DriverManager.getConnection(String url, String user, String password)`. It's worth mentioning that it is a good practice to keep the password encrypted. We are not going to show you how to do this, but there are plenty of guides available online.

Also, the `getConnection()` method throws `SQLException`, so we need to wrap it in a `try...catch` block.

To hide all of this plumbing, it is a good idea to keep the connection-establishing code inside a method:

```
Connection getDbConnection(){
  String url = "jdbc:postgresql://localhost/cookbook";
  try {
    return DriverManager.getConnection(url);
  }
  catch(Exception ex) {
    ex.printStackTrace();
    return null;
  }
}
```

Another way of connecting to a database is to use the `DataSource` interface. Its implementation is typically included in the same `.jar` file as the database driver. In the case of PostgreSQL, there are two classes that implement the `DataSource` interface: `org.postgresql.ds.PGSimpleDataSource` and `org.postgresql.ds.PGPoolingDataSource`. We can use them instead of `DriverManager`. Here is an example of the usage of `PGSimpleDataSource`:

```
Connection getDbConnection(){
   PGSimpleDataSource source = new PGSimpleDataSource();
   source.setServerName("localhost");
   source.setDatabaseName("cookbook");
   source.setLoginTimeout(10);
   try {
     return source.getConnection();
   }
   catch(Exception ex) {
     ex.printStackTrace();
     return null;
   }
}
```

And the following is an example of the usage of `PGPoolingDataSource`:

```
Connection getDbConnection(){
   PGPoolingDataSource source = new PGPoolingDataSource();
   source.setServerName("localhost");
   source.setDatabaseName("cookbook");
   source.setInitialConnections(3);
   source.setMaxConnections(10);
   source.setLoginTimeout(10);
   try {
     return source.getConnection();
   }
   catch(Exception ex) {
     ex.printStackTrace();
     return null;
   }
}
```

The last version of the `getDbConnection()` method is usually the preferred way of connecting because it allows you to use connection pooling and some other features, in addition to those available when connecting via `DriverManager`. Please note though that the class `PGPoolingDataSource` is deprecated, since version `42.0.0` was in favor of the third-party connection-pooling software. One such framework, HikariCP, which we have mentioned previously, will be discussed and demonstrated in the recipe *Using the Hikari Connection Pool*.

Whatever version of the `getDbConnection()` implementation you choose, you can use it in all the code examples the same way.

There's more...

It is good practice to close the connection as soon as you do not need it. The way to do this is by using the `try-with-resources` construct, which ensures that the resource is closed at the end of the `try...catch` block:

```
try (Connection conn = getDbConnection()) {
  // code that uses the connection to access the DB
}
catch(Exception ex) {
  ex.printStackTrace();
}
```

Such a construct can be used with any object that implements the `java.lang.AutoCloseable` or the `java.io.Closeable` interface.

Setting up the tables required for DB interactions

In this recipe, you will learn how to create, change, and delete tables and other logical database constructs that compose a database schema.

Getting ready

The standard SQL statement for table creation looks as follows:

```
CREATE TABLE table_name (
  column1_name data_type(size),
  column2_name data_type(size),
  column3_name data_type(size),
  ....
);
```

Here, `table_name` and `column_name` have to be alphanumeric and unique (inside the schema) identifiers. The limitations for the names and possible data types are database-specific. For example, Oracle allows the table name to have 128 characters, while in PostgreSQL, the maximum length of the table name and column name is 63 characters. There are differences in the data types too, so read the database documentation.

How it works...

Here is an example of a command that creates the `traffic_unit` table in PostgreSQL:

```
CREATE TABLE traffic_unit (
    id SERIAL PRIMARY KEY,
    vehicle_type VARCHAR NOT NULL,
    horse_power integer NOT NULL,
    weight_pounds integer NOT NULL,
    payload_pounds integer NOT NULL,
    passengers_count integer NOT NULL,
    speed_limit_mph double precision NOT NULL,
    traction double precision NOT NULL,
    road_condition VARCHAR NOT NULL,
    tire_condition VARCHAR NOT NULL,
    temperature integer NOT NULL
);
```

The `size` parameter is optional. If not set, as in the previous example code, it means that the column can store values of any length. The `integer` type, in this case, allows you to store numbers from `Integer.MIN_VALUE` (which is -2147483648) to `Integer.MAX_VALUE` (which is +2147483647). The `NOT NULL` type was added because, by default, the column would be nullable and we wanted to make sure that all the columns will be populated.

We also identified the id column as the PRIMARY KEY, which indicates that the column (or the combination of columns) uniquely identifies the record. For example, if there is a table that contains information about all the people of all the countries, the unique combination would *probably* be their full name, address, and date of birth. Well, it is plausible to imagine that in some households, twins are born and given the same name, so we said *probably*. If the chance of such an occasion is high, we would need to add another column to the primary key combination, which is an order of birth, with the default value of 1. Here is how we can do this in PostgreSQL:

```
CREATE TABLE person (
  name VARCHAR NOT NULL,
  address VARCHAR NOT NULL,
  dob date NOT NULL,
  order integer DEFAULT 1 NOT NULL,
  PRIMARY KEY (name,address,dob,order)
);
```

In the case of the traffic_unit table, there is no combination of columns that can serve as a primary key. Many cars have the same values in any combination of columns. But we need to refer to a traffic_unit record so we could know, for example, which units have been selected and processed and which were not. This is why, we added an id column to populate it with a unique generated number, and we would like the database to generate this primary key automatically.

If you issue the command \d traffic_unit to display the table description, you will see the function nextval('traffic_unit_id_seq'::regclass) assigned to the id column. This function generates numbers sequentially, starting with 1. If you need a different behavior, create the sequence number generator manually. Here's an example of how to do this:

```
CREATE SEQUENCE traffic_unit_id_seq
START WITH 1000 INCREMENT BY 1
NO MINVALUE NO MAXVALUE CACHE 10;
ALTER TABLE ONLY traffic_unit ALTER COLUMN id SET DEFAULT
nextval('traffic_unit_id_seq'::regclass);
```

This sequence starts from 1,000, and caches 10 numbers for a better performance, if there is a need to generate numbers in quick succession.

According to the code examples given in the previous chapters, the values of `vehicle_type`, `road_condition`, and `tire_condition` are limited by the `enum` type. That's why when the `traffic_unit` table is populated, we would like to make sure that only the values of the corresponding `enum` type can be set in the column. To accomplish this, we'll create a lookup table called `enums` and populate it with the values from our `enum` types:

```
CREATE TABLE enums (
  id integer PRIMARY KEY,
  type VARCHAR NOT NULL,
  value VARCHAR NOT NULL
);

insert into enums (id, type, value) values
(1, 'vehicle', 'car'),
(2, 'vehicle', 'truck'),
(3, 'vehicle', 'crewcab'),
(4, 'road_condition', 'dry'),
(5, 'road_condition', 'wet'),
(6, 'road_condition', 'snow'),
(7, 'tire_condition', 'new'),
(8, 'tire_condition', 'worn');
```

PostgreSQL has an `enum` data type, but it incurs an overhead if the list of possible values is not fixed and has to be changed over time. We think it is quite possible that the list of values in our application will expand. So, we decided not to use a database `enum` type but create the lookup table ourselves.

Now, we can refer to the values of the `enums` table from the `traffic_unit` table by using their ID as a foreign key. First, we delete the table:

```
drop table traffic_unit;
```

Then, we recreate it with a slightly different SQL command:

```
CREATE TABLE traffic_unit (
    id SERIAL PRIMARY KEY,
    vehicle_type integer REFERENCES enums (id),
    horse_power integer NOT NULL,
    weight_pounds integer NOT NULL,
    payload_pounds integer NOT NULL,
    passengers_count integer NOT NULL,
    speed_limit_mph double precision NOT NULL,
    traction double precision NOT NULL,
    road_condition integer REFERENCES enums (id),
    tire_condition integer REFERENCES enums (id),
    temperature integer NOT NULL
);
```

The columns `vehicle_type`, `road_condition`, and `tire_condition` must now be populated by the values of a primary key of the corresponding record of the `enums` table. This way, we can make sure that our traffic-analyzing code will be able to match the values in these columns to the values of the `enum` types in the code.

There's more...

We would also like to make sure that the `enums` table does not contain a duplicate combination type and value. To ensure this, we can add a unique constraint to the `enums` table:

```
ALTER TABLE enums ADD CONSTRAINT enums_unique_type_value
UNIQUE (type, value);
```

Now, if we try to add a duplicate, the database will not allow it.

Another important consideration of database table creation is whether an index has to be added. An *index* is a data structure that helps to accelerate data searches in the table without having to check every table record. It can include one or more columns of a table. For example, an index for a primary key is created automatically. If you bring up the description of the table we have created already, you will see the following:

```
Indexes: "traffic_unit_pkey" PRIMARY KEY, btree (id)
```

We can also add an index ourselves if we think (and have proven by experimentation) it will help the application performance. In the case of `traffic_unit`, we discovered that our code often searches this table by `vehicle_type` and `passengers_count`. So, we measured the performance of our code during the search and added these two columns to the index:

```
CREATE INDEX idx_traffic_unit_vehicle_type_passengers_count
ON traffic_unit USING btree (vehicle_type,passengers_count);
```

Then, we measure the performance again. If it does improve, we would leave the index in place, but, in our case, we have removed it:

```
drop index idx_traffic_unit_vehicle_type_passengers_count;
```

The index did not improve the performance significantly, probably because an index has an overhead of additional writes and storage space.

In our examples of primary key, constraints, and indexes, we followed the naming convention of PostgreSQL. If you use a different database, we suggest you look up its naming convention and follow it, so that your naming aligns with the names created automatically.

Performing CRUD operations using JDBC

In this recipe, you will learn how to populate, read, change, and delete data in the using JDBC.

Getting ready

We have already seen examples of SQL statements that create (populate) data in the database:

```
INSERT INTO table_name (column1,column2,column3,...)
VALUES (value1,value2,value3,...);
```

We've also seen examples of instances where several table records have to be added:

```
INSERT INTO table_name (column1,column2,column3,...)
VALUES (value1,value2,value3, ... ),
       (value21,value22,value23, ...),
       ( ...                      );
```

If a column has a default value specified, there is no need to list it in the INSERT INTO statement, unless a different value has to be inserted.

The reading of the data from the database is done by a SELECT statement:

```
SELECT column_name,column_name
FROM table_name WHERE some_column=some_value;
```

Here's a general definition of the WHERE clause:

```
WHERE column_name operator value
Operator:
  = Equal
  <> Not equal. In some versions of SQL, !=
  > Greater than
  < Less than
  >= Greater than or equal
  <= Less than or equal
  BETWEEN Between an inclusive range
  LIKE Search for a pattern
  IN To specify multiple possible values for a column
```

The column_name operator value construct can be combined with logical operators AND and OR and grouped with the brackets (and).

The selected values can be returned in a certain order:

```
SELECT * FROM table_name WHERE-clause by some_other_column;
```

The order can be marked as ascending (default) or descending:

```
SELECT * FROM table_name WHERE-clause by some_other_column desc;
```

The data can be changed with the UPDATE statement:

```
UPDATE table_name SET column1=value1,column2=value2,... WHERE-clause;
```

Alternatively, it can be deleted with the DELETE statement:

```
DELETE FROM table_name WHERE-clause;
```

Without the WHERE clause, all the records of the table are going to be affected by the UPDATE or DELETE statement.

How to do it...

We have already seen an INSERT statement. Here is an example of other types of statements:

```
[cookbook=# select * from enums;
 id |      type       |  value
----+-----------------+----------
  1 | vehicle         | car
  2 | vehicle         | truck
  3 | vehicle         | crewcab
  4 | road_condition  | dry
  5 | road_condition  | wet
  6 | road_condition  | snow
  7 | tire_condition  | new
  8 | tire_condition  | worn
(8 rows)
```

The preceding SELECT statement brings up the values from all the columns of all the rows of the table. To limit the amount of returned data, a WHERE clause can be added:

```
cookbook=# select * from enums where (type = 'vehicle' AND value != 'crewcab') OR value = 'new';
 id |      type       | value
----+-----------------+--------
  1 | vehicle         | car
  2 | vehicle         | truck
  7 | tire_condition  | new
(3 rows)
```

The following screenshot captures three statements:

```
[cookbook=# update enums set value = 'NEW' where value = 'new';
UPDATE 1
[cookbook=# delete from enums where value != 'NEW';
DELETE 7
[cookbook=# select * from enums;
 id |      type       | value
----+-----------------+--------
  7 | tire_condition  | NEW
(1 row)
```

The first one is an UPDATE statement that changes values in the value column to NEW, but only in the rows where the value column contains value new (apparently, the value is case-sensitive). The second statement deletes all the rows that do not have the value NEW in the value column. The third statement (SELECT) retrieves values from all the rows of all columns.

It is worth noting that we would not be able to delete the records of the enums table if these records were referred to (as foreign keys) by the traffic_unit table. Only after deleting the corresponding records of the traffic_unit table it is possible to delete the records of the enums table.

To execute any of the CRUD operations in the code, one has to acquire a JDBC connection first, then create and execute a statement:

```
try (Connection conn = getDbConnection()) {
   try (Statement st = conn.createStatement()) {
     boolean res = st.execute("select id, type, value from enums");
     if (res) {
       ResultSet rs = st.getResultSet();
       while (rs.next()) {
         int id = rs.getInt(1);
         String type = rs.getString(2);
         String value = rs.getString(3);
         System.out.println("id = " + id + ", type = "
                            + type + ", value = " + value);
       }
     } else {
       int count = st.getUpdateCount();
       System.out.println("Update count = " + count);
     }
   }
} catch (Exception ex) { ex.printStackTrace(); }
```

It is good practice to use the try-with-resources construct for the Statement object. The closing of the Connection object would close the Statement object automatically. However, when you close the Statement object explicitly, the cleanup happens immediately, instead of you having to wait for the necessary checks and actions to propagate through the layers of the framework.

The `execute()` method is the most generic one among the three methods that can execute a statement. The other two include `executeQuery()` (for `SELECT` statements only) and `executeUpdate()` (for `UPDATE`, `DELETE`, `CREATE`, or `ALTER` statements). As you can see from the preceding example, the `execute()` method returns `boolean`, which indicates whether the result is a `ResultSet` object or just a count. This means that `execute()` acts as `executeQuery()` for the `SELECT` statement and `executeUpdate()` for the other statements that we have listed.

We can demonstrate this by running the preceding code for the following sequence of statements:

```
"select id, type, value from enums"
"insert into enums (id, type, value)" + " values(1,'vehicle','car')"
"select id, type, value from enums"
"update enums set value = 'bus' where value = 'car'"
"select id, type, value from enums"
"delete from enums where value = 'bus'"
"select id, type, value from enums"
```

The result will be as follows:

```
id = 7, type = tire_condition, value = NEW

Update count = 1

id = 7, type = tire_condition, value = NEW
id = 1, type = vehicle, value = car

Update count = 1

id = 7, type = tire_condition, value = NEW
id = 1, type = vehicle, value = bus

Update count = 1

id = 7, type = tire_condition, value = NEW
```

We used the positional extraction of the values from `ResultSet` because this is more efficient than using the column name (as in `rs.getInt("id")` or `rs.getInt("type")`). The difference in performance is very small, though, and becomes important only when the operation happens many times. Only the actual measuring and testing can tell you whether this difference is significant for your application. Bear in mind that getting values by name provides better code readability, which pays well in the long term during application maintenance.

We used the `execute()` method for demonstration purposes. In practice, the `executeQuery()` method is used for `SELECT` statements:

```
try (Connection conn = getDbConnection()) {
  try (Statement st = conn.createStatement()) {
    boolean res = st.execute("select id, type, value from enums");
    ResultSet rs = st.getResultSet();
    while (rs.next()) {
        int id = rs.getInt(1);
        String type = rs.getString(2);
        String value = rs.getString(3);
        System.out.println("id = " + id + ", type = "
                          + type + ", value = " + value);
    }
  }
} catch (Exception ex) { ex.printStackTrace(); }
```

As you can see, the preceding code cannot be generalized as a method that receives the SQL statement as a parameter. The code that extracts the data is specific to the executed SQL statement. By contrast, the call to `executeUpdate()` can be wrapped in a generic method:

```
void executeUpdate(String sql){
  try (Connection conn = getDbConnection()) {
    try (Statement st = conn.createStatement()) {
      int count = st.executeUpdate(sql);
      System.out.println("Update count = " + count);
    }
  } catch (Exception ex) { ex.printStackTrace(); }
}
```

There's more...

SQL is a rich language, and we do not have enough space to cover all of its features. But we would like to enumerate a few of its most popular ones so that you are aware of their existence and can look them up when needed:

- The SELECT statement allows the use of the DISTINCT keyword, to get rid of all the duplicate values
- The keyword LIKE allows you to set the search pattern to the WHERE clause
- The search pattern can use several wildcards—%, _, [charlist], [^charlist], or [!charlist].
- Matching values can be enumerated with the IN keyword
- The SELECT statement can include several tables using the JOIN clause
- SELECT * INTO table_2 from table_1 creates table_2 and copies data from table_1
- TRUNCATE is faster and uses fewer resources when removing all the rows of a table

There are many other useful methods in the ResultSet interface as well. Here is an example of how some of its methods can be used to write generic code that would traverse the returned result and use metadata to print out the column name and the returned value:

```java
void traverseRS(String sql){
  System.out.println("traverseRS(" + sql + "):");
  try (Connection conn = getDbConnection()) {
    try (Statement st = conn.createStatement()) {
      try(ResultSet rs = st.executeQuery(sql)){
        int cCount = 0;
        Map<Integer, String> cName = new HashMap<>();
        while (rs.next()) {
          if (cCount == 0) {
            ResultSetMetaData rsmd = rs.getMetaData();
            cCount = rsmd.getColumnCount();
            for (int i = 1; i <= cCount; i++) {
              cName.put(i, rsmd.getColumnLabel(i));
            }
          }
          List<String> l = new ArrayList<>();
          for (int i = 1; i <= cCount; i++) {
            l.add(cName.get(i) + " = " + rs.getString(i));
          }
          System.out.println(l.stream()
```

```
                                    .collect(Collectors.joining(", ")));
            }
         }
      }
   } catch (Exception ex) { ex.printStackTrace(); }
}
```

We used `ResultSetMetaData` only once to collect the returned column names and the length (number of columns) of one row. Then, we extracted the values from each row by position and created `List<String>` elements with the corresponding column names. To print, we used something you are already familiar with—a programmer's delight—the joining collector (we discussed it in the previous chapter). If we call the `traverseRS("select * from enums")` method, the result will be as follows:

```
id = 7, type = tire_condition, value = NEW
```

Using the Hikari Connection Pool (HikariCP)

In this recipe, you will learn how to set up and use the high-performance HikariCP.

Getting ready

The HikariCP framework was created by Brett Wooldridge, who lives in Japan. *Hikari* in Japanese means *light*. It is a lightweight and relatively small API that is highly optimized and allows for tuning via many properties, some of which are not available in other pools. In addition to standard user, password, maximum pool size, various timeout settings, and cache configuration properties, it also exposes such properties as `allowPoolSuspension`, `connectionInitSql`, `connectionTestQuery`, and many others, even including a property that deals with the not-timely-closed connections, `leakDetectionThreshold`.

To use the latest (at the time of writing this book) version of Hikari pool, add the following dependency to the project:

```
<dependency>
    <groupId>com.zaxxer</groupId>
    <artifactId>HikariCP</artifactId>
    <version>3.2.0</version>
</dependency>
```

For demonstration purposes, we will use the database created in the previous recipe of this chapter, *Connecting to a database using JDBC*. We will also assume that you have studied that recipe and there is no need to repeat what was said there about the database, JDBC, and how they work together.

How to do it...

There are several ways to configure the Hikari connection pool. All of them are based on the usage of the `javax.sql.DataSource` interface:

1. The most obvious and straightforward method is to set the pool properties on the `DataSource` object directly:

```
HikariDataSource ds = new HikariDataSource();
ds.setPoolName("cookpool");
ds.setDriverClassName("org.postgresql.Driver");
ds.setJdbcUrl("jdbc:postgresql://localhost/cookbook");
ds.setUsername( "cook");
//ds.setPassword("123Secret");
ds.setMaximumPoolSize(10);
ds.setMinimumIdle(2);
ds.addDataSourceProperty("cachePrepStmts", Boolean.TRUE);
ds.addDataSourceProperty("prepStmtCacheSize", 256);
ds.addDataSourceProperty("prepStmtCacheSqlLimit", 2048);
ds.addDataSourceProperty("useServerPrepStmts", Boolean.TRUE);
```

We have commented out password because we did not set one for our database. Between properties `jdbcUrl` and `dataSourceClassName`, only one of them can be used at a time, except when using some older drivers that may require setting both of these properties. Also, please notice how we have used the general method `addDataSourceProperty()` when there is no dedicated setter for the particular property.

To switch from PostgreSQL to another relational database, all you need to do is change the driver class name and the database URL. There are also many other properties; some of them are database specific, but we are not going to dive into such details, because this recipe demonstrates how to use HikariCP. Read the database documentation about database-specific pool configuration properties and how to use them for tuning the pool for the best performance, which also very much depends on how the particular application interacts with the database.

2. Another way to configure the Hikari pool is to use the `HikariConfig` class to collect all the properties and then set the `HikariConfig` object in the `HikariDataSource` constructor:

```
HikariConfig config = new HikariConfig();
config.setPoolName("cookpool");
config.setDriverClassName("org.postgresql.Driver");
config.setJdbcUrl("jdbc:postgresql://localhost/cookbook");
config.setUsername("cook");
//conf.setPassword("123Secret");
config.setMaximumPoolSize(10);
config.setMinimumIdle(2);
config.addDataSourceProperty("cachePrepStmts", true);
config.addDataSourceProperty("prepStmtCacheSize", 256);
config.addDataSourceProperty("prepStmtCacheSqlLimit", 2048);
config.addDataSourceProperty("useServerPrepStmts", true);

HikariDataSource ds = new HikariDataSource(config);
```

As you can see, we have used the general method `addDataSourceProperty()` again because there are no dedicated setters for those properties in the `HikariConfig` class either.

3. The `HikariConfig` object, in turn, can be populated with data using the class `java.util.Properties`:

```
Properties props = new Properties();
props.setProperty("poolName", "cookpool");
props.setProperty("driverClassName", "org.postgresql.Driver");
props.setProperty("jdbcUrl",
"jdbc:postgresql://localhost/cookbook");
props.setProperty("username", "cook");
//props.setProperty("password", "123Secret");
props.setProperty("maximumPoolSize", "10");
props.setProperty("minimumIdle", "2");
props.setProperty("dataSource.cachePrepStmts","true");
props.setProperty("dataSource.prepStmtCacheSize", "256");
```

```
props.setProperty("dataSource.prepStmtCacheSqlLimit", "2048");
props.setProperty("dataSource.useServerPrepStmts","true");

HikariConfig config = new HikariConfig(props);
HikariDataSource ds = new HikariDataSource(config);
```

Please, note that we have used the prefix dataSource for the properties that do not have dedicated setters in the HikariConfig class.

4. To make the configuration even easier to load, the HikariConfig class has a constructor that accepts a file with the properties. For example, let's create a file called database.properties in the folder resources with the following content:

```
poolName=cookpool
driverClassName=org.postgresql.Driver
jdbcUrl=jdbc:postgresql://localhost/cookbook
username=cook
password=
maximumPoolSize=10
minimumIdle=2
dataSource.cachePrepStmts=true
dataSource.useServerPrepStmts=true
dataSource.prepStmtCacheSize=256
dataSource.prepStmtCacheSqlLimit=2048
```

Notice how we used the prefix dataSource with the same properties again. Now, we can load the preceding file directly into the HikariConfig constructor:

```
ClassLoader loader = getClass().getClassLoader();
File file =
    new
File(loader.getResource("database.properties").getFile());
HikariConfig config = new
HikariConfig(file.getAbsolutePath());
HikariDataSource ds = new HikariDataSource(config);
```

Behind the scenes, as you could guess, it just loads properties:

```
public HikariConfig(String propertyFileName) {
    this();
    this.loadProperties(propertyFileName);
}
```

5. Alternatively, we can use the following functionality that's included in the `HikariConfig` default constructor:

```
String systemProp =
        System.getProperty("hikaricp.configurationFile");
if (systemProp != null) {
    this.loadProperties(systemProp);
}
```

It means that we can set the system property as follows:

```
-Dhikaricp.configurationFile=src/main/resources/database.properties
```

Then, we can configure HikariCP as follows:

```
HikariConfig config = new HikariConfig();
HikariDataSource ds = new HikariDataSource(config);
```

All the preceding methods of the pool configuration produce the same result, so it is only up to the style, convention, or just your personal preference to decide which of them to use.

How it works...

The following method is using the created `DataSource` object to access the database and select all the values from the table `enums`, which were created in the recipe *Connecting to a database using JDBC*:

```
void readData(DataSource ds) {
    try(Connection conn = ds.getConnection();
      PreparedStatement pst =
        conn.prepareStatement("select id, type, value from enums");
      ResultSet rs = pst.executeQuery()){
      while (rs.next()) {
            int id = rs.getInt(1);
            String type = rs.getString(2);
            String value = rs.getString(3);
            System.out.println("id = " + id + ", type = " +
                                    type + ", value = " + value);
      }
    } catch (SQLException ex){
      ex.printStackTrace();
    }
}
```

If we run the preceding code, the result will be as follows:

```
id = 1, type = vehicle, value = car
id = 3, type = vehicle, value = crewcab
id = 7, type = tire_condition, value = NEW
```

There's more...

You can read more about HikariCP's features on GitHub (`https://github.com/brettwooldridge/HikariCP`).

Using prepared statements

In this recipe, you will learn how to use a **prepared statement**—a statement template that can be stored in the database and executed efficiently with different input values.

Getting ready

An object of `PreparedStatement`—a subinterface of `Statement`—can be precompiled and stored in the database and then used to efficiently execute the SQL statement multiple times for different input values. Similar to an object of `Statement` (created by the `createStatement()` method), it can be created by the `prepareStatement()` method of the same `Connection` object.

The same SQL statement that was used to generate `Statement` can be used to generate `PreparedStatement` too. In fact, it is a good idea to consider using `PrepdaredStatement` for any SQL statement that is called multiple times, because it performs better than `Statement`. To do this, all we need to change are these two lines in the sample code of the previous section:

```
try (Statement st = conn.createStatement()) {
   boolean res = st.execute("select * from enums");
```

We change these lines to the following:

```
try (PreparedStatement st =
          conn.prepareStatement("select * from enums")) {
   boolean res = st.execute();
```

How to do it...

The true usefulness of `PreparedStatement` shines because of its ability to accept parameters—the input values that substitute (in order of appearance) the ? symbol. Here's an example of this:

```
traverseRS("select * from enums");
System.out.println();
try (Connection conn = getDbConnection()) {
  String[][] values = {{"1", "vehicle", "car"},
                       {"2", "vehicle", "truck"}};
  String sql = "insert into enums (id, type, value) values(?, ?, ?)";
  try (PreparedStatement st = conn.prepareStatement(sql) {
    for(String[] v: values){
      st.setInt(1, Integer.parseInt(v[0]));
      st.setString(2, v[1]);
      st.setString(3, v[2]);
      int count = st.executeUpdate();
      System.out.println("Update count = " + count);
    }
  }
} catch (Exception ex) { ex.printStackTrace(); }
System.out.println();
traverseRS("select * from enums");
```

The result of this is as follows:

```
id = 7, type = tire_condition, value = NEW

Update count = 1
Update count = 1

id = 7, type = tire_condition, value = NEW
id = 1, type = vehicle, value = car
id = 2, type = vehicle, value = truck
```

There's more...

It is not a bad idea to always use prepared statements for CRUD operations. They might be slower if executed only once, but you can test and see whether this is the price you are willing to pay. By using prepared statements systematically, you will produce a consistent (better readable) code that provides more security (prepared statements are not vulnerable to SQL injection).

Using transactions

In this recipe, you will learn what a database transaction is and how it can be used in Java code.

Getting ready

A **transaction** is a unit of work that includes one or many operations that change data. If successful, all the data changes are **committed** (applied to the database). If one of the operations errors out, the transaction is **rolled back**, and none of the changes included in the transaction will be applied to the database.

Transaction properties are set up on the `Connection` object. They can be changed without closing the connection, so different transactions can reuse the same `Connection` object.

JDBC allows transaction control only for CRUD operations. Table modification (`CREATE TABLE`, `ALTER TABLE`, and so on) is committed automatically and cannot be controlled from the Java code.

By default, a CRUD operation transaction is set to be **auto-committed**. This means that every data change that was introduced by a SQL statement is applied to the database as soon as the execution of this statement is completed. All the preceding examples in this chapter use this default behavior.

To change this behavior, you have to use the `setAutoCommit(boolean)` method of the `Connection` object. If set to `false`, the data changes will not be applied to the database until the `commit()` method on the `Connection` object is invoked. Also, if the `rollback()` method is called instead, all the data changes since the beginning of the transaction or since the last call to `commit()` will be discarded.

Explicit programmatic transaction management improves performance, but it is insignificant in the case of short atomic operations that are called once and not very often. Taking over transaction control becomes crucial when several operations introduce changes that have to be applied either all together or none of them. It allows for group database changes into atomic units and thus avoids accidental violation of data integrity.

How to do it...

First, let's add an output to the `traverseRS()` method:

```
void traverseRS(String sql){
  System.out.println("traverseRS(" + sql + "):");
  try (Connection conn = getDbConnection()) {
    ...
  }
}
```

This will help you analyze the output when many different SQL statements are executed in the same demo example.

Now, let's run the following code that reads data from the enums table, then inserts a row, and then reads all the data from the table again:

```
traverseRS("select * from enums");
System.out.println();
try (Connection conn = getDbConnection()) {
  conn.setAutoCommit(false);
  String sql = "insert into enums (id, type, value) "
                      + " values(1,'vehicle','car')";
  try (PreparedStatement st = conn.prepareStatement(sql)) {
    System.out.println(sql);
    System.out.println("Update count = " + st.executeUpdate());
  }
  //conn.commit();
} catch (Exception ex) { ex.printStackTrace(); }
System.out.println();
traverseRS("select * from enums");
```

Note that we took over transaction control by calling `conn.setAutoCommit(false)`. The result is as follows:

```
traverseRS(select * from enums):
id = 7, type = tire_condition, value = NEW

insert into enums (id, type, value) values(1,'vehicle','car')
Update count = 1

traverseRS(select * from enums):
id = 7, type = tire_condition, value = NEW
```

As you can see, the changes were not applied because the call to `commit()` was commented out. When we uncomment it, the result changes:

```
traverseRS(select * from enums):
id = 7, type = tire_condition, value = NEW

insert into enums (id, type, value) values(1,'vehicle','car')
Update count = 1

traverseRS(select * from enums):
id = 1, type = vehicle, value = car
id = 7, type = tire_condition, value = NEW
```

Now, let's execute two inserts, but introduce a spelling error in the second insert:

```
traverseRS("select * from enums");
System.out.println();
try (Connection conn = getDbConnection()) {
  conn.setAutoCommit(false);
  String sql = "insert into enums (id, type, value) "
                    + " values(1,'vehicle','car')";
  try (PreparedStatement st = conn.prepareStatement(sql)) {
    System.out.println(sql);
    System.out.println("Update count = " + st.executeUpdate());
  }
  conn.commit();
  sql = "inst into enums (id, type, value) "
                    + " values(2,'vehicle','truck')";
  try (PreparedStatement st = conn.prepareStatement(sql)) {
    System.out.println(sql);
    System.out.println("Update count = " + st.executeUpdate());
  }
  conn.commit();
} catch (Exception ex) { ex.printStackTrace(); } //get exception here
System.out.println();
traverseRS("select * from enums");
```

We get an exception stack trace (we do not show it to save space) and this message:

```
org.postgresql.util.PSQLException: ERROR: syntax error at or near
"inst"
```

Nevertheless, the first insert was executed successfully:

```
traverseRS(select * from enums):
id = 1, type = vehicle, value = car
id = 7, type = tire_condition, value = NEW
```

The second row was not inserted. If there was no `conn.commit()` after the first `INSERT INTO` statement, the first insert would not be applied either. This is the advantage of the programmatic transaction control in the case of many independent data changes—if one fails, we can skip it and continue applying other changes.

Now, let's try to insert three rows with an error (by setting a letter instead of a number as the `id` value) in the second row:

```
traverseRS("select * from enums");
System.out.println();
try (Connection conn = getDbConnection()) {
  conn.setAutoCommit(false);
  String[][] values = { {"1", "vehicle", "car"},
                        {"b", "vehicle", "truck"},
                        {"3", "vehicle", "crewcab"} };
  String sql = "insert into enums (id, type, value) "
                        + " values(?, ?, ?)";
  try (PreparedStatement st = conn.prepareStatement(sql)) {
    for (String[] v: values){
      try {
        System.out.print("id=" + v[0] + ": ");
        st.setInt(1, Integer.parseInt(v[0]));
        st.setString(2, v[1]);
        st.setString(3, v[2]);
        int count = st.executeUpdate();
        conn.commit();
        System.out.println("Update count = "+count);
      } catch(Exception ex){
        //conn.rollback();
        System.out.println(ex.getMessage());
      }
    }
  }
} catch (Exception ex) { ex.printStackTrace(); }
System.out.println();
traverseRS("select * from enums");
```

We put each insert execution in the `try...catch` block and commit the changes before printing out the result (update count or error message). The result is as follows:

```
traverseRS(select * from enums):
id = 7, type = tire_condition, value = NEW

id=1: Update count = 1
id=b: For input string: "b"
id=3: Update count = 1

traverseRS(select * from enums):
id = 7, type = tire_condition, value = NEW
id = 1, type = vehicle, value = car
id = 3, type = vehicle, value = crewcab
```

As you can see, the second row was not inserted, although `conn.rollback()` was commented out. Why? This is because the only SQL statement included in this transaction failed, so there was nothing to roll back.

Now, let's create a `test` table with only one column `name` using the database console:

```
cookbook=# create table test (name varchar not null);
CREATE TABLE
cookbook=# select * from test;
 name
-------
(0 rows)
```

We will insert in the table `test` the vehicle type before inserting a record in the `enums` table:

```
traverseRS("select * from enums");
System.out.println();
try (Connection conn = getDbConnection()) {
  conn.setAutoCommit(false);
  String[][] values = { {"1", "vehicle", "car"},
                        {"b", "vehicle", "truck"},
                        {"3", "vehicle", "crewcab"} };
  String sql = "insert into enums (id, type, value) " +
                                        " values(?, ?, ?)";
  try (PreparedStatement st = conn.prepareStatement(sql)) {
    for (String[] v: values){
      try(Statement stm = conn.createStatement()) {
        System.out.print("id=" + v[0] + ": ");
```

```
        stm.execute("insert into test values('"+ v[2] + "')");
        st.setInt(1, Integer.parseInt(v[0]));
        st.setString(2, v[1]);
        st.setString(3, v[2]);
        int count = st.executeUpdate();
        conn.commit();
        System.out.println("Update count = " + count);
      } catch(Exception ex){
        //conn.rollback();
        System.out.println(ex.getMessage());
      }
    }
  }
} catch (Exception ex) { ex.printStackTrace(); }
System.out.println();
traverseRS("select * from enums");
System.out.println();
traverseRS("select * from test");
```

As you can see, the previous code commits the changes after the second insert, which, as in the previous example, is not successful for the second element of the array `values`. With `conn.rollback()` commented out, the result will be as follows:

```
traverseRS(select * from enums):
id = 7, type = tire_condition, value = NEW

id=1: Update count = 1
id=b: For input string: "b"
id=3: Update count = 1

traverseRS(select * from enums):
id = 7, type = tire_condition, value = NEW
id = 1, type = vehicle, value = car
id = 3, type = vehicle, value = crewcab

traverseRS(select * from test):
name = car
name = truck
name = crewcab
```

The row with `truck` was not inserted in the `enums` table but added to the `test` table. That is, when the usefulness of a rollback was demonstrated. If we uncomment `conn.rollback()`, the result will be as follows:

```
traverseRS(select * from enums):
id = 7, type = tire_condition, value = NEW

id=1: Update count = 1
id=b: For input string: "b"
id=3: Update count = 1

traverseRS(select * from enums):
id = 7, type = tire_condition, value = NEW
id = 1, type = vehicle, value = car
id = 3, type = vehicle, value = crewcab

traverseRS(select * from test):
name = car
name = crewcab
```

This demonstrates that `conn.rollback()` rolls back all the changes not committed yet.

There's more...

Another important property of a transaction is the **transaction isolation level**. It defines the boundaries between database users. For example, can other users see your database changes before they are committed? The higher the isolation (the highest is **serializable**), the more time it takes a transaction to complete in the case of concurrent access to the same records. The less restrictive the isolation (the least restrictive is **read uncommitted**), the dirtier the data is, which means that other users can get the values you have not committed yet (and are maybe never going to commit).

Usually, it is enough to use the default level, which is typically `TRANSACTION_READ_COMMITTED`, although it may be different for different databases. JDBC allows you to get the current transaction isolation level by calling the method `getTransactionIsolation()` on the `Connection` object. The method `setTransactionIsolation()` of the `Connection` object allows you to set any isolation level as needed.

In the case of complex decision-making logic about which changes need to be committed and which need to be rolled back, one can use two other `Connection` methods to create and delete **savepoints**. The `setSavepoint(String savepointName)` method creates a new savepoint and returns a `Savepoint` object, which can later be used to roll back all the changes up to this point using the `rollback(Savepoint savepoint)` method. A savepoint can be deleted by calling `releaseSavepoint(Savepoint savepoint)`.

The most complex types of database transactions are **distributed transactions**. They are sometimes called **global transactions**, **XA transactions**, or **JTA transactions** (the latter is a Java API that consists of two Java packages, namely `javax.transaction` and `javax.transaction.xa`). They allow for the creation and execution of a transaction that spans operations across two different databases. Providing a detailed overview of distributed transactions is outside the scope of this book.

Working with large objects

In this recipe, you will learn how to store and retrieve a LOB that can be one of three types—**Binary Large Object (BLOB)**, **Character Large Object (CLOB)**, and **National Character Large Object (NCLOB)**.

Getting ready

The actual processing of LOB objects inside a database is vendor-specific, but JDBC APIs hide these implementation details from the application by representing the three LOB types as interfaces—`java.sql.Blob`, `java.sql.Clob`, and `java.sql.NClob`.

`Blob` is usually used to store images or other non-alphanumeric data. On the way to the database, an image can be converted into a stream of bytes and stored using the `INSERT INTO` statement. The `Blob` interface allows you to find the length of the object and convert it into an array of bytes that can be processed by Java for the purpose of displaying the image, for example.

`Clob` allows you to store character data. `NClob` stores Unicode character data as a way to support internationalization. It extends the `Clob` interface and provides the same methods. Both interfaces allow you to find the length of LOB and to get a substring inside the value.

The methods in the `ResultSet`, `CallableStatement` (we will discuss this in the next recipe), and `PreparedStatement` interfaces allow an application to store and access the stored value in a variety of ways—some of them via setters and getters of the corresponding objects, while others as `bytes[]`, or as a binary, character, or ASCII stream.

How to do it...

Each database has its specific way of storing a LOB. In the case of PostgreSQL, `Blob` is usually mapped to the `OID` or `BYTEA` data type, while `Clob` and `NClob` are mapped to the `TEXT` type. To demonstrate how to do this, let's create tables that can store each of the large object types. We will write a new method that creates tables programmatically:

```
void execute(String sql){
  try (Connection conn = getDbConnection()) {
    try (PreparedStatement st = conn.prepareStatement(sql)) {
      st.execute();
    }
  } catch (Exception ex) {
    ex.printStackTrace();
  }
}
```

Now, we can create three tables:

```
execute("create table images (id integer, image bytea)");
execute("create table lobs (id integer, lob oid)");
execute("create table texts (id integer, text text)");
```

Look at the JDBC interfaces `PreparedStatement` and `ResultSet` and you'll notice the setters and getters for the objects—`get/setBlob()`, `get/setClob()`, `get/setNClob()`, `get/setBytes()`—and the methods that use `InputStream` and `Reader`—`get/setBinaryStream()`, `get/setAsciiStream()`, or `get/setCharacterStream()`. The big advantage of streaming methods is that they move data between the database and source without storing the whole LOB in memory.

However, the object's setters and getters are closer to our heart being in line with object-oriented coding. So we will start with them, using objects that aren't too big, for demonstration purposes. We expect the following code to work just fine:

```
try (Connection conn = getDbConnection()) {
  String sql = "insert into images (id, image) values(?, ?)";
  try (PreparedStatement st = conn.prepareStatement(sql)) {
    st.setInt(1, 100);
    File file =
      new
File("src/main/java/com/packt/cookbook/ch06_db/image1.png");
    FileInputStream fis = new FileInputStream(file);
    Blob blob = conn.createBlob();
    OutputStream out = blob.setBinaryStream(1);
    int i = -1;
    while ((i = fis.read()) != -1) {
      out.write(i);
    }
    st.setBlob(2, blob);
    int count = st.executeUpdate();
    System.out.println("Update count = " + count);
  }
} catch (Exception ex) { ex.printStackTrace(); }
```

Alternatively, in the case of `Clob`, we write this code:

```
try (Connection conn = getDbConnection()) {
  String sql = "insert into texts (id, text) values(?, ?)";
  try (PreparedStatement st = conn.prepareStatement(sql)) {
    st.setInt(1, 100);
    File file = new File("src/main/java/com/packt/cookbook/" +
                            "ch06_db/Chapter06Database.java");
    Reader reader = new FileReader(file);
    st.setClob(2, reader);
    int count = st.executeUpdate();
    System.out.println("Update count = " + count);
  }
} catch (Exception ex) { ex.printStackTrace(); }
```

It turns out that not all methods that are available in the JDBC API are actually implemented by the drivers of all the databases. For example, `createBlob()` seems to work just fine for Oracle and MySQL, but in the case of PostgreSQL, we get this:

```
traverseRS(select * from images):
java.sql.SQLFeatureNotSupportedException: Method org.postgresql.jdbc.PgConnection.createBlob() is not yet implemented.
    at org.postgresql.Driver.notImplemented(Driver.java:640)
```

For `Clob`, we get the following:

```
traverseRS(select * from texts):

java.sql.SQLFeatureNotSupportedException: Method org.postgresql.jdbc.PgPreparedStatement.setClob(int, Reader) is not yet implemented.
    at org.postgresql.Driver.notImplemented(Driver.java:640)
```

We can try to retrieve an object from `ResultSet` via the getter as well:

```java
String sql = "select image from images";
try (PreparedStatement st = conn.prepareStatement(sql)) {
  st.setInt(1, 100);
  try(ResultSet rs = st.executeQuery()){
    while (rs.next()){
      Blob blob = rs.getBlob(1);
      System.out.println("blob length = " + blob.length());
    }
  }
}
```

The result will be as follows:

```
org.postgresql.util.PSQLException: Bad value for type long : \x89504e470d0a1a0a0000000d49484452000
    at org.postgresql.jdbc.PgResultSet.toLong(PgResultSet.java:2861)
    at org.postgresql.jdbc.PgResultSet.getLong(PgResultSet.java:2072)
    at org.postgresql.jdbc.PgResultSet.getBlob(PgResultSet.java:420)
```

Apparently, knowing the JDBC API is not enough; you have to read the documentation for the database too. Here is what the documentation for PostgreSQL (`https://jdbc.postgresql.org/documentation/80/binary-data.html`) has to say about LOB handling:

> "To use the BYTEA data type you should simply use the `getBytes()`, `setBytes()`, `getBinaryStream()`, or `setBinaryStream()` methods. To use the Large Object functionality you can use either the `LargeObject` class provided by the PostgreSQL JDBC driver, or by using the `getBLOB()` and `setBLOB()` methods."

Also, you must access large objects within an SQL transaction block. You can start a transaction block by calling `setAutoCommit(false)`.

Without knowing such specifics, figuring out a way to handle LOBs would require a lot of time and cause much frustration.

When dealing with LOBs, the streaming methods are preferred because they transfer data directly from the source into the database (or the other way around) and do not consume memory as much as the setters and getters do (which have to load all the LOB in memory first). Here is the code that streams `Blob` in and from PostgreSQL database:

```
traverseRS("select * from images");
System.out.println();
try (Connection conn = getDbConnection()) {
   String sql = "insert into images (id, image) values(?, ?)";
   try (PreparedStatement st = conn.prepareStatement(sql)) {
      st.setInt(1, 100);
      File file =
         new
File("src/main/java/com/packt/cookbook/ch06_db/image1.png");
      FileInputStream fis = new FileInputStream(file);
      st.setBinaryStream(2, fis);
      int count = st.executeUpdate();
      System.out.println("Update count = " + count);
   }
   sql = "select image from images where id = ?";
   try (PreparedStatement st = conn.prepareStatement(sql)) {
      st.setInt(1, 100);
      try(ResultSet rs = st.executeQuery()){
         while (rs.next()){
            try(InputStream is = rs.getBinaryStream(1)){
               int i;
               System.out.print("ints = ");
               while ((i = is.read()) != -1) {
                  System.out.print(i);
               }
            }
         }
      }
   }
} catch (Exception ex) { ex.printStackTrace(); }
System.out.println();
traverseRS("select * from images");
```

Let's look at the result. We have cut the screenshot arbitrarily on the right-hand side; otherwise, it is too long horizontally:

```
traverseRS(select * from images):

Update count = 1
ints = 137807871131026100001373726882001750001748600019173472700122410567678073676732801141111102105

traverseRS(select * from images):
id = 100, image = \x89504e470d0a1a0a0000000d494844520000014b000000ae0806000000bf492f1b00000c1869434
```

Another way to process the retrieved image is to use `byte[]`:

```java
try (Connection conn = getDbConnection()) {
  String sql =  "insert into images (id, image) values(?, ?)";
  try (PreparedStatement st = conn.prepareStatement(sql)) {
    st.setInt(1, 100);
    File file =
      new
File("src/main/java/com/packt/cookbook/ch06_db/image1.png");
    FileInputStream fis = new FileInputStream(file);
    byte[] bytes = fis.readAllBytes();
    st.setBytes(2, bytes);
    int count = st.executeUpdate();
    System.out.println("Update count = " + count);
  }
  sql = "select image from images where id = ?";
  System.out.println();
  try (PreparedStatement st = conn.prepareStatement(sql)) {
    st.setInt(1, 100);
    try(ResultSet rs = st.executeQuery()){
      while (rs.next()){
        byte[] bytes = rs.getBytes(1);
        System.out.println("bytes = " + bytes);
      }
    }
  }
} catch (Exception ex) { ex.printStackTrace(); }
```

PostgreSQL limits the `BYTEA` size to 1 GB. Larger binary objects can be stored as the **object identifier (OID)** data type:

```java
traverseRS("select * from lobs");
System.out.println();
try (Connection conn = getDbConnection()) {
  conn.setAutoCommit(false);
  LargeObjectManager lobm =
        conn.unwrap(org.postgresql.PGConnection.class)
```

```
          .getLargeObjectAPI();
  long lob = lobm.createLO(LargeObjectManager.READ
                            | LargeObjectManager.WRITE);
  LargeObject obj = lobm.open(lob, LargeObjectManager.WRITE);
  File file =
      new
File("src/main/java/com/packt/cookbook/ch06_db/image1.png");
  try (FileInputStream fis = new FileInputStream(file)){
    int size = 2048;
    byte[] bytes = new byte[size];
    int len = 0;
    while ((len = fis.read(bytes, 0, size)) > 0) {
      obj.write(bytes, 0, len);
    }
    obj.close();
    String sql = "insert into lobs (id, lob) values(?, ?)";
    try (PreparedStatement st = conn.prepareStatement(sql)) {
      st.setInt(1, 100);
      st.setLong(2, lob);
      st.executeUpdate();
    }
  }
    conn.commit();
} catch (Exception ex) { ex.printStackTrace(); }
System.out.println();
traverseRS("select * from lobs");
```

The result will be as follows:

```
traverseRS(select * from lobs):


traverseRS(select * from lobs):
id = 100, lob = 304191
```

Please note that the select statement returns a long value from the lob column. This is because the OID column does not store the value itself like BYTEA does. Instead, it stores the reference to the object that is stored somewhere else in the database. Such an arrangement makes deleting the row with the OID type not as straightforward as this:

```
execute("delete from lobs where id = 100");
```

If you do just that, it leaves the actual object an orphan that continues to consume disk space. To avoid this problem, you have to `unlink` the LOB first by executing the following command:

```
execute("select lo_unlink((select lob from lobs " + " where
id=100))");
```

Only after this can you safely execute the `delete from lobs where id = 100` commands.

If you forgot to `unlink` first, or if you created an orphan LOB accidentally (because of an error in the code, for example), there is a way to find orphans in system tables. Again, database documentation should provide you with instructions on how to do this. In the case of PostgreSQL v.9.3 or later, you can check whether you have an orphan LOB by executing the `select count(*) from pg_largeobject` command. If it returns a count that is bigger than 0, then you can delete all the orphans with the following join (assuming that the `lobs` table is the only one that can contain a reference to a LOB):

```
SELECT lo_unlink(pgl.oid) FROM pg_largeobject_metadata pgl
WHERE (NOT EXISTS (SELECT 1 FROM lobs ls" + "WHERE ls.lob = pgl.oid));
```

This is the price one has to pay for storing a LOB in a database.

It's worth noting that although BYTEA does not require such complexity during the delete operation, it has a different kind of overhead. According to the PostgreSQL documentation, when close to 1 GB, *it would require a huge amount of memory to process such a large value.*

To read LOB data, you can use the following code:

```
try (Connection conn = getDbConnection()) {
  conn.setAutoCommit(false);
  LargeObjectManager lobm =
          conn.unwrap(org.postgresql.PGConnection.class)
              .getLargeObjectAPI();
  String sql = "select lob from lobs where id = ?";
  try (PreparedStatement st = conn.prepareStatement(sql)) {
    st.setInt(1, 100);
    try(ResultSet rs = st.executeQuery()){
      while (rs.next()){
        long lob = rs.getLong(1);
        LargeObject obj = lobm.open(lob, LargeObjectManager.READ);
        byte[] bytes = new byte[obj.size()];
        obj.read(bytes, 0, obj.size());
        System.out.println("bytes = " + bytes);
```

```
            obj.close();
        }
    }
}
conn.commit();
} catch (Exception ex) { ex.printStackTrace(); }
```

Alternatively, it is possible to use a simpler code by getting `Blob` directly from the `ResultSet` object if the LOB is not too big:

```
while (rs.next()){
  Blob blob = rs.getBlob(1);
  byte[] bytes = blob.getBytes(1, (int)blob.length());
  System.out.println("bytes = " + bytes);
}
```

To store `Clob` in PostgreSQL, you can use the same code as the preceding one. While reading from the database, you can convert bytes into a `String` data type or something similar (again, if the LOB is not too big):

```
String str = new String(bytes, Charset.forName("UTF-8"));
System.out.println("bytes = " + str);
```

However, `Clob` in PostgreSQL can be stored directly as data type `TEXT` that is unlimited in size. This code reads the file where this code is written and stores/retrieves it in/from the database:

```
traverseRS("select * from texts");
System.out.println();
try (Connection conn = getDbConnection()) {
  String sql = "insert into texts (id, text) values(?, ?)";
  try (PreparedStatement st = conn.prepareStatement(sql)) {
    st.setInt(1, 100);
    File file = new File("src/main/java/com/packt/cookbook/ch06_db/"
                                    + "Chapter06Database.java");
    try (FileInputStream fis = new FileInputStream(file)) {
      byte[] bytes = fis.readAllBytes();
      st.setString(2, new String(bytes, Charset.forName("UTF-8")));
    }
    int count = st.executeUpdate();
    System.out.println("Update count = " + count);
  }
  sql = "select text from texts where id = ?";
  try (PreparedStatement st = conn.prepareStatement(sql)) {
    st.setInt(1, 100);
    try(ResultSet rs = st.executeQuery()){
      while (rs.next()) {
```

```
            String str = rs.getString(1);
            System.out.println(str);
        }
      }
   }
} catch (Exception ex) { ex.printStackTrace(); }
```

The result will be as follows (we have shown only the first few lines of the output):

```
traverseRS(select * from texts):

Update count = 1
package com.packt.cookbook.ch06_db;

import org.postgresql.ds.PGSimpleDataSource;
import org.postgresql.ds.PGPoolingDataSource;
import org.postgresql.largeobject.LargeObject;
import org.postgresql.largeobject.LargeObjectManager;
```

For bigger objects, streaming methods would be a better (if not the only) choice:

```
traverseRS("select * from texts");
System.out.println();
try (Connection conn = getDbConnection()) {
   String sql = "insert into texts (id, text) values (?, ?)";
   try (PreparedStatement st = conn.prepareStatement(sql)) {
     st.setInt(1, 100);
     File file = new File("src/main/java/com/packt/cookbook/ch06_db/"
                                        + "Chapter06Database.java");
     //This is not implemented:
     //st.setCharacterStream(2, reader, file.length());
     st.setCharacterStream(2, reader, (int)file.length());

     int count = st.executeUpdate();
     System.out.println("Update count = " + count);
   }
} catch (Exception ex) { ex.printStackTrace(); }
System.out.println();
traverseRS("select * from texts");
```

Note that, as of the time of writing this book, setCharacterStream(int, Reader, long) is not implemented, while setCharacterStream(int, Reader, int) works just fine.

We can also read the file from the `texts` table as a character stream and limit it to the first 160 characters:

```
String sql = "select text from texts where id = ?";
try (PreparedStatement st = conn.prepareStatement(sql)) {
  st.setInt(1, 100);
  try(ResultSet rs = st.executeQuery()){
    while (rs.next()) {
      try(Reader reader = rs.getCharacterStream(1)) {
        char[] chars = new char[160];
        reader.read(chars);
        System.out.println(chars);
      }
    }
  }
}
```

The result will be as follows:

```
package com.packt.cookbook.ch06_db;

import org.postgresql.ds.PGSimpleDataSource;
import org.postgresql.ds.PGPoolingDataSource;

import java.io.File;
import jav
```

There's more...

Here is another recommendation from the PostgreSQL documentation (you can access it at `https://jdbc.postgresql.org/documentation/80/binary-data.html`):

"The BYTEA data type is not well suited for storing very large amounts of binary data. While a column of type BYTEA can hold up to 1 GB of binary data, it would require a huge amount of memory to process such a large value.
The Large Object method for storing binary data is better suited to storing very large values, but it has its own limitations. Specifically deleting a row that contains a Large Object reference does not delete the Large Object. Deleting the Large Object is a separate operation that needs to be performed. Large Objects also have some security issues since anyone connected to the database can view and/or modify any Large Object, even if they don't have permissions to view/update the row containing the Large Object reference."

While deciding to store LOBs in a database, you need to remember that the bigger the database, the more difficult it is to maintain it. The speed of access—the main advantage of choosing a database as a storage facility—also decreases, and it is not possible to create indices for LOB types to improve the search. Also, you cannot use LOB columns in a WHERE clause, except for a few CLOB cases, or use LOB columns in multiple rows of INSERT or UPDATE statements.

So, before thinking about a database for a LOB, you should always consider whether storing the name of a file, keywords, and some other content properties in the database would be enough for the solution.

Executing stored procedures

In this recipe, you will learn how to execute a database-stored procedure from a Java program.

Getting ready

Once in a while, a Java programmer encounters the need to manipulate and/or select data in/from several tables, and so the programmer comes up with a set of complex SQL statements that are impractical to implement in Java or it is strongly suspected that the Java implementation might not yield an adequate performance. This is when the set of SQL statements can be wrapped into a stored procedure that is compiled and stored in the database and then invoked via the JDBC interface. Or, in another twist of fate, a Java programmer might encounter the need for incorporating a call to an existing stored procedure into the program. To accomplish this, the interface CallableStatement (which extends the PreparedStatement interface) can be used, although some databases allow you to call a stored procedure using either an interface Statement or a PreparedStatement.

CallableStatement can have parameters of three types—IN for an input value, OUT for the result, and IN OUT for either an input or an output value. OUT parameters must be registered by the registerOutParameter() method of CallableStatement. The IN parameters can be set the same way as the parameters of PreparedStatement.

Bear in mind that executing a stored procedure from Java programmatically is one of the least standardized areas. PostgreSQL, for example, does not support stored procedures directly, but they can be invoked as functions, which have been modified for this purpose by interpreting OUT parameters as return values. Oracle, on the other hand, allows OUT parameters for functions too.

This is why the following differences between database functions and stored procedures can serve only as a general guideline and not as a formal definition:

- A function has a return value, but it does not allow OUT parameters (except for some databases) and can be used in a SQL statement.
- A stored procedure does not have a return value (except for some databases); it allows OUT parameters (for most databases) and can be executed using the JDBC interface CallableStatement.

This is why reading the database documentation to learn how to execute a stored procedure is very important.

Since stored procedures are compiled and stored on the database server, the execute() method of CallableStatement performs better for the same SQL statement than the corresponding method of Statement or PreparedStatement. This is one of the reasons a lot of Java code is sometimes replaced by one or several stored procedures that include even the business logic. But there is no right answer for every case and problem, so we will refrain from making specific recommendations, except to repeat the familiar mantra about the value of testing and the clarity of the code you are writing.

How to do it...

As in the previous recipe, we will continue using the PostgreSQL database for demonstration purposes. Before writing custom SQL statements, functions, and stored procedures, you should look at the list of already existing functions first. Usually, they provide a wealth of functionality.

Here is an example of calling the replace(string text, from text, to text) function that searches the first parameter (string text) and replaces it with all the substrings that match the second parameter (from text) with the substring provided by the third parameter (string text):

```
String sql = "{ ? = call replace(?, ?, ? ) }";
try (CallableStatement st = conn.prepareCall(sql)) {
  st.registerOutParameter(1, Types.VARCHAR);
```

```
        st.setString(2, "Hello, World! Hello!");
        st.setString(3, "llo");
        st.setString(4, "y");
        st.execute();
        String res = st.getString(1);
        System.out.println(res);
    }
```

The result is as follows:

```
Hey, World! Hey!
```

We will incorporate this function into our custom functions and stored procedures to show you how this can be done.

A stored procedure can be without any parameters at all, with IN parameters only, with OUT parameters only, or with both. The result may be one or multiple values, or a ResultSet object. Here is an example of creating a stored procedure without any parameters in PostgreSQL:

```
execute("create or replace function createTableTexts() "
        + " returns void as "
        + "$$ drop table if exists texts; "
        + "   create table texts (id integer, text text); "
        + "$$ language sql");
```

In the preceding code, we use the method execute(), which we are already familiar with:

```
void execute(String sql){
    try (Connection conn = getDbConnection()) {
        try (PreparedStatement st = conn.prepareStatement(sql)) {
            st.execute();
        }
    } catch (Exception ex) {
        ex.printStackTrace();
    }
}
```

This stored procedure (it is always a function in PostgreSQL) creates the texts table (after dropping it if the table existed already). You can find the syntax of the SQL for function creation in the database documentation. The only thing we would like to comment on here is that instead of the symbol $$ that denotes the function body, you can use single quotes. We prefer $$, though, because it helps avoid the escaping of single quotes if we need to include them in the body of the function.

After being created and stored in the database, the procedure can be invoked by
`CallableStatement`:

```
String sql = "{ call createTableTexts() }";
try (CallableStatement st = conn.prepareCall(sql)) {
  st.execute();
}
```

Alternatively, it can be invoked with the SQL statement `select
createTableTexts()` or `select * from createTableTexts()`. Both statements
return a `ResultSet` object (which is `null` in the case of the `createTableTexts()`
function), so we can traverse it by our method:

```
void traverseRS(String sql){
   System.out.println("traverseRS(" + sql + "):");
   try (Connection conn = getDbConnection()) {
     try (Statement st = conn.createStatement()) {
       try(ResultSet rs = st.executeQuery(sql)){
         int cCount = 0;
         Map<Integer, String> cName = new HashMap<>();
         while (rs.next()) {
           if (cCount == 0) {
             ResultSetMetaData rsmd = rs.getMetaData();
             cCount = rsmd.getColumnCount();
             for (int i = 1; i <= cCount; i++) {
               cName.put(i, rsmd.getColumnLabel(i));
             }
           }
           List<String> l = new ArrayList<>();
           for (int i = 1; i <= cCount; i++) {
             l.add(cName.get(i) + " = " + rs.getString(i));
           }
           System.out.println(l.stream()
                      .collect(Collectors.joining(", ")));
         }
       }
     }
   } catch (Exception ex) { ex.printStackTrace(); }
}
```

We have already used this method in the previous recipes.

The function can be deleted by using the following statement:

```
drop function if exists createTableTexts();
```

Now, let's put all of this together in Java code, create a function, and invoke it in three different styles:

```
execute("create or replace function createTableTexts() "
        + "returns void as "
        + "$$ drop table if exists texts; "
        + "  create table texts (id integer, text text); "
        + "$$ language sql");
String sql = "{ call createTableTexts() }";
try (Connection conn = getDbConnection()) {
  try (CallableStatement st = conn.prepareCall(sql)) {
    st.execute();
  }
}
traverseRS("select createTableTexts()");
traverseRS("select * from createTableTexts()");
execute("drop function if exists createTableTexts()");
```

The result is as follows:

```
traverseRS(select createTexts()):
createtexts = null
traverseRS(select * from createTexts()):
createtexts = null
```

As was expected, the returned `ResultSet` object is `null`. Note that the name of the function is case-insensitive. We keep it in camel case style for human readability only.

Now, let's create and call another stored procedure (function) with two input parameters:

```
execute("create or replace function insertText(int,varchar)"
        + " returns void "
        + " as $$ insert into texts (id, text) "
        + "   values($1, replace($2,'XX','ext'));"
        + " $$ language sql");
String sql = "{ call insertText(?, ?) }";
try (Connection conn = getDbConnection()) {
  try (CallableStatement st = conn.prepareCall(sql)) {
    st.setInt(1, 1);
    st.setString(2, "TXX 1");
    st.execute();
```

```
        }
    }
    execute("select insertText(2, 'TXX 2')");
    traverseRS("select * from texts");
    execute("drop function if exists insertText()");
```

In the body of the function, the input parameters are referred to by their position as $1 and $2. As was mentioned before, we also used the built-in `replace()` function to manipulate the values of the second input parameter before inserting it into the table. The newly created stored procedure is called twice: first via `CallableStatment` and then via the `execute()` method, with different input values. Then, we looked inside the table using `traverseRS("select * from texts")` and dropped the newly created function to perform a cleanup. We dropped the function just for this demo. In real-life code, the function, once created, stays and takes advantage of being there, compiled and ready to run.

If we run the preceding code, we'll get the following result:

```
traverseRS(select * from texts):
id = 1, text = Text 1
id = 2, text = Text 2
```

Now let's add two rows to the `texts` table and then look into it and create a stored procedure (function) that counts the number of rows in the table and returns the result:

```
    execute("insert into texts (id, text) "
            + "values(3,'Text 3'),(4,'Text 4')");
    traverseRS("select * from texts");
    execute("create or replace function countTexts() "
            + "returns bigint as "
            + "$$ select count(*) from texts; "
            + "$$ language sql");
    String sql = "{ ? = call countTexts() }";
    try (Connection conn = getDbConnection()) {
      try (CallableStatement st = conn.prepareCall(sql)) {
        st.registerOutParameter(1, Types.BIGINT);
        st.execute();
        System.out.println("Result of countTexts() = " + st.getLong(1));
      }
    }
    traverseRS("select countTexts()");
    traverseRS("select * from countTexts()");
    execute("drop function if exists countTexts()");
```

Note the `bigint` value of the returned value and the matching type for
the `OUT` parameter `Types.BIGINT`. The newly created stored procedure is executed
three times and then deleted. The result is as follows:

```
Result of countTexts() = 4
traverseRS(select * from texts):
id = 1, text = Text 1
id = 2, text = Text 2
id = 3, text = Text 3
id = 4, text = Text 4
traverseRS(select countTexts()):
counttexts = 4
traverseRS(select * from countTexts()):
counttexts = 4
```

Now, let's look at an example of a stored procedure with one input parameter of the
type `int` that returns the `ResultSet` object:

```
execute("create or replace function selectText(int) "
        + "returns setof texts as "
        + "$$ select * from texts where id=$1; "
        + "$$ language sql");
traverseRS("select selectText(1)");
traverseRS("select * from selectText(1)");
execute("drop function if exists selectText(int)");
```

Note the return type defined as `setof texts`, where `texts` is the name of the table.
If we run the preceding code, the result will be as follows:

```
traverseRS(select selectText(1)):
selecttext = (1,"Text 1")
traverseRS(select * from selectText(1)):
id = 1, text = Text 1
```

It's worth analyzing the difference in the `ResultSet` content of two different calls to
the stored procedure. Without `select *`, it contains the name of the procedure and
the returned object (of the `ResultSet` type). But with `select *`, it returns the actual
`ResultSet` content from the last SQL statement in the procedure.

Naturally, the question arises why we could not call this stored procedure via
`CallableStatement`, as follows:

```
String sql = "{ ? = call selectText(?) }";
try (CallableStatement st = conn.prepareCall(sql)) {
  st.registerOutParameter(1, Types.OTHER);
  st.setInt(2, 1);
  st.execute();
  traverseRS((ResultSet)st.getObject(1));
}
```

We tried, but it did not work. Here is what the PostgreSQL documentation has to say
about it:

> *"Functions that return data as a set should not be called via the CallableStatement
> interface, but instead should use the normal Statement or PreparedStatement
> interfaces."*

There is a way around this limitation, though. The same database documentation
describes how to retrieve a `refcursor` (a PostgreSQL-specific feature) value that can
then be cast to `ResultSet`:

```
execute("create or replace function selectText(int) "
        + "returns refcursor " +
        + "as $$ declare curs refcursor; "
        + " begin "
        + "    open curs for select * from texts where id=$1;"
        + "      return curs; "
        + " end; "
        + "$$ language plpgsql");
String sql = "{ ? = call selectText(?) }";
try (Connection conn = getDbConnection()) {
  conn.setAutoCommit(false);
  try(CallableStatement st = conn.prepareCall(sql)){
    st.registerOutParameter(1, Types.OTHER);
    st.setInt(2, 2);
    st.execute();
    try(ResultSet rs = (ResultSet) st.getObject(1)){
      System.out.println("traverseRS(refcursor()=>rs):");
      traverseRS(rs);
    }
  }
}
traverseRS("select selectText(2)");
traverseRS("select * from selectText(2)");
execute("drop function if exists selectText(int)");
```

A few comments about the preceding code would probably help you understand how this was done:

- Autocommit has to be turned off.
- Inside the function, $1 refers to the first IN parameter (not counting the OUT parameter).
- The language is set to plpgsql to access the refcursor functionality (PL/pgSQL is a loadable procedural language of the PostgreSQL database).
- To traverse ResultSet, we wrote a new method, as follows:

```
void traverseRS(ResultSet rs) throws Exception {
  int cCount = 0;
  Map<Integer, String> cName = new HashMap<>();
  while (rs.next()) {
    if (cCount == 0) {
      ResultSetMetaData rsmd = rs.getMetaData();
      cCount = rsmd.getColumnCount();
      for (int i = 1; i <= cCount; i++) {
        cName.put(i, rsmd.getColumnLabel(i));
      }
    }
    List<String> l = new ArrayList<>();
    for (int i = 1; i <= cCount; i++) {
      l.add(cName.get(i) + " = " + rs.getString(i));
    }
    System.out.println(l.stream()
            .collect(Collectors.joining(", ")));
  }
}
```

So, our old friend the traverseRS(String sql) method can now be refactored into the following form:

```
void traverseRS(String sql){
  System.out.println("traverseRS(" + sql + "):");
  try (Connection conn = getDbConnection()) {
    try (Statement st = conn.createStatement()) {
      try(ResultSet rs = st.executeQuery(sql)){
        traverseRS(rs);
      }
    }
  } catch (Exception ex) { ex.printStackTrace(); }
}
```

If we run the last example, the result will be as follows:

```
traverseRS(refcursor()=>rs):
id = 2, text = Text 2
traverseRS(select selectText(2)):
selecttext = <unnamed portal 1>
traverseRS(select * from selectText(2)):
selecttext = <unnamed portal 1>
```

You can see that the result-traversing methods that do not extract an object and cast it to `ResultSet` don't show the correct data in this case.

There's more...

We covered the most popular cases of calling stored procedures from Java code. The scope of this book does not allow us to present more complex and potentially useful forms of stored procedures in PostgreSQL and other databases. However, we would like to mention them here, so that you have an idea of other possibilities:

- Functions on composite types
- Functions with parameter names
- Functions with variable numbers of arguments
- Functions with default values for arguments
- Functions as table sources
- Functions returning tables
- Polymorphic SQL functions
- Functions with collations

Using batch operations for a large set of data

In this recipe, you will learn how to create and execute many **batches** of SQL statements with a single call to a database.

Getting ready

Batch processing is required when many SQL statements have to be executed at the same time to insert, update, or read database records. Executing several SQL statements can be done by iterating over them and sending each to the database one by one, but it incurs a network overhead that can be avoided by sending all the queries to the database at the same time.

To avoid this network overhead, all the SQL statements can be combined into one `String` value, and each statement is separated by a semicolon, so they all can be sent to the database in one call. The returned result, if present, is also sent back as a collection of result sets generated by each statement. Such a processing is usually called bulk processing to distinguish it from a batch processing that's available only for `INSERT` and `UPDATE` statements. Batch processing allows you to combine many SQL statements using `addBatch()` method of the interface `java.sql.Statement` or `java.sql.PreparedStatement`.

We will use the PostgreSQL database and the following table, `person`, to insert, update, and read data from it:

```
create table person (
    name VARCHAR NOT NULL,
    age INTEGER NOT NULL
)
```

As you can see, each record of the table can contain two attributes of a person—name and age.

How to do it...

We are going to demonstrate both **bulk processing** and **batch processing**. In order to accomplish it, let's follow these steps:

1. An example of bulk processing is a single `INSERT` statement with multiple `VALUES` clauses:

```
INSERT into <table_name> (column1, column2, ...) VALUES
                         ( value1,  value2, ...),
                         ( value1,  value2, ...),
                          ...
                         ( value1,  value2, ...)
```

The code that constructs such a statement looks as follows:

```
int n = 100000;  //number of records to insert
StringBuilder sb =
 new StringBuilder("insert into person (name,age) values ");
for(int i = 0; i < n; i++){
    sb.append("(")
        .append("'Name").append(String.valueOf(i)).append("',")
        .append(String.valueOf((int)(Math.random() * 100)))
        .append(")");
    if(i < n - 1) {
        sb.append(",");
    }
}
try(Connection conn = getConnection();
    Statement st = conn.createStatement()){
    st.execute(sb.toString());
} catch (SQLException ex){
    ex.printStackTrace();
}
```

As you can see, the preceding code constructs a statement with 100,000 VALUES clauses, which means it inserts 100,000 records in one trip to a database. In our experiment, it took 1,082 milliseconds to complete this job. As the result, the table `person` now contains 100,000 records of persons with names from Name0 to Name99999 and age as a random number from 1 to 99 inclusive.

There are two disadvantages of this method of bulk processing—it is susceptible to the SQL injection attack and can consume too much memory. SQL injection can be addressed by using `PreparedStatement`, but it is limited by the number of bind variables. In the case of PostgreSQL, it cannot be more than 32767. This means that we would need to break the single `PreparedStatement` into several smaller ones, each having no more than 32767 bind variables. Incidentally, it will also address the memory consumption problem, since each statement is now much smaller than the large one. The previous single statement, for example, includes 200,000 values.

2. The following code addresses both problems by breaking the single SQL statement into smaller `PreparedStatement` objects, each with no more than `32766` bind variables:

```
int n = 100000, limit = 32766, l = 0;
List<String> queries = new ArrayList<>();
List<Integer> bindVariablesCount = new ArrayList<>();
String insert = "insert into person (name, age) values ";
StringBuilder sb = new StringBuilder(insert);
for(int i = 0; i < n; i++){
    sb.append("(?, ?)");
    l = l + 2;
    if(i == n - 1) {
        queries.add(sb.toString());
        bindVariablesCount.add(l % limit);
    }
    if(l % limit == 0) {
        queries.add(sb.toString());
        bindVariablesCount.add(limit);
        sb = new StringBuilder(insert);
    } else {
        sb.append(",");
    }
}
try(Connection conn = getConnection()) {
    int i = 0, q = 0;
    for(String query: queries){
        try(PreparedStatement pst =
conn.prepareStatement(query)) {
            int j = 0;
            while (j < bindVariablesCount.get(q)) {
                pst.setString(++j, "Name" +
String.valueOf(i++));
                pst.setInt(++j, (int)(Math.random() * 100));
            }
            pst.executeUpdate();
            q++;
        }
    }
} catch (SQLException ex){
    ex.printStackTrace();
}
```

The previous code executes as quickly as our previous example. It took 1,175 milliseconds to complete this job. But we ran this code on the same computer where the database is installed, so there is no the network overhead from the seven trips to the database (that was how many queries were added to the List queries). But, as you can see, the code is quite complex. It can be substantially simplified by using batch processing.

3. Batch processing is based on the usage of the methods addBatch() and executeBatch(), which are available in both—Statement and PreparedStatement—interfaces. For our demonstration, we will use PreparedStatement for two reasons—it is not susceptible to SQL injection and performs better when executed many times (that is the main purpose of PreparedStatement—to take advantage of multiple executions of the same statement with different values):

```
int n = 100000;
String insert =
          "insert into person (name, age) values (?, ?)";
try (Connection conn = getConnection();
    PreparedStatement pst = conn.prepareStatement(insert)) {
    for (int i = 0; i < n; i++) {
        pst.setString(1, "Name" + String.valueOf(i));
        pst.setInt(2, (int)(Math.random() * 100));
        pst.addBatch();
    }
    pst.executeBatch();
} catch (SQLException ex) {
    ex.printStackTrace();
}
```

It took 2,299 milliseconds to insert 100,000 records in the person table, which is almost twice as long if compared with using a single statement with multiple VALUES clauses (the first example) or using multiple PreparedStatement objects (the second example). Although its execution takes longer, this code has the obvious advantage of being much simpler. And it sends the batch of statements to the database in one trip, which means that the gap in performance between this implementation and the previous one (with seven trips to the database) will be smaller when the database is not collocated with the application.

But this implementation can be improved too.

4. To improve the batch processing, let's add
   the `reWriteBatchedInserts` property to the `DataSource` object and set
   it to `true`:

```
DataSource createDataSource() {
    HikariDataSource ds = new HikariDataSource();
    ds.setPoolName("cookpool");
    ds.setDriverClassName("org.postgresql.Driver");
    ds.setJdbcUrl("jdbc:postgresql://localhost/cookbook");
    ds.setUsername( "cook");
    //ds.setPassword("123Secret");
    ds.setMaximumPoolSize(2);
    ds.setMinimumIdle(2);
    ds.addDataSourceProperty("reWriteBatchedInserts",
                                            Boolean.TRUE);
    return ds;
}
```

Now, if we run the same batch processing code using the connection
`createDataSource().getConnection()`, the time it takes to insert same
100,000 records drops to 750 milliseconds, which is 25% better than any of
the implementations we have tested so far. And the code remains much
simpler than any of the previous implementations.

But what about memory consumption?

5. As the size of the batch grows, at some point, JVM may run out of memory.
   In such a case, batch processing can be broken into several batches, each
   delivered to the database in a separate trip:

```
int n = 100000;
int batchSize = 30000;
boolean execute = false;
String insert =
        "insert into person (name, age) values (?, ?)";
try (Connection conn = getConnection();
    PreparedStatement pst = conn.prepareStatement(insert)) {
    for (int i = 0; i < n; i++) {
        pst.setString(1, "Name" + String.valueOf(i));
        pst.setInt(2, (int)(Math.random() * 100));
        pst.addBatch();
        if((i > 0 && i % batchSize == 0) ||
                            (i == n - 1 && execute)) {
            pst.executeBatch();
            System.out.print(" " + i);
                    //prints: 30000 60000 90000 99999
            if(n - 1 - i < batchSize && !execute){
```

```
                    execute = true;
            }
        }
    }
    pst.executeBatch();
} catch (SQLException ex) {
    ex.printStackTrace();
}
```

We use variable the `execute` as the flag that indicates that we need to call `executeBatch()` one more time when the last statement is added to the batch if this last batch is smaller than the `batchSize` value. As you can see from the comment to the previous code, `executeBatch()` was called four times, including when the last statement was added (when `i=99999`). The performance of this code in our runs was the same as without generating multiple batches, because our database is located on the same computer as the application. Otherwise, the delivery of each batch over the network would add to the time that it took to execute this code.

How it works...

The last example (step 5) of the previous sub-section is an ultimate implementation of a batch process that can be used for inserting and updating records in a database. The method `executeBatch()` returns an array of `int`, which, in the case of success, indicates how many rows were updated by each of the statements in the batch. In the case of an `INSERT` statement, this value equals -2 (negative two), which is the value of the static constant `Statement.SUCCESS_NO_INFO`. The value of -3 (negative three), which is the value of the constant `Statement.EXECUTE_FAILED`, indicates a statement failure.

If the returned updated row count is expected to be bigger than `Integer.MAX_VALUE`, use the method `long[] executeLargeBatch()` to execute the batch.

There is no batch processing for reading data from the database. To read data in bulk, you can send many statements separated by a semicolon as one string to the database and then iterate over the returned multiple result sets. For example, let's submit SELECT statements that count the number of records for each of the age values from 1 to 99 inclusive:

```
int minAge = 0, maxAge = 0, minCount = n, maxCount = 0;
StringBuilder sb = new StringBuilder();
for (int i = 0; i < 100; i++) {
    sb.append("select count(*) from person where age = ")
                                    .append(i).append(";");
}
try (Connection conn = getConnection();
     PreparedStatement pst = conn.prepareStatement(sb.toString())) {
    boolean hasResult = pst.execute();
    int i = 0;
    while (hasResult){
        try (ResultSet rs = pst.getResultSet()) {
            rs.next();
            int c = rs.getInt(1);
            if(c < minCount) {
                minAge = i;
                minCount = c;
            }
            if(c > maxCount) {
                maxAge = i;
                maxCount = c;
            }
            i++;
            hasResult = pst.getMoreResults();
        }
    }
} catch (SQLException ex) {
    ex.printStackTrace();
}
System.out.println("least popular age=" + minAge + "(" + minCount +
            "), most popular age=" + maxAge + "(" + maxCount + ")");
```

In our test run, it took 2,162 milliseconds to execute the preceding code and display the following message:

```
least popular age=14(929), most popular age=10(1080)
```

There's more...

Moving large sets of data to and from PostgreSQL database can also be done using the COPY command, which copies data to and from a file. You can read more about it in the database documentation (https://www.postgresql.org/docs/current/static/sql-copy.html).

Using MyBatis for CRUD operations

In the previous recipes, while using JDBC, we had the write code, which extracts the results of the query from a ResultSet object returned by the query. The disadvantage of this approach is that you have to write quite a bit of boilerplate code to create and populate domain objects that represent records in the database. As we have mentioned already in the introduction to this chapter, there are several ORM frameworks that can do this for you and create the corresponding domain objects automatically (or, in other words, to map database records to the corresponding domain objects). Naturally, every such framework takes away some of the control and flexibility in constructing SQL statements. So, before committing to a particular ORM framework, you need to research and experiment with different frameworks to find the one that provides everything the application needs with respect to the database and does not create too much of an overhead.

In this recipe, you will learn about the SQL Mapper tool MyBatis, which simplifies database programming compared to using JDBC directly.

Getting ready

MyBatis is a lightweight ORM framework that allows not only mapping the results to Java objects but also executing an arbitrary SQL statement. There are principally two ways to describe the mapping:

- Using Java annotations
- Using XML configuration

In this recipe, we are going to use XML configuration. But, whichever style you prefer, you need to create an object of the type `org.apache.ibatis.session.SqlSessionFactory` and then use it to start a MyBatis session by creating an object of the type `org.apache.ibatis.session.SqlSession`:

```
InputStream inputStream =
Resources.getResourceAsStream(configuration);
SqlSessionFactory sqlSessionFactory =
                      new
SqlSessionFactoryBuilder().build(inputStream);
SqlSession session = sqlSessionFactory.openSession();
```

The `SqlSessionFactoryBuilder` object has nine overloaded `build()` methods that create the `SqlSession` object. These methods allow for configuring the SQL execution environment. Using them, you can define the following:

- Whether you prefer to auto-commit database changes or to do them explicitly (we use the latter in our examples)
- Whether you will use the configured datasource (as in our examples) or use the externally provided database connection
- Whether you will use the default database-specific transaction isolation level (as in our example) or would like to set your own
- Which of the following `ExecutorType` values you will use—`SIMPLE` (default, creates a new `PreparedStatement` for each execution of a statement), `REUSE` (reuses `PreparedStatements`), or `BATCH` (batches all update statements and demarcate them as necessary if `SELECT`s are executed between them)
- Which environment (`development`, `test`, or `production`, for example) this code is deployed to, so the corresponding section of the configuration will be used (we will discuss it shortly)
- The `Properties` object that contains the configuration of the datasource

The `SqlSession` object provides methods that allow you to execute `SELECT`, `INSERT`, `UPDATE`, and `DELETE` statements that are defined in the SQL mapping XML files. It also allows you to commit or rollback the current transaction.

The Maven dependency we used for this recipe is as follows:

```
<dependency>
    <groupId>org.mybatis</groupId>
    <artifactId>mybatis</artifactId>
    <version>3.4.6</version>
</dependency>
```

At the time of writing this book, the latest MyBatis documentation can be found here: http://www.mybatis.org/mybatis-3/index.html

How to do it...

We will start with CRUD operations by using the PostgreSQL database and the class Person1:

```
public class Person1 {
    private int id;
    private int age;
    private String name;
    public Person1(){}  //Must be present, used by the framework
    public Person1(int age, String name){
        this.age = age;
        this.name = name;
    }
    public int getId() { return id; }
    public void setName(String name) { this.name = name; }
    @Override
    public String toString() {
        return "Person1{id=" + id + ", age=" + age +
                                  ", name='" + name + "'}";
    }
}
```

We need the previous getId() method to get an ID value (to demonstrate how to find a database record by ID). The method setName() will be used to update the database record, and the method toString() will be used to display the results. We use the name Person1 to distinguish it from another version of the same class, Person2, which we will use to demonstrate how to implement the relationship between classes and the corresponding tables.

The matching database table can be created using the following SQL statement:

```sql
create table person1 (
    id SERIAL PRIMARY KEY,
    age INTEGER NOT NULL,
    name VARCHAR NOT NULL
);
```

Then execute the following steps:

1. Start by creating an XML configuration file. We will call it mb-config1.xml and place it in the folder mybatis under resources. This way, Maven will put it on a classpath. Another option would be to place the file in any other folder along with the Java code and modify pom.xml to tell Maven to put the .xml files from that folder on the classpath too. The content of the mb-config1.xml file looks as follows:

```xml
<?xml version="1.0" encoding="UTF-8" ?>
<!DOCTYPE configuration
        PUBLIC "-//mybatis.org//DTD Config 3.0//EN"
        "http://mybatis.org/dtd/mybatis-3-config.dtd">
<configuration>
  <settings>
    <setting name="useGeneratedKeys" value="true"/>
  </settings>
  <typeAliases>
    <typeAlias
type="com.packt.cookbook.ch06_db.mybatis.Person1"
alias="Person"/>
  </typeAliases>
  <environments default="development">
      <environment id="development">
        <transactionManager type="JDBC"/>
        <dataSource type="POOLED">
            <property name="driver"
value="org.postgresql.Driver"/>
            <property name="url"
value="jdbc:postgresql://localhost/cookbook"/>
            <property name="username" value="cook"/>
            <property name="password" value=""/>
        </dataSource>
      </environment>
  </environments>
  <mappers>
      <mapper resource="mybatis/Person1Mapper.xml"/>
  </mappers>
</configuration>
```

The <settings> tag allows for defining some behavior globally—lazy loading of the values, enable/disable the cache, set auto-mapping behavior (to populate nested data or not), and more. We have chosen to set the usage of auto-generated keys globally because we need the inserted objects to be populated with IDs generated in the database.

The <typeAiases> tag contains aliases of the fully qualified class names, which work similar to the IMPORT statement. The only difference is that an alias can be any word, not just a class name. After the alias is declared, everywhere else in the MyBatis .xml files, the class can be referred by this alias only. We will see how to do this while reviewing the content of the file Person1Mapper.xml shortly.

The <environments> tag contains configuration for different environments. For example, we could have a configuration for the environment env42 (any string would do). Then, while creating a SqlSession object, you can pass this name as the parameter of the method SqlSessionFactory.build() and the configuration included in the tags <environment id="env42"></environment> will be used. It defines the transaction manager to be used and the datasource.

The TransactionManager may be one of two types—JDBC, which uses the connection provided by the datasource to commit, rollback, and manage the scope of the transaction, and MANAGED, which does nothing and allows the container to manage the lifecycle of the transaction—well, it closes the connection by default, but that behavior can be changed by setting the following property:

```
<transactionManager type="MANAGED">
    <property name="closeConnection"
value="false"/>
</transactionManager>
```

The tag <mappers> contains references to all the .xml files that contain SQL statements that map database records and Java objects, which in our case is the file Person1Mapper.xml.

2. Create the `Person1Mapper.xml` file and put it in the same folder as the `mb-config1.xml` file. This file can have any name you like, but it contains all SQL statements that map database records and objects of the class `Person1`, so we have named it `Person1Mapper.xml` just for the sake of clarity:

```xml
<?xml version="1.0" encoding="UTF-8" ?>
<!DOCTYPE mapper
        PUBLIC "-//mybatis.org//DTD Mapper 3.0//EN"
        "http://mybatis.org/dtd/mybatis-3-mapper.dtd">
<mapper namespace="mybatis.Person1Mapper">
    <insert id="insertPerson" keyProperty="id" keyColumn="id"
parameterType="Person">
        insert into Person1 (age, name) values(#{age}, #{name})
    </insert>
    <select id="selectPersonById" parameterType="int"
resultType="Person">
        select * from Person1 where id = #{id}
    </select>
    <select id="selectPersonsByName" parameterType="string"
resultType="Person">
        select * from Person1 where name = #{name}
    </select>
    <select id="selectPersons" resultType="Person">
        select * from Person1
    </select>
    <update id="updatePersonById" parameterType="Person">
        update Person1 set age = #{age}, name = #{name}
                                            where id = #{id}
    </update>
    <delete id="deletePersons">
        delete from Person1
    </delete>
</mapper>
```

As you can see, the `<mapper>` tag has a `namespace` attribute which is used to resolve files with the same name in different locations. It may or may not match the mapper file location. The mapper file location is specified in the configuration file `mb-config1.xml` as the attribute resource of the tag `<mapper>` (see the previous step).

The attributes of the tags `<insert>`, `<select>`, `<update>`, and `<delete>` are self-explanatory for the most part. The attributes `keyProperty`, `keyColumn`, and `useGeneratedKeys` (in the configuration `<settings>`) are added to populate the inserted object with the value generated by the database. If you don't need it globally, the attribute `useGeneratedKeys` can be removed from the settings in the configuration and added only to those insert statements where you would like to take advantage of the auto-generation of some value. We did this because we wanted to get the generated ID and use it in the code later to demonstrate how the record can be retrieved by ID.

The ID attribute of `<select>` and similar tags are used to invoke, them along with the mapper namespace value. We will show you how this is done shortly. The construct `#{id}` refers to the value passed in as a parameter if the value is of a primitive type. Otherwise, the passed in object is expected to have such a field. Having a getter on the object is not required. If a getter is present, it has to comply with the JavaBean method format.

For the return value, by default, the name of a column matches the name of the object field or setter (has to be compliant with JavaBean method format). If the field (or the setter name) and the column name are different, you can provide mapping using the tag `<resultMap>`. For example, if the table `person` has the columns `person_id` and `person_name`, while the domain object `Person` has the fields `id` and `name`, we can create a map:

```
<resultMap id="personResultMap" type="Person">
    <id property="id" column="person_id" />
    <result property="name" column="person_name"/>
</resultMap>
```

This `resultMap` can then used to populate the domain object `Person` as follows:

```
<select id="selectPersonById" parameterType="int"
resultMap="personResultMap">
   select person_id, person_name from Person where id =
#{id}
</select>
```

Alternatively, it is possible to use the standard select clause aliases:

```
<select id="selectPersonById" parameterType="int"
resultType="Person">
   select person_id as "id", person_name as "name" from
Person
                                             where id =
#{id}
</select>
```

3. Write code that inserts a record in the table `person1` and then reads this record by `id`:

```
String resource = "mybatis/mb-config1.xml";
String mapperNamespace = "mybatis.Person1Mapper";
try {
   InputStream inputStream =
                   Resources.getResourceAsStream(resource);
   SqlSessionFactory sqlSessionFactory =
          new SqlSessionFactoryBuilder().build(inputStream);
   try(SqlSession session = sqlSessionFactory.openSession()){
       Person1 p = new Person1(10, "John");
       session.insert(mapperNamespace + ".insertPerson", p);
       session.commit();
       p = session.selectOne(mapperNamespace +
                           ".selectPersonById", p.getId());
       System.out.println("By id " + p.getId() + ": " + p);
   } catch (Exception ex) {
       ex.printStackTrace();
   }
} catch (Exception ex){
   ex.printStackTrace();
}
```

The preceding code will produce an output:

By id 1: Person1{id=1, age=10, name='John'}

The utility `Resources` has ten overloaded methods for reading the configuration file. We have already described how to make sure that Maven places the configuration and mapper files on the classpath.

The `SqlSession` object implements the `AutoCloseable` interface, so we can use the try-with-resources block and not worry about leaking resources. The `SqlSession` interface provides many execution methods, including the overloaded methods `insert()`, `select()`, `selectList()`, `selectMap()`, `selectOne()`, `update()`, and `delete()`, to name the most often used and straightforward ones. We also have used `insert()` and `selectOne()`. The latter makes sure that only one result is returned. Otherwise, it throws an exception. It also throws an exception when the column used to identify a single record by a value does not have a unique constraint. That is why we have added the `PRIMARY KEY` qualification to the column ID. Alternatively, we could just add a unique constraint (marking it as `PRIMARY KEY` does this implicitly).

The `selectList()` method, on the other hand, produces a `List` object, even when only one result is returned. We will demonstrate this now.

4. Write code that reads all the records from the table `person1`:

```
List<Person1> list = session.selectList(mapperNamespace
                                + ".selectPersons");
for(Person1 p1: list) {
    System.out.println("All: " + p1);
}
```

The preceding code will produce the following output:

All: Person1{id=1, age=10, name='John'}

5. To demonstrate an update, let's change the name of `"John"` to `"Bill"` and read it all the records in the `person1` again:

```
List<Person1> list = session.selectList(mapperNamespace
                        + ".selectPersonsByName", "John");
for(Person1 p1: list) {
    p1.setName("Bill");
    int c = session.update(mapperNamespace +
                            ".updatePersonById", p1);
    System.out.println("Updated " + c + " records");
}
session.commit();
list =
  session.selectList(mapperNamespace + ".selectPersons");
for(Person1 p1: list) {
    System.out.println("All: " + p1);
}
```

The preceding code will produce the following output:

```
Updated 1 records
All: Person1{id=1, age=10, name='Bill'}
```

Notice how the change was committed: `session.commit()`. Without this line, the result is the same, but the change does not persist because the transaction is not autocomitted by default. It can be changed by setting autocommit to `true` while opening the session:

```
    SqlSession session =
  sqlSessionFactory.openSession(true);
```

6. Finally, call the `DELETE` statement and remove all the records from the table `person1`:

```
int c = session.delete(mapperNamespace + ".deletePersons");
System.out.println("Deleted " + c + " persons");
session.commit();

List<Person1> list = session.selectList(mapperNamespace +
                                        ".selectPersons");
System.out.println("Total records: " + list.size());
```

The preceding code will produce the following output:

```
Deleted 0 persons
Total records: 0
```

7. To demonstrate how MyBatis supports relationships, create the table `family` and the table `person2`:

```
create table family (
    id SERIAL PRIMARY KEY,
    name VARCHAR NOT NULL
);
create table person2 (
    id SERIAL PRIMARY KEY,
    age INTEGER NOT NULL,
    name VARCHAR NOT NULL,
    family_id INTEGER references family(id)
                        ON DELETE CASCADE
);
```

As you can see, the records in the tables `family` and `person2` have one-to-many relationships. Each record of the table `person2` may belong to a family (refer to a `family` record) or not. Several persons can belong to the same family. We have also added the ON DELETE CASCADE clause so that the `person2` records can be deleted automatically when the family they belong to is deleted.

The corresponding Java classes look as follows:

```java
class Family {
    private int id;
    private String name;
    private final List<Person2> members = new ArrayList<>();
    public Family(){}  //Used by the framework
    public Family(String name){ this.name = name; }
    public int getId() { return id; }
    public String getName() { return name; }
    public List<Person2> getMembers(){ return this.members; }
}
```

As you see, the class `Family` has a collection of `Person2` objects. For the methods `getId()` and `getMembers()`, we need to establish the relationship with the `Person2` class. Will will use the method `getName()` for the demonstration code.

The class `Person2` looks as follows:

```java
class Person2 {
    private int id;
    private int age;
    private String name;
    private Family family;
    public Person2(){}  //Used by the framework
    public Person2(int age, String name, Family family){
        this.age = age;
        this.name = name;
        this.family = family;
    }
    @Override
    public String toString() {
        return "Person2{id=" + id + ", age=" + age +
                ", name='" + name + "', family='" +
          (family == null ? "" : family.getName())+ "'}";
    }
}
```

8. Create a new configuration file called `mb-config2.xml`:

```xml
<?xml version="1.0" encoding="UTF-8" ?>
<!DOCTYPE configuration
        PUBLIC "-//mybatis.org//DTD Config 3.0//EN"
        "http://mybatis.org/dtd/mybatis-3-config.dtd">
<configuration>
    <settings>
        <setting name="useGeneratedKeys" value="true"/>
    </settings>
    <typeAliases>
        <typeAlias type="com.packt.cookbook.ch06_db.mybatis.Family"
                                              alias="Family"/>
        <typeAlias type="com.packt.cookbook.ch06_db.mybatis.Person2"
                                              alias="Person"/>
    </typeAliases>
    <environments default="development">
        <environment id="development">
            <transactionManager type="JDBC"/>
            <dataSource type="POOLED">
                <property name="driver" value="org.postgresql.Driver"/>
                <property name="url"
                        value="jdbc:postgresql://localhost/cookbook"/>
                <property name="username" value="cook"/>
                <property name="password" value=""/>
            </dataSource>
        </environment>
    </environments>
    <mappers>
        <mapper resource="mybatis/FamilyMapper.xml"/>
        <mapper resource="mybatis/Person2Mapper.xml"/>
    </mappers>
</configuration>
```

Notice that we now had two aliases and two mapper `.xml` files.

9. The content of the `Person2Mapper.xml` file is much smaller than the content of the `Person1Mapper.xml` file that we used before:

```xml
<?xml version="1.0" encoding="UTF-8" ?>
<!DOCTYPE mapper
        PUBLIC "-//mybatis.org//DTD Mapper 3.0//EN"
        "http://mybatis.org/dtd/mybatis-3-mapper.dtd">
<mapper namespace="mybatis.Person2Mapper">
    <insert id="insertPerson" keyProperty="id" keyColumn="id"
                                        parameterType="Person">
        insert into Person2 (age, name, family_id)
                values(#{age}, #{name}, #{family.id})
```

```
        </insert>
        <select id="selectPersonsCount" resultType="int">
            select count(*) from Person2
        </select>
    </mapper>
```

That is because we are not going to update or manage these persons directly. We are going to do this via the families they belong to. We have added a new query that returns the count of the records in the `person2` table.

10. The content of the `FamilyMapper.xml` file is as follows:

```xml
<?xml version="1.0" encoding="UTF-8" ?>
<!DOCTYPE mapper
 PUBLIC "-//mybatis.org//DTD Mapper 3.0//EN"
 "http://mybatis.org/dtd/mybatis-3-mapper.dtd">
<mapper namespace="mybatis.FamilyMapper">
 <insert id="insertFamily" keyProperty="id" keyColumn="id"
parameterType="Family">
 insert into Family (name) values(#{name})
 </insert>
 <select id="selectMembersOfFamily" parameterType="int"
resultMap="personMap">
 select * from Person2 where family_id = #{id}
 </select>
 <resultMap id="personMap" type="Person">
 <association property="family" column="family_id"
select="selectFamilyById"/>
 </resultMap>
 <select id="selectFamilyById" parameterType="int"
resultType="Family">
 select * from Family where id = #{id}
 </select>
 <select id="selectFamilies" resultMap="familyMap">
 select * from Family
 </select>
 <resultMap id="familyMap" type="Family">
 <collection property="members" column="id" ofType="Person"
select="selectMembersOfFamily"/>
 </resultMap>
 <select id="selectFamiliesCount" resultType="int">
 select count(*) from Family
 </select>
 <delete id="deleteFamilies">
 delete from Family
 </delete>
```

The family mapper is much more involved because we manage the relationship in it. First, look at the query `selectMembersOfFamily`. If you don't want to populate the field `family` in the object of `Person2`, the SQL would be much simpler, as follows:

```
<select id="selectMembersOfFamily" parameterType="int"
                                   resultType="Person">
    select * from Person2 where family_id = #{id}
</select>
```

But we wanted to set the corresponding `Family` object value in the `Person2` object, so we used the `ResultMap personMap` that describes only the mapping that cannot be done by default—we used the `<association>` tag to associate the field `family` with the column `family_id` a using the query `selectFamilyById`. This last query will not populate the field `members` of the `Family` object, but we decided it is not needed for our demonstration.

We reuse the query `selectMembersOfFamily` in the query `selectFamilies`. To populate the field `members` of the `Family` object, we created a `ResultMap familyMap` that uses `selectMembersOfFamily` to do that.

How it works...

Let's write the code that demonstrates CRUD operations on the `family` table. First, here's how a `family` record can be created and associated with two `person2` records:

```
String resource = "mybatis/mb-config2.xml";
String familyMapperNamespace = "mybatis.FamilyMapper";
String personMapperNamespace = "mybatis.Person2Mapper";
try {
    InputStream inputStream = Resources.getResourceAsStream(resource);
    SqlSessionFactory sqlSessionFactory =
            new SqlSessionFactoryBuilder().build(inputStream);
    try(SqlSession session = sqlSessionFactory.openSession()){
        Family f = new Family("The Jones");
        session.insert(familyMapperNamespace + ".insertFamily", f);
        System.out.println("Family id=" + f.getId()); //Family id=1

        Person2 p = new Person2(25, "Jill", f);
        session.insert(personMapperNamespace + ".insertPerson", p);
        System.out.println(p);
```

```
        //Person2{id=1, age=25, name='Jill', family='The Jones'}

    p = new Person2(30, "John", f);
    session.insert(personMapperNamespace + ".insertPerson", p);
    System.out.println(p);
        //Person2{id=2, age=30, name='John', family='The Jones'}

    session.commit();
    } catch (Exception ex) {
        ex.printStackTrace();
    }
} catch (Exception ex){
    ex.printStackTrace();
}
```

Now, we can read the created records by using the following code:

```
List<Family> fList =
        session.selectList(familyMapperNamespace + ".selectFamilies");
for (Family f1: fList) {
    System.out.println("Family " + f1.getName() + " has " +
                            f1.getMembers().size() + " members:");
    for(Person2 p1: f1.getMembers()){
        System.out.println("    " + p1);
    }
}
```

The preceding code snippet produces the following output:

```
Family The Jones has 2 members:
    Person2{id=1, age=25, name='Jill', family='The Jones'}
    Person2{id=2, age=30, name='John', family='The Jones'}
```

Now, we can delete all `family` records and check if any of the tables for `family` and `person2` contain any records after it:

```
int c = session.delete(familyMapperNamespace + ".deleteFamilies");
System.out.println("Deleted " + c + " families");
session.commit();

c = session.selectOne(familyMapperNamespace + ".selectFamiliesCount");
System.out.println("Total family records: " + c);

c = session.selectOne(personMapperNamespace + ".selectPersonsCount");
System.out.println("Total person records: " + c);
```

The output of the preceding code snippet is as follows:

```
Deleted 1 families
Total family records: 0
Total person records: 0
```

The table `person2` is empty now too because we added the clause ON DELETE CASCADE while creating the table.

There's more...

MyBatis also provides facilities for building a dynamic SQL, a SqlBuilder class, and many other ways to construct and execute SQL of any complexity or a stored procedure. For the details, read the documentation at `http://www.mybatis.org/mybatis-3`.

Using the Java Persistence API and Hibernate

In this recipe, you will learn how to populate, read, change, and delete data in the database using a **Java Persistence API (JPA)** implementation called the **Hibernate Object-Relational Mapping (ORM)** framework.

Getting ready

JPA is a specification that defines a possible solution for ORM. You can find JPA Version 2.2 at the following link:

`http://download.oracle.com/otn-pub/jcp/persistence-2_2-mrel-spec/JavaPersistence.pdf`

The interfaces, enums, annotations, and exceptions described in the specification belong to the package `javax.persistence` (`https://javaee.github.io/javaee-spec/javadocs`) that is included in **Java Enterprise Edition (EE)**. The JPA is implemented by several frameworks, the most popular of them being:

- Hibernate ORM (`http://hibernate.org/orm`)
- EclipseLink (`http://www.eclipse.org/eclipselink`)

- Oracle TopLink (http://www.oracle.com/technetwork/middleware/toplink/overview/index.html)
- jOOQ (https://www.jooq.org)

JPA is designed around entities—the Java beans that are mapped to the database tables using annotations. Alternatively, the mapping can be defined using XML or a combination of both. The mapping defined by XML supersedes the one defined by the annotations. The specification also defines an SQL-like query language for static and dynamic data queries.

Most of the JPA implementations allow for the creation of a database schema using the mapping defined by annotations and XML.

How to do it...

1. Let's start with adding the `javax.persistence` package dependency to the Maven configuration file `pom.xml`:

```
<dependency>
    <groupId>javax.persistence</groupId>
    <artifactId>javax.persistence-api</artifactId>
    <version>2.2</version>
</dependency>
```

We don't need any of the JPA implementations yet. This way, we can make sure that our code does not use any framework-specific code and uses only JPA interfaces.

2. Create the class `Person1`:

```
public class Person1 {
    private int age;
    private String name;
    public Person1(int age, String name){
        this.age = age;
        this.name = name;
    }
    @Override
    public String toString() {
        return "Person1{id=" + id + ", age=" + age +
                        ", name='" + name + "'}";
    }
}
```

We don't add getters, setters, or any other methods; this is so that we can keep our code example short and simple. To convert this class into an entity we need, according to the JPA spec, to add the annotation @Entity to the class declaration (requires importing java.persistence.Entity). This means that we would like this class to represent a record in a database table called person. By default, the name of the entity's class matches the name of the table. But it is possible to map the class to a table with another name using the annotation @Table(name="<another table name>"). Similarly, each class property is mapped to a column with the same name, and it is possible to change the default name by using the annotation @Column (name="<another column name>").

In addition, an entity class must have a primary key—a field depicted by the annotation @Id. A composite key that combines several fields can be defined using the annotation @IdClass too (not used in our examples). If the primary key is auto-generated in the database, the @GeneratedValue annotation can be placed in front of that field.

And, finally, an entity class must have a constructor without arguments. With all these annotations, the entity class Person now looks as follows:

```
import javax.persistence.Entity;
import javax.persistence.GeneratedValue;
import javax.persistence.GenerationType;
import javax.persistence.Id;

@Entity
public class Person1 {
    @Id
    @GeneratedValue(strategy = GenerationType.IDENTITY)
    private int id;
    public int age;
    private String name;
    public Person1(){}
    public Person1(int age, String name){
        this.age = age;
        this.name = name;
    }
}
```

Neither the class nor any of its persistent instance variables can be declared final. This way, the implementing frameworks can extend the entity classes and implement the required functionality.

Alternatively, the persistence annotations can be added to the getters and setters, instead of the instance fields (if the method names follow Java bean conventions). But mixing up fields and methods annotations is not allowed and may lead to unexpected consequences.

It is also possible to use an XML file instead of an annotation to define the mapping between a Java class and a database table and columns, but we are going to stay with field level annotations in order to provide the most compact and clear method to express the intent.

3. Create a database table called `person1` using the following SQL script:

```
create table person1 (
    id SERIAL PRIMARY KEY,
    age INTEGER NOT NULL,
    name VARCHAR NOT NULL
);
```

We have defined the column `id` as `SERIAL`, which means that we ask the database to generate the next integer value automatically every time a new row is inserted into the table `person1`. It matches the annotations of the property `id` of the class `Person1`.

4. Now, let's write some code that inserts a record into the table `person1` and then reads all the records from it. To create, update, and delete an entity (and the corresponding record in the corresponding table), you need to use an entity manager such as `javax.persistence.EntityManager`:

```
EntityManagerFactory emf =
        Persistence.createEntityManagerFactory("jpa-demo");
EntityManager em = emf.createEntityManager();
try {
    em.getTransaction().begin();
    Person1 p = new Person1(10, "Name10");
    em.persist(p);
    em.getTransaction().commit();

    Query q = em.createQuery("select p from Person1 p");
    List<Person1> pList = q.getResultList();
    for (Person1 p : pList) {
        System.out.println(p);
    }
    System.out.println("Size: " + pList.size());
} catch (Exception ex){
    em.getTransaction().rollback();
} finally {
```

```
        em.close();
        emf.close();
    }
```

As you can see, an object of `EntityManagerFactory` is created using some configuration, that is, `jpa-demo`. We will talk about it shortly. The factory allows for the creation of an `EntityManager` object, which controls the persistence process: creates, commits, and rolls back a transaction, stores a new `Person1` object (thus inserting a new record in the table `person1`), supports reading data using **Java Persistence Query Language (JPQL)**, and many other database operations and transaction management processes.

After the entity manager is closed, the managed entities are in a detached state. To synchronize them again with the database, one can use the method `merge()` of `EntityManager`.

In the previous example, we have JPQL to query the database. Alternatively, we could use the Criteria API defined by the JPA specification, too:

```
CriteriaQuery<Person1> cq =
        em.getCriteriaBuilder().createQuery(Person1.class);
cq.select(cq.from(Person1.class));
List<Person1> pList = em.createQuery(cq).getResultList();
System.out.println("Size: " + pList.size());
```

But it seems that JPQL is less verbose and supports the intuition of those programmers who know SQL, so we are going to use JPQL.

5. Define the persistence configuration in the file `persistence.xml` located in the folder `resources/META-INF`. The tag `<persistence-unit>` has an attribute name. We have set the attribute value to `jpa-demo`, but you can use any other name you like. This configuration specifies JPA implementation (provider), database connection properties, and many other persistence-related properties in an XML format:

```
<?xml version="1.0" encoding="UTF-8"?>
<persistence xmlns="http://xmlns.jcp.org/xml/ns/persistence"
    xmlns:xsi="http://www.w3.org/2001/XMLSchema-instance"
    xsi:schemaLocation="http://xmlns.jcp.org/xml/ns/persistence
    http://xmlns.jcp.org/xml/ns/persistence/persistence_2_1.xsd"
                                            version="2.1">
    <persistence-unit name="jpa-demo"
                            transaction-type="RESOURCE_LOCAL">
<provider>org.hibernate.jpa.HibernatePersistenceProvider</provider
```

```
>
    <properties>
      <property name="javax.persistence.jdbc.url"
                value="jdbc:postgresql://localhost/cookbook"/>
      <property name="javax.persistence.jdbc.driver"
                                value="org.postgresql.Driver"/>
      <property name="javax.persistence.jdbc.user" value="cook"/>
      <property name="javax.persistence.jdbc.password" value=""/>
    </properties>
  </persistence-unit>
</persistence>
```

Refer to the Oracle documentation (https://docs.oracle.com/cd/E16439_01/ doc.1013/e13981/cfgdepds005.htm) about the configuration of the persistence.xml file. For this recipe, we used the Hibernate ORM and, thus, specified org.hibernate.jpa.HibernatePersistenceProvider as a provider.

6. Finally, we need to add JPA implementation (Hibernate ORM) as a dependency in pom.xml:

```
<dependency>
    <groupId>org.hibernate</groupId>
    <artifactId>hibernate-core</artifactId>
    <version>5.3.1.Final</version>
    <scope>runtime</scope>
</dependency>
<dependency>
    <groupId>javax.xml.bind</groupId>
    <artifactId>jaxb-api</artifactId>
    <version>2.3.0</version>
</dependency>
```

As you may have noticed, we have marked Hibernate dependencies as scoped for runtime. We did this to avoid using Hibernate-specific features while writing the code. We have also added the jaxb-api dependency, which is used by Hibernate, but this library is not Hibernate-specific, so we did not make it used at runtime only.

7. For better result presentation, we will add the following `toString()` method to the class `Person1`:

```
@Override
public String toString() {
    return "Person1{id=" + id + ", age=" + age +
                        ", name='" + name + "'}";
}
```

8. Now, we can run our JPA code example and observe the output:

```
Person1{id=1, age=10, name='Name10'}
Size: 1
Size: 1
```

The first two lines of the preceding output come from JPQL usage, and the last line comes from the Criteria API usage fragment of our code example.

9. JPA also has a provision for establishing relationships between classes. An entity class (and the corresponding database table) can have one-to-one, one-to-many, many-to-one, and many-to-many relationships with another entity class (and its table). The relationship can be bidirectional or unidirectional. This specification defines the following rules for a bidirectional relationship:

- The inverse side must refer to its owning side using the `mappedBy` attribute of the annotation `@OneToOne`, `@OneToMany`, or `@ManyToMany`.
- The many side of one-to-many and many-to-one relationships must own this relationship, so the `mappedBy` attribute cannot be specified on the `@ManyToOne` annotation.
- In one-to-one relationships, the owning side is the side that contains the foreign key.
- In many-to-many relationships, either side may be the owning side.

With a unidirectional relationship, only one class has a reference to the other class.

To illustrate these rules, let's create a class called `Family` that has a one-to-many relationship with the class `Person2`:

```
@Entity
public class Family {
    @Id
    @GeneratedValue(strategy = GenerationType.IDENTITY)
```

```
private int id;
private String name;
public Family(){}
public Family(String name){ this.name = name;}

@OneToMany(mappedBy = "family")
private final List<Person2> members = new ArrayList<>();

public List<Person2> getMembers(){ return this.members; }
public String getName() { return name; }
}
```

The SQL script that creates the table `family` is straightforward:

```
create table family (
    id SERIAL PRIMARY KEY,
    name VARCHAR NOT NULL
);
```

We need also to add the `Family` field to the class `Person2`:

```
@Entity
public class Person2 {
    @Id
    @GeneratedValue(strategy = GenerationType.IDENTITY)
    private int id;
    private int age;
    private String name;

    @ManyToOne
    private Family family;

    public Person2(){}
    public Person2(int age, String name, Family family){
        this.age = age;
        this.name = name;
        this.family = family;
    }
    @Override
    public String toString() {
      return "Person2{id=" + id + ", age=" + age +
              ", name='" + name + "', family='" +
        (family == null ? "" : family.getName())+ "'}";
    }
}
```

The `Person2` class is a "many" side, so, according to this rule, it owns the relationship, so the table `person2` has to have a foreign key that points to the record of the table `family`:

```
create table person2 (
    id SERIAL PRIMARY KEY,
    age INTEGER NOT NULL,
    name VARCHAR NOT NULL,
    family_id INTEGER references family(id)
                            ON DELETE CASCADE
);
```

Reference to a column requires this column value to be unique. That is why we have marked the column `id` of the table `person2` as `PRIMARY KEY`. Otherwise, an error `ERROR:  42830: there is no unique constraint matching given keys for referenced table` would be raised.

10. Now, we can use the classes `Family` and `Person2` to create the records in the corresponding tables and read from these tables, too:

```
EntityManagerFactory emf =
        Persistence.createEntityManagerFactory("jpa-demo");
EntityManager em = emf.createEntityManager();
try {
    em.getTransaction().begin();
    Family f = new Family("The Jones");
    em.persist(f);

    Person2 p = new Person2(10, "Name10", f);
    em.persist(p);

    f.getMembers().add(p);
    em.getTransaction().commit();

    Query q = em.createQuery("select f from Family f");
    List<Family> fList = q.getResultList();
    for (Family f1 : fList) {
        System.out.println("Family " + f1.getName() + ": "
                    + f1.getMembers().size() + " members:");
        for(Person2 p1: f1.getMembers()){
            System.out.println("    " + p1);
        }
    }
    q = em.createQuery("select p from Person2 p");
    List<Person2> pList = q.getResultList();
    for (Person2 p1 : pList) {
```

```
            System.out.println(p1);
        }
    } catch (Exception ex){
        ex.printStackTrace();
        em.getTransaction().rollback();
    } finally {
        em.close();
        emf.close();
    }
}
```

In the previous code, we created an object of the class Family and persisted it. This way, the object acquires an id value from the database. We then passed it into the constructor of the class Person2 and established the relationship on the many sides. Then, we persisted the Person2 object (so that it acquired an id from the database, too) and added to the collection members of the Family object, so the one side of the relationship is established too. To preserve data, the transaction has to be committed. When the transaction is committed, all the entity objects associated with an EntityManager (such objects are said to be in a **managed** state) are persisted automatically.

How it works...

If we run the preceding code, the result will be as follows:

```
Family The Jones: 1 members:
    Person2{id=1, age=10, name='Name10', family='The Jones'}
Person2{id=1, age=10, name='Name10', family='The Jones'}
```

As you can see, that is exactly what we expected—an object of class Family The Jones has one member—an object of class Person2, and the record in the table person2 refers to the corresponding record of the table family.

Concurrent and Multithreaded Programming

7

Concurrent programming has always been a difficult task. It is a source of many hard-to-solve problems. In this chapter, we will show you different ways to incorporate concurrency and some best practices, such as immutability, which helps to create multithreaded processing. We will also discuss the implementation of some commonly used patterns, such as divide and- conquer and publish-subscribe, using the constructs provided by Java. We will cover the following recipes:

- Using the basic element of concurrency—thread
- Different synchronization approaches
- Immutability as a means of achieving concurrency
- Using concurrent collections
- Using the executor service to execute async tasks
- Using fork/join to implement divide-and-conquer
- Using flow to implement the publish-subscribe pattern

Introduction

Concurrency—the ability to execute several procedures in parallel—becomes increasingly important as big-data analysis moves into the mainstream of modern applications. Having CPUs or several cores in one CPU helps increase the throughput, but the growth rate of the data volume will always outpace hardware advances. Besides, even in a multiple-CPU system, one still has to structure the code and think about resource-sharing to take advantage of the available computational power.

In the previous chapters, we demonstrated how lambdas with functional interfaces and parallel streams made concurrent processing part of the toolkit of every Java programmer. One can easily take advantage of this functionality with minimal, if any, guidance.

In this chapter, we will describe some other—old (before Java 9) and new—Java features and APIs that allow more control over concurrency. The high-level concurrency Java API has been around since Java 5. The JDK Enhancement Proposal (JEP) 266, *More Concurrency Updates* (`http://openjdk.java.net/jeps/266`), introduced, to Java 9 in the `java.util.concurrent` package.

> *"an interoperable publish-subscribe framework, enhancements to the CompletableFuture API, and various other improvements"*

But before we dive into the details of the latest additions, let's review the basics of concurrent programming in Java and see how to use them.

Java has two units of execution—process and thread. A process usually represents the whole JVM, although an application can create another process using `ProcessBuilder`. But since the multiprocess case is outside the scope of this book, we will focus on the second unit of execution, that is, a thread, which is similar to a process but less isolated from other threads and requires fewer resources for execution.

A process can have many threads running and at least one thread called the *main* thread. Threads can share resources, including memory and open files, which allows for better efficiency. But it comes with a price of higher risk of unintended mutual interference and even blocking of the execution. That is where programming skills and an understanding of the concurrency techniques are required. And that is what we are going to discuss in this chapter.

Using the basic element of concurrency – thread

In this chapter, we will look at the `java.lang.Thread` class and see what it can do for concurrency and program performance in general.

Getting ready

A Java application starts as the main thread (not counting system threads that support the process). It can then create other threads and let them run in parallel, sharing the same core via time-slicing or having a dedicated CPU for each thread. This can be done using the `java.lang.Thread` class that implements the `Runnable` functional interface with only one abstract method, `run()`.

There are two ways to create a new thread: creating a subclass of `Thread`, or implementing the `Runnable` interface and passing the object of the implementing class to the `Thread` constructor. We can invoke the new thread by calling the `start()` method of the `Thread` class which, in turn, calls the `run()` method that was implemented.

Then, we can either let the new thread run until its completion or pause it and let it continue again. We can also access its properties or intermediate results if needed.

How to do it...

First, we create a class called `AThread` that extends `Thread` and overrides its `run()` method:

```
class AThread extends Thread {
   int i1,i2;
   AThread(int i1, int i2){
     this.i1 = i1;
     this.i2 = i2;
   }
   public void run() {
     IntStream.range(i1, i2)
             .peek(Chapter07Concurrency::doSomething)
             .forEach(System.out::println);
   }
}
```

In this example, we want the thread to generate a stream of integers in a certain range. Then, we use the `peek()` operation to invoke the `doSomething()` static method of the main class for each stream element in order to make the thread busy for some time. Refer to the following code:

```
int doSomething(int i){
  IntStream.range(i,
100000).asDoubleStream().map(Math::sqrt).average();
```

```
    return i;
  }
```

As you can see, the doSomething() method generates a stream of integers in the range of i to 99999; it then converts the stream into a stream of doubles, calculates the square root of each of the stream elements, and finally calculates an average of the stream elements. We discard the result and return the passed-in parameter as a convenience that allows us to keep the fluent style in the stream pipeline of the thread, which ends by printing out each element. Using this new class, we can demonstrate the concurrent execution of the three threads, as follows:

```
Thread thr1 = new AThread(1, 4);
thr1.start();

Thread thr2 = new AThread(11, 14);
thr2.start();

IntStream.range(21, 24)
        .peek(Chapter07Concurrency::doSomething)
        .forEach(System.out::println);
```

The first thread generates the integers 1, 2, and 3, the second generates the integers 11, 12, and 13, and the third thread (main one) generates 21, 22, and 23.

As mentioned before, we can rewrite the same program by creating and using a class that could implement the Runnable interface:

```
class ARunnable implements Runnable {
  int i1,i2;
  ARunnable(int i1, int i2){
    this.i1 = i1;
    this.i2 = i2;
  }
  public void run() {
    IntStream.range(i1, i2)
            .peek(Chapter07Concurrency::doSomething)
            .forEach(System.out::println);
  }
}
```

One can run the same three threads like this:

```
Thread thr1 = new Thread(new ARunnable(1, 4));
thr1.start();

Thread thr2 = new Thread(new ARunnable(11, 14));
thr2.start();
```

```
IntStream.range(21, 24)
        .peek(Chapter07Concurrency::doSomething)
        .forEach(System.out::println);
```

We can also take advantage of `Runnable` being a functional interface and avoid creating an intermediate class by passing in a lambda expression instead:

```
Thread thr1 = new Thread(() -> IntStream.range(1, 4)
                .peek(Chapter07Concurrency::doSomething)
                .forEach(System.out::println));
thr1.start();

Thread thr2 = new Thread(() -> IntStream.range(11, 14)
                .peek(Chapter07Concurrency::doSomething)
                .forEach(System.out::println));
thr2.start();

IntStream.range(21, 24)
        .peek(Chapter07Concurrency::doSomething)
        .forEach(System.out::println);
```

Which implementation is better depends on your goal and style. Implementing `Runnable` has an advantage (and in some cases, is the only possible option) that allows the implementation to extend another class. It is particularly helpful when you would like to add thread-like behavior to an existing class. You can even invoke the `run()` method directly, without passing the object to the `Thread` constructor.

Using a lambda expression wins over the `Runnable` implementation when only the `run()` method implementation is needed, no matter how big it is. If it is too big, you can isolate it in a separate method:

```
public static void main(String arg[]) {
  Thread thr1 = new Thread(() -> runImpl(1, 4));
  thr1.start();

  Thread thr2 = new Thread(() -> runImpl(11, 14));
  thr2.start();

  runImpl(21, 24);
}

private static void runImpl(int i1, int i2){
  IntStream.range(i1, i2)
          .peek(Chapter07Concurrency::doSomething)
          .forEach(System.out::println);
}
```

One would be hard-pressed to come up with a shorter implementation of the preceding functionality.

If we run any of the preceding versions, we will get an output that looks something like this:

As you can see, the three threads print out their numbers concurrently, but the sequence depends on the particular JVM implementation and underlying operating system. So, you will probably get a different output. Besides, it also may change from run to run.

The `Thread` class has several constructors that allow setting the thread name and the group it belongs to. Grouping threads helps manage them if there are many threads running in parallel. The class also has several methods that provide information about the thread's status and properties, and allow us to control the thread's behavior. Add these two lines to the preceding example:

```
System.out.println("Id=" + thr1.getId() + ", " + thr1.getName() + ",
                priority=" + thr1.getPriority() + ",
                state=" + thr1.getState());
System.out.println("Id=" + thr2.getId() + ", " + thr2.getName() + ",
                priority=" + thr2.getPriority() + ",
                state=" + thr2.getState());
```

The result of the preceding code will look something like this:

```
Id=13, Thread-0, priority=5, state=RUNNABLE
Id=14, Thread-1, priority=5, state=TERMINATED
```

Next, say you add a name to each thread:

```
Thread thr1 = new Thread(() -> runImpl(1, 4), "First Thread");
thr1.start();

Thread thr2 = new Thread(() -> runImpl(11, 14), "Second Thread");
thr2.start();
```

In this case, the output will show the following:

```
Id=13, First Thread, priority=5, state=RUNNABLE
Id=14, Second Thread, priority=5, state=TERMINATED
```

The thread's `id` is generated automatically and cannot be changed, but it can be reused after the thread is terminated. Several threads, on the other hand, can be set with the same name. The execution priority can be set programmatically with a value between `Thread.MIN_PRIORITY` and `Thread.MAX_PRIORITY`. The smaller the value, the more time the thread is allowed to run, which means it has higher priority. If not set, the priority value defaults to `Thread.NORM_PRIORITY`.

The state of a thread can have one of the following values:

- `NEW`: When a thread has not yet started
- `RUNNABLE`: When a thread is being executed
- `BLOCKED`: When a thread is blocked and is waiting for a monitor lock
- `WAITING`: When a thread is waiting indefinitely for another thread to perform a particular action
- `TIMED_WAITING`: When a thread is waiting for another thread to perform an action for up to a specified waiting time
- `TERMINATED`: When a thread has exited

The `sleep()` method can be used to suspend the thread execution for a specified (in milliseconds) period of time. The complementary `interrupt()` method sends `InterruptedException` to the thread that can be used to wake up the *sleeping* thread. Let's work this out in the code and create a new class:

```
class BRunnable implements Runnable {
    int i1, result;
    BRunnable(int i1){ this.i1 = i1; }
    public int getCurrentResult(){ return this.result; }
    public void run() {
        for(int i = i1; i < i1 + 6; i++){
```

```
            //Do something useful here
            this.result = i;
            try{ Thread.sleep(1000);
            } catch(InterruptedException ex){}
        }
    }
}
```

The preceding code produces intermediate results, which are stored in the `result` property. Each time a new result is produced, the thread pauses (sleeps) for one second. In this specific example, written for demonstrative purposes only, the code does not do anything particularly useful. It just iterates over a set of values and considers each of them a result. In real-world code, you would do some calculations based on the current state of the system and assign the calculated value to the `result` property. Now let's use this class:

```
BRunnable r1 = new BRunnable(1);
Thread thr1 = new Thread(r1);
thr1.start();

IntStream.range(21, 29)
        .peek(i -> thr1.interrupt())
        .filter(i ->   {
           int res = r1.getCurrentResult();
           System.out.print(res + " => ");
           return res % 2 == 0;
        })
        .forEach(System.out::println);
```

The preceding code snippet generates a stream of integers—21, 22, ..., 28. After each integer is generated, the main thread interrupts the `thr1` thread and lets it generate the next result, which is then accessed via the `getCurrentResult()` method. If the current result is an even number, the filter allows the generated number flow to be printed out. If not, it is skipped. Here is a possible result:

```
1 => 2 => 22
3 => 3 => 4 => 25
6 => 26
6 => 27
6 => 28
```

The output may look different on different computers, but you get the idea: this way, one thread can control the output of another thread.

There's more...

There are two other important methods that support thread cooperation. The first is the `join()` method, which allows the current thread to wait until another thread is terminated. Overloaded versions of `join()` accept the parameters that define how long the thread has to wait before it can do something else.

The `setDaemon()` method can be used to make the thread terminate automatically after all the non-daemon threads are terminated. Usually, daemon threads are used for background and supporting processes.

Different synchronization approaches

In this recipe, you will learn about the two most popular methods of managing concurrent access to common resources in Java: `synchronized method` and `synchronized block`.

Getting ready

Two or more threads modifying the same value while other threads read it is the most general description of one of the problems of concurrent access. Subtler problems include **thread interference** and **memory consistency errors**, which both produce unexpected results in seemingly benign fragments of code. We are going to demonstrate such cases and ways to avoid them.

At first glance, it seems quite straightforward: just allow only one thread at a time to modify/access the resource and that's it. But if the access takes a long time, it creates a bottleneck that might eliminate the advantage of having many threads working in parallel. Or, if one thread blocks access to one resource while waiting for access to another resource and the second thread blocks access to the second resource while waiting for access to the first one, it creates a problem called a **deadlock**. These are two very simple examples of the possible challenges a programmer has to tackle when dealing with multiple threads.

How to do it...

First, we'll reproduce a problem caused by the concurrent modification of the same value. Let's create a `Calculator` class that has the `calculate()` method:

```
class Calculator {
    private double prop;
    public double calculate(int i){
        DoubleStream.generate(new Random()::nextDouble).limit(50);
        this.prop = 2.0 * i;
        DoubleStream.generate(new Random()::nextDouble).limit(100);
        return Math.sqrt(this.prop);
    }
}
```

This method assigns an input value to a property and then calculates its square root. We also inserted two lines of code that generate streams of 50 and 100 values. We did this to keep the method busy for some time. Otherwise, everything is done so quickly that there will be little chance for any concurrency to occur. Our adding the 100-values-generating code gives another thread a chance to assign the `prop` field another value before the current thread calculates the square root of the value the current thread has just assigned.

Now we are going to use the `calculate()` method in the following code fragment:

```
Calculator c = new Calculator();
Runnable runnable = () -> System.out.println(IntStream.range(1, 40)
                           .mapToDouble(c::calculate).sum());
Thread thr1 = new Thread(runnable);
thr1.start();
Thread thr2 = new Thread(runnable);
thr2.start();
```

The two preceding threads modify the same property of the same `Calculator` object concurrently. Here is the result we got from one of our runs:

```
231.69407148192175
237.44481627598856
```

If you run these examples on your computer and do not see the effect of concurrency, try to increase the number of doubles generated in the *slowing* line by replacing `100` with `1000`, for example. When the results of the threads are different, it means that in the period between setting the value of the `prop` field and returning its square root in the `calculate()` method, the other thread managed to assign a different value to `prop`. This is the case of thread interference.

There are two ways to protect code from such a problem: using `synchronized` method or `synchronized block`—both help to execute code as an atomic operation without any interference from another thread.

Making `synchronized method` is easy and straightforward:

```
class Calculator{
  private double prop;
  synchronized public double calculate(int i){
     DoubleStream.generate(new Random()::nextDouble).limit(50);
     this.prop = 2.0 * i;
     DoubleStream.generate(new Random()::nextDouble).limit(100);
     return Math.sqrt(this.prop);
  }
}
```

We just add the `synchronized` keyword in front of the method definition. Now, the results of both threads are going to always be the same:

```
233.75710300331153
233.75710300331153
```

This is because another thread cannot enter the synchronized method until the current thread (the one that has entered the method already) has exited it. This approach may cause performance degradation if the method takes a long time to execute. In such cases, `synchronized block` can be used, which wraps not the whole method but only several lines of code in an atomic operation. In our case, we can move the *slowing* line of code that generates 50 values outside the synchronized block:

```
class Calculator{
  private double prop;
  public double calculate(int i){
  DoubleStream.generate(new Random()::nextDouble).limit(50);
  synchronized (this) {
      this.prop = 2.0 * i;
      DoubleStream.generate(new Random()::nextDouble).limit(100);
      return Math.sqrt(this.prop);
  }
  }
}
```

This way, the synchronized portion is much smaller, thus it has fewer chances to become a bottleneck.

`synchronized block` acquires a lock on an object—any object, for that matter. In a huge class, you might not notice that the current object (this) is used as a lock for several blocks. And a lock acquired on a class is even more susceptible to unexpected sharing. So, it is better to use a dedicated lock:

```
class Calculator{
   private double prop;
   private Object calculateLock = new Object();
   public double calculate(int i){
      DoubleStream.generate(new Random()::nextDouble).limit(50);
      synchronized (calculateLock) {
         this.prop = 2.0 * i;
         DoubleStream.generate(new Random()::nextDouble).limit(100);
         return Math.sqrt(this.prop);
      }
   }
}
```

A dedicated lock has a higher level of assurance that the lock will be used to access only a particular block.

We did all these examples just to demonstrate synchronization approaches. If they were real code, we would just let each thread create its own `Calculator` object:

```
Runnable runnable = () -> {
    Calculator c = new Calculator();
    System.out.println(IntStream.range(1, 40)
            .mapToDouble(c::calculate).sum());
};
Thread thr1 = new Thread(runnable);
thr1.start();
Thread thr2 = new Thread(runnable);
thr2.start();
```

This would be in line with the general idea of making lambda expressions independent of the context in which they are created. This is because, in a multithreaded environment, one never knows how the context will look during their execution. The cost of creating a new object every time is negligible unless a large amount of data has to be processed, and testing ensures that the object-creation overhead is noticeable.

Memory consistency errors can have many forms and causes in a multithreaded environment. They are well discussed in the Javadoc of the `java.util.concurrent` package. Here, we will mention only the most common case, which is caused by a lack of visibility. When one thread changes a property value, the other might not see the change immediately, and you cannot use the `synchronized` keyword for a primitive type. In such a situation, consider using the `volatile` keyword for the property; it guarantees its read/write visibility between different threads.

There's more...

Different types of locks for different needs and with different behaviors are assembled in the `java.util.concurrent.locks` package.

The `java.util.concurrent.atomic` package provides support for lock-free, thread-safe programming on single variables.

The following classes provide synchronization support too:

- `Semaphore`: This restricts the number of threads that can access a resource
- `CountDownLatch`: This allows one or more threads to wait until a set of operations being performed in other threads are completed
- `CyclicBarrier`: This allows a set of threads to wait for each other to reach a common barrier point
- `Phaser`: This provides a more flexible form of barrier that may be used to control phased computation among multiple threads
- `Exchanger`: This allows two threads to exchange objects at a rendezvous point and is useful in several pipeline designs

Each object in Java inherits the `wait()`, `notify()`, and `notifyAll()` methods from the base object. These methods can also be used to control the threads' behavior and their access to the locks.

The `Collections` class has methods that synchronize various collections. However, this means that only the modifications of the collection could become thread-safe, not the changes to the collection members. Also, while traversing the collection via its iterator, it has to be protected too because an iterator is not thread-safe. Here is a Javadoc example of the correct usage of a synchronized map:

```
Map m = Collections.synchronizedMap(new HashMap());
...
Set s = m.keySet(); // Needn't be in synchronized block
...
synchronized (m) { // Synchronizing on m, not s!
  Iterator i = s.iterator(); //Must be synchronized block
  while (i.hasNext())
  foo(i.next());
}
```

To add more to your plate as a programmer, you have to realize that the following code is not thread-safe:

```
List<String> l = Collections.synchronizedList(new ArrayList<>());
l.add("first");
//... code that adds more elements to the list
int i = l.size();
//... some other code
l.add(i, "last");
```

This is because although `List l` is synchronized, in multithreaded processing, it is quite possible that some other code would add more elements to the list or remove an element.

The concurrency problems are not easy to solve. That is why it is not surprising that more and more developers now take a more radical approach. Instead of managing an object state, they prefer processing data in a set of stateless operations. We saw examples of such code in `Chapter 5`, *Streams and Pipelines*. It seems that Java and many modern languages and computer systems are evolving in this direction.

Immutability as a means of achieving concurrency

In this recipe, you will learn how to use immutability against problems caused by concurrency.

Getting ready

A concurrency problem most often occurs when different threads modify and read data of the same shared resource. Decreasing the number of modifying operations diminishes the risk of concurrency issues. This is where immutability—the condition of read-only values—enters the stage.

Object immutability means an absence of means to change its state after the object has been created. It does not guarantee thread-safety but helps to increase it significantly and provide sufficient protection from concurrency problems in many practical applications.

Creating a new object instead of reusing an existing one (by changing its state via setters and getters) is often perceived as an expensive approach. But with the power of modern computers, there has to be a huge number of object creations done for performance to be affected in any significant way. And even if that is the case, programmers often choose some performance degradation as the price for getting predictable results.

How to do it...

Here is an example of a class that produces mutable objects:

```
class MutableClass{
  private int prop;
  public MutableClass(int prop){
    this.prop = prop;
  }
  public int getProp(){
    return this.prop;
  }
  public void setProp(int prop){
    this.prop = prop;
  }
}
```

To make it immutable, we need to remove the setter and add the `final` keyword to its only property and to the class itself:

```
final class ImmutableClass{
  final private int prop;
  public ImmutableClass(int prop){
    this.prop = prop;
  }
  public int getProp(){
    return this.prop;
  }
}
```

Adding the `final` keyword to a class prevents it from being extended, so its methods cannot be overridden. Adding `final` to a private property is not as obvious. The motivation is somewhat complex and has to do with the way the compiler reorders the fields during object construction. If the field is declared `final`, it is treated by the compiler as synchronized. That is why adding `final` to a private property is necessary to make the object completely immutable.

The challenge mounts up if the class is composed of other classes, especially mutable ones. When this happens, the injected class might bring in code that would affect the containing class. Also, the inner (mutable) class, which is retrieved by references via the getter, could then be modified and propagate the change inside the containing class. The way to close such holes is to generate new objects during the composition of the object retrieval. Here is an example of this:

```
final class ImmutableClass{
  private final double prop;
  private final MutableClass mutableClass;
  public ImmutableClass(double prop, MutableClass mc){
    this.prop = prop;
    this.mutableClass = new MutableClass(mc.getProp());
  }
  public double getProp(){
    return this.prop;
  }
  public MutableClass getMutableClass(){
    return new MutableClass(mutableClass.getProp());
  }
}
```

There's more...

In our examples, we used very simple code. If more complexity is added to any of the methods, especially with parameters (and especially when some of the parameters are objects), it is possible you'll get concurrency issues again:

```
int getSomething(AnotherMutableClass amc, String whatever){
    //... code is here that generates a value "whatever"
    amc.setProperty(whatever);
    //...some other code that generates another value "val"
    amc.setAnotherProperty(val);
    return amc.getIntValue();
}
```

Even if this method belongs to `ImmutableClass` and does not affect the state of the `ImmutableClass` object, it is still a subject of the thread's race and has to be analyzed and protected as needed.

The `Collections` class has methods that make various collections unmodifiable. It means that the modification of the collection itself becomes read-only, not the collection members.

Using concurrent collections

In this recipe, you will learn about the thread-safe collections of the `java.util.concurrent` package.

Getting ready

A collection can be synchronized if you apply one of the `Collections.synchronizeXYZ()` methods to it; here, we have used XYZ as a placeholder that represents either `Set`, `List`, `Map`, or one of the several collection types (see the API of the `Collections` class). We have already mentioned that the synchronization applies to the collection itself, not to its iterator or the collection members.

Such synchronized collections are also called **wrappers** because all of the functionality is still provided by the collections passed as parameters to the `Collections.synchronizeXYZ()` methods, while the wrappers provide only thread-safe access to them. The same effect could be achieved by acquiring a lock on the original collection. Obviously, such a synchronization incurs a performance overhead in a multithreading environment, causing each thread to wait for its turn to access the collection.

A well-tuned application for performance implementation of thread-safe collections is provided by the `java.util.concurrent` package.

How to do it...

Each of the concurrent collections of the `java.util.concurrent` package implements (or extends, if it is an interface) one of the four interfaces of the `java.util` package: `List`, `Set`, `Map`, or `Queue`:

1. The `List` interface has only one implementation: the `CopyOnWriteArrayList` class. The following is taken from the Javadoc of this class:

   "all mutative operations (add, set, and so on) are implemented by making a fresh copy of the underlying array... The "snapshot" style iterator method uses a reference to the state of the array at the point that the iterator was created. This array never changes during the lifetime of the iterator, so interference is impossible and the iterator is guaranteed not to throw `ConcurrentModificationException`. *The iterator will not reflect additions, removals, or changes to the list since the iterator was created. Element-changing operations on iterators themselves (remove, set, and add) are not supported. These methods throw* `UnsupportedOperationException`.*"*

2. To demonstrate the behavior of the `CopyOnWriteArrayList` class, let's compare it with `java.util.ArrayList` (which is not a thread-safe implementation of `List`). Here is the method that adds an element to the list while iterating on the same list:

   ```
   void demoListAdd(List<String> list) {
     System.out.println("list: " + list);
     try {
       for (String e : list) {
         System.out.println(e);
         if (!list.contains("Four")) {
   ```

```
            System.out.println("Calling list.add(Four)...");
            list.add("Four");
        }
    }
} catch (Exception ex) {
    System.out.println(ex.getClass().getName());
}
System.out.println("list: " + list);
}
```

Consider the following code:

```
System.out.println("***** ArrayList add():");
demoListAdd(new ArrayList<>(Arrays
                .asList("One", "Two", "Three")));

System.out.println();
System.out.println("***** CopyOnWriteArrayList add():");
demoListAdd(new CopyOnWriteArrayList<>(Arrays.asList("One",
                                    "Two", "Three")));
```

If we execute this code, the result will be as follows:

```
***** ArrayList add():
list: [One, Two, Three]
One
Calling list.add(Four)...
java.util.ConcurrentModificationException
list: [One, Two, Three, Four]

***** CopyOnWriteArrayList add():
list: [One, Two, Three]
One
Calling list.add(Four)...
Two
Three
list: [One, Two, Three, Four]
```

As you can see, `ArrayList` throws `ConcurrentModificationException` when the list is modified while being iterated (we used the same thread for simplicity and because it leads to the same effect, as in the case of another thread modifying the list). The specification, though, does not guarantee that the exception will be thrown or the list modification applied (as in our case), so a programmer should not base the application logic on such behavior.

The `CopyOnWriteArrayList` class, on the other hand, tolerates the same intervention; however, note that it does not add a new element to the current list because the iterator was created from a snapshot of the fresh copy of the underlying array.

Now let's try to remove a list element concurrently while traversing the list, using this method:

```java
void demoListRemove(List<String> list) {
    System.out.println("list: " + list);
    try {
        for (String e : list) {
            System.out.println(e);
            if (list.contains("Two")) {
                System.out.println("Calling list.remove(Two)...");
                list.remove("Two");
            }
        }
    } catch (Exception ex) {
        System.out.println(ex.getClass().getName());
    }
    System.out.println("list: " + list);
}
```

Consider the following code:

```java
System.out.println("***** ArrayList remove():");
demoListRemove(new ArrayList<>(Arrays.asList("One",
                                "Two", "Three")));
System.out.println();
System.out.println("***** CopyOnWriteArrayList remove():");
demoListRemove(new CopyOnWriteArrayList<>(Arrays
                .asList("One", "Two", "Three")));
```

If we execute this, we will get the following:

```
***** ArrayList remove():
list: [One, Two, Three]
One
Calling list.remove(Two)...
java.util.ConcurrentModificationException
list: [One, Three]

***** CopyOnWriteArrayList remove():
list: [One, Two, Three]
One
Calling list.remove(Two)...
Two
Three
list: [One, Three]
```

The behavior is similar to the previous example. The
CopyOnWriteArrayList class allows the concurrent access to the list but
does not allow modify the current list's copy.

We knew ArrayList would not be thread-safe for a long time, so we used
a different technique to remove an element from the list while traversing it.
Here is how this was done before the Java 8 release:

```java
void demoListIterRemove(List<String> list) {
  System.out.println("list: " + list);
  try {
    Iterator iter = list.iterator();
    while (iter.hasNext()) {
      String e = (String) iter.next();
      System.out.println(e);
      if ("Two".equals(e)) {
        System.out.println("Calling iter.remove()...");
        iter.remove();
      }
    }
  } catch (Exception ex) {
      System.out.println(ex.getClass().getName());
  }
  System.out.println("list: " + list);
}
```

Let's try this and run the code:

```
System.out.println("***** ArrayList iter.remove():");
demoListIterRemove(new ArrayList<>(Arrays
                .asList("One", "Two", "Three")));
System.out.println();
System.out.println("*****"
                + " CopyOnWriteArrayList iter.remove():");
demoListIterRemove(new CopyOnWriteArrayList<>(Arrays
                .asList("One", "Two", "Three")));
```

The result will be as follows:

```
***** ArrayList iter.remove():
list: [One, Two, Three]
One
Two
Calling iter.remove()...
Three
list: [One, Three]

***** CopyOnWriteArrayList iter.remove():
list: [One, Two, Three]
One
Two
Calling iter.remove()...
java.lang.UnsupportedOperationException
list: [One, Two, Three]
```

This is exactly what the Javadoc warned about (https://docs.oracle.com/cd/E17802_01/j2se/j2se/1.5.0/jcp/beta2/apidiffs/java/util/concurrent/CopyOnWriteArrayList.html):

> *"Element-changing operations on iterators themselves (remove, set, and add) are not supported. These methods throw UnsupportedOperationException."*

We should remember this when upgrading an application to make it work in a multithreaded environment—just changing from `ArrayList()` to `CopyOnWriteArrayList` would not be enough if we use an iterator to remove a list element.

Since Java 8, there is a better way to remove an element from a collection using a lambda, which should be used as it leaves the plumbing details to the library code:

```java
void demoRemoveIf(Collection<String> collection) {
    System.out.println("collection: " + collection);
    System.out.println("Calling list.removeIf(e ->"
                            + " Two.equals(e))...");
    collection.removeIf(e -> "Two".equals(e));
    System.out.println("collection: " + collection);
}
```

So let's do this:

```java
System.out.println("***** ArrayList list.removeIf():");
demoRemoveIf(new ArrayList<>(Arrays
                    .asList("One", "Two", "Three")));
System.out.println();
System.out.println("*****"
            + " CopyOnWriteArrayList list.removeIf():");
demoRemoveIf(new CopyOnWriteArrayList<>(Arrays
                    .asList("One", "Two", "Three")));
```

The result of the preceding code is as follows:

```
***** ArrayList list.removeIf():
collection: [One, Two, Three]
Calling list.removeIf(e -> Two.equals(e))...
collection: [One, Three]

***** CopyOnWriteArrayList list.removeIf():
collection: [One, Two, Three]
Calling list.removeIf(e -> Two.equals(e))...
collection: [One, Three]
```

It is short and has no problem with any of the collections and is in line with the general trend of having a stateless parallel computation that uses streams with lambdas and functional interfaces.

Also, after we upgrade an application to use the `CopyOnWriteArrayList` class, we can take advantage of a simpler way of adding a new element to the list (without first checking whether it is already there):

```
CopyOnWriteArrayList<String> list =
  new CopyOnWriteArrayList<>(Arrays.asList("Five","Six","Seven"));
list.addIfAbsent("One");
```

With `CopyOnWriteArrayList`, this can be done as an atomic operation, so one does not need to synchronize the if-not-present-then-add block of code.

2. Let's review the concurrent collections of the `java.util.concurrent` package that implements the `Set` interface. There are three such implementations—`ConcurrentHashMap.KeySetView`, `CopyOnWriteArraySet`, and `ConcurrentSkipListSet`.

The first one is just a view of the keys of `ConcurrentHashMap`. It is backed up by `ConcurrentHashMap` (which can be retrieved by the `getMap()` method). We will review the behavior of `ConcurrentHashMap` later.

The second implementation of `Set` in the `java.util.concurrent` package is the `CopyOnWriteArraySet` class. Its behavior is similar to the `CopyOnWriteArrayList` class. In fact, it uses the `CopyOnWriteArrayList` class's implementation under the hood. The only difference is that it does not allow duplicate elements in the collection.

The third (and last) implementation of `Set` in the `java.util.concurrent` package is `ConcurrentSkipListSet`; it implements a sub-interface of `Set` called `NavigableSet`. According to the Javadoc of the `ConcurrentSkipListSet` class, insertion, removal, and access operations are safely executed concurrently by multiple threads. There are some limitations described in the Javadoc too:

- It does not permit the use of `null` elements.
- The size of the set is calculated dynamically by traversing the collection, so it may report inaccurate results if this collection is modified during the operation.

- The addAll(), removeIf(), and forEach() operations are not guaranteed to be performed atomically. The forEach() operation, if concurrent with an addAll() operation for example, "might observe only some of the added elements."

The implementation of the ConcurrentSkipListSet class is based on the ConcurrentSkipListMap class, which we will discuss shortly. To demonstrate the behavior of the ConcurrentSkipListSet class, let's compare it with the java.util.TreeSet class (non-concurrent implementation of NavigableSet). We start with removing an element:

```
void demoNavigableSetRemove(NavigableSet<Integer> set) {
  System.out.println("set: " + set);
  try {
    for (int i : set) {
      System.out.println(i);
      System.out.println("Calling set.remove(2)...");
      set.remove(2);
    }
  } catch (Exception ex) {
    System.out.println(ex.getClass().getName());
  }
  System.out.println("set: " + set);
}
```

Of course, this code is not very efficient; we've removed the same element many times without checking for its presence. We have done this just for demonstrative purposes. Besides, since Java 8, the same removeIf() method works for Set just fine. But we would like to bring up the behavior of the new ConcurrentSkipListSet class, so let's execute this code:

```
System.out.println("***** TreeSet set.remove(2):");
demoNavigableSetRemove(new TreeSet<>(Arrays
                    .asList(0, 1, 2, 3)));
System.out.println();
System.out.println("*****"
          + " ConcurrentSkipListSet set.remove(2):");
demoNavigableSetRemove(new ConcurrentSkipListSet<>(Arrays
                    .asList(0, 1, 2, 3)));
```

The output will be as follows:

```
***** TreeSet set.remove(2):
set: [0, 1, 2, 3]
0
Calling set.remove(2)...
java.util.ConcurrentModificationException
set: [0, 1, 3]

***** ConcurrentSkipListSet set.remove(2):
set: [0, 1, 2, 3]
0
Calling set.remove(2)...
1
Calling set.remove(2)...
3
Calling set.remove(2)...
set: [0, 1, 3]
```

As expected, the `ConcurrentSkipListSet` class handles the concurrency and even removes an element from the current set, which is helpful. It also removes an element via an iterator without an exception. Consider the following code:

```java
void demoNavigableSetIterRemove(NavigableSet<Integer> set){
    System.out.println("set: " + set);
    try {
        Iterator iter = set.iterator();
        while (iter.hasNext()) {
            Integer e = (Integer) iter.next();
            System.out.println(e);
            if (e == 2) {
                System.out.println("Calling iter.remove()...");
                iter.remove();
            }
        }
    } catch (Exception ex) {
        System.out.println(ex.getClass().getName());
    }
    System.out.println("set: " + set);
}
```

Run this for `TreeSet` and `ConcurrentSkipListSet`:

```
System.out.println("***** TreeSet iter.remove():");
demoNavigableSetIterRemove(new TreeSet<>(Arrays
                                  .asList(0, 1, 2, 3)));

System.out.println();
System.out.println("*****"
              + " ConcurrentSkipListSet iter.remove():");
demoNavigableSetIterRemove(new ConcurrentSkipListSet<>
                              (Arrays.asList(0, 1, 2, 3)));
```

We won't get any exception:

```
***** TreeSet iter.remove():
set: [0, 1, 2, 3]
0
1
2
Calling iter.remove()...
3
set: [0, 1, 3]

***** ConcurrentSkipListSet iter.remove():
set: [0, 1, 2, 3]
0
1
2
Calling iter.remove()...
3
set: [0, 1, 3]
```

This is because, according to the Javadoc, the iterator of
`ConcurrentSkipListSet` is weakly consistent, which means the
following:

- They may proceed concurrently with other operations
- They will never throw
  `ConcurrentModificationException`
- They are guaranteed to traverse elements as they existed
  upon construction exactly once, and may (but are not
  guaranteed to) reflect any modifications subsequent to
  construction (from the Javadoc)

This "not guaranteed" part is somewhat disappointing, but it is better than getting an exception, as with `CopyOnWriteArrayList`.

Adding to a `Set` class is not as problematic as to a `List` class because `Set` does not allow duplicates and handles the necessary checks internally:

```java
void demoNavigableSetAdd(NavigableSet<Integer> set) {
  System.out.println("set: " + set);
  try {
    int m = set.stream().max(Comparator.naturalOrder())
                        .get() + 1;
    for (int i : set) {
      System.out.println(i);
      System.out.println("Calling set.add(" + m + ")");
      set.add(m++);
      if (m > 6) {
        break;
      }
    }
  } catch (Exception ex) {
    System.out.println(ex.getClass().getName());
  }
  System.out.println("set: " + set);
}
```

Consider the following code:

```java
System.out.println("***** TreeSet set.add():");
demoNavigableSetAdd(new TreeSet<>(Arrays
                        .asList(0, 1, 2, 3)));

System.out.println();
System.out.println("*****"
                + " ConcurrentSkipListSet set.add():");
demoNavigableSetAdd(new ConcurrentSkipListSet<>(Arrays
                        .asList(0,1,2,3)));
```

If we run this, we'll get the following result:

```
***** TreeSet set.add():
set: [0, 1, 2, 3]
0
Calling set.add(4)
java.util.ConcurrentModificationException
set: [0, 1, 2, 3, 4]

***** ConcurrentSkipListSet set.add():
set: [0, 1, 2, 3]
0
Calling set.add(4)
1
Calling set.add(5)
2
Calling set.add(6)
set: [0, 1, 2, 3, 4, 5, 6]
```

As before, we observe that the concurrent `Set` version handles concurrency better.

3. Let's turn to the `Map` interface, which has two implementations in the `java.util.concurrent` package: `ConcurrentHashMap` and `ConcurrentSkipListMap`.

   The `ConcurrentHashMap` class from the Javadoc.

   > *"supports full concurrency of retrievals and high concurrency for updates"*

   It is a thread-safe version of `java.util.HashMap` and is analogous to `java.util.Hashtable` in this respect. In fact, the `ConcurrentHashMap` class meets the requirements of the same functional specification as `java.util.Hashtable`, although its implementation is "somewhat different in synchronization details" (from the Javadoc).

Unlike `java.util.HashMap` and `java.util.Hashtable`, `ConcurrentHashMap` supports, according to its Javadoc (https://docs. oracle.com/javase/9/docs/api/java/util/concurrent/ ConcurrentHashMap.html),

> *"a set of sequential and parallel bulk operations that, unlike most Stream methods, are designed to be safely, and often sensibly, applied even with maps that are being concurrently updated by other threads"*

- `forEach()`: This performs a given action on each element
- `search()`: This returns the first available non-null result of applying a given function to each element
- `reduce()`: This accumulates each element (there are five overloaded versions)

These bulk operations accept a `parallelismThreshold` argument that allows deferring parallelization until the map size reaches the specified threshold. Naturally, when the threshold is set to `Long.MAX_VALUE`, there will be no parallelism whatsoever.

There are many other methods in the class API, so refer to its Javadoc for an overview.

Unlike `java.util.HashMap` (and similar to `java.util.Hashtable`), neither `ConcurrentHashMap` nor `ConcurrentSkipListMap` allows null to be used as a key or value.

The second implementation of `Map`—the `ConcurrentSkipListSet` class—is based, as we mentioned before, on the `ConcurrentSkipListMap` class, so all the limitations of the `ConcurrentSkipListSet` class we just described apply to the `ConcurrentSkipListMap` class too. The `ConcurrentSkipListSet` class is practically a thread-safe version of `java.util.TreeMap`. `SkipList` is a sorted data structure that allows fast searches concurrently. All the elements are sorted based on their natural sorting order of keys. The `NavigableSet` functionality we demonstrated for the `ConcurrentSkipListSet` class is present in the `ConcurrentSkipListMap` class too. For many other methods in the class API, refer to its Javadoc.

Now let's demonstrate the difference in the behavior in response to concurrency between the `java.util.HashMap`, `ConcurrentHashMap`, and `ConcurrentSkipListMap` classes. First, we will write the method that generates a test `Map` object:

```
Map createhMap() {
  Map<Integer, String> map = new HashMap<>();
  map.put(0, "Zero");
  map.put(1, "One");
  map.put(2, "Two");
  map.put(3, "Three");
  return map;
}
```

Here is the code that adds an element to a `Map` object concurrently:

```
void demoMapPut(Map<Integer, String> map) {
  System.out.println("map: " + map);
  try {
    Set<Integer> keys = map.keySet();
    for (int i : keys) {
      System.out.println(i);
      System.out.println("Calling map.put(8, Eight)...");
      map.put(8, "Eight");

      System.out.println("map: " + map);
      System.out.println("Calling map.put(8, Eight)...");
      map.put(8, "Eight");

      System.out.println("map: " + map);
      System.out.println("Calling"
                           + " map.putIfAbsent(9, Nine)...");
      map.putIfAbsent(9, "Nine");

      System.out.println("map: " + map);
      System.out.println("Calling"
                           + " map.putIfAbsent(9, Nine)...");
      map.putIfAbsent(9, "Nine");

      System.out.println("keys.size(): " + keys.size());
      System.out.println("map: " + map);
    }
  } catch (Exception ex) {
    System.out.println(ex.getClass().getName());
  }
}
```

Run this for all three implementations of `Map`:

```
System.out.println("***** HashMap map.put():");
demoMapPut(createhMap());

System.out.println();
System.out.println("***** ConcurrentHashMap map.put():");
demoMapPut(new ConcurrentHashMap(createhMap()));

System.out.println();
System.out.println("*****"
                    + " ConcurrentSkipListMap map.put():");
demoMapPut(new ConcurrentSkipListMap(createhMap()));
```

If we do this, we get an output for `HashMap` for the first key only:

```
***** HashMap map.put():
map: {0=Zero, 1=One, 2=Two, 3=Three}
0
Calling map.put(8, Eight)...
map: {0=Zero, 1=One, 2=Two, 3=Three, 8=Eight}
Calling map.put(8, Eight)...
map: {0=Zero, 1=One, 2=Two, 3=Three, 8=Eight}
Calling map.putIfAbsent(9, Nine)...
map: {0=Zero, 1=One, 2=Two, 3=Three, 8=Eight, 9=Nine}
Calling map.putIfAbsent(9, Nine)...
keys.size(): 6
map: {0=Zero, 1=One, 2=Two, 3=Three, 8=Eight, 9=Nine}
java.util.ConcurrentModificationException
```

We also get an output
for `ConcurrentHashMap` and `ConcurrentSkipListMap` for all the keys,
including the newly added ones. Here is the last section of
the `ConcurrentHashMap` output:

```
keys.size(): 6
map: {0=Zero, 1=One, 2=Two, 3=Three, 8=Eight, 9=Nine}
9
Calling map.put(8, Eight)...
map: {0=Zero, 1=One, 2=Two, 3=Three, 8=Eight, 9=Nine}
Calling map.put(8, Eight)...
map: {0=Zero, 1=One, 2=Two, 3=Three, 8=Eight, 9=Nine}
Calling map.putIfAbsent(9, Nine)...
map: {0=Zero, 1=One, 2=Two, 3=Three, 8=Eight, 9=Nine}
Calling map.putIfAbsent(9, Nine)...
keys.size(): 6
map: {0=Zero, 1=One, 2=Two, 3=Three, 8=Eight, 9=Nine}
```

As mentioned already, the appearance of
`ConcurrentModificationException` is not guaranteed. Now we see that
the moment it is thrown (if it is thrown) is the moment when the code
discovers that the modification has taken place. In the case of our example,
it happened in the next iteration. Another point worth noting is that the
current set of keys changes even as we isolate the set in a separate variable:

```
Set<Integer> keys = map.keySet();
```

This reminds us not to dismiss the changes propagated through the objects
via their references.

To save ourselves some space and time, we will not show the code for
concurrent removal and just summarize the results. As expected, `HashMap`
throws the `ConcurrentModificationException` exception when an
element is removed in any of the following ways:

```
String result = map.remove(2);
boolean success = map.remove(2, "Two");
```

The concurrent removal can be done using `Iterator` in one of the
following ways:

```
iter.remove();
boolean result = map.keySet().remove(2);
boolean result = map.keySet().removeIf(e -> e == 2);
```

By contrast, the two concurrent `Map` implementations allow a concurrent
element removal not just using `Iterator`.

Similar behavior is also exhibited by all the concurrent implementations of
the `Queue` interface: `LinkedTransferQueue`, `LinkedBlockingQueue`,
`LinkedBlockingDequeue`, `ArrayBlockingQueue`,
`PriorityBlockingQueue`, `DelayQueue`, `SynchronousQueue`,
`ConcurrentLinkedQueue`, and `ConcurrentLinkedDequeue`, all in the
`java.util.concurrent` package. But to demonstrate all of them would
require a separate volume, so we leave it up to you to browse the Javadoc
and provide an example of `ArrayBlockingQueue` only. The queue will be
represented by the `QueueElement` class:

```
class QueueElement {
  private String value;
  public QueueElement(String value){
    this.value = value;
  }
```

```
      public String getValue() {
        return value;
      }
  }
}
```

The queue producer will be as follows:

```
class QueueProducer implements Runnable {
  int intervalMs, consumersCount;
  private BlockingQueue<QueueElement> queue;
  public QueueProducer(int intervalMs, int consumersCount,
                       BlockingQueue<QueueElement> queue) {
    this.consumersCount = consumersCount;
    this.intervalMs = intervalMs;
    this.queue = queue;
  }
  public void run() {
    List<String> list =
        List.of("One","Two","Three","Four","Five");
    try {
      for (String e : list) {
        Thread.sleep(intervalMs);
        queue.put(new QueueElement(e));
        System.out.println(e + " produced" );
      }
      for(int i = 0; i < consumersCount; i++){
        queue.put(new QueueElement("Stop"));
      }
    } catch (InterruptedException e) {
      e.printStackTrace();
    }
  }
}
```

The following will be the queue consumer:

```
class QueueConsumer implements Runnable{
  private String name;
  private int intervalMs;
  private BlockingQueue<QueueElement> queue;
  public QueueConsumer(String name, int intervalMs,
                       BlockingQueue<QueueElement> queue){
    this.intervalMs = intervalMs;
    this.queue = queue;
    this.name = name;
  }
  public void run() {
    try {
```

```
        while(true){
          String value = queue.take().getValue();
          if("Stop".equals(value)){
            break;
          }
          System.out.println(value + " consumed by " + name);
          Thread.sleep(intervalMs);
        }
      } catch(InterruptedException e) {
        e.printStackTrace();
      }
    }
  }
}
```

Run the following code:

```
BlockingQueue<QueueElement> queue =
            new ArrayBlockingQueue<>(5);
QueueProducer producer = new QueueProducer(queue);
QueueConsumer consumer = new QueueConsumer(queue);
new Thread(producer).start();
new Thread(consumer).start();
```

Its results may look like this:

```
One produced
One consumed by Second
Two produced
Two consumed by First
Three produced
Three consumed by First
Four produced
Four consumed by Second
Five produced
Five consumed by First
```

How it works...

Before we select which collections to use, read the Javadoc to see whether the limitations of the collection are acceptable for your application.

For example, as per the Javadoc, the `CopyOnWriteArrayList` class

> *"is ordinarily too costly, but may be more efficient than alternatives when traversal operations vastly outnumber mutations, and is useful when you cannot or don't want to synchronize traversals, yet need to preclude interference among concurrent threads."*

Use it when you do not need to add new elements at different positions and do not require sorting. Otherwise, use `ConcurrentSkipListSet`.

The `ConcurrentSkipListSet` and `ConcurrentSkipListMap` classes, as per the Javadoc,

> *"provide expected average log(n) time cost for the contains, add, and remove operations and their variants. Ascending ordered views and their iterators are faster than descending ones."*

Use them when you need to iterate quickly through the elements in a certain order.

Use `ConcurrentHashMap` when the concurrency requirements are very demanding and you need to allow locking on the write operation but do not need to lock the element.

`ConcurrentLinkedQueque` and `ConcurrentLinkedDeque` are an appropriate choice when many threads share access to a common collection. `ConcurrentLinkedQueque` employs an efficient non-blocking algorithm.

`PriorityBlockingQueue` is a better choice when a natural order is acceptable and you need fast adding of elements to the tail and fast removing of elements from the head of the queue. Blocking means that the queue waits to become non-empty when retrieving an element and waits for space to become available in the queue when storing an element.

`ArrayBlockingQueue`, `LinkedBlockingQueue`, and `LinkedBlockingDeque` have a fixed size (they are bounded). The other queues are unbounded.

Use these and similar characteristics and recommendations as the guidelines, but execute comprehensive testing and performance-measuring before and after implementing your functionality.

Using the executor service to execute async tasks

In this recipe, you will learn how to use `ExecutorService` to implement controllable thread-execution.

Getting ready

In an earlier recipe, we demonstrated how to create and execute threads using the `Thread` class directly. It is an acceptable mechanism for a small number of threads that run and produce results predictably quickly. For big-scale applications with longer-running threads with complex logic (which might keep them alive for an unpredictably long time) and/or a number of threads growing unpredictably too, a simple create-and-run-until-exit approach might result in an `OutOfMemory` error or require a complex customized system of threads' status maintenance and management. For such cases, `ExecutorService` and related classes of the `java.util.concurrent` package provides an out-of-the-box solution that relieves a programmer of the need to write and maintain a lot of infrastructural code.

At the foundation of the Executor Framework lies an `Executor` interface that has only one `void execute(Runnable command)` method that executes the given command at some time in the future.

Its subinterface, `ExecutorService`, adds methods that allow you to manage the executor:

- The `invokeAny()`, `invokeAll()`, and `awaitTermination()` methods and `submit()` allow you to define how the threads will be executed and whether they are expected to return some values
- The `shutdown()` and `shutdownNow()` methods allow you to shut down the executor
- The `isShutdown()` and `isTerminated()` methods provide the status of the executor

The objects of `ExecutorService` can be created with the static factory methods of the `java.util.concurrent.Executors` class:

- `newSingleThreadExecutor()`: Creates an `Executor` method that uses a single worker thread operating off an unbounded queue. It has an overloaded version with `ThreadFactory` as a parameter.
- `newCachedThreadPool()`: Creates a thread pool that creates new threads as needed, but reuses previously constructed threads when they are available. It has an overloaded version with `ThreadFactory` as a parameter.
- `newFixedThreadPool(int nThreads)`: Creates a thread pool that reuses a fixed number of threads operating off a shared unbounded queue. It has an overloaded version with `ThreadFactory` as a parameter.

The `ThreadFactory` implementation allows you to override the process of creating new threads, enabling applications to use special thread subclasses, priorities, and so on. A demonstration of its usage is outside the scope of this book.

How to do it...

1. One important aspect of the behavior of the `Executor` interface you need to remember is that once created, it keeps running (waiting for new tasks to execute) until the Java process is stopped. So, if you would like to free memory, the `Executor` interface has to be stopped explicitly. If not shut down, forgotten executors will create a memory leak. Here is one possible way to make sure no executor is left behind:

```
int shutdownDelaySec = 1;
ExecutorService execService =
             Executors.newSingleThreadExecutor();
Runnable runnable =  () -> System.out.println("Worker One did
                                             the job.");
execService.execute(runnable);
runnable =   () -> System.out.println("Worker Two did the
                                      job.");
Future future = execService.submit(runnable);
try {
  execService.shutdown();
  execService.awaitTermination(shutdownDelaySec,
                             TimeUnit.SECONDS);
} catch (Exception ex) {
  System.out.println("Caught around"
```

```
              + " execService.awaitTermination(): "
              + ex.getClass().getName());
    } finally {
      if (!execService.isTerminated()) {
        if (future != null && !future.isDone()
                          && !future.isCancelled()){
          System.out.println("Cancelling the task...");
          future.cancel(true);
        }
      }
      List<Runnable> l = execService.shutdownNow();
      System.out.println(l.size()
              + " tasks were waiting to be executed."
              + " Service stopped.");
    }
```

You can pass a worker (an implementation of either
the Runnable or Callable functional interface) for execution to
ExecutorService in a variety of ways, which we will see shortly. In this
example, we executed two threads: one using the execute() method and
another using the submit() method. Both methods accept Runnable or
Callable, but we used only Runnable in this example.
The submit() method returns Future, which represents the result of an
asynchronous computation.

The shutdown() method initiates an orderly shutdown of the previously
submitted tasks and prevents any new tasks from being accepted. This
method does not wait for the task to complete the execution. The
awaitTermination() method does that. But after shutdownDelaySec, it
stops blocking and the code flow gets into the finally block, where
the isTerminated() method returns true if all the tasks are completed
following the shutdown. In this example, we have two tasks executed in
two different statements. But note that other methods of ExecutorService
accept a collection of tasks.

In such a case, when the service is shutting down, we iterate over the
collection of Future objects. We call each task and cancel it if it is not
completed yet, possibly doing something else that had to be done before
canceling the task. How much time to wait (the value of
shutdownDelaySec) has to be tested for each application and the possible
running tasks.

Finally, the `shutdownNow()` method says that it

> *"attempts to stop all actively executing tasks, halts the processing of waiting tasks, and returns a list of the tasks that were awaiting execution"*

(according to the Javadoc).

2. Collect and assess the results. In a real application, we typically do not want to shut down a service often. We just check the status of the tasks and collect the results of those that return true from the `isDone()` method. In the preceding code example, we just show how to make sure that when we do stop the service, we do it in a controlled manner, without leaving behind any runaway process. If we run that code example, we will get the following:

```
Worker One did the job.
Worker Two did the job.
0 tasks were waiting to be executed. Service stopped.
```

3. Generalize the preceding code and create a method that shuts down a service and the task that has returned `Future`:

```
void shutdownAndCancelTask(ExecutorService execService,
            int shutdownDelaySec, String name, Future future) {
  try {
    execService.shutdown();
    System.out.println("Waiting for " + shutdownDelaySec
                + " sec before shutting down service...");
    execService.awaitTermination(shutdownDelaySec,
                                  TimeUnit.SECONDS);
  } catch (Exception ex) {
    System.out.println("Caught around"
                + " execService.awaitTermination():"
                + ex.getClass().getName());
  } finally {
    if (!execService.isTerminated()) {
      System.out.println("Terminating remaining tasks...");
      if (future != null && !future.isDone()
                      && !future.isCancelled()) {
        System.out.println("Cancelling task "
                      + name + "...");
        future.cancel(true);
      }
```

```
        }
        System.out.println("Calling execService.shutdownNow("
                        + name + ")...");
        List<Runnable> l = execService.shutdownNow();
        System.out.println(l.size() + " tasks were waiting"
                        + " to be executed. Service stopped.");
    }
}
```

4. Enhance the example by making `Runnable` (using the lambda expression) sleep for some time (simulating useful work to be done):

```
void executeAndSubmit(ExecutorService execService,
                int shutdownDelaySec, int threadSleepsSec) {
    System.out.println("shutdownDelaySec = "
                    + shutdownDelaySec + ", threadSleepsSec = "
                    + threadSleepsSec);
    Runnable runnable = () -> {
        try {
            Thread.sleep(threadSleepsSec * 1000);
            System.out.println("Worker One did the job.");
        } catch (Exception ex) {
            System.out.println("Caught around One Thread.sleep(): "
                            + ex.getClass().getName());
        }
    };
    execService.execute(runnable);
    runnable = () -> {
        try {
            Thread.sleep(threadSleepsSec * 1000);
            System.out.println("Worker Two did the job.");
        } catch (Exception ex) {
            System.out.println("Caught around Two Thread.sleep(): "
                            + ex.getClass().getName());
        }
    };
    Future future = execService.submit(runnable);
    shutdownAndCancelTask(execService, shutdownDelaySec,
                    "Two", future);
}
```

Note the two parameters, `shutdownDelaySec` (defines how long the service will wait without allowing new tasks to be submitted before moving on and shutting itself down, eventually) and `threadSleepSec` (defines how long the worker is sleeping, indicating that the simulating process is doing its job).

5. Run the new code for different implementations of `ExecutorService` and the `shutdownDelaySec` and `threadSleepSec` values:

```java
System.out.println("Executors.newSingleThreadExecutor():");
ExecutorService execService =
                Executors.newSingleThreadExecutor();
executeAndSubmit(execService, 3, 1);

System.out.println();
System.out.println("Executors.newCachedThreadPool():");
execService = Executors.newCachedThreadPool();
executeAndSubmit(execService, 3, 1);

System.out.println();
int poolSize = 3;
System.out.println("Executors.newFixedThreadPool("
                                 + poolSize + "):");
execService = Executors.newFixedThreadPool(poolSize);
executeAndSubmit(execService, 3, 1);
```

This is how the output may look (it might be slightly different on your computer, depending on the exact timing of the events controlled by the operating system):

```
Executors.newSingleThreadExecutor():
shutdownDelaySec = 3, threadSleepsSec = 1
Waiting for 3 sec before shutting down service...
Worker One did the job.
Worker Two did the job.
Calling execService.shutdownNow(Two)...
0 tasks were waiting to be executed. Service stopped.
```

6. Analyze the results. In the first example, we find no surprise because of the following line:

```java
execService.awaitTermination(shutdownDelaySec,
                            TimeUnit.SECONDS);
```

It is blocking for three seconds, whereas each worker works for one second only. So it is enough time for each worker to complete its work even for a single-thread executor.

Let's make the service wait for one second only:

```
Executors.newSingleThreadExecutor():
shutdownDelaySec = 1, threadSleepsSec = 3
Waiting for 1 sec before shutting down service...
Terminating remaining running tasks...
Cancelling task Two...
Calling execService.shutdownNow(Two)...
1 tasks were waiting to be executed. Service stopped.
Caught around One Thread.sleep(): java.lang.InterruptedException
```

When you do this, you will notice that none of the tasks will be completed. In this case, worker One was interrupted (see the last line of the output), while task Two was canceled.

Let's make the service wait for three seconds:

```
Executors.newSingleThreadExecutor():
shutdownDelaySec = 3, threadSleepsSec = 3
Waiting for 3 sec before shutting down service...
Worker One did the job.
Terminating remaining running tasks...
Cancelling task Two...
Calling execService.shutdownNow(Two)...
0 tasks were waiting to be executed. Service stopped.
Caught around Two Thread.sleep(): java.lang.InterruptedException
```

Now we see that worker One was able to complete its task, while worker Two was interrupted.

The ExecutorService interface produced by newCachedThreadPool() or newFixedThreadPool() performs similarly on a one-core computer. The only significant difference is that if the shutdownDelaySec value is equal to the threadSleepSec value, then they both allow you to complete the threads:

```
Executors.newCachedThreadPool():
shutdownDelaySec = 3, threadSleepsSec = 3
Waiting for 3 sec before shutting down service...
Worker One did the job.
Worker Two did the job.
Calling execService.shutdownNow(Two)...
0 tasks were waiting to be executed. Service stopped.
```

This was the result of using `newCachedThreadPool()`. The output of the example using `newFixedThreadPool()` looks exactly the same on a one-core computer.

7. To have more control over the task, check the returned value of the `Future` object, not just submit a task and wait hoping it will be completed as needed. There is another method, called `submit()`, in the `ExecutorService` interface that allows you to not only return a `Future` object but also include the result that is passed to the method as a second parameter in the return object. Let's check out an example of this:

```
Future<Integer> future = execService.submit(() ->
        System.out.println("Worker 42 did the job."), 42);
int result = future.get();
```

The value of `result` is 42. This method can be helpful when you have submitted many workers (`nWorkers`) and need to know which one is completed:

```
Set<Integer> set = new HashSet<>();
while (set.size() < nWorkers){
   for (Future<Integer> future : futures) {
     if (future.isDone()){
       try {
         String id = future.get(1, TimeUnit.SECONDS);
         if(!set.contains(id)){
           System.out.println("Task " + id + " is done.");
           set.add(id);
         }
       } catch (Exception ex) {
         System.out.println("Caught around future.get(): "
                            + ex.getClass().getName());
       }
     }
   }
}
```

Well, the catch is that `future.get()` is a blocking method. This is why we use a version of the `get()` method that allows us to set the `delaySec` timeout. Otherwise, `get()` blocks the iteration.

How it works...

Let's move a step closer to real-life code and create a class that implements `Callable` and allows you to return a result from a worker as an object of the `Result` class:

```
class Result {
  private int sleepSec, result;
  private String workerName;
  public Result(String workerName, int sleptSec, int result) {
    this.workerName = workerName;
    this.sleepSec = sleptSec;
    this.result = result;
  }
  public String getWorkerName() { return this.workerName; }
  public int getSleepSec() { return this.sleepSec; }
  public int getResult() { return this.result; }
}
```

An actual numeric result is returned by the `getResult()` method. Here, we also included the name of the worker and how long the thread is expected to sleep (to work) just for convenience and to better illustrate the output.

The worker itself is going to be an instance of the `CallableWorkerImpl` class:

```
class CallableWorkerImpl implements CallableWorker<Result>{
  private int sleepSec;
  private String name;
  public CallableWorkerImpl(String name, int sleepSec) {
    this.name = name;
    this.sleepSec = sleepSec;
  }
  public String getName() { return this.name; }
  public int getSleepSec() { return this.sleepSec; }
  public Result call() {
    try {
      Thread.sleep(sleepSec * 1000);
    } catch (Exception ex) {
      System.out.println("Caught in CallableWorker: "
                          + ex.getClass().getName());
    }
    return new Result(name, sleepSec, 42);
  }
}
```

Here, the number `42` is an actual numeric result, which a worker supposedly calculated (while sleeping). The `CallableWorkerImpl` class implemented the `CallableWorker` interface:

```
interface CallableWorker<Result> extends Callable<Result> {
  default String getName() { return "Anonymous"; }
  default int getSleepSec() { return 1; }
}
```

We had to make the methods default and return some data (they will be overridden by the class implementation anyway) to preserve its `functional interface` status. Otherwise, we would not be able to use it in lambda expressions.

We will also create a factory that will generate a list of workers:

```
List<CallableWorker<Result>> createListOfCallables(int nSec){
  return List.of(new CallableWorkerImpl("One", nSec),
                 new CallableWorkerImpl("Two", 2 * nSec),
                 new CallableWorkerImpl("Three", 3 * nSec));
}
```

Now we can use all these new classes and methods to demonstrate the `invokeAll()` method:

```
void invokeAllCallables(ExecutorService execService,
       int shutdownDelaySec, List<CallableWorker<Result>> callables)
{
  List<Future<Result>> futures = new ArrayList<>();
  try {
    futures = execService.invokeAll(callables, shutdownDelaySec,
                                    TimeUnit.SECONDS);
  } catch (Exception ex) {
    System.out.println("Caught around execService.invokeAll(): "
                       + ex.getClass().getName());
  }
  try {
    execService.shutdown();
    System.out.println("Waiting for " + shutdownDelaySec
                       + " sec before terminating all tasks...");
    execService.awaitTermination(shutdownDelaySec,
                                 TimeUnit.SECONDS);
  } catch (Exception ex) {
    System.out.println("Caught around awaitTermination(): "
                       + ex.getClass().getName());
  } finally {
    if (!execService.isTerminated()) {
      System.out.println("Terminating remaining tasks...");
```

```
       for (Future<Result> future : futures) {
          if (!future.isDone() && !future.isCancelled()) {
             try {
                System.out.println("Cancelling task "
                          + future.get(shutdownDelaySec,
                                   TimeUnit.SECONDS).getWorkerName());
                future.cancel(true);
             } catch (Exception ex) {
                System.out.println("Caught at cancelling task: "
                                  + ex.getClass().getName());
             }
          }
       }
    }
    System.out.println("Calling execService.shutdownNow()...");
    execService.shutdownNow();
  }
  printResults(futures, shutdownDelaySec);
}
```

The `printResults()` method outputs the results received from the workers:

```
void printResults(List<Future<Result>> futures, int timeoutSec) {
  System.out.println("Results from futures:");
  if (futures == null || futures.size() == 0) {
    System.out.println("No results. Futures"
                      + (futures == null ? " = null" : ".size()=0"));
  } else {
    for (Future<Result> future : futures) {
       try {
          if (future.isCancelled()) {
             System.out.println("Worker is cancelled.");
          } else {
             Result result = future.get(timeoutSec, TimeUnit.SECONDS);
             System.out.println("Worker "+ result.getWorkerName() +
                             " slept " + result.getSleepSec() +
                             " sec. Result = " + result.getResult());
          }
       } catch (Exception ex) {
          System.out.println("Caught while getting result: "
                            + ex.getClass().getName());
       }
    }
  }
}
```

To get the results, again we use a version of the `get()` method with timeout settings. Run the following code:

```
List<CallableWorker<Result>> callables = createListOfCallables(1);
System.out.println("Executors.newSingleThreadExecutor():");
ExecutorService execService = Executors.newSingleThreadExecutor();
invokeAllCallables(execService, 1, callables);
```

Its output will be as follows:

```
Executors.newSingleThreadExecutor():
Waiting for 1 sec before terminating all tasks...
Calling execService.shutdownNow()...
Results from futures:
Worker is cancelled.
Worker is cancelled.
Worker is cancelled.
```

It's probably worth mentioning that the three workers were created with sleep times of one, two, and three seconds, while the waiting time before the service shuts down is one second. This is why all the workers were canceled.

Now if we set the waiting time to six seconds, the output of the single-thread executor will be as follows:

```
Executors.newSingleThreadExecutor():
Waiting for 6 sec before terminating all tasks...
Caught in CallableWorkerImpl: java.lang.InterruptedException
Calling execService.shutdownNow()...
Results from futures:
Worker One slept 1 sec. Result = 42
Worker Two slept 2 sec. Result = 42
Worker is cancelled.
```

Naturally, if we increase the waiting time again, all the workers will be able to complete their tasks.

The `ExecutorService` interface produced by `newCachedThreadPool()` or `newFixedThreadPool()` performs much better even on a one-core computer:

```
Executors.newCachedThreadPool():
Waiting for 3 sec before terminating all tasks...
Calling execService.shutdownNow()...
Results from futures:
Worker One slept 1 sec. Result = 42
Worker Two slept 2 sec. Result = 42
Worker Three slept 3 sec. Result = 42
```

As you can see, all the threads were able to complete even with three seconds of waiting time.

As an alternative, instead of setting a timeout during the service shutdown, you can possibly set it on the overloaded version of the `invokeAll()` method:

```
List<Future<T>> invokeAll(Collection<? extends Callable<T>> tasks,
                          long timeout, TimeUnit unit)
```

There is one particular aspect of the `invokeAll()` method's behavior that often gets overlooked and causes surprises for first-time users: it returns only after all the tasks are complete (either normally or by throwing an exception). Read the Javadoc and experiment until you recognize that this behavior is acceptable for your application.

By contrast, the `invokeAny()` method blocks only until at least one task is

"completed successfully (without throwing an exception), if any do. Upon normal or exceptional return, tasks that have not completed are cancelled"

The preceding quote is from the Javadoc (https://docs.oracle.com/javase/7/docs/api/java/util/concurrent/ExecutorService.html). Here is an example of the code that does this:

```
void invokeAnyCallables(ExecutorService execService,
        int shutdownDelaySec, List<CallableWorker<Result>> callables)
{
  Result result = null;
  try {
    result = execService.invokeAny(callables, shutdownDelaySec,
TimeUnit.SECONDS);
  } catch (Exception ex) {
    System.out.println("Caught around execService.invokeAny(): "
                       + ex.getClass().getName());
  }
  shutdownAndCancelTasks(execService, shutdownDelaySec,
                         new ArrayList<>());
  if (result == null) {
    System.out.println("No result from execService.invokeAny()");
```

```
    } else {
      System.out.println("Worker " + result.getWorkerName() +
                          " slept " + result.getSleepSec() +
                          " sec. Result = " + result.getResult());
    }
  }
```

You can experiment with it, setting different values for the waiting time (shutdownDelaySec) and sleep time for threads until you are comfortable with how this method behaves. As you can see, we have reused the shutdownAndCancelTasks() method by passing an empty list of Future objects since we do not have them here.

There's more...

There are two more static factory methods in the Executors class that create instances of ExecutorService:

- newWorkStealingPool(): This creates a work-stealing thread pool using the number of available processors as its target parallelism level. It has an overloaded version with a parallelism level as a parameter.
- unconfigurableExecutorService(ExecutorService executor): This returns an object that delegates all the defined ExecutorService methods to the given executor, except for those methods that might otherwise be accessible using casts.

Also, a sub-interface of the ExecutorService interface, called ScheduledExecutorService, enhances the API with the capability to schedule a thread execution in future and/or their periodic execution.

The objects of ScheduledExecutorService can be created using the static factory methods of the java.util.concurrent.Executors class:

- newSingleThreadScheduledExecutor(): Creates a single-threaded executor that can schedule commands to run after a given delay or to execute them periodically. It has an overloaded version with ThreadFactory as a parameter.
- newScheduledThreadPool(int corePoolSize): Creates a thread pool that can schedule commands to run after a given delay or to execute them periodically. It has an overloaded version with ThreadFactory as a parameter.

- unconfigurableScheduledExecutorService(
  ScheduledExecutorService executor): Returns an object that
  delegates all the defined ScheduledExecutorService methods to the
  given executor, but not any other methods that might otherwise be
  accessible using casts.

The Executors class also has several overloaded methods that accept, execute, and
return Callable (which, in contrast with Runnable, contains the result).

The java.util.concurrent package also includes classes that implement
ExecutorService:

- ThreadPoolExecutor: This class executes each submitted task using one
  of the several pooled threads, normally configured using the Executors
  factory methods.
- ScheduledThreadPoolExecutor: This class extends
  the ThreadPoolExecutor class and implements
  the ScheduledExecutorService interface.
- ForkJoinPool: It manages the execution of workers (the ForkJoinTask
  processes) using a work-stealing algorithm. We will discuss it in the next
  recipe.

Instances of these classes can be created via class constructors that accept more
parameters, including the queue that holds the results, for providing more refined
thread-pool management.

Using fork/join to implement divide-and-conquer

In this recipe, you will learn how to use the fork/join framework for the divide-and-
conquer computation pattern.

Getting ready

As mentioned in the previous recipe, the `ForkJoinPool` class is an implementation of the `ExecutorService` interface that manages the execution of workers—the `ForkJoinTask` processes—using the work-stealing algorithm. It takes advantage of multiple processors, if available, and works best on tasks that can be broken down into smaller tasks recursively, which is also called a **divide-and-conquer** strategy.

Each thread in the pool has a dedicated double-ended queue (deque) that stores tasks, and the thread picks up the next task (from the head of the queue) as soon as the current task is completed. When another thread finishes executing all the tasks in its queue, it can take a task (steal it) from the tail of a non-empty queue of another thread.

As with any `ExecutorService` implementation, the fork/join framework distributes tasks to worker threads in a thread pool. This framework is distinct because it uses a work-stealing algorithm. Worker threads that run out of tasks can steal tasks from other threads that are still busy.

Such a design balances the load and allows an efficient use of the resources.

For demonstrative purposes, we are going to use the API created in Chapter 3, *Modular Programming*, the `TrafficUnit`, `SpeedModel`, and `Vehicle` interfaces and the `TrafficUnitWrapper`, `FactoryTraffic`, `FactoryVehicle`, and `FactorySpeedModel` classes. We will also rely on the streams and stream pipelines described in Chapter 3, *Modular Programming*.

Just to refresh your memory, here is the `TrafficUnitWrapper` class:

```
class TrafficUnitWrapper {
  private double speed;
  private Vehicle vehicle;
  private TrafficUnit trafficUnit;
  public TrafficUnitWrapper(TrafficUnit trafficUnit){
    this.trafficUnit = trafficUnit;
    this.vehicle = FactoryVehicle.build(trafficUnit);
  }
  public TrafficUnitWrapper setSpeedModel(SpeedModel speedModel) {
    this.vehicle.setSpeedModel(speedModel);
    return this;
  }
  TrafficUnit getTrafficUnit(){ return this.trafficUnit; }
  public double getSpeed() { return speed; }

  public TrafficUnitWrapper calcSpeed(double timeSec) {
```

```
    double speed = this.vehicle.getSpeedMph(timeSec);
    this.speed = Math.round(speed * this.trafficUnit.getTraction());
    return this;
  }
}
```

We will also slightly modify the existing API interface and make it a bit more compact by introducing a new DateLocation class:

```
class DateLocation {
  private int hour;
  private Month month;
  private DayOfWeek dayOfWeek;
  private String country, city, trafficLight;

  public DateLocation(Month month, DayOfWeek dayOfWeek,
                      int hour, String country, String city,
                      String trafficLight) {
    this.hour = hour;
    this.month = month;
    this.dayOfWeek = dayOfWeek;
    this.country = country;
    this.city = city;
    this.trafficLight = trafficLight;
  }
  public int getHour() { return hour; }
  public Month getMonth() { return month; }
  public DayOfWeek getDayOfWeek() { return dayOfWeek; }
  public String getCountry() { return country; }
  public String getCity() { return city; }
  public String getTrafficLight() { return trafficLight;}
}
```

It will also allow you to hide the details and help you see the important aspects of this recipe.

How to do it...

All computations are encapsulated inside a subclass of one of the two subclasses (RecursiveAction or RecursiveTask<T>) of the abstract ForkJoinTask class. You can extend either RecursiveAction (and implement the void compute() method) or RecursiveTask<T> (and implement the T compute() method). As you may have noticed, you can choose to extend the RecursiveAction class for tasks that do not return any value, and extend RecursiveTask<T> when you need your tasks to return a value. In our demo, we are going to use the latter because it is slightly more complex.

Let's say we would like to calculate the average speed of traffic in a certain location on a certain date and time and driving conditions (all these parameters are defined by the DateLocation property object). Other parameters will be as follows:

- timeSec: The number of seconds during which the vehicles have a chance to accelerate after stopping at the traffic light
- trafficUnitsNumber: The number of vehicles to include in the average speed calculation

Naturally, the more vehicles included in the calculations, the better the prediction. But as this number increases, the number of calculations increases too. This gives rise to the need to break down the number of vehicles into smaller groups and compute the average speed of each group in parallel with the others. Yet, there is a certain minimal number of calculations that is not worth splitting between two threads. Here's what Javadoc (https://docs.oracle.com/javase/8/docs/api/java/util/concurrent/ForkJoinTask.html) has to say about it:

> *"As a very rough rule of thumb, a task should perform more than 100 and less than 10000 basic computational steps, and should avoid indefinite looping. If tasks are too big, then parallelism cannot improve throughput. If too small, then memory and internal task maintenance overhead may overwhelm processing."*

Yet, as always, the determination of the optimal number of calculations without splitting them between parallel threads should be based on testing. This is why we recommend you pass it as a parameter. We will call this parameter threshold. Note that it also serves as a criterion for exiting from the recursion.

We will call our class (task) `AverageSpeed` and extend `RecursiveTask<Double>` because we would like to have as a result of the average speed value of the `double` type:

```
class AverageSpeed extends RecursiveTask<Double> {
  private double timeSec;
  private DateLocation dateLocation;
  private int threshold, trafficUnitsNumber;
  public AverageSpeed(DateLocation dateLocation,
                  double timeSec, int trafficUnitsNumber,
                  int threshold) {
    this.timeSec = timeSec;
    this.threshold = threshold;
    this.dateLocation = dateLocation;
    this.trafficUnitsNumber = trafficUnitsNumber;
  }
  protected Double compute() {
    if (trafficUnitsNumber < threshold) {
      //... write the code here that calculates
      //... average speed trafficUnitsNumber vehicles
      return averageSpeed;
    } else{
      int tun = trafficUnitsNumber / 2;
      //write the code that creates two tasks, each
      //for calculating average speed of tun vehicles
      //then calculates an average of the two results
      double avrgSpeed1 = ...;
      double avrgSpeed2 = ...;
      return (double) Math.round((avrgSpeed1 + avrgSpeed2) / 2);
    }
  }
}
```

Before we finish writing the code for the `compute()` method, let's write the code that will execute this task. There are several ways to do this. We can use `fork()` and `join()`, for example:

```
void demo1_ForkJoin_fork_join() {
  AverageSpeed averageSpeed = createTask();
  averageSpeed.fork();
  double result = averageSpeed.join();
  System.out.println("result = " + result);
}
```

This technique provided the name for the framework. The `fork()` method, according to Javadoc,

> *"arranges to asynchronously execute this task in the pool the current task is running in, if applicable, or using the* `ForkJoinPool.commonPool()` *if not in* `ForkJoinPool().`*"*

In our case, we have not used any pool yet, so `fork()` is going to use `ForkJoinPool.commonPool()` by default. It places the task in the queue of a thread in the pool. The `join()` method returns the result of the computation when it is done.

The `createTask()` method contains the following:

```
AverageSpeed createTask() {
   DateLocation dateLocation = new DateLocation(Month.APRIL,
         DayOfWeek.FRIDAY, 17, "USA", "Denver", "Main103S");
   double timeSec = 10d;
   int trafficUnitsNumber = 1001;
   int threshold = 100;
   return new AverageSpeed(dateLocation, timeSec,
                           trafficUnitsNumber, threshold);
}
```

Note the values of the `trafficUnitsNumber` and `threshold` parameters. This will be important for analyzing the results.

Another way to accomplish this is to use either the `execute()` or `submit()` method—each providing the same functionality—for the execution of the task. The result of the execution can be retrieved by the `join()` method (the same as in the previous example):

```
void demo2_ForkJoin_execute_join() {
   AverageSpeed averageSpeed = createTask();
   ForkJoinPool commonPool = ForkJoinPool.commonPool();
   commonPool.execute(averageSpeed);
   double result = averageSpeed.join();
   System.out.println("result = " + result);
}
```

The last method we are going to review is `invoke()`, which is equivalent to calling the `fork()` method followed by the `join()` method:

```
void demo3_ForkJoin_invoke() {
   AverageSpeed averageSpeed = createTask();
   ForkJoinPool commonPool = ForkJoinPool.commonPool();
   double result = commonPool.invoke(averageSpeed);
   System.out.println("result = " + result);
}
```

Naturally, this is the most popular way to start the divide-and-conquer process.

Now let's get back to the `compute()` method and see how it can be implemented. First, let's implement the `if` block (calculates the average speed of less than `threshold` vehicles). We will use the technique and code we described in Chapter 3, *Modular Programming*:

```
double speed =
    FactoryTraffic.getTrafficUnitStream(dateLocation,
                                                trafficUnitsNumber)
        .map(TrafficUnitWrapper::new)
        .map(tuw -> tuw.setSpeedModel(FactorySpeedModel.
                      generateSpeedModel(tuw.getTrafficUnit())))
        .map(tuw -> tuw.calcSpeed(timeSec))
        .mapToDouble(TrafficUnitWrapper::getSpeed)
        .average()
        .getAsDouble();
System.out.println("speed(" + trafficUnitsNumber + ") = " + speed);
return (double) Math.round(speed);
```

We get `trafficUnitsNumber` of the vehicles from `FactoryTraffic`. We create an object of `TrafficUnitWrapper` for each emitted element and call the `setSpeedModel()` method on it (by passing in the newly generated `SpeedModel` object, based on the emitted `TrafficUnit` object). Then we calculate the speed, get an average of all the speeds in the stream, and get the result as `double` from the `Optional` object (the return type of the `average()` operation). We then print out the result and round to get a more presentable format.

It is also possible to achieve the same result using a traditional `for` loop. But, as mentioned before, it seems that Java follows the general trend of a more fluent and stream-like style, geared toward processing a large amount of data. So, we recommend you get used to it.

In Chapter 14, *Testing*, you will see another version of the same functionality that allows better unit testing of each step in isolation, which again supports the view that unit testing, along with writing code, helps you make your code more testable and decreases the need to rewrite it later.

Now, let's review the options of the else block implementation. The first few lines are always going to be the same:

```
int tun = trafficUnitsNumber / 2;
System.out.println("tun = " + tun);
AverageSpeed as1 =
    new AverageSpeed(dateLocation, timeSec, tun, threshold);
AverageSpeed as2 =
    new AverageSpeed(dateLocation, timeSec, tun, threshold);
```

We divide the trafficUnitsNumber number by 2 (we do not worry about possible loss of one unit in the case of an average across a big set) and create two tasks.

The following—the actual task execution code—can be written in several different ways. Here is the first possible solution, which is familiar to us already, that comes to mind:

```
as1.fork();                        //add to the queue
double res1 = as1.join();  //wait until completed
as2.fork();
double res2 = as2.join();
return (double) Math.round((res1 + res2) / 2);
```

Run the following code:

```
demo1_ForkJoin_fork_join();
demo2_ForkJoin_execute_join();
demo3_ForkJoin_invoke();
```

If we do this, we will see the same output (but with different speed values) three times:

```
tun = 500
tun = 250
tun = 125
tun = 62
speed (62) = 18.548387096774192
speed (62) = 33.483870967741936
tun = 62
speed (62) = 28.532258064516128
speed (62) = 23.64516129032258
tun = 125
tun = 62
speed (62) = 29.306451612903224
speed (62) = 23.112903225806452
tun = 62
speed (62) = 24.919354838709676
speed (62) = 27.322580645161292
tun = 250
tun = 125
tun = 62
speed (62) = 29.112903225806452
speed (62) = 18.903225806451612
tun = 62
speed (62) = 23.193548387096776
speed (62) = 31.85483870967742
tun = 125
tun = 62
speed (62) = 29.451612903225808
speed (62) = 25.580645161290324
tun = 62
speed (62) = 27.14516129032258
speed (62) = 23.532258064516128
result = 27.0
```

You see how the original task of calculating average speed over 1,001 units (vehicles) was first divided by 2 several times until the number of one group (62) fell under the threshold of 100. Then, an average speed of the last two groups was calculated and combined (joined) with the results of other groups.

Another way to implement an `else` block of the `compute()` method could be as follows:

```
as1.fork();                      //add to the queue
double res1 = as2.compute();  //get the result recursively
double res2 = as1.join();     //wait until the queued task ends
return (double) Math.round((res1 + res2) / 2);
```

Here's how the result will look:

```
tun = 500
tun = 250
tun = 125
tun = 62
tun = 250
tun = 125
tun = 125
tun = 62
tun = 125
tun = 62
tun = 62
tun = 62
tun = 62
speed (62) = 22.774193548387096
speed (62) = 31.822580645161292
speed (62) = 27.758064516129032
tun = 62
speed (62) = 27.112903225806452
speed (62) = 28.887096774193548
speed (62) = 28.306451612903224
speed (62) = 26.35483870967742
tun = 62
speed (62) = 25.887096774193548
speed (62) = 29.596774193548388
speed (62) = 32.274193548387096
speed (62) = 32.37096774193548
speed (62) = 27.548387096774192
speed (62) = 22.0
speed (62) = 25.661290322580644
speed (62) = 21.161290322580644
speed (62) = 25.177419354838708
result = 28.0
```

You can see how, in this case, the `compute()` method (of the second task) was called recursively many times until it reached the threshold by the number of elements, then its results were joined with the results of the call to the `fork()` and `join()` methods of the first task.

As mentioned before, all this complexity can be replaced by a call to the `invoke()` method:

```
double res1 = as1.invoke();
double res2 = as2.invoke();
return (double) Math.round((res1 + res2) / 2);
```

It produces a result similar to the one produced by calling `fork()` and `join()` on each of the tasks:

```
tun = 500
tun = 250
tun = 125
tun = 62
speed (62) = 30.467741935483872
speed (62) = 17.14516129032258
tun = 62
speed (62) = 29.93548387096774
speed (62) = 27.70967741935484
tun = 125
tun = 62
speed (62) = 28.85483870967742
speed (62) = 33.45161290322581
tun = 62
speed (62) = 22.419354838709676
speed (62) = 35.645161290322584
tun = 250
tun = 125
tun = 62
speed (62) = 20.338709677419356
speed (62) = 34.064516129032256
tun = 62
speed (62) = 38.854838709677416
speed (62) = 22.387096774193548
tun = 125
tun = 62
speed (62) = 28.14516129032258
speed (62) = 35.725806451612904
tun = 62
speed (62) = 22.161290322580644
speed (62) = 23.20967741935484
result = 29.0
```

Yet, there is an even better way to implement an `else` block of the `compute()` method:

```
return ForkJoinTask.invokeAll(List.of(as1, as2))
        .stream()
        .mapToDouble(ForkJoinTask::join)
        .map(Math::round)
        .average()
        .getAsDouble();
```

If this looks complex to you, just note that it is just a stream-like way to iterate over the results of `invokeAll()`:

```
<T extends ForkJoinTask> Collection<T> invokeAll(Collection<T> tasks)
```

It is also to iterate over the results of calling `join()` on each of the returned tasks (and combining the results into average). The advantage is that we yield to the framework to decide how to optimize the load distribution. The result is as follows:

```
tun = 500
tun = 250
tun = 250
tun = 125
tun = 125
tun = 62
tun = 62
tun = 125
tun = 62
tun = 62
speed (62) = 24.306451612903224
speed (62) = 19.161290322580644
tun = 125
tun = 62
speed (62) = 32.17741935483871
tun = 62
speed (62) = 21.661290322580644
speed (62) = 38.096774193548384
speed (62) = 28.14516129032258
speed (62) = 24.258064516129032
speed (62) = 40.88709677419355
speed (62) = 35.564516129032256
speed (62) = 33.03225806451613
tun = 62
speed (62) = 19.548387096774192
tun = 62
speed (62) = 30.387096774193548
speed (62) = 32.03225806451613
speed (62) = 25.5
speed (62) = 33.91935483870968
speed (62) = 17.20967741935484
result = 29.0
```

You can see that it differs from any of the preceding results and can change depending on the availability and load of the CPUs on your computer.

Using flow to implement the publish-subscribe pattern

In this recipe, you will learn about the new publish-subscribe capability introduced in Java 9.

Getting ready

Among many other features, Java 9 introduced these four interfaces in the `java.util.concurrent.Flow` class:

```
Flow.Publisher<T> - producer of items (messages) of type T
Flow.Subscriber<T> - receiver of messages of type T
Flow.Subscription - links producer and receiver
Flow.Processor<T,R> - acts as both producer and receiver
```

With this, Java stepped into the world of reactive programming—programming with the asynchronous processing of data streams.

We discussed streams in `Chapter 3`, *Modular Programming,* and pointed out that they are not data structures, as they do not keep data in memory. The stream pipeline does nothing until an element is emitted. Such a model allows minimal resource-allocation and uses resources only as needed. The application behaves *in response* to the appearance of the data it reacts to, thus the name.

In a publish-subscribe pattern, the main two actors are `Publisher`, which streams data (publishes), and `Subscriber`, which listens to data (subscribes).

The `Flow.Publisher<T>` interface is a functional interface. It only has one abstract method:

```
void subscribe(Flow.Subscriber<? super T> subscriber)
```

According to the Javadoc (`https://docs.oracle.com/javase/10/docs/api/java/util/concurrent/SubmissionPublisher.html`), this method,

> *"adds the given* `Flow.Subscriber<T>` *if possible. If already subscribed, or the attempt to subscribe fails, the* `onError()` *method of* `Flow.Subscriber<T>` *is invoked with an* `IllegalStateException`. *Otherwise, the* `onSubscribe()` *method of* `Flow.Subscriber<T>` *is invoked with a new* `Flow.Subscription`. *Subscribers may enable receiving items by invoking the* `request()` *method of this* `Flow.Subscription` *and may unsubscribe by invoking its* `cancel()` *method."*

The `Flow.Subscriber<T>` interface has four methods:

- `void onSubscribe(Flow.Subscription subscription)`: Invoked prior to invoking any other `Subscriber` methods for the given `Subscription`
- `void onError(Throwable throwable)`: Invoked upon an unrecoverable error encountered by a `Publisher` or `Subscription`, after which no other `Subscriber` methods are invoked by `Subscription`
- `void onNext(T item)`: Invoked with the next item of `Subscription`
- `void onComplete()`: Invoked when it is known that no additional `Subscriber` method invocations will occur for `Subscription`

The `Flow.Subscription` interface has two methods:

- `void cancel()`: Causes `Subscriber` to (eventually) stop receiving messages
- `void request(long n)`: Adds the given *n* number of items to the current unfulfilled demand for this subscription

The `Flow.Processor<T,R>` interface is outside the scope of this book.

How to do it...

To save some time and space, instead of creating our own implementation of the `Flow.Publisher<T>` interface, we can use the `SubmissionPublisher<T>` class from the `java.util.concurrent` package. But, we will create our own implementation of the `Flow.Subscriber<T>` interface:

```
class DemoSubscriber<T> implements Flow.Subscriber<T> {
  private String name;
  private Flow.Subscription subscription;
  public DemoSubscriber(String name){ this.name = name; }
  public void onSubscribe(Flow.Subscription subscription) {
    this.subscription = subscription;
    this.subscription.request(0);
  }
  public void onNext(T item) {
    System.out.println(name + " received: " + item);
    this.subscription.request(1);
  }
  public void onError(Throwable ex){ ex.printStackTrace();}
  public void onComplete() { System.out.println("Completed"); }
}
```

We will also implement the `Flow.Subscription` interface:

```
class DemoSubscription<T> implements Flow.Subscription {
  private final Flow.Subscriber<T> subscriber;
  private final ExecutorService executor;
  private Future<?> future;
  private T item;
  public DemoSubscription(Flow.Subscriber subscriber,
                          ExecutorService executor) {
    this.subscriber = subscriber;
    this.executor = executor;
  }
  public void request(long n) {
    future = executor.submit(() -> {
      this.subscriber.onNext(item );
    });
  }
  public synchronized void cancel() {
    if (future != null && !future.isCancelled()) {
      this.future.cancel(true);
    }
  }
}
```

As you can see, we just followed Javadoc recommendations and expect the `onSubscribe()` method of a subscriber to be called when the subscriber is added to a publisher.

Another detail to note is that the `SubmissionPublisher<T>` class has the `submit(T item)` method that, according to Javadoc (`https://docs.oracle.com/javase/10/docs/api/java/util/concurrent/SubmissionPublisher.html`):

> *"publishes the given item to each current subscriber by asynchronously invoking its* `onNext()` *method, blocking uninterruptibly while resources for any subscriber are unavailable."*

This way, the `SubmissionPublisher<T>` class submits items to the current subscribers until it is closed. This allows item generators to act as reactive-streams publishers.

To demonstrate this, let's create several subscribers and subscriptions using the `demoSubscribe()` method:

```
void demoSubscribe(SubmissionPublisher<Integer> publisher,
        ExecutorService execService, String subscriberName){
    DemoSubscriber<Integer> subscriber =
                    new DemoSubscriber<>(subscriberName);
    DemoSubscription subscription =
            new DemoSubscription(subscriber, execService);
    subscriber.onSubscribe(subscription);
    publisher.subscribe(subscriber);
}
```

Then use them in the following code:

```
ExecutorService execService = ForkJoinPool.commonPool();
try (SubmissionPublisher<Integer> publisher =
                        new SubmissionPublisher<>()){
    demoSubscribe(publisher, execService, "One");
    demoSubscribe(publisher, execService, "Two");
    demoSubscribe(publisher, execService, "Three");
    IntStream.range(1, 5).forEach(publisher::submit);
} finally {
    //...make sure that execService is shut down
}
```

The preceding code creates three subscribers, connected to the same publisher with a dedicated subscription. The last line generates a stream of numbers, 1, 2, 3, and 4, and submits each of them to the publisher. We expect that every subscriber will get each of the generated numbers as the parameter of the `onNext()` method.

In the `finally` block, we included the code you are already familiar with from the previous recipe:

```
try {
  execService.shutdown();
  int shutdownDelaySec = 1;
  System.out.println("Waiting for " + shutdownDelaySec
                        + " sec before shutting down service...");
  execService.awaitTermination(shutdownDelaySec, TimeUnit.SECONDS);
} catch (Exception ex) {
  System.out.println("Caught around execService.awaitTermination(): "
                                    + ex.getClass().getName());
} finally {
  System.out.println("Calling execService.shutdownNow()...");
  List<Runnable> l = execService.shutdownNow();
  System.out.println(l.size()
          +" tasks were waiting to be executed. Service stopped.");
}
```

If we run the preceding code, the output may look like the following:

```
Waiting for 1 sec before shutting down service...
Three received: null
Two received: null
One received: null
Three received: 1
One received: 1
Two received: 1
One received: 2
Three received: 2
One received: 3
Two received: 2
One received: 4
Three received: 3
Completed
Two received: 3
Three received: 4
Two received: 4
Completed
Completed
Calling execService.shutdownNow()...
0 tasks were waiting to be executed. Service stopped.
```

As you can see, because of asynchronous processing, the control gets to the `finally` block very quickly and waits one second before shutting down the service. This period of waiting is enough for the items to be generated and passed to the subscribers. We also confirmed that every generated item was sent to each of the subscribers. The three `null` values were generated every time the `onSubscribe()` method of each of the subscribers was called.

It is reasonable to expect that, in future Java releases, there will be more support added for reactive (asynchronous and non-blocking) functionality.

Better Management of the OS Process

8

In this chapter, we will cover the following recipes:

- Spawning a new process
- Redirecting the process output and error streams to file
- Changing the working directory of a subprocess
- Setting the environment variable for a subprocess
- Running shell scripts
- Obtaining the process information of the current JVM
- Obtaining the process information of the spawned process
- Managing the spawned process
- Enumerating live processes in the system
- Connecting multiple processes using pipe
- Managing subprocesses

Introduction

How often have you ended up writing code that spawns a new process? Not often. However, there may have been situations that necessitated the writing of such code. In such cases, you had to resort to using a third-party API such as **Apache Commons Exec** (`https://commons.apache.org/proper/commons-exec/`), among others. Why was this? Wasn't the Java API sufficient? No, it wasn't; at least not until Java 9. Now, with Java 9 and above, we have many more features added to the process API.

Until Java 7, redirecting the input, output, and error streams were not trivial. With Java 7, new APIs were introduced, which allowed the redirecting of the input, output, and error to other processes (pipe), to a file, or to a standard input/output. Then, in Java 8, a few more APIs were introduced. In Java 9, there are now new APIs for the following areas:

- Getting the process information, such as **Process ID (PID)**, the user who launched the process, the time it has been running for, and so on
- Enumerating the processes running in the system
- Managing the subprocesses and getting access to the process tree by navigating up the process hierarchy

In this chapter, we will look at a few recipes that will help you explore everything that is new in the process API, and you will also get to know the changes that have been introduced since the time of `Runtime.getRuntime().exec()`. And you all know that using that was a crime.

All these recipes can only be executed on the Linux platform because we will be using Linux-specific commands while spawning a new process from Java code. There are two ways to execute the script `run.sh` on Linux:

- `sh run.sh`
- `chmod +x run.sh && ./run.sh`

Those who are on Windows 10 need not worry, as Microsoft has released Windows Subsystem For Linux, which allows you to run your favorite Linux distributions, such as Ubuntu, OpenSuse, and others, on Windows. For more details, check out this link: `https://docs.microsoft.com/en-in/windows/wsl/install-win10`.

Spawning a new process

In this recipe, we will see how to spawn a new process using `ProcessBuilder`. We will also see how to make use of the input, output, and error streams. This should be a very straightforward and common recipe. However, the aim of introducing this is to make this chapter a bit more complete and not just to focus on Java 9 features.

Getting ready

There is a command in Linux called `free`, which shows the amount of RAM that is free and how much is being used by the system. It accepts an option, `-m`, to show the output in megabytes. So, just running free -m gives us the following output:

```
root@ubuntu-512mb-lon1-01:~/samples/java9-samples/chp8/2_redirect_to_file# free -m
              total        used        free      shared  buff/cache   available
Mem:            488         208          17           5         261         243
Swap:             0           0           0
```

We will be running the preceding code from within the Java program.

How to do it...

Follow these steps:

1. Create an instance of `ProcessBuilder` by providing the required command and its options:

   ```
   ProcessBuilder pBuilder = new ProcessBuilder("free", "-m");
   ```

   An alternative way to specify the command and options is as follows:

   ```
   pBuilder.command("free", "-m");
   ```

2. Set up the input and output streams for the process builder and other properties, such as the directory of execution and environment variables. After that, invoke `start()` on the `ProcessBuilder` instance to spawn the process and get a reference to the `Process` object:

   ```
   Process p = pBuilder.inheritIO().start();
   ```

   The `inheritIO()` function sets the standard I/O of the spawned subprocess to be the same as that of the current Java process.

3. We then wait for the completion of the process, or for one second (whichever is sooner), as shown in the following code:

```
if(p.waitFor(1, TimeUnit.SECONDS)){
  System.out.println("process completed successfully");
}else{
  System.out.println("waiting time elapsed, process did
                      not complete");
  System.out.println("destroying process forcibly");
  p.destroyForcibly();
}
```

If this doesn't complete in the time specified, then we kill the process by invoking the `destroyForcibly()` method.

4. Compile and run the code by using the following commands:

```
$ javac -d mods --module-source-path src
$(find src -name *.java)
$ java -p mods -m process/com.packt.process.NewProcessDemo
```

5. The output we get is as follows:

	total	used	free	shared	buff/cache	available
Mem:	487	96	30	5	361	370
Swap:	0	0	0			

```
process completed successfully
```

The code for this recipe can be found at `Chapter08/1_spawn_new_process`.

How it works...

There are two ways to let `ProcessBuilder` know which command to run:

- By passing the command and its options to the constructor while creating the `ProcessBuilder` object
- By passing the command and its options as parameters to the `command()` method of the `ProcessBuilder` object

Before spawning the process, we can do the following:

- We can change the directory of execution by using the `directory()` method.
- We can redirect the input stream, output stream, and error streams to file or to another process.
- We can provide the required environment variables for the subprocess.

We will see all these activities in their respective recipes in this chapter.

A new process is spawned when the `start()` method is invoked and the caller gets a reference to this subprocess in the form of an instance of the `Process` class. Using this `Process` object, we can do a lot of things, such as the following:

- Get information about the process, including its PID
- Get the output and error streams
- Check for the completion of the process
- Destroy the process
- Associate the tasks to be performed once the process completes
- Check for the subprocesses spawned by the process
- Find the parent process of the process, if it exists

In our recipe, we `waitFor` one second, or for the process to complete (whichever occurs first). If the process has completed, then `waitFor` returns `true`; otherwise, it returns `false`. If the process doesn't complete, we can kill the process by invoking the `destroyForcibly()` method on the `Process` object.

Redirecting the process output and error streams to file

In this recipe, we will see how to deal with the output and error streams of a process spawned from the Java code. We will write the output or error produced by the spawned process to a file.

Getting ready

In this recipe, we will make use of the `iostat` command. This command is used for reporting the CPU and I/O statistics for different devices and partitions. Let's run the command and see what it reports:

```
$ iostat
```

 In some Linux distributions, such as Ubuntu, `iostat` is not installed by default. You can install the utility by running `sudo apt-get install sysstat`.

The output of the preceding command is as follows:

```
Linux 4.8.0-26-generic (ubuntu-512mb-blr1-01)    12/22/2016     _x86_64_        (1 CPU)

avg-cpu:  %user   %nice %system %iowait  %steal   %idle
           0.17    0.00    0.06    0.01    0.00   99.76

Device:            tps    kB_read/s    kB_wrtn/s    kB_read    kB_wrtn
vda               0.32         1.79         3.95    7844239   17323645
```

How to do it...

Follow these steps:

1. Create a new `ProcessBuilder` object by specifying the command to be executed:

   ```
   ProcessBuilder pb = new ProcessBuilder("iostat");
   ```

2. Redirect the output and error streams to the file's output and error, respectively:

   ```
   pb.redirectError(new File("error"))
     .redirectOutput(new File("output"));
   ```

3. Start the process and wait for it to complete:

   ```
   Process p = pb.start();
   int exitValue = p.waitFor();
   ```

4. Read the content of the output file:

```
Files.lines(Paths.get("output"))
                 .forEach(l -> System.out.println(l));
```

5. Read the content of the error file. This is created only if there is an error in the command:

```
Files.lines(Paths.get("error"))
                 .forEach(l -> System.out.println(l));
```

 Steps 4 and 5 are for our reference. This has nothing to do with `ProcessBuilder` or the process spawned. Using these two lines of code, we can inspect what was written to the output and error files by the process.

The complete code can be found at Chapter08/2_redirect_to_file.

6. Compile the code by using the following command:

```
$ javac -d mods --module-source-path src $(find src -name
*.java)
```

7. Run the code by using the following command:

```
$ java -p mods -m process/com.packt.process.RedirectFileDemo
```

We will get the following output:

```
Output
Linux 4.8.0-26-generic (ubuntu-512mb-blr1-01)    12/22/2016     _x86_64_       (1 CPU)

avg-cpu:  %user   %nice %system %iowait  %steal   %idle
           0.17    0.00    0.06    0.01    0.00   99.76

Device:           tps    kB_read/s    kB_wrtn/s    kB_read    kB_wrtn
vda              0.32         1.79         3.95    7874939   17335285

Error
                                                         _
```

We can see that as the command executed successfully, there is nothing in the error file.

There's more...

You can provide an erroneous command to `ProcessBuilder` and then see the error get written to the error file and nothing in the output file. You could do this by changing the `ProcessBuilder` instance creation as follows:

```
ProcessBuilder pb = new ProcessBuilder("iostat", "-Z");
```

Compile and run by using the commands given earlier in the *How to do it...* section.

You will see that there is an error reported in the error file but nothing in the output file:

```
Output
Error
Usage: iostat [ options ] [ <interval> [ <count> ] ]
Options are:
[ -c ] [ -d ] [ -h ] [ -k | -m ] [ -N ] [ -t ] [ -V ] [ -x ] [ -y ] [ -z ]
[ -j { ID | LABEL | PATH | UUID | ... } ]
[ [ -H ] -g <group_name> ] [ -p [ <device> [,...] | ALL ] ]
[ <device> [...] | ALL ]
```

Changing the working directory of a subprocess

Often, you'll want a process to be executed in the context of a path, such as listing the files in a directory. To do so, we will have to tell `ProcessBuilder` to launch the process in the context of a given location. We can achieve this by using the `directory()` method. This method serves two purposes:

- It returns the current directory of execution when we don't pass any parameters.
- It sets the current directory of execution to the passed value when we pass a parameter.

In this recipe, we will see how to execute the

`tree` command to recursively traverse all the directories from the current directory and print it in the form of a tree.

Getting ready

Generally, the `tree` command doesn't come preinstalled, so you will have to install the package that contains the command. To install on an Ubuntu/Debian-based system, run the following command:

```
$ sudo apt-get install tree
```

To install on Linux, which supports the `yum` package manager, run the following command:

```
$ yum install tree
```

To verify your installation, just run the `tree` command, and you should be able to see the current directory structure printed. For me, it's something like this:

```
├── 1_spawn_new_process
│   ├── mods
│   │   └── process
│   │       ├── com
│   │       │   └── packt
│   │       │       └── process
│   │       │           └── NewProcessDemo.class
│   │       └── module-info.class
│   └── src
│       └── process
│           ├── com
│           │   └── packt
│           │       └── process
│           │           └── NewProcessDemo.java
│           └── module-info.java
└── 2_redirect_to_file
    ├── error
    ├── mods
    │   └── process
    │       ├── com
    │       │   └── packt
    │       │       └── process
    │       │           └── RedirectFileDemo.class
    │       └── module-info.class
    ├── output
    └── src
        └── process
            ├── com
            │   └── packt
            │       └── process
            │           ├── input
            │           └── RedirectFileDemo.java
            └── module-info.java

22 directories, 11 files
```

There are multiple options supported by the `tree` command. It's for you to explore.

How to do it...

Follow these steps:

1. Create a new `ProcessBuilder` object:

```
ProcessBuilder pb = new ProcessBuilder();
```

2. Set the command to `tree` and the output and error to the same as that of the current Java process:

```
pb.command("tree").inheritIO();
```

3. Set the directory to whatever directory you want. I set it as the root folder:

```
pb.directory(new File("/root"));
```

4. Start the process and wait for it to exit:

```
Process p = pb.start();
int exitValue = p.waitFor();
```

5. Compile and run using the following commands:

```
$ javac -d mods --module-source-path src $(find src -name
*.java)
$ java -p mods -m
process/com.packt.process.ChangeWorkDirectoryDemo
```

6. The output will be the recursive contents of the directory, specified in the `directory()` method of the `ProcessBuilder` object, printed in a tree-like format.

The complete code can be found at `Chapter08/3_change_work_directory`.

How it works...

The `directory()` method accepts the path of the working directory for `Process`. The path is specified as an instance of `File`.

Setting the environment variable for a subprocess

Environment variables are just like any other variables that we have in our programming languages. They have a name and hold some value, which can be varied. These are used by the Linux/Windows commands or the shell/batch scripts to perform different operations. These are called **environment variables** because they are present in the environment of the process/command/script being executed. Generally, the process inherits the environment variables from the parent process.

They are accessed in different ways in different operating systems. In Windows, they are accessed as %ENVIRONMENT_VARIABLE_NAME%, and in Unix-based operating systems, they are accessed as $ENVIRONMENT_VARIABLE_NAME.

In Unix-based systems, you can use the printenv command to print all the environment variables available for the process, and in Windows-based systems, you can use the SET command.

In this recipe, we will pass some environment variables to our subprocess and make use of the printenv command to print all the environment variables available.

How to do it...

Follow these steps:

1. Create an instance of ProcessBuilder:

   ```
   ProcessBuilder pb = new ProcessBuilder();
   ```

2. Set the command to printenv and the output and error streams to the same as that of the current Java process:

   ```
   pb.command("printenv").inheritIO();
   ```

3. Provide the environment variables COOKBOOK_VAR1 with the value First variable, COOKBOOK_VAR2 with the value Second variable, and COOKBOOK_VAR3 with the value Third variable:

   ```
   Map<String, String> environment = pb.environment();
   environment.put("COOKBOOK_VAR1", "First variable");
   environment.put("COOKBOOK_VAR2", "Second variable");
   environment.put("COOKBOOK_VAR3", "Third variable");
   ```

4. Start the process and wait for it to complete:

```
Process p = pb.start();
int exitValue = p.waitFor();
```

The complete code for this recipe can be found at
`Chapter08/4_environment_variables`.

5. Compile and run the code by using the following commands:

```
$ javac -d mods --module-source-path src $(find src -name
*.java)
$ java -p mods -m
 process/com.packt.process.EnvironmentVariableDemo
```

The output you get is as follows:

```
XDG_SESSION_ID=2412
MAIL=/var/mail/root
COOKBOOK_VAR1=First variable
COOKBOOK_VAR2=Second variable
LOGNAME=root
COOKBOOK_VAR3=Third variable
PWD=/root/java9-samples/chp8/4_environment_variables
```

You can see the three variables printed among other variables.

How it works...

When you invoke the `environment()` method on the instance of `ProcessBuilder`,
it copies the environment variables of the current process, populates them in an
instance of `HashMap`, and returns it to the caller code.

 All the work of loading the environment variables is done by a
package private final class, `ProcessEnvironment`, which actually
extends `HashMap`.

We then make use of this map to populate our own environment variables, but we
need not set the map back to `ProcessBuilder` because we will have a reference to
the map object and not a copy. Any changes made to the map object will be reflected
in the actual map object held by the `ProcessBuilder` instance.

Running shell scripts

We generally collect a set of commands used in performing an operation in a file, called a **shell script** in the Unix world and a **batch file** in Windows. The commands present in these files are executed sequentially, with the exceptions being when you have conditional blocks or loops in the scripts.

These shell scripts are evaluated by the shell in which they get executed. Different types of shells available are bash, csh, ksh, and so on. The bash shell is the most commonly used shell.

In this recipe, we will write a simple shell script and then invoke the same from the Java code using the ProcessBuilder and Process objects.

Getting ready

First, let's write our shell script. This script does the following:

1. Prints the value of the environment variable, MY_VARIABLE
2. Executes the tree command
3. Executes the iostat command

Let's create a shell script file by the name, script.sh, with the following commands in it:

```
echo $MY_VARIABLE;
echo "Running tree command";
tree;
echo "Running iostat command"
iostat;
```

You can place the script.sh in your home folder; that is, in the /home/<username>. Now let's see how we can execute this from Java.

How to do it...

Follow these steps:

1. Create a new instance of `ProcessBuilder`:

   ```
   ProcessBuilder pb = new ProcessBuilder();
   ```

2. Set the directory of execution to point to the directory of the shell script file:

   ```
   pb.directory(new File("/root"));
   ```

   Note that the previous path passed, while creating the `File` object will depend on where you have placed your script `script.sh`. In our case, we had it placed in `/root`. You might have copied the script in `/home/yourname` and, accordingly, the `File` object will be created as `newFile("/home/yourname")`.

3. Set an environment variable that would be used by the shell script:

   ```
   Map<String, String> environment = pb.environment();
   environment.put("MY_VARIABLE", "Set by Java process");
   ```

4. Set the command to be executed, and also the arguments to be passed to the command. Also, set the output and error streams for the process to same as that of the current Java process:

   ```
   pb.command("/bin/bash", "script.sh").inheritIO();
   ```

5. Start the process and wait for it to execute completely:

   ```
   Process p = pb.start();
   int exitValue = p.waitFor();
   ```

You can get the complete code from `Chapter08/5_running_shell_script`.

You can compile and run the code by using the following commands:

```
$ javac -d mods --module-source-path src $(find src -name *.java)
$ java -p mods -m process/com.packt.process.RunningShellScriptDemo
```

The output we get is as follows:

```
From your parent Java process
Running tree command

├── mods
│   └── process
│       ├── com
│       │   └── packt
│       │       └── process
│       │           └── RunningShellScriptDemo.class
│       └── module-info.class
├── script.sh
├── src
│   └── process
│       ├── com
│       │   └── packt
│       │       └── process
│       │           └── RunningShellScriptDemo.java
│       └── module-info.java

10 directories, 5 files
Running iostat command
Linux 4.8.0-26-generic (ubuntu-512mb-blr1-01)    12/25/2016        _x86_64_        (1 CPU)

avg-cpu:  %user   %nice %system %iowait  %steal   %idle
           0.17    0.00    0.06    0.01    0.00   99.76

Device:            tps    kB_read/s    kB_wrtn/s    kB_read    kB_wrtn
vda               0.32         1.85         3.90    8584787   18137805
```

How it works...

You must make a note of two things in this recipe:

- Change the working directory of the process to the location of the shell script.
- Use /bin/bash to execute the shell script.

If you don't make a note of step 1, then you'll have to use the absolute path for the shell script file. However, in this recipe, we did do this, and hence we just use the shell script name for the /bin/bash command.

Step 2 is basically how you would want to execute the shell script. The way to do so is to pass the shell script to the interpreter, which will interpret and execute the script. That is what the following line of code does:

```
pb.command("/bin/bash", "script.sh")
```

Obtaining the process information of the current JVM

A running process has a set of attributes associated with it, such as the following:

- **PID**: This uniquely identifies the process
- **Owner**: This is the name of the user who launched the process
- **Command**: This is the command that runs under the process
- **CPU time**: This indicates the time for which the process has been active
- **Start time**: This indicates the time when the process was launched

These are a few attributes that we are generally interested in. Perhaps we would also be interested in CPU usage or memory usage. Now, getting this information from within Java was not possible prior to Java 9. However, in Java 9, a new set of APIs has been introduced, which enables us to get the basic information about the process.

In this recipe, we will see how to get the process information for the current Java process; that is, the process that is executing your code.

How to do it...

Follow these steps:

1. Create a simple class and use `ProcessHandle.current()` to get `ProcessHandle` for the current Java process:

   ```
   ProcessHandle handle = ProcessHandle.current();
   ```

2. We have added some code, which will add some running time to the code:

```
for ( int i = 0 ; i < 100; i++){
  Thread.sleep(1000);
}
```

3. Use the `info()` method on the instance of `ProcessHandle` to get an instance of `ProcessHandle.Info`:

```
ProcessHandle.Info info = handle.info();
```

4. Use the instance of `ProcessHandle.Info` to get all the information made available by the interface:

```
System.out.println("Command line: " +
                         info.commandLine().get());
System.out.println("Command: " + info.command().get());
System.out.println("Arguments: " +
            String.join(" ", info.arguments().get()));
System.out.println("User: " + info.user().get());
System.out.println("Start: " + info.startInstant().get());
System.out.println("Total CPU Duration: " +
        info.totalCpuDuration().get().toMillis() +"ms");
```

5. Use the `pid()` method of `ProcessHandle` to get the process ID of the current Java process:

```
System.out.println("PID: " + handle.pid());
```

6. We will also print the end time using the time at which the code is about to end. This will give us an idea of the execution time of the process:

```
Instant end = Instant.now();
System.out.println("End: " + end);
```

You can get the complete code from `Chapter08/6_current_process_info`.

Compile and run the code by using the following commands:

```
$ javac -d mods --module-source-path src $(find src -name *.java)
$ java -p mods -m process/com.packt.process.CurrentProcessInfoDemo
```

The output you see will be something like this:

```
Started main...
Command line: /usr/lib/jdk-9-b146/jdk-9/bin/java -p mods -m process/com.packt.process.CurrentProcessInfoDemo
Command: /usr/lib/jdk-9-b146/jdk-9/bin/java
Arguments: -p mods -m process/com.packt.process.CurrentProcessInfoDemo
User: root
Start: 2016-12-28T21:05:20.490Z
Total CPU Duration: 350ms
PID: 13487
End: 2016-12-28T21:07:00.995953Z
```

 It will take some time until the program completes execution. One observation to be made is that even if the program ran for around two minutes, the total CPU duration was 350 millisecond. This is the time period during which the CPU was busy.

How it works...

To give more control to the native processes and get its information, a new interface called `ProcessHandle` has been added to the Java API. Using `ProcessHandle`, you can control the process execution as well as get some information about the process. The interface has another inner interface called `ProcessHandle.Info`. This interface provides APIs to get information about the process.

There are multiple ways to get hold of the `ProcessHandle` object for a process. Some of the ways are as follows:

- `ProcessHandle.current()`: This is used to get the `ProcessHandle` instance for the current Java process.
- `Process.toHandle()`: This is used to get the `ProcessHandle` for a given `Process` object.
- `ProcessHandle.of(pid)`: This is used to get `ProcessHandle` for a process identified by the given PID.

In our recipe, we make use of the first approach, that is, we use `ProcessHandle.current()`. This gives us a handle on the current Java process. Invoking the `info()` method on the `ProcessHandle` instance will give us an instance of the implementation of the `ProcessHandle.Info` interface, which we can make use of to get the process information, as shown in the recipe code.

`ProcessHandle` and `ProcessHandle.Info` are interfaces. The JDK provide either Oracle JDK or Open JDK, will provide implementations for these interfaces. Oracle JDK has a class called `ProcessHandleImpl`, which implements `ProcessHandle` and another inner class within `ProcessHandleImpl` called `Info`, which implements the `ProcessHandle.Info` interface. So, whenever you call one of the aforementioned methods to get a `ProcessHandle` object, an instance of `ProcessHandleImpl` is returned.

The same goes with the `Process` class as well. It is an abstract class and Oracle JDK provides an implementation called `ProcessImpl`, which implements the abstract methods in the `Process` class.

In all the recipes in this chapter, any mention of the instance of `ProcessHandle` or the `ProcessHandle` object will refer to the instance or object of `ProcessHandleImpl` or any other implementation class provided by the JDK you are using.

Also, any mention of the instance of `ProcessHandle.Info` or the `ProcessHandle.Info` object will refer to the instance or object of `ProcessHandleImpl.Info` or any other implementation class provided by the JDK you are using.

Obtaining the process information of the spawned process

In our previous recipe, we saw how to get the process information for the current Java process. In this recipe, we will look at how to get the process information for a process spawned by the Java code; that is, by the current Java process. The APIs used will be the same as we saw in the previous recipe, except for the way the instance of `ProcessHandle` is implemented.

Getting ready

In this recipe, we will make use of a Unix command, `sleep`, which is used to pause the execution for a period of time in seconds.

How to do it...

Follow these steps:

1. Spawn a new process from the Java code, which runs the `sleep` command:

```
ProcessBuilder pBuilder = new ProcessBuilder("sleep", "20");
Process p = pBuilder.inheritIO().start();
```

2. Get the `ProcessHandle` instance for this spawned process:

```
ProcessHandle handle = p.toHandle();
```

3. Wait for the spawned process to complete execution:

```
int exitValue = p.waitFor();
```

4. Use `ProcessHandle` to get the `ProcessHandle.Info` instance, and use its APIs to get the required information. Alternatively, we can even use the `Process` object directly to get `ProcessHandle.Info` by using the `info()` method in the `Process` class:

```
ProcessHandle.Info info = handle.info();
System.out.println("Command line: " +
                                info.commandLine().get());
System.out.println("Command: " + info.command().get());
System.out.println("Arguments: " + String.join(" ",
                                info.arguments().get()));
System.out.println("User: " + info.user().get());
System.out.println("Start: " + info.startInstant().get());
System.out.println("Total CPU time(ms): " +
                    info.totalCpuDuration().get().toMillis());
System.out.println("PID: " + handle.pid());
```

You can get the complete code from `Chapter08/7_spawned_process_info`.

Compile and run the code by using the following commands:

```
$ javac -d mods --module-source-path src $(find src -name *.java)
$ java -p mods -m process/com.packt.process.SpawnedProcessInfoDemo
```

Alternatively, there is a `run.sh` script in `Chapter08/7_spawned_process_info`, which you can run from any Unix-based system as `/bin/bash run.sh`.

The output you see will be something like this:

```
Started main
Command line: /bin/sleep 20
Command: /bin/sleep
Arguments: 20
User: root
Start: 2016-12-28T21:18:17.130Z
Total CPU time(ms): 0
PID: 13589
```

Managing the spawned process

There are a few methods, such as `destroy()`, `destroyForcibly()` (added in Java 8), `isAlive()` (added in Java 8), and `supportsNormalTermination()` (added in Java 9), which can be used to control the process spawned. These methods are available on the `Process` object as well as on the `ProcessHandle` object. Here, controlling would be just to check whether the process is alive, and if it is, then destroy the process.

In this recipe, we will spawn a long-running process and do the following:

- Check for its liveliness
- Check whether it can be stopped normally; that is, depending on the platform, the process has to be stopped by just using destroy or by using force destroy
- Stop the process

How to do it...

1. Spawn a new process from the Java code, which runs the `sleep` command for, say, one minute, or 60 seconds:

```
ProcessBuilder pBuilder = new ProcessBuilder("sleep", "60");
Process p = pBuilder.inheritIO().start();
```

2. Wait for, say, 10 seconds:

```
p.waitFor(10, TimeUnit.SECONDS);
```

3. Check whether the process is alive:

```
boolean isAlive = p.isAlive();
System.out.println("Process alive? " + isAlive);
```

4. Check whether the process can be stopped normally:

```
boolean normalTermination = p.supportsNormalTermination();
System.out.println("Normal Termination? " +
normalTermination);
```

5. Stop the process and check for its liveliness:

```
p.destroy();
isAlive = p.isAlive();
System.out.println("Process alive? " + isAlive);
```

You can get the complete code from `Chapter08/8_manage_spawned_process`.

We have provided a utility script called `run.sh`, which you can use to compile and run the code—`sh run.sh`.

The output we get is as follows:

```
Started main
Process alive? true
Normal Termination? true
Process alive? false
```

If we run the program on Windows, `supportsNormalTermination()` returns `false`, but on Unix `supportsNormalTermination()` returns `true` (as seen in the preceding output as well).

Enumerating live processes in the system

In Windows, you open the **Windows Task Manager** to view the processes currently active, and in Linux you use the ps command with its varied options to view the processes along with other details, such as user, time spent, command, and so on.

In Java 9, a new API was added, called ProcessHandle, which deals with controlling and getting information about the processes. One of the methods of the API is allProcesses(), which returns a snapshot of all the processes visible to the current process. In this recipe, we will look at how the method works and what information we can extract from the API.

How to do it...

Follow these steps:

1. Use the allProcesses() method on the ProcessHandle interface to get a stream of the currently active processes:

```
Stream<ProcessHandle> liveProcesses =
                ProcessHandle.allProcesses();
```

2. Iterate over the stream using forEach(), and pass a lambda expression to print the details available:

```
liveProcesses.forEach(ph -> {
  ProcessHandle.Info phInfo = ph.info();
  System.out.println(phInfo.command().orElse("") +" " +
                  phInfo.user().orElse(""));
});
```

You can get the complete code from Chapter08/9_enumerate_all_processes.

We have provided a utility script called run.sh, which you can use to compile and run the code—sh run.sh.

The output we get is as follows:

```
/lib/systemd/systemd-timesyncd systemd-timesync
/lib/systemd/systemd-logind root
/usr/sbin/cron root
/lib/systemd/systemd-resolved systemd-resolve
/usr/sbin/rsyslogd syslog
/usr/bin/dbus-daemon (deleted) messagebus
/usr/sbin/atd daemon
/usr/lib/snapd/snapd root
/usr/bin/lxcfs root
/usr/sbin/acpid root
/usr/lib/accountsservice/accounts-daemon root
/sbin/iscsid root
/sbin/iscsid root
/sbin/agetty root
/sbin/agetty root
/usr/lib/policykit-1/polkitd root
/usr/sbin/sshd root
```

In the preceding output, we are printing the command name as well as the user of the process. We have shown a small part of the output.

Connecting multiple processes using pipe

In Unix, it's common to pipe a set of commands together using the | symbol to create a pipeline of activities, where the input for the command is the output from the previous command. This way, we can process the input to get the desired output.

A common scenario is when you want to search for something or a pattern in the log files, or for an occurrence of some text in the log file. In such scenarios, you can create a pipeline, wherein you pass the required log file data via a series of commands, namely, cat, grep, wc -l, and so on.

In this recipe, we will make use of the Iris dataset from the UCI machine learning repository available at https://archive.ics.uci.edu/ml/datasets/Iris to create a pipeline, wherein we will count the number of occurrences of each type of flower.

Getting ready

We have already downloaded the Iris Flower Dataset (`https://archive.ics.uci.edu/ml/datasets/iris`), which can be found at `Chapter08/10_connecting_process_pipe/iris.data` of the code download for this book.

If you happen to look at the `Iris` data, you will see there are 150 rows in the following format:

```
4.7,3.2,1.3,0.2,Iris-setosa
```

Here, there are multiple attributes separated by a comma (,), and the attributes are as follows:

- Sepal length in cm
- Sepal width in cm
- Petal length in cm
- Petal width in cm
- Class:
  - Iris setosa
  - Iris versicolour
  - Iris virginica

In this recipe, we will find the total number of flowers in each class, namely setosa, versicolour, and virginica.

We will make use of a pipeline with the following commands (using a Unix-based operating system):

```
$ cat iris.data.txt | cut -d',' -f5 | uniq -c
```

The output we get is as follows:

```
50 Iris-setosa
50 Iris-versicolor
50 Iris-virginica
1
```

The 1 at the end is for the new line available at the end of the file. So, there are 50 flowers of each class. Let's dissect the above shell command pipeline and understand the function of each of them:

- `cat`: This command reads the file given as the argument.
- `cut`: This splits each line by using the character given in the `-d` option and returns the value in the column identified by the `-f` option.
- `uniq`: This returns a unique list from the given values, and when the `-c` option is used, it returns how many times each unique value is present in the list.

How to do it...

1. Create a list of `ProcessBuilder` objects, which will hold the `ProcessBuilder` instances participating in our pipeline. Also, redirect the output of the last process in the pipeline to the standard output of the current Java process:

```
List<ProcessBuilder> pipeline = List.of(
  new ProcessBuilder("cat", "iris.data.txt"),
  new ProcessBuilder("cut", "-d", ",", "-f", "5"),
  new ProcessBuilder("uniq", "-c")
      .redirectOutput(ProcessBuilder.Redirect.INHERIT)
);
```

2. Use the `startPipeline()` method of `ProcessBuilder` and pass the list of `ProcessBuilder` objects to start the pipeline. It will return a list of `Process` objects, each representing a `ProcessBuilder` object in the list:

```
List<Process> processes = ProcessBuilder.startPipeline(pipeline);
```

3. Get the last process in the list and `waitFor` it to complete:

```
int exitValue = processes.get(processes.size() - 1).waitFor();
```

You can get the complete code from `Chapter08/10_connecting_process_pipe`.

We have provided a utility script called `run.sh`, which you can use to compile and run the code—`sh run.sh`.

The output we get is as follows:

```
50 Iris-setosa
50 Iris-versicolor
50 Iris-virginica
 1
```

How it works...

The `startPipeline()` method starts a `Process` for each `ProcessBuilder` object in the list. Except for the first and the last processes, it redirects the output of one process to the input of another process by using `ProcessBuilder.Redirect.PIPE`. If you have provided `redirectOutput` for any intermediate process as something other than `ProcessBuilder.Redirect.PIPE`, then there will be an error thrown; something similar to the following:

```
Exception in thread "main" java.lang.IllegalArgumentException: builder
redirectOutput() must be PIPE except for the last builder: INHERIT.
```

It states that any builder except for the last should redirect its output to the next process. The same is applicable for `redirectInput`.

Managing subprocesses

When a process launches another process, the launched process becomes the subprocess of the launching process. The launched process, in turn, can launch another process, and this chain can continue. This results in a process tree. Often, we would have to deal with a buggy subprocess and might want to kill that subprocess, or we might want to know the subprocesses that are launched and might want to get some information about them.

In Java 9, two new APIs in the `Process` class were added—`children()` and `descendants()`. The `children()` API allows you to get a list of the snapshot of processes that are the immediate children of the current process, and the `descendants()` API provides a snapshot of processes that are recursively `children()` of the current process; that is, they are invoking `children()` recursively on each child process.

In this recipe, we will look at both the `children()` and `descendants()` APIs and see what information we can gather from the snapshot of the process.

Getting ready

Let's create a simple shell script, which we will be using in the recipe. This script can be found at `Chapter08/11_managing_sub_process/script.sh`:

```
echo "Running tree command";
tree;
sleep 60;
echo "Running iostat command";
iostat;
```

In the preceding script, we are running the commands, `tree` and `iostat`, separated by a sleep time of one minute. If you want to know about these commands, please refer to the *Running shell scripts* recipe of this chapter. The sleep command, when executed from within the bash shell, creates a new subprocess each time it is invoked.

We will create, say, 10 instances of `ProcessBuilder` to run the preceding shell script and launch them simultaneously.

How to do it...

1. We will create 10 instances of `ProcessBuilder` to run our shell script (available at `Chapter08/11_managing_sub_process/script.sh`). We are not concerned with its output, so let's discard the output of the commands by redirecting the output to a predefined redirect called `ProcessHandle.Redirect.DISCARD`:

```
for ( int i = 0; i < 10; i++){
  new ProcessBuilder("/bin/bash", "script.sh")
    .redirectOutput(ProcessBuilder.Redirect.DISCARD)
    .start();
}
```

2. Get the handle for the current process:

```
ProcessHandle currentProcess = ProcessHandle.current();
```

3. Use the current process to get its children using the `children()` API and iterate over each of its children to print their information. Once we have an instance of `ProcessHandle`, we can do multiple things, such as destroy the process, get its process information, and so on:

```
System.out.println("Obtaining children");
currentProcess.children().forEach(pHandle -> {
  System.out.println(pHandle.info());
});
```

4. Use the current process to get all the subprocesses that are its descendants by using the `descendants()` API and iterate over each of them to print their information:

```
currentProcess.descendants().forEach(pHandle -> {
  System.out.println(pHandle.info());
});
```

You can get the complete code from `Chapter08/11_managing_sub_process`.

We have provided a utility script called `run.sh`, which you can use to compile and run the code—`sh run.sh`.

The output we get is as follows:

```
Obtaining children
[user: Optional[root], cmd: /bin/bash, args: [script.sh], startTime: Optional[2017-01-07T08:05:15.800Z], totalTime: Optional[PT0S]]
[user: Optional[root], cmd: /bin/bash, args: [script.sh], startTime: Optional[2017-01-07T08:05:15.850Z], totalTime: Optional[PT0S]]
[user: Optional[root], cmd: /bin/bash, args: [script.sh], startTime: Optional[2017-01-07T08:05:15.850Z], totalTime: Optional[PT0S]]
[user: Optional[root], cmd: /bin/bash, args: [script.sh], startTime: Optional[2017-01-07T08:05:15.850Z], totalTime: Optional[PT0S]]
[user: Optional[root], cmd: /bin/bash, args: [script.sh], startTime: Optional[2017-01-07T08:05:15.860Z], totalTime: Optional[PT0S]]
[user: Optional[root], cmd: /bin/bash, args: [script.sh], startTime: Optional[2017-01-07T08:05:15.860Z], totalTime: Optional[PT0S]]
[user: Optional[root], cmd: /bin/bash, args: [script.sh], startTime: Optional[2017-01-07T08:05:15.860Z], totalTime: Optional[PT0S]]
[user: Optional[root], cmd: /bin/bash, args: [script.sh], startTime: Optional[2017-01-07T08:05:15.870Z], totalTime: Optional[PT0S]]
[user: Optional[root], cmd: /bin/bash, args: [script.sh], startTime: Optional[2017-01-07T08:05:15.870Z], totalTime: Optional[PT0S]]
[user: Optional[root], cmd: /bin/bash, args: [script.sh], startTime: Optional[2017-01-07T08:05:15.870Z], totalTime: Optional[PT0S]]
Obtaining descendants
[user: Optional[root], cmd: /bin/bash, args: [script.sh], startTime: Optional[2017-01-07T08:05:15.800Z], totalTime: Optional[PT0S]]
[user: Optional[root], cmd: /bin/bash, args: [script.sh], startTime: Optional[2017-01-07T08:05:15.850Z], totalTime: Optional[PT0S]]
[user: Optional[root], cmd: /bin/bash, args: [script.sh], startTime: Optional[2017-01-07T08:05:15.850Z], totalTime: Optional[PT0S]]
[user: Optional[root], cmd: /bin/bash, args: [script.sh], startTime: Optional[2017-01-07T08:05:15.850Z], totalTime: Optional[PT0S]]
[user: Optional[root], cmd: /bin/bash, args: [script.sh], startTime: Optional[2017-01-07T08:05:15.860Z], totalTime: Optional[PT0S]]
[user: Optional[root], cmd: /bin/bash, args: [script.sh], startTime: Optional[2017-01-07T08:05:15.860Z], totalTime: Optional[PT0S]]
[user: Optional[root], cmd: /bin/bash, args: [script.sh], startTime: Optional[2017-01-07T08:05:15.870Z], totalTime: Optional[PT0S]]
[user: Optional[root], cmd: /bin/bash, args: [script.sh], startTime: Optional[2017-01-07T08:05:15.870Z], totalTime: Optional[PT0S]]
[user: Optional[root], cmd: /bin/bash, args: [script.sh], startTime: Optional[2017-01-07T08:05:15.870Z], totalTime: Optional[PT0S]]
[user: Optional[root], cmd: /bin/sleep, args: [5], startTime: Optional[2017-01-07T08:05:15.820Z], totalTime: Optional[PT0S]]
[user: Optional[root], cmd: /bin/sleep, args: [5], startTime: Optional[2017-01-07T08:05:15.860Z], totalTime: Optional[PT0S]]
[user: Optional[root], cmd: /bin/sleep, args: [5], startTime: Optional[2017-01-07T08:05:15.860Z], totalTime: Optional[PT0S]]
[user: Optional[root], cmd: /bin/sleep, args: [5], startTime: Optional[2017-01-07T08:05:15.860Z], totalTime: Optional[PT0S]]
[user: Optional[root], cmd: /bin/sleep, args: [5], startTime: Optional[2017-01-07T08:05:15.860Z], totalTime: Optional[PT0S]]
[user: Optional[root], cmd: /bin/sleep, args: [5], startTime: Optional[2017-01-07T08:05:15.870Z], totalTime: Optional[PT0S]]
[user: Optional[root], cmd: /bin/sleep, args: [5], startTime: Optional[2017-01-07T08:05:15.870Z], totalTime: Optional[PT0S]]
[user: Optional[root], cmd: /bin/sleep, args: [5], startTime: Optional[2017-01-07T08:05:15.880Z], totalTime: Optional[PT0S]]
```

How it works...

The APIs `children()` and `descendants()` return the `Stream` of the `ProcessHandler` for each of the processes, which are either direct children or descendants of the current process. Using the instance of `ProcessHandler`, we can perform the following operations:

- Get the process information
- Check the status of the process
- Stop the process

RESTful Web Services Using Spring Boot

9

In this chapter, we are going to cover the following recipes:

- Creating a simple Spring Boot application
- Interacting with the database
- Creating a RESTful web service
- Creating multiple profiles for Spring Boot
- Deploying RESTful web services to Heroku
- Containerizing the RESTful web service using Docker
- Monitoring the Spring Boot 2 application using Micrometer and Prometheus

Introduction

In recent years, the drive for microservice-based architectures has gained wide adoption, thanks to the simplicity and ease of maintenance it provides when done the right way. A lot of companies, such as Netflix and Amazon, have moved from monolithic systems to more focused and lighter systems, all talking with each other via RESTful web services. The advent of RESTful web services and its straightforward approach to creating web services using the known HTTP protocol has made it easier for communication between applications than the older SOAP-based web services.

In this chapter, we will look at the **Spring Boot** framework, which provides a convenient way to create production-ready microservices using Spring libraries. Using Spring Boot, we will develop a simple RESTful web service and deploy it to the cloud.

Creating a simple Spring Boot application

Spring Boot helps in creating production-ready, Spring-based applications easily. It provides support for working with almost all Spring libraries, without any need to configure them explicitly. There are auto-configuration classes provided for easy integration with most commonly-used libraries, databases, and message queues.

In this recipe, we will look at creating a simple Spring Boot application with a controller that prints a message when opened in the browser.

Getting ready

Spring Boot supports Maven and Gradle as its build tools, and we will be using Maven in our recipes. The following URL, http://start.spring.io/, provides a convenient way to create an empty project with the required dependencies. We will use it to download an empty project. Follow these steps to create and download an empty Spring Boot-based project:

1. Navigate to http://start.spring.io/ to see something similar to the following screenshot:

2. You can select the dependency-management and build tool, selecting the appropriate option in the dropdown after the **Generate a** text.

3. Spring Boot supports Java, Kotlin, and Groovy. You can choose the language by changing the dropdown after the **with** text.

4. Select the Spring Boot version by choosing its value from the dropdown after the **and Spring Boot** text. For this recipe, we'll use the latest stable edition of Spring Boot 2, that is 2.0.4.

5. On the left-hand side, under **Project Metadata**, we have to provide Maven-related information, that is, the group ID and artifact ID. We'll use **Group** as `com.packt` and **Artifact** as `boot_demo`.

6. On the right-hand side, under **Dependencies**, you can search for the dependencies you want to add. For this recipe, we need web and Thymeleaf dependencies. This means that we want to create a web application that uses Thymeleaf UI templates and would want all the dependencies, such as Spring MVC and Embedded Tomcat, to be part of the application.

7. Click on the **Generate Project** button to download the empty project. You can load this empty project in any IDE of your choice, just like any other Maven project.

At this point, you will have your empty project loaded into an IDE of your choice and will be ready to explore further. In this recipe, we will make use of the Thymeleaf template engine to define our web pages and create a simple controller to render the web page.

The complete code for this recipe can be found at `Chapter09/1_boot_demo`.

How to do it...

1. If you have followed the group ID and artifact ID naming convention as mentioned in the *Getting ready* section, you will have a package structure, `com.packt.boot_demo`, and a `BootDemoApplication.java` main class already created for you. There will be an equivalent package structure and a `BootDemoApplicationTests.java` main class under the `tests` folder.

2. Create a new class, `SimpleViewController`, under
   the `com.packt.boot_demo` package, with the following code:

```
@Controller
public class SimpleViewController{
  @GetMapping("/message")
  public String message(){
    return "message";
  }
}
```

3. Create a web page, `message.html`,
   under `src/main/resources/templates`, with the following code:

```
<h1>Hello, this is a message from the Controller</h1>
<h2>The time now is [[${#dates.createNow()}]]</h2>
```

4. From the command prompt, navigate to the project root folder and issue
   the `mvn spring-boot:run` command; you'll see the application being
   launched. Once it completes the initialization and starts, it will be running
   on the default port, `8080`. Navigate to
   `http://localhost:8080/message` to see the message.

We are using Spring Boot's Maven plugin, which provides us with convenient tools to launch the application during development. But for production, we will create a fat JAR, that is, a JAR comprising all the dependencies, and deploy it as a Linux or Windows service. We can even run the fat JAR using the `java -jar` command.

How it works...

We will not go into the working of Spring Boot or the other Spring libraries. Spring Boot creates an embedded Tomcat running on the default port, that is, `8080`. It then registers all the controllers, components, and services that are available in the packages and sub-packages of the class with the `@SpringBootApplication` annotation.

In our recipe, the `BootDemoApplication` class in the `com.packt.boot_demo` package is annotated with `@SpringBootApplication`. So, all the classes that are annotated with `@Controller`, `@Service`, `@Configuration`, and `@Component` get registered with the Spring framework as beans and are managed by it. Now, these can be injected into the code by using the `@Autowired` annotation.

There are two ways we can create a web controller:

- Annotating with @Controller
- Annotating with @RestController

In the first approach, we create a controller that can serve both raw data and HTML data (generated by template engines such as Thymeleaf, Freemarker, and JSP). In the second approach, the controller supports endpoints that can only serve raw data in the form of JSON or XML. In our recipe, we used the former approach, as follows:

```
@Controller
public class SimpleViewController{
  @GetMapping("/message")
  public String message(){
    return "message";
  }
}
```

We can annotate the class with @RequestMapping, say, @RequestMapping("/api"). In this case, any HTTP endpoints exposed in the controller are prepended by /api. There is a specialized annotation mapping for the HTTP GET, POST, DELETE, and PUT methods, which are @GetMapping, @PostMapping, @DeleteMapping, and @PutMapping, respectively. We can also rewrite our controller class as follows:

```
@Controller
@RequestMapping("/message")
public class SimpleViewController{
  @GetMapping
  public String message(){
    return "message";
  }
}
```

We can modify the port by providing server.port = 9090 in the application.properties file. This file can be found in src/main/resources/application.properties. There is a whole set of properties (http://docs.spring.io/spring-boot/docs/current/reference/html/common-application-properties.html) that we can use to customize and connect with different components.

Interacting with the database

In this recipe, we will look at how to integrate with a database to create, read, modify, and delete the data. For this, we will set up a MySQL database with the required table. Subsequently, we will update the data in a table from our Spring Boot application.

We will be using Windows as the development platform for this recipe. You can perform a similar action on Linux as well, but you would first have to set up your MySQL database.

Getting ready

Before we start integrating our application with the database, we need to set up the database locally on our development machines. In the subsequent sections, we will download and install MySQL tools and then create a sample table with some data, which we will use with our application.

Installing MySQL tools

First, download the MySQL installer from `https://dev.mysql.com/downloads/windows/installer/5.7.html`. This MySQL bundle is for Windows only. Follow the onscreen instructions to successfully install MySQL along with other tools such as MySQL Workbench. To confirm that the MySQL daemon (`mysqld`) is running, open the task manager and you should be able to see a process similar to the following:

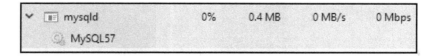

You should remember the password you set for the root user.

Let's run the MySQL workbench; on starting up, you should be able to see something similar to the following screenshot, among other things provided by the tool:

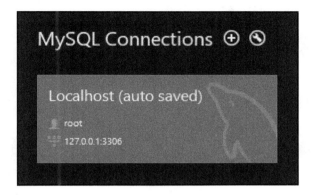

If you don't find a connection like in the preceding image, you can add one using the (+) sign. When you click on (+), you will see the following dialog. Fill it in and click on **Test Connection** to get a success message:

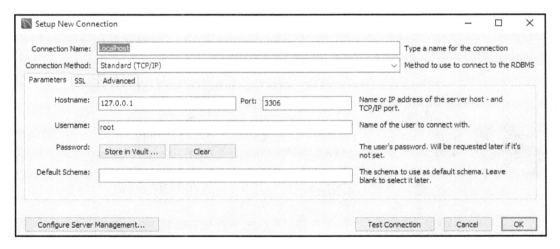

A successful **Test Connection** will result in the following message:

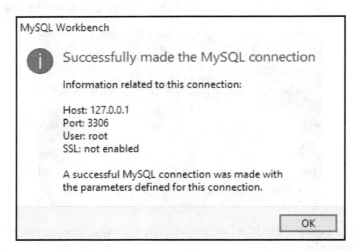

Double-click on the connection to connect to the database, and you should see a list of DBs on the left-hand side, an empty area on the right-hand side, and a menu and toolbars on the top. From the **File** menu, click on **New Query Tab**, or press *Ctrl + T* to get a new query window. Here, we will write our queries to create a database and create a table within that database.

> The bundled installer downloaded from `https://dev.mysql.com/downloads/windows/installer/5.7.html` is for Windows only. Linux users have to download the MySQL Server and MySQL Workbench (GUI for interacting with DB) separately.
> The MySQL server can be downloaded from `https://dev.mysql.com/downloads/mysql/`.
> The MySQL Workbench can be downloaded from `https://dev.mysql.com/downloads/workbench/`.

Creating a sample database

Run the following SQL statement to create a database:

```
create database sample;
```

Creating a person table

Run the following SQL statements to use the newly created database and create a simple person table:

```
create table person(
    id int not null auto_increment,
    first_name varchar(255),
    last_name varchar(255),
    place varchar(255),
    primary key(id)
);
```

Populating sample data

Let's go ahead and insert some sample data in the table we just created:

```
insert into person(first_name, last_name, place)
values('Raj', 'Singh', 'Bangalore');

insert into person(first_name, last_name, place)
values('David', 'John', 'Delhi');
```

Now that we have our database ready, we will go ahead and download the empty Spring Boot project from http://start.spring.io/ with the following options:

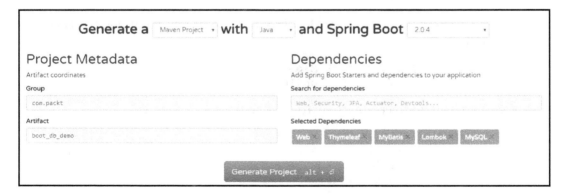

How to do it...

1. Create a model class, `com.packt.boot_db_demo.Person`, to represent a person. We will make use of Lombok annotations to generate the getters and setters for us:

```
@Data
public class Person{
  private Integer id;
  private String firstName;
  private String lastName;
  private String place;
}
```

2. Create `com.packt.boot_db_demo.PersonMapper` to map the data from the database into our model class, `Person`:

```
@Mapper
public interface PersonMapper {
}
```

3. Let's add a method to get all the rows from the table. Note that the next few methods will be written inside the `PersonMapper` interface:

```
@Select("SELECT * FROM person")
public List<Person> getPersons();
```

4. Another method to get the details of a single person identified by ID is as follows:

```
@Select("SELECT * FROM person WHERE id = #{id}")
public Person getPerson(Integer id);
```

5. The method to create a new row in the table is as follows:

```
@Insert("INSERT INTO person(first_name, last_name, place) "
        + " VALUES (#{firstName}, #{lastName}, #{place})")
@Options(useGeneratedKeys = true)
public void insert(Person person);
```

6. The method to update an existing row in the table, identified by the ID, is as follows:

```
@Update("UPDATE person SET first_name = #{firstName},last_name =
          #{lastName}, "+ "place = #{place}  WHERE id = #{id} ")
public void save(Person person);
```

7. The method to delete a row from the table, identified by the ID, is as follows:

```
@Delete("DELETE FROM person WHERE id = #{id}")
public void delete(Integer id);
```

8. Let's create a `com.packt.boot_db_demo.PersonController` class, which we will use to write our web endpoints:

```
@Controller
@RequestMapping("/persons")
public class PersonContoller {
  @Autowired PersonMapper personMapper;
}
```

9. Let's create an endpoint to list all the entries in the `person` table:

```
@GetMapping
public String list(ModelMap model){
  List<Person> persons = personMapper.getPersons();
  model.put("persons", persons);
  return "list";
}
```

10. Let's create an endpoint to add a new row in the `person` table:

```
@GetMapping("/{id}")
public String detail(ModelMap model, @PathVariable Integer id){
    System.out.println("Detail id: " + id);
    Person person = personMapper.getPerson(id);
    model.put("person", person);
    return "detail";
}
```

11. Let's create an endpoint to add a new row or edit an existing row in the `person` table:

```
@PostMapping("/form")
public String submitForm(Person person){
    System.out.println("Submiting form person id: " +
                          person.getId());
    if ( person.getId() != null ){
      personMapper.save(person);
    }else{
      personMapper.insert(person);
    }
    return "redirect:/persons/";
}
```

12. Let's create an endpoint to delete a row from the `person` table:

```
@GetMapping("/{id}/delete")
public String deletePerson(@PathVariable Integer id){
    personMapper.delete(id);
    return "redirect:/persons";
}
```

13. Update the `src/main/resources/application.properties` file to provide the configuration related to our data source, that is, our MySQL database:

```
spring.datasource.driver-class-name=com.mysql.jdbc.Driver
spring.datasource.url=jdbc:mysql://localhost/sample?useSSL=fal
se
spring.datasource.username=root
spring.datasource.password=mohamed
mybatis.configuration.map-underscore-to-camel-case=true
```

You can run the application from the command line using `mvn spring-boot:run`. This application starts up on the default port, that is, `8080`. Navigate to `http://localhost:8080/persons` in your browser.

The complete code for this recipe can be found at `Chapter09/2_boot_db_demo`.

On visiting `http://localhost:8080/persons`, this is what you will find:

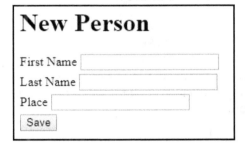

Persons!

New Person

- **David rere John** lives in **Delhi** Edit Delete
- **Raj Singh** lives in **Bangalore** Edit Delete

On clicking on **New Person**, you'll get the following:

New Person

First Name [   ]
Last Name [   ]
Place [   ]
[Save]

On clicking on **Edit**, you'll get the following:

Edit Person

First Name [Raj   ]
Last Name [Singh   ]
Place [Bangalore   ]
[Save]

How it works...

Firstly, `com.packt.boot_db_demo.PersonMapper` annotated with `org.apache.ibatis.annotations.Mapper` knows how to execute the query provided within the `@Select`, `@Update`, and `@Delete` annotations and to return relevant results. This is all managed by the MyBatis and Spring Data libraries.

You must be wondering how the connection to the database was achieved. One of the Spring Boot auto-configuration classes, `DataSourceAutoConfiguration`, does the work of setting up by making use of the `spring.datasource.*` properties defined in your `application.properties` file to give us an instance of `javax.sql.DataSource`. This `javax.sql.DataSource` object is then used by the MyBatis library to provide you with an instance of `SqlSessionTemplate`, which is what is used by our `PersonMapper` under the hood.

Then, we make use of `com.packt.boot_db_demo.PersonMapper` by injecting it into the `com.packt.boot_db_demo.PersonController` class by using `@AutoWired`. The `@AutoWired` annotation looks for any Spring managed beans, which are either instances of the exact type or its implementation. Take a look at the *Creating a simple Spring Boot application* recipe in this chapter to understand the `@Controller` annotation.

With very little configuration, we have been able to quickly set up simple CRUD operations. This is the flexibility and agility that Spring Boot provides to developers!

Creating a RESTful web service

In our previous recipe, we interacted with data using web forms. In this recipe, we will see how to interact with data using RESTful web services. These web services are a means to interact with other applications using the known HTTP protocol and its methods, namely GET, POST, and PUT. The data can be exchanged in the form of XML, JSON, or even plain text. We will be using JSON in our recipe.

So, we will create RESTful APIs to support retrieving data, creating new data, editing data, and deleting data.

Getting ready

As usual, download the starter project from `http://start.spring.io/` by selecting the dependencies shown in the following screenshot:

How to do it...

1. Copy the `Person` class from the previous recipe:

```
public class Person {
    private Integer id;
    private String firstName;
    private String lastName;
    private String place;
    //required getters and setters
}
```

2. We will do the `PersonMapper` part in a different way. We will write all our SQL queries in a mapper XML file and then refer to them from the `PersonMapper` interface. We will place the mapper XML under the `src/main/resources/mappers` folder. We'll set the value of the `mybatis.mapper-locations` property to `classpath*:mappers/*.xml`. This way, the `PersonMapper` interface can discover the SQL queries corresponding to its methods.

3. Create the `com.packt.boot_rest_demo.PersonMapper` interface:

```
@Mapper
public interface PersonMapper {
  public List<Person> getPersons();
  public Person getPerson(Integer id);
  public void save(Person person);
  public void insert(Person person);
  public void delete(Integer id);
}
```

4. Create the SQL in `PersonMapper.xml`. Make sure that the `namespace` attribute of the `<mapper>` tag is the same as the fully qualified name of the `PersonMapper` mapper interface:

```
<!DOCTYPE mapper PUBLIC "-//mybatis.org//DTD Mapper 3.0//EN"
  "http://mybatis.org/dtd/mybatis-3-mapper.dtd">
<mapper namespace="com.packt.boot_rest_demo.PersonMapper">
  <select id="getPersons"
   resultType="com.packt.boot_rest_demo.Person">
    SELECT id, first_name firstname, last_name lastname, place
    FROM person
  </select>

  <select id="getPerson"
   resultType="com.packt.boot_rest_demo.Person"
   parameterType="long">
    SELECT id, first_name firstname, last_name lastname, place
    FROM person
    WHERE id = #{id}
  </select>
  <update id="save"
   parameterType="com.packt.boot_rest_demo.Person">
    UPDATE person SET
      first_name = #{firstName},
      last_name = #{lastName},
      place = #{place}
    WHERE id = #{id}
  </update>

  <insert id="insert"
   parameterType="com.packt.boot_rest_demo.Person"
   useGeneratedKeys="true" keyColumn="id" keyProperty="id">
    INSERT INTO person(first_name, last_name, place)
    VALUES (#{firstName}, #{lastName}, #{place})
  </insert>

  <delete id="delete" parameterType="long">
```

```
    DELETE FROM person WHERE id = #{id}
   </delete>
</mapper>
```

5. Define the application properties in the
   `src/main/resources/application.properties` file:

   ```
   spring.datasource.driver-class-name=com.mysql.jdbc.Driver
   spring.datasource.url=jdbc:mysql://localhost/sample?
   useSSL=false
   spring.datasource.username=root
   spring.datasource.password=mohamed
   mybatis.mapper-locations=classpath*:mappers/*.xml
   ```

6. Create an empty controller for the REST APIs. This controller will be
   marked with the `@RestController` annotation because all the APIs in it
   are going to deal solely with data:

   ```
   @RestController
   @RequestMapping("/api/persons")
   public class PersonApiController {
     @Autowired PersonMapper personMapper;
   }
   ```

7. Add an API to list all the rows in the `person` table:

   ```
   @GetMapping
   public ResponseEntity<List<Person>> getPersons(){
     return new ResponseEntity<>(personMapper.getPersons(),
                          HttpStatus.OK);
   }
   ```

8. Add an API to get the details of a single person:

```
@GetMapping("/{id}")
public ResponseEntity<Person> getPerson(@PathVariable Integer id){
   return new ResponseEntity<>(personMapper.getPerson(id),
                                          HttpStatus.OK);

}
```

9. Add an API to add new data to the table:

```
@PostMapping
public ResponseEntity<Person> newPerson
                (@RequestBody Person person){
  personMapper.insert(person);
  return new ResponseEntity<>(person, HttpStatus.OK);
}
```

10. Add an API to edit the data in the table:

```
@PostMapping("/{id}")
public ResponseEntity<Person> updatePerson
                (@RequestBody Person person,
  @PathVariable Integer id){
    person.setId(id);
    personMapper.save(person);
    return new ResponseEntity<>(person, HttpStatus.OK);
}
```

11. Add an API to delete the data in the table:

```
@DeleteMapping("/{id}")
public ResponseEntity<Void> deletePerson
                (@PathVariable Integer id){
  personMapper.delete(id);
  return new ResponseEntity<>(HttpStatus.OK);
}
```

You can find the complete code at `Chapter09/3_boot_rest_demo`. You can launch the application by using `mvn spring-boot:run` from the project folder. Once the application has started, navigate to `http://localhost:8080/api/persons` to view all the data in the person table.

To test the other APIs, we will make use of the Postman REST client app for Google Chrome.

This is what adding a new person looks like. Look at the request body, that is, the person detail specified in JSON:

This is how we edit a person's details:

This is what deleting a person looks like:

How it works...

First, let's look at how the `PersonMapper` interface discovers the SQL statements to execute. If you look at `src/main/resources/mappers/PersonMapper.xml`, you will find that the `<mapper>` `namespace` attribute is `org.packt.boot_rest_demo.PersonMapper`. This is a requirement that the value of the `namespace` attribute should be the fully qualified name of the mapper interface, which, in our case, is `org.packt.boot_rest_demo.PersonMapper`.

Next, the `id` attributes of the individual SQL statements defined within `<select>`, `<insert>`, `<update>`, and `<delete>` should match the name of the method in the mapper interface. For example, the `getPersons()` method in the `PersonMapper` interface looks for a SQL statement with `id="getPersons"`.

Now, the MyBatis library discovers the location of this mapper XML by reading the value of the `mybatis.mapper-locations` property.

Coming to the controller, we have introduced a new annotation, `@RestController`. This special annotation indicates, in addition to it being a web controller, that all the methods defined in the class return a response that is sent via the HTTP response body; so do all the REST APIs. They just work with the data.

As usual, you can launch your Spring Boot application either by using the Maven Spring Boot plugin, `mvn spring-boot:run`, or by executing the JAR created by the Maven package, `java -jar my_jar_name.jar`.

Creating multiple profiles for Spring Boot

Generally, web applications are deployed on different environments – first, they are run locally on a developer's machine, then deployed on test servers, and finally deployed on production servers. We would have the application interacting with components located in different places for each environment. The best approach for this is to maintain different profiles for each environment. One way to do this is by creating different versions of the `application.properties` file, that is, different versions of the file that stores the application-level properties. These property files in Spring Boot can also be YML files, such as `application.yml`. Even if you create different versions, you need a mechanism to tell your applications to pick the relevant version of the file, based on the environment it has been deployed to.

Spring Boot provides amazing support for such a feature. It allows you to have multiple configuration files, each representing a specific profile, and then, you can launch your application in different profiles, depending on the environment it is being deployed to. Let's see this in action, and then we will explain how it works.

Getting ready

For this recipe, there are two options to host another instance of your MySQL database:

1. Use a cloud provider such as AWS and use its Amazon **Relational Database Service** (**RDS**) (https://aws.amazon.com/rds/). They have a certain free usage limit.
2. Use a cloud provider such as DigitalOcean (https://www.digitalocean.com/) to purchase a droplet (that is, a server) for as little as $5 per month. Install the MySQL server on it.
3. Use VirtualBox to install Linux on your machine, assuming we are using Windows, or vice versa if you are using Linux. Install the MySQL server on it.

The options are much more, right from hosted database services to servers, which give you complete root access to install the MySQL server. For this recipe, we did the following:

1. We purchased a basic droplet from DigitalOcean.
2. We installed MySQL using `sudo apt-get install mysql-server-5.7` with a password for the root user.
3. We created another user, `springboot`, so that we can use this user to connect from our RESTful web service application:

```
$ mysql -uroot -p
Enter password:
mysql> create user 'springboot'@'%' identified by 'springboot';
```

4. We modified the MySQL configuration file so that the MySQL allows remote connections. This can be done by editing the `bind-address` property in the `/etc/mysql/mysql.conf.d/mysqld.cnf` file for the IP of the server.
5. From the MySQL workbench, we added the new MySQL connection by using `IP = <Digital Ocean droplet IP>`, `username = springboot`, and `password = springboot`.

The location for the MySQL configuration file in Ubuntu OS is
`/etc/mysql/mysql.conf.d/mysqld.cnf`. One way to find out
the location of a configuration file specific to your OS is to do the
following:

1. Run `mysql --help`.
2. In the output, search for `Default options are read
   from the following files in the given order:`.
   What follows is the possible locations for the MySQL
   configuration file.

We will create the required table and populate some data. But before that, we will
create the `sample` database as `root` and grant all privileges on it to the `springboot`
user:

```
mysql -uroot
Enter password:

mysql> create database sample;

mysql> GRANT ALL ON sample.* TO 'springboot'@'%';
Query OK, 0 rows affected (0.00 sec)

mysql> flush privileges;
```

Now, let's connect to the database as the `springboot` user, create the required table,
and populate it with some sample data:

```
mysql -uspringboot -pspringboot

mysql> use sample
Database changed
mysql> create table person(
-> id int not null auto_increment,
-> first_name varchar(255),
-> last_name varchar(255),
-> place varchar(255),
-> primary key(id)
-> );
Query OK, 0 rows affected (0.02 sec)

mysql> INSERT INTO person(first_name, last_name, place)
VALUES('Mohamed', 'Sanaulla', 'Bangalore');
mysql> INSERT INTO person(first_name, last_name, place) VALUES('Nick',
'Samoylov', 'USA');
```

```
mysql> SELECT * FROM person;
+----+------------+-----------+-----------+
| id | first_name | last_name | place     |
+----+------------+-----------+-----------+
| 1  | Mohamed    | Sanaulla  | Bangalore |
| 2  | Nick       | Samoylov  | USA       |
+----+------------+-----------+-----------+
2 rows in set (0.00 sec)
```

Now, we have our cloud instance of the MySQL DB ready. Let's look at how to manage the information of two different connections based on the profile the application is running in.

The initial sample app required for this recipe can be found at `Chapter09/4_boot_multi_profile_incomplete`. We will convert this app to make it run on different environments.

How to do it...

1. In the `src/main/resources/application.properties` file, add a new springboot property, `spring.profiles.active = local`.

2. Create a new file, `application-local.properties`, in `src/main/resources/`.

3. Add the following properties to `application-local.properties` and remove them from the `application.properties` file:

```
spring.datasource.url=jdbc:mysql://localhost/sample?useSSL=false
spring.datasource.username=root
spring.datasource.password=mohamed
```

4. Create another file, `application-cloud.properties`, in `src/main/resources/`.

5. Add the following properties to `application-cloud.properties`:

```
spring.datasource.url=
        jdbc:mysql://<digital_ocean_ip>/sample?useSSL=false
spring.datasource.username=springboot
spring.datasource.password=springboot
```

The complete code for the complete application can be found at
Chapter09/4_boot_multi_profile_incomplete. You can run the application
using the mvn spring-boot:run command. Spring Boot reads the
spring.profiles.active property from the application.properties file and
runs the application in a local profile. Open
the http://localhost:8080/api/persons URL in the browser to find the
following data:

```
[
  {
    "id": 1,
    "firstName": "David ",
    "lastName": "John",
    "place": "Delhi"
  },
  {
    "id": 2,
    "firstName": "Raj",
    "lastName": "Singh",
    "place": "Bangalore"
  }
]
```

Now, run the application on the cloud profile by using the mvn spring-boot:run -
Dspring.profiles.active=cloud command. Then, open
http://localhost:8080/api/persons in the browser to find the following data:

```
[
  {
    "id": 1,
    "firstName": "Mohamed",
    "lastName": "Sanaulla",
    "place": "Bangalore"
  },
  {
    "id": 2,
    "firstName": "Nick",
    "lastName": "Samoylov",
    "place": "USA"
  }
]
```

You can see that there is a different set of data returned by the same API and the
preceding data was inserted in our MySQL database running on the cloud. So, we
have been able to successfully run the app in two different profiles: local and cloud.

How it works...

There are multiple ways Spring Boot can read the configuration for the application. Some significant ones are listed here in the order of their relevance (the property defined in the earlier source overrides the property defined in the later sources):

- From the command line. The properties are specified using the `-D` option, like we did while launching the app in the cloud profile, `mvn spring-boot:run -Dspring.profiles.active=cloud`. Or, if you are using JAR, it would be `java -Dspring.profiles.active=cloud -jar myappjar.jar`.

- From the Java system properties, using `System.getProperties()`.

- OS environment variables.

- Profile-specific application properties, `application-{profile}.properties`, or the `application-{profile}.yml` files, outside of the packaged JAR.

- Profile-specific application properties, the `application-{profile}.properties` or `application-{profile}.yml` files, packaged within the JAR.

- Application properties, `application.properties`, or `application.yml` defined outside of the packaged JAR.

- Application properties, `application.properties`, or `application.yml` packaged within the JAR.

- Configuration classes (that is, annotated with `@Configuration`) serving as property sources (annotated with `@PropertySource`).

- Spring Boot's default properties.

In our recipe, we specified all the generic properties, such as the following, in the `application.properties` file, and any profile-specific properties were specified in the profile-specific application properties file:

```
spring.profiles.active=local
spring.datasource.driver-class-name=com.mysql.jdbc.Driver

mybatis.mapper-locations=classpath*:mappers/*.xml
mybatis.configuration.map-underscore-to-camel-case=true
```

From the preceding list, we can find that the `application.properties` or `application-{profile}.properties` file can be defined outside the application JAR. There are default locations where Spring Boot will search for the properties file, and one such path is the `config` subdirectory of the current directory the app is running from.

The complete list of Spring Boot-supported application properties can be found at `http://docs.spring.io/spring-boot/docs/current/reference/html/common-application-properties.html`. In addition to these, we can create our own properties, which will be required for our application.

The complete code for this recipe can be found at `Chapter09/4_boot_multi_profile_complete`.

There's more...

We can create a configuration server using Spring Boot, which will act as a repository for all the properties for all the apps in all the profiles. The client apps can then connect with the configuration server to read the relevant properties based on the app name and the app profile.

In the configuration server, the application properties can be read from the filesystem using the classpath or a GitHub repository. The advantage of using a GitHub repository is that the property files can be versioned. The property files in the configuration server can be updated, and these updates can be pushed to the client apps by setting up a message queue to relay the changes downstream. Another way is to use the `@RefreshScope` beans and then invoke the `/refresh` API whenever we need the client apps to pull the configuration changes.

Deploying RESTful web services to Heroku

Platform as a Service (Paas) is one of the cloud computing models (the other two being **Software as a Service (SaaS)** and **Infrastructure as a Service (IaaS)**) where the cloud computing provider provides managed computing platforms, which includes OS, programming language runtime, database, and other add-ons such as queues, log management, and alerting. They also provide you with tools to ease the deployment and dashboards to monitor your applications.

Heroku is one of the earliest players in the field of PaaS providers. It supports the following programming languages: Ruby, Node.js, Java, Python, Clojure, Scala, Go, and PHP. Heroku supports multiple data stores, such as MySQL, MongoDB, Redis, and Elastic search. It provides integration with logging tools, network utilities, email services, and monitoring tools.

Heroku provides a command-line tool called heroku-cli (`cli.heroku.com`), which can be used to create Heroku applications, deploy, monitor, add resources, and more. The functionality provided by their web dashboard is supported by the CLI as well. It uses Git to store the application's source code. So, when you push the application code to Heroku's Git repository, it triggers a build, based on the build pack you are using. Then, it either uses the default way to spawn the application or `ProcFile` to execute your application.

In this recipe, we will deploy our Spring Boot-based RESTful web service to Heroku. We will continue to use the database we created on another cloud provider in the previous recipe, *Creating multiple profiles for Spring Boot*.

Getting ready

Before we proceed with deploying our sample application on Heroku, we need to sign up for a Heroku account and install its tools, which will enable us to work from the command line. In the subsequent sections, we will guide you through the signup process, creating a sample app via the web UI, and via the Heroku **command-line interface (CLI)**.

Setting up a Heroku account

Visit `http://www.heroku.com` and sign up if you don't have an account. If you have an account, you can log in. To sign up, visit `https://signup.heroku.com`:

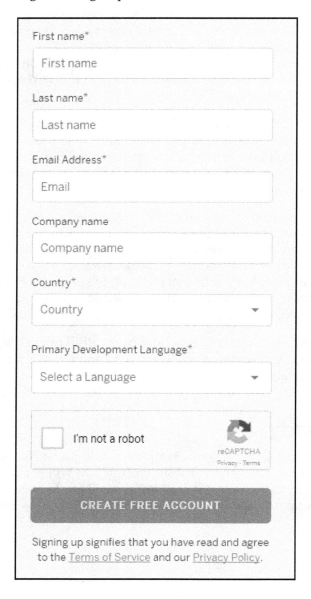

To log in, the URL is `https://id.heroku.com/login`:

Once you log in successfully, you will see a dashboard with the list of apps, if you have any:

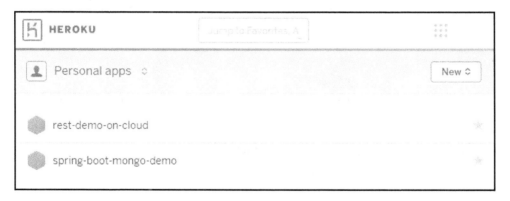

Creating a new app from the UI

Click on **New** | **Create new app**, fill in the details, and click on **Create App**:

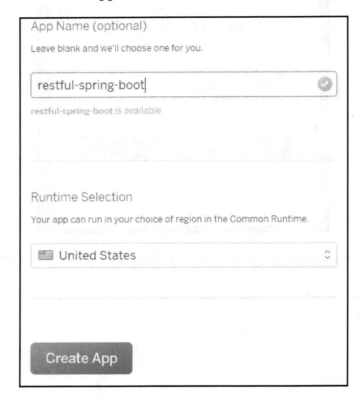

Creating a new app from the CLI

Perform the following steps to create a new app from the CLI:

1. Install the Heroku CLI from `https://cli.heroku.com`.
2. Once installed, Heroku should be in your system's `PATH` variable.
3. Open a command prompt and run `heroku create`. You will see an output similar to the following:

```
Creating app... done, glacial-beyond-27911
https://glacial-beyond-27911.herokuapp.com/ |
https://git.heroku.com/glacial-beyond-27911.git
```

4. The app name is generated dynamically and a remote Git repository is created. You can specify the app name and region (as done via the UI) by running the following command:

```
$ heroku create test-app-9812 --region us
Creating test-app-9812... done, region is us
https://test-app-9812.herokuapp.com/ |
https://git.heroku.com/test-app-9812.git
```

The deployment to Heroku is done via `git push` to the remote Git repository created on Heroku. We will see this in the next section.

We have the source code for the app at `Chapter09/5_boot_on_heroku`. So, copy this application and go ahead and deploy on Heroku.

 You have to log into the Heroku account before running any of the commands in Heroku's cli. You can log in by running the `heroku login` command.

How to do it...

1. Run the following command to create a Heroku application:

```
$ heroku create <app_name> -region us
```

2. Initialize the Git repository in the project folder:

```
$ git init
```

3. Add the Heroku Git repository as a remote to your local Git repository:

```
$ heroku git:remote -a <app_name_you_chose>
```

4. Push the source code, that is, the master branch, to the Heroku Git repository:

```
$ git add .
$ git commit -m "deploying to heroku"
$ git push heroku master
```

5. When the code is pushed to the Heroku Git repository, it triggers a build. As we are using Maven, it runs the following command:

```
./mvnw -DskipTests clean dependency:list install
```

6. Once the code has completed the build and deployed, you can open the application by using the `heroku open` command. This will open the application in a browser.

7. You can monitor the logs of the application using the `heroku logs --tail` command.

Once the app has been successfully deployed, and after you run the `heroku open` command, you should see the URL being loaded by the browser:

Spring Boot App on Heroku

RESTful APIs supported

- Persons

Clicking on the **Persons** link will display the following information:

```
[
  {
    "id":1,
    "firstName":"Mohamed",
    "lastName":"Sanaulla",
    "place":"Bangalore"
  },
  {
    "id":2,
    "firstName":"Nick",
    "lastName":"Samoylov",
    "place":"USA"
  }
]
```

The interesting thing here is that we have our app running on Heroku, which is connecting to a MySQL database on a DigitalOcean server. We can even provision a database along with the Heroku app and connect to that database. Check out how to do this in the *There's more...* section.

There's more...

1. Add a new DB add-on to the application:

   ```
   $ heroku addons:create jawsdb:kitefin
   ```

   Here, `addons:create` takes the add-on name and the service plan name, both separated by a colon (`:`). You can learn more about the add-on details and plans at `https://elements.heroku.com/addons/jawsdb-maria`. Also, the Heroku CLI command to add the add-on to your application is given toward the end of the add-on details page for all add-ons.

2. Open the **DB** dashboard to view the connection details, such as URL, username, password, and the database name:

   ```
   $ heroku addons:open jawsdb
   ```

   The `jawsdb` dashboard looks something similar to the following:

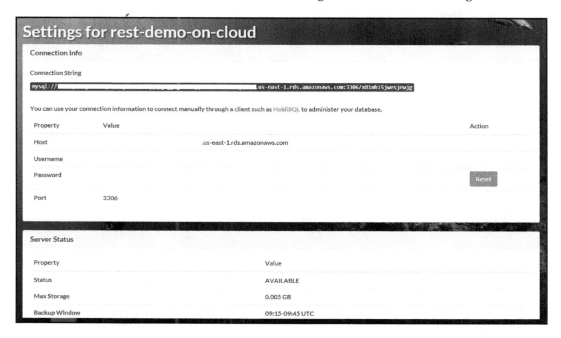

3. You can even get the MySQL connection string from the `JAWSDB_URL` configuration property. You can list the configuration for your app by using the following command:

```
$ heroku config
=== rest-demo-on-cloud Config Vars
JAWSDB_URL: <URL>
```

4. Copy the connection details, create a new connection in MySQL Workbench, and connect to this connection. The database name is also created by the add-on. Run the following SQL statements after connecting to the database:

```
use x81mhi5jwesjewjg;
create table person(
  id int not null auto_increment,
  first_name varchar(255),
  last_name varchar(255),
  place varchar(255),
  primary key(id)
);

INSERT INTO person(first_name, last_name, place)
VALUES('Heroku First', 'Heroku Last', 'USA');

INSERT INTO person(first_name, last_name, place)
VALUES('Jaws First', 'Jaws Last', 'UK');
```

5. Create a new properties file for the Heroku profile, `application-heroku.properties`, at `src/main/resources`, with the following properties:

```
spring.datasource.url=jdbc:mysql://
<URL DB>:3306/x81mhi5jwesjewjg?useSSL=false
spring.datasource.username=zzu08pc38j33h89q
spring.datasource.password=<DB password>
```

You can find the connection-related details in the add-on dashboard.

6. Update the `src/main/resources/application.properties` file to replace the value of the `spring.profiles.active` property to `heroku`.

7. Commit and push the changes to the Heroku remote:

```
$ git commit -am"using heroky mysql addon"
$ git push heroku master
```

8. Once the deployment succeeds, run the `heroku open` command. Once the page loads in the browser, click on the **Persons** link. This time, you will see a different set of data, the one we entered in our Heroku add-on:

```
[
    {
        "id":1,
        "firstName":"Heroku First",
        "lastName":"Heroku Last",
        "place":"USA"
    },
    {
        "id":2,
        "firstName":"Jaws First",
        "lastName":"Jaws Last",
        "place":"UK"
    }
]
```

With this, we have integrated with a database that we created in Heroku.

Containerizing the RESTful web service using Docker

We have advanced a lot from the time when an app would be installed across servers, to each server being virtualized and the app then being installed on these smaller virtual machines. Scalability issues for the applications were resolved by adding more virtual machines, with the app running to the load balancer.

In virtualization, a large server is divided into multiple virtual machines by allocating the computing power, memory, and storage among the multiple virtual machines. This way, each of the virtual machines is in itself capable of all those things that a server was, albeit on a smaller scale. With this virtualization has helped us a lot in judiciously making use of the server's computing, memory, and storage resources.

However, virtualization needs some setup, that is, you need to create the virtual machine, install the required dependencies, and then run the app. Moreover, you may not be 100% sure if the app would run successfully. The reason for failure may be due to the incompatible OS versions or even due to some configuration missed while setting up or some missing dependency. This setup also leads to some difficulty in horizontal scaling because there is some time spent in the provisioning of the virtual machine and then deploying the app.

Using tools such as Puppet and Chef does help in provisioning, but then the setting up of the app can often result in issues that might be due to a missing or incorrect configuration. This led to the introduction of another concept, called containerization.

In the world of virtualization, we have the host OS and then the virtualization software, that is, the hypervisor. We then end up creating multiple machines, where each machine has its own OS on which apps are deployed. However, in containerization, we don't divide the resources of the server. Instead, we have the server with its host OS, and above that, we have a containerization layer which is a software abstraction layer. We package apps as containers, where a container is packaged with just enough OS functions required to run the app, the software dependencies for the app, and then the app itself. The following image, taken from `https://docs.docker.com/get-started/#container-diagram`, best depicts this:

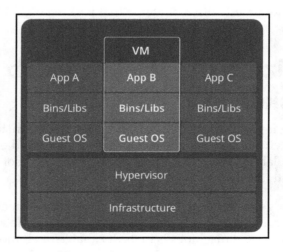

The preceding image illustrates a typical architecture of virtualization systems. The following image illustrates a typical architecture of containerization systems:

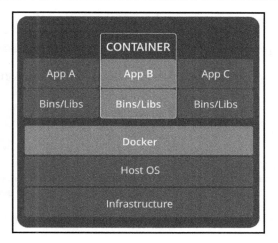

The biggest advantage of containerization is that you bundle all the dependencies of the app into a container image. This image is then run on the containerization platform, leading to the creation of a container. We can have multiple containers running simultaneously on the server. If there is a need to add more instances, we can just deploy the image, and this deployment can be automated to support high scalability in an easy way.

Docker is one of the popular software-containerization platform. In this recipe, we will package our sample app found at the location `Chapter09/6_boot_with_docker` into a Docker image and run the Docker image to launch our application.

Getting ready

For this recipe, we will use a Linux server running Ubuntu 16.04.2 x64:

1. Download the latest `.deb` file from `https://download.docker.com/linux/ubuntu/dists/xenial/pool/stable/amd64/`. For other Linux distros, you can find the packages at `https://download.docker.com/linux/`:

   ```
   $ wget https://download.docker.com/linux/ubuntu/dists/xenial
   /pool/stable/amd64/docker-ce_17.03.2~ce-0~ubuntu-
   xenial_amd64.deb
   ```

2. Install the Docker package using the `dpkg` package manager:

```
$  sudo dpkg -i docker-ce_17.03.2~ce-0~ubuntu-xenial_amd64.deb
```

The name of the package will vary based on the version you have downloaded.

3. After successful installation, the Docker service starts running. You can verify this by using the `service` command:

```
$ service docker status
   docker.service - Docker Application Container Engine
   Loaded: loaded (/lib/systemd/system/docker.service; enabled;
   vendor preset: enabled)
Active: active (running) since Fri 2017-07-28 13:46:50 UTC;
          2min 3s ago
Docs: https://docs.docker.com
Main PID: 22427 (dockerd)
```

The application to be dockerized is available at `Chapter09/6_boot_with_docker`, in the source code downloaded for this book.

How to do it...

1. Create `Dockerfile` at the root of the application with the following content:

```
FROM ubuntu:17.10
FROM openjdk:9-b177-jdk
VOLUME /tmp
ADD target/boot_docker-1.0.jar restapp.jar
ENV JAVA_OPTS="-Dspring.profiles.active=cloud"
ENTRYPOINT [ "sh", "-c", "java $JAVA_OPTS -jar /restapp.jar" ]
```

2. Run the following command to build a Docker image using the `Dockerfile` we created in the preceding step:

```
$ docker build --tag restapp-image .

Sending build context to Docker daemon 18.45 MB
Step 1/6 : FROM ubuntu:17.10
---> c8cdcb3740f8
Step 2/6 : FROM openjdk:9-b177-jdk
---> 38d822ff5025
Step 3/6 : VOLUME /tmp
```

```
---> Using cache
---> 38367613d375
Step 4/6 : ADD target/boot_docker-1.0.jar restapp.jar
---> Using cache
---> 54ad359f53f7
Step 5/6 : ENV JAVA_OPTS "-Dspring.profiles.active=cloud"
---> Using cache
---> dfa324259fb1
Step 6/6 : ENTRYPOINT sh -c java $JAVA_OPTS -jar /restapp.jar
---> Using cache
---> 6af62bd40afe
Successfully built 6af62bd40afe
```

3. You can view the images that were installed by using the following command:

```
$ docker images
```

```
REPOSITORY      TAG         IMAGE ID        CREATED       SIZE
restapp-image   latest      6af62bd40afe  4 hours ago  606 MB
openjdk         9-b177-jdk  38d822ff5025  6 days ago   588 MB
ubuntu          17.10       c8cdcb3740f8  8 days ago   93.9 MB
```

You will see that there are OpenJDK and Ubuntu images as well. These were downloaded to build the image for our app, which is listed first.

4. Run the image to create a container that contains our running application:

```
docker run -p 8090:8080 -d --name restapp restapp-image
d521b9927cec105d8b69995ef6d917121931c1d1f0b1f4398594bd1f1fcbee55
```

The large string printed after the run command is the identifier of the container. You can use the initial few characters to uniquely identify the container. Alternatively, you can use the container name, restapp.

5. The app will have already started. You can view the logs by running the following command:

```
docker logs restapp
```

6. You can view the Docker containers created by using the following command:

```
docker ps
```

The output for the preceding command looks similar to the following:

```
CONTAINER ID    IMAGE           COMMAND            CREATED        STATUS         PORTS                    NAMES
d521b9927cec    restapp-image   "sh -c 'java $JAVA..."  2 minutes ago  Up 2 minutes   0.0.0.0:8090->8080/tcp   restapp
```

7. You can manage the container by using the following command:

```
$ docker stop restapp
$ docker start restapp
```

Once the app is running, open `http://<hostname>:8090/api/persons`.

How it works...

You define the container structure and its contents by defining `Dockerfile`. `Dockerfile` follows a structure, where each line is of the `INSTRUCTION arguments` form. There is a predefined set of instructions, namely FROM, RUN, CMD, LABEL, ENV, ADD, and COPY. A complete list can be found at `https://docs.docker. com/engine/reference/builder/#from`. Let's look at our defined `Dockerfile`:

```
FROM ubuntu:17.10
FROM openjdk:9-b177-jdk
VOLUME /tmp
ADD target/boot_docker-1.0.jar restapp.jar
ENV JAVA_OPTS="-Dspring.profiles.active=cloud"
ENTRYPOINT [ "sh", "-c", "java $JAVA_OPTS -jar /restapp.jar" ]
```

The first two lines, using the FROM instruction, specified the base image for our Docker image. We use the Ubuntu OS image as the base image and then combine it with the OpenJDK 9 image. The VOLUME instruction is used to specify the mount point for the image. This is usually a path in the host OS.

The ADD instruction is used to copy the file from the source to the destination directory under the working directory. The ENV instruction is used to define the environment variables.

The ENTRYPOINT instruction is used to configure the container to run as an executable. For this instruction, we pass an array of arguments, which we would otherwise have executed directly from the command line. In our scenario, we are using the bash shell to run `java -$JAVA_OPTS -jar <jar name>`.

Once we have defined `Dockerfile`, we instruct the Docker tool to build an image using `Dockerfile`. We also provide a name for the image using the `--tag` option. When building our app image, it will download the required base images, which, in our case, are the Ubuntu and OpenJDK images. So, if you list the Docker images, you will see the base images along with our app image.

This Docker image is a reusable entity. If we need more instances of the app, we spawn a new container using the `docker run` command. When we run the Docker image, we have multiple options, where one of them is a `-p` option, which maps the ports from within the container to the host OS. In our case, we map the `8080` port of our Spring Boot app to `8090` of the host OS.

Now, to check the status of our running app, we can check the logs using `docker logs restapp`. Apart from this, the `docker` tool supports multiple commands. It's highly recommended to run `docker help` and explore the commands that are supported.

Docker, the company behind Docker containerization platform, has created a set of base images, which can be used to create containers. There are images for MySQL DB, Couchbase, Ubuntu, and other operating systems. You can explore the packages at `https://store.docker.com/`.

Monitoring the Spring Boot 2 application using Micrometer and Prometheus

Monitoring and collecting performance metrics is an important part of application development and maintenance. One would be interested in metrics such as memory usage, response time of the various endpoints, CPU usage, load on the machine, garbage-collection frequency, and pauses. There are different ways to enable capturing metrics, such as using Dropwizard Metrics (`https://metrics.dropwizard.io/4.0.0/`) or Spring Boot's metrics framework.

The instrumentation of code in Spring Boot 2 onward is done using a library called Micrometer (`https://micrometer.io/`). Micrometer provides a vendor-neutral code-instrumentation so that you can use any monitoring tool and have Micrometer provide the metrics data in the format understood by the tool. This is like SLF4J for logging. It is a facade over the metrics endpoints that produces output in a vendor-neutral way.

Micrometer supports tools such as Prometheus (`https://prometheus.io/`), Netflix Atlas (`https://github.com/Netflix/atlas`), Datadog (`https://www.datadoghq.com/`) and upcoming support for InfluxDB (`https://www.influxdata.com/`), statsd (`https://github.com/etsy/statsd`), and Graphite (`https://graphiteapp.org/`). Applications using earlier version of Spring Boot, such as 1.5, can also make use of this new instrumentation library, as shown in the *There's more...* section.

In this recipe, we will use Micrometer to instrument our code and ship the metrics to Prometheus. So, first, we will start by setting up Prometheus in the *Getting ready* section.

Getting ready

Prometheus (`https://prometheus.io/`) is a monitoring system and time-series database that allows us to store time-series data, which includes the metrics of an application over time, a simple way to visualize the metrics, or setting up alerts on different metrics.

Let's perform the following steps to get Prometheus running on our machines (in our case, we will be running on Windows. Similar steps will be applicable for Linux as well):

1. Download the Prometheus distribution from `https://github.com/prometheus/prometheus/releases/download/v2.3.2/prometheus-2.3.2.windows-amd64.tar.gz`.

2. Extract it using 7-Zip (`https://www.7-zip.org/`) on Windows to a location that we will call `PROMETHEUS_HOME`.

3. Add `%PROMETHEUS_HOME%` to your PATH variables (on Linux, it would be `$PROMETHEUS_HOME` to the PATH variable).

4. Run Prometheus using the `prometheus --config "%PROMETHEUS_HOME%/prometheus.yml"` command. You will see the following output:

```
level=info ts=2018-08-09T17:30:54.8401736Z caller=main.go:222 msg="Starting Prometheus" version="(version=2.3.2, branch=HEAD, revision=71af5e29e815795e9dd14742ee7725682fa14b7b)"
level=info ts=2018-08-09T17:30:54.8441709Z caller=main.go:223 build_context="(go=go1.10.3, user=root@5258e0bd9cc1, date=20180712-14:13:08)"
level=info ts=2018-08-09T17:30:54.8451704Z caller=main.go:224 host_details=(windows)
level=info ts=2018-08-09T17:30:54.8451704Z caller=main.go:225 fd_limits=N/A
level=info ts=2018-08-09T17:30:54.8471695Z caller=main.go:533 msg="Starting TSDB ..."
level=info ts=2018-08-09T17:30:54.8471695Z caller=web.go:415 component=web msg="Start listening for connections" address=0.0.0.0:9090
level=info ts=2018-08-09T17:30:54.7815242Z caller=main.go:543 msg="TSDB started"
level=info ts=2018-08-09T17:30:54.8821489Z caller=main.go:603 msg="Loading configuration file" filename=G:\prometheus-2.3.2.windows-amd64/prometheus.yml
level=info ts=2018-08-09T17:30:54.8901447Z caller=main.go:629 msg="Completed loading of configuration file" filename=G:\prometheus-2.3.2.windows-amd64/prometheus.yml
level=info ts=2018-08-09T17:30:54.8901447Z caller=main.go:502 msg="Server is ready to receive web requests."
```

5. Open `http://localhost:9090` in your browser to see the Prometheus console. Enter `go_gc_duration_seconds` in the empty text box and click on the **Execute** button to show the metrics captured. You can switch the tab to a **Graph** version to visualize the data:

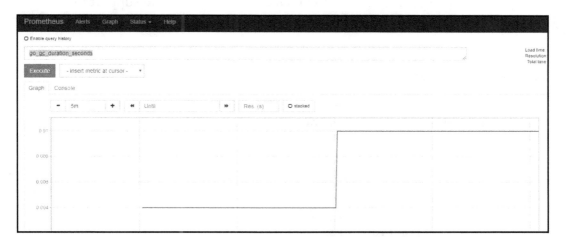

The preceding metrics are for Prometheus itself. You can navigate to `http://localhost:9090/targets` to find out the targets monitored by the Promethues shown as follows:

When you open the `http://localhost:9090/metrics` in your browser, you will see the metric value at the current time instant. It's difficult to understand without visualization. Such metrics are helpful when collected over time and visualized using graphs.

Now, we have Prometheus up and running. Let's enable the Micrometer and metrics publishing in the format understood by Prometheus. For this, we will be reusing the code used in the *Interacting with the database* recipe in this chapter. This recipe is available at `Chapter09/2_boot_db_demo`. So, we will just copy the same code into `Chapter09/7_boot_micrometer` and then enhance parts to add support for Micrometer and Prometheus, as seen in the next section.

How to do it...

1. Update `pom.xml` to include the Spring boot actuator and Micrometer Prometheus registry dependencies:

```
<dependency>
  <groupId>org.springframework.boot</groupId>
  <artifactId>spring-boot-starter-actuator</artifactId>
</dependency>
<dependency>
  <groupId>io.micrometer</groupId>
  <artifactId>micrometer-registry-prometheus</artifactId>
  <version>1.0.6</version>
</dependency>
```

In Spring Boot 2 onwards, Micrometer comes configured with actuator, so we just need to add actuator as the dependency and then the `micrometer-registry-prometheus` dependency produces a metrics representation that is understood by Prometheus.

2. When we run the application (one of the ways is to run `mvn spring-boot:run`) and open the actuator endpoint, by default it will be `<root_url>/actuator`. We will find that there are few actuator endpoints available by default, but the Prometheus metrics endpoint is not part of it:

```json
{
    "_links": {
        "self": {
            "href": "http://localhost:8080/actuator",
            "templated": false
        },
        "health": {
            "href": "http://localhost:8080/actuator/health",
            "templated": false
        },
        "info": {
            "href": "http://localhost:8080/actuator/info",
            "templated": false
        }
    }
}
```

3. To enable the Prometheus endpoint in actuator, we need to add the following property in the `src/main/resources/application.properties` file:

   `management.endpoints.web.exposure.include=prometheus`

4. Restart the app and browse to `http://localhost:8080/actuator/`. Now, you will see that only the Prometheus endpoint is available:

```json
{
    "_links": {
        "self": {
            "href": "http://localhost:8080/actuator",
            "templated": false
        },
        "prometheus": {
            "href": "http://localhost:8080/actuator/prometheus",
            "templated": false
        }
    }
}
```

5. Open `http://localhost:8080/actuator/prometheus` to see the metrics in a format understood by Prometheus:

```
# HELP tomcat_cache_hit_total
# TYPE tomcat_cache_hit_total counter
tomcat_cache_hit_total 0.0
# HELP tomcat_sessions_rejected_total
# TYPE tomcat_sessions_rejected_total counter
tomcat_sessions_rejected_total 0.0
# HELP tomcat_sessions_expired_total
# TYPE tomcat_sessions_expired_total counter
tomcat_sessions_expired_total 0.0
# HELP jvm_memory_max_bytes The maximum amount of memory in bytes that can be used for memory management
# TYPE jvm_memory_max_bytes gauge
jvm_memory_max_bytes{area="nonheap",id="CodeHeap 'non-nmethods'",} 5832704.0
jvm_memory_max_bytes{area="nonheap",id="Metaspace",} -1.0
jvm_memory_max_bytes{area="nonheap",id="CodeHeap 'profiled nmethods'",} 1.2288E8
jvm_memory_max_bytes{area="nonheap",id="Compressed Class Space",} 1.073741824E9
jvm_memory_max_bytes{area="heap",id="G1 Eden Space",} -1.0
jvm_memory_max_bytes{area="heap",id="G1 Old Gen",} 4.26770432E9
jvm_memory_max_bytes{area="heap",id="G1 Survivor Space",} -1.0
jvm_memory_max_bytes{area="nonheap",id="CodeHeap 'non-profiled nmethods'",} 1.22945536E8
# HELP jvm_classes_unloaded_total The total number of classes unloaded since the Java virtual machine has started execution
# TYPE jvm_classes_unloaded_total counter
```

6. Configure Prometheus to call `http://localhost:8080/actuator/prometheus` at a specific frequency, which can be configured. This can be done by updating the `%PROMETHEUS_HOME%/prometheus.yml` configuration file with a new job under the `scrape_configs` property:

```
- job_name: 'spring_apps'
    metrics_path: '/actuator/prometheus'
    static_configs:
      - targets: ['localhost:8080']
```

You will see that, by default, there is a job to scrap the Prometheus metrics itself.

7. Restart Prometheus server and visit `http://localhost:9090/targets`. You will see a new section, `spring_apps`, with the target we have added:

8. We can plot a metric from the metrics captured by visiting `http://localhost:9090/graph`, typing `jvm_memory_max_bytes` in the text box, and clicking on **Execute** to get a graph:

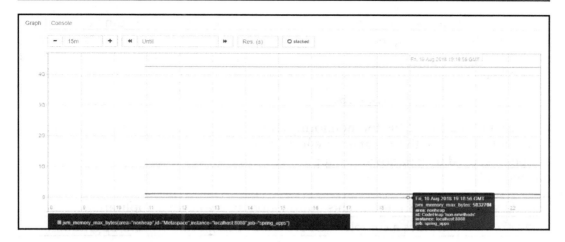

So, we have finally set up the ingestion of metrics in Prometheus and creating charts on Prometheus out of the metric values.

How it works...

Spring Boot provides a library called actuator with features to help you monitor and manage the application when deployed to production. This out-of-the-box functionality doesn't require any setup from the developers' side. So you get auditing, health checks, and metrics-gathering all without any work.

As mentioned before, actuator uses Micrometer to instrument and capture different metrics from the code, such as:

- JVM memory usage
- Connection-pooling information
- Response time of different HTTP endpoints in the app
- Frequency of invocation of different HTTP endpoints

To enable your application to have these production-ready features, you need to add the following dependency to your pom.xml if you are using Maven (there is an equivalent for Gradle):

```
<dependency>
    <groupId>org.springframework.boot</groupId>
    <artifactId>spring-boot-starter-actuator</artifactId>
</dependency>
```

By default, actuator is available at the `/actuator` endpoint, but this can be configured by overriding the `management.endpoints.web.base-path` property in the `src/main/resources/application.properties` file with a different value, as shown here:

```
management.endpoints.web.base-path=/metrics
```

All the endpoints available for monitoring and auditing the application are enabled by default except for the `/shutdown` endpoint, which is disabled by default. This endpoint is used to shut down the application. Here are some of the endpoints that are available:

`auditevents`	Exposes audit events information for the current application
`beans`	Displays a complete list of all the Spring beans in your application
`env`	Exposes properties from Spring's `ConfigurableEnvironment`
`health`	Shows application health information
`info`	Displays arbitrary application info
`metrics`	Shows metrics information for the current application
`mappings`	Displays a collated list of all `@RequestMapping` paths
`prometheus`	Exposes metrics in a format that can be scraped by a Prometheus server

You can see that these are very sensitive endpoints that need to be secured. The good thing is that Spring Boot actuator integrates well with Spring Security to secure these endpoints. So if Spring Security is on the classpath, it secures these endpoints by default.

These endpoints can be accessed by JMX or via the web. Not all of the actuator endpoints are enabled for access by the web by default instead they are enabled by default for access using JMX. Only the following properties are enabled for access by default from the web:

- `health`
- `info`

And this is the reason we had to add the following configuration property to make the Prometheus endpoint, along with health, information, and metrics, available on the web:

```
management.endpoints.web.exposure.include=prometheus,health,info,metrics
```

Even if we enable Prometheus, we need to have the `micrometer-registry-prometheus` library on our classpath. Only then will we be able to view the metrics in the Prometheus format. So, we added the following dependency to our pom:

```
<dependency>
  <groupId>io.micrometer</groupId>
  <artifactId>micrometer-registry-prometheus</artifactId>
  <version>1.0.6</version>
</dependency>
```

The output format processed by Prometheus is simple: it takes in `<property_name value>` with each property in a new line. Spring Boot actuator doesn't push the metrics to Prometheus; instead, we configure Prometheus to pull the metrics from a given URL at a frequency defined in its configuration. The default configuration of Prometheus, which is available in its home directory, is as follows:

```
# my global config
global:
  scrape_interval: 15s # Set the scrape interval to every 15 seconds.
Default is every 1 minute.
  evaluation_interval: 15s # Evaluate rules every 15 seconds. The
default is every 1 minute.
  # scrape_timeout is set to the global default (10s).

# Alertmanager configuration
alerting:
  alertmanagers:
  - static_configs:
    - targets:
      # - alertmanager:9093

# Load rules once and periodically evaluate them according to the
global 'evaluation_interval'.
rule_files:
  # - "first_rules.yml"
  # - "second_rules.yml"

# A scrape configuration containing exactly one endpoint to scrape:
# Here it's Prometheus itself.
scrape_configs:
```

```
    # The job name is added as a label `job=<job_name>` to any
timeseries scraped from this config.
    - job_name: 'prometheus'

        # metrics_path defaults to '/metrics'
        # scheme defaults to 'http'.

        static_configs:
        - targets: ['localhost:9090']
```

So it is configured with default values for intervals at which Prometheus will fetch the metrics and for intervals at which it will evaluate the rules defined under `rule_files`. Scrape is the activity of pulling the metrics from different targets defined under the `scrape_configs` option, and evaluate is the act of evaluating different rules defined in `rule_files`. To enable Prometheus to scrap the metrics from our Spring Boot app, we add a new job under `scrape_configs` by providing the job name, the path of the metrics relative to the application URL, and the URL of the application:

```
    - job_name: 'spring_apps'
        metrics_path: '/actuator/prometheus'
        static_configs:
          - targets: ['localhost:8080']
```

We also saw how we can view the values of these metrics from `http://localhost:9090/graph` and how these can be visualized using the simple graph support provided by Prometheus.

There's more

Alerting can be enabled in Prometheus by configuring another service, called Alertmanager (`https://prometheus.io/docs/alerting/alertmanager/`). This service can be used to send alerts to emails, pagers, and so on.

The graphing support in Prometheus is naive. You can use Grafana (`https://grafana.com/`), which is one of the leading open source software in analyzing time-series data, such as the one stored in Prometheus. This way you can configure Grafana to read the time-series data from Prometheus and build dashboards with predefined metrics plotted on different types of charts.

10
Networking

In this chapter, we will cover the following recipes:

- Making an HTTP GET request
- Making an HTTP POST request
- Making an HTTP request for a protected resource
- Making an asynchronous HTTP request
- Making an HTTP request using Apache HttpClient
- Making an HTTP request using the Unirest HTTP client library

Introduction

Java's support for interacting with HTTP-specific features has been very primitive. The `HttpURLConnection` class, available since JDK 1.1, provides APIs for interacting with URLs with HTTP-specific features. Since this API has been there even before HTTP/1.1, it lacked advanced features and was a pain to use. This is why developers mostly resorted to using third-party libraries, such as **Apache HttpClient**, Spring framework, and HTTP APIs.

In JDK 9, a new HTTP Client API was introduced under JEP 110 (`http://openjdk.java.net/jeps/110`) as an incubator module (`http://openjdk.java.net/jeps/11`). The same incubator module has been promoted as a standard module by the name of `java.net.http` under JEP 321 (`http://openjdk.java.net/jeps/321`), which is part of the latest JDK 11 release.

A note on incubator modules: An incubator module contains non-final APIs, which are significantly larger and not mature enough to be included in Java SE. This is a form of beta release of the API so that the developers get to use the APIs much earlier. But the catch is that there is no backward compatibility support for these APIs in the newer versions of JDK. This means that code that is dependent on the incubator modules might break with the newer versions of JDK. This might be due to the incubator module being promoted to Java SE or being silently dropped from the incubator modules.

In this chapter, we will cover a few recipes showing how to use the HTTP client APIs in JDK 11, and then a few other APIs, which make use of the Apache HttpClient (http://hc.apache.org/httpcomponents-client-ga/) API and the Unirest Java HTTP library (http://unirest.io/java.html).

Making an HTTP GET request

In this recipe, we will look at using the JDK 11 HTTP Client API to make a GET request to http://httpbin.org/get.

How to do it...

1. Create an instance of java.net.http.HttpClient using its builder, java.net.http.HttpClient.Builder:

```
HttpClient client = HttpClient.newBuilder().build();
```

2. Create an instance of java.net.http.HttpRequest using its builder, java.net.http.HttpRequest.Builder. The requested URL should be provided as an instance of java.net.URI:

```
HttpRequest request = HttpRequest
            .newBuilder(new URI("http://httpbin.org/get"))
            .GET()
            .version(HttpClient.Version.HTTP_1_1)
            .build();
```

3. Send the HTTP request using the `send` API of `java.net.http.HttpClient`. This API takes an instance of `java.net.http.HttpRequest` and an implementation of `java.net.http.HttpResponse.BodyHandler`:

```
HttpResponse<String> response = client.send(request,
                    HttpResponse.BodyHandlers.ofString());
```

4. Print the `java.net.http.HttpResponse` status code and the response body:

```
System.out.println("Status code: " + response.statusCode());
System.out.println("Response Body: " + response.body());
```

The complete code for this can be found in `Chapter10/1_making_http_get`. You can make use of the run scripts, `run.bat` or `run.sh`, to compile and run the code:

```
Status code: 200
Response Body: {
  "args": {},
  "headers": {
    "Connection": "close",
    "Host": "httpbin.org",
    "User-Agent": "Java-http-client/11-ea"
  },
  "origin": "188.249.34.11",
  "url": "http://httpbin.org/get"
}

'Bye!!'
```

How it works...

There are two main steps in making an HTTP call to a URL:

- Creating an HTTP client to initiate the call
- Setting up the destination URL, required HTTP headers, and the HTTP method type, that is, GET, POST, or PUT

The Java HTTP Client API provides a builder class, `java.net.http.HttpClient.Builder`, which can be used to build an instance of `java.net.http.HttpClient` at the same time, making use of the builder APIs to set up `java.net.http.HttpClient`. The following code snippet shows how to get an instance of `java.net.http.HttpClient` with the default configuration:

```
HttpClient client = HttpClient.newHttpClient();
```

The following code snippet uses the builder to configure and then create an instance of `java.net.http.HttpClient`:

```
HttpClient client = HttpClient
                    .newBuilder()
                    //redirect policy for the client. Default is NEVER
                    .followRedirects(HttpClient.Redirect.ALWAYS)
                    //HTTP client version. Defabult is HTTP_2
                    .version(HttpClient.Version.HTTP_1_1)
                    //few more APIs for more configuration
                    .build();
```

There are more APIs in the builder, such as for setting authentication, proxy, and providing SSL context, which we will look at in different recipes.

Setting up the destination URL is nothing but creating an instance of `java.net.http.HttpRequest` using its builder and its APIs to configure it. The following code snippet shows how to create an instance of `java.net.http.HttpRequest`:

```
HttpRequest request = HttpRequest
                .newBuilder()
                .uri(new URI("http://httpbin.org/get"))
                .headers("Header 1", "Value 1", "Header 2", "Value 2")
                .timeout(Duration.ofMinutes(5))
                .version(HttpClient.Version.HTTP_1_1)
                .GET()
                .build();
```

The `java.net.http.HttpClient` object provides two APIs to make an HTTP call:

- You can send synchronously using the `HttpClient#send()` method
- You can send asynchronously using the `HttpClient#sendAsync()` method

The `send()` method takes in two parameters: the HTTP request and the handler for the HTTP response. The handler for the response is represented by the implementation of the `java.net.http.HttpResponse.BodyHandlers` interface. There are a few implementations available, such as `ofString()`, which reads the response body as `String`, and `ofByteArray()`, which reads the response body as a byte array. We will use the `ofString()` method, which returns the response `Body` as a string:

```
HttpResponse<String> response = client.send(request,
                            HttpResponse.BodyHandlers.ofString());
```

The instance of `java.net.http.HttpResponse` represents the response from the HTTP server. It provides APIs for the following:

- Getting the response body (`body()`)
- HTTP headers (`headers()`)
- The initial HTTP request (`request()`)
- The response status code (`statusCode()`)
- The URL used for the request (`uri()`)

The `HttpResponse.BodyHandlers` implementation passed to the `send()` method helps to convert the HTTP response into a compatible format, such as `String` or a `byte` array.

Making an HTTP POST request

In this recipe, we will look at posting some data to an HTTP service via the request body. We will post the data to the `http://httpbin.org/post` URL.

 We will skip the package prefix for the classes, as it is assumed to be `java.net.http`.

How to do it...

1. Create an instance of `HttpClient` using its `HttpClient.Builder` builder:

```
HttpClient client = HttpClient.newBuilder().build();
```

2. Create the required data to be passed into the request body:

```
Map<String, String> requestBody =
            Map.of("key1", "value1", "key2", "value2");
```

3. Create a `HttpRequest` object with the request method as POST and by providing the request body data as `String`. We will make use of Jackson's `ObjectMapper` to convert the request body, `Map<String, String>`, into a plain JSON `String` and then make use of `HttpRequest.BodyPublishers` to process the `String` request body:

```
ObjectMapper mapper = new ObjectMapper();
HttpRequest request = HttpRequest
            .newBuilder(new URI("http://httpbin.org/post"))
            .POST(
    HttpRequest.BodyPublishers.ofString(
      mapper.writeValueAsString(requestBody)
    )
)
.version(HttpClient.Version.HTTP_1_1)
.build();
```

4. The request is sent and the response is obtained using the `send(HttpRequest, HttpRequest.BodyHandlers)` method:

```
HttpResponse<String> response = client.send(request,
                    HttpResponse.BodyHandlers.ofString());
```

5. We then print the response status code and the response body sent by the server:

```
System.out.println("Status code: " + response.statusCode());
System.out.println("Response Body: " + response.body());
```

The complete code for this can be found at `Chapter10/2_making_http_post`. Make sure that there are the following Jackson JARs in `Chapter10/2_making_http_post/mods`:

- `jackson.databind.jar`
- `jackson.core.jar`
- `jackson.annotations.jar`

Also, take note of the module definition, `module-info.java`, available in `Chapter10/2_making_http_post/src/http.client.demo`.

 To understand how Jackson JARs are used in this modular code, please refer to the *Bottom-up migration* and *Top-down migration* recipes in `Chapter 3`, *Modular Programming*.

Run scripts, `run.bat` and `run.sh`, are provided to facilitate the compilation and execution of the code:

```
Status code: 200
Response Body: {
  "args": {},
  "data": "{\"key1\":\"value1\",\"key2\":\"value2\"}",
  "files": {},
  "form": {},
  "headers": {
    "Connection": "close",
    "Content-Length": "33",
    "Host": "httpbin.org",
    "User-Agent": "Java-http-client/11-ea"
  },
  "json": {
    "key1": "value1",
    "key2": "value2"
  },
  "origin": "188.249.34.11",
  "url": "http://httpbin.org/post"
}

'Bye!!'
```

Making an HTTP request for a protected resource

In this recipe, we will look at invoking an HTTP resource that has been protected by user credentials. `http://httpbin.org/basic-auth/user/passwd` has been protected by HTTP basic authentication. Basic authentication requires a username and a password to be provided in plain text, which is then used by the HTTP resources to decide whether the user authentication is successful.

If you open `http://httpbin.org/basic-auth/user/passwd` in the browser, it will prompt you for the username and password:

Enter the username as `user` and password as `passwd`, and you will be authenticated to be shown a JSON response:

```
{
    "authenticated": true,
    "user": "user"
}
```

Let's achieve the same thing using the `HttpClient` API.

How to do it...

1. We need to extend `java.net.Authenticator` and override its `getPasswordAuthentication()` method. This method should return an instance of `java.net.PasswordAuthentication`. Let's create a class, `UsernamePasswordAuthenticator`, which extends `java.net.Authenticator`:

```
public class UsernamePasswordAuthenticator
   extends Authenticator{
}
```

2. We will create two instance variables in the `UsernamePasswordAuthenticator` class to store the username and password, and we'll provide a constructor to initialize it:

```
private String username;
private String password;

public UsernamePasswordAuthenticator(){}
public UsernamePasswordAuthenticator ( String username,
                                       String password){
  this.username = username;
  this.password = password;
}
```

3. We will then override the `getPasswordAuthentication()` method to return an instance of `java.net.PasswordAuthentication`, initialized with the username and password:

```
@Override
protected PasswordAuthentication getPasswordAuthentication(){
  return new PasswordAuthentication(username,
                                    password.toCharArray());
}
```

4. We will then create an instance of `UsernamePasswordAuthenticator`:

```
String username = "user";
String password = "passwd";
UsernamePasswordAuthenticator authenticator =
        new UsernamePasswordAuthenticator(username, password);
```

5. We provide the instance of `UsernamePasswordAuthenticator` when initializing `HttpClient`:

```
HttpClient client = HttpClient.newBuilder()
                              .authenticator(authenticator)
                              .build();
```

6. A corresponding `HttpRequest` object is created to call the protected HTTP resource, `http://httpbin.org/basic-auth/user/passwd`:

```
HttpRequest request = HttpRequest.newBuilder(new URI(
  "http://httpbin.org/basic-auth/user/passwd"
))
.GET()
.version(HttpClient.Version.HTTP_1_1)
.build();
```

7. We obtain the `HttpResponse` by executing the request, and print the status code and the request body:

```
HttpResponse<String> response = client.send(request,
HttpResponse.BodyHandlers.ofString());
System.out.println("Status code: " + response.statusCode());
System.out.println("Response Body: " + response.body());
```

The complete code for this is available in `Chapter10/3_making_http_request_protected_res`. You can run the code by using the run scripts, `run.bat` or `run.sh`:

```
Status code: 200
Response Body: {
   "authenticated": true,
   "user": "user"
}

'Bye!!'
```

How it works...

The `Authenticator` object is used by the network calls to obtain the authentication information. Developers generally extend the `java.net.Authenticator` class and override its `getPasswordAuthentication()` method. The username and password are read either from the user input or from the configuration and are used by the extended class to create an instance of `java.net.PasswordAuthentication`.

In the recipe, we created an extension of `java.net.Authenticator`, as follows:

```
public class UsernamePasswordAuthenticator
  extends Authenticator{
    private String username;
    private String password;
    public UsernamePasswordAuthenticator(){}
    public UsernamePasswordAuthenticator ( String username,
                                           String password){
        this.username = username;
        this.password = password;
    }
    @Override
    protected PasswordAuthentication getPasswordAuthentication(){
      return new PasswordAuthentication(username,
                  password.toCharArray());
    }
  }
```

The instance of `UsernamePasswordAuthenticator` is then provided to the `HttpClient.Builder` API. The `HttpClient` instance makes use of this authenticator to get the username and password while invoking the protected HTTP request.

Making an asynchronous HTTP request

In this recipe, we will look at how to make an asynchronous GET request. In an asynchronous request, we don't wait for the response; instead, we handle the response whenever it is received by the client. In jQuery, we will make an asynchronous request and provide a callback that takes care of processing the response, while in the case of Java, we get an instance of `java.util.concurrent.CompletableFuture`, and then we invoke the `thenApply` method to process the response. Let's see this in action.

How to do it...

1. Create an instance of `HttpClient` using its builder, `HttpClient.Builder`:

```
HttpClient client = HttpClient.newBuilder().build();
```

2. Create an instance of `HttpRequest` using its `HttpRequest.Builder` builder, representing the URL and the corresponding HTTP method to be used:

```
HttpRequest request = HttpRequest
                .newBuilder(new URI("http://httpbin.org/get"))
                .GET()
                .version(HttpClient.Version.HTTP_1_1)
                .build();
```

3. Use the `sendAsync` method to make an asynchronous HTTP request and keep a reference to the `CompletableFuture<HttpResponse<String>>` object we obtained. We will use this to process the response:

```
CompletableFuture<HttpResponse<String>> responseFuture =
        client.sendAsync(request,
                HttpResponse.BodyHandlers.ofString());
```

4. We provide `CompletionStage` to process the response once the previous stage completes. For this, we make use of the `thenAccept` method, which takes a lambda expression:

```
CompletableFuture<Void> processedFuture =
            responseFuture.thenAccept(response -> {
    System.out.println("Status code: " + response.statusCode());
    System.out.println("Response Body: " + response.body());
});
```

5. Wait for the future to complete:

```
CompletableFuture.allOf(processedFuture).join();
```

The complete code for this recipe can be found in `Chapter10/4_async_http_request`. We have provided the `run.bat` and `run.sh` scripts to compile and run the recipe:

```
Status code: 200
Response Body: {
  "args": {},
  "headers": {
    "Connection": "close",
    "Host": "httpbin.org",
    "User-Agent": "Java-http-client/11-ea"
  },
  "origin": "188.249.34.11",
  "url": "http://httpbin.org/get"
}

'Bye!!'
```

Making an HTTP request using Apache HttpClient

In this recipe, we will make use of the Apache HttpClient (`https://hc.apache.org/httpcomponents-client-4.5.x/index.html`) library to make a simple HTTP `GET` request. As we are using Java 9, we want to make use of the module path and not the classpath. Hence, we need to modularize the Apache HttpClient library. One way to achieve this is to use the concept of automatic modules. Let's see how to set up the dependencies for the recipe.

Getting ready

All the required JARs are already present in `Chapter10/5_apache_http_demo/mods`:

Once these JARs are on the module path, we can declare a dependency on these JARs in `module-info.java`, which is present in `Chapter10/5_apache_http_demo/src/http.client.demo`, as shown in the following code snippet:

```
module http.client.demo{
    requires httpclient;
    requires httpcore;
    requires commons.logging;
    requires commons.codec;
}
```

How to do it...

1. Create a default instance of `org.http.client.HttpClient` using its `org.apache.http.impl.client.HttpClients` factory:

   ```
   CloseableHttpClient client = HttpClients.createDefault();
   ```

2. Create an instance of `org.apache.http.client.methods.HttpGet` along with the required URL. This represents both the HTTP method type and the requested URL:

   ```
   HttpGet request = new HttpGet("http://httpbin.org/get");
   ```

3. Execute the HTTP request using the `HttpClient` instance to obtain an instance of `CloseableHttpResponse`:

   ```
   CloseableHttpResponse response = client.execute(request);
   ```

   The `CloseableHttpResponse` instance returned after executing the HTTP request can be used to obtain details such as the response status code and other contents of the response embedded within the instance of an implementation of `HttpEntity`.

4. We make use of `EntityUtils.toString()` to obtain the response body embedded within the instance of an implementation of `HttpEntity`, and print both the status code and response body:

   ```
   int statusCode = response.getStatusLine().getStatusCode();
   String responseBody =
                   EntityUtils.toString(response.getEntity());
   System.out.println("Status code: " + statusCode);
   System.out.println("Response Body: " + responseBody);
   ```

The complete code for this recipe can be found in `Chapter10/5_apache_http_demo`. We have provided `run.bat` and `run.sh` to compile and execute the recipe code:

```
Status code: 200
Response Body: {
  "args": {},
  "headers": {
    "Accept-Encoding": "gzip,deflate",
    "Connection": "close",
    "Host": "httpbin.org",
    "User-Agent": "Apache-HttpClient/4.5.3 (Java/9-ea)"
  },
  "origin": "188.248.77.76",
  "url": "http://httpbin.org/get"
}

'Bye!!'
```

There's more...

We can provide a custom response handler while invoking the `HttpClient.execute` method, as follows:

```
String responseBody = client.execute(request, response -> {
    int status = response.getStatusLine().getStatusCode();
    HttpEntity entity = response.getEntity();
    return entity != null ? EntityUtils.toString(entity) : null;
});
```

In this case, the response is processed by the response handler and returns the response body string. The complete code for this can be found in `Chapter10/5_1_apache_http_demo_response_handler`.

Making an HTTP request using the Unirest HTTP client library

In this recipe, we will make use of the Unirest HTTP (`http://unirest.io/java.html`) Java library to access HTTP services. Unirest Java is a library based on Apache's HTTP client library and provides a fluent API for making HTTP requests.

Getting ready

As the Java library is not modular, we will make use of the concept of automatic modules, as explained in Chapter 3, *Modular Programming*. The JARs belonging to the library are placed on the module path of the application, and the application then declares a dependency on the JARs by using the name of the JAR as its module name. This way, a JAR file automatically becomes a module and is hence called an automatic module.

The Maven dependency for the Java library is as follows:

```xml
<dependency>
  <groupId>com.mashape.unirest</groupId>
  <artifactId>unirest-java</artifactId>
  <version>1.4.9</version>
</dependency>
```

As we are not using Maven in our samples, we have downloaded the JARs into the Chapter10/6_unirest_http_demo/mods folder.

The module definition is as follows:

```
module http.client.demo{
   requires httpasyncclient;
   requires httpclient;
   requires httpmime;
   requires json;
   requires unirest.java;
   requires httpcore;
   requires httpcore.nio;
   requires commons.logging;
   requires commons.codec;
}
```

How to do it...

Unirest provides a very fluid API for making HTTP requests. We can make a GET request as follows:

```java
HttpResponse<JsonNode> jsonResponse =
  Unirest.get("http://httpbin.org/get")
        .asJson();
```

The response status and response body can be obtained from the `jsonResponse` object, as follows:

```
int statusCode = jsonResponse.getStatus();
JsonNode jsonBody = jsonResponse.getBody();
```

We can make a `POST` request and pass some data, as follows:

```
jsonResponse = Unirest.post("http://httpbin.org/post")
                    .field("key1", "val1")
                    .field("key2", "val2")
                    .asJson();
```

We can make a call to a protected HTTP resource, as follows:

```
jsonResponse =
Unirest.get("http://httpbin.org/basic-auth/user/passwd")
                    .basicAuth("user", "passwd")
                    .asJson();
```

The code for this can be found in `Chapter10/6_unirest_http_demo`.

We have provided the `run.bat` and `run.sh` scripts to execute the code.

There's more...

The Unirest Java library provides much more advanced functionality, such as making async requests, file uploads, and using proxies. It's advisable that you try out these different features of the library.

11
Memory Management and Debugging

In this chapter, we will cover the following recipes:

- Understanding the G1 garbage collector
- Unified logging for JVM
- Using the `jcmd` command for JVM
- Try-with-resources for better resource handling
- Stack walking for improved debugging
- Using the memory-aware coding style
- Best practices for better memory usage
- Understand Epsilon, a low-overhead garbage collector

Introduction

Memory management is the process of memory allocation for program execution and memory reuse after some of the allocated memory is not used anymore. In Java, this process is called **garbage collection** (**GC**). The effectiveness of GC affects two major application characteristics—responsiveness and throughput.

Responsiveness is measured by how quickly an application responds to the request. For example, how quickly a website returns a page or how quickly a desktop application responds to an event. Naturally, the lower the response time, the better the user experience, which is the goal for many applications.

Throughput indicates the amount of work an application can do in a unit of time. For example, how many requests a web application can serve or how many transactions a database can support. The bigger the number, the more value the application can potentially generate and the greater number of users it can accommodate.

Not every application needs to have the minimal possible responsiveness and the maximum achievable throughput. An application may be an asynchronous submit-and-go-do-something-else, which does not require much user interaction. There may be a few potential application users too, so a lower-than-average throughput could be more than enough. Yet, there are applications that have high requirements to one or both of these characteristics and cannot tolerate long pauses imposed by the GC process.

GC, on the other hand, needs to stop any application execution once in a while to reassess the memory usage and to release it from data no longer used. Such periods of GC activity are called stop-the-world. The longer they are, the quicker the GC does its job and the longer an application freeze lasts, which can eventually grow big enough to affect both the application responsiveness and throughput. If that is the case, the GC tuning and JVM optimization become important and require an understanding of the GC principles and their modern implementations.

Unfortunately, this step is often missed by programmers. Trying to improve responsiveness and/or throughput, they just add memory and other computing capacities, thereby providing the originally-small existing problem with the space to grow. The enlarged infrastructure, in addition to hardware and software costs, requires more people to maintain it and eventually justifies the building of a whole new organization dedicated to keeping up the system. By then, the problem reaches the scale of becoming virtually unsolvable and feeds on those who have created it by forcing them to do the routine—almost menial—work for the rest of their professional lives.

In this chapter, we will focus on the **Garbage-First (G1)** garbage collector, which is the default one since Java 9. However, we'll also refer to a few other available GC implementations to contrast and explain some design decisions that have brought G1 to life. Besides, they might be more appropriate than G1 for some of the applications.

Memory organization and management are very specialized and complex areas of expertise in JVM development. This book is not intended to address the implementation details on such a level. Our focus is on those aspects of GC that can help an application developer to tune it for the application needs by setting the corresponding parameters of JVM runtime.

There are two memory areas that are used by GC—heap and stack. The first one is used by JVM to allocate memory and store objects created by the program. When an object is created with the `new` keyword, it is located in the heap, and the reference to it is stored in the stack. The stack also stores primitive variables and references to heap objects that are used by the current method or thread. The stack operates in **Last-In-First-Out** (**LIFO**). The stack is much smaller than the heap.

The slightly simplistic, but good enough for our purpose, high-level view of the main activity of any GC is the following—walking through objects in the heap and removing those that don't have any references in the stack.

Understanding the G1 garbage collector

The previous GC implementations include the **Serial GC**, **Parallel GC**, and **Concurrent Mark-Sweep** (**CMS**) collector. They divide the heap into three sections—young generation, old or tenured generation, and humongous regions for holding the objects that are 50% of the size of a standard region or larger. The young generation contains most of the newly created objects; this is the most dynamic area because a majority of the objects are short-lived and soon (as they age) become eligible for collection. The term age refers to the number of collection cycles the object has survived. The young generation has three collection cycles— an *Eden space* and two survivor spaces, such as survivor 0 (*S0*) and survivor 1 (*S1*). The objects are moved through them (according to their age and some other characteristics) until they are eventually discarded or placed in the old generation.

The old generation contains objects that are older than a certain age. This area is bigger than the young generation, and because of this, the garbage collection here is more expensive and happens not as often as in the young generation.

The permanent generation contains metadata that describes the classes and methods used in applications. It also stores strings, library classes, and methods.

When JVM starts, the heap is empty and then the objects are pushed into Eden. When it is filling up, a minor GC process starts. It removes the unreferenced and circular referred objects and moves the others to the *S0* area.

The next minor GC process migrates the referenced objects to *S1* and increments the age of those that survived the previous minor collection. After all the surviving objects (of different ages) are moved to *S1*, both *S0* and Eden become empty.

In the next minor collection, *S0* and *S1* switch their roles. The referenced objects are moved from Eden to *S1* and from *S1* to *S0*.

In each of the minor collections, the objects that have reached a certain age are moved to the old generation. As we mentioned earlier, the old generation is checked eventually (after several minor collections), the unreferenced objects are removed from there, and the memory is defragmented. This cleaning of the old generation is considered a major collection.

The permanent generation is cleaned at different times by different GC algorithms.

The G1 GC does it somewhat differently. It divides the heap into equal-sized regions and assigns each of them one of the same roles—Eden, survivor, or old—but changes the number of regions with the same role dynamically, depending on the need. It makes the memory-cleaning process and the memory defragmentation more predictable.

Getting ready

The serial GC cleans the young and the old generations in the same cycle (serially, thus the name). During the task, it stops the world. That is why it is used for non-server applications with one CPU and a heap size of a few hundred MB.

The parallel GC works in parallel on all available cores, although the number of threads can be configured. It also stops the world and is appropriate only for applications that can tolerate long freezing times.

The CMS collector was designed to address this issue of long pauses. It does it at the expense of not defragmenting the old generation and doing some analysis in parallel to the application execution (typically using 25% of CPU). The collection of the old generation starts when it is 68% full (by default, but this value can be configured).

The G1 GC algorithm is similar to the CMS collector. First, it concurrently identifies all the referenced objects in the heap and marks them correspondingly. Then it collects the emptiest regions first, thereby releasing a lot of free space. That's why it is called *Garbage-First*. Because it uses many small dedicated regions, it has a better chance of predicting the amount of time it needs to clean one of them and in fitting a user-defined pause time (G1 may exceed it occasionally, but it is pretty close most of the times).

The main beneficiaries of G1 are applications that require large heaps (6 GB or more) and do not tolerate long pauses (0.5 seconds or less). If an application encounters an issue of too many and/or too-long pauses, it can benefit from switching from the CMS or parallel GC (especially the parallel GC of the old generation) to the G1 GC. If that is not the case, switching to the G1 collector is not a requirement when using JDK 9 or higher.

The G1 GC starts with the young generation collection using stop-the-world pauses for evacuation (moving objects inside the young generation and out to the old generation). After the occupancy of the old generation reaches a certain threshold, it is collected too. The collection of some of the objects in the old generation is done concurrently and some objects are collected using stop-the-world pauses. The steps include the following:

- The initial marking of the survivor regions (root regions), which may have references to objects in the old generation, done using stop-the-world pauses
- The scanning of survivor regions for references to the old generation, done concurrently while the application continues to run
- The concurrent marking of live objects over the entire heap, done concurrently while the application continues to run
- The remark step completes the marking of live objects, done using stop-the-world pauses
- The cleanup process calculates the age of live objects, frees the regions (using stop-the-world pauses), and returns them to the free list (concurrently)

The preceding sequence might be interspersed with young generation evacuations because most of the objects are short-lived and it is easier to free a lot of memory by scanning the young generation more often.

There is also a mixed phase when G1 collects the regions already marked as mostly garbage in both the young and old generations, and humongous allocation when large objects are moved to or evacuated from humongous regions.

There are a few occasions when full GC is performed, using stop-the-world pauses:

- **Concurrent failure**: This happens if the old generation gets full during the marking phase
- **Promotion failure**: This happens if the old generation runs out of space during the mixed phase

- **Evacuation failure**: This happens when the collector cannot promote objects to the survivor space and the old generation
- **Humongous allocation**: This happens when an application tries to allocate a very big object

If tuned properly, your applications should avoid full GC.

To help with GC tuning, JVM documentation (`https://docs.oracle.com/javase/8/docs/technotes/guides/vm/gctuning/ergonomics.html`) describes ergonomics as follows:

> *"Ergonomics is the process by which JVM and garbage collection tuning, such as behavior-based tuning, improve application performance. The JVM provides platform-dependent default selections for the garbage collector, heap size, and runtime compiler. These selections match the needs of different types of applications while requiring less command-line tuning. In addition, behavior-based tuning dynamically tunes the sizes of the heap to meet a specified behavior of the application."*

How to do it...

1. To see how GC works, write the following program:

```
public class Chapter11Memory {
    public static void main(String... args) {
        int max = 99_888_999;
        System.out.println("Chapter11Memory.main() for "
                                + max + " is running...");
        List<AnObject> list = new ArrayList<>();
        IntStream.range(0, max)
                .forEach(i -> list.add(new AnObject(i)));
    }

    private static class AnObject {
        private int prop;
        AnObject(int i){ this.prop = i; }
    }
}
```

As you can see, it creates 99,888,999 objects and adds them to the `List<AnObject>` `list` collection. You might tune it by decreasing the maximum number of objects (`max`) to match the configuration of your computer.

2. The G1 GC is the default collector since Java 9, so you don't have to set anything if it is good enough for your application. Nevertheless, you can explicitly enable G1 by providing `-XX:+UseG1GC` on the command line:

```
java -XX:+UseG1GC -cp ./cookbook-1.0.jar
com.packt.cookbook.ch11_memory.Chapter11Memory
```

Note that we assume you can build an executable `.jar` file and understand the basic Java execution command. If not, please refer to the JVM documentation.

Other available GCs can be used by setting one of the following options:

- `-XX:+UseSerialGC` for using a serial collector.
- `-XX:+UseParallelGC` for using a parallel collector with parallel compaction (which enables the parallel collector to perform major collections in parallel). Without parallel compaction, major collections are performed using a single thread, which can significantly limit the scalability. Parallel compaction is disabled by the `-XX:+UseParallelOldGC` option.
- `-XX:+UseConcMarkSweepGC` for using the CMS collector.

3. To see the log messages of GC, set `-Xlog:gc`. You can also use the Unix utility, `time`, to measure the time it took to do the job (the utility publishes the last three lines of the output, so you do not need to use it if you cannot or do not want to do it):

```
time java -Xlog:gc -cp ./cookbook-1.0.jar
com.packt.cookbook.ch11_memory.Chapter11Memory
```

4. Run the preceding command. The output may look as follows (the actual values may be different on your computer):

```
[5.584s][info][gc] GC(14) Concurrent Cycle 3357.727ms
[5.912s][info][gc] GC(19) Pause Young (G1 Evacuation Pause) 2112M->2114M(3378M) 223.731ms
[6.231s][info][gc] GC(20) Pause Initial Mark (G1 Evacuation Pause) 2261M->2263M(3378M) 188.743ms
[6.231s][info][gc] GC(21) Concurrent Cycle
[9.387s][info][gc] GC(21) Pause Remark 2408M->2408M(3378M) 0.659ms
[9.873s][info][gc] GC(21) Pause Cleanup 2408M->1961M(3378M) 1.316ms
[9.884s][info][gc] GC(21) Concurrent Cycle 3652.662ms

real    0m10.096s
user    0m36.037s
sys     0m1.694s
```

As you can see, the GC went through most of the steps we have described. It has started with collecting the young generation. Then, when the List<AnObject> list object (see the preceding code) becomes too big (more than 50% of a young generation region), the memory for it is allocated in the *humongous* region. You can also see the initial mark step, the following remark, and other steps described earlier.

Each line starts with the time (in seconds) the JVM was running for and ends with the time (in milliseconds) that every step took. At the bottom of the screenshot, we see three lines printed by the time utility:

- real is the amount of wall clock time spent—all the time elapsed (should align with the first column of the JVM uptime value) since the command was run
- user is the amount of time all the CPUs spent in the user-mode code (outside the kernel) within the process; it is bigger because GC worked concurrently with the application
- sys is the amount of time the CPU spent in the kernel within the process
- user+sys is the amount of CPU time the process used

5. Set the -XX:+PrintGCDetails option (or just add * to the log option, -Xlog:gc*) to see more details about GC activity. In the following screenshot, we provide only the beginning of the log related to GC step 0:

```
Chapter12Memory.main() for 99888999 is running...
[0.195s][info][gc,start      ] GC(0) Pause Young (G1 Evacuation Pause)
[0.196s][info][gc,task       ] GC(0) Using 8 workers of 8 for evacuation
[0.258s][info][gc,phases     ] GC(0)    Evacuate Collection Set: 62.1ms
[0.258s][info][gc,phases     ] GC(0)    Code Roots: 0.0ms
[0.258s][info][gc,phases     ] GC(0)    Clear Card Table: 0.0ms
[0.258s][info][gc,phases     ] GC(0)    Expand Heap After Collection: 0.0ms
[0.258s][info][gc,phases     ] GC(0)    Free Collection Set: 0.1ms
[0.258s][info][gc,phases     ] GC(0)    Merge Per-Thread State: 0.0ms
[0.258s][info][gc,phases     ] GC(0)    Other: 0.4ms
[0.258s][info][gc,heap       ] GC(0) Eden regions: 24->0(9)
[0.258s][info][gc,heap       ] GC(0) Survivor regions: 0->3(3)
[0.258s][info][gc,heap       ] GC(0) Old regions: 0->18
[0.258s][info][gc,heap       ] GC(0) Humongous regions: 23->23
[0.258s][info][gc,metaspace  ] GC(0) Metaspace: 5493K->5493K(1056768K)
[0.258s][info][gc            ] GC(0) Pause Young (G1 Evacuation Pause) 47M->43M(256M) 62.699ms
[0.258s][info][gc,cpu        ] GC(0) User=0.40s Sys=0.03s Real=0.07s
```

Now the log has more than a dozen entries for each of the GC steps and ends up with logging the User, Sys, and Real amount of time (the amounts accumulated by the time utility) each step took. You can modify the program by adding more short-lived objects, for example, and see how the GC activity changes.

6. Get even more information with the `-Xlog:gc*=debug` option. The following is only a fragment of an output:

		elapsed	—strong roots—		————termination————			—————waste (KiB)—————		
[gc,task,stats] GC(0)	GC Termination Stats									
[gc,task,stats] GC(0)		elapsed	—strong roots—		————termination————			—————waste (KiB)—————		
[gc,task,stats] GC(0) thr	ms	ms	%	ms	%	attempts	total	alloc	undo
[gc,task,stats] GC(0) ——									
[gc,task,stats] GC(0) 2	53.48	16.96	31.71	0.03	0.06	94	25	25	0
[gc,task,stats] GC(0) 3	53.52	17.07	31.90	0.03	0.05	94	15	15	0
[gc,task,stats] GC(0) 4	53.53	17.08	31.90	0.02	0.04	63	15	15	0
[gc,task,stats] GC(0) 0	53.55	16.89	31.54	0.02	0.04	83	20	20	0
[gc,task,stats] GC(0) 1	53.56	17.10	31.93	0.00	0.00	1	23	23	0
[gc,task,stats] GC(0) 7	53.52	17.02	31.80	0.03	0.06	93	21	21	0
[gc,task,stats] GC(0) 5	53.54	16.83	31.43	0.03	0.06	102	11	11	0
[gc,task,stats] GC(0) 6	53.54	17.03	31.81	0.03	0.06	106	23	23	0
[gc,ref,start] GC(0) SoftReference									
[gc,ref] GC(0) SoftReference 0.014ms									

So, it is up to you to choose how much info you need for the analysis.

We will discuss more details of the logging format and other log options in the *Unified logging for the JVM* recipe.

How it works...

As we have mentioned earlier, the G1 GC uses default ergonomic values that probably would be good enough for most applications. Here is the list of the most important ones (`<ergo>` means that the actual value is determined ergonomically depending on the environment):

- `-XX:MaxGCPauseMillis=200`: Holds the value for the maximum pause time
- `-XX:GCPauseTimeInterval=<ergo>`: Holds the maximum pause time between GC steps (not set by default, allowing G1 to perform garbage collections back to back if needs be)
- `-XX:ParallelGCThreads=<ergo>`: Holds the maximum number of threads used for parallel work during garbage collection pauses (by default, derived from the number of available threads; if the number of CPU threads available to the process is less than or equal to eight, it uses this number; otherwise, it adds five-eighths of the threads greater than eight to the final number of threads)
- `-XX:ConcGCThreads=<ergo>`: Holds the maximum number of threads used for concurrent work (set by default as -XX:ParallelGCThreads divided by four).
- `-XX:+G1UseAdaptiveIHOP`: Indicates that the initiating heap occupancy should be adaptive
- `-XX:InitiatingHeapOccupancyPercent=45`: Sets the first few collection cycles; G1 will use an occupancy of 45% of the old generation as the mark start threshold
- `-XX:G1HeapRegionSize=<ergo>`: Holds the heap region size based on the initial and maximum heap sizes (by default, because the heap contains roughly 2,048 heap regions, the size of a heap region can vary from 1 to 32 MB and must be a power of 2)
- `-XX:G1NewSizePercent=5` and `-XX:XX:G1MaxNewSizePercent=60`: Define the size of the young generation in total, which varies between these two values as percentages of the current JVM heap in use
- `-XX:G1HeapWastePercent=5`: Holds the allowed unreclaimed space in the collection-set candidates as a percentage (G1 stops the space reclamation if the free space in the collection-set candidates is lower than that)

- `-XX:G1MixedGCCountTarget=8`: Holds the expected length of the space-reclamation phase in a number of collections)
- `-XX:G1MixedGCLiveThresholdPercent=85`: Holds the percentage of the live object occupancy of the old generation regions, after which a region won't be collected in this space-reclamation phase

In general, the G1 goals in the default configuration are "to provide relatively small, uniform pauses at high throughput" (from the G1 documentation). If these default settings do not fit your application, you can change the pause time (using `-XX:MaxGCPauseMillis`) and the maximum Java heap size (using the `-Xmx` option). Note, though, that the actual pause time will not be an exact match at runtime, but G1 will try its best to meet the goal.

If you would like to increase the throughput, decrease the pause time goal or request a larger heap. To increase responsiveness, change the pause time value. Note, though, that the limiting of the young generation size (using `-Xmn`, `-XX:NewRatio`, or other options) can impede the pause-time control because "the young generation size is the main means for G1 to allow it to meet the pause time" (from the G1 documentation).

One of the first possible causes of poor performance can be full GC triggered by a too-high heap occupancy in the old generation. This situation can be detected by the presence of *Pause Full (Allocation failure)* in the log. It usually happens when too many objects are created in a quick succession (and cannot be collected quickly enough) or many large (humongous) objects cannot be allocated in a timely manner. There are several recommended ways to handle this condition:

- In the case of an excessive number of humongous objects, try to reduce their count by increasing the region size, using the `-XX:G1HeapRegionSize` option (the currently selected heap region size is printed at the beginning of the log).
- Increase the size of the heap.
- Increase the number of concurrent marking threads by setting `-XX:ConcGCThreads`.
- Facilitate the beginning of marking earlier (using the fact that G1 makes the decisions based on earlier application behavior). Increase the buffer used in an adaptive IHOP calculation by modifying `-XX:G1ReservePercent`, or disable the adaptive calculation of the IHOP by setting it manually using `-XX:-G1UseAdaptiveIHOP` and `-XX:InitiatingHeapOccupancyPercent`.

Only after addressing full GC can one start tuning the JVM for better responsiveness and/or throughput. The JVM documentation identifies the following cases for responsiveness tuning:

- Unusual system or real-time usage
- Reference processing takes too long
- Young-only collections take too long
- Mixed collections take too long
- High update RS and scan RS times

Better throughput can be achieved by decreasing the overall pause times and the frequency of the pauses. Refer to the JVM documentation for the identification and recommendations of mitigating the issues.

Unified logging for JVM

The main components of JVM include the following:

- Classloader
- JVM memory where the runtime data is stored; it is broken down into the following areas:
    - Stack area
    - Method area
    - Heap area
    - PC registers
    - Native method stack
- Execution engine, which consists of the following parts:
    - Interpreter
    - The JIT compiler
    - Garbage collection
    - Native method interface JNI
    - Native method library

The log message of all these components can now be captured and analyzed using unified logging, turned on by the -Xlog option.

The main features of the new logging system are as follows:

- Usage of the log levels—trace, debug, info, warning, error
- Message tags that identify the JVM component, action, or message of a specific interest
- Three output types—stdout, stderr, and file
- The enforcement of the one-message-per-line limit

Getting ready

To see all the logging possibilities at a glance, you can run the following command:

```
java -Xlog:help
```

Here is the output:

```
-Xlog Usage: -Xlog[:[what][:[output][:[decorators][:output-options]]]]
        where 'what' is a combination of tags and levels on the form tag1[+tag2...][*][=level][,...]
        Unless wildcard (*) is specified, only log messages tagged with exactly the tags specified will be matched.

Available log levels:
 off, trace, debug, info, warning, error

Available log decorators:
 time (t), uptime (u), timemillis (tm), uptimemillis (um), timenanos (tn), uptimenanos (un), hostname (hn), pid (p), tid
 (ti), level (l), tags (tg)
 Decorators can also be specified as 'none' for no decoration.

Available log tags:
 add, age, alloc, annotation, arguments, attach, barrier, biasedlocking, blocks, bot, breakpoint, census, class, classhi
 sto, cleanup, compaction, constraints, constantpool, coops, cpu, cset, data, defaultmethods, dump, ergo, exceptions, exi
 t, freelist, gc, heap, humongous, ihop, iklass, init, itables, jni, jvmti, liveness, load, loader, logging, mark, markin
 g, methodcomparator, metadata, metaspace, mmu, modules, monitorinflation, monitormismatch, nmethod, normalize, objecttag
 ging, obsolete, oopmap, os, pagesize, path, phases, plab, promotion, preorder, protectiondomain, ref, redefine, refine,
 region, remset, purge, resolve, safepoint, scavenge, scrub, stacktrace, stackwalk, start, startuptime, state, stats, str
 ingdedup, stringtable, stackmap, subclass, survivor, sweep, task, thread, tlab, time, timer, update, unload, verificatio
 n, verify, vmoperation, vtables, workgang, jfr, instrumentation, setting, types
 Specifying 'all' instead of a tag combination matches all tag combinations.

Described tag combinations:
 logging: Logging for the log framework itself

Available log outputs:
 stdout, stderr, file=<filename>
 Specifying %p and/or %t in the filename will expand to the JVM's PID and startup timestamp, respectively.
```

As you can see, the format of the -Xlog option is defined as follows:

```
-Xlog[:[what][:[output][:[decorators][:output-options]]]]
```

Let's explain the option in detail:

- `what` is a combination of tags and levels of the `tag1[+tag2...][*][=level][,...]` form. We have already demonstrated how this construct works when we used the `gc` tag in the `-Xlog:gc*=debug` option. The wildcard (*) indicates that you'd like to see all the messages that have the `gc` tag (maybe among other tags). An absence of the `-Xlog:gc=debug` wildcard indicates that you would like to see messages marked by one tag (`gc`, in this case) only. If only `-Xlog` is used, the log will show all the messages at the `info` level.
- The `output` sets the type of output (the default is `stdout`).
- The `decorators` indicate what will be placed at the beginning of each line of the log (before the actual log message comes from a component). Default decorators are `uptime`, `level`, and `tags`, each included in square brackets.
- `output_options` may include `filecount=file count` and/or `filesize=file size` with optional K, M or G suffix.

To summarize, the default log configuration is as follows:

```
-Xlog:all=info:stdout:uptime,level,tags
```

How to do it...

Let's run some of the log settings:

1. Run the following command:

```
java -Xlog:cpu -cp ./cookbook-1.0.jar
            com.packt.cookbook.ch11_memory.Chapter11Memory
```

There are no messages because the JVM does not log messages with the `cpu` tag only. The tag is used in combination with other tags.

2. Add a * sign and run the command again:

```
java -Xlog:cpu* -cp ./cookbook-1.0.jar
            com.packt.cookbook.ch11_memory.Chapter11Memory
```

The result will look as follows:

```
Chapter12Memory.main() for 99888999 is running...
[0.241s][info][gc,cpu] GC(0) User=0.33s Sys=0.03s Real=0.05s
[0.291s][info][gc,cpu] GC(1) User=0.23s Sys=0.00s Real=0.03s
[0.316s][info][gc,cpu] GC(2) User=0.11s Sys=0.01s Real=0.01s
[0.355s][info][gc,cpu] GC(3) User=0.13s Sys=0.00s Real=0.01s
[0.391s][info][gc,cpu] GC(4) User=0.14s Sys=0.01s Real=0.03s
[0.598s][info][gc,cpu] GC(6) User=0.45s Sys=0.03s Real=0.06s
[0.673s][info][gc,cpu] GC(7) User=0.33s Sys=0.01s Real=0.05s
[0.676s][info][gc,cpu] GC(5) User=0.01s Sys=0.00s Real=0.00s
[0.703s][info][gc,cpu] GC(5) User=0.00s Sys=0.00s Real=0.00s
[0.793s][info][gc,cpu] GC(8) User=0.33s Sys=0.00s Real=0.04s
```

As you can see, the cpu tag brings only messages about how long it took a garbage collection to execute. Even if we set the log level to trace or debug (-Xlog:cpu*=debug, for example), no other messages will be shown.

3. Run the command with the heap tag:

```
java -Xlog:heap* -cp ./cookbook-1.0.jar
          com.packt.cookbook.ch11_memory.Chapter11Memory
```

You will only get heap-related messages:

```
Chapter12Memory.main() for 99888999 is running...
[0.240s][info][gc,heap     ] GC(0) Eden regions: 24->0(9)
[0.240s][info][gc,heap     ] GC(0) Survivor regions: 0->3(3)
[0.240s][info][gc,heap     ] GC(0) Old regions: 0->18
[0.240s][info][gc,heap     ] GC(0) Humongous regions: 23->23
[0.293s][info][gc,heap     ] GC(1) Eden regions: 9->0(10)
[0.293s][info][gc,heap     ] GC(1) Survivor regions: 3->2(2)
[0.293s][info][gc,heap     ] GC(1) Old regions: 18->29
[0.293s][info][gc,heap     ] GC(1) Humongous regions: 34->34
```

But let's look closer at the first line. It starts with three decorators—uptime, log level, and tags—and then with the message itself, which starts with the collection cycle number (0 in this case) and the information that the number of Eden regions dropped from 24 to 0 (and their count now is 9). It happened because (as we see in the next line) the count of survivor regions grew from 0 to 3 and the count of the old generation (the third line) grew to 18, while the count of humongous regions (23) did not change. These are all the heap-related messages in the first collection cycle. Then, the second collection cycle starts.

4. Add the cpu tag again and run:

```
java -Xlog:heap*,cpu* -cp ./cookbook-1.0.jar
            com.packt.cookbook.ch11_memory.Chapter11Memory
```

As you can see, the cpu message shows how long each cycle took:

```
Chapter12Memory.main() for 99888999 is running...
[0.469s][info][gc,heap    ] GC(0) Eden regions: 24->0(9)
[0.469s][info][gc,heap    ] GC(0) Survivor regions: 0->3(3)
[0.469s][info][gc,heap    ] GC(0) Old regions: 0->18
[0.469s][info][gc,heap    ] GC(0) Humongous regions: 23->23
[0.469s][info][gc,cpu     ] GC(0) User=0.68s Sys=0.06s Real=0.10s
[0.572s][info][gc,heap    ] GC(1) Eden regions: 9->0(10)
```

5. Try to use two tags combined via the + sign (-Xlog:gc+heap, for example). It brings up only the messages that have both tags (similar to the binary AND operation). Note that a wildcard will not work together with the + sign (-Xlog:gc*+heap, for example, does not work).

6. You can also select the output type and decorators. In practice, the decorator level does not seem very informative and can be easily omitted by explicitly listing only the decorators that are needed. Consider the following example:

```
java -Xlog:heap*,cpu*::uptime,tags -cp ./cookbook-1.0.jar
            com.packt.cookbook.ch11_memory.Chapter11Memory
```

Note how the two colons (::) were inserted to preserve the default setting of the output type. We could also show it explicitly:

```
java -Xlog:heap*,cpu*:stdout:uptime,tags -cp ./cookbook-1.0.jar
            com.packt.cookbook.ch11_memory.Chapter11Memory
```

To remove any decoration, one can set them to `none`:

```
java -Xlog:heap*,cpu*::none -cp ./cookbook-1.0.jar
             com.packt.cookbook.ch11_memory.Chapter11Memory
```

The most useful aspect of a new logging system is tag selection. It allows a better analysis of the memory evolution of each JVM component and its subsystems or to find the performance bottleneck, analyzing the time spent in each collection phase—both are critical for the JVM and application tuning.

Using the jcmd command for the JVM

If you open the `bin` folder of the Java installation, you can find quite a few command-line utilities there that can be used to diagnose issues and monitor an application deployed with the **Java Runtime Environment** (**JRE**). They use different mechanisms to get the data they report. The mechanisms are specific to the **Virtual Machine** (**VM**) implementation, operating systems, and release. Typically, only a subset of the tools is applicable to a given issue.

In this recipe, we will focus on the diagnostic command introduced with Java 9 as a command-line utility, `jcmd`. If the `bin` folder is on the path, you can invoke it by typing `jcmd` on the command line. Otherwise, you have to go to the `bin` directory or prepend the `jcmd` in our examples with the full or relative (to the location of your command line window) path to the `bin` folder.

If you do type it and there is no Java process currently running on the machine, you will get back only one line, which looks as follows:

```
87863 jdk.jcmd/sun.tools.jcmd.JCmd
```

It shows that only one Java process is currently running (the `jcmd` utility itself) and it has the **process identifier** (**PID**) of 87863 (which will be different with each run).

Let's run a Java program, for example:

```
java -cp ./cookbook-1.0.jar
             com.packt.cookbook.ch11_memory.Chapter11Memory
```

The output of `jcmd` will show (with different PIDs) the following:

```
87864 jdk.jcmd/sun.tools.jcmd.JCmd
87785 com.packt.cookbook.ch11_memory.Chapter11Memory
```

As you can see, if entered without any options, the jcmd utility reports the PIDs of all the currently running Java processes. After getting the PID, you can then use jcmd to request data from the JVM that runs the process:

```
jcmd 88749 VM.version
```

Alternatively, you can avoid using PID (and calling jcmd without parameters) by referring to the process by the main class of the application:

```
jcmd Chapter11Memory VM.version
```

You can read the JVM documentation for more details about the jcmd utility and how to use it.

How to do it...

jcmd is a utility that allows us to issue commands to the specified Java process:

1. Get the full list of the jcmd commands available for a particular Java process by executing the following line:

```
jcmd PID/main-class-name help
```

Instead of PID/main-class, put the process identifier or the main class name. The list is specific to JVM, so each listed command requests the data from the specific process.

2. In JDK 8, the following jcmd commands were available:

```
JFR.stop
JFR.start
JFR.dump
JFR.check
VM.native_memory
VM.check_commercial_features
VM.unlock_commercial_features
ManagementAgent.stop
ManagementAgent.start_local
ManagementAgent.start
GC.rotate_log
Thread.print
GC.class_stats
GC.class_histogram
GC.heap_dump
GC.run_finalization
```

```
GC.run
VM.uptime
VM.flags
VM.system_properties
VM.command_line
VM.version
```

The JDK 9 introduced the following `jcmd` commands (JDK 18.3 and JDK 18.9 did not add new commands):

- `Compiler.queue`: Prints the methods queued for compilation with either C1 or C2 (separate queues)
- `Compiler.codelist`: Prints n-methods (compiled) with full signature, address range, and state (alive, non-entrant, and zombie), and allows the selection of printing to `stdout`, a file, XML, or text printout
- `Compiler.codecache`: Prints the content of the code cache, where the JIT compiler stores the generated native code to improve performance
- `Compiler.directives_add file`: Adds compiler directives from a file to the top of the directives stack
- `Compiler.directives_clear`: Clears the compiler directives stack (leaves the default directives only)
- `Compiler.directives_print`: Prints all the directives on the compiler directives stack from top to bottom
- `Compiler.directives_remove`: Removes the top directive from the compiler directives stack
- `GC.heap_info`: Prints the current heap parameters and status
- `GC.finalizer_info`: Shows the status of the finalizer thread, which collects objects with a finalizer (that is, a `finalize()` method)
- `JFR.configure`: Allows us to configure the Java Flight Recorder
- `JVMTI.data_dump`: Prints the Java Virtual Machine Tool Interface data dump
- `JVMTI.agent_load`: Loads (attaches) the Java Virtual Machine Tool Interface agent

- `ManagementAgent.status`: Prints the status of the remote JMX agent
- `Thread.print`: Prints all the threads with stack traces
- `VM.log [option]`: Allows us to set the JVM log configuration (which we described in the previous recipe) at runtime, after the JVM has started (the availability can be seen by using `VM.log list`)
- `VM.info`: Prints the unified JVM info (version and configuration), a list of all threads and their state (without thread dump and heap dump), heap summary, JVM internal events (GC, JIT, safepoint, and so on), memory map with loaded native libraries, VM arguments and environment variables, and details of the operation system and hardware
- `VM.dynlibs`: Prints information about dynamic libraries
- `VM.set_flag`: Allows us to set the JVM *writable* (also called *manageable*) flags (see the JVM documentation for a list of the flags)
- `VM.stringtable` and `VM.symboltable`: Prints all UTF-8 string constants
- `VM.class_hierarchy [full-class-name]`: Prints all the loaded classes or just a specified class hierarchy
- `VM.classloader_stats`: Prints information about the classloader
- `VM.print_touched_methods`: Prints all the methods that have been touched (have been read at least) at runtime

As you can see, these new commands belong to several groups, denoted by the prefix compiler, **garbage collector (GC)**, **Java Flight Recorder (JFR)**, **Java Virtual Machine Tool Interface (JVMTI)**, **Management Agent** (related to remote JMX agent), **thread**, and **VM**. In this book, we do not have enough space to go through each command in detail. We will only demonstrate the usage of a few practical ones.

How it works...

1. To get help for the `jcmd` utility, run the following command:

```
jcmd -h
```

Here is the result of the command:

```
Usage: jcmd <pid | main class> <command ...|PerfCounter.print|-f file>
   or: jcmd -l
   or: jcmd -h

command must be a valid jcmd command for the selected jvm.
Use the command "help" to see which commands are available.
If the pid is 0, commands will be sent to all Java processes.
The main class argument will be used to match (either partially
or fully) the class used to start Java.
If no options are given, lists Java processes (same as -l).

PerfCounter.print display the counters exposed by this process
-f   read and execute commands from the file
-l   list JVM processes on the local machine
-h   this help
```

It tells us that the commands can also be read from the file specified after –
f and that there is a `PerfCounter.print` command, which prints all the
performance counters (statistics) of the process.

2. Run the following command:

    jcmd Chapter11Memory GC.heap_info

The output may look like this screenshot:

```
garbage-first heap   total 262144K, used 3072K [0x00000006c0000000, 0x00000006c0100800
   region size 1024K, 4 young (4096K), 0 survivors (0K)
Metaspace       used 5171K, capacity 5280K, committed 5504K, reserved 1056768K
   class space  used 517K, capacity 558K, committed 640K, reserved 1048576K
```

It shows the total heap size and how much of it was used, the size of a
region in the young generation and how many regions are allocated, and
the parameters of `Metaspace` and `class space`.

3. The following command is very helpful in case you are looking for
    runaway threads or would like to know what else is going on behind the
    scenes:

    jcmd Chapter11Memory Thread.print

Here is a fragment of the possible output:

```
"main" #1 prio=5 os_prio=31 tid=0x00007ff803002800 nid=0xb07 waiting on condition [0x0000700000219000]
    java.lang.Thread.State: TIMED_WAITING (sleeping)
        at java.lang.Thread.sleep(java.base@9-ea/Native Method)
        at com.packt.cookbook.ch12_memory.Chapter12Memory.demo2_ProcessForJcmd(Chapter12Memory.java:32)
        at com.packt.cookbook.ch12_memory.Chapter12Memory.main(Chapter12Memory.java:10)

"VM Thread" os_prio=31 tid=0x00007ff803098000 nid=0x5203 runnable

"GC Thread#0" os_prio=31 tid=0x00007ff803807800 nid=0x2803 runnable
```

4. This command is probably used most often, as it produces a wealth of information about the hardware, the JVM process as a whole, and the current state of its components:

```
jcmd Chapter11Memory VM.info
```

It starts with a summary, as follows:

```
# JRE version: Java(TM) SE Runtime Environment (9.0+143) (build 9-ea+143)
# Java VM: Java HotSpot(TM) 64-Bit Server VM (9-ea+143, mixed mode, tiered, compressed

---------------- S U M M A R Y ------------

Command Line: com.packt.cookbook.ch12_memory.Chapter12Memory

Host: MacBookPro11,5 x86_64 2500 MHz, 8 cores, 16G, Darwin 15.6.0
Time: Mon May 15 21:34:45 2017 MDT elapsed time: 388 seconds (0d 0h 6m 28s)
```

The general process description follows:

```
---------------- P R O C E S S ----------------

Heap address: 0x00000006c0000000, size: 4096 MB, Compressed Oops mode: Zero based,
Narrow klass base: 0x0000000000000000, Narrow klass shift: 3
Compressed class space size: 1073741824 Address: 0x00000007c0000000
```

Then come the details of the heap (this is only a tiny fragment of it):

```
Heap:
 garbage-first heap   total 262144K, used 3072K [0x00000006c0000000, 0x00000006c01008
  region size 1024K, 4 young (4096K), 0 survivors (0K)
 Metaspace       used 5172K, capacity 5280K, committed 5504K, reserved 1056768K
  class space    used 518K, capacity 558K, committed 640K, reserved 1048576K
Heap Regions: E=young(eden), S=young(survivor), O=old, HS=humongous(starts), HC=humon
p, AC=allocation context, TAMS=top-at-mark-start (previous, next)
 |   0|0x00000006c0000000, 0x00000006c0000000, 0x00000006c0100000|  0%| F|  ITS  0|AC
 |   1|0x00000006c0100000, 0x00000006c0100000, 0x00000006c0200000|  0%| F|  ITS  0|AC
```

It then prints the compilation events, GC heap history, deoptimization events, internal exceptions, events, dynamic libraries, logging options, environment variables, VM arguments, and many parameters of the system running the process.

The `jcmd` commands give a deep insight into the JVM process, which helps to debug and tune the process for best performance and optimal resource usage.

Try-with-resources for better resource handling

Managing resources is important. Any mishandling (not releasing) of the resources—database connections and file descriptors left opened, for example—can exhaust the system's capability to operate. That's why, in JDK 7, the *try-with-resources* statement was introduced. We have used it in the examples of Chapter 6, *Database Programming*:

```
try (Connection conn = getDbConnection();
Statement st = createStatement(conn)) {
  st.execute(sql);
} catch (Exception ex) {
  ex.printStackTrace();
}
```

As a reminder, here is the `getDbConnection()` method:

```
Connection getDbConnection() {
  PGPoolingDataSource source = new PGPoolingDataSource();
  source.setServerName("localhost");
  source.setDatabaseName("cookbook");
  try {
    return source.getConnection();
```

```
      } catch(Exception ex) {
        ex.printStackTrace();
        return null;
      }
  }
```

And here is the `createStatement()` method:

```
Statement createStatement(Connection conn) {
  try {
    return conn.createStatement();
  } catch(Exception ex) {
    ex.printStackTrace();
    return null;
  }
}
```

This was very helpful, but in some cases, we were still required to write extra code in the old style, for example, if there is an `execute()` method that accepts a `Statement` object as a parameter, and we would like to release (close) it as soon as it was used. In such a case, the code will look as follows:

```
void execute(Statement st, String sql){
  try {
    st.execute(sql);
  } catch (Exception ex) {
    ex.printStackTrace();
  } finally {
    if(st != null) {
      try{
        st.close();
      } catch (Exception ex) {
        ex.printStackTrace();
      }
    }
  }
}
```

As you can see, most of it is just boilerplate copy-and-paste code.

The new *try-with-resources* statement, introduced with Java 9, addresses this case by allowing effectively final variables to be used as the resources.

How to do it...

1. Rewrite the previous example using the new *try-with-resources* statement:

    ```
    void execute(Statement st, String sql){
      try (st) {
        st.execute(sql);
      } catch (Exception ex) {
        ex.printStackTrace();
      }
    }
    ```

    As you can see, it is much more concise and focused, without the need to repeatedly write trivial code that closes the resource. No more `finally` and additional `try...catch` in it.

2. If the connection is passed in too, it also can be put in the same try-block and closed as soon as it is no longer needed:

    ```
    void execute(Connection conn, Statement st, String sql) {
      try (conn; st) {
        st.execute(sql);
      } catch (Exception ex) {
        ex.printStackTrace();
      }
    }
    ```

    It may or may not fit your application's connection-handling, but often, this capability is handy.

3. Try a different combination, such as the following:

    ```
    Connection conn = getDbConnection();
    Statement st = conn.createStatement();
    try (conn; st) {
      st.execute(sql);
    } catch (Exception ex) {
      ex.printStackTrace();
    }
    ```

And this combination is allowed too:

```
Connection conn = getDbConnection();
try (conn; Statement st = conn.createStatement()) {
  st.execute(sql);
} catch (Exception ex) {
  ex.printStackTrace();
}
```

The new statement provides more flexibility to write code that fits the needs without writing the lines that close the resource.

The only requirements are as follows:

- The variable included in the `try` statement has to be final or effectively final
- The resource has to implement the `AutoCloseable` interface, which includes only one method:

```
void close() throws Exception;
```

How it works...

To demonstrate how the new statement works, let's create our own resources that implement `AutoCloseable` and use them in a fashion similar to the resources of the previous examples.

Here is one resource:

```
class MyResource1 implements AutoCloseable {
  public MyResource1(){
    System.out.println("MyResource1 is acquired");
  }
  public void close() throws Exception {
    //Do what has to be done to release this resource
    System.out.println("MyResource1 is closed");
  }
}
```

Here is the second resource:

```
class MyResource2 implements AutoCloseable {
  public MyResource2(){
    System.out.println("MyResource2 is acquired");
  }
  public void close() throws Exception {
    //Do what has to be done to release this resource
    System.out.println("MyResource2 is closed");
  }
}
```

Let's use them in the code example:

```
MyResource1 res1 = new MyResource1();
MyResource2 res2 = new MyResource2();
try (res1; res2) {
  System.out.println("res1 and res2 are used");
} catch (Exception ex) {
  ex.printStackTrace();
}
```

If we run it, the result will be as follows:

```
MyResource1 is acquired
MyResource2 is acquired
res1 and res2 are used
MyResource2 is closed
MyResource1 is closed
```

Note that the resource listed first in the `try` statement is closed last. Let us make only one change and switch the order of the references in the `try` statement:

```
MyResource1 res1 = new MyResource1();
MyResource2 res2 = new MyResource2();
try (res2; res1) {
  System.out.println("res1 and res2 are used");
} catch (Exception ex) {
  ex.printStackTrace();
}
```

The output confirms that the sequence of the references closing changes too:

```
MyResource1 is acquired
MyResource2 is acquired
res1 and res2 are used
MyResource1 is closed
MyResource2 is closed
```

This rule of closing the resources in the reverse order addresses the most important possible issue of dependency between resources, but it is up to the programmer to define the sequence of closing the resources (by listing them in the `try` statement in the correct order). Fortunately, the closing of most standard resources is handled by the JVM gracefully, and the code does not break if the resources are listed in incorrect order. Still, it is a good idea to list them in the same sequence as they were created.

Stack walking for improved debugging

Stack trace can be very helpful in figuring out the source of a problem. When an automatic correction is possible, the need arises to read it programmatically.

Since Java 1.4, the current stack trace can be accessed via the `java.lang.Thread` and `java.lang.Throwable` classes. You can add the following line to any method of your code:

```
Thread.currentThread().dumpStack();
```

You can also add the following line:

```
new Throwable().printStackTrace();
```

It will print the stack trace to the standard output. Alternatively, since Java 8, you can use any of the following lines for the same effect:

```
Arrays.stream(Thread.currentThread().getStackTrace())
      .forEach(System.out::println);

Arrays.stream(new Throwable().getStackTrace())
      .forEach(System.out::println);
```

Or you can extract the fully qualified name of the caller class, using one of these lines:

```
System.out.println("This method is called by " +
Thread.currentThread()
.getStackTrace()[1].getClassName());

System.out.println("This method is called by " + new Throwable()
.getStackTrace()[0].getClassName());
```

All the aforementioned solutions are possible because of
the `java.lang.StackTraceElement` class, which represents a stack frame in a stack
trace. This class provides other methods that describe the execution point represented
by this stack-trace element, which allows programmatic access to the stack-trace
information. For example, you can run this code snippet from anywhere in your
program:

```
Arrays.stream(Thread.currentThread().getStackTrace())
    .forEach(e -> {
      System.out.println();
      System.out.println("e="+e);
      System.out.println("e.getFileName()="+ e.getFileName());
      System.out.println("e.getMethodName()="+ e.getMethodName());
      System.out.println("e.getLineNumber()="+ e.getLineNumber());
});
```

Or you can run the following from anywhere in the program:

```
Arrays.stream(new Throwable().getStackTrace())
    .forEach(x -> {
      System.out.println();
      System.out.println("x="+x);
      System.out.println("x.getFileName()="+ x.getFileName());
      System.out.println("x.getMethodName()="+ x.getMethodName());
      System.out.println("x.getLineNumber()="+ x.getLineNumber());
});
```

Unfortunately, this wealth of data comes with a price. The JVM captures the entire
stack (except for hidden stack frames), and—in those cases when the programmatic
analysis of the stack trace is embedded in the main application flow—it may affect the
application performance. Meanwhile, you only need a fraction of this data to make a
decision.

This is where the new Java 9 class, `java.lang.StackWalker`, with its nested
`Option` class and `StackFrame` interface, comes in handy.

Getting ready

The `StackWalker` class has four overloaded `getInstance()` static factory methods:

- `StackWalker getInstance()`: This is configured to skip all the hidden frames and no caller class reference is retained. The hidden frames contain JVM internal implementation-specific information. Not retaining the caller class reference means that calling the `getCallerClass()` method on the `StackWalker` object throws `UnsupportedOperationException`.
- `StackWalker getInstance(StackWalker.Option option)`: This creates an instance with the given option, specifying the stack frame information it can access.
- `StackWalker getInstance(Set<StackWalker.Option> options)`: This creates an instance with the given set of options, specifying the stack frame information it can access. If the given set is empty, the instance is configured exactly like the instance created by `StackWalker getInstance()`.
- `StackWalker getInstance(Set<StackWalker.Option> options, int estimatedDepth)`: This creates a similar instance as the preceding one and accepts the `estimatedDepth` parameter, which allows us to estimate the buffer size it might need.

The following are the values of `enum StackWalker.Option`:

- `StackWalker.Option.RETAIN_CLASS_REFERENCE`: Configures the `StackWalker` instance to support the `getCallerClass()` method, and the `StackFrame` to support the `getDeclaringClass()` method
- `StackWalker.Option.SHOW_HIDDEN_FRAMES`: Configures the `StackWalker` instance to show all reflection frames and implementation-specific frames
- `StackWalker.Option.SHOW_REFLECT_FRAMES`: Configures the `StackWalker` instance to show all reflection frames

The `StackWalker` class also has three methods:

- `T walk(Function<Stream<StackWalker.StackFrame>, T> function)`: This applies the given function to the stream of `StackFrames` for the current thread, traversing the frames from the top of the stack. The top frame contains the method that has called this `walk()` method.
- `void forEach(Consumer<StackWalker.StackFrame> action)`: This performs the given action on each element of the `StackFrame` stream of the current thread, traversing from the top frame of the stack, which is the method calling the `forEach` method. This method is equivalent to calling `walk(s -> { s.forEach(action); return null; })`.
- `Class<?> getCallerClass()`: This gets the `Class` object of the caller that invoked the method that called `getCallerClass()`. This method throws `UnsupportedOperationException` if this `StackWalker` instance is not configured with the `RETAIN_CLASS_REFERENCE` option.

How to do it...

Create several classes and methods that will call each other, so you can perform stack-trace processing:

1. Create a `Clazz01` class:

```
public class Clazz01 {
  public void method(){
    new Clazz03().method("Do something");
    new Clazz02().method();
  }
}
```

2. Create a `Clazz02` class:

```
public class Clazz02 {
  public void method(){
    new Clazz03().method(null);
  }
}
```

3. Create a `Clazz03` class:

```
public class Clazz03 {
  public void method(String action){
    if(action != null){
      System.out.println(action);
      return;
    }
    System.out.println("Throw the exception:");
    action.toString();
  }
}
```

4. Write a `demo4_StackWalk()` method:

```
private static void demo4_StackWalk(){
  new Clazz01().method();
}
```

Call this method from the main method of the `Chapter11Memory` class:

```
public class Chapter11Memory {
  public static void main(String... args) {
    demo4_StackWalk();
  }
}
```

If we now run the `Chapter11Memory` class, the result will be as follows:

```
Do something

Throw the exception:
Exception in thread "main" java.lang.NullPointerException
    at com.packt.cookbook.ch12_memory.walk.Clazz03.method(Clazz03.java:13)
    at com.packt.cookbook.ch12_memory.walk.Clazz02.method(Clazz02.java:6)
    at com.packt.cookbook.ch12_memory.walk.Clazz01.method(Clazz01.java:7)
    at com.packt.cookbook.ch12_memory.Chapter12Memory.demo4_StackWalk(Chapter12Memory.java:194)
    at com.packt.cookbook.ch12_memory.Chapter12Memory.main(Chapter12Memory.java:17)
```

The `Do something` message is passed from `Clazz01` and printed out in `Clazz03`. Then `Clazz02` passes null to `Clazz03`, and the `Throw the exception` message is printed out before the stack trace caused by `NullPointerException` from the `action.toString()` line.

How it works...

For a deeper understanding of the concepts here, let's modify `Clazz03`:

```java
public class Clazz03 {
  public void method(String action){
    if(action != null){
      System.out.println(action);
      return;
    }
    System.out.println("Print the stack trace:");
    Thread.currentThread().dumpStack();
  }
}
```

The result will be the following:

```
Do something

Print the stack trace:
java.lang.Exception: Stack trace
    at java.lang.Thread.dumpStack(java.base@9-ea/Thread.java:1435)
    at com.packt.cookbook.ch12_memory.walk.Clazz03.method(Clazz03.java:21)
    at com.packt.cookbook.ch12_memory.walk.Clazz02.method(Clazz02.java:7)
    at com.packt.cookbook.ch12_memory.walk.Clazz01.method(Clazz01.java:8)
    at com.packt.cookbook.ch12_memory.Chapter12Memory.demo4_StackWalk(Chapter12Memory.java:195)
    at com.packt.cookbook.ch12_memory.Chapter12Memory.main(Chapter12Memory.java:17)
```

Alternatively, we can get a similar output by using `Throwable` instead of `Thread`:

```java
new Throwable().printStackTrace();
```

The preceding line produces this output:

```
Do something

Print the stack trace:
java.lang.Throwable
    at com.packt.cookbook.ch12_memory.walk.Clazz03.method(Clazz03.java:16)
    at com.packt.cookbook.ch12_memory.walk.Clazz02.method(Clazz02.java:6)
    at com.packt.cookbook.ch12_memory.walk.Clazz01.method(Clazz01.java:7)
    at com.packt.cookbook.ch12_memory.Chapter12Memory.demo4_StackWalk(Chapter12Memory.java:194)
    at com.packt.cookbook.ch12_memory.Chapter12Memory.main(Chapter12Memory.java:17)
```

A similar result will produce each of the following two lines:

```
Arrays.stream(Thread.currentThread().getStackTrace())
                        .forEach(System.out::println);
Arrays.stream(new Throwable().getStackTrace())
                        .forEach(System.out::println);
```

Since Java 9, the same output can be achieved using the `StackWalker` class. Let's look at what happens if we modify `Clazz03` as follows:

```
public class Clazz03 {
  public void method(String action){
    if(action != null){
      System.out.println(action);
      return;
    }
    StackWalker stackWalker = StackWalker.getInstance();
    stackWalker.forEach(System.out::println);
  }
}
```

The result is this:

```
Do something

Print the stack trace:
com.packt.cookbook.ch12_memory.walk.Clazz03.method(Clazz03.java:15)
com.packt.cookbook.ch12_memory.walk.Clazz02.method(Clazz02.java:6)
com.packt.cookbook.ch12_memory.walk.Clazz01.method(Clazz01.java:7)
com.packt.cookbook.ch12_memory.Chapter12Memory.demo4_StackWalk(Chapter12Memory.java:194)
com.packt.cookbook.ch12_memory.Chapter12Memory.main(Chapter12Memory.java:17)
```

It contains all the information the traditional methods produced. However, contrary to the full stack trace generated and stored as an array in the memory, the `StackWalker` class only brings the requested elements. This is already a big plus. Yet the biggest advantage of `StackWalker` is that, when we need the caller class name only, instead of getting all the array and using only one element, we can now get the info we need by using the following two lines:

```
System.out.println("Print the caller class name:");
System.out.println(StackWalker.getInstance(StackWalker
                        .Option.RETAIN_CLASS_REFERENCE)
                        .getCallerClass().getSimpleName());
```

The result of the preceding code snippet is the following:

```
Print the caller class name:
Clazz02
```

Using the memory-aware coding style

When writing code, a programmer has two main objectives in mind:

- To implement the required functionality
- To write code that is easy to read and understand

Yet, while doing that, they also have to make many other decisions, one of them being which of the standard library classes and methods with similar functionality to use. In this recipe, we will walk you through a few considerations that help to avoid the wasting of memory and make your code style memory-aware:

- Pay attention to the object created inside the loop
- Use lazy initialization and create an object just before the usage, especially if there is a good chance that, this need may never materialize at all
- Don't forget to clean the cache and remove unnecessary entries
- Use `StringBuilder` instead of the + operator
- Use `ArrayList` if it fits your needs, before using `HashSet` (the memory usage increases from `ArrayList` to `LinkedList`, `HashTable`, `HashMap`, and `HashSet`, in this sequence)

How to do it...

1. Pay attention to the object created inside the loop.

   This recommendation is pretty obvious. Creating and discarding many objects in quick succession may consume too much memory before the garbage collector catches up with reusing the space. Consider reusing objects instead of creating a new one every time. Here is an example:

   ```
   class Calculator {
       public  double calculate(int i) {
           return Math.sqrt(2.0 * i);
   ```

```
        }
    }

class SomeOtherClass {
    void reuseObject() {
        Calculator calculator = new Calculator();
        for(int i = 0; i < 100; i++ ){
            double r = calculator.calculate(i);
            //use result r
        }
    }
}
```

The preceding code can be improved by making the `calculate()` method static. Another solution would be to create a static property, `Calculator calculator = new Calculator()`, of the `SomeOtherClass` class. But the static property is initialized as soon as the class is loaded the first time. If the `calculator` property is not used, its initialization would be unnecessary overhead. In such cases, lazy initialization has to be added.

2. Use lazy initialization and create an object just before the usage, especially if there is a good chance this need may never materialize for some requests.

In the previous step, we talked about lazy initialization of the `calculator` property:

```
class Calculator {
    public  double calculate(int i) {
        return Math.sqrt(2.0 * i);
    }
}

class SomeOtherClass {
    private static Calculator calculator;
    private static Calculator getCalculator(){
        if(this.calculator == null){
            this.calculator = new Calculator();
        }
        return this.calculator;
    }
    void reuseObject() {
        for(int i = 0; i < 100; i++ ){
            double r = getCalculator().calculate(i);
            //use result r
        }
    }
}
```

In the preceding example, the `Calculator` object is a singleton—once created, only one instance of it exists in the application. If we know that calculator property is always going to be used, then there is no need for the lazy initialization. In Java, we can take advantage of the static-property initialization the first time the class is loaded by any of the application threads:

```
class SomeOtherClass {
    private static Calculator calculator = new Calculator();
    void reuseObject() {
        for(int i = 0; i < 100; i++ ){
            double r = calculator.calculate(i);
            //use result r
        }
    }
}
```

But if there is a good chance the initialized object will never be used, we are back to the lazy initialization that can be implemented as was discussed earlier (using the `getCalculator()` method) in a single thread or when the shared object is stateless and its initialization does not consume many resources.

In the case of a multi-threaded application and complex object initialization with substantial resource consumption, some additional measures have to be taken to avoid the conflict of a concurrent access and make sure only one instance is created. For example, consider the following class:

```
class ExpensiveInitClass {
    private Object data;
    public ExpensiveInitClass() {
        //code that consumes resources
        //and assignes value to this.data
    }

    public Object getData(){
        return this.data;
    }
}
```

If the preceding constructor requires an extensive time to complete object creation, there is a chance that the second thread enters the constructor before the first thread has completed the object creation. To avoid this concurrent creation of the second object, we need to synchronize the initialization process:

```
class LazyInitExample {
  public ExpensiveInitClass expensiveInitClass
  public Object getData(){  //can synchrnonize here
    if(this.expensiveInitClass == null){
      synchronized (LazyInitExample.class) {
        if (this.expensiveInitClass == null) {
          this.expensiveInitClass = new ExpensiveInitClass();
        }
      }
    }
    return expensiveInitClass.getData();
  }
}
```

As you can see, we could synchronize access to the `getData()` method, but this synchronization is not needed after the object is created and can cause a bottleneck in a highly concurrent multithreaded environment. Similarly, we could have only one check for null—inside the synchronized block—but this synchronization is not needed after the object is initialized, so we surround it with another check for null to decrease the chance for the bottleneck.

3. Don't forget to clean the cache and remove unnecessary entries.

Caching helps to decrease the time for accessing the data. But the cache consumes memory, so it makes sense to keep it as small as possible, while still being useful. How to do it very much depends on the pattern of the cached data usage. For example, if you know that, once used, the object stored in the cache is not going to be used again, you can put it in the cache at the application startup time (or periodically, according to the pattern of the usage) and remove it from the cache after it was used:

```
static HashMap<String, Object> cache = new HashMap<>();
static {
    //populate the cache here
}
public Object getSomeData(String someKey) {
    Object obj = cache.get(someKey);
    cache.remove(someKey);
```

```
    return obj;
}
```

Alternatively, if you expect a high level of reusability for each object, you can put it in the cache after it was requested the first time:

```
static HashMap<String, Object> cache = new HashMap<>();
public Object getSomeData(String someKey) {
    Object obj = cache.get(someKey);
    if(obj == null){
        obj = getDataFromSomeSource();
        cache.put(someKey, obj);
    }
    return obj;
}
```

The preceding case may lead to an uncontrollable growth of the cache that consumes too much memory and eventually causes the OutOfMemoryError condition. To prevent it, you can implement an algorithm that keeps the cache's size limited—after a certain size, every time a new object is added, some other object (used the most, for example, or used the least) is removed. The following is an example of limiting the cache size to 10 by removing the most-used cached object:

```
static HashMap<String, Object> cache = new HashMap<>();
static HashMap<String, Integer> count = new HashMap<>();
public static Object getSomeData(String someKey) {
    Object obj = cache.get(someKey);
    if(obj == null){
        obj = getDataFromSomeSource();
        cache.put(someKey, obj);
        count.put(someKey, 1);
        if(cache.size() > 10){
            Map.Entry<String, Integer> max =
                count.entrySet().stream()
.max(Map.Entry.comparingByValue(Integer::compareTo))
                    .get();
                cache.remove(max.getKey());
                count.remove(max.getKey());
        }
    } else {
        count.put(someKey, count.get(someKey) + 1);
    }
    return obj;
}
```

Alternatively, one can use the `java.util.WeakHashMap` class to implement the cache:

```java
private static WeakHashMap<Integer, Double> cache
                                = new WeakHashMap<>();
void weakHashMap() {
    int last = 0;
    int cacheSize = 0;
    for(int i = 0; i < 100_000_000; i++) {
        cache.put(i, Double.valueOf(i));
        cacheSize = cache.size();
        if(cacheSize < last){
            System.out.println("Used memory=" +
                usedMemoryMB()+" MB, cache="  + cacheSize);
        }
        last = cacheSize;
    }
}
```

If you run the preceding example, you will see that the memory usage and the cache size first increase, then drop down, then increase, and drop down again. Here is an excerpt from an output:

```
Used memory=1895 MB,  cache=2100931
Used memory=189 MB,  cache=95658
Used memory=296 MB,  cache=271
Used memory=408 MB,  cache=153
Used memory=519 MB,  cache=350
Used memory=631 MB,  cache=129
Used memory=745 MB,  cache=2079710
Used memory=750 MB,  cache=69590
Used memory=858 MB,  cache=213
```

The memory usage calculation we used was as follows:

```java
long usedMemoryMB() {
    return Math.round(
        Double.valueOf(Runtime.getRuntime().totalMemory() -
Runtime.getRuntime().freeMemory())/1024/1024
    );
}
```

The `java.util.WeakHashMap` class is a Map implementation with keys of the `java.lang.ref.WeakReference` type. The objects that are referenced only by weak references are garbage-collected any time the garbage collector decides there is more memory needed. This means that an entry in a `WeakHashMap` object will be removed when there is no reference to that key. When the garbage collection removes the key from the memory, the corresponding value is removed from the map too.

In our preceding example, none of the cache keys was used outside the map, so the garbage collector removed them at its discretion. The code behaves the same way even when we add an explicit reference to a key outside the map:

```
private static WeakHashMap<Integer, Double> cache
                                = new WeakHashMap<>();
void weakHashMap() {
    int last = 0;
    int cacheSize = 0;
    for(int i = 0; i < 100_000_000; i++) {
        Integer iObj = i;
        cache.put(iObj, Double.valueOf(i));
        cacheSize = cache.size();
        if(cacheSize < last){
            System.out.println("Used memory=" +
                usedMemoryMB()+" MB, cache="  + cacheSize);
        }
        last = cacheSize;
    }
}
```

That is because the `iObj` reference shown in the earlier code block gets abandoned after each iteration and collected, so the corresponding key in the cache is left without external reference, and the garbage collector removes it too. To prove this point, let's modify the preceding code again:

```
private static WeakHashMap<Integer, Double> cache
                                = new WeakHashMap<>();
void weakHashMap() {
    int last = 0;
    int cacheSize = 0;
    List<Integer> list = new ArrayList<>();
    for(int i = 0; i < 100_000_000; i++) {
        Integer iObj = i;
        cache.put(iObj, Double.valueOf(i));
        list.add(iObj);
        cacheSize = cache.size();
```

```
            if(cacheSize < last){
                System.out.println("Used memory=" +
                    usedMemoryMB()+" MB, cache="  + cacheSize);
            }
            last = cacheSize;
        }
    }
```

We have created a list and added each of the map keys to it. If we run the preceding code, we will eventually get OutOfMemoryError because the cache's keys had strong references outside the map. We can weaken the external references too:

```
private static WeakHashMap<Integer, Double> cache
                                = new WeakHashMap<>();
void weakHashMap() {
    int last = 0;
    int cacheSize = 0;
    List<WeakReference<Integer>> list = new ArrayList<>();
    for(int i = 0; i < 100_000_000; i++) {
        Integer iObj = i;
        cache.put(iObj, Double.valueOf(i));
        list.add(new WeakReference(iObj));
        cacheSize = cache.size();
        if(cacheSize < last){
            System.out.println("Used memory=" +
                usedMemoryMB()+" MB, cache="  + cacheSize +
                ", list size=" + list.size());
        }
        last = cacheSize;
    }
}
```

The preceding code now runs as if the cache keys do not have external references. The used memory and cache size grow and drop down again. But the list size does not drop down, because the garbage collector does not remove values from the list. So, eventually, the application may run out of memory.

Yet, whether you limit the size of the cache or let it grow uncontrollably, there may be a situation when the application needs as much memory as possible. So, if there are big objects that are not critical to the application's main functionality, sometimes it makes sense to remove them from memory in order for the application to survive and not get into the OutOfMemoryError condition.

If there is a cache, it is typically a good candidate for removing and freeing the memory, so we can wrap the cache itself with the WeakReference class:

```
private static WeakReference<Map<Integer, Double[]>> cache;
void weakReference() {
    Map<Integer, Double[]> map = new HashMap<>();
    cache = new WeakReference<>(map);
    map = null;
    int cacheSize = 0;
    List<Double[]> list = new ArrayList<>();
    for(int i = 0; i < 10_000_000; i++) {
        Double[] d = new Double[1024];
        list.add(d);
        if (cache.get() != null) {
            cache.get().put(i, d);
            cacheSize = cache.get().size();
            System.out.println("Cache="+cacheSize +
                    ", used memory=" + usedMemoryMB()+" MB");
        } else {
            System.out.println(i +":
cache.get()=="+cache.get());
            break;
        }
    }
}
```

In the preceding code, we have wrapped up the map (cache) inside the WeakReference class, which means we tell the JVM that it can collect this object as soon as there is no reference to it. Then, in each iteration of the for-loop, we create new Double[1024] object and save it in the list. We do it in order to use up all the available memory quicker. Then we put the same object in the cache. When we run this code, it quickly ends up with the following output:

```
Cache=4582, used memory=25 MB
4582: cache.get()==null
```

This means that the garbage collector decided to collect cache object after 25 MB of memory was used. If such an approach, you think, is too aggressive and you do not need to renew the cache often, you can wrap it in the `java.lang.ref.SoftReference` class instead. If you do, the cache will be collected only when all the memory is used up—just on the brink of throwing `OutOfMemoryError`. Here is the code snippet that demonstrates it:

```
private static SoftReference<Map<Integer, Double[]>> cache;
void weakReference() {
    Map<Integer, Double[]> map = new HashMap<>();
    cache = new SoftReference<>(map);
    map = null;
    int cacheSize = 0;
    List<Double[]> list = new ArrayList<>();
    for(int i = 0; i < 10_000_000; i++) {
        Double[] d = new Double[1024];
        list.add(d);
        if (cache.get() != null) {
            cache.get().put(i, d);
            cacheSize = cache.get().size();
            System.out.println("Cache="+cacheSize +
                    ", used memory=" + usedMemoryMB()+"
MB");
        } else {
            System.out.println(i +":
cache.get()=="+cache.get());
            break;
        }
    }
}
```

If we run it, the output will be the following:

```
Cache=1004737, used memory=4096 MB
1004737: cache.get()==null
```

That's right, on our test computer, there is 4 GB of RAM, so the cache was removed only when almost all of it was used.

3. Use `StringBuilder` instead of the + operator.

You can find many such recommendations on the internet. There are also quite a few statements saying that this recommendation is obsolete because modern Java uses `StringBuilder` to implement the + operator for strings. Here is the result of our experimentation. First, we have run the following code:

```
long um = usedMemoryMB();
String s = "";
for(int i = 1000; i < 10_1000; i++ ){
    s += Integer.toString(i);
    s += " ";
}
System.out.println("Used memory: "
        + (usedMemoryMB() - um) + " MB");   //prints: 71 MB
```

The implementation of `usedMemoryMB()`:

```
long usedMemoryMB() {
    return Math.round(
      Double.valueOf(Runtime.getRuntime().totalMemory() -
                Runtime.getRuntime().freeMemory())/1024/1024
    );
}
```

Then we used `StringBuilder` for the same purpose:

```
long um = usedMemoryMB();
StringBuilder sb = new StringBuilder();
for(int i = 1000; i < 10_1000; i++ ){
    sb.append(Integer.toString(i)).append(" ");
}
System.out.println("Used memory: "
        + (usedMemoryMB() - um) + " MB");   //prints: 1 MB
```

As you can see, using the + operator consumed 71 MB of memory, while `StringBuilder` used only 1 MB for the same task. We have tested `StringBuffer`, too. It consumed 1 MB as well but performed slightly slower than `StringBuilder`, because it is thread-safe, while `StringBuilder` can be used in a single-thread environment only.

All this does not apply to the long `String` value that was broken into several substrings with the plus sign for better readability. The compiler collects the substring back into one long value. For example, the `s1` and `s2` strings occupy the same amount of memory:

```
String s1 = "this " +
            "string " +
            "takes " +
            "as much memory as another one";
String s2 = "this string takes as much memory as another one";
```

4. If you need to use a collection, select `ArrayList` if it fits your needs. The memory usage increases
   from `ArrayList` to `LinkedList`, `HashTable`, `HashMap`, and `HashSet`, in this sequence.

The `ArrayList` object stores its elements in an `Object[]` array and uses an `int` field for tracking the list size (in addition to `array.length`). Because of such a design, it is not recommended to allocate an `ArrayList` of a large capacity while declaring it, if there is a chance that this capacity will not be fully used. As new elements are added to the list, the backend array's capacity is incremented in blocks of 10 elements, which is a possible source of wasted memory. If it is significant for the application, it is possible to shrink the `ArrayList` capacity to the one currently utilized by calling on it the `trimToSize()` method. Please, note that the `clear()` and `remove()` methods do not affect the `ArrayList` capacity, they change only its size.

Other collections have more overhead because they provide more service. The `LinkedList` elements carry references to the previous and next elements as well as a reference to the data value. Most implementations of hash-based collections are focused on better performance, which often comes at the expense of memory footprint.

The choice of Java collection class may be irrelevant if its size is going to be small. However, programmers usually use the same coding pattern, and one can identify the code's author by its style. That's why it pays, in the long run, to figure out the most efficient constructs and use them routinely. However, try to avoid making your code difficult to understand; readability is an important aspect of code quality.

Best practices for better memory usage

Memory management may never become an issue for you, it might your every waking moment, or you might find yourself in between these two polarities. Most of the time, it is a non-issue for the majority of programmers, especially with the constantly improving garbage-collection algorithms. The G1 garbage collector (default in JVM 9) is definitely a step in the right direction. But there is also a chance you will be called (or will notice yourself) about the application's degrading performance, and that is when you'll learn how well you are equipped to meet the challenge.

This recipe is an attempt to help you avoid such a situation or to get out of it successfully.

How to do it...

The first line of defense is the code itself. In the previous recipes, we discussed the need to release resources as soon as they are no longer needed and the usage of StackWalker to consume less memory. There are plenty of recommendations on the internet, but they might not apply to your application. You'll have to monitor the memory consumption and test your design decisions, especially if your code handles a lot of data, before deciding where to concentrate your attention.

Test and profile your code as soon as it starts doing what it was supposed to do. You might need to change your design or some details of implementation. It will also inform your future decisions. There are many profilers and diagnostic tools available for any environment. We described one of them, jcmd, in the *Using the jcmd command for the JVM* recipe.

Learn how your garbage collector works (see the *Understanding the G1 garbage collector* recipe) and do not forget to use JVM logging (described in the *Unified logging for JVM* recipe).

After that, you might need to tune the JVM and garbage collector. Here are a few frequently used `java` command-line parameters (the size is specified in bytes by default, but you can append the letter k or K to indicate kilobytes, m or M to indicate megabytes, g or G to indicate gigabytes):

- `-Xms size`: This option allows us to set the initial heap size (has to be greater than 1 MB and a multiple of 1,024).
- `-Xmx size`: This option allows us to set the maximum heap size (has to be greater than 2 MB and a multiple of 1,024).
- `-Xmn size` or a combination of `-XX:NewSize=size` and `-XX:MaxNewSize=size`: This option allows us to set the initial and maximum size of the young generation. For efficient GC, it has to be lower than `-Xmx size`. Oracle recommends you set it at more than 25% and less than 50% of the heap size.
- `-XX:NewRatio=ratio`: This option allows us to set the ratio between the young and old generations (two, by default).
- `-Xss size`: This option allows us to set the thread stack size. The following are the default values for different platforms:
  - Linux/ARM (32-bit): 320 KB
  - Linux/ARM (64-bit): 1,024 KB
  - Linux/x64 (64-bit): 1,024 KB
  - macOS (64-bit): 1,024 KB
  - Oracle Solaris/i386 (32-bit): 320 KB
  - Oracle Solaris/x64 (64-bit): 1,024 KB
  - Windows: Depends on virtual memory
- `-XX:MaxMetaspaceSize=size`: This option allows us to set the upper limit of the class metadata area (no limit, by default).

The tell-tale sign of a memory leak is the growing of the old generation causing the full GC to run more often. To investigate, you can use the JVM parameters that dump heap memory into a file:

- `-XX:+HeapDumpOnOutOfMemoryError`: Allows us to save the JVM heap content into a file, but only when a `java.lang.OutOfMemoryError` exception is thrown. By default, the heap dump is saved in the current directory with the `java_pid<pid>.hprof` name where `<pid>` is the process ID. Use the `-XX:HeapDumpPath=<path>` option to customize the dump file location. The `<path>` value must include filename.

- `-XX:OnOutOfMemoryError="<cmd args>;<cmd args>"`: Allows us to provide a set of commands (separated by a semicolon) that will be executed when an `OutOfMemoryError` exception is thrown.

- `-XX:+UseGCOverheadLimit`: Regulates the size of the proportion of time GC takes before an `OutOfMemoryError` exception is thrown. For example, the parallel GC will throw an `OutOfMemoryError` exception when GC takes more than 98% of the time and recovers less than 2% of the heap. This option is particularly useful when the heap is small because it prevents JVM from running with little or no progress. It is turned on by default. To disable it, use `-XX:-UseGCOverheadLimit`.

Understanding Epsilon, a low-overhead garbage collector

One of the popular Java interview questions is, *can you enforce garbage collection?* Java runtime memory management remains outside a programmer's control and sometimes acts as an unpredictable Joker it interrupts the otherwise well-performing application and initiates a stop-the-world full-memory scan. It typically happens at the *worst possible time*. It is especially annoying when you try to measure your application performance under the load using a short run and realize afterward that a lot of time and resources were spent on the garbage collection process and that the pattern of the garbage collection, after you changed the code, became different than before the code change.

In this chapter, we described quite a few programming tricks and solutions that help to ease pressure on the garbage collector. Yet, it remains an independent and unpredictable contributor (or detractor) of the application performance. Wouldn't it be nice if the garbage collector was better controlled, at least for test purposes, or could be turned off? In Java 11, a garbage collector, Epsilon, called a no-op garbage collector, was introduced.

At first glance, it looks strange—a garbage collector that doesn't collect anything. But it is predictable (that's for sure) because it does nothing, and that feature allows us to test algorithms in short runs without worrying about unpredictable pauses. Besides, there is a whole category of small short-lived applications that need all the resources they can muster for a brief period of time and it is preferable to restart the JVM and let the load balancer perform failover than to try factoring in an unpredictable Joker of the garbage-collection process.

It was also envisioned as a benchmark process that allows us to estimate a regular garbage collector overhead.

How to do it...

To invoke the no-op garbage collector, use the -XX:+UseEpsilonGC option. At the time of writing, it requires an -XX:+UnlockExperimentalVMOptions option to access the new capability.

We will use the following program for the demonstration:

```
package com.packt.cookbook.ch11_memory;
import java.util.ArrayList;
import java.util.List;
public class Epsilon {
    public static void main(String... args) {
        List<byte[]> list = new ArrayList<>();
        int n = 4 * 1024 * 1024;
        for(int i=0; i < n; i++){
            list.add(new byte[1024]);
            byte[] arr = new byte[1024];
        }
    }
}
```

As you can see, in this program, we are trying to allocate 4 GB of memory by adding a 1 KB array to the list at each iteration. At the same time, we also create a 1 K array, arr, at each iteration but do not use the reference to it, so the traditional garbage collector can collect it.

First, we will run the preceding program with the default garbage collector:

```
time java -cp cookbook-1.0.jar -Xms4G -Xmx4G -Xlog:gc
com.packt.cookbook.ch11_memory.Epsilon
```

Please note that we have limited the JVM heap memory to 4 GB because, for demonstrative purposes, we would like the program to exit with OutOfMemoryError. And we have wrapped the call with the time command to capture three values:

- **Real time**: How long the program was running
- **User time**: How long CPU was used by the program
- **Sys time**: How long the operating system worked for the program

We used JDK 11:

```
java -version
java version "11-ea" 2018-09-25
Java(TM) SE Runtime Environment 18.9 (build 11-ea+22)
Java HotSpot(TM) 64-Bit Server VM 18.9 (build 11-ea+22, mixed mode)
```

The output of the preceding commands may be different on your computer. During our test run, when we executed the preceding program with the specified `java` command parameters, the output started with the following four lines:

```
Using G1
GC(0) Pause Young (Normal) (G1 Evacuation Pause) 204M->101M(4096M)
GC(1) Pause Young (Normal) (G1 Evacuation Pause) 279M->191M(4096M)
GC(2) Pause Young (Normal) (G1 Evacuation Pause) 371M->280M(4096M)
```

As you can see, the G1 garbage collector is the default in JDK 11, and it started collecting unreferenced `arr` objects right away. As we have expected, the program exited after `OutOfMemoryError`:

```
GC(50) Pause Full (G1 Evacuation Pause) 4090M->4083M(4096M)
GC(51) Concurrent Cycle 401.931ms
GC(52) To-space exhausted
GC(52) Pause Young (Concurrent Start) (G1 Humongous Allocation)
GC(53) Concurrent Cycle
GC(54) Pause Young (Normal) (G1 Humongous Allocation)
4088M->4088M(4096M)
GC(55) Pause Full (G1 Humongous Allocation) 4088M->4085M(4096M)
GC(56) Pause Full (G1 Humongous Allocation) 4085M->4085M(4096M)
GC(53) Concurrent Cycle 875.061ms
Exception in thread "main" java.lang.OutOfMemoryError: Java heap space
  at java.base/java.util.Arrays.copyOf(Arrays.java:3720)
  at java.base/java.util.Arrays.copyOf(Arrays.java:3689)
  at java.base/java.util.ArrayList.grow(ArrayList.java:237)
  at java.base/java.util.ArrayList.grow(ArrayList.java:242)
  at java.base/java.util.ArrayList.add(ArrayList.java:485)
  at java.base/java.util.ArrayList.add(ArrayList.java:498)
  at com.packt.cookbook.ch11_memory.Epsilon.main(Epsilon.java:12)
```

The time utility produced the following results:

```
real 0m11.549s    //How long the program ran
user 0m35.301s    //How much time the CPU was used by the program
sys 0m19.125s     //How much time the OS worked for the program
```

Our computer is multicore, so the JVM was able to utilize several cores in parallel, most likely for the garbage collection. That is why user time is bigger than real time, and the system time is bigger than real time for the same reason.

Now let's run the same program with the following command:

```
time java -cp cookbook-1.0.jar -XX:+UnlockExperimentalVMOptions -
XX:+UseEpsilonGC -Xms4G -Xmx4G -Xlog:gc
com.packt.cookbook.ch11_memory.Epsilon
```

Note that we have added the `-XX:+UnlockExperimentalVMOptions -XX:+UseEpsilonGC` options, which requires Epsilon garbage collector. The result looks as follows:

```
Non-resizeable heap; start/max: 4096M
Using TLAB allocation; max: 4096K
Elastic TLABs enabled; elasticity: 1.10x
Elastic TLABs decay enabled; decay time: 1000ms
Using Epsilon
Heap: 4096M reserved, 4096M (100.00%) committed, 205M (5.01%) used
Heap: 4096M reserved, 4096M (100.00%) committed, 410M (10.01%) used
Heap: 4096M reserved, 4096M (100.00%) committed, 614M (15.01%) used
Heap: 4096M reserved, 4096M (100.00%) committed, 820M (20.02%) used
Heap: 4096M reserved, 4096M (100.00%) committed, 1025M (25.02%) used
Heap: 4096M reserved, 4096M (100.00%) committed, 1230M (30.03%) used
Heap: 4096M reserved, 4096M (100.00%) committed, 1435M (35.04%) used
Heap: 4096M reserved, 4096M (100.00%) committed, 1640M (40.04%) used
Heap: 4096M reserved, 4096M (100.00%) committed, 1845M (45.05%) used
Heap: 4096M reserved, 4096M (100.00%) committed, 2050M (50.05%) used
Heap: 4096M reserved, 4096M (100.00%) committed, 2255M (55.06%) used
Heap: 4096M reserved, 4096M (100.00%) committed, 2460M (60.06%) used
Heap: 4096M reserved, 4096M (100.00%) committed, 2665M (65.07%) used
Heap: 4096M reserved, 4096M (100.00%) committed, 2870M (70.07%) used
Heap: 4096M reserved, 4096M (100.00%) committed, 3075M (75.08%) used
Heap: 4096M reserved, 4096M (100.00%) committed, 3280M (80.08%) used
Heap: 4096M reserved, 4096M (100.00%) committed, 3485M (85.09%) used
Heap: 4096M reserved, 4096M (100.00%) committed, 3690M (90.09%) used
Heap: 4096M reserved, 4096M (100.00%) committed, 3895M (95.10%) used
Terminating due to java.lang.OutOfMemoryError: Java heap space
```

As you can see, the garbage collector did not even try to collect the abandoned objects. The usage of the heap space grew steadily until it was consumed completely, and the JVM exited with `OutOfMemoryError`. Using the `time` utility allowed us to measure three following time parameters:

```
real  0m4.239s
user  0m1.861s
sys 0m2.132s
```

Naturally, it took much less time to exhaust all the heap memory, and the user time is much less than real time. That is why, as we have mentioned already, the no-op Epsilon garbage collector can be useful to the programs that have to be as fast as possible but do not consume all the heap memory or can be stopped at any time. There are probably other use cases where the garbage collector that does not do anything can be helpful.

12
The Read-Evaluate-Print Loop (REPL) Using JShell

In this chapter, we will cover the following recipes:

- Getting familiar with REPL
- Navigating JShell and its commands
- Evaluating code snippets
- Object-oriented programming in JShell
- Saving and restoring the JShell command history
- Using the JShell Java API

Introduction

REPL stands for the **Read-Evaluate-Print Loop** and, as the name states, it reads the command entered on the command line, evaluates it, prints the result of evaluation, and continues this process on any command entered.

All the major languages, such as Ruby, Scala, Python, JavaScript, and Groovy, have REPL tools. Java was missing the much-needed REPL. If we had to try out some sample code, say using `SimpleDateFormat` to parse a string, we had to write a complete program with all the ceremonies, including creating a class, adding a main method, and then the single line of code we want to experiment with. Then, we have to compile and run the code. These ceremonies make it harder to experiment and learn the features of the language.

With a REPL, you can type only the line of code that you are interested in experimenting with and you will get immediate feedback on whether the expression is syntactically correct and gives the desired results. REPL is a very powerful tool, especially for people coming to the language for the first time. Suppose you want to show how to print *Hello World* in Java; for this, you'd have to start writing the class definition, then the `public static void main(String [] args)` method, and by the end of it, you would have explained or tried to explain a lot of concepts that would otherwise be difficult for a newbie to comprehend.

Anyways, with Java 9 and onward, Java developers can now stop whining about the absence of a REPL tool. A new REPL, called JShell, is being bundled with the JDK installation. So, we can now proudly write *Hello World* as our first *Hello World* code.

In this chapter, we will explore the features of JShell and write code that will truly amaze us and appreciate the power of REPL. We will also see how we can create our own REPLs using the JShell Java API.

Getting familiar with REPL

In this recipe, we will look at a few basic operations to help us get familiar with the JShell tool.

Getting ready

Make sure you have the latest JDK version installed, which has JShell. JShell is available from JDK 9 onward.

How to do it...

1. You should have `%JAVA_HOME%/bin` (on Windows) or `$JAVA_HOME/bin` (on Linux) added to your `PATH` variable. If not, please visit the *Installing JDK 18.9 on Windows and setting up the PATH variable* and *Installing JDK 18.9 on Linux (Ubuntu, x64) and configuring the PATH variable* recipes in `Chapter 1`, *Installation and a Sneak Peek into Java 11*.
2. On the command line, type `jshell` and press *Enter*.

3. You will see a message and then a `jshell>` prompt:

```
G:\java9\java9-samples\chp15\3_jshell_script>jshell
|  Welcome to JShell -- Version 11-ea
|  For an introduction type: /help intro
```

4. Forward slash (/), followed by the JShell-supported commands, help you
   in interacting with JShell. Just like we try `/help intro` to get the
   following:

```
jshell> /help intro
|
|                              intro
|                              =====
|
|  The jshell tool allows you to execute Java code, getting immediate results.
|  You can enter a Java definition (variable, method, class, etc), like:   int x = 8
|  or a Java expression, like:  x + x
|  or a Java statement or import.
|  These little chunks of Java code are called 'snippets'.
|
|  There are also the jshell tool commands that allow you to understand and
|  control what you are doing, like:  /list
|
|  For a list of commands: /help
```

5. Let's print a `Hello World` message:

```
jshell> "Hello World"
$1 ==> "Hello World"
```

6. Let's print a customized `Hello World` message:

```
jshell> String name = "Sanaulla"
name ==> "Sanaulla"

jshell> String.format("Hello %s", name)
$3 ==> "Hello Sanaulla"

jshell>
```

7. You can navigate through the executed commands using the up and down
   arrow keys.

How it works...

The code snippets entered at the `jshell` prompt are wrapped with just enough code to execute them. So, variable, method, and class declarations get wrapped within a class, and expressions get wrapped within a method which is in turn wrapped within the class. Other things, such as imports and class definitions, remain as they are because they are top-level entities, that is, wrapping a class definition within another class is not required as a class definition is a top-level entity that can exist by itself. Similarly, in Java, import statements can occur by themselves and they occur outside of a class declaration and hence need not be wrapped inside a class.

In the subsequent recipes, we will see how to define a method, import additional packages, and define classes.

In the preceding recipe, we saw `$1 ==> "Hello World"`. If we have some value without any variable associated with it, `jshell` gives it a variable name, such as `$1` or `$2`.

Navigating JShell and its commands

In order to leverage a tool, we need to be familiar with how to use it, the commands it provides, and the various shortcut keys that we can use to be productive. In this recipe, we will look at the different ways we can navigate through JShell and also at the different keyboard shortcuts it provides to be productive while using it.

How to do it...

1. Spawn JShell by typing `jshell` on the command line. You will be greeted with a welcome message that contains the instructions to get started.

2. Type `/help intro` to get a brief introduction to JShell:

```
jshell> /help intro

                                intro
                                =====

  The jshell tool allows you to execute Java code, getting immediate results.
  You can enter a Java definition (variable, method, class, etc), like:  int x = 8
  or a Java expression, like:  x + x
  or a Java statement or import.
  These little chunks of Java code are called 'snippets'.

  There are also the jshell tool commands that allow you to understand and
  control what you are doing, like:  /list

  For a list of commands: /help
```

3. Type `/help` to get a list of the supported commands:

```
jshell> /help
  Type a Java language expression, statement, or declaration.
  Or type one of the following commands:
  /list [<name or id>|-all|-start]
        list the source you have typed
  /edit <name or id>
        edit a source entry referenced by name or id
  /drop <name or id>
        delete a source entry referenced by name or id
  /save [-all|-history|-start] <file>
        Save snippet source to a file.
  /open <file>
        open a file as source input
```

4. To get more information about a command, type `/help <command>`. For example, to get information about `/edit`, type `/help /edit`:

```
jshell> /help /edit
|
|                           /edit
|                           =====
|
|   Edit a snippet or snippets of source in an external editor.
|   The editor to use is set with /set editor. If no editor is set, then the
|   following environment variables are checked in order: JSHELLEDITOR, VISUAL,
|   and EDITOR. If no editor has been set and none of the editor environment
|   variables is set, a simple editor will be launched.
|
|   /edit <name>
|       Edit the snippet or snippets with the specified name (preference for active snippets)
|
|   /edit <id>
|       Edit the snippet with the specified snippet ID.
|       One or more IDs or ID ranges may used, see '/help id'
|
|   /edit -start
|       Edit the startup snippets. Any changes are in this session, and do not
|       affect the startup setting
|
|   /edit -all
|       Edit all snippets including failed, overwritten, dropped, and startup
|
|   /edit
|       Edit the currently active snippets of code that you typed or read with /open
```

5. There is autocompletion support in JShell. This makes Java developers feel at home. You can invoke auto-completion using the *Tab* key:

```
jshell> System.out.
append(          checkError()     close()          equals(          flush()
format(          getClass()       hashCode()       notify()         notifyAll()
print(           printf(          println(         toString()       wait(
write(

jshell> System.out.
append(          checkError()     close()          equals(          flush()
format(          getClass()       hashCode()       notify()         notifyAll()
print(           printf(          println(         toString()       wait(
write(

jshell> System.out.print
print(      printf(      println(

jshell> System.out.println(
println(

jshell> System.out.println(String.format(
format(

jshell> System.out.println(String.
CASE_INSENSITIVE_ORDER    class                          copyValueOf(
format(                   join(                          valueOf(

jshell> System.out.println(String.format|
```

6. You can use `/ !` to execute a previously executed command, and `/line_number` to re-execute an expression at the line number.

7. To navigate the cursor through the command line, use *Ctrl + A* to reach the beginning of the line and *Ctrl + E* to reach the end of the line.

Evaluating code snippets

In this recipe, we will look at executing the following code snippets:

- Import statements
- Class declarations
- Interface declarations
- Method declarations
- Field declarations
- Statements

How to do it...

1. Open the command line and launch JShell.
2. By default, JShell imports a few libraries. We can check that by issuing the /imports command:

```
jshell> /imports
|    import java.io.*
|    import java.math.*
|    import java.net.*
|    import java.nio.file.*
|    import java.util.*
|    import java.util.concurrent.*
|    import java.util.function.*
|    import java.util.prefs.*
|    import java.util.regex.*
|    import java.util.stream.*
```

3. Let's import java.text.SimpleDateForm by issuing the import java.text.SimpleDateFormat command. This imports the SimpleDateFormat class.
4. Let's declare an Employee class. We will issue one statement in each line so that it's an incomplete statement, and we'll proceed in the same way as we do in any ordinary editor. The following illustration will clarify this:

```
class Employee{
  private String empId;
  public String getEmpId() {
    return empId;
  }
  public void setEmpId ( String empId ) {
    this.empId = empId;
  }
}
```

You will get the following output:

```
jshell> class Employee {
   ...>     private String empId;
   ...>     public String getEmpId() {
   ...>         return empId;
   ...>     }
   ...>     public void setEmpId (String empId ) {
   ...>         this.empId = empId;
   ...>     }
   ...> }
|  created class Employee
```

5. Let's declare an `Employability` interface, which defines a method, `employable()`, as shown in the following code snippet:

```
interface Employability {
  public boolean employable();
}
```

The preceding interface, when created via `jshell`, is shown in the following screenshot:

```
jshell> interface Employability {
   ...>     public boolean employable();
   ...> }
|  created interface Employability
```

6. Let's declare a `newEmployee(String empId)` method, which constructs an `Employee` object with the given `empId`:

```
public Employee newEmployee(String empId ) {
  Employee emp = new Employee();
  emp.setEmpId(empId);
  return emp;
}
```

The preceding method defined in JShell is shown here:

```
jshell> public Employee newEmployee(String empId) {
   ...>     Employee emp = new Employee();
   ...>     emp.setEmpId(empId);
   ...>     return emp;
   ...> }
```

7. We will use the method defined in the previous step to create a statement that declares an `Employee` variable:

```
Employee e = newEmployee("1234");
```

The preceding statement and its output when executed from within JShell are shown in the following screenshot. The snippet `e.get` + `Tab` key generates autocompletion as supported by the IDEs:

```
jshell> Employee e = newEmployee("1234");
e ==> Employee@5ec0a365

jshell> e.get
getClass()    getEmpId()

jshell> e.getEmpId();
$18 ==> "1234"
```

There's more...

We can invoke an undefined method. Take a look at the following example:

```
public void newMethod(){
   System.out.println("New  Method");
   undefinedMethod();
}
```

The image below shows the definition of `newMethod()` invoking `undefinedMethod()`:

```
jshell> public void newMethod(){
   ...>    System.out.println("New Method");
   ...>    undefinedMethod();
   ...> }
|  created method newMethod(), however, it cannot be invoked until method undefinedMethod() is declared

jshell> newMethod()
|  attempted to call method newMethod() which cannot be invoked until method undefinedMethod() is declared
```

However, the method cannot be invoked before the method being used has been defined:

```
public void undefinedMethod(){
   System.out.println("Now defined");
}
```

The below image shows the method `undefinedMethod()` being defined and then `newMethod()` can be successfully invoked:

```
jshell> public void undefinedMethod(){
   ...>    System.out.println("Now defined");
   ...> }
|  created method undefinedMethod()

jshell> newMethod()
New Method
Now defined
```

We can invoke `newMethod()` only after we have defined `undefinedMethod()`.

Object-oriented programming in JShell

In this recipe, we will make use of predefined Java class definition files and import them into JShell. Then, we will play around with those classes in JShell.

How to do it...

1. The class definition files we will use in this recipe are available in `Chapter12/4_oo_programming`, in the code downloads for this book.
2. There are three class definition files: `Engine.java`, `Dimensions.java`, and `Car.java`.
3. Navigate to the directory where these three class definition files are available.
4. The `/open` command allows us to load the code from within a file.
5. Load the `Engine` class definition and create an `Engine` object:

```
jshell> /open Engine.java

jshell> Engine e = new Engine("Petrol", 4, 1400)
e ==> Engine@28d25987
```

6. Load the `Dimensions` class definition and create a `Dimensions` object:

```
jshell> /open Dimensions.java

jshell> Dimensions d = new Dimensions(
Dimensions(

jshell> Dimensions d = new Dimensions(4370, 1720, 1455)
d ==> Dimensions@61832929
```

7. Load the `Car` class definition and create a `Car` object:

```
shell> /open Car.java

shell> Car c = new Car(e, d, "Kia", "Rio", 2017)
  ==> Car@26653222
```

Saving and restoring the JShell command history

We will want to try out some code snippets in `jshell` as a means to explain Java programming to someone who is new to it. Moreover, some form of record of what code snippets were executed will be useful for the person who is learning the language.

In this recipe, we will execute a few code snippets and save them into a file. We will then load the code snippets from the saved file.

How to do it...

1. Let's execute a series of code snippets, as follows:

```
"Hello World"
String msg = "Hello, %s. Good Morning"
System.out.println(String.format(msg, "Friend"))
int someInt = 10
boolean someBool = false
if ( someBool ) {
  System.out.println("True block executed");
```

```
}
if ( someBool ) {
  System.out.println("True block executed");
}else{
  System.out.println("False block executed");
}
for ( int i = 0; i < 10; i++ ){
  System.out.println("I is : " + i );
}
```

You will get the following output:

```
jshell> "Hello World"
$1 ==> "Hello World"

jshell> String msg = "Hello, %s. Good Morning"
msg ==> "Hello, %s. Good Morning"

jshell> System.out.println(String.format(msg, "Friend"))
Hello, Friend. Good Morning

jshell> int someInt = 10
someInt ==> 10

jshell> boolean someBool = false
someBool ==> false

jshell> if ( someBool ) {
   ...> System.out.println("True block executed");
   ...> }

jshell> if ( someBool ) {
   ...> System.out.println("True block executed");
   ...> }else{
   ...> System.out.println("False block executed");
   ...> }
False block executed

jshell> for ( int i = 0; i < 10; i++){
   ...> System.out.println("I is : " + i);
   ...> }
I is : 0
I is : 1
I is : 2
I is : 3
I is : 4
I is : 5
I is : 6
I is : 7
I is : 8
I is : 9
```

2. Save the code snippets executed into a file called `history` using the `/save history` command.

3. Exit the shell using `/exit` and list the files in the directory by using `dir` or `ls`, depending on the OS. There will be a `history` file in the listing.

4. Open `jshell` and check for the history of code snippets executed using `/list`. You will see that there are no code snippets executed.

5. Load the `history` file using `/open history` and then check for the history of the code snippets executed using `/list`. You will see all the previous code snippets being executed and added to the history:

```
jshell> /list

jshell> /open history
Hello, Friend. Good Morning
False block executed
I is : 0
I is : 1
I is : 2
I is : 3
I is : 4
I is : 5
I is : 6
I is : 7
I is : 8
I is : 9

jshell> /list

   1 : "Hello World"
   2 : String msg = "Hello, %s. Good Morning";
   3 : System.out.println(String.format(msg, "Friend"))
   4 : int someInt = 10;
   5 : boolean someBool = false;
   6 : if ( someBool ) {
       System.out.println("True block executed");
       }
   7 : if ( someBool ) {
       System.out.println("True block executed");
       }else{
       System.out.println("False block executed");
       }
   8 : for ( int i = 0; i < 10; i++){
       System.out.println("I is : " + i);
       }
```

Using the JShell Java API

JDK 11 provides the Java API for creating tools such as `jshell` for evaluating Java code snippets. This Java API is present in the `jdk.jshell` module (`http://cr.openjdk.java.net/~rfield/arch/doc/jdk/jshell/package-summary.html`). So, if you want to use the API in your application, you need to declare a dependency on the `jdk.jshell` module.

In this recipe, we will use the JShell JDK API to evaluate simple code snippets, and you'll also see different APIs to get the state of JShell. The idea is not to recreate JShell but to show how to make use of its JDK API.

 For this recipe, we will not be using JShell; instead, we will follow the usual way of compiling using `javac` and running using `java`.

How to do it...

1. Our module will depend on the `jdk.jshell` module. So, the module definition will look like the following:

```
module jshell{
    requires jdk.jshell;
}
```

2. Create an instance of the `jdk.jshell.JShell` class by using its `create()` method or the builder API in `jdk.jshell.JShell.Builder`:

```
JShell myShell = JShell.create();
```

3. Read the code snippet from `System.in` using `java.util.Scanner`:

```
try(Scanner reader = new Scanner(System.in)){
    while(true){
        String snippet = reader.nextLine();
        if ( "EXIT".equals(snippet)){
            break;
        }
        //TODO: Code here for evaluating the snippet using JShell
API
    }
}
```

4. Use the `jdk.jshell.JShell#eval(String snippet)` method to evaluate the input. The evaluation will result in a list of `jdk.jshell.SnippetEvent`, which contains the status and output of the evaluation. The TODO in the preceding code snippet will be replaced by the following lines:

```
List<SnippetEvent> events = myShell.eval(snippet);
events.stream().forEach(se -> {
    System.out.print("Evaluation status: " + se.status());
    System.out.println(" Evaluation result: " + se.value());
});
```

5. When the evaluation is completed, we will print the snippets processed by using the `jdk.jshell.JShell.snippets()` method, which will return `Stream` of `Snippet` processed.

```
System.out.println("Snippets processed: ");
myShell.snippets().forEach(s -> {
    String msg = String.format("%s -> %s", s.kind(),
s.source());
    System.out.println(msg);
});
```

6. Similarly, we can print the active method and variables, as follows:

```
System.out.println("Methods: ");
myShell.methods().forEach(m ->
    System.out.println(m.name() + " " + m.signature()));

System.out.println("Variables: ");
myShell.variables().forEach(v ->
    System.out.println(v.typeName() + " " + v.name()));
```

7. Before the application exits, we close the `JShell` instance by invoking its `close()` method:

```
myShell.close();
```

The code for this recipe can be found in `Chapter12/6_jshell_api`. You can run the sample by using the `run.bat` or `run.sh` scripts available in the same directory. The sample execution and output are shown here:

```
Welcome to JShell Java API Demo
Please Enter a Snippet. Enter EXIT to exit:
int i = 10;
Evaluation status: VALID Evaluation result: 10
void test() { System.out.println("Test called"); }
Evaluation status: VALID Evaluation result: null
int sum(int a, int b){ return a + b; }
Evaluation status: VALID Evaluation result: null
sum(4,5)
Evaluation status: VALID Evaluation result: 9
EXIT
Snippets processed:
VAR -> int i = 10;
METHOD -> void test() { System.out.println("Test called"); }
METHOD -> int sum(int a, int b){ return a + b; }
VAR -> sum(4,5)
Methods:
test ()void
sum (int,int)int
Variables:
int i
int $1
'Bye!!'
```

How it works...

The central class in the API is the `jdk.jshell.JShell` class. This class is the evaluation state engine, whose state is modified with every evaluation of the snippet. As we saw earlier, the snippets are evaluated using the `eval(String snippet)` method. We can even drop the previously-evaluated snippet using the `drop(Snippet snippet)` method. Both these methods result in a change of the internal state maintained by `jdk.jshell.JShell`.

The code snippets passed to the `JShell` evaluation engine are categorized as follows:

- **Erroneous**: Syntactically incorrect input
- **Expressions**: An input that might or might not result in some output
- **Import**: An import statement
- **Method**: A method declaration
- **Statement**: A statement
- **Type declaration**: A type, that is, class/interface declaration
- **Variable declaration**: A variable declaration

All these categories are captured in the `jdk.jshell.Snippet.Kind` enum.

We also saw different APIs to execute the evaluated snippets, created methods, variable declarations, and other specific snippet types. Each snippet type is backed by a class that extends the `jdk.jshell.Snippet` class.

13
Working with New Date and Time APIs

In this chapter, we will cover the following recipes:

- How to construct time zone-independent date and time instances
- How to construct time zone-dependent time instances
- How to create a date-based period between date instances
- How to create a time-based period between time instances
- How to represent epoch time
- How to manipulate date and time instances
- How to compare date and time
- How to work with different calendar systems
- How to format dates using `DateTimeFormatter`

Introduction

Working with `java.util.Date` and `java.util.Calendar` was a pain for Java developers until Stephen Colebourne (http://www.joda.org/) introduced Joda-Time (http://www.joda.org/joda-time/), a library for working with date and time in Java. Joda-Time provided the following advantages over the JDK API:

- Richer API for getting date components, such as the day of a month, the day of a week, the month, and the year, and time components, such as the hour, minutes, and seconds.
- Ease of manipulation and comparison of dates and time.
- Both time zone-independent and time zone-dependent APIs are available. Most of the time, we will be using time zone-independent APIs, which makes it easier to use the API.

- Amazing APIs to compute duration between dates and times.
- Date formatting and duration computation follow ISO standards by default.
- Supports multiple calendars such as Gregorian, Buddhist, and Islamic.

Joda-Time inspired JSR-310 (`https://jcp.org/en/jsr/detail?id=310`), which ported the API to JDK under the `java.time` package and was released as part of Java 8. As the new Date/Time API is based on ISO standards, it makes it dead simple to integrate date/time libraries across different layers of your application. For example, at the JavaScript layer, we can use moment.js (`https://momentjs.com/docs/`) to work with date and time and use its default formatting style (which is ISO-compliant) to send data to the server. At the server layer, we can use the new Date/Time API to obtain date and time instances as required. So we are interacting between the client and server using standard date representations.

In this chapter, we will look at different ways we can leverage the new Date/Time API.

How to work with time zone-independent date and time instances

Prior to JSR-310, it was not straightforward to create date and time instances for any point in time or any day in a calendar. The only way was to use the `java.util.Calendar` object to set the required dates and time, and then invoke the `getTime()` method to get an instance of `java.util.Date`. And those date and time instances contained time zone information as well, which sometimes led to bugs in the application.

In new APIs, it's far simpler to get date and time instances, and these date and time instances do not have any time zone information associated with them. In this recipe, we will show you how to work with date-only instances represented by `java.time.LocalDate`, time-only instances represented by `java.time.LocalTime`, and date/time instances represented by `java.time.LocalDateTime`. These date and time instances are time zone-independent and represent the information in the current time zone of the machine.

Getting ready

You need to have at least JDK 8 installed to be able to use these newer libraries, and the samples in this chapter use the syntax that is supported on Java 10 and onward. If you want, you can run these code snippets directly in JShell. You can visit Chapter 12, *The Read-Evaluate-Print Loop (REPL) Using JShell,* to learn more about JShell.

How to do it...

1. The current date wrapped in java.time.LocalDate can be obtained using the now() method, as follows:

```
var date = LocalDate.now();
```

2. We can get individual fields of the java.time.LocalDate instance using the generic get(fieldName) method or specific methods such as getDayOfMonth(), getDayOfYear(), getDayOfWeek(), getMonth(), and getYear(), as follows:

```
var dayOfWeek = date.getDayOfWeek();
var dayOfMonth = date.getDayOfMonth();
var month = date.getMonth();
var year = date.getYear();
```

3. We can get an instance of java.time.LocalDate for any date in the calendar using the of() method, as follows:

```
var date1 = LocalDate.of(2018, 4, 12);
var date2 = LocalDate.of(2018, Month.APRIL, 12);
date2 = LocalDate.ofYearDay(2018, 102);
date2 = LocalDate.parse("2018-04-12");
```

4. There is the java.time.LocalTime class, which is used to represent any time instance irrespective of the date. The current time can be obtained using the following:

```
var time = LocalTime.now();
```

5. The `java.time.LocalTime` class also comes with the `of()` factory method, which can be used to create an instance representing any time. Similarly, there are methods to get different components of the time, as follows:

```
time = LocalTime.of(23, 11, 11, 11);
time = LocalTime.ofSecondOfDay(3600);

var hour = time.getHour();
var minutes = time.getMinute();
var seconds = time.get(ChronoField.SECOND_OF_MINUTE);
```

6. `java.time.LocalDateTime` is used to represent an entity containing both time and date. It is made up of `java.time.LocalDate` and `java.time.LocalTime` to represent date and time respectively. Its instance can be created using `now()` and different flavors of the `of()` factory method, as follows:

```
var dateTime1 = LocalDateTime.of(2018, 04, 12, 13, 30, 22);
var dateTime2 = LocalDateTime.of(2018, Month.APRIL, 12, 13,
30, 22);
dateTime2 = LocalDateTime.of(date2, LocalTime.of(13, 30, 22));
```

How it works...

The following three classes in the `java.time` package represent date and time values in the default time zone (the system's time zone):

- `java.time.LocalDate`: Contains only date information
- `java.time.LocalTime`: Contains only time information
- `java.time.LocalDateTime`: Contains both date and time information

Each of the classes is made up of fields, namely the following:

- Day
- Month
- Year
- Hour
- Minutes
- Seconds
- Milliseconds

All classes contain the `now()` method, which returns the current date and time values. There are `of()` factory methods provided to build the date and time instances from their fields, such as day, month, year, hour, and minute. `java.time.LocalDateTime` is made up of `java.time.LocalDate` and `java.time.LocalTime`, so one can build `java.time.LocalDateTime` from `java.time.LocalDate` and `java.time.LocalTime`.

The important APIs learned from this recipe are the following:

- `now()`: This gives the current date and time
- `of()`: This factory method is used to construct the required date, time and date/time instances

There's more...

In Java 9, there's a new API, `datesUntil`, which takes the end date and returns a stream of sequential dates (in other words, `java.time.LocalDate`) from the date of the current object until the end date (but excluding it). Using this API groups all the dates for the given month and year into their respective days of the week, namely, Monday, Tuesday, Wednesday, and so forth.

Let's accept the month and year and store it in the `month` and `year` variables respectively. The start of the range will be the first day of the month and year, as follows:

```
var startDate = LocalDate.of(year, month, 1);
```

The end date of the range will be the number of days in the month, as shown in the following snippet:

```
var endDate = startDate.plusDays(startDate.lengthOfMonth());
```

We are making use of the `lengthOfMonth` method to fetch the number of days in the month. We then use the `datesUntil` method to get a stream of `java.time.LocalDate` and then we perform some stream operations:

- Grouping `java.time.LocalDate` instances by day of the week.
- Collecting the grouped instances into `java.util.ArrayList`. But before that, we are applying a transformation to convert the `java.time.LocalDate` instances into a simple day of the month, which gives us a list of integers representing the day of the month.

The preceding two operations in the code are shown in the following snippet:

```
var dayBuckets = startDate.datesUntil(endDate).collect(
Collectors.groupingBy(date -> date.getDayOfWeek(),
    Collectors.mapping(LocalDate::getDayOfMonth,
        Collectors.toList())
));
```

The code for this can be found at `Chapter13/1_2_print_calendar` of the downloaded code.

How to construct time zone-dependent time instances

In the previous recipe, *How to construct time zone-independent date and time instances,* we constructed date and time objects that didn't contain any time zone information. They implicitly represented the values in the system's time zone; these classes were `java.time.LocalDate`, `java.time.LocalTime`, and `java.time.LocalDateTime`.

Often we would need to represent the time with respect to some time zone; in such scenarios we will make use of `java.time.ZonedDateTime`, which contains time zone information along with `java.time.LocalDateTime`. The time zone information is embedded using `java.time.ZoneId` or `java.time.ZoneOffset` instances. There are two other classes, `java.time.OffsetTime` and `java.time.OffsetDateTime`, which are also time zone-specific variants for `java.time.LocalTime` and `java.time.LocalDateTime`.

In this recipe, we will show you how to make use of `java.time.ZonedDateTime`, `java.time.ZoneId`, `java.time.ZoneOffset`, `java.time.OffsetTime`, and `java.time.OffsetDateTime`.

Getting ready

We will make use of Java 10 syntax that uses `var` for local variable declarations and modules. Apart from Java 10 and higher, there is no other prerequisite.

How to do it...

1. We will make use of the `now()` factory method to get the current date, time, and time zone information based on the system's time zone, as follows:

   ```
   var dateTime = ZonedDateTime.now();
   ```

2. We will make use of `java.time.ZoneId` to get the current date and time information based on any given time zone:

   ```
   var indianTz = ZoneId.of("Asia/Kolkata");
   var istDateTime = ZonedDateTime.now(indianTz);
   ```

3. `java.time.ZoneOffset` can also be used to provide time zone information for the date and time, as follows:

   ```
   var indianTzOffset = ZoneOffset.ofHoursMinutes(5, 30);
   istDateTime = ZonedDateTime.now(indianTzOffset);
   ```

4. We make use of the `of()` factory method to build an instance of `java.time.ZonedDateTime`:

   ```
   ZonedDateTime dateTimeOf = ZonedDateTime.of(2018, 4, 22, 14,
   30, 11, 33, indianTz);
   ```

5. We can even extract `java.time.LocalDateTime` from `java.time.ZonedDateTime`:

   ```
   var localDateTime = dateTimeOf.toLocalDateTime();
   ```

How it works...

First, let's look at how the time zone information is captured. It's captured based on the number of hours and minutes from **Greenwich Mean Time (GMT)**, also known as Coordinated Universal Time (UTC). For example, Indian Standard Time (IST), also known as Asia/Kolkata, is 5:30 hours ahead of GMT.

Java provides `java.time.ZoneId` and `java.time.ZoneOffset` to represent time zone information. `java.time.ZoneId` captures time zone information based on the time zone name, such as Asia/Kolkata, US/Pacific, and US/Mountain. There are around 599 zone IDs. This has been computed using the following line of code:

```
jshell> ZoneId.getAvailableZoneIds().stream().count()
$16 ==> 599
```

We will print 10 of the zone IDs:

```
jshell>
ZoneId.getAvailableZoneIds().stream().limit(10).forEach(System.out::pr
intln)
Asia/Aden
America/Cuiaba
Etc/GMT+9
Etc/GMT+8
Africa/Nairobi
America/Marigot
Asia/Aqtau
Pacific/Kwajalein
America/El_Salvador
Asia/Pontianak
```

Time zone names, such as Asia/Kolkata, Africa/Nairobi, and America/Cuiaba, are based on the time zone database released by International Assigned Numbers Authority (IANA). The time zone region names provided by IANA are the default for Java.

Sometimes time zone region names are also represented as GMT+02:30 or simply +02:30, which indicates the offset (ahead or behind) of the current time zone from the GMT zone.

This `java.time.ZoneId` captures `java.time.zone.ZoneRules`, which contains rules for obtaining the time zone offset transitions and other information, such as the daylight savings time. Let's investigate the zone rules for US/Pacific:

```
jshell>
ZoneId.of("US/Pacific").getRules().getDaylightSavings(Instant.now())
$31 ==> PT1H

jshell>
ZoneId.of("US/Pacific").getRules().getOffset(LocalDateTime.now())
$32 ==> -07:00

jshell>
```

```
ZoneId.of("US/Pacific").getRules().getStandardOffset(Instant.now())
$33 ==> -08:00
```

The `getDaylightSavings()` method returns a `java.time.Duration` object, which represents some duration in terms of hours, minutes, and seconds. The default `toString()` implementation returns the duration represented using ISO 8601 seconds-based representation where a duration of 1 hour, 20 minutes, and 20 seconds is represented as `PT1H20M20S`. More about this will be covered in the *How to create a time-based period between time instances* recipe in this chapter.

We are not going into the details of how it's been calculated. For those interested to know more about `java.time.zone.ZoneRules` and `java.time.ZoneId`, visit the documentation at https://docs. oracle.com/javase/10/docs/api/java/time/zone/ZoneRules. html and https://docs.oracle.com/javase/10/docs/api/java/ time/ZoneId.html respectively.

The `java.time.ZoneOffset` class captures the time zone information in terms of the number of hours and minutes the time zone is ahead of or behind GMT. Let's create an instance of the `java.time.ZoneOffset` class using the `of*()` factory method:

```
jshell> ZoneOffset.ofHoursMinutes(5,30)
$27 ==> +05:30
```

The `java.time.ZoneOffset` class extends from `java.time.ZoneId` and adds a few new methods. The important thing to remember is to construct the right instance of `java.time.ZoneOffset` and `java.time.ZoneId` based on the required time zone to be used in your applications.

Now that we have an understanding of time zone representation, `java.time.ZonedDateTime` is nothing but `java.time.LocalDateTime` along with `java.time.ZoneId` or `java.time.ZoneOffset`. There are two other classes, `java.time.OffsetTime` and `java.time.OffsetDateTime`, which wraps `java.time.LocalTime` and `java.time.LocalDateTime` respectively, along with `java.time.ZoneOffset`.

Let's see some ways to construct instances of `java.time.ZonedDateTime`.

The first way is using `now()`:

```
Signatures:
ZonedDateTime ZonedDateTime.now()
ZonedDateTime ZonedDateTime.now(ZoneId zone)
ZonedDateTime ZonedDateTime.now(Clock clock)

jshell> ZonedDateTime.now()
jshell> ZonedDateTime.now(ZoneId.of("Asia/Kolkata"))
$36 ==> 2018-05-04T21:58:24.453113900+05:30[Asia/Kolkata]
jshell>
ZonedDateTime.now(Clock.fixed(Instant.ofEpochSecond(1525452037),
ZoneId.of("Asia/Kolkata")))
$54 ==> 2018-05-04T22:10:37+05:30[Asia/Kolkata]
```

The first usage of `now()` uses the system's clock, as well as the system time zone to print the current date and time. The second usage of `now()` uses the system's clock, but the time zone is provided by `java.time.ZoneId`, which in this case is Asia/Kolkata. The third usage of `now()` uses the fixed clock provided and the time zone provided by `java.time.ZoneId`.

The fixed clock is created using the `java.time.Clock` class and its static method, `fixed()`, which takes an instance of `java.time.Instant` and `java.time.ZoneId`. The instance of `java.time.Instant` has been built using some static number of seconds after epoch. `java.time.Clock` is used to represent a clock which can be used by the new Date/Time API to determine the current time. The clock can be fixed, as we have seen earlier, then we can create a clock which is one hour ahead of the current system time in the Asia/Kolkata time zone, as follows:

```
var hourAheadClock =
Clock.offset(Clock.system(ZoneId.of("Asia/Kolkata")),
Duration.ofHours(1));
```

We can use this new clock to build instances of `java.time.LocalDateTime` and `java.time.ZonedDateTime`, as follows:

```
jshell> LocalDateTime.now(hourAheadClock)
$64 ==> 2018-05-04T23:29:58.759973700
jshell> ZonedDateTime.now(hourAheadClock)
$65 ==> 2018-05-04T23:30:11.421913800+05:30[Asia/Kolkata]
```

Both date and time values are based on the same time zone, that is, `Asia/Kolkata`, but as we have already learned, `java.time.LocalDateTime` doesn't have any time zone information and it bases the values on the time zone of the system or the `java.time.Clock` provided in this case. On the other hand, `java.time.ZonedDateTime` contains and displays the time zone information as [Asia/Kolkata].

The other approach for creating an instance of `java.time.ZonedDateTime` is using its `of()` factory method:

```
Signatures:
ZonedDateTime ZonedDateTime.of(LocalDate date, LocalTime time, ZoneId
zone)
ZonedDateTime ZonedDateTime.of(LocalDateTime localDateTime, ZoneId
zone)
ZonedDateTime ZonedDateTime.of(int year, int month, int dayOfMonth,
int hour, int minute, int second, int nanoOfSecond, ZoneId zone)

jshell> ZonedDateTime.of(LocalDateTime.of(2018, 1, 1, 13, 44, 44),
ZoneId.of("Asia/Kolkata"))
$70 ==> 2018-01-01T13:44:44+05:30[Asia/Kolkata]

jshell> ZonedDateTime.of(LocalDate.of(2018,1,1), LocalTime.of(13, 44,
44), ZoneId.of("Asia/Kolkata"))
$71 ==> 2018-01-01T13:44:44+05:30[Asia/Kolkata]

jshell> ZonedDateTime.of(LocalDate.of(2018,1,1), LocalTime.of(13, 44,
44), ZoneId.of("Asia/Kolkata"))
$72 ==> 2018-01-01T13:44:44+05:30[Asia/Kolkata]

jshell> ZonedDateTime.of(2018, 1, 1, 13, 44, 44, 0,
ZoneId.of("Asia/Kolkata"))
$73 ==> 2018-01-01T13:44:44+05:30[Asia/Kolkata]
```

There's more...

We mentioned the `java.time.OffsetTime` and `java.time.OffsetDateTime` classes. Both contain time zone-specific time values. Let's play around with those classes before we wrap up this recipe:

- Using the `of()` factory method:

```
jshell> OffsetTime.of(LocalTime.of(14,12,34),
ZoneOffset.ofHoursMinutes(5, 30))
```

```
$74 ==> 14:12:34+05:30

jshell> OffsetTime.of(14, 34, 12, 11,
ZoneOffset.ofHoursMinutes(5, 30))
$75 ==> 14:34:12.000000011+05:30
```

- Using the `now()` factory method:

```
Signatures:
OffsetTime OffsetTime.now()
OffsetTime OffsetTime.now(ZoneId zone)
OffsetTime OffsetTime.now(Clock clock)

jshell> OffsetTime.now()
$76 ==> 21:49:16.895192800+03:00

jshell> OffsetTime.now(ZoneId.of("Asia/Kolkata"))

jshell> OffsetTime.now(ZoneId.of("Asia/Kolkata"))
$77 ==> 00:21:04.685836900+05:30

jshell> OffsetTime.now(Clock.offset(Clock.systemUTC(),
Duration.ofMinutes(330)))
$78 ==> 00:22:00.395463800Z
```

It's worth noting the way we built a `java.time.Clock` instance, which is 330 minutes (5 hours and 30 minutes) ahead of the UTC clock. The other class, `java.time.OffsetDateTime`, is the same as `java.time.OffsetTime`, except that it uses `java.time.LocalDateTime`. So you will be passing the date information, namely, year, month, and day, along with the time information to its factory method, `of()`.

How to create a date-based period between date instances

There are times in the past when we tried to measure the period between two date instances but, due to the lack of an API prior to Java 8 and also lack of proper support to capture this information, we resorted to different means. We remember using SQL-based approaches to process such information. But from Java 8 and onward, we have a new class, `java.time.Period`, which can be used to capture a period between two date instances in terms of the number of years, months, and days.

Also, this class supports parsing ISO 8601 standard-based strings for representing the period. The standard states that any period can be represented in the form of PnYnMnD, where **P** is a fixed character to represent the period, **nY** stands for the number of years, **nM** for the number of months, and **nD** for the number of days. For example, a period of 2 years, 4 months, and 10 days is represented as P2Y4M10D.

Getting ready

You need at least JDK8 to play around with java.time.Period, JDK 9 to be able to make use of JShell, and at least JDK 10 to make use of the examples used in this recipe.

How to do it...

1. Let's create an instance of java.time.Period using its of() factory method, which has the signature Period.of(int years, int months, int days):

```
jshell> Period.of(2,4,30)
$2 ==> P2Y4M30D
```

2. There are specific variants of the of*() method, namely, ofDays(), ofMonths(), and ofYears(), which can be used as well:

```
jshell> Period.ofDays(10)
$3 ==> P10D
jshell> Period.ofMonths(4)
$4 ==> P4M
jshell> Period.ofWeeks(3)
$5 ==> P21D
jshell> Period.ofYears(3)
$6 ==> P3Y
```

Note that the ofWeeks() method is a helper method to build java.time.Period based on days by accepting the number of weeks.

3. The period can also be constructed using the period string, which is generally of the form P<x>Y<y>M<z>D where x, y, and z represent the number of years, months, and days respectively:

```
jshell> Period.parse("P2Y4M23D").getDays()
$8 ==> 23
```

4. We can also compute the period between two instances of
   `java.time.ChronoLocalDate` (one of its implementations is
   `java.time.LocalDate`):

```
jshell> Period.between(LocalDate.now(), LocalDate.of(2018, 8,
23))
$9 ==> P2M2D
jshell> Period.between(LocalDate.now(), LocalDate.of(2018, 2,
23))
$10 ==> P-3M-26D
```

These are the most useful ways to create an instance of `java.time.Period`. The start
date is inclusive and the end date is exclusive.

How it works...

We make use of the factory methods in `java.time.Period` to create its instance. The
`java.time.Period` has three fields to hold the values for year, month, and day
respectively, as follows:

```
/**
 * The number of years.
 */
private final int years;
/**
 * The number of months.
 */
private final int months;
/**
 * The number of days.
 */
private final int days;
```

There is an interesting set of methods, namely, `withDays()`, `withMonths()`,
and `withYears()`. These methods return the same instance if the field that it's trying
to update has the same value; otherwise, it returns a new instance with updated
values, as follows:

```
jshell> Period period1 = Period.ofWeeks(2)
period1 ==> P14D

jshell> Period period2 = period1.withDays(15)
period2 ==> P15D

jshell> period1 == period2
```

```
$19 ==> false

jshell> Period period3 = period1.withDays(14)
period3 ==> P14D

jshell> period1 == period3
$21 ==> true
```

There's more...

We can even compute `java.time.Period` between the two date instances using the `until()` method present in `java.time.ChronoLocalDate`:

```
jshell> LocalDate.now().until(LocalDate.of(2018, 2, 23))
$11 ==> P-3M-26D

jshell> LocalDate.now().until(LocalDate.of(2018, 8, 23))
$12 ==> P2M2D
```

Given an instance of `java.time.Period`, we can use it to manipulate a given date instance. There are two possible ways:

- Using the `addTo` or `subtractFrom` method of the period object
- Using the `plus` or `minus` method of the date object

Both of the approaches are shown in the following snippets:

```
jshell> Period period1 = Period.ofWeeks(2)
period1 ==> P14D

jshell> LocalDate date = LocalDate.now()
date ==> 2018-06-21

jshell> period1.addTo(date)
$24 ==> 2018-07-05

jshell> date.plus(period1)
$25 ==> 2018-07-05
```

On similar lines, you can try out the subtractFrom and minus methods. There is another set of methods used to manipulate the java.time.Period instance, namely, the following:

- minus, minusDays, minusMonths, and minusYears: Subtract the given value from the period.
- plus, plusDays, plusMonths, and plusYears: Add the given value to the period.
- negated: Returns the new period with each of its values negated.
- normalized: Returns a new period by normalizing its higher-order fields, such as months and days. For example, 15 months is normalized to 1 year and 3 months.

We will show you these methods in action as follows, starting with the minus methods:

```
jshell> period1.minus(Period.of(1,3,4))
$28 ==> P2Y12M25D

jshell> period1.minusDays(4)
$29 ==> P3Y15M25D

jshell> period1.minusMonths(3)
$30 ==> P3Y12M29D

jshell> period1.minusYears(1)
$31 ==> P2Y15M29D
```

Then, we will see the plus methods:

```
jshell> Period period1 = Period.of(3, 15, 29)
period1 ==> P3Y15M29D

jshell> period1.plus(Period.of(1, 3, 4))
$33 ==> P4Y18M33D

jshell> period1.plusDays(4)
$34 ==> P3Y15M33D

jshell> period1.plusMonths(3)
$35 ==> P3Y18M29D

jshell> period1.plusYears(1)
$36 ==> P4Y15M29D
```

Finally, here are the `negated()` and `normalized()` methods:

```
jshell> Period period1 = Period.of(3, 15, 29)
period1 ==> P3Y15M29D

jshell> period1.negated()
$38 ==> P-3Y-15M-29D

jshell> period1
period1 ==> P3Y15M29D

jshell> period1.normalized()
$40 ==> P4Y3M29D

jshell> period1
period1 ==> P3Y15M29D
```

Observe that, in both of the earlier cases, it is not mutating the existing period, instead of returning a new instance.

How to create a time-based period between time instances

In our previous recipe, we created a date-based period, which is represented by `java.time.Period`. In this recipe, we will look at creating a time-based difference between time instances in terms of seconds and nanoseconds using the `java.time.Duration` class.

We will look at different ways to create an instance of `java.time.Duration`, manipulate the duration instance, and obtain the duration in terms of different units, such as hours and minutes. The ISO 8601 standard specifies one of the possible patterns for representing duration to be `PnYnMnDTnHnMnS`, where the following applies:

- `Y`, `M`, and `D` represent the date component fields, namely, year, month, and day
- `T` separates the date with the time information
- `H`, `M`, and `S` represent the time component fields, namely, hour, minutes, and seconds

The string representation implementation of `java.time.Duration` is loosely based on the ISO 8601. There is more on this in the *How it works* section.

Getting ready

You need at least JDK 8 to play around with `java.time.Duration` and JDK 9 to be able to make use of JShell.

How to do it...

1. `java.time.Duration` instances can be created using the `of*()` factory methods. We will show using a few of them, as follows:

```
jshell> Duration.of(56, ChronoUnit.MINUTES)
$66 ==> PT56M
jshell> Duration.of(56, ChronoUnit.DAYS)
$67 ==> PT1344H
jshell> Duration.ofSeconds(87)
$68 ==> PT1M27S
jshell> Duration.ofHours(7)
$69 ==> PT7H
```

2. They can also be created by parsing the duration string, as follows:

```
jshell> Duration.parse("P12D")
$70 ==> PT288H
jshell> Duration.parse("P12DT7H5M8.009S")
$71 ==> PT295H5M8.009S
jshell> Duration.parse("PT7H5M8.009S")
$72 ==> PT7H5M8.009S
```

3. They can be constructed by finding the span between two `java.time.Temporal` instances, which support time information (that is, instances of `java.time.LocalDateTime` and the likes), as follows:

```
jshell> LocalDateTime time1 = LocalDateTime.now()
time1 ==> 2018-06-23T10:51:21.038073800
jshell> LocalDateTime time2 = LocalDateTime.of(2018, 6, 22,
11, 00)
time2 ==> 2018-06-22T11:00
jshell> Duration.between(time1, time2)
$77 ==> PT-23H-51M-21.0380738S
jshell> ZonedDateTime time1 = ZonedDateTime.now()
```

```
time1 ==> 2018-06-23T10:56:57.965606200+03:00[Asia/Riyadh]
jshell> ZonedDateTime time2 =
ZonedDateTime.of(LocalDateTime.now(),
ZoneOffset.ofHoursMinutes(5, 30))
time2 ==> 2018-06-23T10:56:59.878712600+05:30
jshell> Duration.between(time1, time2)
$82 ==> PT-2H-29M-58.0868936S
```

How it works...

The data required for `java.time.Duration` is stored in two fields representing seconds and nanoseconds respectively. There are convenience methods provided to get the duration in terms of minutes, hours, and days, namely, `toMinutes()`, `toHours()`, and `toDays()`.

Let's discuss the string representation implementation. `java.time.Duration` supports parsing the ISO string representation containing only the day component in the date part and hours, minutes, seconds, and nanoseconds in the time part. For example, `P2DT3M` is acceptable, whereas parsing `P3M2DT3M` results in `java.time.format.DateTimeParseException` because the string contains the month component in the date part.

The `toString()` method of `java.time.Duration` always returns a string of the `PTxHyMz.nS` form, where x represents the number of hours, y represents the number of minutes, and z.n represents the number of seconds to nanosecond precision. Let's see some examples:

```
jshell> Duration.parse("P2DT3M")
$2 ==> PT48H3M

jshell> Duration.parse("P3M2DT3M")
| Exception java.time.format.DateTimeParseException: Text cannot be
parsed to a Duration
| at Duration.parse (Duration.java:417)
| at (#3:1)

jshell> Duration.ofHours(4)
$4 ==> PT4H

jshell> Duration.parse("PT3H4M5.6S")
$5 ==> PT3H4M5.6S

jshell> Duration d = Duration.parse("PT3H4M5.6S")
d ==> PT3H4M5.6S
```

```
jshell> d.toDays()
$7 ==> 0

jshell> d.toHours()
$9 ==> 3
```

There's more...

Let's look at the manipulation methods provided, which allow adding/subtracting a value from the specific unit of time, such as days, hours, minutes, seconds, or nanoseconds. Each of these methods is immutable, so a new instance is returned each time, as follows:

```
jshell> Duration d = Duration.parse("PT1H5M4S")
d ==> PT1H5M4S

jshell> d.plusDays(3)
$14 ==> PT73H5M4S

jshell> d
d ==> PT1H5M4S

jshell> d.plusDays(3)
$16 ==> PT73H5M4S

jshell> d.plusHours(3)
$17 ==> PT4H5M4S

jshell> d.plusMillis(4)
$18 ==> PT1H5M4.004S

jshell> d.plusMinutes(40)
$19 ==> PT1H45M4S
```

Similarly, you can try out the `minus*()` methods, which does the subtraction. Then there are methods that manipulate the instances of `java.time.LocalDateTime`, `java.time.ZonedDateTime`, and their like. These methods add/subtract the duration to/from the date/time information. Let's see some examples:

```
jshell> Duration d = Duration.parse("PT1H5M4S")
d ==> PT1H5M4S

jshell> d.addTo(LocalDateTime.now())
$21 ==> 2018-06-25T21:15:53.725373600
```

```
jshell> d.addTo(ZonedDateTime.now())
$22 ==> 2018-06-25T21:16:03.396595600+03:00[Asia/Riyadh]

jshell> d.addTo(LocalDate.now())
| Exception java.time.temporal.UnsupportedTemporalTypeException:
Unsupported unit: Seconds
| at LocalDate.plus (LocalDate.java:1272)
| at LocalDate.plus (LocalDate.java:139)
| at Duration.addTo (Duration.java:1102)
| at (#23:1)
```

You can observe in the preceding example that we got an exception when we tried to add the duration to the entity containing only date information.

How to represent epoch time

In this recipe, we will look at using `java.time.Instant` to represent a point in time, as well as convert that point in time to epoch seconds/milliseconds. The Java epoch is used to refer to the time instant 1970-01-01 to 0:00:00Z and `java.time.Instant` stores the number of seconds from the Java epoch. A positive value indicates the time is ahead of the epoch and negative indicates the time is behind the epoch. It uses the system clock in UTC to compute the current time instant value.

Getting ready

You need to have JDK supporting new Date/Time APIs and JShell installed to be able to try out the solution provided.

How to do it...

1. We will just create an instance of `java.time.Instant` and print out the epoch seconds, which will give the time in UTC after the Java epoch:

    ```
    jshell> Instant.now()
    $40 ==> 2018-07-06T07:56:40.651529300Z

    jshell> Instant.now().getEpochSecond()
    $41 ==> 1530863807
    ```

2. We can also print out the epoch milliseconds, which shows the number of milliseconds after the epoch. This is a bit more precise than just seconds:

```
jshell> Instant.now().toEpochMilli()
$42 ==> 1530863845158
```

How it works...

The `java.time.Instant` class stores the time information in its two fields:

- Seconds, which is of the `long` type: This stores the number of seconds from the epoch of 1970-01-01T00:00:00Z.
- Nanos, which is of the `int` type: This stores the number of nanoseconds

When you invoke the `now()` method, `java.time.Instant` uses the system clock in UTC to represent that time instant. And then we can use `atZone()` or `atOffset()` to convert it into the required time zone, as we will see in the next section.

Use this class if you want to just represent the timeline of actions in UTC; that way, the timestamp stored for different events will be based on UTC and you can then convert it into your required time zone as and when required.

There's more...

We can manipulate the `java.time.Instant` by adding/subtracting nanoseconds, milliseconds, and seconds, as follows:

```
jshell> Instant.now().plusMillis(1000)
$43 ==> 2018-07-06T07:57:57.092259400Z

jshell> Instant.now().plusNanos(1991999)
$44 ==> 2018-07-06T07:58:06.097966099Z

jshell> Instant.now().plusSeconds(180)
$45 ==> 2018-07-06T08:01:15.824141500Z
```

Similarly, you can try out the `minus*()` methods. We can also obtain the time zone-dependent date time using the `java.time.Instant` methods, `atOffset()` and `atZone()`, as follows:

```
jshell> Instant.now().atZone(ZoneId.of("Asia/Kolkata"))
$36 ==> 2018-07-06T13:15:13.820694500+05:30[Asia/Kolkata]

jshell> Instant.now().atOffset(ZoneOffset.ofHoursMinutes(2,30))
$37 ==> 2018-07-06T10:15:19.712039+02:30
```

How to manipulate date and time instances

The date and time classes, `java.time.LocalDate`, `java.time.LocalTime`, `java.time.LocalDateTime`, and `java.time.ZonedDateTime`, provide methods to add and subtract values from their components, namely, days, hours, minutes, seconds, weeks, months, years, and others.

In this recipe, we will look at a few such methods, which can be used to manipulate date and time instances by adding and subtracting different values.

Getting ready

You will need a JDK installation that supports the new Date/Time APIs and the JShell console.

How to do it...

1. Let's manipulate `java.time.LocalDate`:

```
jshell> LocalDate d = LocalDate.now()
d ==> 2018-07-27

jshell> d.plusDays(3)
$5 ==> 2018-07-30

jshell> d.minusYears(4)
$6 ==> 2014-07-27
```

2. Let's manipulate the date and time instance, `java.time.LocalDateTime`:

```
jshell> LocalDateTime dt = LocalDateTime.now()
dt ==> 2018-07-27T15:27:40.733389700

jshell> dt.plusMinutes(45)
$8 ==> 2018-07-27T16:12:40.733389700

jshell> dt.minusHours(4)
$9 ==> 2018-07-27T11:27:40.733389700
```

3. Let's manipulate the time zone-dependent date and time, `java.time.ZonedDateTime`:

```
jshell> ZonedDateTime zdt = ZonedDateTime.now()
zdt ==> 2018-07-27T15:28:28.309915200+03:00[Asia/Riyadh]

jshell> zdt.plusDays(4)
$11 ==> 2018-07-31T15:28:28.309915200+03:00[Asia/Riyadh]

jshell> zdt.minusHours(3)
$12 ==> 2018-07-27T12:28:28.309915200+03:00[Asia/Riyadh]
```

There's more...

We just looked at a few of the add and subtract APIs represented by `plus*()` and `minus*()`. There are different methods provided to manipulate different components of date and time, such as years, days, months, hours, minutes, seconds, and nanoseconds. You can try those APIs as an exercise.

How to compare date and time

Often, we would want to compare date and time instances with others to check if they are before, after, or the same as that of the other. To achieve this, JDK provides `isBefore()`, `isAfter()`, and `isEqual()` methods in the `java.time.LocalDate`, `java.time.LocalDateTime`, and `java.time.ZonedDateTime` classes. In this recipe, we will look at using these methods to compare date and time instances.

Getting ready

You will need a JDK installation that has the new Date/Time APIs and supports JShell.

How to do it...

1. Let's try out comparing two `java.time.LocalDate` instances:

```
jshell> LocalDate d = LocalDate.now()
d ==> 2018-07-28

jshell> LocalDate d2 = LocalDate.of(2018, 7, 27)
d2 ==> 2018-07-27

jshell> d.isBefore(d2)
$4 ==> false

jshell> d.isAfter(d2)
$5 ==> true

jshell> LocalDate d3 = LocalDate.of(2018, 7, 28)
d3 ==> 2018-07-28

jshell> d.isEqual(d3)
$7 ==> true

jshell> d.isEqual(d2)
$8 ==> false
```

2. We can also compare the time zone-dependent date and time instances:

```
jshell> ZonedDateTime zdt1 = ZonedDateTime.now();
zdt1 ==> 2018-07-28T14:49:34.778006400+03:00[Asia/Riyadh]

jshell> ZonedDateTime zdt2 = zdt1.plusHours(4)
zdt2 ==> 2018-07-28T18:49:34.778006400+03:00[Asia/Riyadh]

jshell> zdt1.isBefore(zdt2)
$11 ==> true

jshell> zdt1.isAfter(zdt2)
$12 ==> false
jshell> zdt1.isEqual(zdt2)
$13 ==> false
```

There's more...

The comparison can be performed on `java.time.LocalTime` and `java.time.LocalDateTime`. This is left to the reader to explore.

How to work with different calendar systems

So far in our recipes, we worked with the ISO calendar system, which is the de facto calendar system followed in the world. There are other regional calendar systems followed in the world, such as Hijrah, Japanese, and Thai. JDK provides support for such calendar systems as well.

In this recipe, we will look at working with two calendar systems: Japanese and the Hijri.

Getting ready

You should have a JDK installed that supports the new Date/Time APIs and the JShell tool.

How to do it...

1. Let's print the current date in the different calendar systems supported by JDK:

```
jshell> Chronology.getAvailableChronologies().forEach(chrono
->
System.out.println(chrono.dateNow()))
2018-07-30
Minguo ROC 107-07-30
Japanese Heisei 30-07-30
ThaiBuddhist BE 2561-07-30
Hijrah-umalqura AH 1439-11-17
```

2. Let's play around with the date represented in the Japanese calendar system:

```
jshell> JapaneseDate jd = JapaneseDate.now()
jd ==> Japanese Heisei 30-07-30

jshell> jd.getChronology()
$7 ==> Japanese

jshell> jd.getEra()
$8 ==> Heisei

jshell> jd.lengthOfYear()
$9 ==> 365

jshell> jd.lengthOfMonth()
$10 ==> 31
```

3. Different eras supported in the Japanese calendar can be enumerated using `java.time.chrono.JapeneseEra`:

```
jshell> JapaneseEra.values()
$42 ==> JapaneseEra[5] { Meiji, Taisho, Showa, Heisei, NewEra
}
```

4. Let's create a date in the Hijrah calendar system:

```
jshell> HijrahDate hd = HijrahDate.of(1438, 12, 1)
hd ==> Hijrah-umalqura AH 1438-12-01
```

5. We can even convert the ISO date/time into date/time in the Hijrah calendar system as follows:

```
jshell>
HijrahChronology.INSTANCE.localDateTime(LocalDateTime.now())
$23 ==> Hijrah-umalqura AH 1439-11-17T19:56:52.056465900

jshell>
HijrahChronology.INSTANCE.localDateTime(LocalDateTime.now()).t
oLocalDate()
$24 ==> Hijrah-umalqura AH 1439-11-17

jshell>
HijrahChronology.INSTANCE.localDateTime(LocalDateTime.now()).t
oLocalTime()
$25 ==> 19:57:07.705740500
```

How it works...

The calendar system is represented by `java.time.chrono.Chronology` and its implementations, a few of which are `java.time.chrono.IsoChronology`, `java.time.chrono.HijrahChronology`, and `java.time.chrono.JapaneseChronology`. `java.time.chrono.IsoChronology` is the ISO-based de facto calendar system used in the world. The date in each of these calendar systems is represented by `java.time.chrono.ChronoLocalDate` and its implementations, some of which are `java.time.chrono.HijrahDate`, `java.time.chrono.JapaneseDate`, and the well-known `java.time.LocalDate`.

To be able to use these APIs in JShell, you need to import the relevant packages, as follows:

```
jshell> import java.time.*

jshell> import java.time.chrono.*
```

This is applicable to all the recipes that use JShell.

We can directly play with the implementations of `java.time.chrono.ChronoLocalDate`, such as `java.time.chrono.JapaneseDate`, or use the implementation of `java.time.chrono.Chronology` to obtain relevant date representations, as follows:

```
jshell> JapaneseDate jd = JapaneseDate.of(JapaneseEra.SHOWA, 26, 12,
25)
jd ==> Japanese Showa 26-12-25

jshell> JapaneseDate jd = JapaneseDate.now()
jd ==> Japanese Heisei 30-07-30

jshell> JapaneseDate jd = JapaneseChronology.INSTANCE.dateNow()
jd ==> Japanese Heisei 30-07-30

jshell> JapaneseDate jd =
JapaneseChronology.INSTANCE.date(LocalDateTime.now())
jd ==> Japanese Heisei 30-07-30

jshell> ThaiBuddhistChronology.INSTANCE.date(LocalDate.now())
$41 ==> ThaiBuddhist BE 2561-07-30
```

From the preceding code snippets, we can see that one can convert the ISO system date into dates in the required calendar system by using their calendar system's `date(TemporalAccessor temporal)` method.

There's more...

You can play around with the other calendar systems supported in JDK, namely, Thai, Buddhist, and Minguo (Chinese) calendar systems. It's also worth exploring to create our custom calendar systems by writing an implementation of `java.time.chrono.Chronology`, `java.time.chrono.ChronoLocalDate`, and `java.time.chrono.Era`.

How to format dates using the DateTimeFormatter

While working with `java.util.Date`, we made use of `java.text.SimpleDateFormat` to format the date into different text representations and vice versa. Formatting a date means, given a date or a time object representing it in different formats, such as the following:

- 23 Jun 2018
- 23-08-2018
- 2018-08-23
- 23 Jun 2018 11:03:33 AM

These formats are controlled by format strings, such as the following:

- `dd MMM yyyy`
- `dd-MM-yyyy`
- `yyyy-MM-DD`
- `dd MMM yyyy hh:mm:ss`

In this recipe, we will look at `java.time.format.DateTimeFormatter` to format the date and time instances in the new date and time API and also look at the most commonly used pattern letters.

Getting ready

You will need a JDK that has the new Date/Time APIs as well as the `jshell` tool.

How to do it...

1. Let's use the built-in formats to format the date and time:

```
jshell> LocalDate ld = LocalDate.now()
ld ==> 2018-08-01

jshell> ld.format(DateTimeFormatter.ISO_DATE)
$47 ==> "2018-08-01"

jshell>
LocalDateTime.now().format(DateTimeFormatter.ISO_DATE_TIME)
$49 ==> "2018-08-01T17:24:49.1985601"
```

2. Let's create a custom date/time format:

```
jshell> DateTimeFormatter dtf =
DateTimeFormatter.ofPattern("dd MMM yyyy hh:mm:ss a")
dtf ==> Value(DayOfMonth,2)' 'Text(MonthOfYear,SHORT)' 'V ...
2)' 'Text(AmPmOfDay,SHORT)
```

3. Let's use the custom `java.time.format.DateTimeFormatter` for formatting the current date/time:

```
jshell> LocalDateTime ldt = LocalDateTime.now()
ldt ==> 2018-08-01T17:36:22.442159

jshell> ldt.format(dtf)
$56 ==> "01 Aug 2018 05:36:22 PM"
```

How it works...

Let's understand the most commonly used format letters:

Symbol	Meaning	Example
d	day of the month	1,2,3,5
M, MMM, MMMM	month of the year	M: 1,2,3, MMM: Jun, Jul, Aug MMMM: July, August
y, yy	year	y, yyyy: 2017, 2018 yy: 18, 19
h	hour of the day (1-12)	1, 2, 3
k	hour of the day (0-23)	0, 1, 2, 3

m	minutes	1, 2, 3
s	seconds	1, 2, 3
a	AM/PM of the day	AM, PM
VV	Time zone ID	Asia/Kolkata
zz	Time zone name	IST, PST, AST
O	Time zone offset	GMT+5:30, GMT+3

Based on the preceding format letters, let's format `java.time.ZonedDateTime`:

```
jshell> DateTimeFormatter dtf = DateTimeFormatter.ofPattern("dd MMMM
yy h:mm:ss a VV")
dtf ==> Value(DayOfMonth,2)' 'Text(MonthOfYear)' 'Reduced ...
mPmOfDay,SHORT)' 'ZoneId()

jshell> ZonedDateTime.now().format(dtf)
$67 ==> "01 August 18 6:26:04 PM Asia/Kolkata"

jshell> DateTimeFormatter dtf = DateTimeFormatter.ofPattern("dd MMMM
yy h:mm:ss a zz")
dtf ==> Value(DayOfMonth,2)' 'Text(MonthOfYear)' 'Reduced ...
y,SHORT)' 'ZoneText(SHORT)

jshell> ZonedDateTime.now().format(dtf)
$69 ==> "01 August 18 6:26:13 PM IST"

jshell> DateTimeFormatter dtf = DateTimeFormatter.ofPattern("dd MMMM
yy h:mm:ss a O")
dtf ==> Value(DayOfMonth,2)' 'Text(MonthOfYear)' 'Reduced ... )'
'LocalizedOffset(SHORT)

jshell> ZonedDateTime.now().format(dtf)
$72 ==> "01 August 18 6:26:27 PM GMT+5:30"
```

`java.time.format.DateTimeFormatter` comes shipped with plenty of default formatting based on the ISO standards. These formats should be more than enough when you are dealing with the date manipulation without any user being involved, that is, when the date and time is being exchanged between different layers of the application.

But for presenting the date and time information to an end user, we would need to format it in a readable format and, for that, we would need a custom `DateTimeFormatter`. If you need a custom `java.time.format.DateTimeFormatter`, here are two ways of creating one:

- Using a pattern, such as dd MMMM yyyy and the `ofPattern()` method in `java.time.format.DateTimeFormatter`
- Using `java.time.DateTimeFormatterBuilder`

Using Pattern:

We create an instance of `java.time.format.DateTimeFormatter`, as follows:

```
jshell> DateTimeFormatter dtf = DateTimeFormatter.ofPattern("dd MMMM
yy h:mm:ss a VV")
dtf ==> Value(DayOfMonth,2)' 'Text(MonthOfYear)' 'Reduced ...
mPmOfDay,SHORT)' 'ZoneId()
```

And then we apply the format to a date and time instance:

```
jshell> ZonedDateTime.now().format(dtf)
$92 ==> "01 August 18 7:25:00 PM Asia/Kolkata"
```

The pattern approach also uses `DateTimeFormatterBuilder` wherein the builder parses the given format string to build a `DateTimeFormatter` object.

Using `java.time.format.DateTimeFormatterBuilder`:

Let's build `DateTimeFormatter` using `DateTimeFormatterBuilder`, as follows:

```
jshell> DateTimeFormatter dtf = new DateTimeFormatterBuilder().
   ...> appendValue(DAY_OF_MONTH, 2).
   ...> appendLiteral(" ").
   ...> appendText(MONTH_OF_YEAR).
   ...> appendLiteral(" ").
   ...> appendValue(YEAR, 4).
   ...> toFormatter()
dtf ==> Value(DayOfMonth,2)' 'Text(MonthOfYear)' 'Value(Year,4)

jshell> LocalDate.now().format(dtf) E$106 ==> "01 August 2018"
```

You can observe that a `DateTimeFormatter` object consists of a set of instructions on how to represent the date and time. These instructions are presented in form of `Value()`, `Text()`, and delimiters.

14
Testing

This chapter shows how to test your application—how to capture and automate the testing of use cases, how to unit test your APIs before they are integrated with other components, and how to integrate all of the units. We will introduce you to **Behavior-Driven Development** (**BDD**) and show how it can become the starting point of your application development. We will also demonstrate how JUnit framework can be used for unit testing. Sometimes, during unit testing, we would have to stub dependencies with some dummy data, and this can be done by mocking the dependencies. We will show you how to do this using a mocking library. We will also show you how to write fixtures to populate test data and then how you can test the behavior of your application by integrating different APIs and testing them together. We will cover the following recipes:

- Behavioral testing using Cucumber
- Unit testing of an API using JUnit
- Unit testing by mocking dependencies
- Using fixtures to populate data for testing
- Integration testing

Introduction

Well-tested code provides peace of mind to the developer. If you get a feeling that writing a test for the new method you are developing is too much of an overhead, then you usually don't get it right the first time. You have to test your method anyway, and it is less time-consuming in the long run to set up or write a unit test than to build and start up the application many times—every time the code changes and for every logical pass through.

One of the reasons we often feel pressed for time is that we do not include in our estimates the time needed for writing the test. One reason is that we sometimes just forget to do it. Another reason is that we shy away from giving a higher estimate because we do not want to be perceived as not skilled enough. Whatever the reason, it happens. Only after years of experience, we learn to include tests in our estimates and earn enough respect and clout to be able to assert publicly that doing things right requires more time up front, but saves much more time in the long run. Besides, doing it right leads to a robust code with far less stress, which means a better quality of life overall.

Another advantage of testing early—before the main code is completed—is that the code weaknesses are discovered during the phase when fixing it is easy. If need be, you can even restructure code for better testability.

If you are still not convinced, make note of the date when you read this and check back every year until this advice becomes obvious to you. Then, please share your experiences with others. This is how humanity makes progress—by passing knowledge from one generation to the next.

Methodologically, the content of this chapter is applicable to other languages and professions too, but the examples are written primarily for Java developers.

Behavioral testing using Cucumber

The following are three recurring complaints of programmers:

- Lack of requirements
- Ambiguity of requirements
- Requirements are changing all the time

There are quite a few recommendations and processes that help alleviate these problems, but none of them were able to eliminate them completely. The most successful, in our opinion, was an agile process methodology in conjunction with BDD, using Cucumber or another similar framework. Short iterations allow quick adjustment and coordination between businesses (customers) and programmers, while BDD with Cucumber captures the requirements in a formal language called Gherkin, but without the overhead of maintaining extensive documentation.

The requirements written in Gherkin have to be broken into **features**. Each feature is stored in a file with a `.feature` extension and consists of one or more **scenarios** that describe different aspects of the feature. Each scenario consists of steps that describe user actions or just input data and how the application responds to it.

A programmer implements the necessary application functionality and then uses it to implement the scenarios in one or many `.java` files. Each step is implemented in a method.

After their implementation, the scenarios become a suite of tests that can be as fine-grained as a unit test or as high-level as an integration test, and anything in between. It all depends on who writes the scenario and how the application code is structured. If the authors of the scenarios are business folk, the scenarios tend to be higher-level use cases. But if the application is structured so that each scenario (with possibly multiple permutations of input data) is implemented as a method, then it serves effectively as a unit test. Alternatively, if a scenario spans several methods or even subsystems, it can serve as an integration test, while programmers may complement it with finer-grained (more unit test-like) scenarios. Later, after the code is delivered, all the scenarios can serve as regression tests.

The price you pay is an overhead of the scenarios, maintenance, but the reward is the formal system that captures the requirements and provides an assurance that the application does exactly what is required. That said, one qualification is in order: capturing scenarios for the UI layer is usually more problematic because the UI tends to change more often, especially at the beginning of application development. Yet, as soon as UI has stabilized, the requirements to it can also be captured in Cucumber scenarios using Selenium or a similar framework.

How to do it...

1. Install Cucumber. The Cucumber installation is nothing more than adding the framework to the project as a Maven dependency. Since we are going to add several Cucumber JAR files and all of them have to be of the same version, it makes sense to add the `cucumber.version` property in `pom.xml` first:

   ```
   <properties>
       <cucumber.version>3.0.2</cucumber.version>
   </properties>
   ```

Now we can add the Cucumber main JAR file in `pom.xml` as a dependency:

```
<dependency>
    <groupId>io.cucumber</groupId>
    <artifactId>cucumber-java</artifactId>
    <version>${cucumber.version}</version>
    <scope>test</scope>
</dependency>
```

Alternatively, if you prefer a fluent stream-based style of coding, you can add a different Cucumber main JAR file:

```
<dependency>
    <groupId>io.cucumber</groupId>
    <artifactId>cucumber-java8</artifactId>
    <version>${cucumber.version}</version>
    <scope>test</scope>
</dependency>
```

If your project does not have JUnit set up as a dependency yet, you may add it as follows along with another `cucumber-junit` JAR file:

```
<dependency>
    <groupId>junit</groupId>
    <artifactId>junit</artifactId>
    <version>4.12</version>
    <scope>test</scope>
</dependency>
<dependency>
    <groupId>io.cucumber</groupId>
    <artifactId>cucumber-junit</artifactId>
    <version>${cucumber.version}</version>
    <scope>test</scope>
</dependency>
```

The above is necessary if you plan to take advantage of JUnit assertions. Note that, at the time of writing, Cucumber does not support JUnit 5.

Alternatively, you can use assertions from TestNG (`https://testng.org`):

```
<dependency>
    <groupId>org.testng</groupId>
    <artifactId>testng</artifactId>
    <version>6.14.2</version>
    <scope>test</scope>
</dependency>
<dependency>
    <groupId>io.cucumber</groupId>
```

```
            <artifactId>cucumber-testng</artifactId>
            <version>${cucumber.version}</version>
            <scope>test</scope>
        </dependency>
```

As you can see, in this case, you need to add the `cucumber-testng` JAR file instead of the `cucumber-junit` JAR file. TestNG offers a rich variety of assertion methods, including deep collections and other object comparisons.

2. Run Cucumber. The `cucumber-junit` JAR file also provides an `@RunWith` annotation that designates a class as a test runner:

```
package com.packt.cookbook.ch16_testing;

import cucumber.api.CucumberOptions;
import cucumber.api.junit.Cucumber;
import org.junit.runner.RunWith;

@RunWith(Cucumber.class)
public class RunScenariousTest {
}
```

Execution of the preceding class will execute all scenarios in the same package where the runner is located. Cucumber reads each `.feature` file and the scenarios in it. For each step of each scenario, it tries to find its implementation in the same package as the runner and the `.feature` file. It executes each implemented step in the sequence they are listed in a scenario.

3. Create a `.feature` file. As we have mentioned already, a `.feature` file contains one or more scenarios. The name of the file does not mean anything for Cucumber. The content of the file starts with the `Feature` keyword (with the colon : after it). The following text describes the feature and, similar to the filename, does not mean anything to Cucumber. The feature description ends when the `Scenario` keyword (with the colon : after it) starts a new line. That is when the first scenario description begins. Here is an example:

```
Feature: Vehicle speed calculation
    The calculations should be made based on the assumption
    that a vehicle starts moving, and driving conditions are
    always the same.

Scenario: Calculate speed
    This the happy path that demonstrates the main case
```

The scenario description ends when one of the following keywords starts a new line: `Given`, `When`, `Then`, `And`, or `But`. Each of these keywords, when it starts a new line, indicates the beginning of a step definition. For Cucumber, such a keyword means nothing except the beginning of the step definition. But for humans, it is easier to read if the scenario starts with the keyword `Given`—the step that describes the initial state of the system—prerequisite. Several other steps (prerequisites) may follow; each step starts with a new line and the keyword `And` or `But`, for example, as follows:

```
Given the vehicle has 246 hp engine and weighs 4000 pounds
```

After that, the group of steps describes the actions or events. For human readability, the group typically starts with the `When` keyword at a new line. Other actions or events follow, and each starts with a new line and the `And` or `But` keyword. It is recommended to keep the number of steps in this group to a minimum, so each scenario is well focused, for example, as follows:

```
When the application calculates its speed after 10.0 sec
```

The last group of steps in a scenario starts with the `Then` keyword in the new line. They describe the expected results. As in the previous two groups of steps, each subsequent step in this group starts with a new line and the `And` or `But` keyword too, for example, as follows:

```
Then the result should be 117.0 mph
```

To summarize the previous, the feature looks as follows:

```
Feature: Vehicle speed calculation
    The calculations should be made based on the assumption
    that a vehicle starts moving, and driving conditions are
    always the same.

Scenario: Calculate speed
    This the happy path that demonstrates the main case

    Given the vehicle has 246 hp engine and weighs 4000 pounds
    When the application calculates its speed after 10.0 sec
    Then the result should be 117.0 mph
```

We put it in the `CalculateSpeed.feature` file in the following folder: `src/test/resources/com/packt/cookbook/Chapter14_testing,`

Note that, it has to be in the `test/resources` folder and the path to it has to match the package name where the `RunScenariosTest` test runner belongs.

The test runner is executed as any JUnit test, using the `mvn test` command, for example, or just by running it in JDE. When executed, it looks for all `.feature` files in the same package (Maven copies them from the `resources` folder to the `target/classes` folder, hence setting them on the classpath). It then reads the steps of each scenario sequentially and tries to find the implementation of each step in the same package.

As we have mentioned already, names of the file do not have any meaning for Cucumber. It looks for the `.feature` extension first, then finds the first step and, in the same directory, tries to find a class that has a method in it annotated by the same wording as the step.

To illustrate what it means, let's run the created feature by executing the test runner. The results are going to be as follows:

```
cucumber.runtime.junit.UndefinedThrowable:
The step "the vehicle has 246 hp engine and weighs 4000 pounds"
                                                    is undefined
cucumber.runtime.junit.UndefinedThrowable:
The step "the application calculates its speed after 10.0 sec"
                                                    is undefined
cucumber.runtime.junit.UndefinedThrowable:
The step "the result should be 117.0 mph" is undefined

Undefined scenarios:
com/packt/cookbook/ch16_testing/CalculateSpeed.feature:6
                                          # Calculate speed

1 Scenarios (1 undefined)
3 Steps (3 undefined)
0m0.081s


You can implement missing steps with the snippets below:

@Given("the vehicle has {int} hp engine and weighs {int} pounds")
public void the_vehicle_has_hp_engine_and_weighs_pounds(Integer
                                        int1, Integer int2) {
  // Write code here that turns the phrase above
  // into concrete actions
  throw new PendingException();
}

@When("the application calculates its speed after {double} sec")
```

```
public void the_application_calculates_its_speed_after_sec(Double
                                                           double1)
{
 // Write code here that turns the phrase above
 // into concrete actions
 throw new PendingException();
}

@Then("the result should be {double} mph")
public void the_result_should_be_mph(Double double1) {
 // Write code here that turns the phrase above
 // into concrete actions
 throw new PendingException();
}
```

As you can see, Cucumber not only tells us which and how many features and scenarios are `undefined`, it even provides a possible way to implement them. Please note how Cucumber allows passing in parameters using a type in curly braces. The following are built-in types: `int`, `float`, `word`, `string`, `biginteger`, `bigdecimal`, `byte`, `short`, `long`, and `double`. The difference between `word` and `string` is that the latter allows spaces. But Cucumber also allows us to define custom types.

4. Write and run step definitions. Cucumber's term `undefined` may be confusing because we did define the feature and scenarios. We just did not implement them. So, the `undefined` in the Cucumber message actually means `not implemented`.

   To start the implementation, we first create a class, `CalculateSpeedSteps`, in the same directory with the test runner. The class name has no meaning for Cucumber, so you can name it any other way you prefer. Then, we copy the three methods suggested previously with annotations and put them in that class:

```
package com.packt.cookbook.ch16_testing;

import cucumber.api.PendingException;
import cucumber.api.java.en.Given;
import cucumber.api.java.en.Then;
import cucumber.api.java.en.When;

public class Calc {
  @Given("the vehicle has {int} hp engine and weighs {int}
pounds")
  public void the_vehicle_has_hp_engine_and_weighs_pounds(Integer
```

```
                                          int1, Integer int2)
{
    // Write code here that turns the phrase above
    // into concrete actions
    throw new PendingException();
}

@When("the application calculates its speed after {double} sec")
public void
the_application_calculates_its_speed_after_sec(Double
                                          double1)
{
    // Write code here that turns the phrase above
    // into concrete actions
    throw new PendingException();
}

@Then("the result should be {double} mph")
  public void the_result_should_be_mph(Double double1) {
    // Write code here that turns the phrase above
    // into concrete actions
    throw new PendingException();
  }
}
```

If we execute the test runner again, the output will be as follows:

```
cucumber.api.PendingException: TODO: implement me
 at
com.packt.cookbook.ch16_testing.CalculateSpeedSteps.the_vehicle
_has_hp_engine_and_weighs_pounds(CalculateSpeedSteps.java:13)
 at *.the vehicle has 246 hp engine and weighs 4000
pounds(com/packt/cookbook/ch16_testing/CalculateSpeed.feature:9)

Pending scenarios:
com/packt/cookbook/ch16_testing/CalculateSpeed.feature:6
                                          # Calculate speed

1 Scenarios (1 pending)
3 Steps (2 skipped, 1 pending)
0m0.055s

cucumber.api.PendingException: TODO: implement me
 at
com.packt.cookbook.ch16_testing.CalculateSpeedSteps.the_vehicle
has_hp_engine_and_weighs_pounds(CalculateSpeedSteps.java:13)
 at *.the vehicle has 246 hp engine and weighs 4000
pounds(com/packt/cookbook/ch16_testing/CalculateSpeed.feature:9)
```

The runner stopped executing at the first `PendingException`, so the other two steps were skipped. If BDD methodology is applied systematically, then the feature is written first—before any code of the application is written. So, every feature produces the previous result.

As the application gets developed, each new feature is implemented and does not fail anymore.

How it works...

Immediately after the requirements are expressed as features, the application gets implemented feature by feature. For example, we could start by creating the `Vehicle` class:

```
class Vehicle {
    private int wp, hp;
    public Vehicle(int weightPounds, int hp){
        this.wp = weightPounds;
        this.hp = hp;
    }
    protected double getSpeedMpH(double timeSec){
        double v = 2.0 * this.hp * 746 ;
        v = v*timeSec * 32.174 / this.wp;
        return Math.round(Math.sqrt(v) * 0.68);
    }
}
```

Then the steps of the first feature shown previously can be implemented as follows:

```
package com.packt.cookbook.ch16_testing;

import cucumber.api.java.en.Given;
import cucumber.api.java.en.Then;
import cucumber.api.java.en.When;
import static org.junit.Assert.assertEquals;

public class CalculateSpeedSteps {
    private Vehicle vehicle;
    private double speed;

    @Given("the vehicle has {int} hp engine and weighs {int} pounds")
    public void the_vehicle_has_hp_engine_and_weighs_pounds(Integer
                                          wp, Integer hp) {
        vehicle = new Vehicle(wp, hp);
    }
```

```
@When("the application calculates its speed after {double} sec")
public void
      the_application_calculates_its_speed_after_sec(Double t) {
      speed = vehicle.getSpeedMpH(t);
}

@Then("the result should be {double} mph")
public void the_result_should_be_mph(Double speed) {
      assertEquals(speed, this.speed, 0.0001 * speed);
}
}
```

If we run the test runner in the `com.packt.cookbook.ch16_testing`
package again, the steps will be executed successfully.

Now, if the requirements change and the `.feature` file is modified correspondingly,
the test will fail, unless the application code is changed too and matches the
requirements. That is the power of BDD. It keeps requirements in sync with the code.
It also allows the Cucumber tests to serve as regression tests. If the code changes
violate the requirements, the test fails.

Unit testing of an API using JUnit

According to Wikipedia, more than 30% of the projects hosted on GitHub include
JUnit—one of a family of unit testing frameworks collectively known as xUnit that
originated with SUnit. It is linked as a JAR at compile time and resides (since JUnit 4)
in the `org.junit` package.

In object-oriented programming, a unit can be an entire class but could be an
individual method. We've found the last part—a unit as an individual method—the
most useful in practice. It serves as the basis for the examples of the recipes of this
chapter.

Getting ready

At the time of writing, the latest stable version of JUnit is 4.12, which can be used by adding the following Maven dependency to the `pom.xml` project level:

```
<dependency>
  <groupId>junit</groupId>
  <artifactId>junit</artifactId>
  <version>4.12</version>
  <scope>test</scope>
</dependency>
```

After this, you can write your first JUnit test. Let's assume you have the `Vehicle` class created in the `src/main/java/com/packt/cookbook.ch02_oop.a_classes` folder (this is the code we discussed in `Chapter 2`, *Fast Track to OOP - Classes and Interfaces*):

```
package com.packt.cookbook.ch02_oop.a_classes;
public class Vehicle {
  private int weightPounds;
  private Engine engine;
  public Vehicle(int weightPounds, Engine engine) {
    this.weightPounds = weightPounds;
    if(engine == null){
      throw new RuntimeException("Engine value is not set.");
    }
    this.engine = engine;
  }
  protected double getSpeedMph(double timeSec){
    double v = 2.0*this.engine.getHorsePower()*746;
    v = v*timeSec*32.174/this.weightPounds;
    return Math.round(Math.sqrt(v)*0.68);
  }
}
```

Now you can create the `src/test/java/com/packt/cookbook.ch02_oop.a_classes` folder and a new file in it called `VehicleTest.java`, which contains the `VehicleTest` class:

```
package com.packt.cookbook.ch02_oop.a_classes;
import org.junit.Test;
public class VehicleTest {
  @Test
  public void testGetSpeedMph(){
    System.out.println("Hello!" + " I am your first test method!");
  }
}
```

Run it using your favorite IDE or just with the `mvn test` command. You will see output that will include the following:

```
T E S T S

Running com.packt.cookbook.ch02_oop.a_classes.VehicleTest
Hello! I am your first test method!
Tests run: 1, Failures: 0, Errors: 0, Skipped: 0, Time elapsed: 0.037 sec

Results :

Tests run: 1, Failures: 0, Errors: 0, Skipped: 0
```

Congratulations! You have created your first test class. It does not test anything yet, but it is an important setup—the overhead that is necessary for doing things the right way. In the next section, we will start with the actual testing.

How to do it...

Let's look at the `Vehicle` class closer. Testing the getters would be of little value, but we can still do it, making sure that the value passed to the constructor is returned by the corresponding getter. The exception in the constructor belongs to the must-test features as well as the `getSpeedMph()` method. There is also an object of the `Engine` class that has the `getHorsePower()` method. Can it return `null`? To answer this question, let's look at the `Engine` class:

```
public class Engine {
  private int horsePower;
  public int getHorsePower() {
    return horsePower;
  }
  public void setHorsePower(int horsePower) {
    this.horsePower = horsePower;
  }
}
```

The `getHorsePower()` method cannot return `null`. The `horsePower` field will be initiated to the value zero by default if not set explicitly by the `setHorsePower()` method. But returning a negative value is a definite possibility, which in turn can cause problems for the `Math.sqrt()` function of the `getSpeedMph()` method. Should we make sure that the horsepower value will never be negative? It depends on how limited the method's usage is and the source of the input data for it.

Similar considerations are applicable to the value of the `weightPounds` field of the `Vehicle` class. It can stop the application with `ArithmeticException` caused by the division by zero in the `getSpeedMph()` method.

However, in practice, there is little chance that the values of an engine's horsepower and vehicle weight will be negative or close to zero, so we will assume this and will not add these checks to the code.

Such analysis is the daily routine and the background thoughts of every developer, and that is the first step in the right direction. The second step is to capture all these thoughts and doubts in the unit tests and verify the assumptions.

Let's go back to the test class we have created. As you may have noticed, the `@Test` annotation makes a certain method a test method. This means it will be run by your IDE or Maven every time you issue a command to run tests. The method can be named any way you like, but a best practice advises to indicate which method (of the `Vehicle` class, in this case) you are testing. So, the format usually looks like `test<methodname><scenario>`, where `scenario` indicates a particular test case: a happy path, a failure, or some other condition you would like to test. In the first example, though we do not use the suffix, just to keep the code simple. We will show examples of methods that test other scenarios later.

In a test, you can call the application method you are testing, provide it with the data, and assert the result. You can create your own assertions (methods that compare the actual results with the expected ones) or you can use assertions provided by JUnit. To do the latter, just add the `static` import:

```
import static org.junit.Assert.assertEquals;
```

If you use a modern IDE, you can type `import static org.junit.Assert` and see how many different assertions are available (or go to JUnit's API documentation and see it there). There are a dozen or more overloaded methods available: `assertArrayEquals()`, `assertEquals()`, `assertNotEquals()`, `assertNull()`, `assertNotNull()`, `assertSame()`, `assertNotSame()`, `assertFalse()`, `assertTrue()`, `assertThat()`, and `fail()`. It would be helpful if you spend a few minutes reading what these methods do. You can also guess their purpose by their name. Here is an example of the usage of the `assertEquals()` method:

```
import org.junit.Test;
import static org.junit.Assert.assertEquals;
public class VehicleTest {
  @Test
  public void testGetSpeedMph(){
    System.out.println("Hello!" + " I am your first test method!");
    assertEquals(4, "Hello".length());
  }
}
```

We compare the actual length of the word `Hello` and the expected length of 4. We know that the correct number would be 5, but we would like the test to fail to demonstrate the failing behavior. If you run the preceding test, you'll get the following result:

```
Running com.packt.cookbook.ch02_oop.a_classes.VehicleTest
Hello! I am your first test method!
Tests run: 1, Failures: 1, Errors: 0, Skipped: 0, Time elapsed: 0.04 sec <<< FAILURE!
testGetSpeedMph(com.packt.cookbook.ch02_oop.a_classes.VehicleTest)  Time elapsed: 0.006 sec
java.lang.AssertionError: expected:<4> but was:<5>
```

As you can see, the last line tells you what went wrong: the expected value was 4, while the actual was 5. Say you switch the order of the parameters like this:

```
assertEquals("Assert Hello length:","Hello".length(), 4);
```

The result will be as follows:

```
Running com.packt.cookbook.ch02_oop.a_classes.VehicleTest
Hello! I am your first test method!
Tests run: 1, Failures: 1, Errors: 0, Skipped: 0, Time elapsed: 0.041 sec <<< FAILURE!
testGetSpeedMph(com.packt.cookbook.ch02_oop.a_classes.VehicleTest)  Time elapsed: 0.007 sec
java.lang.AssertionError: expected:<5> but was:<4>
```

The last message is misleading now.

 It is important to remember that, in each of the asserting methods, the parameter with the expected value is located (in the signature of an assertion) **before** the actual one.

After the test is written, you will do something else, and months later, you will probably forget what each assertion actually evaluated. But it may well be that one day the test will fail (because the application code was changed). You will see the test method name, expected value, and the actual value, but you will have to dig through the code to figure out which of the assertions failed (there are often several of them in each test method). You will probably be forced to add a debug statement and run the test several times in order to figure it out.

To help you avoid this extra digging, each of the JUnit assertions allows you to add a message that describes the particular assertion. For example, run this version of the test:

```java
public class VehicleTest {
  @Test
  public void testGetSpeedMph(){
    System.out.println("Hello!" + " I am your first test method!");
    assertEquals("Assert Hello length:", 4, "Hello".length());
  }
}
```

If you do this, the result will be much more readable:

```
Running com.packt.cookbook.ch02_oop.a_classes.VehicleTest
Hello! I am your first test method!
Tests run: 1, Failures: 1, Errors: 0, Skipped: 0, Time elapsed: 0.04 sec <<< FAILURE!
testGetSpeedMph(com.packt.cookbook.ch02_oop.a_classes.VehicleTest)  Time elapsed: 0.006 sec
java.lang.AssertionError: Assert Hello length: expected:<4> but was:<5>
```

To complete this demonstration, we change the expected value to 5:

```java
    assertEquals("Assert Hello length:", 5, "Hello".length());
```

Now the test results show no failures:

```
Running com.packt.cookbook.ch02_oop.a_classes.VehicleTest
Hello! I am your first test method!
Tests run: 1, Failures: 0, Errors: 0, Skipped: 0, Time elapsed: 0.038 sec
```

How it works...

Equipped with the basic understanding of the usage of the JUnit framework, we can now write a real test method for the main case of the calculation of the speed of a vehicle with a certain weight and an engine of certain horsepower to determine. We take the formula we use for the speed calculations and calculate the expected value manually first. For example, if the vehicle has an engine of 246 hp and weight of 4,000 lb, then in 10 seconds, its speed can reach 117 mph. Since the speed is of the `double` type, we will use the assertion with some delta. Otherwise, two `double` values may never be equal due to the way a `double` value is represented in the computer. Here is the assertion method of the `org.junit.Assert` class:

```
void assertEquals(String message, double expected,
                      double actual, double delta)
```

The `delta` value is allowable precision. The resultant implementation of the `test` method will look as follows:

```
@Test
public void testGetSpeedMph(){
   double timeSec = 10.0;
   int engineHorsePower = 246;
   int vehicleWeightPounds = 4000;

   Engine engine = new Engine();
   engine.setHorsePower(engineHorsePower);

   Vehicle vehicle = new Vehicle(vehicleWeightPounds, engine);
   double speed = vehicle.getSpeedMph(timeSec);
   assertEquals("Assert vehicle (" + engineHorsePower
           + " hp, " + vehicleWeightPounds + " lb) speed in "
           + timeSec + " sec: ", 117, speed, 0.001 * speed);
}
```

As you can see, we have decided that one-tenth of one percent of the value is a good enough precision for our purposes. If we run the preceding test, the output will be as follows:

```
Running com.packt.cookbook.ch02_oop.a_classes.VehicleTest
Tests run: 1, Failures: 0, Errors: 0, Skipped: 0, Time elapsed: 0.081 sec
```

To make sure the test is working, we can set the expected value to 119 mph (more than one percent different from the actual one) and run the test again. The result will be as follows:

```
Running com.packt.cookbook.ch02_oop.a_classes.VehicleTest
Tests run: 1, Failures: 1, Errors: 0, Skipped: 0, Time elapsed: 0.075 sec <<< FAILURE!
testGetSpeedMph(com.packt.cookbook.ch02_oop.a_classes.VehicleTest)  Time elapsed: 0.045 sec  <<< FAILURE!
java.lang.AssertionError: Assert vehicle (246 hp, 4000 lb) speed in 10.0 sec:  expected:<119.0> but was:<117.0>
```

We change the expected value back to 117 and continue writing other test cases we discussed while analyzing the code.

Let's make sure that the exception is thrown when expected. To do that, we add another import:

```
import static org.junit.Assert.fail;
```

Then, we can write the code that tests the case when the value passed in the constructor of the `Vehicle` class is null (so the exception should be thrown):

```
@Test
public void testGetSpeedMphException(){
  int vehicleWeightPounds = 4000;
  Engine engine = null;
  try {
    Vehicle vehicle = new Vehicle(vehicleWeightPounds, engine);
    fail("Exception was not thrown");
  } catch (RuntimeException ex) {}
}
```

This test runs successfully, which means that the `Vehicle` constructor had thrown an exception and the code has never reached the line:

```
fail("Exception was not thrown");
```

To make sure that the test works correctly, we temporarily pass a non-null value into the `Vehicle` constructor:

```
Engine engine = new Engine();
```

Then, we observe the output:

```
Running com.packt.cookbook.ch02_oop.a_classes.VehicleTest
Tests run: 2, Failures: 1, Errors: 0, Skipped: 0, Time elapsed: 0.074 sec <<< FAILURE!
testGetSpeedMphException(com.packt.cookbook.ch02_oop.a_classes.VehicleTest)  Time elapsed: 0.004 sec
java.lang.AssertionError: Exception was not thrown
```

This way, we get a level of confidence that our test works as expected. Alternatively, we can create another test that fails when an exception is thrown:

```
@Test
public void testGetSpeedMphException(){
   int vehicleWeightPounds = 4000;
   Engine engine = new Engine();
   try {
     Vehicle vehicle = new Vehicle(vehicleWeightPounds, engine);
   } catch (RuntimeException ex) {
     fail("Exception was thrown");
   }
}
```

The best way to write such tests is in the process of writing application code, so you can test the code as it grows in complexity. Otherwise, especially in more complex code, you might have problems debugging it after all of the code is written already.

There are quite a few other annotations and JUnit features that can be helpful to you, so please refer to the JUnit documentation for a more in-depth understanding of all the framework capabilities.

Unit testing by mocking dependencies

Writing a unit test requires controlling all the input data. In case a method receives its input from other objects, there arises a need to limit the depth of testing so that each layer can be tested in isolation as a unit. This is when the need for mocking the lower level comes into focus.

Mocking can be done not only vertically, but also horizontally at the same level. If a method is big and complicated, you might consider breaking it into several smaller methods so you can test only one of them while mocking the others. This is another advantage of unit testing code along with its development; it is easier to redesign code for better testability at the earlier stages of its development.

Getting ready

Mocking other methods and classes is straightforward. Coding to an interface (as described in Chapter 2, *Fast Track to OOP - Classes and Interfaces*) makes it much easier, although there are mocking frameworks that allow you to mock classes that do not implement any interface (we will see examples of such framework usage in the next section of this recipe). Also, using object and method factories helps you create test-specific implementations of such factories so they can generate objects with methods that return the expected hardcoded values.

For example, in Chapter 4, *Going Functional*, we introduced FactoryTraffic, which produced one or many objects of TrafficUnit. In a real system, this factory would draw data from some external system. Using the real system as the source could complicate the code setup. As you could see, to get around this problem, we mocked the data by generating it according to the distribution that somewhat resembles the real one: a bit more cars than trucks, the weight of the vehicle depending on the type of the car, the number of passengers and weight of the payload, and similar. What is important for such a simulation is that the range of values (minimum and maximum) should reflect those coming from the real system, so the application would be tested on the full range of possible real data.

The important constraint for mocking code is that it should not be too complicated. Otherwise, its maintenance would require an overhead that would either decrease the team productivity or decrease the test coverage.

How to do it...

The mock of FactoryTraffic may look like the following:

```
public class FactoryTraffic {
  public static List<TrafficUnit> generateTraffic(int
    trafficUnitsNumber, Month month, DayOfWeek dayOfWeek,
    int hour, String country, String city, String trafficLight){
    List<TrafficUnit> tms = new ArrayList();
    for (int i = 0; i < trafficUnitsNumber; i++) {
      TrafficUnit trafficUnit =
        FactoryTraffic.getOneUnit(month, dayOfWeek,  hour, country,
                                  city, trafficLight);
      tms.add(trafficUnit);
    }
    return tms;
  }
}
```

It assembles a collection of `TrafficUnit` objects. In a real system, these objects would be created from the rows of the result of some database query, for example. But in our case, we just hardcode the values:

```
public static TrafficUnit getOneUnit(Month month,
             DayOfWeek dayOfWeek, int hour, String country,
             String city, String trafficLight) {
   double r0 = Math.random();
   VehicleType vehicleType = r0 < 0.4 ? VehicleType.CAR :
   (r0 > 0.6 ? VehicleType.TRUCK : VehicleType.CAB_CREW);
   double r1 = Math.random();
   double r2 = Math.random();
   double r3 = Math.random();
   return new TrafficModelImpl(vehicleType, gen(4,1),
             gen(3300,1000), gen(246,100), gen(4000,2000),
             (r1 > 0.5 ? RoadCondition.WET : RoadCondition.DRY),
             (r2 > 0.5 ? TireCondition.WORN : TireCondition.NEW),
             r1 > 0.5 ? ( r3 > 0.5 ? 63 : 50 ) : 63 );
}
```

As you can see, we used a random number generator to pick up the value from a range for each of the parameters. The range is in line with the ranges of the real data. This code is very simple and it does not require much maintenance, but it provides the application with the flow of data similar to the real one.

You can use another technique. For example, let's revisit the `VechicleTest` class. Instead of creating a real `Engine` object, we can mock it using one of the mocking frameworks. In this case, we use Mockito. Here is the Maven dependency for it:

```
<dependency>
   <groupId>org.mockito</groupId>
   <artifactId>mockito-core</artifactId>
   <version>2.7.13</version>
   <scope>test</scope>
</dependency>
```

 The test method now looks like this (the two lines that were changed are highlighted):

```
@Test
public void testGetSpeedMph(){
   double timeSec = 10.0;
   int engineHorsePower = 246;
   int vehicleWeightPounds = 4000;

   Engine engine = Mockito.mock(Engine.class);
   Mockito.when(engine.getHorsePower()).thenReturn(engineHorsePower);
```

```
    Vehicle vehicle =  new Vehicle(vehicleWeightPounds, engine);
    double speed = vehicle.getSpeedMph(timeSec);
    assertEquals("Assert vehicle (" + engineHorsePower
                + " hp, " + vehicleWeightPounds + " lb) speed in "
                + timeSec + " sec: ", 117, speed, 0.001 * speed);
  }
```

As you can see, we instruct the `mock` object to return a fixed value when the `getHorsePower()` method is called. We can even go as far as creating a mock object for the method we want to test:

```
Vehicle vehicleMock = Mockito.mock(Vehicle.class);
Mockito.when(vehicleMock.getSpeedMph(10)).thenReturn(30d);

double speed = vehicleMock.getSpeedMph(10);
System.out.println(speed);
```

So, it always returns the same value:

However, this would defeat the purpose of testing because we would like to test the code that calculates the speed, not to mock it.

For testing a stream's pipeline methods, yet another technique can be used. Let's assume we need to test the `trafficByLane()` method in the `TrafficDensity1` class (we are going to have `TrafficDensity2` and `TrafficDensity3`, too):

```
public class TrafficDensity1 {
  public Integer[] trafficByLane(Stream<TrafficUnit> stream,
  int trafficUnitsNumber, double timeSec,
  SpeedModel speedModel, double[] speedLimitByLane) {

    int lanesCount = speedLimitByLane.length;

    Map<Integer, Integer> trafficByLane = stream
      .limit(trafficUnitsNumber)
      .map(TrafficUnitWrapper::new)
      .map(tuw -> tuw.setSpeedModel(speedModel))
      .map(tuw -> tuw.calcSpeed(timeSec))
      .map(speed ->  countByLane(lanesCount, speedLimitByLane, speed))
      .collect(Collectors.groupingBy(CountByLane::getLane,
              Collectors.summingInt(CountByLane::getCount)));

    for(int i = 1; i <= lanesCount; i++){
```

```
      trafficByLane.putIfAbsent(i, 0);
    }
    return trafficByLane.values()
      .toArray(new Integer[lanesCount]);
  }

  private CountByLane countByLane(int lanesCount,
              double[] speedLimit, double speed) {
    for(int i = 1; i <= lanesCount; i++){
      if(speed <= speedLimit[i - 1]){
        return new CountByLane(1, i);
      }
    }
    return new CountByLane(1, lanesCount);
  }
}
```

It uses two support classes:

```
private class CountByLane{
  int count, lane;
  private CountByLane(int count, int lane){
    this.count = count;
    this.lane = lane;
  }
  public int getLane() { return lane; }
  public int getCount() { return count; }
}
```

It also uses the following:

```
private static class TrafficUnitWrapper {
  private Vehicle vehicle;
  private TrafficUnit trafficUnit;
  public TrafficUnitWrapper(TrafficUnit trafficUnit){
    this.vehicle = FactoryVehicle.build(trafficUnit);
    this.trafficUnit = trafficUnit;
  }
  public TrafficUnitWrapper setSpeedModel(SpeedModel speedModel) {
    this.vehicle.setSpeedModel(speedModel);
    return this;
  }
  public double calcSpeed(double timeSec) {
    double speed = this.vehicle.getSpeedMph(timeSec);
    return Math.round(speed * this.trafficUnit.getTraction());
  }
}
```

We demonstrated the use of such support classes in Chapter 3, *Modular Programming,* while talking about streams. Now we realize that testing this class might not be easy.

Because the SpeedModel object is an input parameter for the trafficByLane() method, we could test its getSpeedMph() method in isolation:

```
@Test
public void testSpeedModel(){
  double timeSec = 10.0;
  int engineHorsePower = 246;
  int vehicleWeightPounds = 4000;
  double speed = getSpeedModel().getSpeedMph(timeSec,
                vehicleWeightPounds, engineHorsePower);
  assertEquals("Assert vehicle (" + engineHorsePower
                + " hp, " + vehicleWeightPounds + " lb) speed in "
                + timeSec + " sec: ", 117, speed, 0.001 * speed);
}

private SpeedModel getSpeedModel(){
  //FactorySpeedModel possibly
}
```

Refer to the following code:

```
public class FactorySpeedModel {
  public static SpeedModel generateSpeedModel(TrafficUnit
trafficUnit){
    return new SpeedModelImpl(trafficUnit);
  }
  private static class SpeedModelImpl implements SpeedModel{
    private TrafficUnit trafficUnit;
    private SpeedModelImpl(TrafficUnit trafficUnit){
      this.trafficUnit = trafficUnit;
    }
    public double getSpeedMph(double timeSec,
                          int weightPounds, int horsePower) {
      double traction = trafficUnit.getTraction();
      double v = 2.0 * horsePower * 746
              * timeSec * 32.174 / weightPounds;
      return Math.round(Math.sqrt(v) * 0.68 * traction);
    }
  }
}
```

As you can see, the current implementation of `FactorySpeedModel` requires the `TrafficUnit` object in order to get the traction value. To get around this problem, we can modify the preceding code and remove the `SpeedModel` dependency on `TrafficUnit`. We can do it by moving the traction application to the `calcSpeed()` method. The new version of `FactorySpeedModel` can look like this:

```
public class FactorySpeedModel {
  public static SpeedModel generateSpeedModel(TrafficUnit
                                             trafficUnit) {
    return new SpeedModelImpl(trafficUnit);
  }
  public static SpeedModel getSpeedModel(){
    return SpeedModelImpl.getSpeedModel();
  }
  private static class SpeedModelImpl implements SpeedModel{
    private TrafficUnit trafficUnit;
    private SpeedModelImpl(TrafficUnit trafficUnit){
      this.trafficUnit = trafficUnit;
    }
    public double getSpeedMph(double timeSec,
                    int weightPounds, int horsePower) {
      double speed = getSpeedModel()
              .getSpeedMph(timeSec, weightPounds, horsePower);
      return Math.round(speed *trafficUnit.getTraction());
    }
    public static SpeedModel getSpeedModel(){
      return  (t, wp, hp) -> {
        double weightPower = 2.0 * hp * 746 * 32.174 / wp;
        return Math.round(Math.sqrt(t * weightPower) * 0.68);
      };
    }
  }
}
```

The test method can now be implemented as follows:

```
@Test
public void testSpeedModel(){
  double timeSec = 10.0;
  int engineHorsePower = 246;
  int vehicleWeightPounds = 4000;
  double speed = FactorySpeedModel.generateSpeedModel()
              .getSpeedMph(timeSec, vehicleWeightPounds,
                          engineHorsePower);
  assertEquals("Assert vehicle (" + engineHorsePower
              + " hp, " + vehicleWeightPounds + " lb) speed in "
```

```
                      + timeSec + " sec: ", 117, speed, 0.001 * speed);
  }
```

However, the `calcSpeed()` method in `TrafficUnitWrapper` remains untested. We could test the `trafficByLane()` method as a whole:

```
@Test
public void testTrafficByLane() {
  TrafficDensity1 trafficDensity = new TrafficDensity1();
  double timeSec = 10.0;
  int trafficUnitsNumber = 120;
  double[] speedLimitByLane = {30, 50, 65};
  Integer[] expectedCountByLane = {30, 30, 60};
  Integer[] trafficByLane =
    trafficDensity.trafficByLane(getTrafficUnitStream2(
      trafficUnitsNumber), trafficUnitsNumber, timeSec,
      FactorySpeedModel.getSpeedModel(),speedLimitByLane);
  assertArrayEquals("Assert count of "
              + trafficUnitsNumber + " vehicles by "
              + speedLimitByLane.length +" lanes with speed limit "
              + Arrays.stream(speedLimitByLane)
                  .mapToObj(Double::toString)
                  .collect(Collectors.joining(", ")),
                  expectedCountByLane, trafficByLane);
  }
```

But this would require creating a stream of objects of `TrafficUnit` with fixed data:

```
TrafficUnit getTrafficUnit(int engineHorsePower,
                           int vehicleWeightPounds) {
  return new TrafficUnit() {
    @Override
    public Vehicle.VehicleType getVehicleType() {
      return Vehicle.VehicleType.TRUCK;
    }
    @Override
    public int getHorsePower() {return engineHorsePower;}
    @Override
    public int getWeightPounds() { return vehicleWeightPounds; }
    @Override
    public int getPayloadPounds() { return 0; }
    @Override
    public int getPassengersCount() { return 0; }
    @Override
    public double getSpeedLimitMph() { return 55; }
    @Override
    public double getTraction() { return 0.2; }
    @Override
```

```
    public SpeedModel.RoadCondition getRoadCondition(){return null;}
    @Override
    public SpeedModel.TireCondition getTireCondition(){return null;}
    @Override
    public int getTemperature() { return 0; }
  };
}
```

Such a solution does not provide a variety of test data for different vehicle types and other parameters. We need to revisit the design of the trafficByLane() method.

How it works...

If you look closely at the trafficByLane() method, you will notice that the problem is caused by the location of the calculation—inside the private class, TrafficUnitWrapper. We can move it out of there and create a new method, calcSpeed(), in the TrafficDensity class:

```
double calcSpeed(double timeSec) {
  double speed = this.vehicle.getSpeedMph(timeSec);
  return Math.round(speed * this.trafficUnit.getTraction());
}
```

Then, we can change its signature and include the Vehicle object and traction coefficient as parameters:

```
double calcSpeed(Vehicle vehicle, double traction, double timeSec){
  double speed = vehicle.getSpeedMph(timeSec);
  return Math.round(speed * traction);
}
```

Let's also add two methods to the TrafficUnitWrapper class (you will see in a moment why we need them):

```
public Vehicle getVehicle() { return vehicle; }
public double getTraction() { return trafficUnit.getTraction(); }
```

The preceding changes allow us to rewrite the stream pipeline as follows (the changed line is in bold):

```
Map<Integer, Integer> trafficByLane = stream
  .limit(trafficUnitsNumber)
  .map(TrafficUnitWrapper::new)
  .map(tuw -> tuw.setSpeedModel(speedModel))
  .map(tuw -> calcSpeed(tuw.getVehicle(), tuw.getTraction(), timeSec))
```

```
        .map(speed -> countByLane(lanesCount, speedLimitByLane, speed))
      .collect(Collectors.groupingBy(CountByLane::getLane,
            Collectors.summingInt(CountByLane::getCount)));
```

By making the `calcSpeed()` method protected and assuming that the `Vehicle` class is tested in its own test class, `VehicleTest`, we can now write the `testCalcSpeed()` method:

```java
@Test
public void testCalcSpeed(){
   double timeSec = 10.0;
   TrafficDensity2 trafficDensity = new TrafficDensity2();

   Vehicle vehicle = Mockito.mock(Vehicle.class);
   Mockito.when(vehicle.getSpeedMph(timeSec)).thenReturn(100d);
   double traction = 0.2;
   double speed = trafficDensity.calcSpeed(vehicle, traction, timeSec);
   assertEquals("Assert speed (traction=" + traction + ") in "
            + timeSec + " sec: ",20,speed,0.001 *speed);
}
```

The remaining functionality can be tested by mocking the `calcSpeed()` method:

```java
@Test
public void testCountByLane() {
  int[] count ={0};
  double[] speeds =
                  {1, 2, 3, 4, 5, 6, 7, 8, 9, 10, 11, 12};
  TrafficDensity2 trafficDensity = new TrafficDensity2() {
    @Override
    protected double calcSpeed(Vehicle vehicle,
                  double traction, double timeSec) {
      return speeds[count[0]++];
    }
  };
  double timeSec = 10.0;
  int trafficUnitsNumber = speeds.length;

  double[] speedLimitByLane = {4.5, 8.5, 12.5};
  Integer[] expectedCountByLane = {4, 4, 4};

  Integer[] trafficByLane = trafficDensity.trafficByLane(
    getTrafficUnitStream(trafficUnitsNumber),
    trafficUnitsNumber, timeSec, FactorySpeedModel.getSpeedModel(),
    speedLimitByLane );
  assertArrayEquals("Assert count of " + speeds.length
        + " vehicles by " + speedLimitByLane.length
        + " lanes with speed limit "
```

```
    + Arrays.stream(speedLimitByLane)
        .mapToObj(Double::toString).collect(Collectors
        .joining(", ")), expectedCountByLane, trafficByLane);
}
```

There's more...

This experience has made us aware that using an inner private class can make the functionality untestable in isolation. Let's try to get rid of the `private` class, `CountByLane`. This leads us to the third version of the `TrafficDensity3` class (the changed code is highlighted):

```
Integer[] trafficByLane(Stream<TrafficUnit> stream,
int trafficUnitsNumber, double timeSec,
SpeedModel speedModel, double[] speedLimitByLane) {
  int lanesCount = speedLimitByLane.length;
  Map<Integer, Integer> trafficByLane = new HashMap<>();
  for(int i = 1; i <= lanesCount; i++){
    trafficByLane.put(i, 0);
  }
  stream.limit(trafficUnitsNumber)
    .map(TrafficUnitWrapper::new)
    .map(tuw -> tuw.setSpeedModel(speedModel))
    .map(tuw -> calcSpeed(tuw.getVehicle(), tuw.getTraction(),
                                                 timeSec))
    .forEach(speed -> trafficByLane.computeIfPresent(
      calcLaneNumber(lanesCount,
                       speedLimitByLane, speed), (k, v) -> ++v));
    return trafficByLane.values().toArray(new Integer[lanesCount]);
}
protected int calcLaneNumber(int lanesCount,
  double[] speedLimitByLane, double speed) {
    for(int i = 1; i <= lanesCount; i++){
      if(speed <= speedLimitByLane[i - 1]){
        return i;
      }
    }
    return lanesCount;
}
```

This change allows us to extend the class in our test:

```
class TrafficDensityTestCalcLaneNumber extends TrafficDensity3 {
  protected int calcLaneNumber(int lanesCount,
    double[] speedLimitByLane, double speed){
    return super.calcLaneNumber(lanesCount,
    speedLimitByLane, speed);
  }
}
```

It also allows us to change the `calcLaneNumber()` test method in isolation:

```
@Test
public void testCalcLaneNumber() {
  double[] speeds = {1, 2, 3, 4, 5, 6, 7, 8, 9, 10, 11, 12};
  double[] speedLimitByLane = {4.5, 8.5, 12.5};
  int[] expectedLaneNumber = {1, 1, 1, 1, 2, 2, 2, 2, 3, 3, 3, 3};

  TrafficDensityTestCalcLaneNumber trafficDensity =
            new TrafficDensityTestCalcLaneNumber();
  for(int i = 0; i < speeds.length; i++){
    int ln = trafficDensity.calcLaneNumber(
            speedLimitByLane.length,
            speedLimitByLane, speeds[i]);
    assertEquals("Assert lane number of speed "
            + speeds + " with speed limit "
            + Arrays.stream(speedLimitByLane)
                   .mapToObj(Double::toString).collect(
                        Collectors.joining(", ")),
            expectedLaneNumber[i], ln);
  }
}
```

Using fixtures to populate data for testing

In more complex applications (that use a database, for example), there is often the
need to set up the data before each test and clean it up after the test is completed.
Some parts of the data need to be set before each test method and/or cleaned after
each test method has completed. Other data may need to be set up before any test
method of the test class was run and/or cleaned up after the last test method of the
test class has completed.

How to do it...

To accomplish this, you add an `@Before` annotation in front of it, which indicates that this method has to run before every test method. The corresponding cleaning method is identified by the `@After` annotation. Similarly, the class-level setup methods are annotated by `@BeforeClass` and `@AfterClass`, which means these setup methods are going to be executed only once—before any test method of this class is executed (`@BeforeClass`) and after the last test method of this class has been executed (`@AfterClass`). Here is a quick demo of this:

```
public class DatabaseRelatedTest {
  @BeforeClass
  public static void setupForTheClass(){
    System.out.println("setupForTheClass() is called");
  }
  @AfterClass
  public static void cleanUpAfterTheClass(){
    System.out.println("cleanAfterClass() is called");
  }
  @Before
  public void setupForEachMethod(){
    System.out.println("setupForEachMethod() is called");
  }
  @After
  public void cleanUpAfterEachMethod(){
    System.out.println("cleanAfterEachMethod() is called");
  }
  @Test
  public void testMethodOne(){
    System.out.println("testMethodOne() is called");
  }
  @Test
  public void testMethodTwo(){
    System.out.println("testMethodTwo() is called");
  }
}
```

If you run the tests now, you'll get the following result:

```
Running com.packt.cookbook.ch06_db.DatabaseRelatedTest
setupForTheClass() is called
setupForEachMethod() is called
testMethodOne() is called
cleanAfterEachMethod() is called
setupForEachMethod() is called
testMethodTwo() is called
cleanAfterEachMethod() is called
cleanAfterClass() is called
Tests run: 2, Failures: 0, Errors: 0, Skipped: 0, Time elapsed: 0.003 sec
```

Such methods that *fix* the test context are called **fixtures**. Note that they have to be public, and the class-level setup/cleanup fixtures have to be static. The upcoming JUnit version 5 plans to lift these constraints, though.

How it works...

A typical example of such a usage would be creating necessary tables before the first test method is run and removing them after the last method of the test class is finished. The setup/cleanup methods can also be used to create/close a database connection unless your code does it in the try-with-resources construct (refer to Chapter 11, *Memory Management and Debugging*).

Here is an example of the usage of fixtures (refer to Chapter 6, *Database Programming*, for more on *how to set up a database for running it,* section). Let's assume we need to test the DbRelatedMethods class:

```java
class DbRelatedMethods{
  public void updateAllTextRecordsTo(String text){
    executeUpdate("update text set text = ?", text);
  }
  private void executeUpdate(String sql, String text){
    try (Connection conn = getDbConnection();
      PreparedStatement st = conn.prepareStatement(sql)){
        st.setString(1, text);
        st.executeUpdate();
      } catch (Exception ex) {
        ex.printStackTrace();
      }
  }
  private Connection getDbConnection(){
```

```
        //... code that creates DB connection
    }
}
```

We would like to make sure that the previous
method, `updateAllTextRecordsTo()`, always updates all the records of the `text`
table with the provided value. Our first test, `updateAllTextRecordsTo1()`, is to
update one existing record:

```
@Test
public void updateAllTextRecordsTo1(){
    System.out.println("updateAllTextRecordsTo1() is called");
    String testString = "Whatever";
    System.out.println("  Update all records to " + testString);
    dbRelatedMethods.updateAllTextRecordsTo(testString);
    int count = countRecordsWithText(testString);
    assertEquals("Assert number of records with "
                            + testString + ": ", 1, count);
    System.out.println("All records are updated to " + testString);
}
```

This means that the table has to exist in the test database and should have one record
in it.

Our second test, `updateAllTextRecordsTo2()`, makes sure that two records are
updated even if each record contains a different value:

```
@Test
public void updateAllTextRecordsTo2(){
    System.out.println("updateAllTextRecordsTo2() is called");
    String testString = "Unexpected";
    System.out.println("Update all records to " + testString);
    dbRelatedMethods.updateAllTextRecordsTo(testString);
    executeUpdate("insert into text(id,text) values(2, ?)","Text 01");

    testString = "Whatever";
    System.out.println("Update all records to " + testString);
    dbRelatedMethods.updateAllTextRecordsTo(testString);
    int count = countRecordsWithText(testString);
    assertEquals("Assert number of records with "
                + testString + ": ", 2, count);
    System.out.println("  " + count + " records are updated to " +
                                            testString);
}
```

Both the preceding tests use the same table, that is, `text`. Therefore, there is no need to drop the table after each test. This is why we create and drop it at the class level:

```
@BeforeClass
public static void setupForTheClass(){
   System.out.println("setupForTheClass() is called");
   execute("create table text (id integer not null,
         text character varying not null)");
}
@AfterClass
public static void cleanUpAfterTheClass(){
   System.out.println("cleanAfterClass() is called");
   execute("drop table text");
}
```

This means that all we need to do is populate the table before each test and clean it up after each test is completed:

```
@Before
public void setupForEachMethod(){
   System.out.println("setupForEachMethod() is called");
   executeUpdate("insert into text(id, text) values(1,?)", "Text 01");
}
@After
public void cleanUpAfterEachMethod(){
   System.out.println("cleanAfterEachMethod() is called");
   execute("delete from text");
}
```

Also, since we can use the same object, `dbRelatedMethods`, for all the tests, let's create it on the class level too (as the test class's property), so it's created only once:

```
private DbRelatedMethods dbRelatedMethods = new DbRelatedMethods();
```

If we run all the tests of the `test` class now, the output will look like this:

```
Running com.packt.cookbook.ch06_db.DbRelatedMethodsTest
setupForTheClass() is called
   create table text (id integer not null, text character varying not null)
setupForEachMethod() is called
   insert into text(id, text) values(1, ?), params=Text 01
updateAllTextRecordsTo1() is called
   Update all records to Whatever
   1 record is updated to Whatever
cleanAfterEachMethod() is called
   delete from text
setupForEachMethod() is called
   insert into text(id, text) values(1, ?), params=Text 01
updateAllTextRecordsTo2() is called
   Update all records to Unexpected
   insert into text(id, text) values(2, ?), params=Text 01
   Update all records to Whatever
   2 records are updated to Whatever
cleanAfterEachMethod() is called
   delete from text
cleanAfterClass() is called
   drop table text
Tests run: 2, Failures: 0, Errors: 0, Skipped: 0, Time elapsed: 0.36 sec
```

The printed messages allow you to trace the sequence of all the method calls and see that they are executed as expected.

Integration testing

If you have read all the chapters and have looked at the code examples, you may have noticed that, by now, we have discussed and built all the components necessary for a typical distributed application. It is the time to put all the components together and see whether they cooperate as expected. This process is called **integration**.

While doing this, we will look closely at assessing whether the application behaves according to the requirements. In cases where functional requirements are presented in an executable form (using the Cucumber framework, for example), we can run them and check whether all the checks pass. Many software companies follow a Behavior-Driven Development process and perform testing very early, sometimes even before any substantial amount of code is written (such tests fail, of course, but succeed as soon as the expected functionality is implemented). As mentioned already, early testing can be very helpful for writing a focused, clear, and well-testable code.

However, even without strict adherence to the *test-first* process, the integration phase naturally includes some kind of behavioral testing too. In this recipe, we will see several possible approaches and specific examples related to this.

Getting ready

You might have noticed that, in the course of this book, we have built several classes that compose an application that analyzes and models traffic. For your convenience, we have included all of them in the `com.packt.cookbook.ch16_testing` package.

From the earlier chapters, you're already familiar with the five interfaces in the `api` folder—`Car`, `SpeedModel`, `TrafficUnit`, `Truck`, and `Vehicle`. Their implementations are encapsulated inside classes called **factories** in the folder with the same name: `FactorySpeedModel`, `FactoryTraffic`, and `FactoryVehicle`. These factories produce input for the functionality of the `AverageSpeed` class (Chapter 7, *Concurrent and Multithreaded Programming*) and the `TrafficDensity` class (based on Chapter 5, *Streams and Pipelines*, but created and discussed in this chapter)—the core classes of our demo application. They produce the values that motivated the development of this particular application in the first place.

The main functionality of the application is straightforward. For a given number of lanes and speed limit for each lane, `AverageSpeed` calculates (estimates) the actual speed of each lane (assuming all the drivers are behaving rationally, taking the lane according to their speed), while `TrafficDensity` calculates the number of vehicles in each lane after 10 seconds (assuming all the cars start at the same time after the traffic light). The calculations are done based on the data from the `numberOfTrafficUnits` vehicles collected at a certain location and time of the year. It does not mean that all the 1,000 vehicles were racing at the same time. These 1,000 measuring points have been collected over 50 years for approximately 20 vehicles that drove at the specified intersection during the specified hour (which means one vehicle every three minutes, on average).

The overall infrastructure of the application is supported by the classes in the `process` folder: `Dispatcher`, `Processor`, and `Subscription`. We discussed their functionality and demonstrated them in Chapter 7, *Concurrent and Multithreaded Programming*. These classes allow distributing the processing.

The `Dispatcher` class sends a request for processing to the population of `Processors` in a pool, using the `Subscription` class. Each `Processor` class performs the task according to the request (using the `AverageSpeed` and `TraffciDensity` classes) and stores the results in the database (using the `DbUtil` class in the `utils` folder, based on the functionality discussed in `Chapter 6`, *Database Programming*).

We have tested most of these classes as units. Now we are going to integrate them and test the application as a whole for correct behavior.

The requirements were made up just for demonstrative purposes. The goal of the demonstration was to show something well motivated (resembling real data) and at the same time simple enough to understand without special knowledge of traffic analysis and modeling.

How to do it...

There are several levels of integration. We need to integrate the classes and subsystems of the application and also integrate our application with the external system (the source of the traffic data developed and maintained by a third party).

Here is an example of class-level integration using the `demo1_class_level_integration()` method in the `Chapter14Testing` class:

```
String result = IntStream.rangeClosed(1,
   speedLimitByLane.length).mapToDouble(i -> {
     AverageSpeed averageSpeed =
       new AverageSpeed(trafficUnitsNumber, timeSec,
                        dateLocation, speedLimitByLane, i,100);
     ForkJoinPool commonPool = ForkJoinPool.commonPool();
     return commonPool.invoke(averageSpeed);
}).mapToObj(Double::toString).collect(Collectors.joining(", "));
System.out.println("Average speed = " + result);

TrafficDensity trafficDensity = new TrafficDensity();
Integer[] trafficByLane =
     trafficDensity.trafficByLane(trafficUnitsNumber,
                   timeSec, dateLocation, speedLimitByLane );
System.out.println("Traffic density = "+Arrays.stream(trafficByLane)
                               .map(Object::toString)
                               .collect(Collectors.joining(", ")));
```

In this example, we integrated each of the two main classes, namely `AverageSpeed` and `TrafficDensity`, with factories and implementations of their interfaces.

The results are as follows:

```
Average speed = 8.5, 23.5, 44.0
Traffic density = 345, 315, 340
```

Note that the results are slightly different from one run to another. This is because the data produced by `FactoryTraffic` varies from one request to another. But, at this stage, we just have to make sure that everything works together and produces some more or less accurate-looking results. We have tested the code by units and have a level of confidence that each unit is doing what it is supposed to do. We will get back to the results' validation during the actual integration *testing* process, not during integration.

After finishing the integration at the class level, see how the subsystems work together using the `demo1_subsystem_level_integration()` method in the `Chapter14Testing` class:

```
DbUtil.createResultTable();
Dispatcher.dispatch(trafficUnitsNumber, timeSec, dateLocation,
                    speedLimitByLane);
try { Thread.sleep(2000L); }
catch (InterruptedException ex) {}
Arrays.stream(Process.values()).forEach(v -> {
  System.out.println("Result " + v.name() + ": "
                    + DbUtil.selectResult(v.name())));
});
```

In this code, we used `DBUtil` to create the necessary table that holds the input data and the results produced and recorded by `Processor`. The `Dispatcher` class sends a request and inputs data to the objects of the `Processor` class, as shown here:

```
void dispatch(int trafficUnitsNumber, double timeSec,
        DateLocation dateLocation, double[] speedLimitByLane) {
  ExecutorService execService = ForkJoinPool.commonPool();
  try (SubmissionPublisher<Integer> publisher =
                           new SubmissionPublisher<>()){
    subscribe(publisher, execService,Process.AVERAGE_SPEED,
            timeSec, dateLocation, speedLimitByLane);
    subscribe(publisher,execService,Process.TRAFFIC_DENSITY,
            timeSec, dateLocation, speedLimitByLane);
    publisher.submit(trafficUnitsNumber);
```

```
    } finally {
      try {
        execService.shutdown();
        execService.awaitTermination(1, TimeUnit.SECONDS);
      } catch (Exception ex) {
        System.out.println(ex.getClass().getName());
      } finally {
        execService.shutdownNow();
      }
    }
  }
}
```

The Subscription class is used to send/get the message (refer to Chapter 7,
Concurrent and Multithreaded Programming, for a description of this functionality):

```
void subscribe(SubmissionPublisher<Integer> publisher,
               ExecutorService execService, Process process,
               double timeSec, DateLocation dateLocation,
               double[] speedLimitByLane) {
  Processor<Integer> subscriber =  new Processor<>(process, timeSec,
                                    dateLocation, speedLimitByLane);
  Subscription subscription =
                    new Subscription(subscriber, execService);
  subscriber.onSubscribe(subscription);
  publisher.subscribe(subscriber);
}
```

The processors are doing their job; we just need to wait for a few seconds (you might
adjust this time if the computer you are using requires more time to finish the job)
before we get the results. We use DBUtil for reading the results from the database:

```
AVERAGE_SPEED: 8.5, 23.0, 43.0
TRAFFIC_DENSITY: 370, 314, 316
```

The names of the Process enum class point to the corresponding records in the
result table in the database. Again, at this stage, we are primarily looking for
getting any results at all, not at how correct the values are.

After the successful integration between the subsystems of our application based on the generated data from `FactoryTraffic`, we can try to connect to the external system that provides real traffic data. Inside `FactoryTraffic`, we would now switch from generating `TrafficUnit` objects to getting data from a real system:

```
public class FactoryTraffic {
   private static boolean switchToRealData = true;
   public static Stream<TrafficUnit>
   getTrafficUnitStream(DateLocation dl, int trafficUnitsNumber){
     if(switchToRealData){
       return getRealData(dL,  trafficUnitsNumber);
     } else {
       return IntStream.range(0, trafficUnitsNumber)
       .mapToObj(i -> generateOneUnit());
     }
   }

   private static Stream<TrafficUnit>
   getRealData(DateLocation dl, int trafficUnitsNumber) {
     //connect to the source of the real data
     // and request the flow or collection of data
     return new ArrayList<TrafficUnit>().stream();
   }
}
```

The switch can be implemented as a `Boolean` property in the class (as seen in the preceding code) or the project configuration property. We leave out the details of the connection to a particular source of real traffic data as this is not relevant to the purpose of this book.

The main focus at this stage has to be the performance and having a smooth data flow between the external source of real data and our application. After we have made sure that everything works and produces realistic results with satisfactory performance, we can turn to integration *testing* with the actual results' assertion.

How it works...

For testing, we need to set the expected values, which we can compare with the actual values produced by the application that processes real data. But real data changes slightly from run to run, and an attempt to predict the resultant values either makes the test fragile or forces the introduction of a huge margin of error, which may effectively defeat the purpose of testing.

We cannot even mock the generated data (as we did in the case of unit testing) because we are at the integration stage and have to use the real data.

One possible solution would be to store the incoming real data and the result our application produced in the database. Then, a domain specialist can walk through each record and assert whether the results are as expected.

To accomplish this, we introduced a `boolean` switch in the `TrafficDensity` class, so it records the input along with each unit of the calculations:

```
public class TrafficDensity {
  public static Connection conn;
  public static boolean recordData = false;
  //...
  private double calcSpeed(TrafficUnitWrapper tuw, double timeSec){
    double speed = calcSpeed(tuw.getVehicle(),
    tuw.getTrafficUnit().getTraction(), timeSec);
    if(recordData) {
      DbUtil.recordData(conn, tuw.getTrafficUnit(), speed);
    }
    return speed;
  }
  //...
}
```

We also introduced a static property to keep the same database connection across all the class instances. Otherwise, the connection pool should be very big because, as you may recall from Chapter 7, *Concurrent and Multithreaded Programming*, the number of workers that execute the task in parallel grows as the amount of work to do increases.

If you look at `DbUtils`, you will see a new method that creates the `data` table designed to hold `TrafficUnits` coming from `FactoryTraffic` and the `data_common` table that keeps the main parameters used for data requests and calculations: requested numbers of traffic units, the date and geolocation of the traffic data, the time in seconds (the point when the speed is calculated), and the speed limit for each lane (its size defines how many lanes we plan to use while modeling the traffic). Here is the code that we configure to do the recording:

```
private static void demo3_prepare_for_integration_testing(){
  DbUtil.createResultTable();
  DbUtil.createDataTables();
  TrafficDensity.recordData = true;
  try(Connection conn = DbUtil.getDbConnection()){
    TrafficDensity.conn = conn;
    Dispatcher.dispatch(trafficUnitsNumber, timeSec,
                 dateLocation, speedLimitByLane);
```

```
      } catch (SQLException ex){
        ex.printStackTrace();
      }
   }
```

After the recording is completed, we can turn the data over to a domain specialist who can assert the correctness of the application behavior.

The verified data can now be used for integration testing. We can add another switch to `FactoryTrafficUnit` and force it to read the recorded data instead of the unpredictable real data:

```
public class FactoryTraffic {
   public static boolean readDataFromDb = false;
   private static boolean switchToRealData = false;
   public static Stream<TrafficUnit>
      getTrafficUnitStream(DateLocation dl, int trafficUnitsNumber){
    if(readDataFromDb){
      if(!DbUtil.isEnoughData(trafficUnitsNumber)){
        System.out.println("Not enough data");
        return new ArrayList<TrafficUnit>().stream();
      }
      return readDataFromDb(trafficUnitsNumber);
    }
    //....
  }
```

As you may have noticed, we have also added the `isEnoughData()` method which checks whether there is enough recorded data:

```
public static boolean isEnoughData(int trafficUnitsNumber){
   try (Connection conn = getDbConnection();
   PreparedStatement st =
      conn.prepareStatement("select count(*) from data")){
     ResultSet rs = st.executeQuery();
     if(rs.next()){
       int count = rs.getInt(1);
       return count >= trafficUnitsNumber;
     }
   } catch (Exception ex) {
     ex.printStackTrace();
   }
   return false;
}
```

This will help avoid the unnecessary frustration of debugging the test problem, especially in the case of testing a more complex system.

Now we control not only the input values but also the expected results that we can use to assert the application behavior. Both are now included in the `TrafficUnit` object. To be able to do this, we took advantage of the new Java interface feature discussed in Chapter 2, *Fast Track to OOP - Classes and Interfaces*, which is the interface default method:

```
public interface TrafficUnit {
  VehicleType getVehicleType();
  int getHorsePower();
  int getWeightPounds();
  int getPayloadPounds();
  int getPassengersCount();
  double getSpeedLimitMph();
  double getTraction();
  RoadCondition getRoadCondition();
  TireCondition getTireCondition();
  int getTemperature();
  default double getSpeed(){ return 0.0; }
}
```

So, we can attach the result to the input data. See the following method:

```
List<TrafficUnit> selectData(int trafficUnitsNumber){...}
```

We can attach the result to the `DbUtil` class and the `TrafficUnitImpl` class inside `DbUtil` too:

```
class TrafficUnitImpl implements TrafficUnit{
  private int horsePower, weightPounds, payloadPounds,
              passengersCount, temperature;
  private Vehicle.VehicleType vehicleType;
  private double speedLimitMph, traction, speed;
  private RoadCondition roadCondition;
  private TireCondition tireCondition;
  ...
  public double getSpeed() { return speed; }
}
```

And we can attach it inside the `DbUtil` class too.

The preceding changes allow us to write an integration test. First, we will test the speed model using the recorded data:

```
void demo1_test_speed_model_with_real_data(){
  double timeSec = DbUtil.getTimeSecFromDataCommon();
  FactoryTraffic.readDataFromDb = true;
  TrafficDensity trafficDensity = new TrafficDensity();
```

```
FactoryTraffic.
            getTrafficUnitStream(dateLocation,1000).forEach(tu -> {
    Vehicle vehicle = FactoryVehicle.build(tu);
    vehicle.setSpeedModel(FactorySpeedModel.getSpeedModel());
    double speed = trafficDensity.calcSpeed(vehicle,
                            tu.getTraction(), timeSec);
    assertEquals("Assert vehicle (" + tu.getHorsePower()
                + " hp, " + tu.getWeightPounds() + " lb) speed in "
                + timeSec + " sec: ", tu.getSpeed(), speed,
                speed * 0.001);
});
}
```

A similar test can be written for testing the speed calculation of the `AverageSpeed` class with real data.

Then, we can write an integration test for the class level:

```
private static void demo2_class_level_integration_test() {
    FactoryTraffic.readDataFromDb = true;
    String result = IntStream.rangeClosed(1,
                speedLimitByLane.length).mapToDouble(i -> {
        AverageSpeed averageSpeed = new AverageSpeed(trafficUnitsNumber,
                timeSec, dateLocation, speedLimitByLane, i,100);
        ForkJoinPool commonPool = ForkJoinPool.commonPool();
        return commonPool.invoke(averageSpeed);
    }).mapToObj(Double::toString).collect(Collectors.joining(", "));
    String expectedResult = "7.0, 23.0, 41.0";
    String limits = Arrays.stream(speedLimitByLane)
                        .mapToObj(Double::toString)
                        .collect(Collectors.joining(", "));
    assertEquals("Assert average speeds by "
                + speedLimitByLane.length
                + " lanes with speed limit "
                + limits, expectedResult, result);
```

Similar code can be written for the class-level testing of the `TrafficDensity` class too:

```
TrafficDensity trafficDensity = new TrafficDensity();
String result = Arrays.stream(trafficDensity.
        trafficByLane(trafficUnitsNumber, timeSec,
                    dateLocation, speedLimitByLane))
        .map(Object::toString)
        .collect(Collectors.joining(", "));
expectedResult = "354, 335, 311";
assertEquals("Assert vehicle count by " + speedLimitByLane.length +
        " lanes with speed limit " + limits, expectedResult, result);
```

Finally, we can write the integration test for the subsystem level as well:

```
void demo3_subsystem_level_integration_test() {
  FactoryTraffic.readDataFromDb = true;
  DbUtil.createResultTable();
  Dispatcher.dispatch(trafficUnitsNumber, 10, dateLocation,
                      speedLimitByLane);
  try { Thread.sleep(30001); }
  catch (InterruptedException ex) {}
  String result = DbUtil.selectResult(Process.AVERAGE_SPEED.name());
  String expectedResult = "7.0, 23.0, 41.0";
  String limits = Arrays.stream(speedLimitByLane)
                       .mapToObj(Double::toString)
                       .collect(Collectors.joining(", "));
  assertEquals("Assert average speeds by " + speedLimitByLane.length
        + " lanes with speed limit " + limits, expectedResult,
result);
  result = DbUtil.selectResult(Process.TRAFFIC_DENSITY.name());
  expectedResult = "354, 335, 311";
  assertEquals("Assert vehicle count by " + speedLimitByLane.length
        + " lanes with speed limit " + limits, expectedResult,
result);
}
```

All of the preceding tests are run successfully now and may be used for application regression testing any time later.

An automated integration test between our application and the source of the real traffic data can be created only if the latter has a test mode from where the same flow of data can be sent our way so we can use it in the same manner we use recorded data (which is essentially the same thing).

One parting thought—all of this integration testing is possible when the amount of processing data is statistically significant. This is because we do not have full control over the number of workers and how the JVM decides to split the load. It is quite possible that, on a particular occasion, the code demonstrated in this chapter would not work. In such a case, try to increase the number of requested traffic units. This will ensure more space for the load-distributing logic.

15
The New Way of Coding with Java 10 and Java 11

In this chapter, we will cover the following recipes:

- Using local-variable type inference
- Using local-variable syntax for lambda parameters

Introduction

This chapter gives you a quick introduction to new features that affect your coding. Many other languages, including JavaScript, have this feature—the ability to declare a variable using a `var` keyword (in Java, it is actually a **reserved type name**, not a keyword). It has many advantages but is not without controversy. If used excessively, especially with short non-descriptive identifiers, it can make the code less readable and the added value may be drowned out by the increased code obscurity.

That is why in the following recipe, we explain the reasons the reserved `var` type was introduced. Try to avoid using `var` in the other cases.

Using local-variable type inference

In this recipe, you will learn about local-variable type inference, which was introduced in Java 10, where it can be used, and its limitations.

Getting ready

A local-variable type inference is the ability of a compiler to identify the type of the local variable using the correct side of an expression. In Java, a local variable with an inferred type is declared using the `var` identifier. For example:

```
var i = 42;          //int
var s = "42";        //String
var list1 = new ArrayList();         //ArrayList of Objects;
var list2 = new ArrayList<String>(); //ArrayList of Strings
```

The type of each of the preceding variables is clearly identifiable. We captured their types in comments.

 Note that `var` is not a keyword, but an identifier, with a special meaning as the type of a local variable declaration.

It definitely saves typing and makes the code less cluttered with repeated code. Let's look at this example:

```
Map<Integer, List<String>> idToNames = new HashMap<>();
//...
for(Map.Entry<Integer, List<String>> e: idToNames.entrySet()){
    List<String> names = e.getValue();
    //...
}
```

That was the only way to implement such a loop. But since Java 10, it can be written as follows:

```
var idToNames = new HashMap<Integer, List<String>>();
//...
for(var e: idToNames.entrySet()){
    var names = e.getValue();
    //...
}
```

As you can see, the code becomes clearer, but using more descriptive variable names (such as `idToNames` and `names`) is helpful. Well, it is helpful anyway. But if you do not pay attention to the variable names,it is easy to make the code not easy to understand. For example, look at the following code:

```
var names = getNames();
```

Looking at the preceding line, you have no idea what type the `names` variable is. Changing it to `idToNames` makes it easier to guess. Nevertheless, many programmers do not do it. They prefer short variable names and figure out the type of each variable using the IDE context support (adding a dot after the variable name). But at the end of the day, it's just a matter of style and personal preferences.

Another potential problem comes from the fact that the new style may violate encapsulation and coding to an interface principle if no extra care is taken. For example, consider this interface and its implementation:

```
interface A {
    void m();
}

static class AImpl implements A {
    public void m(){}
    public void f(){}
}
```

Note that the `AImpl` class has more public methods than the interface it implements. The traditional style of creating the `AImpl` object would be as follows:

```
A a = new AImpl();
a.m();
//a.f();   //does not compile
```

This way, we expose only the methods present in the interface, while the new style allows access to all the methods:

```
var a = new AImpl();
a.m();
a.f();
```

To limit the reference to the methods of the interface only, one needs to add the typecasting as follows:

```
var a = (A) new AImpl();
a.m();
//a.f();   //does not compile
```

So, like many powerful tools, the new style can make your code easier to write and much more readable or, if special care is not taken, less readable and more difficult to debug.

How to do it...

You can use a local variable type in the following ways:

- With a right-hand initializer:

```
var i = 1;
var a = new int[2];
var l = List.of(1, 2);
var c = "x".getClass();
var o = new Object() {};
var x = (CharSequence & Comparable<String>) "x";
```

The following declarations and assignments are illegal and will not compile:

```
var e;                   // no initializer
var g = null;            // null type
var f = { 6 };           // array initializer
var g = (g = 7);         // self reference is not allowed
var b = 2, c = 3.0;      // multiple declarators re not allowed
var d[] = new int[4];    // extra array dimension brackets
var f = () -> "hello";   // lambda requires an explicit target-
type
```

By extension, with an initializer in the loop:

```
for(var i = 0; i < 10; i++){
    //...
}
```

And we have talked already about this example:

```
var idToNames = new HashMap<Integer, List<String>>();
//...
for(var e: idToNames.entrySet()){
    var names = e.getValue();
    //...
}
```

- As an anonymous class reference:

```
interface A {
 void m();
}

var aImpl = new A(){
 @Override
 public void m(){
```

```
    //...
    }
};
```

- As an identifier:

```
var var = 1;
```

- As a method name:

```
public void var(int i){
    //...
}
```

But `var` cannot be used as a class or an interface name.

- As a package name:

```
package com.packt.cookbook.var;
```

Using local-variable syntax for lambda parameters

In this recipe, you will learn how to use the local-variable syntax (discussed in the previous recipe) for lambda parameters and the motivation for introducing this feature. It was introduced in Java 11.

Getting ready

Until the release of Java 11, there were two ways to declare parameter types—explicit and implicit. Here is an explicit version:

```
BiFunction<Double, Integer, Double> f = (Double x, Integer y) -> x /
y;
System.out.println(f.apply(3., 2));    //prints: 1.5
```

And the following is an implicit parameter type definition:

```
BiFunction<Double, Integer, Double> f = (x, y) -> x / y;
System.out.println(f.apply(3., 2));    //prints: 1.5
```

In the preceding code, the compiler figures the type of the parameters by the interface definition.

With Java 11, another way of parameter type declaration was introduced—using the var identifier.

How to do it...

1. The following parameter declaration is exactly the same as the implicit one before Java 11:

```
BiFunction<Double, Integer, Double> f = (var x, var y) -> x /
y;
System.out.println(f.apply(3., 2));        //prints: 1.5
```

2. The new local variable style syntax allows us to add annotations without defining the parameter type explicitly:

```
import org.jetbrains.annotations.NotNull;
...
BiFunction<Double, Integer, Double> f =
  (@NotNull var x, @NotNull var y) -> x / y;
System.out.println(f.apply(3., 2));        //prints: 1.5
```

The annotations tell the tools that process the code (the IDE, for example) about the programmer's intent, so they can warn the programmer during compilation or execution in case the declared intent is violated. For example, we have tried to run the following code inside IntelliJ IDEA:

```
BiFunction<Double, Integer, Double> f = (x, y) -> x / y;
System.out.println(f.apply(null, 2));
```

It failed with NullPointerException at runtime. Then we have run the following code (with annotations):

```
BiFunction<Double, Integer, Double> f4 =
            (@NotNull var x, @NotNull var y) -> x / y;
Double j = 3.;
Integer i = 2;
System.out.println(f4.apply(j, i));
```

The result was the following:

```
Exception in thread "main" java.lang.IllegalArgumentException:
Argument for @NotNull parameter 'x' of
com/packt/cookbook/ch17_new_way/b_lambdas/Chapter15Var.lambda$
main$4 must not be null
```

The lambda expression was not even executed.

3. The advantage of local-variable syntax in the case of lambda parameters becomes clear if we need to use annotations when the parameters are the objects of a class with a really long name. Before Java 11, the code may look like the following:

```
BiFunction<SomeReallyLongClassName,
   AnotherReallyLongClassName, Double> f4 =
      (@NotNull SomeReallyLongClassName x,
       @NotNull AnotherReallyLongClassName y) ->
x.doSomething(y);
```

We had to declare the type of the variable explicitly because we wanted to add annotations and the following implicit version would not even compile:

```
BiFunction<SomeReallyLongClassName,
   AnotherReallyLongClassName, Double> f4 =
      (@NotNull x, @NotNull y) -> x.doSomething(y);
```

With Java 11, the new syntax allows us to use the implicit parameter type inference using the `var` identifier:

```
BiFunction<SomeReallyLongClassName,
   AnotherReallyLongClassName, Double> f4 =
      (@NotNull var x, @NotNull var y) -> x.doSomething(y);
```

That is the advantage of and the motivation behind introducing a local-variable syntax for the lambda parameter's declaration.

16
GUI Programming Using JavaFX

In this chapter, we will cover the following recipes:

- Creating a GUI using JavaFX controls
- Using FXML markup to create a GUI
- Using CSS to style elements in JavaFX
- Creating a bar chart
- Creating a pie chart
- Embedding HTML in an application
- Embedding media in an application
- Adding effects to controls
- Using the Robot API

Introduction

GUI programming has been in Java since JDK 1.0, via the API called the **Abstract Window Toolkit (AWT)**. This was a remarkable thing during those times, but it had its own limitations, a few of which are as follows:

- It had a limited set of components.
- You couldn't create custom reusable components because AWT was using native components.
- The look and feel of the components couldn't be controlled, and they took the look and feel of the host OS.

Then, in Java 1.2, a new API for GUI development called **Swing** was introduced, which worked on the deficiencies of AWT by providing the following:

- A richer components library.
- Support for creating custom components.
- A native look and feel, and support for plugging in a different look and feel. Some well-known Java looks and feel themes are Nimbus, Metal, Motif, and the system default.

A lot of desktop applications that make use of Swing have been built, and a lot of them are still being used. However, with time, technology has to evolve; otherwise, it will eventually be outdated and seldom used. In 2008, Adobe's **Flex** started gaining attention. It was a framework for building **Rich Internet applications** (**RIAs**). The desktop applications were always rich component-based UIs, but the web applications were not that amazing to use. Adobe introduced a framework called Flex, which enabled web developers to create rich, immersive UIs on the web. So the web applications were no longer boring.

Adobe also introduced a rich internet application runtime environment for the desktop called **Adobe AIR**, which allowed the running of Flex applications on the desktop. This was a major blow to the age-old Swing API. But let's go back to the market: In 2009, Sun Microsystems introduced something called **JavaFX**. This framework was inspired by Flex (which used XML for defining the UI) and introduced its own scripting language called **JavaFX script**, which was somewhat closer to JSON and JavaScript. You could invoke Java APIs from the JavaFX script. There was a new architecture introduced, which had a new Windowing toolkit and a new graphics engine. It was a much better alternative to Swing, but it had a drawback—developers had to learn JavaFX script to develop JavaFX-based applications. In addition to Sun Microsystems not being able to invest more on JavaFX and the Java platform, in general, JavaFX never took off as envisioned.

Oracle (after acquiring Sun Microsystems) announced a new JavaFX Version 2.0, which was an entire rewrite of JavaFX, thereby eliminating the scripting language and making JavaFX an API within the Java platform. This has made using the JavaFX API similar to using Swing APIs. Also, you can embed JavaFX components within Swing, thereby making Swing-based applications more functional. Since then, there has been no looking back for JavaFX.

JavaFX is no longer being bundled with JDK 11 onward (neither Oracle JDK nor OpenJDK builds). And it's also no longer being bundled with the OpenJDK 10 build. They have to be downloaded separately from the OpenJFX Project page (`https://wiki.openjdk.java.net/display/OpenJFX/Main`). A new community website has been launched for OpenJFX (`https://openjfx.io/`)

In this chapter, we will focus entirely on the recipes around JavaFX. We will try to cover as many recipes as possible to give you all a good experience of using JavaFX.

Creating a GUI using JavaFX controls

In this recipe, we will look at creating a simple GUI application, using JavaFX controls. We will build an app that will help you compute your age, after you provide your date of birth. Optionally, you can even enter your name, and the app will greet you and display your age. It is a pretty simple example that tries to show how you can create a GUI by using layouts, components, and event handling.

Getting ready

The following are the modules part of JavaFX:

- `javafx.base`
- `javafx.controls`
- `javafx.fxml`
- `javafx.graphics`
- `javafx.media`
- `javafx.swing`
- `javafx.web`

If you are using Oracle JDK 10 and 9, it comes with the previously mentioned JavaFX modules as part of the setup; that is to say, you can find them in the `JAVA_HOME`/`jmods` directory. And if you are using OpenJDK 10 onward and JDK 11 onward, you need to download the JavaFX SDK from `https://gluonhq.com/products/javafx/` and make the JARs at the location `JAVAFX_SDK_PATH/libs` available on your modulepath, as follows:

```
javac -p "PATH_TO_JAVAFX_SDK_LIB" <other parts of the command line>

#Windows
java -p "PATH_TO_JAVAFX_SDK_LIB;COMPILED_CODE" <other parts of the
command line>
#Linux
java -p "PATH_TO_JAVAFX_SDK_LIB:COMPILED_CODE" <other parts of the
command line>
```

In our recipe, we will be using a few modules as and when required from the preceding list.

How to do it...

1. Create a class that extends `javafx.application.Application`. The `Application` class manages the life cycle of the JavaFX application. The `Application` class has an abstract method, `start(Stage stage)`, which you have to implement. This would be the starting point for the JavaFX UI:

```java
public class CreateGuiDemo extends Application{
  public void start(Stage stage){
    //to implement in new steps
  }
}
```

The class can also be the starting point for the application by providing a `public static void main(String [] args) {}` method:

```java
public class CreateGuiDemo extends Application{
  public void start(Stage stage){
    //to implement in new steps
  }
  public static void main(String[] args){
    //launch the JavaFX application
  }
}
```

The code for the subsequent steps has to be written within the `start(Stage stage)` method.

2. Let's create a container layout to properly align the components that we will be adding. In this case, we will use `javafx.scene.layout.GridPane` to lay out the components in the form of a grid of rows and columns:

```
GridPane gridPane = new GridPane();
gridPane.setAlignment(Pos.CENTER);
gridPane.setHgap(10);
gridPane.setVgap(10);
gridPane.setPadding(new Insets(25, 25, 25, 25));
```

Along with creating the `GridPane` instance, we are setting its layout properties, such as the alignment of `GridPane`, the horizontal and vertical spaces between the rows and columns, and the padding within each cell of the grid.

3. Create a new label, which will show the name of our application, specifically, `Age calculator`, and add it to `gridPane`, which we created in the preceding step:

```
Text appTitle = new Text("Age calculator");
appTitle.setFont(Font.font("Arial", FontWeight.NORMAL, 15));
gridPane.add(appTitle, 0, 0, 2, 1);
```

4. Create a label and a text input combination, which will be used for accepting the user's name. Then add these two components to `gridPane`:

```
Label nameLbl = new Label("Name");
TextField nameField = new TextField();
gridPane.add(nameLbl, 0, 1);
gridPane.add(nameField, 1, 1);
```

5. Create a label and a date-picker combination, which will be used for accepting the user's date of birth:

```
Label dobLbl = new Label("Date of birth");
gridPane.add(dobLbl, 0, 2);
DatePicker dateOfBirthPicker = new DatePicker();
gridPane.add(dateOfBirthPicker, 1, 2);
```

6. Create a button, which will be used by the user to trigger the age calculation, and add it to `gridPane`:

```
Button ageCalculator = new Button("Calculate");
gridPane.add(ageCalculator, 1, 3);
```

7. Create a component to hold the result of the computed age:

```
Text resultTxt = new Text();
resultTxt.setFont(Font.font("Arial", FontWeight.NORMAL, 15));
gridPane.add(resultTxt, 0, 5, 2, 1);
```

8. Now we need to bind an action to the button created in step 6. The action will be to get the name entered in the name field and the date of birth entered in the date-picker field. If the date of birth is provided, then use the Java time APIs to compute the period between now and the date of birth. If there is a name provided, then prepend a greeting, `Hello, <name>`, to the result:

```
ageCalculator.setOnAction((event) -> {
  String name = nameField.getText();
  LocalDate dob = dateOfBirthPicker.getValue();
  if ( dob != null ){
    LocalDate now = LocalDate.now();
    Period period = Period.between(dob, now);
    StringBuilder resultBuilder = new StringBuilder();
    if ( name != null && name.length() > 0 ){
      resultBuilder.append("Hello, ")
                  .append(name)
                  .append("n");
    }
    resultBuilder.append(String.format(
      "Your age is %d years %d months %d days",
      period.getYears(),
      period.getMonths(),
      period.getDays())
    );
    resultTxt.setText(resultBuilder.toString());
  }
});
```

9. Create an instance of the `Scene` class by providing the `gridPane` object we created in step 2 and the dimensions, the width, and height of the scene:

```
Scene scene = new Scene(gridPane, 300, 250);
```

An instance of `Scene` holds the graph of the UI components, which is called a **scene graph**.

10. We have seen that the `start()` method provides us with a reference to a `Stage` object. The `Stage` object is the top-level container in JavaFX, something like a JFrame. We set the `Scene` object to the `Stage` object and use its `show()` method to render the UI:

```
stage.setTitle("Age calculator");
stage.setScene(scene);
stage.show();
```

11. Now we need to launch this JavaFX UI from the main method. We use the `launch(String[] args)` method of the `Application` class to launch the JavaFX UI:

```
public static void main(String[] args) {
  Application.launch(args);
}
```

The complete code can be found at `Chapter16/1_create_javafx_gui`.

We have provided two scripts, `run.bat` and `run.sh`, in `Chapter16/1_create_javafx_gui`. The `run.bat` script will be for running the application on Windows, and `run.sh` will be for running the application on Linux.

Run the application using `run.bat` or `run.sh`, and you will see the GUI, as shown in the following screenshot:

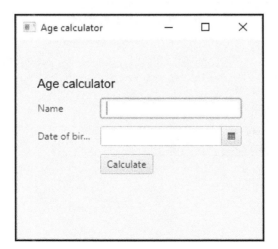

Enter the name and the date of birth and click on `Calculate` to view the age:

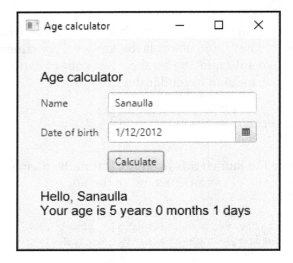

How it works...

Before going into the other details, let's give you a brief overview of the JavaFX architecture. We have taken the following diagram describing the architecture stack from the JavaFX documentation (`http://docs.oracle.com/javase/8/javafx/get-started-tutorial/jfx-architecture.htm#JFXST788`):

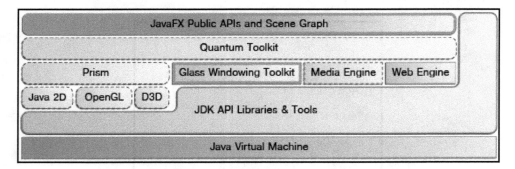

Let's start from the top of the stack:

- **The JavaFX APIs and Scene graph**: This is the starting point of the application, and most of our focus will be around this part. This provides APIs for different components, layout, and other utilities, to facilitate developing a JavaFX-based UI. The scene graph holds the visual elements of the application.
- **Prism, Quantum Toolkit, and the other stuff in blue**: These components manage the rendering of the UI and provide a bridge between the underlying operating system and JavaFX. This layer provides software rendering in cases where the graphics hardware is unable to provide hardware-accelerated rendering of rich UI and 3D elements.
- **The Glass Windowing Toolkit**: This is the windowing toolkit, just like the AWT used by Swing.
- **The media engine**: This supports media in JavaFX.
- **The web engine**: This supports the web component, which allows complete HTML rendering.
- **The JDK APIs and JVM**: These integrate with the Java API and compile the code down to bytecode to run on the JVM.

Let's get back to explaining the recipe. The `javafx.application.Application` class is the entry point for launching the JavaFX applications. It has the following methods that map to the life cycle of the application (in their invocation order):

- `init()`: This method is invoked immediately after the instantiation of `javafx.application.Application`. You can override this method to do some initialization before the start of the application. By default, this method does nothing.
- `start(javafx.stage.Stage)`: This method is called immediately after `init()` and after the system has done the required initialization to run the application. This method is passed with a `javafx.stage.Stage` instance, which is the primary stage on which the components are rendered. You can create other `javafx.stage.Stage` objects, but the one provided by the application is the primary stage.
- `stop()`: This method is called when the application should stop. You can do the necessary exit-related operations.

A *stage* is a top-level JavaFX container. The primary stage passed as an argument to the `start()` method is created by the platform, and the application can create other `Stage` containers as and when required.

The other important method related to `javafx.application.Application` is the `launch()` method. There are two variants of this:

- `launch(Class<? extends Application> appClass, String... args)`
- `launch(String... args)`

This method is called from the main method, and should be called only once. The first variant takes the name of the class that extends the `javafx.application.Application` class along with the arguments passed to the main method, and the second variant doesn't take the name of the class and, instead, should be invoked from within the class that extends the `javafx.application.Application` class. In our recipe, we have made use of the second variant.

We have created a class, `CreateGuiDemo`, extends `javafx.application.Application`. This will be the entry point for JavaFX UI, and we also added a main method to the class, making it an entry point for our application.

A layout construct determines how your components are laid out. There are multiple layouts supported by JavaFX, as follows:

- `javafx.scene.layout.HBox` and `javafx.scene.layout.VBox`: These are used to align the components horizontally and vertically.
- `javafx.scene.layout.BorderPane`: This allows the placing of the components in the top, right, bottom, left, and center positions.
- `javafx.scene.layout.FlowPane`: This layout allows the placing of the components in a flow, that is, besides each other, wrapping at the flow pane's boundary.
- `javafx.scene.layout.GridPane`: This layout allows the placing of the components in a grid of rows and columns.

- `javafx.scene.layout.StackPane`: This layout places the components in a back-to-front stack.
- `javafx.scene.layout.TilePane`: This layout places the components in a grid of uniformly sized tiles.

In our recipe, we have made use of `GridPane` and configured the layout so that we can achieve the following:

- The grid placed at the center (`gridPane.setAlignment(Pos.CENTER);`)
- Set the gap between the columns to 10 (`gridPane.setHgap(10);`)
- Set the gap between the rows to 10 (`gridPane.setVgap(10);`)
- Set the padding within the cell of the grid (`gridPane.setPadding(new Insets(25, 25, 25, 25));`)

A `javafx.scene.text.Text` component's font can be set using the `javafx.scene.text.Font` object as shown here: `appTitle.setFont(Font.font("Arial", FontWeight.NORMAL, 15));`

While adding the component to `javafx.scene.layout.GridPane`, we have to mention the column number, row number, and column span, that is, how many columns the component occupies, and the row span, that is, how many rows the component occupies in that order. The column span and the row span are optional. In our recipe, we have placed `appTitle` in the first row and column, and it occupies two column spaces and one-row space, as shown in the code here: `appTitle.setFont(Font.font("Arial", FontWeight.NORMAL, 15));`

The other important part in this recipe is the setting of the event for the `ageCalculator` button. We make use of the `setOnAction()` method of the `javafx.scene.control.Button` class to set the action performed when the button is clicked. This accepts an implementation of the `javafx.event.EventHandler<ActionEvent>` interface. As `javafx.event.EventHandler` is a functional interface, its implementation can be written in the form of a lambda expression, as shown here:

```
ageCalculator.setOnAction((event) -> {
  //event handling code here
});
```

The preceding syntax looks similar to your anonymous inner classes widely used during the times of Swing. You can learn more about functional interfaces and lambda expressions in the recipes in `Chapter 4`, *Going Functional*.

In our event-handling code, we get the values from `nameField` and `dateOfBirthPicker` by using the `getText()` and `getValue()` methods respectively. `DatePicker` returns the date selected as an instance of `java.time.LocalDate`. This is one of the new date-time APIs added to Java 8. It represents a date, that is, the year, the month, and the day, without any timezone-related information. We then make use of the `java.time.Period` class to find the duration between the current date and the selected date, as follows:

```
LocalDate now = LocalDate.now();
Period period = Period.between(dob, now);
```

`Period` represents the date-based duration in terms of years, months, and days, for example, three years, two months, and three days. This is exactly what we are trying to extract with this line of code: `String.format("Your age is %d years %d months %d days", period.getYears(), period.getMonths(), period.getDays())`.

We have already mentioned that the UI components in JavaFX are represented in the form of a scene graph, and this scene graph is then rendered onto a container, called `Stage`. The way to create a scene graph is by using the `javafx.scene.Scene` class. We create a `javafx.scene.Scene` instance by passing the root of the scene graph and also by providing the dimensions of the container in which the scene graph is going to be rendered.

We make use of the container provided to the `start()` method, which is nothing but an instance of `javafx.stage.Stage`. Setting the scene for the `Stage` object and then calling its `show()` methods makes the complete scene graph rendered on the display:

```
stage.setScene(scene);
stage.show();
```

Using the FXML markup to create a GUI

In our first recipe, we looked at using Java APIs to build a UI. It often happens that a person who is adept at Java might not be a good UI designer; that is, they may be poor at identifying the best user experience for their app. In the world of web development, we have developers working on the frontend, based on the designs given by the UX designer, and the other set of developers working on the backend, to build services that are consumed by the frontend.

Both developer parties agree to a set of APIs and a common data interchange model. Front-end developers work by using some mock data based on the data interchange model and also integrate the UI with the required APIs. On the other hand, backend developers work on implementing APIs so that they return the data in the interchange model agreed upon. So, both parties work simultaneously, using their expertise in their work areas.

It would be amazing if the same could be replicated (at least to some extent) on desktop applications. A step in this direction was the introduction of an XML-based language, called **FXML**. This enables a declarative method of UI development, where the developer can independently develop the UI using the same JavaFX components but available as XML tags. The different properties of the JavaFX components are available as attributes of the XML tags. Event handlers can be declared and defined in the Java code and then referred from FXML.

In this recipe, we will guide you through building the UI using FXML and then integrating FXML with the Java code for binding the action and for launching the UI defined in the FXML.

Getting ready

As we know that JavaFX libraries are not shipped in the JDK installation from Oracle JDK 11 onwards and Open JDK 10 onwards, we will have to download the JavaFX SDK from `https://gluonhq.com/products/javafx/` and include the JARs present in the SDK's `lib` folder on the modular path using the `-p` option, as shown here:

```
javac -p "PATH_TO_JAVAFX_SDK_LIB" <other parts of the command line>

#Windows
java -p "PATH_TO_JAVAFX_SDK_LIB;COMPILED_CODE" <other parts of the
command line>
#Linux
java -p "PATH_TO_JAVAFX_SDK_LIB:COMPILED_CODE" <other parts of the
command line>
```

We will develop a simple age calculator app. This app will ask for the user's name (which is optional) and their date of birth, and calculate the age from the given date of birth and display it to the user.

How to do it...

1. All the FXML files should end with the `.fxml` extension. Let's create an empty `fxml_age_calc_gui.xml` file in the location `src/gui/com/packt`. In the subsequent steps, we will update this file with the XML tags for the JavaFX components.

2. Create a `GridPane` layout, which will hold all the components in a grid of rows and columns. We will also provide the required spacing between the rows and the columns using the `vgap` and `hgap` attributes. Also, we will provide `GridPane`, which is our root component, with the reference to the Java class, where we will add the required event handling. This Java class will be like the controller for the UI:

```
<GridPane alignment="CENTER" hgap="10.0" vgap="10.0"
  xmlns:fx="http://javafx.com/fxml"
  fx:controller="com.packt.FxmlController">
</GridPane>
```

3. We will provide the padding within each cell of the grid by defining a `padding` tag with `Insets` within `GridPane`:

```
<padding>
  <Insets bottom="25.0" left="25.0" right="25.0" top="25.0" />
</padding>
```

4. Next is to add a `Text` tag, which displays the title of the application—`Age Calculator`. We provide the required style information in the `style` attribute and the placement of the `Text` component within `GridPane` using the `GridPane.columnIndex` and `GridPane.rowIndex` attributes. The cell occupancy information can be provided using the `GridPane.columnSpan` and `GridPane.rowSpan` attributes:

```
<Text style="-fx-font: NORMAL 15 Arial;" text="Age calculator"
  GridPane.columnIndex="0" GridPane.rowIndex="0"
  GridPane.columnSpan="2" GridPane.rowSpan="1">
</Text>
```

5. We then add the `Label` and `TextField` components for accepting the name. Note the use of the `fx:id` attribute in `TextField`. This helps in binding this component in the Java controller by creating a field with the same name as that of the `fx:id` value:

```
<Label text="Name" GridPane.columnIndex="0"
  GridPane.rowIndex="1">
</Label>
<TextField fx:id="nameField" GridPane.columnIndex="1"
  GridPane.rowIndex="1">
</TextField>
```

6. We add the `Label` and `DatePicker` components for accepting the date of birth:

```
<Label text="Date of Birth" GridPane.columnIndex="0"
  GridPane.rowIndex="2">
</Label>
<DatePicker fx:id="dateOfBirthPicker" GridPane.columnIndex="1"
  GridPane.rowIndex="2">
</DatePicker>
```

7. Then, we add a `Button` object and set its `onAction` attribute to the name of the method in the Java controller that handles the click event of this button:

```
<Button onAction="#calculateAge" text="Calculate"
  GridPane.columnIndex="1" GridPane.rowIndex="3">
</Button>
```

8. Finally, we add a `Text` component to display the calculated age:

```
<Text fx:id="resultTxt" style="-fx-font: NORMAL 15 Arial;"
  GridPane.columnIndex="0" GridPane.rowIndex="5"
  GridPane.columnSpan="2" GridPane.rowSpan="1">
</Text>
```

9. The next step is to implement the Java class, which is directly related to the XML-based UI components created in the preceding steps. Create a class named `FxmlController`. This will contain the code that is relevant to the FXML UI; that is, it will contain the references to the components created in the FXML action handlers for the components created in the FXML:

```
public class FxmlController {
  //to implement in next few steps
}
```

10. We need references to the `nameField`, `dateOfBirthPicker`, and `resultText` components. We use the first two to get the entered name and date of birth, respectively, and the third to display the result of the age calculation:

```
@FXML private Text resultTxt;
@FXML private DatePicker dateOfBirthPicker;
@FXML private TextField nameField;
```

11. The next step is to implement the `calculateAge` method, which is registered as the action event handler for the `Calculate` button. The implementation is similar to the one in the previous recipe. The only difference is that it is a method, unlike the previous recipe, where it was a lambda expression:

```
@FXML
public void calculateAge(ActionEvent event){
    String name = nameField.getText();
    LocalDate dob = dateOfBirthPicker.getValue();
    if ( dob != null ){
        LocalDate now = LocalDate.now();
        Period period = Period.between(dob, now);
        StringBuilder resultBuilder = new StringBuilder();
        if ( name != null && name.length() > 0 ){
            resultBuilder.append("Hello, ")
                         .append(name)
                         .append("n");
        }
        resultBuilder.append(String.format(
            "Your age is %d years %d months %d days",
            period.getYears(),
            period.getMonths(),
            period.getDays())
        );
        resultTxt.setText(resultBuilder.toString());
    }
}
```

12. In both steps 10 and 11, we have used an annotation, @FXML. This annotation indicates that the class or the member is accessible to the FXML-based UI.

13. Next, we'll create another Java class, FxmlGuiDemo, which is responsible for rendering the FXML-based UI and which would also be the entry point for launching the application:

```
public class FxmlGuiDemo extends Application{
  //code to launch the UI + provide main() method
}
```

14. Now we need to create a scene graph from the FXML UI definition by overriding the start(Stage stage) method of the javafx.application.Application class and then render the scene graph within the passed javafx.stage.Stage object:

```
@Override
public void start(Stage stage) throws IOException{
  FXMLLoader loader = new FXMLLoader();
  Pane pane = (Pane)loader.load(getClass()
    .getModule()
    .getResourceAsStream("com/packt/fxml_age_calc_gui.fxml")
  );
  Scene scene = new Scene(pane,300, 250);
  stage.setTitle("Age calculator");
  stage.setScene(scene);
  stage.show();
}
```

15. Finally, we provide the main() method implementation:

```
public static void main(String[] args) {
  Application.launch(args);
}
```

The complete code can be found at the location Chapter16/2_fxml_gui.

We have provided two-run scripts, run.bat and run.sh, in Chapter16/2_fxml_gui. The run.bat script will be for running the application on Windows, and run.sh will be for running the application on Linux.

Run the application using `run.bat` or `run.sh`, and you will see the GUI as shown in the following screenshot:

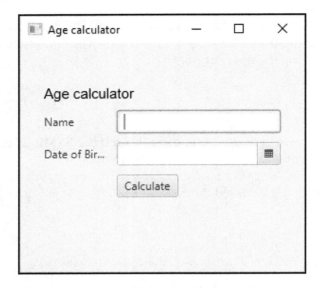

Enter the name and the date of birth and click on `Calculate` to view the age:

How it works...

There is no XSD defining the schema for the FXML document. So, to know the tags to be used, they follow a simple naming convention. The Java class name of the component is also the name of the XML tag. For example, the XML tag for the `javafx.scene.layout.GridPane` layout is `<GridPane>`, and for `javafx.scene.control.TextField` it is `<TextField>`, and for `javafx.scene.control.DatePicke` it is `<DatePicker>`:

```
Pane pane = (Pane)loader.load(getClass()
    .getModule()
    .getResourceAsStream("com/packt/fxml_age_calc_gui.fxml")
);
```

The preceding line of code makes use of an instance of `javafx.fxml.FXMLLoader` to read the FXML file and get the Java representation of the UI components. `FXMLLoader` uses an event-based SAX parser to parse the FXML file. Instances of the respective Java classes for the XML tags are created via reflection, and the values of attributes of the XML tags are populated into the respective properties of the Java classes.

As the root of our FXML is `javafx.scene.layout.GridPane`, which extends `javafx.scene.layout.Pane`, we can cast the return value from `FXMLoader.load()` to `javafx.scene.layout.Pane`.

The other interesting thing in this recipe is the `FxmlController` class. This class acts as an interface to FXML. We indicate the same in the FXML by using the `fx:controller` attribute to the `<GridPane>` tag. We can get hold of the UI components defined in FXML by using the `@FXML` annotation against the member fields of the `FxmlController` class, as we did in this recipe:

```
@FXML private Text resultTxt;
@FXML private DatePicker dateOfBirthPicker;
@FXML private TextField nameField;
```

The name of the member is the same as that of the `fx:id` attribute value in FXML, and the type of the member is the same as that of the tag in FXML. For example, the first member is bound to the following:

```
<Text fx:id="resultTxt" style="-fx-font: NORMAL 15 Arial;"
  GridPane.columnIndex="0" GridPane.rowIndex="5"
  GridPane.columnSpan="2" GridPane.rowSpan="1">
</Text>
```

On similar lines, we created an event handler in `FxmlController` and annotated it with `@FXML`, and the same has been referenced in FXML with the `onAction` attribute of `<Button>`. Note that we have added # to the beginning of the method name in the `onAction` attribute value.

Using CSS to the style elements in JavaFX

Those from a web development background will be able to appreciate the usefulness of the **Cascading Style Sheets** (**CSS**), and for those who are not, we will provide an overview of what they are and how they are useful, before diving into CSS application in JavaFX.

The elements or the components that you see on web pages are often styled according to the theme of the website. This styling is made possible by using a language called **CSS**. CSS consists of a group of `name:value` pairs, separated by semicolons. These `name:value` pairs, when associated with an HTML element, say, `<button>`, give it the required styling.

There are multiple ways to associate these `name:value` pairs to the element, the simplest being when you put this `name:value` pair within the style attribute of your HTML element. For example, to give the button a blue background, we can do the following:

```
<button style="background-color: blue;"></button>
```

There are predefined names for different styling properties, and these take a specific set of values; that is, the property, `background-color`, will only take valid color values.

The other approach is to define these groups of `name:value` pairs in a different file with a `.css` extension. Let's call this group of `name:value` pairs **CSS properties**. We can associate these CSS properties with different selectors, that is, selectors for choosing the elements on the HTML page to apply the CSS properties too. There are three different ways of providing the selectors:

1. By directly giving the name of the HTML element, that is, whether it is an anchor tag (`<a>`), button, or input. In such cases, the CSS properties are applied to all the types of HTML elements in the page.

2. By using the `id` attribute of the HTML element. Suppose, we have a button with `id="btn1"`, then we can define a selector, `#btn1`, against which we provide the CSS properties. Take a look at the following example:

```
#btn1 { background-color: blue; }
```

3. By using the class attribute of the HTML element. Suppose we have a button with `class="blue-btn"`, then we can define a selector, `.blue-btn`, against which we provide the CSS properties. Check out the following example:

```
.blue-btn { background-color: blue; }
```

The advantage of using a different CSS file is that we can independently evolve the appearance of the web pages without getting tightly coupled to the location of the elements. Also, this encourages the reuse of CSS properties across different pages, thereby giving them a uniform look across all the pages.

When we apply a similar approach to JavaFX, we can leverage the CSS knowledge already available with our web designers to build CSS for JavaFX components, and this helps in styling the components more easily than with the use of Java APIs. When this CSS is mixed with FXML, then it becomes a known domain for web developers.

In this recipe, we will look at styling a few JavaFX components using an external CSS file.

Getting ready

As we know that JavaFX libraries are not shipped in the JDK installation from Oracle JDK 11 onwards and Open JDK 10 onwards, we will have to download the JavaFX SDK from `https://gluonhq.com/products/javafx/` and include the JARs present in the SDK's `lib` folder on the modular path using the `-p` option, as shown here:

```
javac -p "PATH_TO_JAVAFX_SDK_LIB" <other parts of the command line>

#Windows
java -p "PATH_TO_JAVAFX_SDK_LIB;COMPILED_CODE" <other parts of the
command line>
#Linux
java -p "PATH_TO_JAVAFX_SDK_LIB:COMPILED_CODE" <other parts of the
command line>
```

There is a small difference in defining the CSS properties for the JavaFX components. All the properties must be prefixed with `-fx-`, that is, `background-color` becomes `-fx-background-color`. The selectors, that is, `#id` and `.class-name` still remain the same in the JavaFX world as well. We can even provide multiple classes to the JavaFX components, thereby applying all these CSS properties to the components.

The CSS that I have used in this recipe is based on a popular CSS framework called **Bootstrap** (`http://getbootstrap.com/css/`).

How to do it...

1. Let's create `GridPane`, which will hold the components in a grid of rows and columns:

```
GridPane gridPane = new GridPane();
gridPane.setAlignment(Pos.CENTER);
gridPane.setHgap(10);
gridPane.setVgap(10);
gridPane.setPadding(new Insets(25, 25, 25, 25));
```

2. First, we will create a button and add two classes, `btn`, and `btn-primary`, to it. In the next step, we will define these selectors with the required CSS properties:

```
Button primaryBtn = new Button("Primary");
primaryBtn.getStyleClass().add("btn");
primaryBtn.getStyleClass().add("btn-primary");
gridPane.add(primaryBtn, 0, 1);
```

3. Now let's provide the required CSS properties for the classes, `btn` and `btn-primary`. The selector for the classes are of the form `.<class-name>`:

```
.btn{
  -fx-border-radius: 4px;
  -fx-border: 2px;
  -fx-font-size: 18px;
  -fx-font-weight: normal;
  -fx-text-align: center;
}
.btn-primary {
  -fx-text-fill: #fff;
  -fx-background-color: #337ab7;
  -fx-border-color: #2e6da4;
}
```

4. Let's create another button with a different CSS class:

```
Button successBtn = new Button("Sucess");
successBtn.getStyleClass().add("btn");
successBtn.getStyleClass().add("btn-success");
gridPane.add(successBtn, 1, 1);
```

5. Now we define the CSS properties for the `.btn-success` selector as follows:

```
.btn-success {
  -fx-text-fill: #fff;
  -fx-background-color: #5cb85c;
  -fx-border-color: #4cae4c;
}
```

6. Let's create yet another button with a different CSS class:

```
Button dangerBtn = new Button("Danger");
dangerBtn.getStyleClass().add("btn");
dangerBtn.getStyleClass().add("btn-danger");
gridPane.add(dangerBtn, 2, 1);
```

7. We will define the CSS properties for the selector `.btn-danger`:

```
.btn-danger {
  -fx-text-fill: #fff;
  -fx-background-color: #d9534f;
  -fx-border-color: #d43f3a;
}
```

8. Now, let's add some labels with different selectors, namely `badge` and `badge-info`:

```
Label label = new Label("Default Label");
label.getStyleClass().add("badge");
gridPane.add(label, 0, 2);

Label infoLabel = new Label("Info Label");
infoLabel.getStyleClass().add("badge");
infoLabel.getStyleClass().add("badge-info");
gridPane.add(infoLabel, 1, 2);
```

9. The CSS properties for the previous selectors are as follows:

```
.badge{
  -fx-label-padding: 6,7,6,7;
  -fx-font-size: 12px;
  -fx-font-weight: 700;
  -fx-text-fill: #fff;
  -fx-text-alignment: center;
  -fx-background-color: #777;
  -fx-border-radius: 4;
}

.badge-info{
  -fx-background-color: #3a87ad;
}
.badge-warning {
  -fx-background-color: #f89406;
}
```

10. Let's add `TextField` with a `big-input` class:

```
TextField bigTextField = new TextField();
bigTextField.getStyleClass().add("big-input");
gridPane.add(bigTextField, 0, 3, 3, 1);
```

11. We define CSS properties so that the content of the textbox is large in size and red in color:

```
.big-input{
  -fx-text-fill: red;
  -fx-font-size: 18px;
  -fx-font-style: italic;
  -fx-font-weight: bold;
}
```

12. Let's add some radio buttons:

```
ToggleGroup group = new ToggleGroup();
RadioButton bigRadioOne = new RadioButton("First");
bigRadioOne.getStyleClass().add("big-radio");
bigRadioOne.setToggleGroup(group);
bigRadioOne.setSelected(true);
gridPane.add(bigRadioOne, 0, 4);
RadioButton bigRadioTwo = new RadioButton("Second");
bigRadioTwo.setToggleGroup(group);
bigRadioTwo.getStyleClass().add("big-radio");
gridPane.add(bigRadioTwo, 1, 4);
```

13. We define CSS properties so that the labels of the radio buttons are large in size and green in color:

```
.big-radio{
  -fx-text-fill: green;
  -fx-font-size: 18px;
  -fx-font-weight: bold;
  -fx-background-color: yellow;
  -fx-padding: 5;
}
```

14. Finally, we add `javafx.scene.layout.GridPane` to the scene graph and render the scene graph on `javafx.stage.Stage`. We also need to associate the `stylesheet.css` with the `Scene`:

```
Scene scene = new Scene(gridPane, 600, 500);
scene.getStylesheets().add("com/packt/stylesheet.css");
stage.setTitle("Age calculator");
stage.setScene(scene);
stage.show();
```

15. Add a `main()` method to launch the GUI:

```
public static void main(String[] args) {
  Application.launch(args);
}
```

The complete code can be found here: `Chapter16/3_css_javafx`.

We have provided two run scripts, `run.bat` and `run.sh`, under `Chapter16/3_css_javafx`. The `run.bat` will be for running the application on Windows, and `run.sh` will be for running the application on Linux.

Run the application using `run.bat` or `run.sh`, and you will see the following GUI:

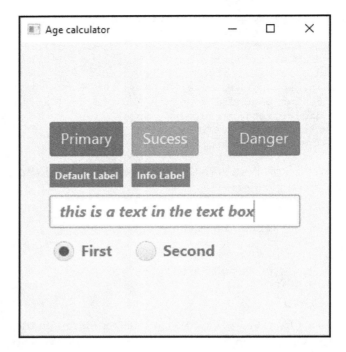

How it works...

In this recipe, we make use of class names and their corresponding CSS selectors to associate components with different styling properties. JavaFX supports a subset of CSS properties, and there are different properties applicable to different types of JavaFX components. The JavaFX CSS reference guide (`http://docs.oracle.com/javase/8/javafx/api/javafx/scene/doc-files/cssref.html`) will help you identify the supported CSS properties.

All the scene graph nodes extend from an abstract class, `javax.scene.Node`. This abstract class provides an API, `getStyleClass()`, that returns a list of class names (which are plain `String`) added to the node or to the JavaFX component. As this is a simple list of class names, we can even add more class names to it by using `getStyleClass().add("new-class-name")`.

The advantage of using class names is that it allows us to group similar components by a common class name. This technique is widely used in the web development world. Suppose I have a list of buttons on the HTML page and I want a similar action to be performed on the click of each button. To achieve this, I will assign each of the buttons the same class, say, `my-button`, and then use `document.getElementsByClassName('my-button')` to get an array of these buttons. Now we can loop through the array of buttons obtained and add the required action handlers.

After assigning a class to the component, we need to write the CSS properties for the given class name. These properties then get applied to all the components with the same class name.

Let's pick one of the components from our recipe and see how we went about styling it. Consider the following component with two classes, `btn` and `btn-primary`:

```
primaryBtn.getStyleClass().add("btn");
primaryBtn.getStyleClass().add("btn-primary");
```

We have used the selectors, `.btn` and `.btn-primary`, and we have grouped all the CSS properties under these selectors, as follows:

```
.btn{
  -fx-border-radius: 4px;
  -fx-border: 2px;
  -fx-font-size: 18px;
  -fx-font-weight: normal;
  -fx-text-align: center;
}

.btn-primary {
  -fx-text-fill: #fff;
  -fx-background-color: #337ab7;
  -fx-border-color: #2e6da4;
}
```

Note that, in CSS, we have a `color` property, and its equivalent in JavaFX is `-fx-text-fill`. The rest of the CSS properties, namely `border-radius`, `border`, `font-size`, `font-weight`, `text-align`, `background-color`, and `border-color`, are prefixed with `-fx-`.

The important part is how you associate the style sheet with the `Scene` component.

The `scene.getStylesheets().add("com/packt/stylesheet.css");` line of code associates stylesheets with the scene component. As `getStylesheets()` returns a list of strings, we can add multiple strings to it, which means that we can associate multiple stylesheets to a Scene.

The documentation of `getStylesheets()` states the following:

> *"The URL is a hierarchical URI of the form [scheme:][//authority][path]. If the URL does not have a [scheme:] component, the URL is considered to be the [path] component only. Any leading '/' character of the [path] is ignored and the [path] is treated as a path relative to the root of the application's classpath."*

In our recipe, we are using the `path` component only, and hence it looks for the file in the classpath. This is the reason we have added the stylesheet to the same package as that of the scene. This is an easier way of making it available on the classpath.

Creating a bar chart

Data, when represented in the form of tables, is very hard to understand, but when data is represented graphically by using charts, it is comfortable for the eyes and easy to understand. We have seen a lot of charting libraries for web applications. However, the same support was lacking on the desktop application front. Swing didn't have native support for creating charts, and we had to rely on third-party applications such as **JFreeChart** (`http://www.jfree.org/jfreechart/`). With JavaFX, though, we have native support for creating charts, and we are going to show you how to represent the data in the form of charts using the JavaFX chart components.

JavaFX supports the following chart types:

- Bar chart
- Line chart
- Pie chart
- Scatter chart
- Area chart
- Bubble chart

In the next few recipes, we will cover the construction of each chart type. The segregation of each chart type into a recipe of its own will help us in explaining the recipes in a simpler way and will aid better understanding.

This recipe will be all about bar charts. A sample bar chart looks something like this:

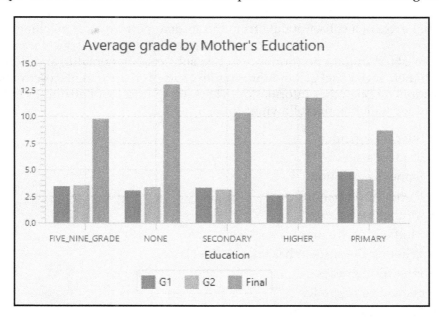

Bar charts can have a single bar or multiple bars (as in the preceding diagram) for each value on the x axis. Multiple bars help us in comparing multiple value points for each value on the x axis.

Getting ready

As we know that JavaFX libraries are not shipped in the JDK installation from Oracle JDK 11 onwards and Open JDK 10 onwards, we will have to download the JavaFX SDK from here `https://gluonhq.com/products/javafx/` and include the JARs present in the SDK's `lib` folder on the modular path using the `-p` option, as shown here:

```
javac -p "PATH_TO_JAVAFX_SDK_LIB" <other parts of the command line>

#Windows
java -p "PATH_TO_JAVAFX_SDK_LIB;COMPILED_CODE" <other parts of the
command line>
#Linux
java -p "PATH_TO_JAVAFX_SDK_LIB:COMPILED_CODE" <other parts of the
command line>
```

We will make use of a subset of data from the student performance machine learning repository (`https://archive.ics.uci.edu/ml/datasets/Student+Performance`). The dataset consists of student performance in two subjects, Mathematics and Portuguese, along with their social background information, such as their parents' occupations and education, among other information. There are quite a lot of attributes in the dataset, but we will pick the following:

- Student's gender
- Student's age
- Father's education
- Father's occupation
- Mother's education
- Mother's occupation
- Whether the student has taken extra classes
- First-term grades
- Second-term grades
- Final grades

As we mentioned earlier, there are a lot of attributes captured in the data, but we should be good with a few important attributes that will help us plot some useful charts. Due to this, we have extracted the information from the dataset available in the machine learning repository into a separate file, which can be found at `Chapter16/4_bar_charts/src/gui/com/packt/students`, in the code download for the book. An excerpt from the students file follows:

```
"F";18;4;4;"at_home";"teacher";"no";"5";"6";6
"F";17;1;1;"at_home";"other";"no";"5";"5";6
"F";15;1;1;"at_home";"other";"yes";"7";"8";10
"F";15;4;2;"health";"services";"yes";"15";"14";15
"F";16;3;3;"other";"other";"yes";"6";"10";10
"M";16;4;3;"services";"other";"yes";"15";"15";15
```

The entries are separated by semicolons (;). Each entry has been explained for what it represents. The education information (fields 3 and 4) is a numeric value, where each number represents the level of education, as follows:

- 0: None
- 1: Primary education (fourth grade)
- 2: Fifth to ninth grade
- 3: Secondary education
- 4: Higher education

We have created a module for processing the student file. The module name is `student.processor` and its code can be found at `Chapter16/101_student_data_processor`. So, if you want to change any code there, you can rebuild the JAR by running the `build-jar.bat` or `build-jar.sh` file. This will create a modular JAR, `student.processor.jar`, in the `mlib` directory. Then, you have to replace this modular JAR with the one present in the `mlib` directory of this recipe, that is, `Chapter16/4_bar_charts/mlib`.

We recommend that you build the `student.processor` modular jar from the source available in `Chapter16/101_student_data_processor`. We have provided `build-jar.bat` and `build-jar.sh` scripts to help you build the JAR. You just have to run the script relevant to your platform and then copy the jar build in `101_student_data_processor/mlib` to `4_bar_charts/mlib`.

This way, we can reuse this module across all the recipes involving charts.

How to do it...

1. First, create `GridPane` and configure it to place the charts that we will be creating:

```
GridPane gridPane = new GridPane();
gridPane.setAlignment(Pos.CENTER);
gridPane.setHgap(10);
gridPane.setVgap(10);
gridPane.setPadding(new Insets(25, 25, 25, 25));
```

2. Use the `StudentDataProcessor` class from the `student.processor` module to parse the student file and load the data into `List` of `Student`:

```
StudentDataProcessor sdp = new StudentDataProcessor();
List<Student> students = sdp.loadStudent();
```

3. The raw data, that is, the list of `Student` objects, is not useful for plotting a chart, so we need to process the students' grades by grouping the students according to their mothers' and fathers' education and computing the average of those students' grades (all three terms). For this, we will write a simple method that accepts `List<Student>`, a grouping function, that is, the value on which the students need to be grouped, and a mapping function, that is, the value that has to be used to compute the average:

```
private Map<ParentEducation, IntSummaryStatistics> summarize(
    List<Student> students,
    Function<Student, ParentEducation> classifier,
    ToIntFunction<Student> mapper
){
    Map<ParentEducation, IntSummaryStatistics> statistics =
        students.stream().collect(
            Collectors.groupingBy(
                classifier,
                Collectors.summarizingInt(mapper)
            )
        );
    return statistics;
}
```

The preceding method uses the new Stream-based APIs. These APIs are so powerful that they group the students by using `Collectors.groupingBy()` and then compute the statistics of their grades by using `Collectors.summarizingInt()`.

4. The data for the bar chart is provided as an instance of `XYChart.Series`. Each series results in one *y* value for a given *x* value, which is one bar for a given *x* value. We will have multiple series, one for each term, that is, first-term grades, second-term grades, and the final grades. Let's create a method that takes in the statistics of each term grades and the `seriesName` and returns a `series` object:

```
private XYChart.Series<String,Number> getSeries(
    String seriesName,
    Map<ParentEducation, IntSummaryStatistics> statistics
){
 XYChart.Series<String,Number> series = new
XYChart.Series<>();
    series.setName(seriesName);
    statistics.forEach((k, v) -> {
      series.getData().add(
        new XYChart.Data<String, Number>(
          k.toString(),v.getAverage()
        )
      );
    });
    return series;
}
```

5. We will create two bar charts—one for the average grade from the mother's education and the other for the average grade from the father's education. For this, we will create a method that will take `List<Student>` and a classifier, that is, a function that will return the value to be used to group the students. This method will do the necessary computations and return a `BarChart` object:

```
private BarChart<String, Number>
getAvgGradeByEducationBarChart(
      List<Student> students,
      Function<Student, ParentEducation> classifier
    ){
      final CategoryAxis xAxis = new CategoryAxis();
      final NumberAxis yAxis = new NumberAxis();
      final BarChart<String,Number> bc =
          new BarChart<>(xAxis,yAxis);
      xAxis.setLabel("Education");
      yAxis.setLabel("Grade");
      bc.getData().add(getSeries(
        "G1",
        summarize(students, classifier,
Student::getFirstTermGrade)
```

```
            ));
          bc.getData().add(getSeries(
            "G2",
           summarize(students, classifier,
   Student::getSecondTermGrade)
          ));
          bc.getData().add(getSeries(
            "Final",
            summarize(students, classifier,
   Student::getFinalGrade)
          ));
          return bc;
        }
```

6. Create `BarChart` for the average grades from the mother's education, and add it to `gridPane`:

```
BarChart<String, Number> avgGradeByMotherEdu =
    getAvgGradeByEducationBarChart(
        students,
        Student::getMotherEducation
    );
avgGradeByMotherEdu.setTitle(
    "Average grade by Mother's Education"
);
gridPane.add(avgGradeByMotherEdu, 1,1);
```

7. Create `BarChart` for the average grades from the father's education and add it to `gridPane`:

```
BarChart<String, Number> avgGradeByFatherEdu =
    getAvgGradeByEducationBarChart(
        students,
        Student::getFatherEducation
    );
avgGradeByFatherEdu.setTitle(
    "Average grade by Father's Education");
gridPane.add(avgGradeByFatherEdu, 2,1);
```

8. Create a scene graph using `gridPane` and set it to `Stage`:

```
Scene scene = new Scene(gridPane, 800, 600);
stage.setTitle("Bar Charts");
stage.setScene(scene);
stage.show();
```

The complete code can be found at `Chapter16/4_bar_charts`.

We have provided two run scripts: `run.bat` and `run.sh`, under `Chapter16/4_bar_charts`. The `run.bat` script will be for running the application on Windows, and `run.sh` will be for running the application on Linux.

Run the application using `run.bat` or `run.sh`, and you will see the following GUI:

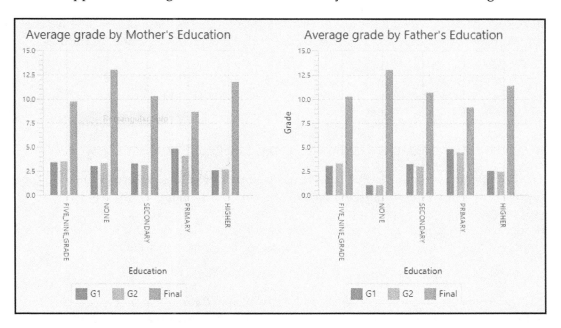

How it works...

Let's first see what it takes to create `BarChart`. `BarChart` is a two axes-based chart, where the data is plotted on two axes, namely the *x* axis (horizontal axis) and the *y* axis (vertical axis). The other two axes-based charts are area chart, bubble chart, and line chart.

In JavaFX, there are two types of axes supported:

- `javafx.scene.chart.CategoryAxis`: This supports string values on the axes
- `javafx.scene.chart.NumberAxis`: This supports numeric values on the axes

In our recipe, we created `BarChart` with `CategoryAxis` as the *x* axis, where we plot the education, and `NumberAxis` as the *y* axis, where we plot the grade, as follows:

```
final CategoryAxis xAxis = new CategoryAxis();
final NumberAxis yAxis = new NumberAxis();
final BarChart<String,Number> bc = new BarChart<>(xAxis,yAxis);
xAxis.setLabel("Education");
yAxis.setLabel("Grade");
```

In the next few paragraphs, we show you how the plotting of `BarChart` works.

The data to be plotted on `BarChart` should be a pair of values, where each pair represents *(x, y)* values, that is, a point on the *x* axis and a point on the *y* axis. This pair of values is represented by `javafx.scene.chart.XYChart.Data`. `Data` is a nested class within `XYChart`, which represents a single data item for a two axes-based chart. An `XYChart.Data` object can be created quite simply, as follows:

```
XYChart.Data item = new XYChart.Data("Cat1", "12");
```

This is just a one-data item. A chart can have multiple data items, that is, a series of data items. To represent a series of data items, JavaFX provides a class called `javafx.scene.chart.XYChart.Series`. This `XYChart.Series` object is a named series of `XYChart.Data` items. Let's create a simple series, as follows:

```
XYChart.Series<String,Number> series = new XYChart.Series<>();
series.setName("My series");
series.getData().add(
  new XYChart.Data<String, Number>("Cat1", 12)
);
series.getData().add(
  new XYChart.Data<String, Number>("Cat2", 3)
);
series.getData().add(
  new XYChart.Data<String, Number>("Cat3", 16)
);
```

BarChart can have multiple series of data items. If we provide it with multiple series, then there will be multiple bars for each data point on the *x* axis. For our demonstration of how this works, we will stick with one series. But the BarChart class in our recipe uses multiple series. Let's add the series to the BarChart and then render it onto the screen:

```
bc.getData().add(series);
Scene scene = new Scene(bc, 800, 600);
stage.setTitle("Bar Charts");
stage.setScene(scene);
stage.show();
```

This results in the following chart:

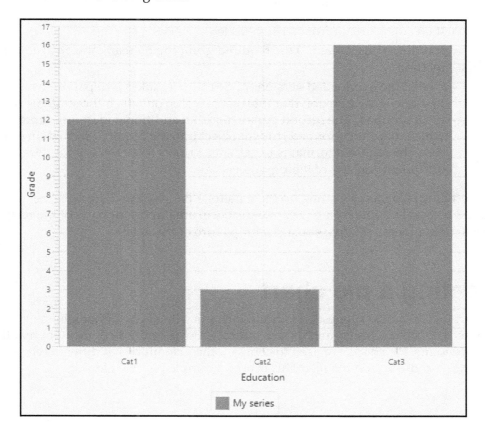

The other interesting part of this recipe is the grouping of students based on the education of the mother and father and then computing the average of their first-term, second-term, and final grades. The code that does the grouping and average computation are as follows:

```
Map<ParentEducation, IntSummaryStatistics> statistics =
        students.stream().collect(
  Collectors.groupingBy(
    classifier,
    Collectors.summarizingInt(mapper)
  )
);
```

The preceding code does the following:

- It creates a stream from `List<Student>`.
- It reduces this stream to the required grouping by using the `collect()` method.
- One of the overloaded versions of `collect()` takes two parameters. The first one is the function that returns the value on which the students need to be grouped. The second parameter is an additional mapping function, which maps the grouped student object into the required format. In our case, the required format is to get `IntSummaryStatistics` for the group of students on any of their grade values.

The preceding two pieces (setting up the data for a bar chart and creating the required objects to populate a `BarChart` instance) are important parts of the recipe; understanding them will give you a clearer picture of the recipe.

Creating a pie chart

Pie charts, as the name suggests, are circular charts with slices (either joined or separated), where each slice and its size indicates the magnitude of the item that the slice represents. Pie charts are used to compare the magnitudes of different classes, categories, products, and the like. This is how a sample pie chart looks:

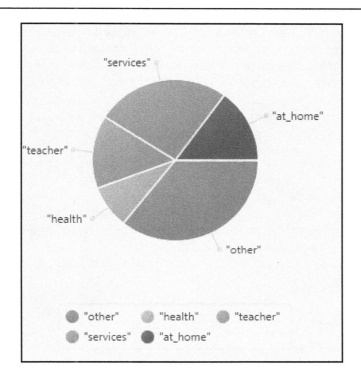

Getting ready

As we know that JavaFX libraries are not shipped in the JDK installation from Oracle JDK 11 onwards and Open JDK 10 onwards, we will have to download the JavaFX SDK from here https://gluonhq.com/products/javafx/ and include the JARs present in the SDK's lib folder on the modular path using the -p option, as shown here:

```
javac -p "PATH_TO_JAVAFX_SDK_LIB" <other parts of the command line>

#Windows
java -p "PATH_TO_JAVAFX_SDK_LIB;COMPILED_CODE" <other parts of the
command line>
#Linux
java -p "PATH_TO_JAVAFX_SDK_LIB:COMPILED_CODE" <other parts of the
command line>
```

We will make use of the same student data (taken from the machine learning repository and processed at our end) that we had discussed in the recipe, *Creating a bar chart* recipe. For this, we have created a module, `student.processor`, which will read the student data and provide us with a list of `Student` objects. The source code for the module can be found at `Chapter16/101_student_data_processor`. We have provided the modular jar for the `student.processor` module at `Chapter16/5_pie_charts/mlib` of this recipe's code.

> We recommend you to build the `student.processor` modular jar from the source available in `Chapter16/101_student_data_processor`. We have provided `build-jar.bat` and `build-jar.sh` scripts to help you with building the jar. You just have to run the script relevant to your platform and then copy the jar build in `101_student_data_processor/mlib` to `4_bar_charts/mlib`.

How to do it...

1. Let's first create and configure `GridPane` to hold our pie charts:

```
GridPane gridPane = new GridPane();
gridPane.setAlignment(Pos.CENTER);
gridPane.setHgap(10);
gridPane.setVgap(10);
gridPane.setPadding(new Insets(25, 25, 25, 25));
```

2. Create an instance of `StudentDataProcessor` (which comes from the `student.processor` module) and use it to load `List` of `Student`:

```
StudentDataProcessor sdp = new StudentDataProcessor();
List<Student> students = sdp.loadStudent();
```

3. Now we need to get the count of students by their mothers' and fathers' professions. We will write a method that will take a list of students and a classifier, that is, the function that returns the value on which the students need to be grouped. The method returns an instance of `PieChart`:

```
private PieChart getStudentCountByOccupation(
    List<Student> students,
    Function<Student, String> classifier
){
  Map<String, Long> occupationBreakUp =
          students.stream().collect(
```

```
        Collectors.groupingBy(
          classifier,
          Collectors.counting()
        )
    );
    List<PieChart.Data> pieChartData = new ArrayList<>();
    occupationBreakUp.forEach((k, v) -> {
      pieChartData.add(new PieChart.Data(k.toString(), v));
    });
    PieChart chart = new PieChart(
      FXCollections.observableList(pieChartData)
    );
    return chart;
}
```

4. We will invoke the preceding method twice—one with the mother's occupation as the classifier and the other with the father's occupation as the classifier. We then add the returned `PieChart` instance to `gridPane`. This should be done from within the `start()` method:

```
PieChart motherOccupationBreakUp =
getStudentCountByOccupation(
  students, Student::getMotherJob
);
motherOccupationBreakUp.setTitle("Mother's Occupation");
gridPane.add(motherOccupationBreakUp, 1,1);

PieChart fatherOccupationBreakUp =
getStudentCountByOccupation(
  students, Student::getFatherJob
);
fatherOccupationBreakUp.setTitle("Father's Occupation");
gridPane.add(fatherOccupationBreakUp, 2,1);
```

5. The next step is to create the scene graph using `gridPane` and add it to `Stage`:

```
Scene scene = new Scene(gridPane, 800, 600);
stage.setTitle("Pie Charts");
stage.setScene(scene);
stage.show();
```

6. The UI can be launched from the main method by invoking the `Application.launch` method:

```
public static void main(String[] args) {
  Application.launch(args);
}
```

The complete code can be found at `Chapter16/5_pie_charts`.

We have provided two run scripts, `run.bat` and `run.sh`, under `Chapter16/5_pie_charts`. The `run.bat` script will be for running the application on Windows, and `run.sh` will be for running the application on Linux.

Run the application using `run.bat` or `run.sh` and you will see the following GUI:

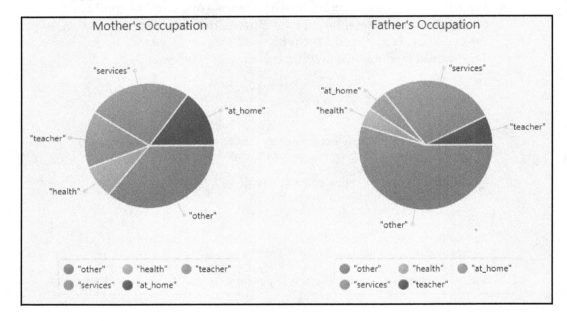

How it works...

The most important method which does all the work in this recipe is
`getStudentCountByOccupation()`. It does the following:

1. It groups the number of students by profession. This can be done in a single
    line of code using the power of the new streaming APIs (added as part of
    Java 8):

    ```
    Map<String, Long> occupationBreakUp =
                students.stream().collect(
      Collectors.groupingBy(
        classifier,
        Collectors.counting()
      )
    );
    ```

2. Build data required for `PieChart`. The `PieChart` instance's data is
    `ObservableList` of `PieChart.Data`. We first make use of `Map` obtained
    in the preceding step to create `ArrayList` of `PieChart.Data`. Then, we
    use the `FXCollections.observableList()` API to obtain
    `ObservableList<PieChart.Data>` from `List<PieChart.Data>`:

    ```
    List<PieChart.Data> pieChartData = new ArrayList<>();
    occupationBreakUp.forEach((k, v) -> {
      pieChartData.add(new PieChart.Data(k.toString(), v));
    });
    PieChart chart = new PieChart(
      FXCollections.observableList(pieChartData)
    );
    ```

The other important thing in the recipe is the classifiers we
use: `Student::getMotherJob` and `Student::getFatherJob`. These are the two
method references that invoke the `getMotherJob` and `getFatherJob` methods on
the different instances of `Student` in the list of `Student`.

Once we get the `PieChart` instances, we add them to `GridPane` and then construct
the scene graph using `GridPane`. The scene graph has to be associated with `Stage` for
it to be rendered on the screen.

The main method launches the UI by invoking the `Application.launch(args);`
method.

JavaFX provides APIs for creating different types of charts, such as the following ones:

- Area charts
- Bubble charts
- Line charts
- Scatter charts

All of these charts are *x* and *y* axis-based charts and can be constructed like a bar chart. We have provided some sample implementations to create these types of charts, and they can be found at these locations: `Chapter16/5_2_area_charts`, `Chapter16/5_3_line_charts`, `Chapter16/5_4_bubble_charts`, and `Chapter16/5_5_scatter_charts`.

Embedding HTML in an application

JavaFX provides support for managing web pages via the classes defined in the `javafx.scene.web` package. It supports loading the web page, either by accepting the web page URL or by accepting the web page content. It also manages the document model of the web page, applies the relevant CSS, and runs the relevant JavaScript code. It also extends support for a two-way communication between JavaScript and the Java code.

In this recipe, we will build a very primitive and simple web browser that supports the following:

- Navigating through the history of the pages visited
- Reloading the current page
- An address bar for accepting the URL
- A button for loading the entered URL
- Showing the web page
- Showing the status of loading of the web page

Getting ready

As we know that JavaFX libraries are not shipped in the JDK installation from Oracle JDK 11 onward and Open JDK 10 onward, we will have to download the JavaFX SDK from here `https://gluonhq.com/products/javafx/` and include the JARs present in the SDK's `lib` folder on the modular path using the -p option, as shown here:

```
javac -p "PATH_TO_JAVAFX_SDK_LIB" <other parts of the command line>

#Windows
java -p "PATH_TO_JAVAFX_SDK_LIB;COMPILED_CODE" <other parts of the
command line>
#Linux
java -p "PATH_TO_JAVAFX_SDK_LIB:COMPILED_CODE" <other parts of the
command line>
```

We will require an internet connection to test the loading of pages. So, make sure you are connected to the internet. Apart from this, there is nothing specific required to work with this recipe.

How to do it...

1. Let's first create a class with empty methods, which would represent the main application for launching the application as well as the JavaFX UI:

```java
public class BrowserDemo extends Application{
  public static void main(String[] args) {
    Application.launch(args);
  }
  @Override
  public void start(Stage stage) {
    //this will have all the JavaFX related code
  }
}
```

In the subsequent steps, we will write all our code within the start(Stage stage) method.

2. Let's create a javafx.scene.web.WebView component, which will render our web page. This has the required javafx.scene.web.WebEngine instance, which manages the loading of the web page:

```java
WebView webView = new WebView();
```

3. Get the instance of `javafx.scene.web.WebEngine` used by `webView`. We will use this instance of `javafx.scene.web.WebEngine` to navigate through the history and load other web pages. Then we will, by default, load the URL, `http://www.google.com`:

```
WebEngine webEngine = webView.getEngine();
webEngine.load("http://www.google.com/");
```

4. Now let's create a `javafx.scene.control.TextField` component, which will act as our browser's address bar:

```
TextField webAddress = new
TextField("http://www.google.com/");
```

5. We want to change the title of the browser and the web page in the address bar, based on the title and URL of the completely loaded web page. This can be done by listening to the change in the `stateProperty` of `javafx.concurrent.Worker` obtained from the `javafx.scene.web.WebEngine` instance:

```
webEngine.getLoadWorker().stateProperty().addListener(
  new ChangeListener<State>() {
    public void changed(ObservableValue ov,
                        State oldState, State newState) {
      if (newState == State.SUCCEEDED) {
        stage.setTitle(webEngine.getTitle());
        webAddress.setText(webEngine.getLocation());
      }
    }
  }
);
```

6. Let's create a `javafx.scene.control.Button` instance, which, upon clicking, will load the web page identified by the URL entered in the address bar:

```
Button goButton = new Button("Go");
goButton.setOnAction((event) -> {
  String url = webAddress.getText();
  if ( url != null && url.length() > 0){
    webEngine.load(url);
  }
});
```

7. Let's create a `javafx.scene.control.Button` instance, which, upon clicking, will go to the previous web page in the history. To achieve this, we will execute the JavaScript code, `history.back()`, from within the action handler:

```
Button prevButton = new Button("Prev");
prevButton.setOnAction(e -> {
  webEngine.executeScript("history.back()");
});
```

8. Let's create a `javafx.scene.control.Button` instance, which, upon clicking, will go to the next entry in the history maintained by `javafx.scene.web.WebEngine` instance. For this, we will make use of the `javafx.scene.web.WebHistory` API:

```
Button nextButton = new Button("Next");
nextButton.setOnAction(e -> {
  WebHistory wh = webEngine.getHistory();
  Integer historySize = wh.getEntries().size();
  Integer currentIndex = wh.getCurrentIndex();
  if ( currentIndex < (historySize - 1)){
    wh.go(1);
  }
});
```

9. Next is the button for reloading the current page. Again, we will make use of `javafx.scene.web.WebEngine` to reload the current page:

```
Button reloadButton = new Button("Refresh");
reloadButton.setOnAction(e -> {
  webEngine.reload();
});
```

10. Now we need to group all the components created so far, namely, `prevButton`, `nextButton`, `reloadButton`, `webAddress`, and `goButton`, so that they align horizontally with one another. To achieve this, we will make use of `javafx.scene.layout.HBox` with relevant spacing and padding to make the components look well spaced:

```
HBox addressBar = new HBox(10);
addressBar.setPadding(new Insets(10, 5, 10, 5));
addressBar.setHgrow(webAddress, Priority.ALWAYS);
addressBar.getChildren().addAll(
  prevButton, nextButton, reloadButton, webAddress, goButton
);
```

11. We would want to know whether the web page is loading and whether it has finished. Let's create a `javafx.scene.layout.Label` field to update the status if the web page is loaded. Then, we listen to the updates to `workDoneProperty` of the `javafx.concurrent.Worker` instance, which we can get from the `javafx.scene.web.WebEngine` instance:

```
Label websiteLoadingStatus = new Label();
webEngine
  .getLoadWorker()
  .workDoneProperty()
  .addListener(
    new ChangeListener<Number>(){
      public void changed(
        ObservableValue ov,
        Number oldState,
        Number newState
      ) {
        if (newState.doubleValue() != 100.0){
          websiteLoadingStatus.setText(
            "Loading " + webAddress.getText());
        }else{
          websiteLoadingStatus.setText("Done");
        }
      }
    }
  );
```

12. Let's align the entire address bar (with its navigation buttons), `webView`, and `websiteLoadingStatus` vertically:

```
VBox root = new VBox();
root.getChildren().addAll(
  addressBar, webView, websiteLoadingStatus
);
```

13. Create a new `Scene` object with the `VBox` instance created in the preceding step as the root:

```
Scene scene = new Scene(root);
```

14. We want the `javafx.stage.Stage` instance to occupy the complete screen size; for this, we will make use of `Screen.getPrimary().getVisualBounds()`. Then, as usual, we will render the scene graph on the stage:

```
Rectangle2D primaryScreenBounds =
```

```
                    Screen.getPrimary().getVisualBounds();
    stage.setTitle("Web Browser");
    stage.setScene(scene);
    stage.setX(primaryScreenBounds.getMinX());
    stage.setY(primaryScreenBounds.getMinY());
    stage.setWidth(primaryScreenBounds.getWidth());
    stage.setHeight(primaryScreenBounds.getHeight());
    stage.show();
```

The complete code can be found at the location, `Chapter16/6_embed_html`.

We have provided two run scripts, `run.bat` and `run.sh`, under `Chapter16/6_embed_html`. The `run.bat` script will be for running the application on Windows, and `run.sh` will be for running the application on Linux.

Run the application using `run.bat` or `run.sh`, and you will see the following GUI:

How it works...

The web-related APIs are available in the `javafx.web` module, so we will have to require it in `module-info`:

```
module gui{
  requires javafx.controls;
  requires javafx.web;
  opens com.packt;
}
```

The following are the important classes in the `javafx.scene.` web package when dealing with web pages in JavaFX:

- `WebView`: This UI component uses `WebEngine` to manage the loading, rendering, and interaction with the web page.
- `WebEngine`: This is the main component that deals with loading and managing the web page.
- `WebHistory`: This records the web pages visited in the current `WebEngine` instance.
- `WebEvent`: These are the instances passed to the event handlers of `WebEngine` invoked by the JavaScript event.

In our recipe, we make use of the first three classes.

We don't directly create an instance of `WebEngine`; instead, we make use of `WebView` to get a reference to the `WebEngine` instance managed by it. The `WebEngine` instance loads the web page asynchronously by submitting the task of loading the page to `javafx.concurrent.Worker` instances. Then, we register change listeners on these worker instance properties to track the progress of loading the web page. We have made use of two such properties in this recipe, namely, `stateProperty` and `workDoneProperty`. The former tracks the change of the state of the worker, and the latter tracks the percentage of the work done.

A worker can go through the following states (as listed in
the `javafx.concurrent.Worker.State` enum):

- CANCELLED
- FAILED
- READY
- RUNNING
- SCHEDULED
- SUCCEEDED

In our recipe, we are only checking for SUCCEEDED, but you can enhance it to check
for FAILED as well. This will help us report invalid URLs or even get the message
from the event object and show it to the user.

The way we add the listeners to track the change in the properties is by using
the `addListener()` method on `*Property()`, where * can be `state`, `workDone`, or
any other attribute of the worker that has been exposed as a property:

```
webEngine
  .getLoadWorker()
  .stateProperty()
  .addListener(
    new ChangeListener<State>() {
      public void changed(ObservableValue ov,
        State oldState, State newState) {
          //event handler code here
        }
    }
);

webEngine
  .getLoadWorker()
  .workDoneProperty()
  .addListener(
    new ChangeListener<Number>(){
      public void changed(ObservableValue ov,
        Number oldState, Number newState) {
          //event handler code here
        }
    }
);
```

Then the `javafx.scene.web.WebEngine` component also supports the following:

- Reloading the current page
- Getting the history of the pages loaded by it
- Executing the JavaScript code
- Listening to JavaScript properties, such as showing an alert box or a confirmation box
- Interacting with the document model of the web page using the `getDocument()` method

In this recipe, we also looked at using `WebHistory` obtained from `WebEngine`. `WebHistory` stores the web pages loaded by the given `WebEngine` instance, which means one `WebEngine` instance will have one `WebHistory` instance. `WebHistory` supports the following:

- Getting the list of entries by using the `getEntries()` method. This will also get us the number of entries in the history. This is required while navigating forward and backward in history; otherwise, we will end up with an index out of bounds exception.
- Getting `currentIndex`, that is, its index within the `getEntries()` list.
- Navigating to the specific entry in the entries list of `WebHistory`. This can be achieved by using the `go()` method, which accepts an offset. This offset indicates which web page to load, relative to the current position. For example, *+1* indicates the next entry, and *-1* indicates the previous entry. It's important to check for the boundary conditions; otherwise, you will end up going before *0*, that is, *-1*, or going past the entry list size.

There's more...

In this recipe, we showed you a basic approach to creating a web browser, using the support provided by JavaFX. You can enhance this to support the following:

- Better error handling and user messages, that is, to show whether the web address is valid by tracking the state change of the worker
- Multiple tabs
- Bookmarking
- Storing the state of the browser locally so that the next time it is run it loads all the bookmarks and the history

Embedding media in an application

JavaFX provides a component, `javafx.scene.media.MediaView`, for viewing videos and listening to audios. This component is backed by a media engine, `javafx.scene.media.MediaPlayer`, which loads and manages the playback of the media.

In this recipe, we will look at playing a sample video and controlling its playback by using the methods on the media engine.

Getting ready

As we know that JavaFX libraries are not shipped in the JDK installation from Oracle JDK 11 onward and Open JDK 10 onward, we will have to download the JavaFX SDK from here `https://gluonhq.com/products/javafx/` and include the JARs present in the SDK's `lib` folder on the modular path using the `-p` option shown here:

```
javac -p "PATH_TO_JAVAFX_SDK_LIB" <other parts of the command line>

#Windows
java -p "PATH_TO_JAVAFX_SDK_LIB;COMPILED_CODE" <other parts of the
command line>
#Linux
java -p "PATH_TO_JAVAFX_SDK_LIB:COMPILED_CODE" <other parts of the
command line>
```

We will make use of the sample video available at `Chapter16/7_embed_audio_video/sample_video1.mp4`.

How to do it...

1. Let's first create a class with empty methods, which would represent the main application for launching the application as well as the JavaFX UI:

```
public class EmbedAudioVideoDemo extends Application{
  public static void main(String[] args) {
    Application.launch(args);
  }
  @Override
  public void start(Stage stage) {
    //this will have all the JavaFX related code
  }
}
```

2. Create a `javafx.scene.media.Media` object for the video located at `Chapter16/7_embed_audio_video/sample_video1.mp4`:

```
File file = new File("sample_video1.mp4");
Media media = new Media(file.toURI().toString());
```

3. Create a new media engine, `javafx.scene.media.MediaPlayer`, using the `javafx.scene.media.Media` object created in the previous step:

```
MediaPlayer mediaPlayer = new MediaPlayer(media);
```

4. Let's track the status of the media player by registering a change listener on `statusProperty` of the `javafx.scene.media.MediaPlayer` object:

```
mediaPlayer.statusProperty().addListener(
        new ChangeListener<Status>() {
  public void changed(ObservableValue ov,
                  Status oldStatus, Status newStatus) {
    System.out.println(oldStatus +"->" + newStatus);
  }
});
```

5. Let's now create a media viewer using the media engine created in the previous step:

```
MediaView mediaView = new MediaView(mediaPlayer);
```

6. We will restrict the width and height of the media viewer:

```
mediaView.setFitWidth(350);
mediaView.setFitHeight(350);
```

7. Next, we create three buttons to pause the video playback, resume the playback, and stop the playback. We will make use of the relevant methods in the `javafx.scene.media.MediaPlayer` class:

```
Button pauseB = new Button("Pause");
pauseB.setOnAction(e -> {
  mediaPlayer.pause();
});

Button playB = new Button("Play");
playB.setOnAction(e -> {
  mediaPlayer.play();
});

Button stopB = new Button("Stop");
stopB.setOnAction(e -> {
  mediaPlayer.stop();
});
```

8. Align all these buttons horizontally using `javafx.scene.layout.HBox`:

```
HBox controlsBox = new HBox(10);
controlsBox.getChildren().addAll(pauseB, playB, stopB);
```

9. Align the media viewer and the buttons bar vertically using `javafx.scene.layout.VBox`:

```
VBox vbox = new VBox();
vbox.getChildren().addAll(mediaView, controlsBox);
```

10. Create a new scene graph using the `VBox` object as the root and set it to the stage object:

```
Scene scene = new Scene(vbox);
stage.setScene(scene);
// Name and display the Stage.
stage.setTitle("Media Demo");
```

11. Render the stage on the display:

```
stage.setWidth(400);
stage.setHeight(400);
stage.show();
```

The complete code can be found at `Chapter16/7_embed_audio_video`.

We have provided two run scripts, `run.bat` and `run.sh`, under `Chapter16/7_embed_audio_video`. The `run.bat` script will be for running the application on Windows and `run.sh` will be for running the application on Linux.

Run the application using `run.bat` or `run.sh`, and you will see the following GUI:

How it works...

The important classes, in the `javafx.scene.media` package for media playback are the following:

- `Media`: This represents the source of the media, that is, either video or audio. This accepts the source in the form of HTTP/HTTPS/FILE and JAR URLs.
- `MediaPlayer`: This manages the playback of the media.
- `MediaView`: This is the UI component that allows viewing the media.

There are a few other classes, but we haven't covered them in this recipe. The media-related classes are in the `javafx.media` module. So, do not forget to require a dependency on it, as shown here:

```
module gui{
    requires javafx.controls;
    requires javafx.media;
    opens com.packt;
}
```

In this recipe, we have a sample video at `Chapter16/7_embed_audio_video/sample_video1.mp4`, and we make use of the `java.io.File` API to build `File` URL to locate the video:

```
File file = new File("sample_video1.mp4");
Media media = new Media(file.toURI().toString());
```

The media playback is managed by using the API exposed by the `javafx.scene.media.MediaPlayer` class. In this recipe, we made use of a few of its methods, namely `play()`, `pause()`, and `stop()`. The `javafx.scene.media.MediaPlayer` class is initialized by using the `javafx.scene.media.Media` object:

```
MediaPlayer mediaPlayer = new MediaPlayer(media);
```

Rendering the media on the UI is managed by the `javafx.scene.media.MediaView` class, and it is backed by a `javafx.scene.media.MediaPlayer` object:

```
MediaView mediaView = new MediaView(mediaPlayer);
```

We can set the height and width of the viewer by using the `setFitWidth()` and `setFitHeight()` methods.

There's more...

We gave a basic demo of media support in JavaFX. There's a lot more to explore. You can add volume control options, options to seek forward or backward, play audios, and audio equalizer.

Adding effects to controls

Adding effects in a controlled way gives a good appearance to the user interface. There are multiple effects such as blurring, shadows, reflection, blooming, and so on. JavaFX provides a set of classes under the `javafx.scene.effects` package, which can be used to add effects to enhance the look of the application. This package is available in the `javafx.graphics` module.

In this recipe, we will look at a few effects—blur, shadow, and reflection.

Getting ready

As we know that JavaFX libraries are not shipped in the JDK installation from Oracle JDK 11 onward and Open JDK 10 onward, we will have to download the JavaFX SDK from here `https://gluonhq.com/products/javafx/` and include the JARs present in the SDK's `lib` folder on the modular path using the `-p` option shown as follows:

```
javac -p "PATH_TO_JAVAFX_SDK_LIB" <other parts of the command line>

#Windows
java -p "PATH_TO_JAVAFX_SDK_LIB;COMPILED_CODE" <other parts of the
command line>
#Linux
java -p "PATH_TO_JAVAFX_SDK_LIB:COMPILED_CODE" <other parts of the
command line>
```

How to do it...

1. Let's first create a class with empty methods, which would represent the main application for launching the application as well as the JavaFX UI:

    ```
    public class EffectsDemo extends Application{
      public static void main(String[] args) {
        Application.launch(args);
      }
      @Override
      public void start(Stage stage) {
        //code added here in next steps
      }
    }
    ```

2. The subsequent code will be written within the `start(Stage stage)` method. Create and configure `javafx.scene.layout.GridPane`:

```
GridPane gridPane = new GridPane();
gridPane.setAlignment(Pos.CENTER);
gridPane.setHgap(10);
gridPane.setVgap(10);
gridPane.setPadding(new Insets(25, 25, 25, 25));
```

3. Create rectangles required for applying the blur effects:

```
Rectangle r1 = new Rectangle(100,25, Color.BLUE);
Rectangle r2 = new Rectangle(100,25, Color.RED);
Rectangle r3 = new Rectangle(100,25, Color.ORANGE);
```

4. Add `javafx.scene.effect.BoxBlur` to Rectangle r1, `javafx.scene.effect.MotionBlur` to Rectangle r2, and `javafx.scene.effect.GaussianBlur` to Rectangle r3:

```
r1.setEffect(new BoxBlur(10,10,3));
r2.setEffect(new MotionBlur(90, 15.0));
r3.setEffect(new GaussianBlur(15.0));
```

5. Add the rectangles to `gridPane`:

```
gridPane.add(r1,1,1);
gridPane.add(r2,2,1);
gridPane.add(r3,3,1);
```

6. Create three circles, required for applying shadows:

```
Circle c1 = new Circle(20, Color.BLUE);
Circle c2 = new Circle(20, Color.RED);
Circle c3 = new Circle(20, Color.GREEN);
```

7. Add `javafx.scene.effect.DropShadow` to c1 and `javafx.scene.effect.InnerShadow` to c2:

```
c1.setEffect(new DropShadow(0, 4.0, 0, Color.YELLOW));
c2.setEffect(new InnerShadow(0, 4.0, 4.0, Color.ORANGE));
```

8. Add these circles to `gridPane`:

```
gridPane.add(c1,1,2);
gridPane.add(c2,2,2);
gridPane.add(c3,3,2);
```

9. Create a simple text, `Reflection Sample`, on which we will apply the reflection effect:

```
Text t = new Text("Reflection Sample");
t.setFont(Font.font("Arial", FontWeight.BOLD, 20));
t.setFill(Color.BLUE);
```

10. Create a `javafx.scene.effect.Reflection` effect and add it to the text:

```
Reflection reflection = new Reflection();
reflection.setFraction(0.8);
t.setEffect(reflection);
```

11. Add the text component to `gridPane`:

```
gridPane.add(t, 1, 3, 3, 1);
```

12. Create a scene graph using `gridPane` as the root node:

```
Scene scene = new Scene(gridPane, 500, 300);
```

13. Set the scene graph to the stage and render it on the display:

```
stage.setScene(scene);
stage.setTitle("Effects Demo");
stage.show();
```

The complete code can be found at `Chapter16/8_effects_demo`.

We have provided two run scripts, `run.bat` and `run.sh`, under `Chapter16/8_effects_demo`. The `run.bat` script will be for running the application on Windows and `run.sh` will be for running the application on Linux.

Run the application using `run.bat` or `run.sh` and you will see the following GUI:

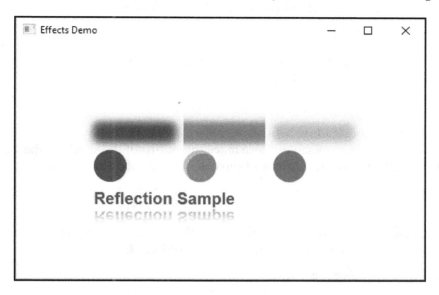

How it works...

In this recipe, we have made use of the following effects:

- `javafx.scene.effect.BoxBlur`
- `javafx.scene.effect.MotionBlur`
- `javafx.scene.effect.GaussianBlur`
- `javafx.scene.effect.DropShadow`
- `javafx.scene.effect.InnerShadow`
- `javafx.scene.effect.Reflection`

The `BoxBlur` effect is created by specifying the width and height of the blur effect, and also the number of times the effect needs to be applied:

```
BoxBlur boxBlur = new BoxBlur(10,10,3);
```

The `MotionBlur` effect is created by providing the angle of the blur and its radius. This gives an effect of something captured while in motion:

```
MotionBlur motionBlur = new MotionBlur(90, 15.0);
```

The `GaussianBlur` effect is created by providing the radius of the effect, and the effect uses the Gaussian formula to apply the effect:

```
GaussianBlur gb = new GaussianBlur(15.0);
```

`DropShadow` adds the shadow behind the object, whereas `InnerShadow` adds the shadow within the object. Each of these takes the radius of the shadow, the x and y location of the start of the shadow, and the color of the shadow:

```
DropShadow dropShadow = new DropShadow(0, 4.0, 0, Color.YELLOW);
InnerShadow innerShadow = new InnerShadow(0, 4.0, 4.0, Color.ORANGE);
```

`Reflection` is a pretty simple effect that adds the reflection of the object. We can set the fraction of how much of the original object is reflected:

```
Reflection reflection = new Reflection();
reflection.setFraction(0.8);
```

There's more...

There are quite a few more effects:

- The blend effect, which blends two different inputs with a predefined blending approach
- The bloom effect, which makes the brighter portions appear brighter
- The glow effect, which makes the object glow
- The lighting effect, which simulates a light source on the object, thereby giving it a 3D appearance.

We would recommend that you try out these effects in the same way as we have tried them out.

Using the Robot API

Robot API is used to simulate keyboard and mouse actions on the screen, which means you would instruct the code to type some text in the text field, choose an option, and then click on a button. People coming from the Web UI-testing background can relate this to the Selenium Testing Library. **Abstract Window Toolkit** (**AWT**), which is an older windowing toolkit in JDK, provides Robot API, but using the same API on JavaFX is not straightforward and requires some hacks. The JavaFX window toolkit called **Glass** has its own Robot APIs (`https://openjfx.io/javadoc/11/javafx.graphics/javafx/scene/robot/Robot.html`), but these are not public. So, as part of the OpenJFX 11 release, new public APIs were introduced for the same.

In this recipe, we will look at using the Robot API to simulate some actions on JavaFX UI.

Getting ready

As we know that JavaFX libraries are not shipped in the JDK installation from Oracle JDK 11 onward and Open JDK 10 onward, we will have to download the JavaFX SDK from here (`https://gluonhq.com/products/javafx/`) and include the JARs present in the SDK's `lib` folder on the modular path, using the `-p` option, shown as follows:

```
javac -p "PATH_TO_JAVAFX_SDK_LIB" <other parts of the command line>

#Windows
java -p "PATH_TO_JAVAFX_SDK_LIB;COMPILED_CODE" <other parts of the
command line>
#Linux
java -p "PATH_TO_JAVAFX_SDK_LIB:COMPILED_CODE" <other parts of the
command line>
```

In this recipe, we will create a simple application that accepts a name from the user and, on clicking a button, prints a message to the user. This entire operation will be simulated using the Robot API, and, finally, before exiting the application, we will capture the screen using the Robot API.

How to do it...

1. Create a simple class, `RobotApplication` that extends `javafx.application.Application` and sets up the UI required for testing the Robot API and also creates an instance of `javafx.scene.robot.Robot`. This class will be defined as a static inner class to the `RobotAPIDemo` main class :

```
public static class RobotApplication extends Application{

  @Override
  public void start(Stage stage) throws Exception{
    robot = new Robot();
    GridPane gridPane = new GridPane();
    gridPane.setAlignment(Pos.CENTER);
    gridPane.setHgap(10);
    gridPane.setVgap(10);
    gridPane.setPadding(new Insets(25, 25, 25, 25));

    Text appTitle = new Text("Robot Demo");
    appTitle.setFont(Font.font("Arial",
        FontWeight.NORMAL, 15));
    gridPane.add(appTitle, 0, 0, 2, 1);

    Label nameLbl = new Label("Name");
    nameField = new TextField();
    gridPane.add(nameLbl, 0, 1);
    gridPane.add(nameField, 1, 1);

    greeting = new Button("Greet");
    gridPane.add(greeting, 1, 2);

    Text resultTxt = new Text();
    resultTxt.setFont(Font.font("Arial",
        FontWeight.NORMAL, 15));
    gridPane.add(resultTxt, 0, 5, 2, 1);

    greeting.setOnAction((event) -> {
      String name = nameField.getText();
      StringBuilder resultBuilder = new StringBuilder();
      if ( name != null && name.length() > 0 ){
        resultBuilder.append("Hello, ")
            .append(name).append("\n");
      }else{
        resultBuilder.append("Please enter the name");
      }
```

```
        resultTxt.setText(resultBuilder.toString());
        btnActionLatch.countDown();
    });


    Scene scene = new Scene(gridPane, 300, 250);
    stage.setTitle("Age calculator");
    stage.setScene(scene);
    stage.setAlwaysOnTop(true);
    stage.addEventHandler(WindowEvent.WINDOW_SHOWN, e ->
        Platform.runLater(appStartLatch::countDown));
    stage.show();
    appStage = stage;
  }
}
```

2. As the JavaFX UI will be launched in a different JavaFX application thread and there will be some delays in rendering the UI completely before we execute the commands to interact with the UI, we will make use of `java.util.concurrent.CountDownLatch` to indicate different events. To work with `CountDownLatch`, we create a simple static helper method with the following definition in the `RobotAPIDemo` class:

```
public static void waitForOperation(
    CountDownLatch latchToWaitFor,
    int seconds, String errorMsg) {
  try {
    if (!latchToWaitFor.await(seconds,
        TimeUnit.SECONDS)) {
      System.out.println(errorMsg);
    }
  } catch (Exception ex) {
    ex.printStackTrace();
  }
}
```

3. The `typeName()` method is the helper method that types the name of the person in the text field:

```
public static void typeName(){
  Platform.runLater(() -> {
    Bounds textBoxBounds = nameField.localToScreen(
      nameField.getBoundsInLocal());
    robot.mouseMove(textBoxBounds.getMinX(),
      textBoxBounds.getMinY());
    robot.mouseClick(MouseButton.PRIMARY);
    robot.keyType(KeyCode.CAPS);
```

```
      robot.keyType(KeyCode.S);
      robot.keyType(KeyCode.CAPS);
      robot.keyType(KeyCode.A);
      robot.keyType(KeyCode.N);
      robot.keyType(KeyCode.A);
      robot.keyType(KeyCode.U);
      robot.keyType(KeyCode.L);
      robot.keyType(KeyCode.L);
      robot.keyType(KeyCode.A);
    });
  }
```

4. The `clickButton()` method is the helper method; it clicks on the correct button to trigger the greeting message display:

```
public static void clickButton(){
  Platform.runLater(() -> {
    //click the button
    Bounds greetBtnBounds = greeting
      .localToScreen(greeting.getBoundsInLocal());
    robot.mouseMove(greetBtnBounds.getCenterX(),
      greetBtnBounds.getCenterY());
    robot.mouseClick(MouseButton.PRIMARY);
  });
}
```

5. The `captureScreen()` method is the helper method to take a screenshot of the application and save it to the filesystem:

```
public static void captureScreen(){
  Platform.runLater(() -> {
    try{
      WritableImage screenCapture =
        new WritableImage(
          Double.valueOf(appStage.getWidth()).intValue(),
          Double.valueOf(appStage.getHeight()).intValue()
        );
      robot.getScreenCapture(screenCapture,
        appStage.getX(), appStage.getY(),
        appStage.getWidth(), appStage.getHeight());

      BufferedImage screenCaptureBI =
        SwingFXUtils.fromFXImage(screenCapture, null);
      String timePart = LocalDateTime.now()
        .format(DateTimeFormatter.ofPattern("yyyy-dd-M-m-H-
ss"));
      ImageIO.write(screenCaptureBI, "png",
        new File("screenCapture-" + timePart +".png"));
```

```
            Platform.exit();
        }catch(Exception ex){
            ex.printStackTrace();
        }
    });
}
```

6. We will bind the launching of the UI and the created helper methods in the `main()` method, as follows:

```
public static void main(String[] args)
    throws Exception{
    new Thread(() -> Application.launch(
        RobotApplication.class, args)).start();
    waitForOperation(appStartLatch, 10,
        "Timed out waiting for JavaFX Application to Start");
    typeName();
    clickButton();
    waitForOperation(btnActionLatch, 10,
        "Timed out waiting for Button to complete operation");
    Thread.sleep(1000);
    captureScreen();
}
```

The complete code for this can be found at `Chapter16/9_robot_api`. You can run the sample either by using `run.bat` or `run.sh`. Running the application will launch the UI, execute the actions, take a screenshot, and exit the app. The screenshot will be placed in the folder from which the application was launched, and it would follow the naming convention—`screenCapture-yyyy-dd-M-m-H-ss.png`. Here is a sample screenshot:

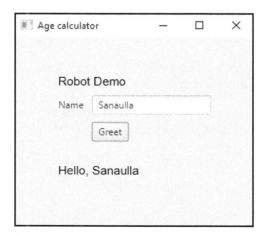

How it works...

As JavaFX application is run in a different thread, we need to ensure that the operations of the Robot API are ordered correctly and the actions of the Robot API are executed only when the complete UI has been displayed. To ensure this, we have made use of `java.util.concurrent.CountDownLatch` to communicate about events such as the following ones:

- Complete loading of the UI
- Completion of the execution of the action defined for the button

The communication about the completion of the loading of the UI is achieved by using a `CountDownLatch`, as follows:

```
# Declaration of the latch
static public CountDownLatch appStartLatch = new CountDownLatch(1);

# Using the latch
stage.addEventHandler(WindowEvent.WINDOW_SHOWN, e ->
                Platform.runLater(appStartLatch::countDown));
```

The `countDown()` method is invoked in the `Stage` event handler when the window is shown thereby releasing the latch and triggering the execution of the following block of code in the main method:

```
typeName();
clickButton();
```

The main thread then again gets blocked from waiting for the `btnActionLatch` to be released. The `btnActionLatch` is released after the completion of the action in the button greeting. Once the `btnActionLatch` is released, the main thread continues execution to invoke the `captureScreen()` method.

Let's discuss some of the methods we have used from the `javafx.scene.robot.Robot` class:

`mouseMove()`: This method is used to move the mouse cursor to a given location identified from its *x* and *y* co-ordinates. We have used the following line of code to get the bounds of the component:

```
Bounds textBoxBounds =
nameField.localToScreen(nameField.getBoundsInLocal());
```

The bounds of a component contain the following:

- The upper-left x and y coordinates
- The lower-right x and y coordinates
- The width and the height of the component

So, for our Robot API use case, we make use of the upper-left x and y coordinates, shown as follows:

```
robot.mouseMove(textBoxBounds.getMinX(), textBoxBounds.getMinY());
```

`mouseClick()`: This method is used to click the buttons on the mouse. The mouse buttons are identified by the following `enums` in `javafx.scene.input.MouseButton` enum:

- `PRIMARY`: Represents the mouse's left click
- `SECONDARY`: Represents the mouse's right click
- `MIDDLE`: Represents the mouse's scroll, or the middle, button.

So, to be able to use `mouseClick()`, we need to move the location of the component on which we need to perform the click operation. In our case, as seen in the implementation of the method `typeName()`, we move to the location of the text field using `mouseMove()` and then invoke the `mouseClick()`, shown as follows:

```
robot.mouseMove(textBoxBounds.getMinX(),
    textBoxBounds.getMinY());
robot.mouseClick(MouseButton.PRIMARY);
```

`keyType()`: This method is used to type characters into components that accept text input. The characters to be typed are represented by the enums in the `javafx.scene.input.KeyCode` enum. In our `typeName()` method implementation, we type the string `Sanaulla`, shown as follows:

```
robot.keyType(KeyCode.CAPS);
robot.keyType(KeyCode.S);
robot.keyType(KeyCode.CAPS);
robot.keyType(KeyCode.A);
robot.keyType(KeyCode.N);
robot.keyType(KeyCode.A);
robot.keyType(KeyCode.U);
robot.keyType(KeyCode.L);
robot.keyType(KeyCode.L);
robot.keyType(KeyCode.A);
```

getScreenCapture(): This method is used to take the screenshot of the application. The area for capturing the screenshot is determined by the *x* and *y* coordinates and the width and the height information passed to the method. The image captured is then converted to java.awt.image.BufferedImage and saved onto the file system, as shown in the following code:

```
WritableImage screenCapture = new WritableImage(
    Double.valueOf(appStage.getWidth()).intValue(),
    Double.valueOf(appStage.getHeight()).intValue()
  );
robot.getScreenCapture(screenCapture,
  appStage.getX(), appStage.getY(),
  appStage.getWidth(), appStage.getHeight());

BufferedImage screenCaptureBI =
  SwingFXUtils.fromFXImage(screenCapture, null);
String timePart = LocalDateTime.now().format(
  DateTimeFormatter.ofPattern("yyyy-dd-M-m-H-ss"));
ImageIO.write(screenCaptureBI, "png",
  new File("screenCapture-" + timePart +".png"));
```

Other Books You May Enjoy

If you enjoyed this book, you may be interested in these other books by Packt:

Design Patterns and Best Practices in Java
Kamalmeet Singh, Adrian Ianculescu, Lucian-Paul Torje

ISBN: 9781786463593

- Understand the OOP and FP paradigms
- Explore the traditional Java design patterns
- Get to know the new functional features of Java
- See how design patterns are changed and affected by the new features
- Discover what reactive programming is and why is it the natural augmentation of FP
- Work with reactive design patterns and find the best ways to solve common problems using them
- See the latest trends in architecture and the shift from MVC to serverless applications
- Use best practices when working with the new features

Beginning Java Data Structures and Algorithms
James Cutajar

ISBN: 9781789537178

- Understand some of the fundamental concepts behind key algorithms
- Express space and time complexities using Big O notation.
- Correctly implement classic sorting algorithms such as merge and quicksort
- Correctly implement basic and complex data structures
- Learn about different algorithm design paradigms, such as greedy, divide and conquer, and dynamic programming
- Apply powerful string matching techniques and optimize your application logic
- Master graph representations and learn about different graph algorithms

Leave a review - let other readers know what you think

Please share your thoughts on this book with others by leaving a review on the site that you bought it from. If you purchased the book from Amazon, please leave us an honest review on this book's Amazon page. This is vital so that other potential readers can see and use your unbiased opinion to make purchasing decisions, we can understand what our customers think about our products, and our authors can see your feedback on the title that they have worked with Packt to create. It will only take a few minutes of your time, but is valuable to other potential customers, our authors, and Packt. Thank you!

Index